THE BOOK OF
ENGLISH INTERNATIONAL RUGBY
1871–1982

The BOOK OF ENGLISH INTERNATIONAL RUGBY

1871-1982

Compiled and edited by
JOHN GRIFFITHS

WILLOW BOOKS
Collins
St James's Place, London
1982

Willow Books
William Collins Sons & Co Ltd
London · Glasgow · Sydney · Auckland
Toronto · Johannesburg

First published 1982
© John Griffiths 1982

Griffiths, John
The book of English international rugby 1871–1982
1. Rugby football – England – History
I. Title
796.33'375   GV945.5

ISBN 00 218006 5

Filmset in Times Roman
by Filmtype Services Limited, Scarborough, North Yorkshire
Printed and bound in Great Britain by
Wm Collins Sons & Co Ltd, Glasgow

CONTENTS

PICTURE ACKNOWLEDGEMENTS

The author and publishers would like to thank the following for permission to reproduce the illustrations included in this book:

The Rugby Football Union – pages 16 and 27;
The British Library – pages 59 (top), 79, 123, 140 (bottom) and 146;
Central News – page 130 (bottom);
Sport & General Press Agency – pages 179, 190, 199, 211, 220 (bottom), 226, 234, 264, 282, 294, 308, 353 (bottom right) and 400 (bottom left);
Colorsport – pages 353 (bottom left) and 400 (top, and bottom right).

At the time of going to press, it proved difficult to determine the copyright holders of a number of the early photographs – interested parties should contact the publishers.

PREFACE

The idea for a book of international Rugby records came as a result of one match. In 1967, when Keith Jarrett scored 19 points against England, it was surprising to learn that there was no single source available to confirm whether or not Jarrett had created an individual scoring record. So, in a modest attempt to fill this gap in the records of the game, I began to collate facts concerning international matches from such invaluable references as *The Rugby Football Annual* and the *Playfair Rugby Football Annual*. Later, at the Colindale Newspaper Museum, I was able to check these details, extend the records back to the first international played in 1871 and, thanks to the Rugby correspondents, past and present, enlarge the scope of the work by adding brief descriptions for each game.

This volume covers the 370 full internationals played by England up to April 1982, but it is not intended as a history of English Rugby. Rev. F. Marshall in *Football: The Rugby Union Game* (1894); L.R. Tosswill in his revision of *Marshall* (1925); O.L. Owen in *The History of the Rugby Football Union* (1955); U.A. Titley and Ross McWhirter in *Centenary History of the Rugby Football Union* (1970); and Barry Bowker in *England Rugby* (1976), have already published detailed accounts of the subject, and I acknowledge the debts owed to these authors for their accurate and lively histories. Furthermore, the reminiscences of A.A. Thomson, E.H.D. Sewell and W.J.T. Collins, and the books of J.B.G. Thomas, have been essential background reading to this work.

The search for photographs to complement the text was one of the most interesting aspects of the project and my sincere thanks for their assistance go to Mr Alfred Wright, archivist of the R.F.U. at Twickenham; Timothy Auty of Leeds; and my father, who travelled many miles to make excellent prints of some of the more unusual items. Historical significance and rarity – sometimes at the expense of quality – were the important factors determining selection, particularly for the older pictures.

To the many Rugby correspondents, enthusiasts and former internationals who have been extremely helpful answering my questions or confirming facts, I offer grateful thanks. Above all, I am indebted to my friend Tim Auty, who has given his unselfish support throughout the stages leading to publication, suggesting many improvements and corrections; while the encouragement of Vivian Jenkins, editor of *Rothmans Rugby Yearbook*, and the backing of Alan Smith at Collins, were factors which finally influenced the appearance of this edition. Tim Jollands, editor of Willow Books, handled the manuscript skilfully and competently organised the whole exercise; to him I give special thanks.

JOHN GRIFFITHS
July 1982

ABBREVIATIONS

The following abbreviations are used to denote Rugby clubs

Acads.	Academicals	O.B.	Old Boys
A.C.T.	Australian Capital Territory	O.F.S.	Orange Free State
A.S.F.	Association Sportive Française	O.M.Ts.	Old Merchant Taylors
		P.U.C.	Paris Université Club
C.A.S.G.	Club Athlétique des Sports Généraux	R.A.F.	Royal Air Force
		R.C.F.	Racing Club de France
C.I.Y.M.S.	Church of Ireland Young Men's Society	R.I.E.	Royal Indian Engineering
		R.M.A.	Royal Military Academy
Const.	Constitution	R.N.	Royal Navy
E.C.	(Bordeaux) Etudiants Club	R.N.E.	Royal Naval Engineering
E.R.	(Hull) and East Riding	R.U.C.	Royal Ulster Constabulary
F.P.	Former Pupils	S.B.U.C.	Stade Bordelais Université Club
G.S.	Grammar School		
G.S.F.P.	Grammar School Former Pupils	S.C.U.F.	Sporting Club Universitaire de France
H.	Hospital	T.C.	Training College
H.S.F.P.	High School Former Pupils	T.O.E.C.	Toulouse Olympique Employés Club
Inst.F.P.	Institution Former Pupils		
K.C.H.	King's College Hospital	U.	University
N.I.F.C.	North of Ireland Football Club	U.C.	University College
		U.C.H.	University College Hospital
N.S.W.	New South Wales	U.S.	United Services
O.	Old	Wands.	Wanderers

Symbols used: † for a New Cap (England only)
* for a Captain

English International Match Summaries
1871–1982

This section contains the summaries, teams and scorers for the 370 international matches played by England up to 30 April, 1982.

The principal source for reports was *The Times*, though occasionally other sources were consulted in attempts to resolve difficulties over the names of scorers. Before 1920, for instance, it was uncommon for teams to be numbered and sometimes reporters disagreed about the identity of a scorer. Nevertheless, the *Times's* version has been generally accepted for details of England players and scorers.

In the other Home Unions and France, the following publications have been consulted to verify details of England's opponents: *The Scotsman* and *History of Scottish Rugby* (by A.M.C. Thorburn, published 1980); *The Irish Times*; the *Western Mail* and *History of Welsh International Rugby* (by J.D. Billot, published 1970); and *Les Capes du Matin* (by G. Pastre, published 1970). *Men in Black* (by R.H. Chester and N.A. McMillan, published 1978), *Springbok Annals* (by Dr D.H. Craven, published 1959) and *The Springboks* (by A.C. Parker, published 1970) have been invaluable references for England matches against overseas teams. Furthermore, the reviews and records of *The Rugby Football Annual* (1913–1940); *Playfair Rugby Annual* (1948–1973), and *Rothmans Rugby Yearbook* (1972–) have been indispensable general aids. Two other books, *International . . . . . . Rugby Teams* (by L.M. Holden, published 1912) and *Rugby Football Today* (by E.H.D. Sewell, published 1931) contained useful sections on international matches. The casual researcher should be warned, however, that these last two sources were not infallible.

The team line-ups have been listed in blocks to show clearly, in any formation from 20- to 15-a-side, the full-backs, three-quarters, halves and forwards, in that order. An effort has been made to list three-quarters from wing to wing; to place the fly-half before the scrum-half; and to list the forwards from front row to back row. However, specialised positions have not always existed in the game. In England, for instance, halves did not usually specialise until the first decade of the present century, and forwards did not generally have fixed places in the scrummage until the era between the two wars. So, only since about 1930 has it been possible to list the forwards in the prop/hooker/prop/lock/lock/flanker/number-eight/flanker formation so familiar today. (Note, too, that New Zealand have always played two five-eighths with their scrum-half: these are shown in the half-back blocks in the summaries, as is the 'rover' or wing-forward employed by the New Zealanders to work their 2-3-2 diamond scrummage in matches up to 1931.)

As far as possible the club shown adjacent to a player's name is that for which the man was playing at the time of the match under review.

Referees did not control international matches before 1875. Disputes and points arising over the laws of the game were resolved by captains and umpires (i.e. touch-judges) prior to this date.

The England XX, 1871: *standing* J. E. Bentley, A. S. Gibson, F. Tobin, D. P. Turner,
F. Stokes (captain), J. H. Clayton, R. R. Osborne, H. J. C. Turner;
middle right J. H. Luscombe, R. H. Birkett, J. F. Green; *sitting* A. St G. Hamersley,
W. MacLaren, C. W. Sherrard, A. Lyon, C. A. Crompton; *front* A. Davenport,
A. G. Guillemard, J. M. Dugdale, B. H. Burns.

The cap of one of England's first internationals, A. G. Guillemard. When caps were
awarded no dates were given and the players would embroider them themselves.
The caps have changed little in design to this day: the colour is plum with a silver tassel.

SCOTLAND v ENGLAND 1871

Played at Raeburn Place, Edinburgh, 27 March 1871
Scotland won by 1G, 1T to 1T

The first ever international Rugby match was played in perfect conditions on a bright, sunny afternoon before an attendance of 4000 spectators. The pitch, measuring 120 yards by 55, was small by English standards and consequently the visiting half-backs were unable to display the excellent running of which they were capable. The first half was a prolonged forward battle and after 50 minutes the teams changed ends, neither side having scored. In the second period, the Scottish forwards dominated and the scoring opened with a pushover try which Cross, the Scottish half, converted. England fought back and Birkett scored a try near the corner which Stokes, the English captain, could not convert. In the closing minutes of the game, the fitter Scottish combination secured another try when Cross scored.

For England, Tobin and Green were the outstanding players in an uncoordinated team, while the Scottish victory stemmed from a well-drilled pack of forwards. Cross was the best back on the field though Osborne, one of the English full-backs, made a memorable tackle on Finlay during the course of the match. While the Scottish forward was sprinting towards the English goal-line, Osborne folded his arms across his chest and charged into Finlay, both players recoiling yards before falling to the ground.

SCOTLAND		ENGLAND	
W.D. Brown	(Glasgow Acads.)	†A.G. Guillemard	(West Kent)
T.Chalmers	(Glasgow Acads.)	†R.R. Osborne	(Manchester)
A.C. Ross	(St Andrew's U.)	†A. Lyon	(Liverpool)
T.R. Marshall	(Edinburgh Acads.)	†W. MacLaren	(Manchester)
W. Cross	(Merchistonians)		
J.W. Arthur	(Glasgow Acads.)	†J.E. Bentley	(Gipsies)
		†F. Tobin	(Liverpool)
		†J.F. Green	(West Kent)
*F.J. Moncreiff	(Edinburgh Acads.)		
A. Buchanan	(Royal H.S.F.P.)	†R.H. Birkett	(Clapham Rovers)
A.G. Colville	(Merchistonians)	†B.H. Burns	(Blackheath)
D. Drew	(Glasgow Acads.)	†J.H. Clayton	(Liverpool)
J. Forsyth	(Edinburgh U.)	†C.A. Crompton	(Blackheath)
J.F. Finlay	(Edinburgh Acads.)	†A. Davenport	(Ravenscourt Park)
R.W. Irvine	(Edinburgh Acads.)	†J.M. Dugdale	(Ravenscourt Park)
W.J.C. Lyall	(Edinburgh Acads.)	†A.S. Gibson	(Manchester)
J.A.W. Mein	(Edinburgh Acads.)	†A.St G. Hamersley	(Marlborough Nomads)
J.L.H McFarlane	(Edinburgh U.)	†J.H. Luscombe	(Gipsies)
R. Munro	(St Andrew's U.)	†C.W. Sherrard	(Blackheath)
G. Ritchie	(Merchistonians)	*†F. Stokes	(Blackheath)
A.H. Robertson	(West of Scotland)	†D.P. Turner	(Richmond)
J.S. Thomson	(St Andrew's U.)	†H.J.C. Turner	(Manchester)

Tries: Buchanan, Cross
Conversion: Cross

Try: Birkett

ENGLAND v SCOTLAND 1872
Played at The Oval, London, 5 February 1872
England won by 1G, 1DG, 2T to 1DG

The teams for this match were selected after a series of trials and as a result both sides showed considerable qualities in combined movements. On a wider pitch than that of the previous season, the English backs ran and handled with skill, though their forwards were the architects of victory.

After a long period of rain the turf was in excellent condition when Stokes, captaining England for the second time, kicked off towards the gasworks end of the ground. England possessed the heavier pack, but the nimbler Scottish forwards immediately took play to the English line and despite relieving runs by Wilkinson and Bentley, the English half-backs, Scotland took the lead after ten minutes when Cathcart dropped a neat goal. Following this initial set-back the English forwards discovered their true form and, after a period of sustained pressure, Turner charged over the Scottish goal-line for Hamersley to touch down after a maul in goal. Isherwood converted with a fine kick.

England went ahead midway through the second half when Freeman dropped a magnificent goal with his left foot; soon after, D'Aguilar scored a try. Scotland rallied and Balfour narrowly failed to equalise with an attempted goal from a mark. The English forwards continued to dominate, however, with Stokes, Hamersley, Turner and Isherwood particularly outstanding. Just before no-side, Finney, who had played brilliantly, scored a try.

F. Luscombe's brother had played for England in the 1871 match.

ENGLAND		SCOTLAND	
A.G. Guillemard	(West Kent)	W.D. Brown	(Glasgow Acads.)
†F.W. Mills	(Marlborough Nomads)	T. Chalmers	(Glasgow Acads.)
†W.O. Moberley	(Ravenscourt Park)	L.M. Balfour	(Edinburgh Acads.)
†H. Freeman	(Marlborough Nomads)	T.R. Marshall	(Edinburgh Acads.)
		R.P. Maitland	(Royal Artillery)
J.E. Bentley	(Gipsies)		
†S. Finney	(R.I.E. College)	J.W. Arthur	(Glasgow Acads.)
†P. Wilkinson	(Law Club)	*F.J. Moncreiff	(Edinburgh Acads.)
		W. Cross	(Merchistonians)
†T. Batson	(Blackheath)		
†J.A. Body	(Gipsies)	J. Anderson	(West of Scotland)
†J.A. Bush	(Clifton)	E.M. Bannerman	(Edinburgh Acads.)
†F.I. Currey	(Marlborough Nomads)	C.W. Cathcart	(Edinburgh U.)
†F.B.G. D'Aguilar	(Royal Engineers)	A.G. Colville	(Merchistonians)
A.St G. Hamersley	(Marlborough Nomads)	J.F. Finlay	(Edinburgh Acads.)
†F.W. Isherwood	(Ravenscourt Park)	R.W. Irvine	(Edinburgh Acads.)
†F. Luscombe	(Gipsies)	W. Marshall	(Edinburgh Acads.)
†J.E.H. Mackinlay	(St George's H.)	J.L.H. McFarlane	(Edinburgh U.)
†W.W. Pinching	(Guy's H.)	J.H. McClure	(West of Scotland)
C.W. Sherrard	(Royal Engineers)	F.T. Maxwell	(Royal Engineers)
*F. Stokes	(Blackheath)	J.A.W. Mein	(Edinburgh Acads.)
D.P. Turner	(Richmond)	H.W. Renny-Tailyour	(Royal Engineers)

Tries: D'Aguilar, Finney, Hamersley
Conversion: Isherwood
Dropped goal: Freeman

Dropped goal: Cathcart

SCOTLAND v ENGLAND 1873

Played at West of Scotland Club, Glasgow, 3 March 1873
Drawn, neither side scoring

Melting snow and incessant rain turned the ground into a morass and seriously affected the running and handling of the backs. A crowd of 5000 saw this game end as a draw (the first in international Rugby) with neither side scoring.

The forwards were very evenly matched and in the heavy conditions neither pack was able to maintain any advantage. Behind the scrummage McFarlane, who, interestingly, had played as a forward in the previous internationals, made many strong dashes and was the most enterprising of the Scottish backs, while Finney and Boyle were the outstanding Englishmen. Indeed, Finney very nearly won the match for England when he executed a 'poster' with a prodigious drop kick from a mark 50 yards from the goal. (A 'poster' was a kick which sailed so high above the uprights that it was impossible for the umpires to decide if the ball had crossed the bar.) Scotland were forced to touch down in defence on five occasions.

Before the contest, Stokes advised his team to alter the soles of their boots in order to overcome the wet, muddy conditions. However, after a cobbler had completed the necessary modifications, Freeman and Boyle, two of the key men in the English back division, discovered that their footwear had not been returned and, consequently, they were forced to play in 'dress-boots'.

SCOTLAND		ENGLAND	
W.D. Brown	(Glasgow Acads.)	F.W. Mills	(Marlborough Nomads)
T. Chalmers	(Glasgow Acads.)	†C.H.R. Vanderspar	(Richmond)
J.L.P. Sanderson	(Edinburgh Acads.)	†S. Morse	(Law Club)
G.B. McClure	(West of Scotland)	H. Freeman	(Marlborough Nomads)
J.L.H. McFarlane	(Edinburgh Acads.)		
		†C.W. Boyle	(Oxford U.)
W.St Clair Grant	(Craigmount School)	S. Finney	(R.I.E. College)
T.R. Marshall	(Edinburgh Acads.)		
		J.A. Body	(Gipsies)
H.W. Allen	(Glasgow Acads.)	J.A. Bush	(Clifton)
P. Anton	(St Andrew's U.)	†E.C. Cheston	(Law Club)
E.M. Bannerman	(Edinburgh Acads.)	†W.R.B. Fletcher	(Marlborough Nomads)
C.C. Bryce	(Glasgow Acads.)	A.St G. Hamersley	(Marlborough Nomads)
C.W. Cathcart	(Edinburgh U.)	†Hon. H.A. Lawrence	(Richmond)
J.P. Davidson	(R.I.E. College)	F. Luscombe	(Gipsies)
R.W. Irvine	(Edinburgh Acads.)	J.E.H. Mackinlay	(St George's H.)
J.A.W. Mein	(Edinburgh Acads.)	†H. Marsh	(R.I.E. College)
*F.J. Moncreiff	(Edinburgh Acads.)	†M.W. Marshall	(Blackheath)
A.G. Petrie	(Royal H.S.F.P.)	†C.H. Rickards	(Gipsies)
T.P. Whittington	(Merchistonians)	†E.R. Still	(Ravenscourt Park)
R.W. Wilson	(West of Scotland)	*F. Stokes	(Blackheath)
A. Wood	(Royal H.S.F.P.)	D.P. Turner	(Richmond)

ENGLAND v SCOTLAND 1874

Played at The Oval, London, 23 February 1874
England won by 1DG to 1T

Fog, mist and a heavy shower which lasted for half an hour made conditions miserable, as in the previous match. Scotland kicked off, defending the gasworks end of the ground, and their lively forwards rushed play to the English goal-posts where Finlay, the Edinburgh Academical, scored an unconverted try before the home team could clear its line. Until half-time, the game was evenly contested and there was no further scoring.

In the second half, England dominated the play, admirably mastering the unfavourable conditions which resulted in the muddy jerseys of the two teams becoming indistinguishable. The forwards, who combined excellently, twice forced the Scots to touch down in defence, while a feature of this match was the superb drop-kicking of the English backs. Morse and Milton just failed with two long attempts at goal but a successful kick by Freeman gave England victory ten minutes from no-side. Despite a late Scottish effort, the scores remained unchanged and England registered a narrow win.

This match was played on a Monday afternoon before a crowd of 4000 spectators and *The Times*, in an account of the proceedings, recorded that there were 'fewer ladies present than usual'.

W.H. Milton, later Sir William Milton, had two sons, C.H. Milton and J.G. Milton, capped for England in the 1900s; H.A. Bryden's brother was capped in 1876.

ENGLAND		SCOTLAND	
†J.M. Batten	(Cambridge U.)	*W.D. Brown	(Glasgow Acads.)
†M.J. Brooks	(Oxford U.)	T. Chalmers	(Glasgow Acads.)
H. Freeman	(Marlborough Nomads)	H.M. Hamilton	(West of Scotland)
		T.R. Marshall	(Edinburgh Acads.)
†W.E. Collins	(Old Cheltonians)	W.H. Kidston	(West of Scotland)
S. Morse	(Marlborough Nomads)		
†W.H. Milton	(Marlborough Nomads)	W.St Clair Grant	(Craigmount School)
		A.K. Stewart	(Edinburgh U.)
T. Batson	(Blackheath)		
†H.A. Bryden	(Clapham Rovers)	C.C. Bryce	(Glasgow Acads.)
E.C. Cheston	(Richmond)	J.P. Davidson	(R.I.E. College)
†C.W. Crosse	(Oxford U.)	J.F. Finlay	(Edinburgh Acads.)
†F.L. Cunliffe	(R.M.A.)	G. Heron	(Glasgow Acads.)
†J.S.M. Genth	(Manchester)	R.W. Irvine	(Edinburgh Acads.)
*A.St G. Hamersley	(Marlborough Nomads)	J.A.W. Mein	(Edinburgh Acads.)
†E. Kewley	(Liverpool)	T. Neilson	(West of Scotland)
Hon. H.A. Lawrence	(Richmond)	A.G. Petrie	(Royal H.S.F.P.)
M.W. Marshall	(Blackheath)	J. Reid	(Edinburgh Wands.)
†Hon. S. Parker	(Liverpool)	J.K. Todd	(Glasgow Acads.)
†W.F.H. Stafford	(Royal Engineers)	R.W. Wilson	(West of Scotland)
D.P. Turner	(Richmond)	A. Wood	(Royal H.S.F.P.)
†R. Walker	(Manchester)	A.H. Young	(Edinburgh Acads.)

Dropped goal: Freeman

Try: Finlay

ENGLAND v IRELAND 1875

Played at The Oval, London, 15 February 1875
England won by 1G, 1DG, 1T to Nil

A crowd of 3000 spectators witnessed this first international between England and Ireland. The match was played on a Monday afternoon, heavy rain during the previous weekend having turned the pitch, which measured 130 yards by 75, into a quagmire.

The visiting team had been selected from the Northern and Southern Irish Unions and, consequently, many of the players had never seen one another before. Two of those chosen to play did not even appear and backs were put to play in forward positions and *vice-versa*: it was no surprise that England dominated the game from the kick-off. Some astute kicking by Stokes and Milton pushed England to the Irish goal-line and, after 20 minutes' play, Michell scored a try near the corner which Fraser failed to convert. In the second half England added two goals, Nash dropping a splendid goal and Pearson converting a try by Cheston. But for the atrocious ground conditions, England's obvious superiority would have been rewarded by a far greater margin of victory.

The outstanding Irish player was Cronyn who tackled bravely and ran cleverly but the general positional play and kicking of the Irish backs was deplorable. Even though the Irish forwards often out-pushed the English pack in the scrummages, their poor loose-play and lack of stamina prevented them from pressurising their opponents.

W.H.H. Hutchinson was the first Yorkshire county player to represent England, although R.R. Osborne of Rochdale, Manchester and Lancashire, who had appeared in the 1871 match against Scotland, was born at Middleham, North Yorkshire.

ENGLAND		IRELAND	
†A.W. Pearson	(Guy's H.)	H.L. Cox	(Dublin U.)
†L. Stokes	(Blackheath)	R.B. Walkington	(North of Ireland)
W.H. Milton	(Marlborough Nomads)	R.J. Bell	(North of Ireland)
		A.P. Cronyn	(Dublin U.)
W.E. Collins	(St George's H.)		
†A.T. Michell	(Oxford U.)	R. Galbraith	(Dublin U.)
†E.H. Nash	(Oxford U.)	J. Myles	(Dublin U.)
		E.N. McIlwaine	(North of Ireland)
†F.R. Adams	(Richmond)		
T. Batson	(Blackheath)	W.S. Allen	(Wanderers)
E.C. Cheston	(Richmond)	G. Andrews	(North of Ireland)
C.W. Crosse	(Oxford U.)	W.H. Ash	(North of Ireland)
†E.C. Fraser	(Oxford U.)	M. Barlow	(Wanderers)
†H.J. Graham	(Wimbledon Hornets)	B.N. Casement	(Dublin U.)
†W.H.H. Hutchinson	(Hull)	A. Combe	(North of Ireland)
*Hon. H.A. Lawrence	(Richmond)	W. Gaffikin	(Windsor)
F. Luscombe	(Gipsies)	E. Galbraith	(Dublin U.)
J.E.H. Mackinlay	(St George's H.)	F.T. Hewson	(Wanderers)
M.W. Marshall	(Blackheath)	J.A. McDonald	(Methodist College)
†E.S. Perrott	(Old Cheltonians)	R.M. Maginess	(Dublin U.)
D.P. Turner	(Richmond)	*G. Stack	(Dublin U.)
R. Walker	(Manchester)	H.D. Walsh	(Dublin U.)

Tries: Cheston, Michell
Conversion: Pearson
Dropped goal: Nash

The first England team to play Ireland: *standing* C. W. Crosse, E. H. Nash, A. T. Michell, E. C. Fraser, H. J. Graham, W. H. H. Hutchinson, E. S. Perrott, R. Walker, L. Stokes, A. W. Pearson, T. Batson, W. H. Milton; *sitting* J. E. H. Mackinlay, F. Luscombe, F. R. Adams, Hon. H. A. Lawrence (captain), D. P. Turner, W. E. Collins, M. W. Marshall, E. C. Cheston.

SCOTLAND v ENGLAND 1875

Played at Raeburn Place, Edinburgh, 8 March 1875
Drawn, neither side scoring

Raeburn Place, where the first international had been settled in 1871, was again the scene for the England–Scotland match. 7000 spectators were present on a beautiful afternoon to witness a fast, closely-contested game played on a pitch in excellent condition.

As in the match of 1873, a scoreless draw resulted, though the visiting team forced their opponents to touch down in defence on six occasions. Both sides narrowly failed with attempted drops at goal – Ninian Finlay and Chalmers for Scotland, and Marshall and A.T. Michell for England, displaying particularly outstanding abilities in this aspect of the game.

L.H. Birkett and R.H. Birkett were brothers, the latter being father of John Birkett, an England centre in the first decade of the 1900s. The English line-up is taken from A.G. Guillemard's records, shown in Marshall [1892]. *However, it is known that the English backs adopted several different formations during the match: a report in* Bell's Life, *for example, which notes how the Englishmen copied the Scottish system during part of the match, places Morse amongst the backs, and lists R.H. Birkett and A.T. Michell as three-quarters for a while. Furthermore, Evanson spent the latter stages of the match as a three-quarter, changing positions with Michell.*

SCOTLAND		ENGLAND	
*W.D. Brown	(Glasgow Acads.)	†L.H. Birkett	(Clapham Rovers)
T. Chalmers	(Glasgow Acads.)	A.W. Pearson	(Guy's H.)
M. Cross	(Merchistonians)	S. Morse	(Marlborough Nomads)
N.J. Finlay	(Edinburgh Acads.)		
H.M. Hamilton	(West of Scotland)	W.E. Collins	(Old Cheltonians)
		A.T. Michell	(Oxford U.)
J.K. Todd	(Glasgow Acads.)	†W.A.D. Evanson	(Civil Service)
J.R. Hay-Gordon	(Edinburgh Acads.)		
		F.R. Adams	(Richmond)
A. Arthur	(Glasgow Acads.)	R.H. Birkett	(Clapham Rovers)
J.W. Dunlop	(West of Scotland)	J.A. Bush	(Clifton)
A.B. Finlay	(Edinburgh Acads.)	E.C. Cheston	(Richmond)
J.F. Finlay	(Edinburgh Acads.)	W.R.B. Fletcher	(Marlborough Nomads)
G.R. Fleming	(Glasgow Acads.)	J.S.M. Genth	(Manchester)
G. Heron	(Glasgow Acads.)	H.J. Graham	(Wimbledon Hornets)
R.W. Irvine	(Edinburgh Acads.)	E. Kewley	(Liverpool)
A. Marshall	(Edinburgh Acads.)	*Hon. H.A. Lawrence	(Richmond)
J.A.W. Mein	(Edinburgh Acads.)	F. Luscombe	(Gipsies)
A.G. Petrie	(Royal H.S.F.P.)	M.W. Marshall	(Blackheath)
J. Reid	(Edinburgh Wands.)	Hon. S. Parker	(Liverpool)
D. Robertson	(Edinburgh Acads.)	†J.E. Paul	(R.I.E. College)
A. Wood	(Royal H.S.F.P.)	D.P. Turner	(Richmond)

17

IRELAND v ENGLAND 1876[1]

Played at Leinster Cricket Ground, Rathmines, 13 December 1875

England won by 1G, 1T to Nil

A long period of hard frost during the week before the game had put the prospect of the first international match in Ireland in some jeopardy, but a late thaw enabled the fixture to go ahead as planned. As in the previous season England were the victors, but on this occasion Ireland showed a considerable improvement in their handling and kicking, and tackling was once again the strength of their general play. The match was played on the same day as the first fifteen-a-side University match between Oxford and Cambridge.

In the opening quarter of the game England scrummaged powerfully, while Ireland appeared most dangerous when their backs were breaking down the flanks. The visitors scored first when Clark crossed the Irish line for a try but Pearson failed to convert. Ireland retaliated and, after excellent work by Moore, England were forced to touch down in defence. Before half-time, Bulteel and Kewley led a dribble almost the entire length of the pitch, only for Luscombe to lose control of the ball and sacrifice a certain try. In addition, Gunner narrowly failed to drop a goal.

In the initial attack of the second half the Irish backs brought play to the English goal-line, but Marshall and Graham averted the potential danger with some good relieving kicks. Then Cronyn ran from his own 25 and dodged most of the English team before Pearson foiled him a yard short of glory. Just before no-side England scored their winning goal, Kewley running in for Pearson to convert.

The Graham brothers were capped for England in the same match. E.B. Turner's brother played against Scotland three months later.

IRELAND		ENGLAND	
R.B. Walkington	(North of Ireland)	†S.H.M. Login	(Royal Naval College)
H. Moore	(Windsor)	A.W. Pearson	(Blackheath)
B.N. Casement	(Wanderers)	†C.R. Gunner	(Marlborough Nomads)
E.W. Hobson	(Dublin U.)	A.T. Michell	(Oxford U.)
*R.J. Bell	(North of Ireland)	†C.W.H. Clark	(Liverpool)
A.P. Cronyn	(Dublin U.)	W.E. Collins	(St George's H.)
G. Andrews	(North of Ireland)	†J. Brewer	(Gipsies)
D.T. Arnott	(Lansdowne)	†C.C. Bryden	(Clapham Rovers)
W.H. Ash	(North of Ireland)	†A.J. Bulteel	(Manchester)
H.L. Cox	(Lansdowne)	J.A. Bush	(Clifton)
W.A. Cuscaden	(Bray)	H.J. Graham	(Wimbledon Hornets)
W. Finlay	(Windsor)	†J.D.G. Graham	(Wimbledon Hornets)
R. Galbraith	(Dublin U.)	†W. Greg	(Manchester)
R. Greer	(Kingstown)	W.H.H. Hutchinson	(Hull)
J. Ireland	(Windsor)	E. Kewley	(Liverpool)
J.A. McDonald	(Methodist College)	*F. Luscombe	(Gipsies)
R.M. Maginess	(Dublin U.)	†E.E. Marriott	(Manchester)
E.N. McIlwaine	(North of Ireland)	M.W. Marshall	(Blackheath)
H.D. Walsh	(Dublin U.)	†E.B. Turner	(St George's H.)
A.J. Westby	(Dublin U.)	†C.L. Verelst	(Liverpool)

Tries: Clark, Kewley *Conversion:* Pearson

[1] i.e. 1875–76 season, the match taking place in Dec 1875.

ENGLAND v SCOTLAND 1876

Played at The Oval, London, 6 March 1876
England won by 1G, 1T to Nil

An exciting, fast game with plenty of good running and handling by the back divisions was anticipated by the 4000 spectators who assembled to watch the sixth England–Scotland international match. The ground, which had not been used during the previous fortnight, was firm and in good condition and Scotland, winning the toss, elected to defend the gasometer goal. An even first half followed in which neither pack was able to create any advantage, and the opening score of the match did not come until early in the second period of play. Collins, gathering the ball in his own half, dodged several Scotsmen before passing to his half-back partner, Hutchinson, who ran almost the entire length of the pitch. Beating the Scottish halves with sheer pace and crashing through the three-quarter backs as though they were non-existent, he was grounded just 20 yards from the goal, whereupon Lee, following up at speed, collected the loose ball and ran behind the Scottish posts for a try which Stokes converted with a simple kick.

The Scottish forwards were combining well, but they lacked enterprise and England scored again when Collins touched down for a try after a brilliant run. On this occasion, however, Stokes could not convert, and there was no further scoring. Victory for England had been due to the wonderful running of their backs and the crowd was satisfied with the performance. Of the Scottish backs, Cross alone showed any flair.

T.S. Tetley was the first England international capped from the Bradford club, and W.H. Hunt was the first of three brothers (R. Hunt and J.T. Hunt were the others) to represent England.

ENGLAND		SCOTLAND	
†A.H. Heath	(Oxford U.)	J.S. Carrick	(Glasgow Acads.)
A.W. Pearson	(Blackheath)	T. Chalmers	(Glasgow Acads.)
R.H. Birkett	(Clapham Rovers)	M. Cross	(Glasgow Acads.)
†T.S. Tetley	(Bradford)	N.J. Finlay	(Edinburgh Acads.)
L. Stokes	(Blackheath)	A.K. Stewart	(Edinburgh U.)
W.E. Collins	(St George's H.)	G.Q. Paterson	(Edinburgh Acads.)
†W.C. Hutchinson	(R.I.E. College)	D.H. Watson	(Glasgow Acads.)
F.R. Adams	(Richmond)	A. Arthur	(Glasgow Acads.)
J.A. Bush	(Clifton)	W.H. Bolton	(West of Scotland)
E.C. Cheston	(Richmond)	N.T. Brewis	(Edinburgh Inst.F.P.)
H.J. Graham	(Wimbledon Hornets)	C.W. Cathcart	(Edinburgh U.)
W. Greg	(Manchester)	D. Drew	(Glasgow Acads.)
†W.H. Hunt	(Preston Grasshoppers)	G.R. Fleming	(Glasgow Acads.)
E. Kewley	(Liverpool)	J.H.S. Graham	(Edinburgh Acads.)
†F.H. Lee	(Oxford U.)	*R.W. Irvine	(Edinburgh Acads.)
*F. Luscombe	(Gipsies)	J.E. Junor	(Glasgow Acads.)
M.W. Marshall	(Blackheath)	D. Lang	(Paisley)
†W.C.W. Rawlinson	(Blackheath)	A.G. Petrie	(Royal H.S.F.P.)
†G.R. Turner	(St George's H.)	J. Reid	(Edinburgh Wands.)
R. Walker	(Manchester)	C. Villar	(Edinburgh Wands.)

Tries: Collins, Lee
Conversion: Stokes

Referee: Mr A. Rutter (England)

ENGLAND v IRELAND 1877
Played at The Oval, London, 5 February 1877
England won by 2G, 2T to Nil[1]

Following the example set by Oxford and Cambridge in the 1875 University match, England and Ireland met at The Oval to play in the first international match between teams of fifteen players. England selected a fast, lightweight pack for the occasion, but the Irish forwards were even lighter and, as a result, the home side were able to register a comfortable win.

England, playing with the wind to their advantage in the first half, took the lead early in the match when Hutchinson scored a try after a scrummage near the Irish goal-line and Stokes converted. The Irish backs then displayed their ability to run with the ball, making several useful breaks. Their failure to kick intelligently or drop at goal, however, meant that they were unable to put the opposing backs in any difficulty. Consequently, England dominated the rest of the match. Hornby, playing his first match for England a week before his thirtieth birthday, was often conspicuous with some good kicking and then, after a long run, scored a try before half-time.

In the second half Adams, one of the finest forwards in the game, increased England's lead with another try but the conversion attempt was an unusually poor effort so no goal resulted. England's last try, converted by Stokes, was scored by Hutchinson.

ENGLAND		IRELAND	
L.H. Birkett	(Clapham Rovers)	R.B. Walkington	(North of Ireland)
L. Stokes	(Blackheath)	*R. Galbraith	(Dublin U.)
†A.N. Hornby	(Preston Grasshoppers)	H. Brown	(Windsor)
R.H. Birkett	(Clapham Rovers)	F.W. Kidd	(Lansdowne)
W.C. Hutchinson	(R.I.E. College)	A.M. Whitestone	(Dublin U.)
†P.L.A. Price	(R.I.E. College)	T.G. Gordon	(North of Ireland)
*E. Kewley	(Liverpool)	H.W. Jackson	(Dublin U.)
F.R. Adams	(Richmond)	H.L. Cox	(Dublin U.)
†R.H. Fowler	(Leeds)	W. Finlay	(North of Ireland)
M.W. Marshall	(Blackheath)	J. Ireland	(Windsor)
†G. Harrison	(Hull)	W.H. Wilson	(Dublin U.)
W.H. Hunt	(Preston Grasshoppers)	H.G. Edwards	(Dublin U.)
†C.J.C. Touzel	(Cambridge U.)	H.C. Kelly	(North of Ireland)
F.H. Lee	(Oxford U.)	T. Brown	(Windsor)
E.B. Turner	(St George's H.)	W.J. Hamilton	(Dublin U.)

Tries: Hutchinson (2), Adams, Hornby
Conversions: Stokes (2)

Referee: Mr A.G. Guillemard (England)

[1] Some records neglect Adams's try and give this result as 2G, 1T to Nil.

SCOTLAND v ENGLAND 1877

Played at Raeburn Place, Edinburgh, 5 March 1877
Scotland won by 1DG to Nil

This was the seventh encounter between Scotland and England, and the first fifteen-a-side contest between the teams.

Scotland, cheered on by 5000 spectators, won for the second time in the series. The first half was evenly contested but the second half saw Scotland dominate. Only some relieving dashes and determined tackling by Hornby and Stokes saved England in a dour struggle and Scotland's winning score did not come until the last ten minutes of the match when Malcolm Cross dropped an excellent goal. His kick, from half-way, was helped by a healthy breeze.

SCOTLAND		ENGLAND	
J.S. Carrick	(Glasgow Acads.)	A.W. Pearson	(Blackheath)
H.H. Johnston	(Edinburgh Collegians)	L.H. Birkett	(Clapham Rovers)
M. Cross	(Glasgow Acads.)	A.N. Hornby	(Preston Grasshoppers)
R.C. MacKenzie	(Glasgow Acads.)	L. Stokes	(Blackheath)
J.R. Hay-Gordon	(Edinburgh Acads.)	W.A.D. Evanson	(Richmond)
E.J. Pocock	(Edinburgh Wands.)	P.L.A. Price	(R.I.E. College)
J.H.S. Graham	(Edinburgh Acads.)	C.C. Bryden	(Clapham Rovers)
*R.W. Irvine	(Edinburgh Acads.)	†H.W.T. Garnett	(Bradford)
J.E. Junor	(Glasgow Acads.)	G. Harrison	(Hull)
H.M. Napier	(West of Scotland)	W.H. Hunt	(Preston Grasshoppers)
A.G. Petrie	(Royal H.S.F.P.)	*E. Kewley	(Liverpool)
J. Reid	(Edinburgh Wands.)	†A.F. Law	(Richmond)
T.J. Torrie	(Edinburgh Acads.)	M.W. Marshall	(Blackheath)
C. Villar	(Edinburgh Wands.)	†R. Todd	(Manchester)
D.H. Watson	(Glasgow Acads.)	C.J.C. Touzel	(Cambridge U.)

Dropped goal: Cross

Referee: Mr W. Cross (Scotland)

ENGLAND v SCOTLAND 1878
Played at The Oval, London, 4 March 1878
Drawn, neither side scoring

A disappointing attendance saw the third scoreless draw in this series of matches. The weather was delightful, though a strong wind swept the length of the pitch, and it was thought that the English fifteen, which was reported to be one of the best ever fielded, would win.

Scotland proved otherwise and their mobile forwards dictated the play in the first half when England faced into the wind. In fact, Napier almost scored a try – only a fine tackle by Pearson forcing him into touch in goal – while for England, Kewley ran the length of the field in the best move of the match. In the second half the play swung from goal to goal and the English backs, Hornby and Stokes, each went near to scoring with drops at goal. The Richmond forward, Adams, actually ran in for a try but Mr Guillemard, the referee, disallowed the score. During the game, England were forced to touch down in defence seven times, while the Scots did so four times.

For England, Marshall and Kewley were the outstanding forwards with Cross and Finlay, both backs, the pick of the Scottish team.

G.T. Thomson was the first England international from the Halifax club.

ENGLAND		SCOTLAND	
†H.E. Kayll	(Sunderland)	W.E. MacLagan	(Edinburgh Acads.)
A.W. Pearson	(Blackheath)		
		M. Cross	(Glasgow Acads.)
A.N. Hornby	(Preston Grasshoppers)	N.J. Finlay	(Edinburgh Acads.)
L. Stokes	(Blackheath)		
		J.A. Campbell	(Merchistonians)
W.A.D. Evanson	(Richmond)	J.A. Neilson	(West of Scotland)
P.L.A. Price	(R.I.E. College)		
		L.J. Auldjo	(Abertay)
F.R. Adams	(Richmond)	N.T. Brewis	(Edinburgh Inst.F.P.)
†J.M. Biggs	(U.C.H.)	J.H.S. Graham	(Edinburgh Acads.)
†F.D. Fowler	(R.I.E. College)	D.R. Irvine	(Edinburgh Acads.)
†H. Fowler	(Oxford U.)	*R.W. Irvine	(Edinburgh Acads.)
†E.T. Gurdon	(Old Haileyburians)	G. Macleod	(Edinburgh Acads.)
*E. Kewley	(Liverpool)	H.M. Napier	(West of Scotland)
M.W. Marshall	(Blackheath)	A.G. Petrie	(Royal H.S.F.P.)
†G.T. Thomson	(Halifax)	S.H. Smith	(Glasgow Acads.)
†G.F. Vernon	(Blackheath)	J.E. Junor	(Glasgow Acads.)

Referee: Mr A.G. Guillemard (England)

IRELAND v ENGLAND 1878

Played at Lansdowne Road, Dublin, 11 March 1878
England won by 2G, 1T to Nil

One week after their drawn game with Scotland, England crossed St George's Channel to meet the Irish – the fourth match in this series. Once again, the inability to master the arts of punting and drop-kicking let Ireland down badly, giving England a fairly easy match even though the home pack gave its usual sterling performance.

England took the lead early on when Matier, one of the Irish three-quarters, misjudged a wind-assisted kick ahead and Gardner followed up to snatch a try which Pearson converted from the touch-line. There are conflicting reports as to what happened next. A.G. Guillemard, writing in *Marshall*, describes Penny as scoring a similar try shortly afterwards with Pearson again converting from the touch-line, before Turner obtained his try. However, the *Times*'s report of the match states that the second score followed a run by Bell, who actually crossed the line but failed to ground the ball. The eventual try was credited to Turner and not converted. Then, continued *The Times*, play changed from goal to goal before Hornby scored a try which Pearson converted. All of the scoring took place in the first half.

Clearly, then, a difficult sequence of scoring remains to be resolved, but let us follow other Rugby historians and give Penny the credit of scoring the try which led to England's second goal – the first try obtained by a full-back in international Rugby football.

This was the first international at Lansdowne Road, venue of all England's subsequent matches in Ireland (except in 1905 and 1924). England were the only regular visitors to Dublin in the early days – Scotland first played in Ireland in 1877 but did not visit Dublin until 1894.

IRELAND		ENGLAND	
*R.B. Walkington	(North of Ireland)	†W.J. Penny	(K.C.H.)
		A.W. Pearson	(Blackheath)
R.N. Matier	(North of Ireland)		
F.W. Kidd	(Lansdowne)	A.N. Hornby	(Preston Grasshoppers)
		†H.J. Enthoven	(Richmond)
G.L. Fagan	(Kingstown School)		
T.G. Gordon	(North of Ireland)	†A.H. Jackson	(Guy's H.)
		†J.L. Bell	(Darlington)
E.W.D. Croker	(Limerick)		
W. Moore	(Windsor)	†H.P. Gardner	(Richmond)
F. Schute	(Wanderers)	C.L. Verelst	(Liverpool)
H.W. Murray	(Dublin U.)	†T. Blatherwick	(Manchester)
W. Finlay	(North of Ireland)	*M.W. Marshall	(Blackheath)
J.A. McDonald	(Windsor)	†A. Budd	(Blackheath)
H.G. Edwards	(Dublin U.)	G.F. Vernon	(Blackheath)
H.C. Kelly	(North of Ireland)	W.H. Hunt	(Manchester)
R.W. Hughes	(Windsor)	†E.F. Dawson	(R.I.E. College)
W. Griffiths	(Limerick)	E.B. Turner	(St George's H.)

Tries: Gardner, Penny, Turner
Conversions: Pearson (2)

Referee: Mr E. Swainston (England)

SCOTLAND v ENGLAND 1879
Played at Raeburn Place, Edinburgh, 10 March 1879
Drawn: Scotland 1DG, England 1G

Once again, England and Scotland played a drawn game, England scoring a converted try to a Scottish dropped goal. Scotland kicked off into a strong wind before a crowd of 8000 people and the English forwards began strongly. Evanson made a good run early in the game but it was Burton, playing in his first international match, who opened the scoring when he ran in behind the Scottish posts to give Stokes a simple conversion. In the second half a good dropped goal by Finlay levelled the scores and there were no further goals, though Stokes once struck an upright with a long drop attempt. Other features of the play were the running of the English backs and the steady defensive play of MacLagan – the sole Scottish full-back.

This was the fourth draw in the series of matches and the first game for the Calcutta Cup, which had been presented to the R.F.U. on the dissolution of the Calcutta club in India.

Harry Huth, one of three brothers who played county Rugby for Yorkshire, was the first Huddersfield international.

SCOTLAND		ENGLAND	
W.E. MacLagan	(Edinburgh Acads.)	†H. Huth	(Huddersfield)
		W.J. Penny	(United Hs./K.C.H.)
M. Cross	(Glasgow Acads.)		
N.J. Finlay	(Edinburgh Acads.)	L. Stokes	(Blackheath)
J.A. Campbell	(Glasgow Acads.)	W.A.D. Evanson	(Richmond)
J.A. Neilson	(Glasgow Acads.)	†H.H. Taylor	(St George's H.)
R. Ainslie	(Edinburgh Inst.F.P.)	*F.R. Adams	(Richmond)
N.T. Brewis	(Edinburgh Inst.F.P.)	A. Budd	(Blackheath)
J.B. Brown	(Glasgow Acads.)	†G.W. Burton	(Blackheath)
E.N. Ewart	(Glasgow Acads.)	F.D. Fowler	(Manchester)
J.H.S. Graham	(Edinburgh Acads.)	G. Harrison	(Hull)
D.R. Irvine	(Edinburgh Acads.)	†N.F. McLeod	(R.I.E. College)
*R.W. Irvine	(Edinburgh Acads.)	†S. Neame	(Old Cheltonians)
J.E. Junor	(Glasgow Acads.)	†H.C. Rowley	(Manchester)
H.M. Napier	(West of Scotland)	†H.H. Springman	(Liverpool)
A.G. Petrie	(Royal H.S.F.P.)	R. Walker	(Manchester)

Dropped goal: Finlay   *Try:* Burton   *Conversion:* Stokes

Referee: Mr G.R. Fleming (Scotland)

ENGLAND v IRELAND 1879

Played at The Oval, London, 24 March 1879
England won by 2G, 1DG, 2T to Nil

This match was postponed from 3 February because of a hard frost, and late changes meant that Ireland were unable to field their strongest fifteen. On a bitterly cold afternoon, Ireland defended the gasworks end of the ground after winning the toss and were forced to touch down soon after Adams kicked off, Stokes putting in a dangerous run. For most of the first half, Ireland's backs tackled bravely and attacked strongly – Pike was frequently prominent in both these respects, once stopping Twynam from scoring with a grand tackle. Stokes nearly kicked a goal from a mark when Penny claimed a fair catch from a kick by Casement, and then England took the lead just before half-time when Evanson scored a try which Stokes failed to goal.

In the second half, with the wind behind them, England completely dominated the game and a score resulted from their first attack – Rowley running under the posts for a try converted by Stokes. The Blackheath three-quarter then attempted another goal from a mark, the fair catch this time claimed by Twynam, before dropping a goal to increase England's lead. The Irish forwards worked hard for the next 20 minutes but the pressure on them was too great and, in a final flurry, England added a try by Adams and a goal from a try by Twynam.

This was the seventh and last international match staged at The Oval. In the summer of the following year, the first in a long sequence of Test cricket matches was played at the ground.

J.M. Biggs, a doctor, was the first international to play for Wasps, captaining the club between 1877 and 1879.

ENGLAND		IRELAND	
W.J. Penny	(United Hs./K.C.H.)	W.W. Pike	(Kingstown)
W.A.D. Evanson	(Richmond)	W.J. Willis	(Lansdowne)
L. Stokes	(Blackheath)	J.C. Bagot	(Dublin U.)
†H.T. Twynam	(Richmond)	A.M. Whitestone	(Dublin U.)
†W.E. Openshaw	(Manchester)	J. Heron	(North of Ireland)
†H.D. Bateson	(Liverpool)	B.N. Casement	(Dublin U.)
S. Neame	(Old Cheltonians)	J.R. Bristow	(North of Ireland)
*F.R. Adams	(Richmond)	F. Schute	(Wanderers)
J.M. Biggs	(United Hs./U.C.H.)	H.W. Murray	(Dublin U.)
A. Budd	(Blackheath)	W. Finlay	(North of Ireland)
G. Harrison	(Hull)	J.J. Keon	(Limerick)
G.W. Burton	(Blackheath)	J.L. Cuppaidge	(Dublin U.)
H.C. Rowley	(Manchester)	*W.C. Neville	(Dublin U.)
E.T. Gurdon	(Richmond)	G. Scriven	(Dublin U.)
N.F. McLeod	(R.I.E. College)	H. Purdon	(North of Ireland)

Tries: Adams, Evanson, Rowley, Twynam
Conversions: Stokes (2)
Dropped goal: Stokes

Referee: Mr A.G. Guillemard (England)

IRELAND v ENGLAND 1880

Played at Lansdowne Road, Dublin, 30 January 1880
England won by 1G, 1T to 1T

This was an exciting day for Irish supporters as their team registered their first try in matches against England. This was the seventh match in the series between the countries and for a long time it seemed possible that Ireland could even secure their first victory in international Rugby. To be fair to England, however, one should add that the R.F.U. had great difficulty raising a fifteen for this match, and Lennard Stokes, in his first appearance as captain of England, had to work hard to obtain a victory.

Ireland started the match with the strong wind in their favour and the forwards, as ever, stormed off at a tremendous rate, forcing England to defend. Cuppaidge was the man to make history for Ireland, scoring his try in the first half, but Walkington could not improve the situation, missing the goal.

England had the elements in their favour in the second half, but Ireland started where they had left off at the interval and kept England on the defensive. Slowly, however, England forced their way back into the game, Stokes giving his men encouragement with some huge kicks into the Irish half. Eventually, a period of concentrated pressure resulted in a disastrous five-minute spell for Ireland, during which Markendale and then Ellis scored tries. Hunt failed to convert the first try, but Stokes made no mistake in improving Ellis's effort.

Charles Gurdon followed his brother E. T. Gurdon into the England XV.

Woodhead, a Dublin student, was a late replacement in the England team for a player suffering from the effects of sea sickness.

IRELAND		ENGLAND	
R.B. Walkington	(North of Ireland)	†T.W. Fry	(Queen's House)
		A.N. Hornby	(Manchester)
A.M. Whitestone	(Dublin U.)		
J.C. Bagot	(Dublin U.)	*L. Stokes	(Blackheath)
		†R. Hunt	(Manchester)
W.T. Heron	(North of Ireland)		
M. Johnston	(Dublin U.)	H.T. Twynam	(Richmond)
		A.H. Jackson	(Blackheath)
A.J. Forrest	(Wanderers)		
F. Kennedy	(Wanderers)	S. Neame	(Old Cheltonians)
A. Millar	(Kingstown)	†C. Gurdon	(Richmond)
*H.C. Kelly	(North of Ireland)	†B. Kilner	(Wakefield Trinity)
J.W. Taylor	(North of Ireland)	G.F. Vernon	(Blackheath)
J.A. McDonald	(Wanderers)	†E. Woodhead	(Huddersfield/Dublin U.)
J.L. Cuppaidge	(Wanderers)	†S.S. Ellis	(Queen's House)
R.W. Hughes	(North of Ireland)	H.C. Rowley	(Manchester)
G. Scriven	(Dublin U.)	†J.W. Schofield	(Manchester Rangers)
H. Purdon	(North of Ireland)	†E.T. Markendale	(Manchester Rangers)

Try: Cuppaidge

Tries: Ellis, Markendale
Conversion: Stokes

Referee: Mr G.P. Nugent (Ireland)

Lennard Stokes's makeshift team against Ireland, 1880, heralded a decade of
unparalleled success in which England lost only two of their 22 matches:
standing B. Kilner; *middle* C. Gurdon, S. Neame, G. F. Vernon, A. H. Jackson,
A. N. Hornby, L. Stokes, H. C. Rowley, E. T. Markendale, R. Hunt;
front E. Woodhead, T. W. Fry, S. S. Ellis, J. W. Schofield, H. T. Twynam.
(Woodhead, a student at Dublin U., stood in for a player suffering from the
effects of sea-sickness.)

ENGLAND v SCOTLAND 1880

Played at Whalley Range, Manchester, 28 February 1880
England won by 2G, 3T to 1G

England, fielding one of their strongest-ever combinations, registered their largest victory over Scotland since the beginning of matches between the countries, and thus became the first holders of the Calcutta Cup. Weather conditions were fine for the game but the playing surface was wet and slippery.

Scotland began with the fresh breeze and slope of the ground to their advantage, but the English forwards immediately pushed the Scots deep into their own territory and, after only ten minutes of play, Taylor scored a try from a short burst. Stokes could not convert. Before half-time, Taylor added another English try, but again the captain was unable to convert. The second half began at a tremendous pace and the superior play of the English backs proved decisive – there being little to choose between the two packs. Fry became the first full-back to score a try in England–Scotland matches when he ran in for Stokes to goal with a good kick. But Scotland fought back and Sorley Brown obtained a try which Cross converted into a goal to narrow England's lead. Then, in the last quarter of the match, the English team dominated and E.T. Gurdon and Burton scored further tries, one of which Stokes converted to complete a fine game of Rugby football.

ENGLAND		SCOTLAND	
T.W. Fry	(Queen's House)	W.E. MacLagan	(Edinburgh Acads.)
*L. Stokes	(Blackheath)	M. Cross	(Glasgow Acads.)
†C.M. Sawyer	(Broughton)	N.J. Finlay	(Edinburgh Acads.)
†R.T. Finch	(Cambridge U.)	W.S. Brown	(Edinburgh Inst.F.P.)
H.H. Taylor	(St George's H.)	W.H. Masters	(Edinburgh Inst.F.P.)
G.W. Burton	(Blackheath)	R. Ainslie	(Edinburgh Inst.F.P.)
†C.H. Coates	(Cambridge U.)	N.T. Brewis	(Edinburgh Inst.F.P.)
C. Gurdon	(Richmond)	J.B. Brown	(Glasgow Acads.)
E.T. Gurdon	(Richmond)	D.Y. Cassells	(West of Scotland)
G. Harrison	(Hull)	E.N. Ewart	(Glasgow Acads.)
S. Neame	(Old Cheltonians)	J.H.S. Graham	(Edinburgh Acads.)
†C. Phillips	(Oxford U.)	*R.W. Irvine	(Edinburgh Acads.)
H.C. Rowley	(Manchester)	D. McCowan	(West of Scotland)
G.F. Vernon	(Blackheath)	A.G. Petrie	(Royal H.S.F.P.)
R. Walker	(Manchester)	C.A.R. Stewart	(West of Scotland)

Tries: Taylor (2), Burton, Fry, E.T. Gurdon
Conversions: Stokes (2)

Try: W.S. Brown
Conversion: Cross

Referee: Mr A.G. Guillemard (England)

ENGLAND v IRELAND 1881

Played at Whalley Range, Manchester, 5 February 1881
England won by 2G, 2T to Nil

It was disappointing to record that Ireland, after such a sterling performance in the corresponding fixture of 1880, gave an inept display on English soil. Part of the blame for this disappointment rested with the selection: unfortunately there had been a rift in the Irish Union and as a result the team was not fully representative of the country. In fact, fourteen of the Irish side were from Southern Ireland, and Purdon, the only Northerner in the ranks, was made to play out of position at forward. By contrast, England fielded a very strong combination.

England began by defending the pavilion end of the ground, though in the early stages the pack appeared rather sluggish. Spunner made some clever runs for Ireland, as did Sawyer for England. The only score of the first half was a try by Taylor which was not goaled.

In the second half the Irish were outplayed and three more tries resulted. *Marshall* credits another two scores to Lancastrians – Hornby the back and Sawyer the three-quarter – while the report of the match which appeared in the Monday edition of *The Times* records the try by Sawyer (the third of the match) but gives the other to Taylor. Both reports add that Taylor scored the final try too – giving him either two or three for the match. The goals were placed by Stokes, captaining England for the third time, off the last two tries.

Phillips and Ravenscroft were the first players capped direct from Birkenhead Park club. Both had played in the Varsity match of 1878–79, while Phillips had captained Oxford University in 1879–80 at the time of his initial appearance for England.

ENGLAND		IRELAND	
A.N. Hornby	(Manchester)	T. Harrison	(Cork)
C.M. Sawyer	(Broughton)	W. Peirce	(Cork)
*L. Stokes	(Blackheath)	W.W. Pike	(Kingstown)
†W.R. Richardson	(Manchester)	H.F. Spunner	(Tipperary)
H.H. Taylor	(Blackheath)	M. Johnston	(Dublin U.)
†J.I. Ward	(Richmond)	*A.J. Forrest	(Dublin U.)
†C.W.L. Fernandes	(Leeds)	D.R. Browning	(Wanderers)
C. Gurdon	(Richmond)	J.C.S. Burkitt	(Cork)
C. Phillips	(Birkenhead Park)	F. Kennedy	(Wanderers)
G.F. Vernon	(Blackheath)	H.B. Morell	(Dublin U.)
†J. Ravenscroft	(Birkenhead Park)	W.E.A. Cummins	(Cork)
G.W. Burton	(Blackheath)	W.A. Wallis	(Dublin U.)
H.C. Rowley	(Manchester)	A.R. McMullen	(Cork)
E.T. Gurdon	(Richmond)	G. Scriven	(Dublin U.)
†W.W. Hewitt	(Queen's House)	H. Purdon	(North of Ireland)

Tries: Taylor (3), Sawyer
Conversions: Stokes (2)

Referee: Mr A.G. Guillemard (England)

ENGLAND v WALES 1881

Played at Richardson's Field, Blackheath, 19 February 1881
England won by 7G, 1DG, 6T to Nil

After several creditable performances against the county sides of English Rugby, including Gloucestershire and Somerset, Wales, the youngest of the four home countries, were awarded their first fixture in international Rugby against the strong English team. The result – the largest win by any team in an official international match – was regarded as a disaster in Wales and, as a consequence, was directly responsible for the formation of the W.F.U. in March 1881.

England completely overwhelmed the Welsh, who later claimed that this team was not fully representative of the strong South Wales clubs. Two of the English forwards – Vassall, in his first international, and Burton – scored seven tries between them, and Burton's four remain a record for a forward in matches at this level (although Cornelsen, an Australian forward, obtained four against New Zealand in 1978).

Reports of the match give little attention to the deeds of the visiting team, but one record does mention that Treharne of Pontypridd was the best of the Welsh forwards. There was also an unusual incident in this match: a long pass by Stokes to Hunt enabled the three-quarter to score a try without a Welshman laying a hand on him, but the English referee ruled that such a tactic was 'not football' and the try was disallowed.

This was the first international match to be played in Blackheath, though the only one staged at Richardson's Field, for the land was later acquired by a builder and the Blackheath Club was forced to move to the Rectory Field shortly afterwards. The teams changed at the Princess of Wales, a hostelry on the Heath, and walked the half-mile to the ground. Today, the Princess of Wales is still a popular public-house.

ENGLAND		WALES	
T.W. Fry	(Queen's House)	R.H.B. Summers	(Haverfordwest)
		C.H. Newman	(Newport)
*L. Stokes	(Blackheath)		
R. Hunt	(Manchester)	*J.A. Bevan	(Grosmont)
		E. Peake	(Chepstow)
H.H. Taylor	(Blackheath)		
H.T. Twynam	(Richmond)	E.J. Lewis	(Llandovery)
		L. Watkins	(Llandaff)
H. Fowler	(Walthamstow)		
H.C. Rowley	(Manchester)	E. Treharne	(Pontypridd)
†C.P. Wilson	(Cambridge U.)	G. Darbishire	(Bangor)
W.W. Hewitt	(Queen's House)	W.D. Phillips	(Cardiff)
C. Gurdon	(Richmond)	B.B. Mann	(Cardiff)
E.T. Gurdon	(Richmond)	B.E. Girling	(Cardiff)
C.W.L. Fernandes	(Leeds)	G.F. Harding	(Newport)
G.W. Burton	(Blackheath)	F. Purdon	(Newport)
A. Budd	(Blackheath)	T.A. Rees	(Llandovery)
†H. Vassall	(Oxford U.)	R.D.G. Williams	(Newport)

Tries: Burton (4), Vassall (3), Budd,
Fernandes, Hunt, Rowley,
Taylor, Twynam
Conversions: Stokes (6), Hunt
Dropped goal: Hunt

Referee: Mr A.G. Guillemard (England)

SCOTLAND v ENGLAND 1881

Played at Raeburn Place, Edinburgh, 19 March 1881
Drawn: Scotland 1G, 1T, England 1DG, 1T

This match was played in perfect conditions before a crowd of more than 10,000 spectators. England had to rearrange their line-up when H.H. Taylor missed the train to Scotland – his place was occupied by Wright, who was a pupil at Edinburgh Academy – and Rowley, usually a forward, strengthened the halves in the absence of C.M. Sawyer.

Scotland had the advantage of the wind in the first half and the scoring opened when R. Ainslie crossed for a try after making a determined run: Begbie's conversion attempt struck an upright. After this, the contest became a battle between the English forwards and the Scottish backs, Fowler and the Gurdon brothers leading many threatening foot rushes only to be repulsed by splendid relieving runs out of defence by the Scottish backs. Reid actually crossed the English line on one occasion but could not ground the ball to give his side a greater lead. In the second half, Stokes put England ahead with an 80-yards dropped goal – a colossal effort by all accounts – and this so stirred the English forwards that they became unstoppable and Rowley scored a try. This was not goaled and Scotland, encouraged by the large crowd, slowly came back into the game. In the last five minutes, Finlay narrowly missed a drop at goal and Brown, following up, gathered the loose ball and touched down beneath the posts. The English players thought that Brown was off-side and had not challenged him. A dispute followed but the try stood, Begbie converted, and the game was left drawn.

The outstanding Scottish performers in this match were R. Ainslie, Brown and Campbell, while Rowley for England completely outplayed Don Wauchope, Scotland's famous half-back.

This was Len Stokes's last match for England. His career record of 17 conversions in internationals remains an England record 100 years later. He was the brother of Fred Stokes.

Edinburgh Academy had a pupil in each team – a unique distinction for a school.

SCOTLAND		ENGLAND	
T.A. Begbie	(Edinburgh Wands.)	A.N. Hornby	(Manchester)
W.E. MacLagan	(Edinburgh Acads.)	*L. Stokes	(Blackheath)
N.J. Finlay	(Edinburgh Acads.)	R. Hunt	(Manchester)
R.C. MacKenzie	(Glasgow Acads.)		
		†F.T. Wright	(Manchester/ Edinburgh Academy)
A.R. Don Wauchope	(Cambridge U.)	H.C. Rowley	(Manchester)
J.A. Campbell	(Glasgow Acads.)		
		G.W. Burton	(Blackheath)
*J.H.S. Graham	(Edinburgh Acads.)	C.H. Coates	(Leeds)
C. Reid	(Edinburgh Academy)	C.W.L. Fernandes	(Leeds)
J.W. Fraser	(Edinburgh Inst.F.P.)	H. Vassall	(Oxford U.)
D. McCowan	(West of Scotland)	C. Phillips	(Birkenhead Park)
R. Maitland	(Edinburgh Inst.F.P.)	H. Fowler	(Walthamstow)
J.B. Brown	(Glasgow Acads.)	W.W. Hewitt	(Queen's House)
T. Ainslie	(Edinburgh Inst.F.P.)	C. Gurdon	(Richmond)
R. Ainslie	(Edinburgh Inst.F.P.)	E.T. Gurdon	(Richmond)
W.A. Peterkin	(Edinburgh U.)	A. Budd	(Blackheath)

Tries: R. Ainslie, Brown
Conversion: Begbie

Try: Rowley
Dropped goal: Stokes

Referee: Mr D.H. Watson (Scotland)

IRELAND v ENGLAND 1882

Played at Lansdowne Road, Dublin, 6 February 1882
Drawn: Ireland 2T, England 2T

This was Ireland's most successful effort against England since the inception of matches in 1875. The match was played on a Monday, as were most of the early internationals, and 5000 were present to see an evenly-contested game with Ireland the unluckier of the sides. The pitch, as usual in Dublin, was in fine condition and a fast match took place.

Ireland made an encouraging start because Stokes scored a try almost from the kick-off, though Walkington was unable to convert. England had quite a strong combination in the field, but many criticised the standard of play in the open. There were several brilliant individual runs, but the combined work of the visitors was well below their usual level. Nevertheless, England led as the game entered its closing stages, tries by Hunt and Bolton, the latter on his debut for England, giving them a rather undeserved lead.

Ireland then appeared to have won the contest, for Johnston scored a try after some excellent work by Taylor and McLean kicked a 'winning goal'. To the dismay and amazement of the teams, Dr Nugent, the umpire, disallowed the kick, and thus the scoring stood even.

The Irish were unlucky again when Morell crossed for a seemingly valid try, but because the referee and the umpire were unsighted, the score could not be allowed. Thus Ireland held the English for the first time in a draw which the famous Irish Rugby commentator, Jacques McCarthy, described as 'altogether in favour of Ireland'.

IRELAND		ENGLAND	
R.B. Walkington	(N.I.F.C.)	A.N. Hornby	(Manchester)
R.E. McLean	(Dublin U.)	†W.N. Bolton	(Blackheath)
E.J. Wolfe	(N.I.F.C.)	†E. Beswick	(Swinton)
W.W. Pike	(Kingstown)	R. Hunt	(Manchester)
M. Johnston	(Dublin U.)	H.T. Twynam	(Richmond)
G.C. Bent	(Dublin U.)	H.C. Rowley	(Manchester)
A.J. Forrest	(Wanderers)	J.I. Ward	(Richmond)
*J.W. Taylor	(N.I.F.C.)	*C. Gurdon	(Richmond)
R. Nelson	(Queen's U.)	†B.B. Middleton	(Birkenhead Park)
H.B. Morell	(Dublin U.)	H. Vassall	(Oxford U.)
W.E.A. Cummins	(Cork)	†H.G. Fuller	(Cambridge U.)
J.A. McDonald	(Queen's U.)	†J.T. Hunt	(Manchester)
R.W. Hughes	(N.I.F.C.)	G.T. Thomson	(Halifax)
O.S. Stokes	(Cork Bankers)	†A. Spurling	(Blackheath)
T.R. Johnstone-Smythe	(Lansdowne)	W.W. Hewitt	(Queen's House)

Tries: Johnston, Stokes   *Tries:* Bolton, R. Hunt

Referee: Dr W.C. Neville (Ireland)

ENGLAND v SCOTLAND 1882
Played at Whalley Range, Manchester, 4 March 1882
Scotland won by 2T to Nil

Scotland became the first team to win away from home in the England–Scotland series of matches with this victory on a wet, heavy ground which slowed an English pack that was heavier than the Scots. A huge crowd overlapped the by-lines; but for this fact, Payne would probably have scored a try for England after making the best run of the match.

The Scottish halves were responsible for the English downfall in the match, adopting some clever tactics, and there was excellent combined play by the Scottish forwards. One of them, R. Ainslie, opened the scoring after Don Wauchope had run almost the length of the pitch; and just before the interval, Scotland nearly increased their lead when MacLagan had a dropped goal from a mark disallowed. Soon after half-time, however, Scotland made victory complete when Ainslie crossed for his second try of the match, which Walker failed to convert.

The English skipper, Hornby, was below his best form at back; and without Lennard Stokes, who had retired from the game, this was the weakest English back division for years. Scotland had thoroughly deserved their first win on English soil, dominating at forward and at back throughout the match.

This was the first international match controlled by a neutral referee.

ENGLAND		SCOTLAND	
*A.N. Hornby	(Manchester)	J.P. Veitch	(Royal H.S.F.P.)
W.N. Bolton	(Blackheath)	W.E. MacLagan	(Edinburgh Acads.)
E. Beswick	(Swinton)	A. Philp	(Edinburgh Inst.F.P.)
H.H. Taylor	(Blackheath)	W.S. Brown	(Edinburgh Inst.F.P.)
†J.H. Payne	(Broughton)	A.R. Don Wauchope	(Cambridge U.)
C.H. Coates	(Yorkshire Wands.)	R. Ainslie	(Edinburgh Inst.F.P.)
H.G. Fuller	(Cambridge U.)	T. Ainslie	(Edinburgh Inst.F.P.)
C. Gurdon	(Richmond)	J.B. Brown	(Glasgow Acads.)
E.T. Gurdon	(Richmond)	*D.Y. Cassels	(West of Scotland)
J.T. Hunt	(Manchester)	R. Maitland	(Edinburgh Inst.F.P.)
†P.A. Newton	(Blackheath)	D. McCowan	(West of Scotland)
H.C. Rowley	(Manchester)	C. Reid	(Edinburgh Acads.)
†W.M. Tatham	(Oxford U.)	A. Walker	(West of Scotland)
G.T. Thomson	(Halifax)	J.G. Walker	(West of Scotland)
H. Vassall	(Oxford U.)	W.A. Walls	(Glasgow Acads.)

Tries: R. Ainslie (2)

Referee: Mr. H.L. Robinson (Ireland)

WALES v ENGLAND 1883[1]

Played at St Helen's, Swansea, 16 December 1882
England won by 2G, 4T to Nil

After their disastrous entry to international Rugby at Blackheath in 1881, Wales were not granted a full international with the English side in the 1882 season, though a Welsh national XV was chosen for a sequence of matches against the North of England, the English Midlands and Ireland in January 1882. The good performances of the Welsh team in these three matches earned them another full international against the English in 1882–83, and this game at St Helen's was the first such match to be played in Wales.

3000 spectators were present to see Wales make a promising start. Gwynn nearly dropped a goal, but before half-time England had established a convincing lead. Tatham sent Bolton over for the first try and Evanson landed the opening goal of the match off a try scored by Wade and made by Rotherham. Wade, a late replacement for Newton in the English XV, was the outstanding player of the match and a run of his created the next try (by Thomson). Evanson's conversion was declared a 'poster'. Wade then completed his hat-trick with a try under the posts, which Evanson failed to make into a goal, just before the interval; and another in the second half from a scrummage on the Welsh 25. Excellent runs by Bolton and Fuller set up England's last try – by Henderson – and Evanson kicked his second goal.

The English side was a strong one and their combined play was spectacular. Accounts of the match also refer to the general improvement shown by the Welsh, who frequently pressed their opponents.

Evanson's brother had been capped for England earlier, in 1875; Taylor's brother in 1879.

WALES		ENGLAND	
*C.P. Lewis	(Llandovery)	†A.S. Taylor	(Blackheath)
D.H. Bowen	(Llanelli)		
		W.N. Bolton	(Blackheath/R.M.A.)
W.B. Norton	(Cardiff/Carmarthen)	†A.M. Evanson	(Oxford U.)
J. Clare	(Cardiff)	†C.G. Wade	(Oxford U.)
D. Gwynn	(Swansea)		
		†A. Rotherham	(Oxford U.)
C.H. Newman	(Newport)	J.H. Payne	(Broughton)
E. Treharne	(Pontypridd)		
		*E.T. Gurdon	(Richmond)
T. Baker-Jones	(Newport)	H. Vassall	(Oxford U.)
T.J.S. Clapp	(Nantyglo/Newport)	G.T. Thomson	(Halifax)
R. Gould	(Newport)	W.M. Tatham	(Oxford U.)
J.H. Judson	(Llandovery/Llanelli)	H.G. Fuller	(Cambridge U.)
G.F. Harding	(Newport)	†G. Standing	(Blackheath)
F. Purdon	(Swansea)	†R.S.F. Henderson	(Blackheath)
G.L. Morris	(Swansea)	†C.S. Wooldridge	(Oxford U.)
A. Cattell	(Llanelli)	†R.S. Kindersley	(Oxford U.)

Tries: Wade (3), Bolton, Henderson, Thomson
Conversions: Evanson (2)

Referee: Mr Herbert (Wales)

[1] i.e. 1882–83 season, the match taking place in Dec 1882.

ENGLAND v IRELAND 1883

Played at Whalley Range, Manchester, 5 February 1883
England won by 1G, 3T to 1T

Ireland were not without their problems when they travelled to Manchester to face England. For a start, the accounts of the Irish R.F.U. had been described as 'quite unintelligible' at the A.G.M. of the Union on 20 January and, as a result, no travelling expenses were allowed for the journey. In addition, the sea crossing was apparently appalling , and one of the players, Hughes, was so ill en-route that it was necessary to carry him to the team's hotel when the ship eventually docked. He was forced to retire at an early stage in the game – Ireland playing with fourteen men against a strong English XV.

Ireland played into bright sunshine in the first half and Morrow, the Irish full-back, had an unfortunate time. The English three-quarters began in entertaining fashion, passing and running skilfully. Wade and Bolton scored fine tries and Evanson added a conversion to an effort by Tatham – the best of the English forwards. (The *Irish Times* account of the match awarded the first try to Payne (28th minute); the second to Taylor in the 38th minute. Tatham's try was scored immediately before the pause).

Some inspired play by Forrest gave the Irish fresh hope, and their scrummaging and dribbling proved superior to that of the English pack, who generally disappointed the Manchester crowd. In fact, the scores were even in the second half with Forrest securing a good try for Ireland and Twynam getting the last score of the match just on no-side.

It was predicted, correctly, that several changes would be made to the English combination before the match with Scotland.

ENGLAND		IRELAND	
A.S. Taylor	(Blackheath)	R.W. Morrow	(Queen's U.)
W.N. Bolton	(Blackheath)	R.E. McLean	(N.I.F.C.)
A.M. Evanson	(Oxford U.)	R.H. Scovell	(Kingstown)
C.G. Wade	(Oxford U.)		
		W.W. Fletcher	(Kingstown)
J.H. Payne	(Broughton)	J.P. Warren	(Kingstown)
H.T. Twynam	(Richmond)		
		S.A.M. Bruce	(N.I.F.C.)
W.M. Tatham	(Oxford U.)	A.J. Forrest	(Wanderers)
G. Standing	(Blackheath)	J.W. Taylor	(Queen's U.)
C.S. Wooldridge	(Oxford U.)	A. Millar	(Kingstown)
B.B. Middleton	(Birkenhead Park)	D.F. Moore	(Wanderers)
H.G. Fuller	(Cambridge U.)	H. King	(Dublin U.)
†R.M. Pattisson	(Cambridge U.)	J.A. McDonald	(Queen's U.)
G.T. Thomson	(Halifax)	R.W. Hughes	(N.I.F.C.)
*E.T. Gurdon	(Richmond)	F.S. Heuston	(Kingstown)
†E.J. Moore	(Oxford U.)	*G. Scriven	(Dublin U.)

Tries: Bolton, Tatham, Twynam, Wade
Conversion: Evanson

Try: Forrest

Referee: Mr A.S. Pattisson (Scotland)

SCOTLAND v ENGLAND 1883

Played at Raeburn Place, Edinburgh, 3 March 1883
England won by 2T to 1T

England gained revenge for their defeat of the previous season with their first victory on Scottish soil. The game was an excellent display of Rugby football, both packs of forwards foraging relentlessly and the backs running and handling cleverly.

Scotland won the toss and immediately their ten forwards rushed the nine members of the English pack back into their 25. England overcame this initial onslaught and began to play the scientific passing game which former international, H. Vassall, had evolved at Oxford University. Slowly, English pressure built up and Rotherham, one of the seven Oxford men in the team, scored a try which Evanson failed to convert. The game continued evenly until the interval, Scotland preferring to use their traditional rush-and-break tactics to the organised passing between backs and forwards adopted by the English. Only the brave, steady tackling of the new English full-back prevented Scotland scoring. After half-time, the game was confined to the forwards and both packs scrummaged well. Scotland equalised when Reid touched down for a try after following a kick ahead, but MacLagan missed the conversion. Then, in an exciting finish, Bolton settled the issue with a try beneath the posts after a good run. Though the simple conversion failed, it did not matter for there was no further scoring.

Both teams played attractive football. Outstanding for England were Tristram, Allan Rotherham, the Gurdons and Bolton; while Reid, the try-scorer, was the best Scotsman.

By defeating Wales, Ireland and Scotland, England had become the first 'holders' of the mythical trophy known as the Triple Crown.

SCOTLAND		ENGLAND	
D.W. Kidston	(Glasgow Acads.)	†H.B. Tristram	(Oxford U.)
W.E. MacLagan	(London Scottish)	W.N. Bolton	(Blackheath)
M.F. Reid	(Loretto)	A.M. Evanson	(Oxford U.)
		C.G. Wade	(Oxford U.)
P.W. Smeaton	(Edinburgh Acads.)		
W.S. Brown	(Edinburgh Inst.F.P.)	A. Rotherham	(Oxford U.)
		J.H. Payne	(Broughton)
T. Ainslie	(Edinburgh Inst.F.P.)		
J.B. Brown	(Glasgow Acads.)	H.G. Fuller	(Cambridge U.)
*D.Y. Cassels	(West of Scotland)	C. Gurdon	(Richmond)
D. McCowan	(West of Scotland)	*E.T. Gurdon	(Richmond)
J.G. Mowat	(Glasgow Acads.)	R.S.F. Henderson	(Blackheath)
C. Reid	(Edinburgh Acads.)	E.J. Moore	(Oxford U.)
D. Somerville	(Edinburgh Inst.F.P.)	R.M. Pattisson	(Cambridge U.)
J. Jamieson	(West of Scotland)	W.M. Tatham	(Oxford U.)
A. Walker	(West of Scotland)	G.T. Thomson	(Halifax)
W.A. Walls	(Glasgow Acads.)	C.S. Wooldridge	(Oxford U.)

Try: C. Reid *Tries:* Bolton, Rotherham

Referee: Mr H.C. Kelly (Ireland)

ENGLAND v WALES 1884

Played at Cardigan Fields, Leeds, 5 January 1884
England won by 1G, 2T to 1G

Conditions were wet for this first international match to be played in Yorkshire and handling was difficult. Despite the conditions, however, the English backs posed many problems to their opponents and frequently ran the ball along the threequarter line. Chapman tended to overlook his wings, but Wade still managed to open the scoring with the only try of the first half. In the second half Bolton ran 75 yards to send Rotherham in for a try (converted by Bolton) and a dribble by Charles Gurdon led to a try by Twynam.

Gwynn and Newman, the Welsh halves, worked efficiently behind a very light pack and, at length, their industry was rewarded when Wales registered their first score in England–Wales matches, Allen touching down for a try after a kick ahead and chase. Lewis converted and Wales very nearly beat the English when C.G. Taylor, described by his contemporaries as the finest drop-kicker in the British Isles, narrowly failed with a drop at goal during the match. (At this time a match could be won by a majority of goals, tries counting only when the tally of goals was equal.)

ENGLAND		WALES	
H.B. Tristram	(Oxford U.)	C.P. Lewis	(Llandovery)
C.G. Wade	(Oxford U.)	C.P. Allen	(Beaumaris)
†C.E. Chapman	(Cambridge U.)	W.B. Norton	(Cardiff)
W.N. Bolton	(Blackheath)	C.G. Taylor	(Ruabon)
A. Rotherham	(Oxford U.)	W.H. Gwynn	(Swansea)
H.T. Twynam	(Richmond)	*C.H. Newman	(Newport)
J.T. Hunt	(Manchester)	F.L. Margrave	(Llanelli)
C.S. Wooldridge	(Blackheath)	W.D. Phillips	(Cardiff)
†C.J.B. Marriott	(Cambridge U.)	H.J. Simpson	(Cardiff)
H.G. Fuller	(Cambridge U.)	F.G. Andrews	(Swansea)
†E.L. Strong	(Oxford U.)	T.J.S. Clapp	(Newport)
W.M. Tatham	(Oxford U.)	R. Gould	(Newport)
R.S.F. Henderson	(Blackheath)	H.S. Lyne	(Newport)
C. Gurdon	(Richmond)	G.L. Morris	(Swansea)
*E.T. Gurdon	(Richmond)	J.S. Smith	(Cardiff)

Tries: Rotherham, Twynam, Wade   *Try:* Allen
Conversion: Bolton   *Conversion:* Lewis

Referee: Mr J.A. Gardner (Scotland)

IRELAND v ENGLAND 1884

Played at Lansdowne Road, Dublin, 4 February 1884
England won by 1G to Nil

England had a most unusual side out this day. There were no fewer than eight changes from the side which defeated Wales at Leeds a month earlier, and several of the men who won their English caps on this occasion were never called upon subsequently. Doubtless they never forgot their only appearances for their country, particularly as it was England's fifth consecutive international victory under the captaincy of E.T. Gurdon.

Fine weather and one of Dublin's largest-ever crowds greeted the sides at the start of the game, and Ireland were the first team to attack. In a hectic opening, England were forced to touch down in defence. Fortunately, the English forwards were in sound form and managed to avert the danger. After surviving the early onslaught, England created a few attacks, too, forcing Ireland to touch down before Payne sent Bolton over for a fine try which Sample converted. Ireland were not happy about the circumstances surrounding this score, claiming that the try-scoring pass had been forward, but their objections were overruled.

Ireland suffered a serious setback early in the second half when Bruce broke a leg and was forced to retire. The home side played pluckily for the remainder of the match, however, and only a desperate, but effective, tackle by Payne on Johnston deprived Ireland of a late try. It was reported that the Irish backs lacked penetration on this occasion, otherwise they must surely have won the match.

Henry Bell was New Brighton's first England player.

IRELAND		ENGLAND	
R.W. Morrow	(Belfast Albion)	†C.H. Sample	(Cambridge U.)
R.E. McLean	(N.I.F.C.)	W.N. Bolton	(Blackheath)
R.H. Scovell	(Dublin U.)	†H.J. Wigglesworth	(Thornes)
D.J. Ross	(Belfast Albion)	†H. Fallas	(Wakefield Trinity)
M. Johnston	(Dublin U.)	J.H. Payne	(Broughton)
W.W. Higgins	(N.I.F.C.)	H.T. Twynam	(Richmond)
S.A.M. Bruce	(N.I.F.C.)	W.M. Tatham	(Oxford U.)
F.H. Levis	(Wanderers)	†A. Wood	(Halifax)
H.M. Brabazon	(Dublin U.)	C.S. Wooldridge	(Blackheath)
D.F. Moore	(Wanderers)	†A. Teggin	(Broughton Rangers)
J.B.W. Buchanan	(Dublin U.)	†H. Bell	(New Brighton)
*J.A. McDonald	(Queen's U.)	E.L. Strong	(Oxford U.)
R.W. Hughes	(N.I.F.C.)	G.T. Thomson	(Halifax)
W.G. Rutherford	(Tipperary)	*E.T. Gurdon	(Richmond)
O.S. Stokes	(Cork Bankers)	C.J.B. Marriott	(Cambridge U.)

Try: Bolton
Conversion: Sample

Referee: Mr J. S. Lang (Scotland)

ENGLAND v SCOTLAND 1884
Played at Rectory Field, Blackheath, 1 March 1884
England won by 1G to 1T

A crowd of 8000 saw this game on a cold, sunny day with the pitch in perfect shape. England, playing against the wind and with the sun in their faces at the start of the game, were immediately under pressure from a series of Scottish foot-rushes. MacLagan made a determined run which was halted with a good tackle by Rotherham, the English half, who then put in a run which took his team to the Scottish line for the first time in the match. Veitch cleared his goal with a kick to touch and from the resulting line-out Grant Asher and Don Wauchope made a threatening run. Eventually, Scotland forced a five-yard-scrum and Jamieson followed a short kick ahead to score a try which Berry failed to convert. (The report of this match in *Marshall* credits the try to Charles Reid). Until the interval England attacked incessantly and Wade, Bolton, Twynam and Rotherham almost ran in for tries, MacLagan and Grant Asher defending staunchly for the Scots. Bolton failed to place a simple goal from a mark by Rotherham.

The second half began with a Scottish onslaught; their forwards completely outplayed the English pack and Macfarlan just missed a drop at goal, while both halves constantly tried to run in. England rallied, and from a scrum near the Scottish line Twynam fed C. Gurdon and the ball reached Kindersley, who scored at the posts. A dispute arose delaying play for ten minutes: the Scots claimed that there had been a knock-back on their side but since this would have given the English an advantage anyway, the Scottish appeal was overruled, and at length Bolton converted the try to give England the lead. Scotland tried desperately in the dying moments to snatch the win they deserved, and Roland made an 80-yards sprint down the right wing in the last move of the match. England prevented a score, held on for victory and gained the Triple Crown, once again.

The dispute concerning Kindersley's try ultimately led to the formation of the International Board in 1890 – there being only two further fixtures in this series before that date.

ENGLAND		SCOTLAND	
H.B. Tristram	(Oxford U.)	J.P. Veitch	(Royal H.S.F.P.)
W.N. Bolton	(Blackheath)	*W.E. MacLagan	(London Scottish)
A.M. Evanson	(Richmond)	E.T. Roland	(Edinburgh Wands.)
C.G. Wade	(Oxford U.)	D.J. Macfarlan	(London Scottish)
A. Rotherham	(Oxford U.)	A.G.G. Asher	(Oxford U.)
H.T. Twynam	(Richmond)	A.R. Don Wauchope	(Edinburgh Wands.)
C. Gurdon	(Richmond)	T. Ainslie	(Edinburgh Inst.F.P.)
*E.T. Gurdon	(Richmond)	J.B. Brown	(Glasgow Acads.)
R.S.F. Henderson	(Blackheath)	C.W. Berry	(Oxford U.)
R.S. Kindersley	(Oxford U./Exeter)	J. Jamieson	(West of Scotland)
C.J.B. Marriott	(Cambridge U./Blackheath)	D. McCowan	(West of Scotland)
E.L. Strong	(Oxford U.)	W.A. Peterkin	(Edinburgh U.)
W.M. Tatham	(Oxford U.)	C. Reid	(Edinburgh Acads.)
G.T. Thomson	(Halifax)	J. Tod	(Watsonians)
C.S. Wooldridge	(Blackheath)	W.A. Walls	(Glasgow Acads.)

Try: Kindersley   *Try:* Jamieson
Conversion: Bolton

Referee: Mr G. Scriven (Ireland)

E. T. Gurdon's run of success in the early 1880s is legendary. He captained England to eight victories in a row and never lost a match. This is his Triple Crown winning side against Scotland, 1884:
standing C. G. Wade, W. M. Tatham, E. L. Strong, C. Gurdon, R. S. Kindersley, A. M. Evanson, A. Rotherham, G. T. Thomson, C. S. Wooldridge, W. N. Bolton; *sitting* R. S. F. Henderson, H. T. Twynam, E. T. Gurdon, H. B. Tristram, C. J. B. Marriott.

Charles Gurdon, one of the leading players of the 1880s and brother of E. T. Gurdon.

WALES v ENGLAND 1885

Played at St Helen's, Swansea, 3 January 1885
England won by 1G, 4T to 1G, 1T

England fielded one of their strongest-ever back divisions and showed fine style in overrunning a competent Welsh team. The play of the home side was a little disappointing after the encouraging performance of the previous season at Leeds, for despite holding the English forwards in the tight play, they were totally outclassed in the open and the English halves passed and dodged with precision and speed.

A crowd of 5000 witnessed a very fast match in a driving wind and steady drizzle. The first pressure on the Welsh goal resulted from a determined run by Hawcridge and soon after Payne gathered a loose ball to send Ryalls over for a try which Tristram failed to convert. Jordan was the best of the Welshmen: he had one good run in the first half, stopped a run by Ryalls which looked as if it would yield a try just before the interval, and levelled the scores in the second half with a try after Gwynn and Taylor moved the ball smoothly from a loose scrum. Taylor failed to convert this try and from the restart (on the English 25) the visitors made a tremendous rush down into the Welsh 25, where Teggin was up to take a pass and score.

Hawcridge increased England's lead with a try after clever work by Rotherham and Harrison, and further English pressure provided Kindersley with a try. Payne kicked the goal before the diminutive Jordan raced clear for a Welsh try which Gould converted. A dancing, darting run by Wade led to the last try of the match.

R. S. Kindersley became the first England player capped direct from the Exeter club.

WALES		ENGLAND	
A.J. Gould	(Newport)	H.B. Tristram	(Oxford U.)
H.M. Jordan	(Newport)	C.G. Wade	(Oxford U.)
F.E. Hancock	(Cardiff)	†A.E. Stoddart	(Blackheath)
C.G. Taylor	(Ruabon)	†J.J. Hawcridge	(Bradford)
W.H. Gwynn	(Swansea)	J.H. Payne	(Broughton)
*C.H. Newman	(Newport)	A. Rotherham	(Oxford U.)
J. Rowlands	(Lampeter)	*E.T. Gurdon	(Richmond)
J.S. Smith	(Cardiff)	R.S. Kindersley	(Exeter)
L.C. Thomas	(Cardiff)	†E.D. Court	(Blackheath)
E.S. Richards	(Swansea)	†H.J. Ryalls	(New Brighton)
S.J. Goldsworthy	(Swansea)	†F. Moss	(Broughton)
H.S. Lyne	(Newport)	†A.T. Kemble	(Liverpool)
T. Baker-Jones	(Newport)	R.S.F. Henderson	(Blackheath)
R. Gould	(Newport)	A. Teggin	(Broughton Rangers)
T.J.S. Clapp	(Newport)	G. Harrison	(Hull)

Tries: Jordan (2)
Conversion: A.J. Gould

Tries: Hawcridge, Kindersley, Ryalls, Teggin, Wade
Conversion: Payne

Referee: Mr C.P. Lewis (Wales)

ENGLAND v IRELAND 1885

Played at Whalley Range, Manchester, 7 February 1885
England won by 2T to 1T

England were disappointing in this match, only the backs managing to find their top form and ultimately winning the game. Budd, writing in *Marshall*, observed that the form of the English side was nothing approaching the brilliancy shown in the Welsh match, and added, 'the English forwards were palpably worsted by the Irishmen in the scrummage.'

Indeed, the Irish forwards did play well, though they were rather slow to release the ball and allow the backs to start moving. There was one glorious exception to this, however, in the early stages of the game. Playing against the wind, Ireland began with tremendous pace and pressed England into their 25, where a classical round of passing between Crawford, McLean and Greene resulted in a splendid try by Greene. The conversion failed, but the 7000 spectators cheered England earnestly, and their energies were rewarded soon after when Rotherham created an opening for Bolton to send Hawcridge in for a try. Sample, who played an excellent defensive game at full-back in place of Tristram, could not kick the goal.

Conditions were bright throughout the afternoon, and the second half was played at great pace. The Irish three-quarters had many chances and received plenty of possession from their hard-toiling pack. The tackling of the English backs was cool and accurate, and after a long period under pressure, Sample was able to relieve his colleagues with a series of fine kicks.

The winning score came in the second half when Rotherham made an excellent chance for Bolton, the Blackheath three-quarter, who made fine use of his speed to decide a close match.

ENGLAND		IRELAND	
C.H. Sample	(Cambridge U.)	G.H. Wheeler	(Queen's U.)
J.J. Hawcridge	(Bradford)	R.E. McLean	(N.I.F.C.)
A.E. Stoddart	(Blackheath)	J.P. Ross	(Lansdowne)
W.N. Bolton	(Blackheath)	E.H. Greene	(Dublin U.)
A. Rotherham	(Oxford U.)	E.C. Crawford	(Dublin U.)
J.H. Payne	(Broughton)	R.G. Warren	(Lansdowne)
†C.H. Horley	(Swinton)	H.J. Neill	(N.I.F.C.)
C. Gurdon	(Richmond)	T. Shanahan	(Lansdowne)
C.S. Wooldridge	(Blackheath)	T.H.M. Hobbs	(Dublin U.)
G.T. Thomson	(Halifax)	T.R. Lyle	(Dublin U.)
G. Harrison	(Hull)	F.W. Moore	(Wanderers)
H.J. Ryalls	(New Brighton)	R.M. Bradshaw	(Wanderers)
F. Moss	(Broughton)	R.W. Hughes	(N.I.F.C.)
*E.T. Gurdon	(Richmond)	*W.G. Rutherford	(Tipperary)
A.T. Kemble	(Liverpool)	T.C. Allen	(N.I.F.C.)

Tries: Bolton, Hawcridge *Try:* Greene

Referee: Mr H.S. Lyne (Wales)

ENGLAND v WALES 1886

Played at Rectory Field, Blackheath, 2 January 1886
England won by 1GM, 2T to 1G

6000 were present at this international – the second to be played on the new Blackheath ground at Rectory Field. The match was not a distinguished one, though Wales, the junior Rugby nation of the four home countries, gave a respectable display in fine conditions.

Wade, a dashing three-quarter, opened the scoring after 25 minutes with a try which Stoddart just failed to convert into a goal, and soon afterwards Wilkinson increased England's lead with another unconverted try. Then, just before the interval, came a most unusual score. The Welsh full-back, Bowen of Llanelli, sliced an attempted clearance kick to touch straight into the arms of Elliot, who had a clear path to the Welsh line ahead. To the astonishment of the crowd, and the players, the Sunderland forward claimed a mark. In these days, any player in the side could take the kick so Stoddart, the famous cricketer, was once again entrusted with the important attempt at goal. A renowned place-kicker, he sent the ball between the posts from more than 40 yards to complete the English scoring.

Although Wales lacked skill, they were well endowed with enthusiasm and registered the only points of the second half when, seven minutes from no-side, the wily Welsh half, Stadden, scored a try beneath the English posts. Taylor's conversion made the final score more acceptable.

The English critics were unhappy with the performance of their side, and it was reported that the forwards were particularly disappointing after the opening 15 minutes of the match.

ENGLAND		WALES	
A.S. Taylor	(Blackheath)	D.H. Bowen	(Llanelli)
C.G. Wade	(Richmond)	C.G. Taylor	(Blackheath/Ruabon)
†A.R. Robertshaw	(Bradford)	A.J. Gould	(Newport)
A.E. Stoddart	(Blackheath)	W.M. Douglas	(Cardiff)
A. Rotherham	(Richmond)	W.J.W. Stadden	(Cardiff)
†F. Bonsor	(Bradford)	*C.H. Newman	(Newport)
C. Gurdon	(Richmond)	R. Gould	(Newport)
†W.G. Clibborn	(Richmond)	E.P. Alexander	(Cambridge U.)
*C.J.B. Marriott	(Blackheath)	W.H. Thomas	(Cambridge U.)
†G.L. Jeffery	(Blackheath)	W. Bowen	(Swansea)
†R.E. Inglis	(Blackheath)	D. Morgan	(Swansea)
†P.F. Hancock	(Blackheath)	A.F. Hill	(Cardiff)
†E. Wilkinson	(Bradford)	G.A. Young	(Cardiff)
F. Moss	(Broughton)	D.H. Lewis	(Cardiff)
†C.H. Elliot	(Sunderland)	E. Roberts	(Llanelli)

Tries: Wade, Wilkinson
Goal from mark: Stoddart

Try: Stadden
Conversion: Taylor

Referee: Mr D.F. Moore (Ireland)

IRELAND v ENGLAND 1886

Played at Lansdowne Road, Dublin, 6 February 1886
England won by 1T to Nil

This was probably England's finest side of the season and Ireland were completely outclassed, although the scoreline of a solitary try (and a lucky one at that!) to nil hides this fact. The play of the English three-quarters was a lesson in combination, for the centre, Robertshaw, brought a new dimension to back play. Contemporary reports state that he was the first player to create opportunities for his wings, and in this match both Stoddart and Wade had many electrifying runs. In Morrow, however, Ireland possessed an heroic full-back who time and again thwarted the efforts of the English threes' – tackling continuously and stoically falling on the loose ball.

Fine weather and a large crowd greeted the players and Marriott started the game with a kick which settled play for a while in the Irish 25. Robertshaw and the English halves made several probing runs but Morrow and Warren defended stoutly and got Ireland out of trouble. A period of even play soon gave way to incessant English pressure as the Irish forwards began to wilt. The Irish backs remained resolute in defence, however, and England were unable to score.

Ireland's hopes were raised early in the second half and only a sound tackle by Taylor prevented Warren scoring near the posts after a fine run. Slowly the English forwards regained the initiative and their halves were able to bring play to Irish quarters. A typical break by Robertshaw was halted by a grand tackle, but Wilkinson was at hand in the follow-up, and he gathered the ball to score a try, which Stoddart failed to convert. This proved to be the only score of the match, though Robertshaw nearly landed a dropped goal at the end of the game.

Spurling's brother had appeared for England in 1882.

IRELAND		ENGLAND	
R.W. Morrow	(Lisburn)	A.S. Taylor	(Blackheath)
D.J. Ross	(Belfast Albion)	C.G. Wade	(Richmond)
J.P. Ross	(N.I.F.C.)	A.R. Robertshaw	(Bradford)
E.H. Greene	(Wanderers)	A.E. Stoddart	(Blackheath)
*M. Johnston	(Wanderers)	A. Rotherham	(Richmond)
R.G. Warren	(Lansdowne)	F. Bonsor	(Bradford)
J. Chambers	(Dublin U.)	C. Gurdon	(Richmond)
T. Shanahan	(Lansdowne)	W.G. Clibborn	(Richmond)
V.C. le Fanu	(Cambridge U.)	R.E. Inglis	(Blackheath)
T.R. Lyle	(Dublin U.)	G.L. Jeffery	(Blackheath)
H.M. Brabazon	(Dublin U.)	A. Teggin	(Broughton Rangers)
J. Johnston	(Belfast Albion)	P.F. Hancock	(Blackheath)
R.W. Hughes	(N.I.F.C.)	E. Wilkinson	(Bradford)
W.G. Rutherford	(Tipperary)	*C.J.B. Marriott	(Blackheath)
R.H. Massey-Westropp	(Limerick/Monkstown)	†N. Spurling	(Blackheath)

Try: Wilkinson

Referee: Mr R. Mullock (Wales)

SCOTLAND v ENGLAND 1886
Played at Raeburn Place, Edinburgh, 13 March 1886
Drawn, neither side scoring

This match, which was postponed from the previous week, was played on a windy day on the ground where the first international had been staged. England had first use of the elements and Brown, the Scottish captain, kicked off. Scotland immediately put pressure on the English forwards and, when Bonsor badly injured a knee which handicapped his play for the remainder of the match, the Scottish three-quarters ran threateningly with Morrison constantly outpacing his opposite number Brutton. The English defence remained intact, however, thanks to the tackling and covering of Robertshaw and Rotherham.

The second half continued along the same lines as the first: Scotland attacking through their backs, with Grant Asher in fine form, and England defending desperately, with their forwards making occasional dribbles into Scottish territory. The dour struggle ended as a nil-all draw, Scotland having forced England to touch down in defence twice, and having a try disallowed.

SCOTLAND		ENGLAND	
J.P. Veitch	(Royal H.S.F.P.)	C.H. Sample	(Cambridge U.)
R.H. Morrison	(Edinburgh U.)	A.E. Stoddart	(Blackheath)
G.R. Wilson	(Royal H.S.F.P.)	A.R. Robertshaw	(Bradford)
W.F. Holms	(R.I.E. College)	†E.B. Brutton	(Cambridge U.)
A.G.G. Asher	(Fettes/Lorettonians)	A. Rotherham	(Richmond)
A.R. Don Wauchope	(Fettes/Lorettonians)	F. Bonsor	(Bradford)
*J.B. Brown	(Glasgow Acads.)	*E.T. Gurdon	(Richmond)
C. Reid	(Edinburgh Acads.)	C. Gurdon	(Richmond)
W.A. Walls	(Glasgow Acads.)	R.E. Inglis	(Blackheath)
T.W. Irvine	(Edinburgh Acads.)	E. Wilkinson	(Bradford)
A.T. Clay	(Edinburgh Acads.)	W.G. Clibborn	(Richmond)
C.J.B. Milne	(West of Scotland)	N. Spurling	(Blackheath)
M.C. McEwan	(Edinburgh Acads.)	C.J.B. Marriott	(Blackheath)
D.A. McLeod	(Glasgow U.)	G.L. Jeffery	(Cambridge U.)
J. Tod	(Watsonians)	A. Teggin	(Broughton Rangers)

Referee: Mr H.G. Cook (Ireland)

WALES v ENGLAND 1887
Played at Stradey Park, Llanelli, 8 January 1887
Drawn, neither side scoring

Wales held England to a drawn game – the first between the countries – on a bitterly cold afternoon during which snow and hail added to the difficulties of the play. A severe frost had rendered the main Stradey Park pitch unplayable, and eventually the match was staged on the adjoining cricket ground, where 8000 spectators huddled together around the makeshift touch-lines. A Welsh report of the match described it as brilliant, while an English commentator stated quite categorically that the ground was unfit for football, and that the game demanded 'no serious comment'.

Wales, after unsuccessfully experimenting with four three-quarters in the previous season, reverted to the three-man game which Arthur Gould preferred. The Welsh backs did not distinguish themselves though, for they tended to kick rather than run at moments when running was more likely to produce a score. The English backs, in contrast, were far happier in the open play and showed some good form. The Welsh forwards outplayed the English pack, which included five new caps.

The playing surface was too hard for any heroic tackling but it appears that there was much for the crowd to appreciate, and Wales very nearly won the match when a drop at goal by Gould missed by less than a yard.

Mr Rowland Hill of the R.F.U. controlled the game, the Scottish official nominated as referee becoming snow-bound en-route to Llanelli.

WALES		ENGLAND	
D.H. Bowen	(Llanelli)	†S. Roberts	(Swinton)
C.G. Taylor	(London Welsh)	†J. le Fleming	(B'heath/Cambridge U.)
A.J. Gould	(Newport)	A.R. Robertshaw	(Bradford)
W.M. Douglas	(Cardiff)	†R.E. Lockwood	(Dewsbury)
O.J. Evans	(Cardiff)	*A. Rotherham	(Richmond)
*C.H. Newman	(Newport)	F. Bonsor	(Bradford)
T.W. Lockwood	(Newport)	†J.L. Hickson	(Bradford)
R. Gould	(Newport)	†R.L. Seddon	(Broughton Rangers)
T.J.S. Clapp	(Newport)	G.L. Jeffery	(Blackheath)
E.P. Alexander	(Cambridge U./L. Welsh)	†H.C. Baker	(Clifton)
W.H. Thomas	(Cambridge U./L. Welsh)	W.G. Clibborn	(Richmond)
D. Morgan	(Swansea)	E. Wilkinson	(Bradford)
W. Bowen	(Swansea)	N. Spurling	(Blackheath)
A.J. Hybart	(Cardiff)	†J.H. Dewhurst	(Cambridge U.)
A.F. Bland	(Cardiff)	†C.R. Cleveland	(Oxford U.)

Referee: Mr G.R. Hill (England)

IRELAND v ENGLAND 1887

Played at Lansdowne Road, Dublin, 5 February 1887
Ireland won by 2G to Nil

So Ireland beat England at last, and a well-deserved win it was too. The Irish forwards completely dominated the English pack and the Irish backs demonstrated style in scoring the two winning tries in the second half. The halves, Warren and McLaughlin, paved the way to victory with a well-planned system: the latter played a bustling, charging role while his companion added the elegant touches which created opportunities for his three-quarters.

Many were present on a fine day to witness this historic match. Rotherham kicked off into the wind but Warren gave his side the initiative with some fine attacking kicking which brought the play to English territory. The home side was unlucky not to lead early in the game, for a try was disallowed after some good work by Walkington. The other feature of the half was the outstanding combined play of the Irish three-quarters, and Rambaut and Montgomery produced several moves which only some careful defence by Rotherham and Scott baulked.

England found their form at the beginning of the second half for a short while, but a drop at goal by McLaughlin sent them back into defence. Shortly afterwards, Rambaut created an opening for Tillie to score a converted try. England redoubled their efforts after this setback, but no progress was made and, when Lockwood was injured and forced to retire near the end of the match, hopes of victory faded for the visitors. England had been forced to 'minor' three times during the match (to Ireland's one touch-down) and the final score came in the closing minutes when Rambaut converted a try by Montgomery.

As an indication of the importance this match held to the Irish players, it is told that the forward, Macauley, 'could only devise the expedient of getting married in order to obtain the necessary leave of absence to play'. This was written by an Irish critic, who added that the action 'was truly heroic, and his wife fully endorsed the enthusiasm'.

Frank Pease, the first player capped for England direct from Hartlepool Rovers, became one of England's oldest internationals. He died, aged 93, in 1957.

IRELAND		ENGLAND	
D.B. Walkington	(N.I.F.C.)	S. Roberts	(Swinton)
C.R. Tillie	(Dublin U.)	W.N. Bolton	(Blackheath)
D.F. Rambaut	(Dublin U.)	†A.R.St L. Fagan	(United Hospitals)
R. Montgomery	(Queen's U.)	R.E. Lockwood	(Dewsbury)
J.H. McLaughlin	(Derry)	*A. Rotherham	(Richmond)
*R.G. Warren	(Lansdowne)	†M.T. Scott	(Cambridge U.)
J. Chambers	(Dublin U.)	J.L. Hickson	(Bradford)
J.S. Dick	(Queen's College, Cork)	R.L. Seddon	(Broughton Rangers)
V.C. le Fanu	(Cambridge U.)	G.L. Jeffery	(Blackheath)
T.R. Lyle	(Dublin U.)	A. Teggin	(Broughton Rangers)
E.J. Walsh	(Lansdowne)	W.G. Clibborn	(Richmond)
J. Johnston	(Belfast Albion)	A.T. Kemble	(Liverpool)
R. Stevenson	(Lisburn)	†F.E. Pease	(Hartlepool Rovers)
H.J. Neill	(N.I.F.C.)	J.H. Dewhurst	(Cambridge U.)
J. Macauley	(Limerick)	C.J.B. Marriott	(Blackheath)

Tries: Montgomery, Tillie
Conversions: Rambaut (2)

Referee: Mr W.D. Phillips (Wales)

ENGLAND v SCOTLAND 1887

Played at Whalley Range, Manchester, 5 March 1887
Drawn: England 1T, Scotland 1T

Scotland were favourites to win but it was England who, on the day, called the tune, and a draw was a fortunate result for Scotland (though it still made them champion nation for the season). The match began in mist which became denser as the play proceeded and the 9000 spectators present saw little of the game. Scotland started at a blistering pace and only brave tackling and covering by Bonsor and Rotherham, the English halves, prevented a score. In addition, Tristram (who was educated at Loretto School in Scotland) gave an immaculate display at full-back: twice he saved certain tries with bone-shattering tackles on Lindsay and MacLagan. After continuous Scottish pressure, the English forwards led play to the half-way line with a controlled dribble. Then, after a series of scrummages, G.L. Jeffery, the best forward on the field, ran in for a try which Bolton failed to convert.

Scotland rushed the English lines to begin the second half and Robertshaw was forced to 'minor'. Play was then even for a long period – the English backs running and passing creatively and the Scottish forwards counter-attacking with the ball at their feet. Reid inspired his men with a run which almost brought a try, and a drop at goal narrowly failed. Finally, Scotland equalised when Morton scored, but Berry failed to convert and the seventh draw in the series of England–Scotland matches was registered.

This was one of the best performances given by an English pack – Hickson, Clibborn, Wilkinson and Dewhurst, in addition to Jeffery, were the bulwarks in the scrummage, while Reid, as ever, gave a polished display for the Scots.

ENGLAND		SCOTLAND	
H.B. Tristram	(Richmond)	W.F. Holms	(London Scottish)
W.N. Bolton	(Blackheath)	W.E. MacLagan	(London Scottish)
A.R. Robertshaw	(Bradford)	G.C. Lindsay	(London Scottish)
R.E. Lockwood	(Dewsbury)	A.N. Woodrow	(Glasgow Acads.)
*A. Rotherham	(Richmond)	C.E. Orr	(West of Scotland)
F. Bonsor	(Bradford)	P.H. Don Wauchope	(Edinburgh Wands.)
C.R. Cleveland	(Oxford U.)	C.W. Berry	(Edinburgh Wands.)
J.H. Dewhurst	(Richmond)	A.T. Clay	(Edinburgh Acads.)
W.G. Clibborn	(Richmond)	J. French	(Glasgow Acads.)
H.H. Springman	(Liverpool)	H.T. Ker	(Glasgow Acads.)
E. Wilkinson	(Bradford)	T.W. Irvine	(Edinburgh Acads.)
R.L. Seddon	(Broughton Rangers)	R.G. MacMillan	(West of Scotland)
A. Teggin	(Broughton Rangers)	M.C. McEwan	(Edinburgh Acads.)
J.L. Hickson	(Bradford)	D.S. Morton	(West of Scotland)
G.L. Jeffery	(Blackheath)	*C. Reid	(Edinburgh Acads.)

Try: Jeffery   *Try:* Morton

Referee: Mr T.R. Lyle (Ireland)

The England Team 1888

The try scored by Kindersley for England against Scotland in the 1884 match at Blackheath had been hotly disputed by the Scots, who proposed that a body be appointed to arbitrate on matters arising from international matches, and the 1884 game in particular. The R.F.U. disagreed with the Scottish proposition, although an international meeting did take place in Dublin in 1886, when the Scots (who had refused to play England in 1885) accepted the result of the 1884 match. The Rugby Union refused to participate in a meeting in Manchester (also in 1886) when the International Board, the name of the committee set up to discuss disputes and policies concerning international matches, first met. In the following year, when the Rugby Union boycotted the I.B. meeting again, the other home countries took action against the English, refusing to play the senior Rugby nation until a four-nation board was established. So England played no matches against Ireland, Wales or Scotland in 1888 or 1889. A team was selected by the R.F.U. committee in 1888, however, and caps were awarded to the following members of a team that never played:

A.R. St L. Fagan	(Richmond)
J. Valentine	(Swinton)
P. Robertshaw	(Bradford)
G.C. Hubbard	(Blackheath)
F. Bonsor	(Bradford)
F.H. Fox	(Wellington)
G.L. Jeffery	(Blackheath)
N. Spurling	(Blackheath)
J.H. Dewhurst	(Richmond)
C. Anderton	(Manchester Free Wands.)
J.L. Hickson	(Bradford)
W.G. Clibborn	(Richmond)
A. Robinson	(Cambridge U.)
H. Eagles	(Salford)
P.F. Hancock	(Blackheath)

Two members of the side, Percy Robertshaw and Harry Eagles, never gained caps for playing in a full England international side. (Albert Rawson Robertshaw, Percy's brother, had been capped in 1886). This team has *not* been included in the records section at the end of the book.

In 1889, England had the consolation of a full fixture with the touring New Zealand Native side, and in 1890 the R.F.U. changed its stance with regard to representation on the Board. Finally, on the morning of the Wales–Scotland match of 1890 (1 February), Mr E. McAlister, Honorary Secretary to the International Board, telegraphed the R.F.U. from Cardiff to state that the English agreement had been accepted, except for a minor point which the R.F.U. were prepared to set aside.

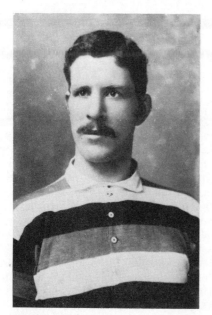

R. L. Seddon and A. E. Stoddart. An unofficial British Rugby tour of Australia and New Zealand took place from March to November 1888, during which 35 matches were played. Seddon, captain of the team, was drowned whilst sculling on the River Hunter at Maitland and Stoddart took over the captaincy. Stoddart, who had made his cricketing debut for England at Sydney in February, went on to captain England in both Rugby and cricket, gaining ten and 16 caps respectively.

England's first Rugby international against overseas opposition, England v New Zealand Natives, 1889: *standing* F. W. Lowrie, D. Jowett, H. Bedford, H. J. Wilkinson, C. Anderton, J. W. Cave, A. V. Royle, A. Budd (touch-judge); *sitting* R. E. Lockwood, W. M. Scott, A. Robinson, W. Yiend, F. Bonsor (captain), F. Evershed, J. W. Sutcliffe, A. E. Stoddart.
(Note that Wilkinson wore his Yorkshire County shirt for this match.)

ENGLAND v NEW ZEALAND NATIVES 1889
Played at Rectory Field, Blackheath, 16 February 1889
England won by 1G, 4T (7) to Nil

Both sides had some caustic comments to make after this match, which was played in wet and unpleasant conditions before a crowd of 12,000 spectators. An English account of the match states that the most memorable incidents of the play were the extremely vigorous exchanges of the 'Maori' players and their protestations against the decisions of Mr Rowland Hill of the R.F.U., who acted as referee.

The New Zealanders wrote later that most of the tries awarded against them in the game were the results of poor refereeing. England's two first-half scores followed punts over the 'Maori' goal-line: Warbrick ran the ball from in-goal in the first instance and then claimed to touch down when he realised he was under pressure from Bedford, who pounced on the ball and was awarded a try; and in the second case, the same English forward was awarded a try after a maul-in-goal in which Lee claimed to have forced a touch-down.

After the interval, Stoddart scored a try and seemed to be set for another when a most extraordinary event took place. He lost a portion of his shorts in a tackle with Ellison. As the players formed the customary guard around Stoddart while he changed, Evershed picked up the ball and claimed a try at the corner. There followed an angry discussion with the referee. During the discussion, Evershed coolly picked up the ball and strolled over to the posts where he touched down, and Mr Hill awarded the try. Sutcliffe converted while three of the disgusted Native side walked off the field!

The manager of the 'Maoris' persuaded his men to retake the field, but England added a later try through Sutcliffe. That, apparently, was perfectly fair, and completed the scoring.

There is some contradiction amongst reports as to the exact 'Maori' line-out for this match. The Times *lists the players as below, but slightly different sides appear in other contemporary publications. Bonsor was the first Yorkshireman to captain England, and Harry Bedford became Morley's first international cap.*

ENGLAND		N.Z. NATIVES	
†A.V. Royle	(Broughton Rangers)	W. Warbrick	(Malata)
†J.W. Sutcliffe	(Heckmondwike)	E. McCausland	(Gordon)
A.E. Stoddart	(Blackheath)	W.T. Wynyard	(North Shore)
R.E. Lockwood	(Dewsbury)	C. Madigan	(Grafton)
†W.M. Scott	(Cambridge U.)	P. Keogh	(Kaikoria)
*F. Bonsor	(Bradford)	D.R. Gage	(Poneke)
		W. Elliott	(Grafton)
†F. Evershed	(Burton)		
†D. Jowett	(Heckmondwike)	T. Rene	(Nelson)
†C. Anderton	(Manchester Free Wands.)	T.R. Ellison	(Poneke)
†H.J. Wilkinson	(Halifax)	H.H. Lee	(Riverton)
†H. Bedford	(Morley)	G.A. Williams	(Poneke)
†W. Yiend	(Hartlepool Rovers)	W. Anderson	(Hokianga)
†J.W. Cave	(Cambridge U.)	R. Taiaroa	(Dunedin)
†F.W. Lowrie	(Wakefield Trinity)	R. Maynard	(North Shore)
†A. Robinson	(Blackheath)	G. Wynyard	(North Shore)

Tries: Bedford (2), Evershed, Stoddart, Sutcliffe *Conversion:* Sutcliffe

Referee: Mr G.R. Hill (England)

ENGLAND v WALES 1890

Played at Crown Flatt, Dewsbury, 15 February 1890
Wales won by 1T (1) to Nil

With the international dispute happily settled, England resumed their home international matches with this game at Dewsbury, and in windy, snowy conditions suffered defeat against Wales for the first time. Wales used four three-quarters and their short, sharp passing was particularly accurate considering the unpleasant weather. The English backs were unable to match their style, and Stoddart had a quiet afternoon.

A Welsh critic of the day reported that the tall English forwards were helpless in the mud and were thoroughly outplayed by the sturdy, thick-set Welshmen. Still, Wales had to work desperately for their victory: only the slick passing of the three-quarters – which gained them much ground – and the intelligent defence and anticipation of the young Bancroft, prevented an English score in the first half. Indeed, Wales were forced to touch down in defence three times before the break.

Two minutes into the second spell, Stadden fooled the English forwards at a line-out by feigning to throw the ball deep, sending them several yards infield. The former Cardiff half then bounced the ball into play just in front of himself, gathered, and sped over for the only score of the match. Curiously Stadden, who was living in Dewsbury at the time of the game and playing on his home ground, was absent from the Welsh team photographed before the match.

England had been unable to field their star half-back, Fred Bonsor of Bradford. He had captained the side the previous season against the 'Maoris', but was thought to have deliberately withdrawn at a late hour from this game so that his Bradford co-half, Wright, could win his cap for England. Well, Wright secured the coveted cap, but neither he nor his colleague ever appeared in England colours again.

J.H. Rogers was the first Moseley international.

ENGLAND		WALES	
†W.G. Mitchell	(Richmond)	W.J. Bancroft	(Swansea)
†P.H. Morrison	(Cambridge U.)	D. Gwynn	(Swansea)
*A.E. Stoddart	(Blackheath)	*A.J. Gould	(Newport)
†J. Valentine	(Swinton)	R.M. Garrett	(Penarth)
		D.P. Lloyd	(Llanelli)
†J.F. Wright	(Bradford)		
†F.H. Fox	(Wellington)	W.J.W. Stadden	(Dewsbury)
		C.J. Thomas	(Newport)
†S.M.J. Woods	(Cambridge U.)		
J.H. Dewhurst	(Richmond)	W. Bowen	(Swansea)
†R.T.D. Budworth	(Blackheath)	A.F. Bland	(Cardiff)
F. Evershed	(Burton)	W.E.O. Williams	(Cardiff)
J.L. Hickson	(Bradford)	D.W. Evans	(Cardiff)
A. Robinson	(Blackheath)	J. Hannan	(Newport)
†J.H. Rogers	(Moseley)	W.H. Thomas	(London Welsh)
P.F. Hancock	(Blackheath)	J. Meredith	(Swansea)
F.W. Lowrie	(Batley)	S. Thomas	(Llanelli)

Try: Stadden

Referee: Mr R.D. Rainie (Scotland)

SCOTLAND v ENGLAND 1890

Played at Raeburn Place, Edinburgh, 1 March 1890
England won by 1G, 1T (6) to Nil

The first match between the nations since the dispute of 1887 was a brilliant exhibition of Rugby before a sporting crowd of 8000. England combined well in attack and defended steadily, while the outstanding features of the Scottish play were the fearsome forward rushes. The English victory was attributed in no small part to the effective teamwork of the forwards, who included five of the successful Yorkshire County pack.

The English three-quarters handled with skill, Aston at centre playing most unselfishly in contrast to his opposite number, Stevenson. MacLagan tackled surely for Scotland and many English moves foundered on his rocklike defence. In the forwards, Toothill and Rogers for the visitors, and McIntyre and Ker for the Scots, were prominent.

Scotland kicked off but Dyson took play to the Scottish half with a punt ahead. Scotland recovered and an interception by Stevenson put Scotland on the attack. Play then continued evenly until a try-giving pass from Toothill to Evershed produced the opening score. Mitchell failed to kick the goal. C.E. Orr and Wilson made a good combined run for Scotland but Mitchell, who played a fine, safe game, halted them with a grand tackle. Both sets of backs ran dangerously, but Mitchell and his adversary, MacGregor, cleared their lines safely.

At length, a burst by Evershed led to a second score when Dyson crossed in the corner for Jowett to convert with a fine kick. In the closing ten minutes of the match, C.E. Orr made a number of runs in a desperate last effort to score, but England held on to win by a goal and a try to nil: a score of 6 points to 0 under the scoring method adopted by the Scottish Union.

Mason Scott, capped earlier at Cambridge University, became the first player capped from Northern R.F.C. A gentleman of considerable wealth, he died in June 1916, leaving £130,000 in his will. His brother, W.M. Scott, also played for England.

SCOTLAND		ENGLAND	
G. MacGregor	(Cambridge U.)	W.G. Mitchell	(Richmond)
*W.E. MacLagan	(London Scottish)	P.H. Morrison	(Cambridge U.)
H.J. Stevenson	(Edinburgh Acads.)	†R.L. Aston	(Cambridge U.)
G.R. Wilson	(Royal H.S.F.P.)	†J.W. Dyson	(Huddersfield)
C.E. Orr	(West of Scotland)	M.T. Scott	(Northern)
D.G. Anderson	(London Scottish)	F.H. Fox	(Wellington)
J.D. Boswell	(West of Scotland)	S.M.J. Woods	(Cambridge U.)
A. Dalgleish	(Gala)	D. Jowett	(Heckmondwike)
F.W.J. Goodhue	(London Scottish)	*J.L. Hickson	(Bradford)
H.T. Ker	(Glasgow Acads.)	J.H. Rogers	(Moseley)
M.C. McEwan	(Edinburgh Acads.)	F. Evershed	(Burton)
J.E. Orr	(West of Scotland)	†J.T. Toothill	(Bradford)
D.S. Morton	(West of Scotland)	A. Robinson	(Blackheath)
R.G. MacMillan	(West of Scotland)	H. Bedford	(Morley)
I. MacIntyre	(Edinburgh Wands.)	†E. Holmes	(Manningham)

Tries: Dyson, Evershed
Conversion: Jowett

Referee: Mr J. Chambers (Ireland)

ENGLAND v IRELAND 1890

Played at Rectory Field, Blackheath, 15 March 1890
England won by 3T (3) to Nil

A crowd of 12,000 saw Stoddart return to the English side to lead the home team to victory and a share with Scotland in the International Championship. Hickson kicked off for England, sending the ball deep into the Irish half where some controlled dribbling by Stevenson, Warren and le Fanu brought play to the half-way line for a while. Le Fanu was outstanding in the visiting pack, and Dunlop and Johnston made some good ground for the Irish backs with a series of astute kicks to touch. The English three-quarters always appeared dangerous, though it was fine play by two forwards, Woods and Evershed, which nearly produced a score for Spence.

Warren and Tuke played competently at half for Ireland, and Walkington was reliable at back, never afraid to fall on the loose balls. But the efforts of these three were unable to prevent England scoring in the first half. Stoddart started the move with a dodging run which confused the Irish defence; then Morrison continued the effort before transferring to Evershed who progressed to the Irish line, where he dropped the ball. Rogers was at hand to open the scoring, but Jowett, with an excellent kick, was narrowly wide with the conversion attempt. Soon afterwards, Scott made an opening for Aston to reach the line and Stoddart was up for the try-scoring pass. Before the interval arrived, both Mitchell and Walkington were called upon to prevent further try-scoring.

The well-organised English pack began with new-found vigour after the break and Stoddart had a clear drop at goal, which forced the Irish to concede a touch-down. Morrison nearly scored shortly after, but Warren led his men out of danger and Ireland next came close to scoring – a rolling ball skidding into touch-in-goal before an Irishman could claim a try. Some fine dribbling by Jowett, Robinson and Rogers ended with Morrison gathering the ball and running through some atrocious Irish tackling to score a try beneath the goal. Jowett hashed the conversion kick.

Ireland really tore into their opponents now, and several times the ball was brought close to the home line – Johnston and Dunlop making penetrative runs. Once, too, they actually rushed the ball over the England line and a mass of bodies fought for possession. However, the referee awarded a drop-out, and thus the score remained at 3–0 in favour of the hosts.

ENGLAND		IRELAND	
W.G. Mitchell	(Richmond)	D.B. Walkington	(Dublin U.)
P.H. Morrison	(Cambridge U.)	R. Dunlop	(Dublin U.)
R.L. Aston	(Cambridge U.)	R.W. Johnston	(Dublin U.)
*A.E. Stoddart	(Blackheath)	T. Edwards	(Lansdowne)
M.T. Scott	(Northern)	B.B. Tuke	(Bective Rangers)
†F.W. Spence	(Birkenhead Park)	*R.G. Warren	(Lansdowne)
F. Evershed	(Burton)	J.N. Lytle	(N.I.F.C.)
J.L. Hickson	(Bradford)	E.G. Forrest	(Wanderers)
S.M.J. Woods	(Cambridge U.)	J. Waites	(Bective Rangers)
J.T. Toothill	(Bradford)	J.H. O'Conor	(Bective Rangers)
J.H. Rogers	(Moseley)	R. Stevenson	(Dungannon)
D. Jowett	(Heckmondwike)	J. Roche	(Wanderers)
H. Bedford	(Morley)	V.C. le Fanu	(Lansdowne)
E. Holmes	(Manningham)	L.C. Nash	(Queen's College Cork)
A. Robinson	(Blackheath)	W.J.N. Davis	(Bective Rangers)

Tries: Rogers, Morrison, Stoddart

Referee: Mr A.R. Don Wauchope (Scotland)

WALES v ENGLAND 1891

Played at Rodney Parade, Newport, 3 January 1891
England won by 2G, 1T (7) to 1G (3)

The English selectors awarded nine new caps for this match, and included Alderson at centre as captain on his debut. There was a high proportion of the Northern-type forward in the English pack and these hardy Yorkshire and Lancashire specimens were more vigorous than their Welsh counterparts. Wales in fact were most unimpressive: Bancroft had a disappointing match and the passing, usually the forte of the Welsh, was so wayward that the four-threequarter system was unable to function at its best. Consequently, England were able to register a decisive victory by 7–3, with a converted try and any goal counting as three points and a try as one.

9000 were present to see England dominate from the start. Leake, who had an excellent debut, caused many problems for the Welsh backs and created the first try. He eluded Ingledew before passing to Christopherson, who outflanked his opponent. Bancroft missed his tackle and the Blackheath man scored, Alderson converting. Christopherson, with a fast, dodging run went over again before half-time.

'Lemons and grapes were handed round in the breathing time' disclosed the *Western Mail* correspondent, before Wales, with their only crisp passing movement of the game, scored. The ball was swiftly transferred across the threequarter line for Pearson to score wide out. Bancroft atoned for his earlier lapse by kicking a splendid goal from the touch-line. Sustained forward pressure by the English pack was the feature of the remaining play and, at length, Woods dribbled the ball over the Welsh line for Budworth, who had learnt the game at a famous Welsh school – Christ College, Brecon – to touch down. Alderson again kicked the goal.

W.R.M. Leake was the first international capped direct from Harlequins.

WALES		ENGLAND	
W.J. Bancroft	(Swansea)	W.G. Mitchell	(Richmond)
D.P.M. Lloyd	(Llanelli)	R.E. Lockwood	(Heckmondwike)
D. Gwynn	(Swansea)	*†F.H.R. Alderson	(Hartlepool Rovers)
C.S. Arthur	(Cardiff)	†P. Christopherson	(Blackheath)
T.W. Pearson	(Cardiff)		
		†W.R.M. Leake	(Harlequins)
H.M. Ingledew	(Cardiff)	†J. Berry	(Tyldesley)
C.J. Thomas	(Newport)		
		S.M.J. Woods	(Cambridge U.)
D.W. Evans	(Cardiff)	†R.P. Wilson	(Liverpool O.B.)
J. Hannan	(Newport)	R.T.D. Budworth	(Blackheath)
E.V. Pegge	(Neath)	†T. Kent	(Salford)
*W. Bowen	(Swansea)	†W.E. Bromet	(Tadcaster)
R.L. Thomas	(London Welsh)	†E.G.H. North	(Oxford U.)
H. Packer	(Newport)	D. Jowett	(Heckmondwike)
P. Bennett	(Cardiff Harlequins)	J.T. Toothill	(Bradford)
W. Rice Evans	(Swansea)	†J. Richards	(Bradford)

Try: Pearson *Conversion:* Bancroft

Tries: Christopherson (2), Budworth
Conversions: Alderson (2)

Referee: Mr R.D. Rainie (Scotland)

IRELAND v ENGLAND 1891
Played at Lansdowne Road, Dublin, 7 February 1891
England won by 2G, 3T (9) to Nil

England's forwards gave the Irish pack a hiding and laid the foundation for this magnificent win by five tries. The Irish selectors made a blunder by selecting C.V. Rooke – a player with a reputation for favouring a wing-forward type role in the pack – when a solid, tight scrummager would have been more appropriate against the marauding English forwards. Both sides made late changes: Christopherson withdrew and Morrison regained his place on the wing; and Lytle replaced Stevenson on the Irish side.

The English backs made an impressive start and Alderson was in action early in the game, making an opening for Lockwood to score after Woods and Wilson had won possession in loose play. Alderson failed to convert but his side continued to play wonderfully attractive football. Lockwood and Berry nearly crossed after some scintillating open play, then Wilson added another try before the break, Jowett striking the posts with the conversion.

Ireland promised much at the beginning of the second half but Mitchell was never found wanting in defence. A run by Bromet and Jowett took play back into Irish quarters where Wilson scored again, Woods missing the kick this time. Two more tries came near the end: Lockwood scoring after outstanding back play and Toothill crossing for the last score. These last efforts were converted by Lockwood who thus contributed six of England's nine points.

This was undoubtedly England's best performance of the season, with powerful forward play complemented by direct running and crisp handling among the backs. Ireland's play was well below international standard and much of the blame must rest on the shoulders of their selectors. J.J. McCarthy, writing about the time of this match, made this perceptive comment on the forward game played in Ireland: 'The almost universal adoption of the detestable wing game left us (Ireland) without a centre to our scrummage.'

IRELAND		ENGLAND	
*D.B. Walkington	(N.I.F.C.)	W.G. Mitchell	(Richmond)
R. Dunlop	(N.I.F.C.)	P.H. Morrison	(Cambridge U.)
S. Lee	(N.I.F.C.)	*F.H.R. Alderson	(Hartlepool Rovers)
R. Montgomery	(N.I.F.C.)	R.E. Lockwood	(Heckmondwike)
A.C. McDonnell	(Dublin U.)	W.R.M. Leake	(Harlequins)
B.B. Tuke	(Bective Rangers)	J. Berry	(Tyldesley)
J.N. Lytle	(N.I.F.C.)	S.M.J. Woods	(Cambridge U.)
E.G. Forrest	(Wanderers)	R.P. Wilson	(Liverpool O.B.)
J. Waites	(Bective Rangers)	D. Jowett	(Heckmondwike)
J.H. O'Conor	(Bective Rangers)	J. Richards	(Bradford)
C.V. Rooke	(Dublin U.)	E.G.H. North	(Oxford U.)
J. Roche	(Wanderers)	W.E. Bromet	(Tadcaster)
V.C. le Fanu	(Lansdowne)	J.T. Toothill	(Bradford)
L.C. Nash	(Queen's College Cork)	T. Kent	(Salford)
W.J.N. Davis	(Bessbrook)	†L.J. Percival	(Oxford U.)

Tries: Lockwood (2), Wilson (2)[1],
Toothill   *Conversions:* Lockwood (2)

Referee: Mr W.M. Douglas (Wales)

[1] *There is a source which credits only one try to Wilson, giving the other to Jowett*

ENGLAND v SCOTLAND 1891

Played at Athletic Ground, Richmond, 7 March 1891
Scotland won by 2G, 1DG (9) to 1G (3)

England were thoroughly outplayed and deserved their defeat. Their forwards were routed and their backs, especially the halves, displayed little enterprise: it was said to be the most disappointing English side since the series of international matches began in 1871. The deplorable play of the English unit, however, must not detract from the spirited Scottish performance. The backs and forwards combined smoothly and the outstanding players were Anderson and MacGregor.

Woods kicked off for England but the Scottish forwards rushed the ball to the home 25 and, after only eight minutes of play, C.E. Orr sent MacGregor away to feed Clauss, who dropped a goal. England were stunned and never recovered from this setback. The Scots continued with their attacks, MacGregor, Anderson and C.E. Orr combining brilliantly, handling and passing with deadly precision. Only the defensive play of Mitchell and Alderson prevented another Scottish score before the interval. The most promising English attack of this period occurred when Leake and Alderson sent Lockwood clear, but the Scottish forwards dribbled their side to safety.

Soon after half-time, J.E. Orr crossed for a try at the posts which MacGregor goaled and another Scottish try was obtained by W. Neilson, following a typical bout of passing between Anderson and MacGregor. The latter kicked Scotland's third goal. Scotland relaxed for a period and England, at last, gave the crowd of about 15,000 something to cheer. After an exchange of punts between Mitchell and Stevenson, Christopherson made a strong run to the Scottish line where Lockwood crossed after the halves had created an opening. With a good kick, Alderson converted the try, restoring a little morale to his team. This proved to be short-lived as the closing ten minutes were dominated by the fitter Scots, though there was no further scoring. The mythical Triple Crown thus went north of the border for the first time.

ENGLAND		SCOTLAND	
W.G. Mitchell	(Richmond)	H.J. Stevenson	(Edinburgh Acads.)
P. Christopherson	(Blackheath)	P.R. Clauss	(Oxford U.)
*F.H.R. Alderson	(Hartlepool Rovers)	G. MacGregor	(Cambridge U.)
R.E. Lockwood	(Heckmondwike)	W. Neilson	(Merchiston)
W.R.M. Leake	(Harlequins)	C.E. Orr	(West of Scotland)
J. Berry	(Tyldesley)	D.G. Anderson	(London Scottish)
J.H. Rogers	(Moseley)	J.D. Boswell	(West of Scotland)
E.G.H. North	(Oxford U.)	H.T.O. Leggatt	(Watsonians)
R.P. Wilson	(Liverpool O.B.)	J.E. Orr	(West of Scotland)
R.T.D. Budworth	(Blackheath)	*M.C. McEwan	(Edinburgh Acads.)
S.M.J. Woods	(Cambridge U.)	G.T. Neilson	(West of Scotland)
J. Richards	(Bradford)	I. MacIntyre	(Edinburgh Wands.)
T. Kent	(Salford)	R.G. MacMillan	(London Scottish)
⁻D. Jowett	(Heckmondwike)	F.W.J. Goodhue	(London Scottish)
†E. Bonham-Carter	(Oxford U.)	W.R. Gibson	(Royal H.S.F.P.)

Try: Lockwood   *Conversion:* Alderson

Tries: W. Neilson, J.E. Orr
Conversions: MacGregor (2)
Dropped goal: Clauss

Referee: Mr J. Chambers (Ireland)

ENGLAND v WALES 1892
Played at Rectory Field, Blackheath, 2 January 1892
England won by 3G, 1T (17) to Nil

The system relating to the scoring of points had again changed before the season's internationals commenced. A try was now worth two points, with the conversion adding another three. Wales were thus beaten by 17 points, a thrashing in most books; but reports of the match were emphatic that this was no easy win for the English. 'It is only fair to state that the score suggests a much greater disparity between the two teams than really existed,' observed the *Western Mail* correspondent.

The Welsh problems lay at half-back, where Rowles and Phillips were unable to inspire their three-quarters to any great heights; much of the Welsh possession, so hard-earned by the driving forward play of an eight-man pack, was frittered away with haphazard and forward passing. Even the return of Arthur Gould at centre – after a season away in the West Indies on business – failed to raise the Welsh back play to any degree. Bancroft played reliably at full-back but he was unable to stop the four English tries. The home forwards handled sharply in the loose and Lockwood, the outstanding back on the field, was a constant threat to the Welsh defence.

10,000 saw England establish a lead of a goal and a try before the interval. Nichol and Hubbard were the scorers, Lockwood converting Hubbard's try from in front of the posts. Early in the second half an eye injury forced Hubbard to retire temporarily and Evershed withdrew from the pack, deputising competently as emergency wing. Then, soon after the Blackheath wing returned, a period of English pressure on the Welsh line ended with a try (and conversion) by Alderson. From the restart, Wales were unlucky to have a try disallowed and, finally, Bromet made a break to send Evershed behind the Welsh posts for a try which Lockwood converted with ease.

G.C. Hubbard's son was capped by England in 1930.

ENGLAND		WALES	
†W.B. Thomson	(Blackheath)	W.J. Bancroft	(Swansea)
R.E. Lockwood	(Heckmondwike)	W.M. McCutcheon	(Swansea)
*F.H.R. Alderson	(Hartlepool Rovers)	*A.J. Gould	(Newport)
†G.C. Hubbard	(Blackheath)	R.M. Garrett	(Penarth)
		T.W. Pearson	(Cardiff)
†C. Emmott	(Bradford)		
†A. Briggs	(Bradford)	H.P. Phillips	(Newport)
		G.R. Rowles	(Penarth)
F. Evershed	(Blackheath)		
†J. Pyke	(St Helens Recreation)	C.B. Nicholl	(Llanelli/Cambridge U.)
†E. Bullough	(Wigan)	A.W. Boucher	(Newport)
T. Kent	(Salford)	J. Deacon	(Swansea)
J.T. Toothill	(Bradford)	T.C. Graham	(Newport)
†A. Allport	(Blackheath)	R.L. Thomas	(Llanelli)
W.E. Bromet	(Tadcaster)	F. Mills	(Swansea)
W. Yiend	(Hartlepool Rovers)	W.H. Watts	(Newport)
†W. Nichol	(Brighouse Rangers)	J. Hannan	(Newport)

Tries: Alderson, Evershed, Hubbard, Nichol *Conversions:* Lockwood (2), Alderson

Referee: Mr M.C. McEwan (Scotland)

A 17-0 win over Wales at Blackheath, followed by victories over Ireland and Scotland, made England undisputed champions in 1892 – a season in which they did not concede a point: *back* J. T. Toothill, J. Pyke, W. Yiend, W. E. Bromet, G. C. Hubbard, F. Evershed; *middle* T. Kent, C. Emmott, F. H. R. Alderson (captain), E. Bullough, R. E. Lockwood, A. Allport; *front* W. Nichol, W. B. Thomson, A. Briggs.

W. E. Bromet, one of England's leading forwards in the early 1890s and a match-winner in the game against Scotland in 1892.

ENGLAND v IRELAND 1892

Played at Whalley Range, Manchester, 6 February 1892
England won by 1G, 1T (7) to Nil

England had many anxious moments early in this match and their forwards were well beaten up front in the initial exchanges. The Irish forwards were particularly proficient at dribbling and played with greater determination than their English counterparts; and Gardiner, Lee and Dunlop gave the defence much work to do with several exciting attacks. All in all, England were fortunate to change ends with the scores level.

For much of the second half play was even, but in the last 15 minutes the stamina of the home pack enabled England to win. Woods, Evershed and Bromet were in the van of several fierce attacks on the Irish line, only brave tackling preventing a score. Although Lockwood was once stopped just short of glory, the greasy surface of the pitch prevented the English backs from showing their finest form and it was left to the pack to secure victory. At length, England took the lead when Woods kicked ahead and the super-fast Evershed outpaced the Irish backs to score a try which his skipper converted. The dynamic-duo were soon in action again. A rush by Woods led to a run by Evershed, and Percival was up with the play to collect a pass and score the second try. The game ended soon after with England conceding no points for the second time, though a report stated that England might not have won but for the inspiring play of Woods and Evershed.

ENGLAND		IRELAND	
†S. Houghton	(Runcorn)	T. Peel	(Limerick)
R.E. Lockwood	(Heckmondwike)	R. Dunlop	(Dublin U.)
†J.H. Marsh	(Swinton)	S. Lee	(N.I.F.C.)
G.C. Hubbard	(Blackheath)	W. Gardiner	(N.I.F.C.)
†E.W. Taylor	(Rockcliff)	T. Thornhill	(Wanderers)
A. Briggs	(Bradford)	B.B. Tuke	(Bective Rangers)
*S.M.J. Woods	(Wellington)	*V.C. le Fanu	(Lansdowne)
L.J. Percival	(Oxford U.)	T.J. Johnston	(Queen's U.)
†A. Ashworth	(Oldham)	E.J. Walsh	(Lansdowne)
T. Kent	(Salford)	A.K. Wallis	(Wanderers)
W.E. Bromet	(Tadcaster)	J.S. Jameson	(Lansdowne)
J.T. Toothill	(Bradford)	R.E. Smith	(Lansdowne)
E. Bullough	(Wigan)	J.H. O'Conor	(Bective Rangers)
F. Evershed	(Blackheath)	W.J.N. Davis	(Bessbrook)
W. Yiend	(Hartlepool Rovers)	C.V. Rooke	(Dublin U.)

Tries: Evershed, Percival
Conversion: Woods

Referee: Mr J.A. Smith (Scotland)

SCOTLAND v ENGLAND 1892
Played at Raeburn Place, Edinburgh, 5 March 1892
England won by 1G (5) to Nil

This was a poor match, there being too much protracted mauling and a number of fights amongst the forwards, which had the effect of breaking up the fluency of the game. There were thirteen Northerners in the English team, but their combined work was disrupted by the tight tactics of the Scottish forwards and the guile and skill of Anderson and Orr at half. The English halves appeared slow and unimaginative in contrast. The outstanding three-quarters were Lockwood for England and Campbell for Scotland, their spectacular running being the only memorable feature of a dull match for the 15,000 spectators.

Scotland kicked off in bright conditions and a punt by Stevenson put England on the defensive. Briggs, Varley and Alderson tackled strongly and England were able to relieve pressure when Lockwood made a run to the half-way line. Play was even for the best part of the first half until Lockwood, again, made a determined run from his own goal. Stevenson halted his progress with a sound tackle but England capitalised on the position thus obtained and Alderson and Evershed almost ran in. Woods actually crossed, but the try was not awarded. England did score, though, when Bromet touched down at the posts after 30 minutes of play and Lockwood kicked the goal. (Another report of this match attributes the try to Woods, and one source gives the conversion to Alderson!)

In the second half, the Scottish halves played with great enterprise and England had to tackle and kick for touch desperately. McEwan ran the length of the pitch in one attempt and Clauss was just wide with a drop at goal. A run by Anderson, who constantly stretched the English defence, would have produced a score but for a tackle by Coop who played rather unsteadily in this, his only appearance for England. The final whistle blew with the Scots still attacking, and England, by winning, registered their third victory on Scottish soil.

SCOTLAND		ENGLAND	
H.J. Stevenson	(Edinburgh Acads.)	†T. Coop	(Leigh)
P.R. Clauss	(Oxford U.)	R.E. Lockwood	(Heckmondwike)
W. Neilson	(Cambridge U.)	*F.H.R. Alderson	(Hartlepool Rovers)
G.T. Campbell	(London Scottish)	J.W. Dyson	(Huddersfield)
*C.E. Orr	(West of Scotland)	A. Briggs	(Bradford)
D.G. Anderson	(London Scottish)	†H. Varley	(Liversedge)
G.T. Neilson	(West of Scotland)	S.M.J. Woods	(Wellington)
F.W.J. Goodhue	(London Scottish)	T. Kent	(Salford)
R.G. MacMillan	(London Scottish)	W. Yiend	(Hartlepool Rovers)
J.E. Orr	(West of Scotland)	E. Bullough	(Wigan)
M.C. McEwan	(Edinburgh Acads.)	F. Evershed	(Blackheath)
J.N. Millar	(West of Scotland)	†H. Bradshaw	(Bramley)
J.D. Boswell	(West of Scotland)	W.E. Bromet	(Tadcaster)
W.R. Gibson	(Royal H.S.F.P.)	W. Nichol	(Brighouse Rangers)
W.A. McDonald	(Glasgow U.)	J.T. Toothill	(Bradford)

Try: Bromet   *Conversion:* Lockwood

Referee: Mr R.G. Warren (Ireland)

WALES v ENGLAND 1893

Played at Cardiff Arms Park, 7 January 1893
Wales won by 1G, 1PG, 2T (12) to 1G, 3T (11)

Severe, cold weather during the three weeks before the match had curtailed fixtures in England to a bare minimum, and many of the visiting forwards showed a distinct lack of fitness in the second half when Wales staged a magnificent revival. The match itself had also been threatened by the hard frosts, and only the efforts of the groundsman and a team of unemployed men made certain that the match proceeded. Some eighteen tons of coal were used to keep braziers going and thus thaw the ground on the eve of the match.

England began in terrific form. Lohden opened the scoring within five minutes of the kick-off and a subsequent try by Marshall, converted by Stoddart, gave the visitors a seven-points lead at the interval. Another Marshall try, soon after, seemed to put the issue beyond doubt, but the Welsh pack fought strongly and an opening made by Nicholl and Hannan, from a line-out, led to a try by Gould near the posts, which Bancroft converted. Some accurate passing amongst the three-quarters led to Biggs getting the next try but England nosed further ahead when Bradshaw led a dribble which allowed Stoddart to send Marshall over for the Blackheath half-back's third try. Gould, who played an inspired game, put his side back in the hunt with the next try after a fine solo effort which Alderson should have checked: 11–9 now and little time remaining.

Then came an interesting and historic score. Wales were awarded a penalty, 30 yards from the English line and near touch. Gould called up Bancroft to kick for goal. The skipper wanted Bancroft to take a place-kick, but the full-back was determined to drop-kick the ball, and, to Gould's disgust, did so – and landed the winning points. This kick, which Bancroft, more than fifty years later, described as his most important kick for Wales, was the first penalty goal landed in an international match.

WALES		ENGLAND	
W.J. Bancroft	(Swansea)	†E. Field	(M'sex Wands/Cambridge U.)
N.M. Biggs	(Cardiff)	R.E. Lockwood	(Heckmondwike)
*A.J. Gould	(Newport)	F.H.R. Alderson	(Hartlepool Rovers)
J.C. Rees	(Oxford U.)	*A.E. Stoddart	(Blackheath)
W.M. McCutcheon	(Swansea)		
		†H. Marshall	(Blackheath)
H.P. Phillips	(Newport)	†R.F.C. de Winton	(Blackheath)
F.C. Parfitt	(Newport)		
		†J.H. Greenwell	(Rockcliff)
F. Mills	(Swansea)	W.E. Bromet	(Richmond)
C.B. Nicholl	(Cambridge U.)	H. Bradshaw	(Bramley)
T.C. Graham	(Newport)	†T. Broadley	(Bingley)
A.F. Hill	(Cardiff)	J.T. Toothill	(Bradford)
J. Hannan	(Newport)	F. Evershed	(Blackheath)
H.T. Day	(Newport)	S.M.J. Woods	(Wellington)
A.W. Boucher	(Newport)	†P. Maud	(Blackheath)
W.H. Watts	(Newport)	†F.C. Lohden	(Blackheath)

Tries: Gould (2), Biggs
Conversion: Bancroft
Penalty: Bancroft

Tries: Marshall (3), Lohden
Conversion: Stoddart

Referee: Mr D.S. Morton (Scotland)

IRELAND v ENGLAND 1893
Played at Lansdowne Road, Dublin, 4 February 1893
England won by 2T (4) to Nil

This was a well-fought game with much excitement for the crowd of 7000 spectators. The features of the match were the fine foraging of the English pack in the loose rushes, and the strong all-round play of the Irish backs. For the latter, the three-quarters passed accurately in attack and Edwards and Lee tackled bravely in defence.

The new English three-quarters brought play to the Irish line early in the match and Bradshaw battled his way over for a try after a forward rush. The attacks were evenly distributed between the sides up to the break and the Irish pack played with pluck and dash against their heavier opponents. In an effort to equalise before half-time, O'Conor actually crossed the line but the score was disallowed. England did increase their lead in the second half when Nicholson, of Rockcliff, made a break which nearly produced a try by Dyson on the other wing. An Irishman succeeded in shepherding him into touch-in-goal, but from a scrum which followed, Taylor, a clubmate of Nicholson, dodged past the Irish cover to register England's second try.

It was reported that the English backs had not played satisfactorily: the experiment of playing Lockwood in the centre after eleven appearances on the wing was not considered a success. The improved play of the forwards, however, after they had shown a marked lack of fitness against Wales, gave English supporters hope for their later encounter with Scotland.

IRELAND		ENGLAND	
S. Gardiner	(Belfast Albion)	E. Field	(Middlesex Wands./Cambridge U.)
T. Edwards	(Lansdowne)	J.W. Dyson	(Huddersfield)
*S. Lee	(N.I.F.C.)	R.E. Lockwood	(Heckmondwike)
W. Gardiner	(N.I.F.C.)	†T. Nicholson	(Rockcliff)
T. Thornhill	(Wanderers)	†H. Duckett	(Bradford)
F.E. Davies	(Lansdowne)	E.W. Taylor	(Rockcliff)
R. Johnston	(Wanderers)	F. Evershed	(Burton/Blackheath)
T.J. Johnston	(Queen's U.)	J.H. Greenwell	(Rockcliff)
E.J. Walsh	(Lansdowne)	*S.M.J. Woods	(Wellington)
A.K. Wallis	(Wanderers)	J.T. Toothill	(Bradford)
H. Lindsay	(Dublin U.)	W.E. Bromet	(Richmond)
M.S. Egan	(Garryowen)	W. Yiend	(Hartlepool Rovers)
J.H. O'Conor	(Bective Rangers)	H. Bradshaw	(Bramley)
R. Stevenson	(Dungannon)	A. Allport	(Blackheath)
C.V. Rooke	(Dublin U.)	P. Maud	(Blackheath)

Tries: Bradshaw, Taylor

Referee: Mr A.R. Don Wauchope (Scotland)

ENGLAND v SCOTLAND 1893
Played at Headingley, Leeds, 4 March 1893
Scotland won by 2DG (8) to Nil

Scotland deserved a larger margin of victory than two dropped goals. Their forwards constantly pushed the English pack back many yards, and the backs were more enterprising in the wet, slippery conditions than Stoddart's men. No tries were scored in the game but there was no doubt that the better team won. The tight play of the Scottish pack, magnificently led by Boswell, was perfect in the set-pieces, though England showed up well in the loose with Broadley, Bromet and Evershed conspicuous. The half-back play of the Scotsmen was superior to that by Duckett and Wells, and their three-quarters were always dangerous.

Despite the heavy ground, the weather was fine and the crowd of 20,000 saw Neilson drop a goal off the upright in the opening minutes of the game. To everyone's astonishment, the referee disallowed the score, ruling that the ball had not actually crossed the bar. MacMillan and Boswell led some Scottish rushes to the English line, but the home halves defended stoutly and the Scots could not cross for a try. Some excellent forward play by the Scottish pack was then complemented by good passing and running amongst the London Scottish three-quarters. England still prevented a score; in fact, a run by the English backs nearly brought a surprise try, the move just breaking down when Stoddart dropped the slippery ball from a Wells pass. On the stroke of half-time, Boswell dropped a goal which, this time, the referee had no hesitation in accepting. Campbell added the second Scottish drop soon after the interval.

F. Soane was the first England international capped from the Bath club, and L.J. Percival, previously capped from Oxford U., became Rugby R.F.C.'s first international player.

ENGLAND		SCOTLAND	
W.G. Mitchell	(Richmond)	H.J. Stevenson	(Edinburgh Acads.)
J.W. Dyson	(Huddersfield)	G.T. Campbell	(London Scottish)
*A.E. Stoddart	(Blackheath)	G. MacGregor	(London Scottish)
†F.P. Jones	(New Brighton)	W. Neilson	(Cambridge U.)
H. Duckett	(Bradford)	J.W. Simpson	(Royal H.S.F.P.)
†C.M. Wells	(Cambridge U.)	W. Wotherspoon	(West of Scotland)
F. Evershed	(Burton)	J.E. Orr	(West of Scotland)
†F. Soane	(Bath)	*J.D. Boswell	(West of Scotland)
W. Yiend	(Hartlepool Rovers)	R.G. MacMillan	(London Scottish)
J.T. Toothill	(Bradford)	T.M. Scott	(Melrose)
H. Bradshaw	(Bramley)	W.R. Gibson	(Royal H.S.F.P.)
L.J. Percival	(Rugby)	H.T.O. Leggatt	(Watsonians)
W.E. Bromet	(Richmond)	R.S. Davidson	(Royal H.S.F.P.)
T. Broadley	(Bingley)	W.B. Cownie	(Watsonians)
†J.J. Robinson	(Cambridge U.)	T.L. Hendry	(Clydesdale)

Dropped goals: Boswell, Campbell

Referee: Mr W. Wilkins (Wales)

ENGLAND v WALES 1894
Played at Birkenhead Park, 6 January 1894
England won by 4G, 1GM (24) to 1T (3)

England followed the Welsh example of playing four three-quarters and overran the Triple Crown holders with a superb display on a hard, frosty pitch. The result astonished followers of Rugby football in Great Britain: the North had beaten the South in the annual match, and the victors supplied nine players to an English side which was not expected to fare well against what was essentially the same Welsh side which had defeated all-comers in the previous season.

Wales had only themselves to blame for defeat. The wrong tactics were adopted, and the spoiling activities of the English pack disrupted the handling of the Welsh backs, who could do nothing right. The Welsh continually dominated in the scrums and Parfitt and Phillips had plenty of opportunities to get their backs away, but only one try was scored, from a classic round of passing near the end of the match. Too often in this game the Welsh three-quarters crowded themselves and, in the view of W.H. Gwynn (who wrote a chapter about the correct way to play the four-threequarter game in *Marshall*) the Welsh centres stood too far from their halves.

Wells set England on the road to victory with a superb run from his own 25 to send Morfitt loping over for the first try. Then Hooper made a mark and Taylor placed the goal. The brawny Bradshaw smashed his way over for the next score before fine play by the new wing, Firth, produced two more tries. Lockwood scored the first when Bancroft was slow to turn after a kick ahead; and then Taylor got in after a run by Firth had been followed by some loose play near the Welsh line.

Sam Morfitt was the first England cap from West Hartlepool club, and W.E. Tucker was the father of W.E. Tucker junior, capped three times 1926–30.

ENGLAND		WALES	
†J.F. Byrne	(Moseley)	W.J. Bancroft	(Swansea)
†F. Firth	(Halifax)	N.M. Biggs	(Cardiff)
†C.A. Hooper	(Middlesex Wands.)	*A.J. Gould	(Newport)
†S. Morfitt	(West Hartlepool)	J.C. Rees	(Oxford U./Llanelli)
*R.E. Lockwood	(Heckmondwike)	W.M. McCutcheon	(Swansea/Oldham)
C.M. Wells	(Harlequins)	H.P. Phillips	(Newport)
E.W. Taylor	(Rockcliff)	F.C. Parfitt	(Newport)
F. Soane	(Bath)	F. Mills	(Swansea)
†J. Hall	(North Durham)	A.F. Hill	(Cardiff)
J.T. Toothill	(Bradford)	C.B. Nicholl	(Llanelli/Cambridge U.)
†H. Speed	(Castleford)	T.C. Graham	(Newport)
†W.E. Tucker	(Cambridge U.)	A.W. Boucher	(Newport)
H. Bradshaw	(Bramley)	W.H. Watts	(Newport)
T. Broadley	(Bingley)	J. Hannan	(Newport)
A. Allport	(Blackheath)	D.J. Daniel	(Llanelli)

Tries: Bradshaw, Lockwood, Morfitt, Taylor   *Conversions:* Lockwood (3), Taylor   *Goal from mark:* Taylor

Try: Parfitt

Referee: Mr J.A. Smith (Scotland)

ENGLAND v IRELAND 1894

Played at Rectory Field, Blackheath, 3 February 1894
Ireland won by 1DG, 1T (7) to 1G (5)

The English forwards made the mistake the Welsh pack had made against them some weeks earlier by concentrating on heeling the ball from the scrummages. Ireland completely upset the balance of the home pack and played an effective spoiling game. Dribbling with great skill, they brought play to the English 25 immediately after the kick-off, and remained there for ninety per cent of the half. It was only after 30 minutes that England managed to reach Ireland's half, their most promising attack being a round of passing between Wood (who had been a late replacement for Wells at half-back), Firth and Taylor. Ireland's opening score came after ten minutes when Tuke fed Gwynn who was brought down near the English goal. From the ensuing mêlée a try was awarded to John Lytle. That Ireland did not increase their lead was due to a failure by the backs to capitalise upon the opportunities with which they were presented. Though the Irish were adopting the four-threequarter system for the first time, it was clear that the handling game, developed so cleverly by the Welsh, had not yet matured in Ireland. Instead, they had to depend upon the individual brilliance of Lee and Gwynn.

An exchange of punts by the opposing backs opened the second spell of the match, and Toothill had to retire with an injury. Morfitt and Wood put in some good runs but the spoiling Irish forwards continued to destroy England's best chances. Then, near the end of the match, the 20,000 crowd had an England score to cheer when Morfitt kicked on, the Irish full-back had a clearing kick charged down, and Lockwood scored. Taylor's conversion, with a fine kick, put England ahead, but the lead was short-lived. Hooper was caught in possession under his own posts, just three minutes later, and Forrest picked up the loose ball and dropped a superb goal. England fought hard in the dying minutes of the match but the Irish defence held out to gain a deserved victory.

ENGLAND		IRELAND	
J.F. Byrne	(Moseley)	W. Sparrow	(Dublin U.)
F. Firth	(Halifax)	H.G. Wells	(Bective Rangers)
C.A. Hooper	(Middlesex Wands.)	S. Lee	(N.I.F.C.)
S. Morfitt	(West Hartlepool)	W. Gardiner	(N.I.F.C.)
*R.E. Lockwood	(Heckmondwike)	L.H. Gwynn	(Dublin U.)
†R. Wood	(Liversedge)	W.S. Brown	(Dublin U.)
E.W. Taylor	(Rockcliff)	B.B. Tuke	(Bective Rangers)
F. Soane	(Bath)	J.N. Lytle	(N.I.F.C.)
J.T. Toothill	(Bradford)	J.H. Lytle	(N.I.F.C.)
W.E. Tucker	(Cambridge U.)	G. Walmsley	(Bective Rangers)
H. Bradshaw	(Bramley)	J.H. O'Conor	(Bective Rangers)
A. Allport	(Blackheath)	H. Lindsay	(Dublin U.)
T. Broadley	(Bingley)	*E.G. Forrest	(Wanderers)
J. Hall	(North Durham)	T.J. Crean	(Wanderers)
H. Speed	(Castleford)	C.V. Rooke	(Dublin U.)

Try: Lockwood *Conversion:* Taylor

Try: J.N. Lytle
Dropped goal: Forrest

Referee: Mr W.M. Douglas (Wales)

SCOTLAND v ENGLAND 1894

Played at Raeburn Place, Edinburgh, 17 March 1894
Scotland won by 2T (6) to Nil

As in the Calcutta Cup match of 1893, Scotland owed their triumph to Boswell's forwards – the outstanding London Scottish threequarter line displayed individual brilliance, but their combined play was disappointing. England were rarely in the game, spending much of the time in their own 25. On the few occasions that the English forwards heeled the ball, their backs, missing the pace and skill of Lockwood, were unable to manufacture any scoring chances.

On a perfect day for Rugby football, England began with the disadvantage of playing into the sun and wind, and kicks by MacGregor and Gowans took Scotland to the English quarters where they remained for most of the half. Taylor defended stoutly for England and many Scottish threequarter movements were checked by his canny anticipation and steady tackling. For the Scots, Gedge and W. Neilson were often dangerous. The most attractive piece of play for the 12,000 spectators was a round of passing in which all of the Scottish backs featured. This gave Gowans an opportunity to score, but he was thwarted by a good English tackle. Alas, the Scottish backs were unable to reproduce this form later in the game when their forwards won an almost continuous supply of good ball.

Scotland lost Wotherspoon before the interval with an injury, and his return after half-time saw a rearrangement of the Scottish back division – Gowans going to full-back, W. Neilson to half and Wotherspoon joining MacGregor in the threes'. Scotland picked up where they had left off at the end of the first half and Boswell, Wotherspoon (twice) and MacGregor had drops at goal. Eventually, Scotland scored the try for which their supporters had waited. Boswell charged over from a set-scrummage near the English line, but there was no conversion. England, for the only time during the match, looked threatening and retaliated with a forward dribble which nearly resulted in a score. Scotland soon stormed back, though, and after a long period of pressure Boswell obtained his second try, in similar vein to his first. There was no conversion and shortly afterwards the referee blew for no-side, giving Scotland a well-deserved victory.

The England centre, Jackson, was the first international player from Gloucester, although he was playing for Halifax at the time of this match.

SCOTLAND

G. MacGregor	(London Scottish)
G.T. Campbell	(London Scottish)
W. Neilson	(London Scottish)
H.T.S. Gedge	(London Scottish/Edinburgh Wands.)
J.J. Gowans	(London Scottish)
J.W. Simpson	(Royal H.S.F.P.)
W. Wotherspoon	(West of Scotland)
H.T.O. Leggatt	(Watsonians)
R.G. MacMillan	(London Scottish)
W.B. Cownie	(Watsonians)
W.R. Gibson	(Royal H.S.F.P.)
W.M.C. McEwan	(Edinburgh Academy)
H.F. Menzies	(West of Scotland)
*J.D. Boswell	(West of Scotland)
W.G. Neilson	(Merchiston)

Tries: Boswell (2)

ENGLAND

J.F. Byrne	(Moseley)
C.A. Hooper	(Middlesex Wands.)
†W.J. Jackson	(Halifax)
S. Morfitt	(West Hartlepool)
F. Firth	(Halifax)
*E.W. Taylor	(Rockcliff)
C.M. Wells	(Harlequins)
A. Allport	(Blackheath)
J. Hall	(North Durham)
†A.E. Elliott	(St. Thomas's H.)
T. Broadley	(Bingley)
H. Bradshaw	(Bramley)
F. Soane	(Bath)
H. Speed	(Castleford)
†W. Walton	(Castleford)

Referee: Mr W. Wilkins (Wales)

WALES v ENGLAND 1895

Played at St Helen's, Swansea, 5 January 1895
England won by 1G, 3T (14) to 2T (6)

As usual, the season began with the meeting between Wales and England, this time at Swansea. The 18–20,000 crowd saw the straw removed from the pitch just before kick-off, and conditions were ideal for fast open Rugby. Heeling out of the scrum to enable the backs to run and handle at speed had become the focal point of the game in Wales by this time, and provided an attractive spectacle for the crowd. On this occasion, however, the brilliant English forwards, after an indifferent start, became the dominating influence on the game and provided the foundation for England's victory.

Wales scored first – after ten minutes – when Biggs, Gould and Pearson figured in a fine passing movement. A kick by Pearson caught the English defence napping and Elsey scored. England equalised just before half-time when a stunning run by Thomson on the left wing, in which he shook off the combined attentions of Pearson and Bancroft, produced a try. The game had thus far taken place at an exhausting rate. Many doubted the English pack's ability to last the pace after the break, but these doubts were soon to be summarily dismissed. After a blatant error by Fegan had allowed Graham to score, the Englishmen combined cleverly and Wales constantly looked vulnerable. Three more English tries were obtained, with Mitchell converting the last, and only some desperate Welsh tackling prevented Woods and his men from running up a huge total in the last quarter of the game.

WALES		ENGLAND	
W.J. Bancroft	(Swansea)	†H. Ward	(Bradford)
T.W. Pearson	(Cardiff)	†J.H.C. Fegan	(Blackheath)
*A.J. Gould	(Newport)	†F.A. Leslie-Jones	(Oxford U.)
O. Badger	(Llanelli)	†E.M. Baker	(Oxford U.)
W.L. Thomas	(Newport)	W.B. Thomson	(Blackheath)
S. Biggs	(Cardiff)	†R.H.B. Cattell	(Moseley)
B. Davies	(Llanelli)	E.W. Taylor	(Rockcliff)
A.W. Boucher	(Newport)	*S.M.J. Woods	(Bridgwater/B'heath)
T.C. Graham	(Newport)	†F.O. Poole	(Oxford U.)
F. Mills	(Cardiff)	W.E. Bromet	(Richmond)
T.H. Jackson	(Swansea)	†F. Mitchell	(Cambridge U.)
C.B. Nicholl	(Llanelli)	W.E. Tucker	(Cambridge U.)
W.J. Elsey	(Cardiff)	†C. Thomas	(Barnstaple)
J. Hannan	(Newport)	†G.M. Carey	(Oxford U.)
W.H. Watts	(Newport)	†H.W. Finlinson	(Blackheath)

Tries: Elsey, Graham

Tries: Carey, Leslie-Jones, Thomson, Woods *Conversion:* Mitchell

Referee: Mr J.A. Smith (Scotland)

IRELAND v ENGLAND 1895
Played at Lansdowne Road, Dublin, 2 February 1895
England won by 2T (6) to 1T (3)

The excellent display by the English forwards against Wales was repeated in this match on a saturated pitch before about 9000 spectators. The Irish forwards played their characteristic game – storming into the Englishmen at the start of the match, but fading away as the hard scrummaging of the fitter English pack wore them down towards the end of the game. Only good play by the Irish backs in the closing quarter of the second half gave the home selectors any pleasure.

Both sides realised early in the match that handling was a futile experiment in such wet conditions. Driving rain added to the problems of a quickly thawing pitch and play was largely a muddy forward battle in which the English pack slowly but surely gained superiority. When the English forwards were unable to take the ball through the scrummage, they would screw the Irish scrummage off-balance with a wheeling shove and break away with the ball at their feet.

No scores were registered before half-time, though Thomson did nearly cross for a try after Taylor had launched an attack. After the interval, prolonged pressure by the English forwards, notably from the scrummages, resulted in near-scores by Cattell, Taylor and Baker. Gardiner temporarily relieved the situation for Ireland but England returned and Thomas scored a try after a scrummage. Mitchell failed to convert, but England stormed back on to the attack and Woods was only just held on the line. A series of scrums and Irish drop-outs followed before Fegan received a short pass and scored the second try.

England were home and dry now, and relaxed in the closing minutes. Tuke and Lee, at last, produced their best form, drawing frequent applause from the Irish crowd, and their efforts were eventually rewarded with a try by Louis Magee. An exciting finish followed but the Irish forwards were unable to match the English pack for stamina and strength, and the visitors thus held on to record their sixteenth victory over Ireland.

IRELAND		ENGLAND	
G.R. Symes	(Monkstown)	J.F. Byrne	(Moseley)
W. Gardiner	(N.I.F.C.)	W.B. Thomson	(Blackheath)
S. Lee	(N.I.F.C.)	E.M. Baker	(Oxford U.)
T.H. Stevenson	(Queen's U.)	F.A. Leslie-Jones	(Oxford U.)
J.T. Magee	(Bective Rangers)	J.H.C. Fegan	(Blackheath)
L.M. Magee	(Bective Rangers)	R.H.B. Cattell	(Moseley)
B.B. Tuke	(Bective Rangers)	E.W. Taylor	(Rockcliff)
T.J. Johnston	(Queen's U.)	G.M. Carey	(Oxford U.)
H. Lindsay	(Armagh)	*S.M.J. Woods	(Bridgwater/B'heath)
A.A. Brunker	(Lansdowne)	H.W. Finlinson	(Blackheath)
*J.H. O'Conor	(Bective Rangers)	W.E. Bromet	(Richmond)
H.C McCoull	(Belfast Albion)	W.E. Tucker	(Cambridge U.)
A.D Clinch	(Wanderers)	F. Mitchell	(Cambridge U.)
T.J. Crean	(Wanderers)	F.O. Poole	(Oxford U.)
C.V. Rooke	(Monkstown)	C. Thomas	(Barnstaple)

Try: L.M. Magee   *Tries:* Fegan, Thomas

Referee: Mr D.G. Findlay (Scotland)

ENGLAND v SCOTLAND 1895

Played at Athletic Ground, Richmond, 9 March 1895
Scotland won by 1PG, 1T (6) to 1PG (3)

A large crowd of 20,000 saw Scotland deservedly win the Triple Crown in a match confined to a mauling forward contest, with the superior fitness of the Scots telling in the closing stages of the game. (A long period of severe frost had forced the postponement of many first-class matches in England, and, as a result, the home players were below their usual condition and clearly out of practice.)

The Scots were impressive in combined play, the forwards favouring the classic Scottish dribbling tactics, and Donaldson was the perfect foil to the pack, preserving their fitness with a series of accurately-placed kicks to touch. The Scottish backs were rarely seen in the open, but Smith defended immaculately. By contrast, the English defence was frequently at sixes-and-sevens in the face of the Scottish foot rushes, and Donaldson gave Byrne, who had a match of mixed fortunes, a thorough examination with a variety of well-directed punts.

The Scots aimed to keep the game tight and dominated territorially throughout. In the few open passages of play, Carey, Thomas and Mitchell led several English rushes, but the home side failed to discover the magnificent form shown earlier in the season. All of the scoring took place before half-time. A dribble by the English pack led to a penalty for off-side and Byrne, much against the run of play, landed England into the lead with a goal from 40 yards. G.T. Neilson soon equalised with a similar score, also from 40 yards. Play was limited to a number of scrummages after this, until Donaldson sent Campbell away. The latter kicked ahead and the English full-back tried to clear to touch, but his kick was charged down by Neilson who scored a try.

England played confidently in the remaining minutes of the first half, but the rock-like defence and siege-gun kicking of Smith prevented a score. In the second half, Scotland completely dominated and Donaldson nursed the touch-line with ease. Many promising Scottish movements threatened the English defence in the last minutes, and the home side were thankful to Cattell, Taylor and Baker for some relieving dashes, and latterly to Byrne for a number of clearing kicks.

ENGLAND		SCOTLAND	
J.F. Byrne	(Moseley)	A.R. Smith	(Oxford U.)
W.B. Thomson	(Blackheath)	J.J. Gowans	(London Scottish)
E.M. Baker	(Oxford U.)	W. Neilson	(London Scottish)
†T.H. Dobson	(Bradford)	G.T. Campbell	(London Scottish)
J.H.C. Fegan	(Blackheath)	R. Welsh	(Watsonians)
R.H.B. Cattell	(Moseley)	J.W. Simpson	(Royal H.S.F.P.)
E.W. Taylor	(Rockcliff)	W.P. Donaldson	(West of Scotland)
G.M. Carey	(Oxford U.)	J.H. Dods	(Edinburgh Acads.)
*S.M.J. Woods	(Bridgwater/B'heath)	J.N. Millar	(West of Scotland)
H.W. Finlinson	(Blackheath)	W.M.C McEwan	(Edinburgh Acads.)
W.E. Bromet	(Richmond)	W.B. Cownie	(Watsonians)
W.E. Tucker	(Cambridge U.)	T.M. Scott	(Hawick)
F. Mitchell	(Cambridge U.)	W.R. Gibson	(Royal H.S.F.P.)
F.O. Poole	(Oxford U.)	G.T. Neilson	(West of Scotland)
C. Thomas	(Barnstaple)	*R.G. MacMillan	(London Scottish)

Penalty: Byrne

Try: G.T. Neilson
Penalty: G.T. Neilson

Referee: Mr W. Wilkins (Wales)

ENGLAND v WALES 1896

Played at Rectory Field, Blackheath, 4 January 1896
England won by 2G, 5T (25) to Nil

A meeting of the R.F.U. on 19 September 1895 outlawed professionalism in any form, and adopted new By-Laws to govern the structure of the game. These laws affected the administration of the clubs in the north of England and the result was the breakaway and formation of a Northern Union – later known as the Rugby League.

This was the first English international since the split, and the result, a rousing victory for the home side, seemed to indicate that England could do without those players who had defected. The annual North–South match had been a triumph for the North, and ten of this English side were from the North: several were later to join their fellow-countrymen in the Rugby League, including Houghton, who returned to Runcorn (now a Northern Union club) soon after this match, although selected to play against Ireland.

Wales were steam-rollered into the Blackheath mud by the hardier English pack, though they were unlucky to lose Badger with a broken collar-bone after only 15 minutes, when the little Llanelli centre was injured tackling Valentine. The Swinton centre went on to send Morfitt in for the opening try and then the flood-gates opened. Cattell added two tries; Mitchell elbowed his way through the middle of the Welsh pack for another – Valentine converting – and Fookes crossed at the corner before the interval.

In the second half, Morfitt slipped through the Welsh defence and ran over from outside the Welsh 25 for his second try and Taylor, the slippery English half-back, created an opportunity for Fookes to score the seventh try. Reports record that this last try was converted: the scorer was either Taylor or Mitchell – accounts vary.

ENGLAND		WALES	
S. Houghton	(Birkenhead Wands.)	W.J. Bancroft	(Swansea)
S. Morfitt	(West Hartlepool)	F.H. Dauncey	(Newport)
J. Valentine	(Swinton)	O. Badger	(Llanelli)
E.M. Baker	(Oxford U.)	*A.J. Gould	(Newport)
†E.F. Fookes	(Sowerby Bridge)	C.A. Bowen	(Llanelli)
R.H.B. Cattell	(Blackheath)	B. Davies	(Llanelli)
*E.W. Taylor	(Rockcliff)	D. Morgan	(Llanelli)
G.M. Carey	(Blackheath)	S.H. Ramsey	(Treorchy)
†J. Pinch	(Lancaster)	C.B. Nicholl	(Llanelli)
F. Mitchell	(B'heath/Cambridge U.)	H. Packer	(Newport)
†L.F. Giblin	(B'heath/Cambridge U.)	E. George	(Pontypridd)
†W. Whiteley	(Bramley)	A.W. Boucher	(Newport)
†J. Rhodes	(Castleford)	W.H. Watts	(Newport)
†J.W. Ward	(Castleford)	A.M. Jenkin	(Swansea)
†A. Starks	(Castleford)	F. Mills	(Swansea)

Tries: Cattell (2), Fookes (2), Morfitt (2), Mitchell
Conversions: Taylor, Valentine

Referee: Mr D.G. Findlay (Scotland)

ENGLAND v IRELAND 1896

Played at Meanwood Road, Leeds, 1 February 1896
Ireland won by 2G (10) to 1DG (4)

The Irish forwards began with their customary dash and the much-fancied English pack had their backs very much to the wall in the opening stages. Rooke kicked off on a windless day, in front of 17,858 spectators, and he sent the ball rolling over the dead-ball line. Play was in the English 25 for much of the first 25 minutes and hard though the English backs tried, they could neither run the ball out of defence nor find touch with kicks ahead. Conversely, the running of the Irish backs was purposeful and penetrative, and their kicking always gained ground. For all their strengths, however, Ireland looked like failing to realise any concrete advantage – points on the board – and only a close drop at goal by Fulton represented a realistic threat to England before the home side counter-attacked, and Cattell nearly scored. Ireland were not to be taken lightly, though, and Magee, Bulger and Lee brought their side storming back to English quarters. Bulger failed with two penalty kicks before Magee punted ahead and Lee produced one of his dazzling runs. Sealy was at hand to score near the posts and Bulger converted.

England were a different side at the beginning of the second half and it looked as though the Irish pack, like many of its predecessors, had shot its bolt and run out of steam. The English heeling in the scrums put pressure on the Irish backs, and it was a desperate kick out by one of the visitors which reached Byrne who dropped a lovely goal from fully 40 yards to reduce Ireland's lead to 5–4. Suddenly the Irishmen, finding their second wind, threw everything into attack. A superb move initiated by the Irish halves created the inevitable score – a try by Stevenson which Bulger goaled. Soon after, constructive combined play nearly resulted in a try for Lee.

With ten minutes remaining, England summoned enough energy for a final fling. One of the most attractive moves of the afternoon featured Baker and Fookes, and the former streaked clear of the defence. However, in crossing for what should have been an easy score, Baker went out of play over the dead-ball line, having attempted to touch down by the posts. This somewhat extravagant act deprived the crowd of a dramatic finish, and Ireland secured her second consecutive victory on English soil. Receipts: £756–10–4.

ENGLAND		IRELAND	
J.F. Byrne	(Moseley)	J. Fulton	(N.I.F.C.)
S. Morfitt	(West Hartlepool)	W. Gardiner	(N.I.F.C.)
J. Valentine	(Swinton)	*S. Lee	(N.I.F.C.)
E.M. Baker	(Oxford U.)	T.H. Stevenson	(Edinburgh U.)
E.F. Fookes	(Sowerby Bridge)	L.Q. Bulger	(Dublin U.)
R.H.B. Cattell	(Blackheath)	L.M. Magee	(Bective Rangers)
*E.W. Taylor	(Rockcliff)	G.G. Allen	(Derry)
G.M. Carey	(Blackheath)	J.H. O'Conor	(Bective Rangers)
J. Pinch	(Lancaster)	J.H. Lytle	(N.I.F.C.)
A. Starks	(Castleford)	W.G. Byron	(N.I.F.C.)
L.F. Giblin	(Cambridge U./B'heath)	H. Lindsay	(Wanderers)
J. Rhodes	(Castleford)	J. Sealy	(Dublin U.)
F. Mitchell	(Cambridge U./B'heath)	A.D. Clinch	(Wanderers)
J.W. Ward	(Castleford)	T.J. Crean	(Wanderers)
W.E. Bromet	(Richmond)	C.V. Rooke	(Monkstown)

Dropped goal: Byrne

Tries: Sealy, Stevenson
Conversions: Bulger (2)

Referee: Mr D.G. Findlay (Scotland)

SCOTLAND v ENGLAND 1896

Played at Old Hampden Park, Glasgow, 14 March 1896
Scotland won by 1G, 2T (11) to Nil

The English selectors included five Yorkshire forwards in their pack, but Scotland did well to offset the power of the Tykes' solid scrummaging with disruptive wheeling and fast dribbling. England were, consequently, rattled up front, and their half-backs had a torrid afternoon throwing themselves at the feet of the marauding Scottish forwards.

The turf was in immaculate condition, and 20,000 gathered, in fine weather, to witness this fifteenth encounter for the Calcutta Cup. The Scottish three-quarters were outstanding and showed their attacking flair early in the match, only a knock-on robbing them of a try. Wells and Cattell defended bravely against the fierce rushes of the Scottish pack, and some fine kicking under pressure by the English backs kept England in the game for most of the first half, but just before the interval Scotland opened their account. Donaldson, who excelled at half, and Elliot initiated a round of passing which saw Fleming clear the defence for Gedge to run to the posts and score a picture-book try. The easy place-kick was missed.

Gedge nearly scored early in the second half after Poole had made a blunder, but Fookes's speed saved the day for the visitors. The Scottish pack continued to pose problems for the Englishmen and only the kicking of Wells, and the occasional bursts by Fookes, halted the progress of the Scots. England then suffered two hammer-blows in the course of five minutes, mid-way through the half. Superb handling and running by Gedge, Donaldson, Dods and Neilson resulted in Gowans adding the final flourish with an unconverted try. England had scarcely recovered when Donaldson launched an attack and Fleming scored after some passing by Campbell and Gedge. This time, Scott kicked the goal. In the last 12 minutes, England could make little in the form of a reply and the Scottish forwards, expertly nursed by Donaldson, kept the match tight until no-side.

SCOTLAND		ENGLAND	
G. MacGregor	(London Scottish)	†R.W. Poole	(Hartlepool Rovers)
G.T. Campbell	(London Scottish)	E.F. Fookes	(Sowerby Bridge)
J.J. Gowans	(London Scottish)	J. Valentine	(Swinton)
C.J.N. Fleming	(Edinburgh Wands.)	E.M. Baker	(Oxford U.)
H.T.S. Gedge	(London Scottish)	S. Morfitt	(West Hartlepool)
M. Elliot	(Hawick)	R.H.B. Cattell	(Blackheath)
W.P. Donaldson	(West of Scotland)	C.M. Wells	(Harlequins)
J.H. Dods	(London Scottish)	†G.E. Hughes	(Barrow)
H.O. Smith	(Watsonians)	†J.H. Barron	(Bingley)
W.M.C. McEwan	(Edinburgh Acads.)	†E. Knowles	(Millom)
T.M. Scott	(Hawick)	H. Speed	(Castleford)
G.O. Turnbull	(West of Scotland)	J. Rhodes	(Castleford)
M.C. Morrison	(Royal H.S.F.P.)	*F. Mitchell	(Cambridge U./B'heath)
*G.T. Neilson	(West of Scotland)	J.W. Ward	(Castleford)
A. Balfour	(Watsonians)	T. Broadley	(Bingley)

Tries: Fleming, Gedge, Gowans
Conversion: Scott

Referee: Mr W.M. Douglas (Wales)

73

WALES v ENGLAND 1897
Played at Rodney Parade, Newport, 9 January 1897
Wales won by 1G, 2T (11) to Nil

In their quest for fast open play, Wales introduced heavier forwards at the expense of skill in the loose. Welsh philosophy was based on the principle of holding the scrummage and heeling out for the halves and three-quarters to handle and run with the maximum of time and space in which to manoeuvre. Thus, in their search for stronger packs, the Welsh selectors turned to the 'Rhondda-type forward', who was, primarily, as hard as nails, and, possibly, a possessor of greater brawn than brain. The effect was never better felt than in this match – Wales's first decisive victory over the English – and subsequent Welsh sides were selected along similar guidelines, though not all were as successful.

Wales gave a wonderful performance on a heavy, wet surface. Pearson, Gould, Nicholls and Biggs each figured prominently in passing movements, and Nicholls nearly scored when, with the line at his mercy, he slipped on the wet surface while veering in to the English goal. Eventually, Pearson scored a classic threequarter try in the corner, and shortly afterwards, just before the interval, Boucher touched down after the Welsh forwards had rushed the ball over the line.

At the start of the second half, the English pack dominated in the tight and it looked, for a while, as if Wales would have to fight hard to retain their lead. Fookes, Taylor and Byrne all made attempts to score, before the home side again took the upper hand and, at length, sealed the victory with a fine try by Dan Jones which was converted by Bancroft.

Gould retired after this match and followers of the game in Wales contributed to a testimonial fund which enabled the Newport man to obtain the title deeds of his home. The other British Unions regarded this as an act of professionalism and a dispute arose, which ultimately led to the isolation of Wales from international competition for twelve months.

Tom Fletcher was the first Cumbrian back to play for England, while J.F. and F.A. Byrne were brothers capped in the same match.

WALES		ENGLAND	
W.J. Bancroft	(Swansea)	J.F. Byrne	(Moseley)
C.A. Bowen	(Llanelli)	E.F. Fookes	(Sowerby Bridge)
E.G. Nicholls	(Cardiff)	E.M. Baker	(Oxford U.)
*A.J. Gould	(Newport)	†F.A. Byrne	(Moseley)
T.W. Pearson	(Newport)	†T. Fletcher	(Seaton)
S. Biggs	(Cardiff)	C.M. Wells	(Harlequins)
D. Jones	(Aberavon)	*E.W. Taylor	(Rockcliff)
F.H. Cornish	(Cardiff)	†F.M. Stout	(Gloucester)
R. Hellings	(Llwynypia)	†R.F. Oakes	(Hartlepool Rovers)
J. Evans	(Llanelli)	†W. Ashford	(Richmond)
H. Packer	(Newport)	†W.B. Stoddart	(Liverpool)
D. Evans	(Penygraig)	†R.H. Mangles	(Richmond)
J. Rhapps	(Penygraig)	†P.J. Ebdon	(Wellington)
W. Morris	(Llanelli)	J.H. Barron	(Bingley)
A.W. Boucher	(Newport)	†F. Jacob	(Cambridge U.)

Tries: Boucher, Jones,
Pearson
Conversion: Bancroft

Referee: Mr J.T. Magee (Ireland)

IRELAND v ENGLAND 1897

Played at Lansdowne Road, Dublin, 6 February 1897
Ireland won by 1GM, 3T (13) to 2PG, 1T (9)

A crowd approaching 15,000 saw Ireland beat England for the third time in four seasons. Conditions were splendid and the match was played at a gruelling pace throughout, taking toll on the players in the closing stages when play was frequently interrupted for attention to injuries.

Ireland's strong, dominating pack carried the day, though the English forwards gave an encouraging account of themselves after the humiliating hammering suffered at Leeds in the previous season. The chief failing of the visiting forwards lay in their dribbling and loose play, but the English selectors could be pleased with the much-improved tight scrummaging. The English backs were restricted in their opportunities to show their pace in open play, however, and only Fookes enhanced his reputation as a running back. The Irish pack swarmed on to the loose ball, and the Irish threes' enjoyed a stream of handsome possession.

The outstanding back on the field, Gardiner, constantly troubled the Englishmen and scored two of the tries – the first after only six minutes of play. Rooke had a try disallowed before Magee and Allen put Gardiner over. England defended stoutly for a period – Taylor stemming the tide of Irish rushes with some canny covering – and Robinson eventually levelled matters with a try near the corner. Ireland's reply was a stylish try by Gardiner and before the break Bulger landed a goal with a drop-kick, after a fair catch had been claimed. (The referee awarded no-charge, enabling Bulger to kick with ease.)

In the second half, Byrne reduced England's deficit with a penalty goal from half-way, but a palpable error by the English backs allowed Rooke to dribble through soon after, and Stevenson lobbed a pass to Bulger who crossed, unchallenged, at the corner. England recovered and in the last 12 minutes of the game, Ebdon, Bunting and Fookes all went close to scoring tries. Robinson just failed with a pot at goal, and Byrne eventually kicked a second penalty, but there was to be no last-minute glory, the referee whistling for no-side soon after Byrne's goal from the touch-line.

G.C. Robinson was the first international capped for England direct from Percy Park R.F.C.

IRELAND		ENGLAND	
J. Fulton	(N.I.F.C.)	J.F. Byrne	(Moseley)
L.Q. Bulger	(Dublin U.)	†G.C. Robinson	(Percy Park)
T.H. Stevenson	(Edinburgh U.)	†W.L. Bunting	(Richmond)
S. Lee	(N.I.F.C.)	†J.T. Taylor	(Castleford)
W. Gardiner	(N.I.F.C.)	E.F. Fookes	(Sowerby Bridge)
L.M. Magee	(Bective Rangers)	†S. Northmore	(Millom)
G.G. Allen	(Liverpool/Derry)	*E.W. Taylor	(Rockcliff)
J.E. McIlwaine	(N.I.F.C.)	F. Jacob	(Cambridge U.)
J.H. Lytle	(N.I.F.C.)	J.H. Barron	(Bingley)
W.G. Byron	(N.I.F.C.)	P.J. Ebdon	(Wellington)
M. Ryan	(Rockwell College)	R.F. Oakes	(Hartlepool Rovers)
J. Ryan	(Rockwell College)	W.B. Stoddart	(Liverpool)
A.D. Clinch	(Wanderers)	F.M. Stout	(Gloucester)
*E.G. Forrest	(Wanderers)	W. Ashford	(Richmond)
C.V. Rooke	(Monkstown)	R.H. Mangles	(Richmond)

Tries: Gardiner (2), Bulger   *Try:* Robinson   *Penalties:* Byrne (2)
Goal from mark: Bulger

Referee: Mr D.G. Findlay (Scotland)

ENGLAND v SCOTLAND 1897

Played at Fallowfield, Manchester, 13 March 1897
England won by 1G, 1DG, 1T (12) to 1T (3)

The Calcutta Cup returned to England for the first time since 1893. The English pack pulled out all the stops and worked brilliantly as a unit to provide the backs with a continuous supply of quality possession. Only tremendous tackling by the Scottish backs prevented the Englishmen tearing the visitors' defence apart, and Smith at full-back was the model of reliability.

15,000 entered the grounds of the Manchester Athletic Club, in favourable conditions, to watch the last international match played in the north of England. Scotland played with the elements in the first half and some adept kicking by Neilson and Scott kept Scotland on the attack during the first 15 minutes, though it was apparent to all that the English side had discovered a verve and purpose which had been lacking in their earlier performances against Wales and Ireland. Their forwards soon created opportunities for the new centre pairing of Mackie and Bunting to show some neat touches, and Robinson made several dashes towards the Scottish line, but there was no scoring in the first half.

England put the first points on the board after a period of Scottish pressure in the second half. Byrne inspired the home side with a gigantic touch-kick from his goal-line to half-way. Robinson made a fine run, Byrne went near with a penalty from touch, and the English forwards got the better of a series of scrums which followed a Scottish drop-out. In fact, the English backs became so dangerous in attack that MacMillan withdrew from the pack to bolster the Scottish defence. His efforts were in vain for Fookes put in a 20-yards run before playing the ball over the Scottish line and squeezing between two defenders to score in the corner. Byrne converted with a beautiful kick. Robinson scored again after a classic round of passing by the three-quarters, but Scotland managed to produce a score after loose play and wild kicking near the English line, ten minutes from no-side. Finally and appropriately, Byrne completed the proceedings with a fine drop-goal: he had played an outstanding game, technically and tactically.

Scotland were so confident of victory that they did not bring the Calcutta Cup to Manchester.

ENGLAND		SCOTLAND	
J.F. Byrne	(Moseley)	A.R. Smith	(Oxford U.)
E.F. Fookes	(Sowerby Bridge)	A.M. Bucher	(Edinburgh Acads.)
W.L. Bunting	(Richmond)	W. Neilson	(London Scottish)
†O.G. Mackie	(Cambridge U.)	A.W. Robertson	(Edinburgh Acads.)
G.C. Robinson	(Percy Park)	T.L. Scott	(Langholm)
*E.W. Taylor	(Rockcliff)	J.W. Simpson	(Royal H.S.F.P.)
C.M. Wells	(Harlequins)	M. Elliot	(Hawick)
†H.W. Dudgeon	(Richmond)	J.H. Dods	(Edinburgh Acads.)
F. Jacob	(Cambridge U.)	A. Balfour	(Cambridge U.)
L.F. Giblin	(Cambridge U.)	W.M.C. McEwan	(Edinburgh Acads.)
†Jas. Davidson	(Aspatria)	T.M. Scott	(Hawick)
E. Knowles	(Millom)	G.O. Turnbull	(London Scottish)
J. Pinch	(Lancaster)	M.C. Morrison	(Royal H.S.F.P.)
W.B. Stoddart	(Liverpool)	R.C. Stevenson	(London Scottish)
R.F. Oakes	(Hartlepool Rovers)	*R.G. MacMillan	(London Scottish)

Tries: Fookes, Robinson
Conversion: Byrne
Dropped goal: Byrne

Try: Bucher

Referee: Mr J.T. Magee (Ireland)

ENGLAND v IRELAND 1898

Played at Athletic Ground, Richmond, 5 February 1898
Ireland won by 1PG, 2T (9) to 1PG, 1T (6)

Ireland's victory was due to the skill and finish of their pack in loose play, with Magee and Allen dictating the tactical aspects of the game at half. Poor passing by Myers from the base of the scrummage wrecked England's back game and the Irish were swift to punish the errors made by the English backs. Magee in fact won the match in the last minute when he snatched the ball after a scrum, left Myers and Mackie clutching at thin air in desperate efforts to halt the Irish wizard, and outpaced Byrne to complete a grand match-winning try.

20,000 were present and the game was staged in ideal conditions. Throughout, play consisted of controlled Irish forward rushes and clever kicking by the Irish backs. The Irish three-quarters were splendid in attack: but for Byrne's careful play at full-back, England must have lost by a far larger margin than three points. Magee and Allen created many Irish attacks, though it was a penalty kicked by Bulger which put the visitors ahead after ten minutes of play. Robinson featured next with an exciting run which nearly produced a score, but Ireland regained their composure and the English halves became swamped by the Irish pack. Lindsay increased the lead before the interval with a try after loose play near the English line.

England played well after half-time and Byrne landed a penalty following a scrummage infringement in front of the Irish posts. Lee then retired with a fractured collar-bone – Lindsay substituting – and England capitalised on this setback when Bunting made an opening for Robinson to equalise. During the closing 15 minutes Ireland gained the initiative and Magee timed his last break to perfection, the referee blowing for no-side soon after the unsuccessful conversion attempt.

Myers was a late replacement for an injured player. Although these were the days before half-backs specialised, he usually 'stood off' from the scrum. In this match he 'worked' the scrum (i.e. played scrum-half) to oblige Jacob, another who normally 'stood off'. Myers died in 1906 from injuries sustained in a Northern Union game.

ENGLAND		IRELAND	
*J.F.Byrne	(Moseley)	P.E. O'Brien-Butler	(Monkstown)
E.F. Fookes	(Sowerby Bridge)	F.C. Purser	(Dublin U.)
W.L. Bunting	(Richmond)	*S. Lee	(N.I.F.C.)
O.G. Mackie	(Cambridge U.)	L.H. Gwynn	(Monkstown)
G.C. Robinson	(Percy Park)	L.Q. Bulger	(Lansdowne)
†P.G. Jacob	(Blackheath)	L.M. Magee	(Bective Rangers)
†H. Myers	(Keighley)	G.G. Allen	(Derry)
F. Jacob	(Richmond)	W.G. Byron	(N.I.F.C.)
†R. Pierce	(Liverpool)	J.E. McIlwaine	(N.I.F.C.)
†F. Shaw	(Cleckheaton)	J.G. Franks	(Dublin U.)
R.F. Oakes	(Hartlepool Rovers)	M. Ryan	(Rockwell College)
H.W. Dudgeon	(Richmond)	J. Ryan	(Rockwell College)
F.M. Stout	(Gloucester)	J.H. Lytle	(N.I.F.C.)
†J.H. Blacklock	(Aspatria)	H. Lindsay	(Wanderers)
†C.E. Wilson	(Blackheath)	J.L. Davis	(Monkstown)

Try: Robinson   *Penalty:* Byrne   *Tries:* Lindsay, Magee   *Penalty:* Bulger

Referee: Mr D.G. Findlay (Scotland)

SCOTLAND v ENGLAND 1898
Played at Powderhall, Edinburgh, 12 March 1898
Drawn: Scotland 1T (3), England 1T (3)

An evenly-contested game ended, fairly enough, in the eighth drawn match between the nations – though *The Times* thought England were lucky to draw. The Scottish forwards played with unabated vigour but the English halves were a brave and resolute pair, turning the scales against the Scotsmen at times by gathering the ball from the toes of the dribbling home forwards and initiating several promising attacks. Byrne, again, was like the Rock of Gibraltar at full-back, and there was a welcome improvement in the English threequarter play, though Pilkington missed one or two opportunities on the right wing.

18,000 were present on a perfect day to see a hard battle. The English forwards took a battering in the early stages, but lasted the pace better than their illustrious opponents. There was an early setback for England too, Unwin having to retire after ten minutes with concussion. Frank Stout replaced him for a quarter of an hour.

There was no scoring until the second half when the English backs repelled one of several fierce Scottish forward attacks. They rushed play to the other end of the field and, in the follow-up, Royds charged down a kick to touch and scored a try in the corner. Byrne failed to convert, and Scotland stormed back on to the attack. One good chance was wasted when Mabon misdirected a kick into touch-in-goal, but shortly after McEwan scored after a succession of scrums along the English goal-line. T.M. Scott failed to kick a simple conversion.

In the remaining 15 minutes of play, Scotland's forwards threatened to break away, but Byrne twice relieved the pressure on his side after the ball had been forced over the English line. Eventually England shoved their way out of defence and no-side was announced as the visitors were putting together a belated attack.

P.W. and F.M. Stout were brothers.

SCOTLAND		ENGLAND	
J.M. Reid	(Edinburgh Acads.)	*J.F. Byrne	(Moseley)
R.T. Neilson	(West of Scotland)	†W.N. Pilkington	(Cambridge U.)
T.A. Nelson	(Oxford U.)	W.L. Bunting	(Richmond)
*A.R. Smith	(Oxford U.)	†P.M.R. Royds	(Blackheath)
T.L. Scott	(Langholm)	†P.W. Stout	(Gloucester)
J.T. Mabon	(Jedforest)	†G.T. Unwin	(Blackheath)
M. Elliot	(Hawick)	†A. Rotherham	(Richmond)
M.C. Morrison	(Royal H.S.F.P.)	F. Jacob	(Richmond)
W.M.C. McEwan	(Edinburgh Acads.)	†J.F. Shaw	(R.N.E. College, Keyham)
T.M. Scott	(Hawick)	†H.E. Ramsden	(Bingley)
G.C. Kerr	(O. Dunelmians)	R.F. Oakes	(Hartlepool Rovers)
H.O. Smith	(Watsonians)	H.W. Dudgeon	(Richmond)
J.M. Dykes	(Glasgow H.S.F.P.)	F.M. Stout	(Gloucester)
A. MacKinnon	(London Scottish)	W. Ashford	(Richmond/Exeter)
R.C. Stevenson	(London Scottish)	Jas. Davidson	(Aspatria)

Try: McEwan   *Try:* Royds

Referee: Mr J. Dodds (Ireland)

England's team which beat Wales in 1898 was the last to do so for 12 years:
back A. Rotherham, H. E. Ramsden, F. M. Stout, J. Davidson, P. M. R. Royds,
F. Jacob, R. F. Oakes, W. L. Bunting; *middle* J. F. Shaw, H. W. Dudgeon,
J. F. Byrne (captain), W. Ashford, P. W. Stout; *front* E. F. Fookes,
R. O'H. Livesay. (The identification of these players has been a matter of
deduction – confirmation from readers would be welcomed.)

ENGLAND v WALES 1898

Played at Rectory Field, Blackheath, 2 April 1898
England won by 1G, 3T (14) to 1DG, 1T (7)

In an exciting game of fluctuating fortunes, England ran out winners, deservedly, on a beautiful spring day. The English halves were the builders of this victory, and, to an extent, prevented the Welshmen from playing their natural short-passing game. Many critics had thought Livesay to be the finest half in England during the season, but it was only through the indispositions of Unwin and Taylor that the Blackheath man won his cap. On this occasion, too, he dispelled any queries the selectors may have held against his defence, for his tackling and kicking were accurate and resourceful.

The English halves and three-quarters had a good game, with Bunting, Royds, Fookes and Stout probably the finest quartette to appear since the 'death' of the three-threequarter system. The English forwards were also lauded for the skilful way they prevented the Welsh pack holding and heeling the scrummages – denying the essential quick possession required by the Welsh threequarter game.

England opened the scoring after ten minutes when Frank Stout crossed, following up a sharp round of passing and dribbling by the home pack. Not long afterwards his brother, Percy, featured prominently in a round of passing with Bunting and Livesay, and scored the second try before Huzzey reduced Wales's deficit just before half-time. Biggs and Nicholls, in one of their rare effective attacks, were the architects of a fine try.

Just after the interval Huzzey put his side ahead with a dropped goal, and, temporarily, Wales appeared to regain her old form up-front. The 20,000 crowd cheered on the home side, however, and in the last 20 minutes of the match, Fookes streaked over twice after Bunting, Stout and Livesay had outwitted the Welsh defence. To complete the scoring, Byrne converted the final try.

ENGLAND		WALES	
*J.F. Byrne	(Moseley)	*W.J. Bancroft	(Swansea)
E.F. Fookes	(Sowerby Bridge)	H.V.P. Huzzey	(Cardiff)
P.M.R. Royds	(Blackheath)	W. Jones	(Cardiff)
W.L. Bunting	(Richmond)	E.G. Nicholls	(Cardiff)
P.W. Stout	(Gloucester)	T.W. Pearson	(Newport)
†R.O'H. Livesay	(Blackheath)	S. Biggs	(Cardiff)
A. Rotherham	(Richmond)	J.E. Elliott	(Cardiff)
H.E. Ramsden	(Bingley)	T. Dobson	(Cardiff)
J.F. Shaw	(R.N.E. College, Keyham)	R. Hellings	(Llwynypia)
H.W. Dudgeon	(Richmond)	F.H. Cornish	(Cardiff)
F.M. Stout	(Gloucester)	W.H. Alexander	(Llwynypia)
R.F. Oakes	(Hartlepool Rovers)	D. Evans	(Penygraig)
W. Ashford	(Exeter)	H. Davies	(Swansea)
F. Jacob	(Richmond)	D.J. Daniel	(Llanelli)
Jas. Davidson	(Aspatria)	G. Boots	(Newport)

Tries: Fookes (2), F.M. Stout, P.W. Stout
Conversion: Byrne

Try: Huzzey   *Dropped goal:* Huzzey

Referee: Mr J.T. Magee (Ireland)

WALES v ENGLAND 1899
Played at St Helen's, Swansea, 7 January 1899
Wales won by 4G, 2T (26) to 1T (3)

This match heralded the Golden Era of Rugby Football for Wales, and eleven years were to pass before England again defeated the men in scarlet. England selected seven new caps for the journey to Swansea: John Daniell was given the pack leadership on his debut, and the great Gamlin had a difficult baptism at full-back.

During the first ten minutes there was no indication of the disastrous defeat England were to sustain. Daniell whipped his forwards into a frenzy and the Welsh pack was, at first, dashed off its feet. Then, a fine passage of play by the backs produced a try by one of the Welsh wings and from that moment England were comprehensively beaten. The *Athletic News Football Annual* reported: 'England's pack was beaten and out-manoeuvred, and the brothers James, with their marvellous legerdemain and their constant change of relative positions, completely fogged and nonplussed Rotherham and Livesay.'

The work of the James brothers enabled the brilliant Welsh three-quarters to entertain the 25,000 spectators with their full repertoire of handling and running skills. In a seven-minutes purple patch during the second half, the Welsh backs clocked 15 points and the poor Englishmen scarcely knew what had hit them. The forwards were overwhelmed in the tight and loose, and the backs were unable to find any rhythm or combination in their play.

It was the largest defeat England had hitherto experienced.

WALES		ENGLAND	
*W.J. Bancroft	(Swansea)	†H.T. Gamlin	(Devonport Albion)
H.V.P. Huzzey	(Cardiff)	G.C. Robinson	(Percy Park)
E.G. Nicholls	(Cardiff)	P.W. Stout	(Gloucester)
R.T. Skrimshire	(Newport)	P.M.R. Royds	(Blackheath)
W.M. Llewellyn	(Llwynypia)	†R. Forrest	(Wellington)
E. James	(Swansea)	R.O'H. Livesay	(Blackheath)
D. James	(Swansea)	*A. Rotherham	(Richmond)
J.J. Hodges	(Newport)	F. Jacob	(Richmond)
D.J. Daniel	(Llanelli)	†G.R. Gibson	(Northern)
W. Parker	(Swansea)	†J. Daniell	(Richmond/Cambridge U.)
A. Brice	(Aberavon)	R.F. Oakes	(Hartlepool Rovers)
J. Blake	(Cardiff)	H.W. Dudgeon	(Richmond)
T. Dobson	(Cardiff)	†W. Mortimer	(Marlborough Nomads)
F. Scrines	(Swansea)	†C.H. Harper	(Oxford U.)
W.H. Alexander	(Llwynypia)	†Jos. Davidson	(Aspatria)

Tries: Llewellyn (4), Huzzey (2)   *Try:* Robinson
Conversions: Bancroft (4)

Referee: Mr A. Turnbull (Scotland)

IRELAND v ENGLAND 1899
Played at Lansdowne Road, Dublin, 4 February 1899
Ireland won by 1PG, 1T (6) to Nil

England failed miserably again, though the margin of defeat was by no means as severe as that suffered at the hands of the Welshmen. Nevertheless, the manner of Ireland's victory – total domination in the tight and loose, backed up by brilliant half-back play – pointed to a titanic encounter at Cardiff in March when the Irish were scheduled to meet Wales.

In this match, the English three-quarters were constantly called upon to fall on the ball, tackle and kick as the Irish mercilessly bore down on the English goal. At the end of the match, it was reported that the English backs were so battered and so covered by mud as to be unrecognisable, while the Irish backs left the field almost unmarked – an interesting and illuminating contrast!

12,000 spectators – including a party from the Viceregal Lodge – witnessed a dull game played in unpleasant conditions. The ground was so wet and heavy that from an early stage the ball was as slippery as a bar of soap. It was understandable that Ireland consequently wished to keep the game close and hard. Under the circumstances, the English pack were rendered useless: they were unable to control the ball in the scrummage, and the Irish were constantly pushing their opponents off the ball.

It was a minor miracle that the English backs kept their opponents from scoring in the first half – the defence of the visitors was the one encouraging point for the English selectors, and Byrne was outstanding. Ireland's opening points came ten minutes into the second half when Magee (another report credits Fulton) kicked a penalty for off-side. The only other score came near the end when Allen bounced the ball in from touch (one of the early tricks of the game) and gathered to touch down wide out.

IRELAND		ENGLAND	
J. Fulton	(N.I.F.C.)	J.F. Byrne	(Moseley)
I.G. Davidson	(N.I.F.C.)	E.F. Fookes	(Sowerby Bridge)
J.B. Allison	(Campbell C., Belfast)	J.T. Taylor	(Castleford)
G.R.A. Harman	(Dublin U.)	†S. Anderson	(Rockcliff)
W.H. Brown	(Dublin U.)	P.W. Stout	(Gloucester)
*L.M. Magee	(Bective Rangers)	E.W. Taylor	(Rockcliff)
G.G. Allen	(Derry)	*A. Rotherham	(Richmond)
M. Ryan	(Rockwell College)	H.W. Dudgeon	(Richmond)
J. Ryan	(Rockwell College)	C. Thomas	(Barnstaple)
W.G. Byron	(N.I.F.C.)	†A.J.L. Darby	(Cambridge U.)
J.E. McIlwaine	(N.I.F.C.)	F. Jacob	(Richmond)
T.M.W. McGown	(N.I.F.C.)	J.H. Blacklock	(Aspatria)
T. Ahearn	(Queen's C., Cork)	Jas. Davidson	(Aspatria)
J. Sealy	(Dublin U.)	F.M. Stout	(Gloucester)
H.C. McCoull	(Belfast Albion)	†J.H. Shooter	(Morley)

Try: Allen *Penalty:* Magee

Referee: Mr D.G. Findlay (Scotland)

ENGLAND v SCOTLAND 1899
Played at Rectory Field, Blackheath, 11 March 1899
Scotland won by 1G (5) to Nil

For England it was the same old story in which the forwards were completely outplayed, with the backs defending for the whole match. Criticism of the English forwards after the match was caustic: Arthur Budd (who died later in the year) called them a 'rustic collection', while *The Times* referred to the northern element in the pack as 'delinquents'!

A fine day dawned at the Rectory Field, the finest ground in the land at this time, but the game itself produced very little except monotonous forward rushes by the Scottish pack. Their dribbling was excellent, and ultimately won the day, but it offered nought as a spectacle for the large crowd of about 25,000.

Scotland were unfortunate to lose the services of Simpson at half-back early in the match. He strained a thigh muscle and was reduced to a limping passenger, acting as an auxiliary full-back. His co-half, Gillespie, played an outstanding game, however, and proved the perfect foil for his forwards by breaking through constantly with the ball at his feet, causing disruption among the English halves.

Scotland registered their only score ten minutes after the interval. The forwards rushed the ball over the English line and Gillespie, ever-present at the heels of his pack, scored the try which Thomson converted with a grand kick. Scott and Gedge showed glimpses of their individual brilliance in the few bouts of open play which followed, while Bunting (still the number-one English back) made a notable break for England. Just as it appeared that the Scottish defence had been drawn, the left wing, Matters, normally a centre for his club, knocked-on Bunting's try-giving pass. England thus ended a season of unrelieved disaster.

The Davidsons were brothers capped in the same match, and R.F.A. Hobbs had a son capped for England in 1932.

ENGLAND		SCOTLAND	
H.T. Gamlin	(Devonport Albion)	H. Rottenburg	(London Scottish)
E.F. Fookes	(Sowerby Bridge)	H.T.S. Gedge	(London Scottish)
P.W. Stout	(Gloucester)	G.A.W. Lamond	(Kelvinside Acads.)
W.L. Bunting	(Richmond)	D.B. Monypenny	(London Scottish)
†J.C. Matters	(R.N.E. College, Keyham)	T.L. Scott	(Langholm)
†R.O. Schwarz	(Richmond)	J.W. Simpson	(Royal H.S.F.P.)
*A. Rotherham	(Richmond)	J.I. Gillespie	(Edinburgh Acads.)
H.W. Dudgeon	(Richmond)	W.J. Thomson	(West of Scotland)
R.F. Oakes	(Hartlepool Rovers)	*M.C. Morrison	(Royal H.S.F.P.)
Jas. Davidson	(Aspatria)	W.M.C. McEwan	(Edinburgh Acads.)
Jos. Davidson	(Aspatria)	H.O. Smith	(Watsonians)
F.M. Stout	(Gloucester)	J.M. Dykes	(London Scottish)
†R.F.A. Hobbs	(Blackheath)	A. MacKinnon	(London Scottish)
J.H. Shooter	(Morley)	R.C. Stevenson	(London Scottish)
†A.O. Dowson	(Moseley)	G.C. Kerr	(O. Dunelmians)

Try: Gillespie   *Conversion:* Thomson

Referee: Mr J.T. Magee (Ireland)

ENGLAND v WALES 1900

Played at Kingsholm, Gloucester, 6 January 1900

Wales won by 2G, 1PG (13) to 1T (3)

There were 15,000 spectators – fewer than expected – to see the only international match to have been played at Gloucester. The English forwards began the game in sterling fashion and looked particularly dangerous with the ball at their feet. Marsden was prominent behind the scrummage in much of the early play. From one of his openings the English three-quarters should have scored a try, but a dreadful error by Coopper on the left wing cost the home side dearly. Slowly, the tide turned and Wales forced their way into the game, opening the scoring after 20 minutes when Hellings, who played for most of the match with a fractured arm, gathered the ball at the rear of a loose maul and drove over for Bancroft to convert. Despite attractive play by the Welsh three-quarters, neither side scored again before ends were changed.

Gamlin had just failed to land some penalty points late in the first half, and the English forwards, sensing that they were still very much in the match, began the second half confidently. Marsden, receiving good possession from the set-pieces, exploited a lapse in the Welsh defence and Nicholson, after some good work, scored. Wales held their narrow lead carefully before producing an exhilarating movement ten minutes from no-side. A wonderful round of passing by the visiting three-quarters gave the crowd a try to remember by Trew, the Swansea man grounding the ball behind the posts. Bancroft kicked the goal and just at the end of the match punished an English offence with a splendid goal from the touch-line.

England introduced 13 new caps for this match, including the entire pack. J.W. Jarman was the first international from the Bristol club.

ENGLAND		**WALES**	
H.T. Gamlin	(Devonport Alb./B'heath)	*W.J. Bancroft	(Swansea)
†E.T. Nicholson	(Birkenhead Park)	W.M. Llewellyn	(Llwynypia)
†A.T. Brettargh	(Liverpool O.B.)	D. Rees	(Swansea)
†G.W. Gordon-Smith	(Blackheath)	G. Davies	(Swansea)
†S.F. Coopper	(Blackheath)	W.J. Trew	(Swansea)
†G.H. Marsden	(Morley)	G.L. Lloyd	(Newport)
*R.H.B. Cattell	(Moseley)	L.A. Phillips	(Newport)
†F.J. Bell	(Northern)	J.J. Hodges	(Newport)
†R.W. Bell	(Cambridge U./Northern)	J. Blake	(Cardiff)
†W. Cobby	(Hull)	W.H. Williams	(Pontymister)
†A. Cockerham	(Bradford Olicana)	F. Miller	(Mountain Ash)
†J. Baxter	(Birkenhead Park)	R. Hellings	(Llwynypia)
†J.W. Jarman	(Bristol)	A. Brice	(Aberavon)
†S. Reynolds	(Richmond)	G. Boots	(Newport)
†C.T. Scott	(Cambridge U./B'heath)	R. Thomas	(Swansea)

Try: Nicholson

Tries: Hellings, Trew
Conversions: Bancroft (2)
Penalty: Bancroft

Referee: Mr A. Turnbull (Scotland)

ENGLAND v IRELAND 1900

Played at Athletic Ground, Richmond, 3 February 1900
England won by 1G, 1DG, 2T (15) to 1DG (4)

England made several changes from the side defeated by Wales and gave the captaincy to John Daniell, the Cambridge forward. It was the first win in an international match for two years and England's first victory against Ireland since 1895. According to *The Times*, 'the fight throughout upheld the high traditions of this England and Ireland match, and the company of 10,000 showed a discrimination and an impartiality that were creditable to every one.'

England's margin of success was rather flattering, for both sides were evenly matched behind the scrummage and Ireland's traditional winging and dribbling forward play posed many problems to the Englishmen. However, the feature of England's improved play was the fine tight-scrummaging, which amply countered the dash of their opponents.

The game remained finely balanced into the last 20 minutes. An exchange of dropped goals, with Ireland scoring first, was followed by a fine English try by Robinson – a prolific try-scorer for club and country. Bell, another new forward from the successful Cambridge XV, led the dribble which enabled the Northumbrian to score his fifth try in this his fifth international match. England thus held a slight advantage at the interval.

The first section of the second half was memorable for the fine tackling of the two sides and Ireland were unfortunate not to score. In the final quarter, though, superior finishing by the home side enabled Gordon-Smith and then Robinson to add two further tries. Alexander converted one of these to give England a win by 11 points.

Owing to snow, it had been doubtful whether the game could be played. However, a party of enthusiasts led by Mr R.S. Whalley of the R.F.U. cleared the pitch in time for the match to go ahead.

ENGLAND		IRELAND	
H.T. Gamlin	(Blackheath)	P.E. O'Brien-Butler	(Monkstown)
G.C. Robinson	(Percy Park)	G.P. Doran	(Lansdowne)
J.T. Taylor	(Castleford)	C. Reid	(N.I.F.C.)
G.W. Gordon-Smith	(Blackheath)	J.B. Allison	(Queen's U.)
E.T. Nicholson	(Birkenhead Park)	E.F. Campbell	(Monkstown)
G.H. Marsden	(Morley)	*L.M. Magee	(Bective Rangers)
†J.C. Marquis	(Birkenhead Park)	J.H. Ferris	(Queen's U.)
*J. Daniell	(Cambridge U./Richmond)	M. Ryan	(Rockwell College)
R.W. Bell	(Cambridge U./Northern)	J.J. Coffey	(Lansdowne)
S. Reynolds	(Richmond)	J. Sealy	(Dublin U.)
J. Baxter	(Birkenhead Park)	C.E. Allen	(Derry)
C.T. Scott	(Cambridge U./B'heath)	F. Gardiner	(N.I.F.C.)
J.H. Shooter	(Morley)	A.W.D. Meares	(Wanderers)
†A.F. Todd	(Blackheath)	S.T. Irwin	(Queen's U.)
†H. Alexander	(Birkenhead Park)	P.C. Nicholson	(Dublin U.)

Tries: Robinson (2), Gordon-Smith   *Conversion:* Alexander   *Dropped goal:* Gordon-Smith

Dropped goal: Allison

Referee: Mr D.G. Findlay (Scotland)

SCOTLAND v ENGLAND 1900
Played at Inverleith, Edinburgh, 10 March 1900
Drawn, neither side scoring

England's first visit to the new Rugby ground of the Scottish Union attracted a crowd of 20,000 to witness a fast but predominantly forward exchange between two well-matched sides. Conditions were excellent for running and handling, but the English tactics were criticised, for it was the view of many that England could have won this game comfortably. The pack, again with Daniell to the fore, succeeded in holding the Scottish eight in the tight and loose, but a peculiar reluctance on the part of the halves to bring their backs into the match cost England this game. It was argued from some quarters that, fearing the reputation of the Scottish three-quarter line, England's tactics of keeping the game tight were justified. From the evidence of the play, however, it was clear that, in Bunting, England had a match-winner who posed the Scottish backs a problem each time he gained possession.

Bunting, in fact, came closest to scoring in the match. During the first half he made a thrilling break which took him away from the Scottish full-back. With the line at his mercy, he elected to pass to Forrest, his wing, when common-sense would have urged him to keep possession and go for the line. Scotland were thus spared defeat, and, as holders of the Calcutta Cup, held the prize for another season. England completed the tournament with three points from three games, a total which placed them second to the invincible Welsh side.

SCOTLAND		ENGLAND	
H. Rottenburg	(London Scottish)	H.T. Gamlin	(Blackheath)
W.H. Welsh	(Edinburgh U.)	G.C. Robinson	(Percy Park)
A.R. Smith	(London Scottish)	G.W. Gordon-Smith	(Blackheath)
G.T. Campbell	(London Scottish)	W.L. Bunting	(Moseley)
T.L. Scott	(Langholm)	R. Forrest	(Wellington)
J.I. Gillespie	(Edinburgh Acads.)	G.H. Marsden	(Morley)
R.T. Neilson	(West of Scotland)	J.C. Marquis	(Birkenhead Park)
*M.C. Morrison	(Royal H.S.F.P.)	*J. Daniell	(Cambridge U.)
W.M.C. McEwan	(Edinburgh Acads.)	R.W. Bell	(Cambridge U.)
H.O. Smith	(Watsonians)	S. Reynolds	(Richmond)
R. Scott	(Hawick)	J. Baxter	(Birkenhead Park)
A. MacKinnon	(London Scottish)	†A.F.C.C. Luxmoore	(Richmond)
L.H.I. Bell	(Edinburgh Acads.)	J.H. Shooter	(Morley)
G.C. Kerr	(Edinburgh Wands.)	A.F. Todd	(Blackheath)
W.P. Scott	(West of Scotland)	H. Alexander	(Birkenhead Park)

Referee: Mr M.G. Delaney (Ireland)

WALES v ENGLAND 1901
Played at Cardiff Arms Park, 5 January 1901
Wales won by 2G, 1T (13) to Nil

On a ground which was hard after frost, with the balder parts of the field quite slippery, about 40,000 assembled to watch what turned out to be an undistinguished match. The Welsh captain, Bancroft, had a poor day and his forwards lacked energy in the loose. Llewellyn Lloyd was given a new scrummage-half-back, but the move did not work for the pair found difficulty in combination. The English side, after disappointing performances in the two previous seasons against Wales, played well and remained in the hunt until the last ten minutes of the match, when the Welsh pack forced two late tries.

The highlight of the first half was a splendid run by Nicholls, who, with the aid of a hand-off, and despite several defenders hanging on to him, forced his way over for a try after 20 minutes.

There appears to be some doubt over the identities of the Welsh scorers in the second half: Welsh authorities (probably most reliable concerning their own players) credit Williams and Hodges with the tries; L.M. Holden records Blake and Hodges; while *The Times* reports that Blake and Williams were the men who finally dashed English hopes!

Sagar, the English full-back, played a reliable game on his debut.

A. O'Neill was the first England player capped from Torquay Athletic R.F.C.

WALES		ENGLAND	
*W.J. Bancroft	(Swansea)	†J.W. Sagar	(Cambridge U.)
W.M. Llewellyn	(Llwynypia)	†C. Smith	(Gloucester)
E.G. Nicholls	(Cardiff)	†E.J. Vivyan	(Devonport Albion)
G. Davies	(Swansea)	*J.T. Taylor	(West Hartlepool)
W.J. Trew	(Swansea)	†E.W. Elliot	(Sunderland)
G.L. Lloyd	(Newport)	R.O. Schwarz	(Richmond)
J. Jones	(Aberavon)	†E.J. Walton	(Castleford/Oxford U.)
J.J. Hodges	(Newport)	A.F.C.C. Luxmoore	(Richmond)
J. Blake	(Cardiff)	†D. Graham	(Aspatria)
F. Miller	(Mountain Ash)	C.T. Scott	(Blackheath)
A. Brice	(Aberavon)	†C.O.P. Gibson	(Northern)
G. Boots	(Newport)	†E.W. Roberts	(R.N.E. College)
R. Hellings	(Llwynypia)	†N.C. Fletcher	(O.M.Ts.)
W.H. Williams	(Pontymister)	†A. O'Neill	(Torquay Athletic)
R. Thomas	(Swansea)	H. Alexander	(Birkenhead Park)

Tries: Hodges, Nicholls, Williams
Conversions: Bancroft (2)

Referee: Mr A. Turnbull (Scotland)

IRELAND v ENGLAND 1901

Played at Lansdowne Road, Dublin, 9 February 1901
Ireland won by 2G (10) to 1PG, 1T (6)

England were again unable to field their strongest pack, with Daniell still absent. Nevertheless, this side showed considerable improvements on the side beaten in Wales, and the crowd of about 8000 witnessed a fast, exciting game, though not a grand match technically. The visitors lacked skill at half-back and, as a result, the three-quarters – the strength of the side – were frequently pushed across the ground and unable to exploit any openings in the Irish defence. By contrast, the play of Magee (though injured early in the match) and Barr was an inspiration to the Irishmen, and their kicking in attack and defence proved to be one of the few attractions for the purists among the crowd.

The Irish forwards played with fire and broke swiftly to disrupt the English halves. It was generally felt that if the halves could get the ball out to their wings quickly enough, then England could win. So it was no surprise when a slick piece of handling by the midfield backs engineered the opening score for Robinson, a fine try behind the posts which Taylor, inexcusably, failed to convert. England looked strong at this stage, but a dreadful clearance by an English forward was charged down by Magee who, making progress along the touch-line, sent Davidson in for a try which Irwin converted.

England could consider themselves a little unlucky to be in arrears at this stage, but in the second half the tendency of the English halves and centres to bunch their wings and delay their passes resulted in the game falling out of England's hands. Another poor kick – this time by Taylor – was charged down to allow Gardiner the easiest of tries and Irwin's conversion gave Ireland a seven-points lead as the game entered the final quarter. England kept to their task, gamely, and Elliot and Taylor were both near scoring when excellent tackles robbed them of tries. At length Alexander kicked a penalty goal, but, by this stage, Ireland were certain winners and play ended with Ireland four points ahead.

Both sides wore black arm-bands, marking their respect for the late Queen Victoria, who had died at Osborne on 22 January.

IRELAND		ENGLAND	
J. Fulton	(N.I.F.C.)	J.W. Sagar	(Cambridge U.)
I.G. Davidson	(N.I.F.C.)	G.C. Robinson	(Percy Park)
J.B. Allison	(Queen's U.)	*W.L. Bunting	(Moseley)
B.R.W. Doran	(Lansdowne)	J.T. Taylor	(West Hartlepool)
A.E. Freear	(Lansdowne)	E.W. Elliot	(Sunderland)
*L.M. Magee	(Bective Rangers)	R.O. Schwarz	(Richmond)
A. Barr	(Methodist College)	E.J. Walton	(Castleford/Oxford U.)
M. Ryan	(Rockwell College)	†C. Hall	(Gloucester)
J. Ryan	(Rockwell College)	†R.D. Wood	(Liverpool O.B.)
C.E. Allen	(Derry)	C.T. Scott	(Blackheath)
S.T. Irwin	(Queen's U.)	S. Reynolds	(Richmond)
F. Gardiner	(N.I.F.C.)	E.W. Roberts	(R.N.E. College)
T.J. Little	(Bective Rangers)	N.C. Fletcher	(O.M.Ts.)
A.G. Heron	(Queen's U.)	A. O'Neill	(Torquay Athletic)
P. Healey	(Limerick)	H. Alexander	(Birkenhead Park)

Tries: Davidson, Gardiner　　　　*Try:* Robinson　*Penalty:* Alexander
Conversions: Irwin (2)

Referee: Mr D.G. Findlay (Scotland)

ENGLAND v SCOTLAND 1901
Played at Rectory Field, Blackheath, 9 March 1901
Scotland won by 3G, 1T (18) to 1T (3)

Scotland's young team set the seal on a remarkably successful season by winning the Triple Crown and retaining the Calcutta Cup in a one-sided match. England's failure was due to a total lack of understanding at half, for the forwards held their own against the lighter Scottish pack and won a reasonable quantity of possession early in the game. Scotland, curiously, made two changes from the successful side which had done duty at Inverleith against Ireland, recalling Stronach and giving Gillespie his club partner at half-back. The latter change proved to be a touch of genius on the part of the Scottish selection committee, for the halves invited their three-quarters to produce backplay to match the brilliant Welsh example. According to *The Times*, 'their combined runs, when going at full speed, could not have been surpassed...'

The scoring opened after 15 minutes, Fell, Turnbull and Gillespie passing accurately at speed for the latter to exploit an opening and score. More quick passing enabled Welsh to beat Gamlin for speed and register the second try, before Fell and Turnbull created an overlap for Timms to score. Each of the tries was converted by Gillespie. For the remainder of the half, and the start of the second half, England tackled bravely and Gamlin enhanced his reputation by stopping many further Scottish attacks.

Despite their large lead, the Scottish forwards still did not have everything their own way in the tight, though the miserable play of the English halves gave the crowd small hope of a try by the English three-quarters. After Alexander had missed a penalty early in the second half, a scoring chance at last came England's way, 15 minutes from time. Cox passed to Robinson and the Northumbrian, with a fine solo effort, made a determined dash for the line to score. Scotland's counter to this was another attractive attack in which Gillespie and the three-quarters featured, Fell crossing the English line to close the scoring.

H.T.F. Weston, at 31, became the first international player from Northampton. His son was an England player in the 1930s.

ENGLAND		SCOTLAND	
H.T. Gamlin	(B'heath/Devonport Alb.)	A.W. Duncan	(Edinburgh U.)
G.C. Robinson	(Percy Park)	W.H. Welsh	(Edinburgh U.)
*W.L. Bunting	(Richmond/Moseley)	A.B. Timms	(Edinburgh U.)
†N.S. Cox	(Sunderland)	P. Turnbull	(Edinburgh Acads.)
E.W. Elliot	(Sunderland)	A.N. Fell	(Edinburgh U.)
†P.D. Kendall	(Birkenhead Park)	J.I. Gillespie	(Edinburgh Acads.)
†B. Oughtred	(Hartlepool Rovers)	R.M. Neill	(Edinburgh Acads.)
C. Hall	(Gloucester)	*M.C. Morrison	(Royal H.S.F.P.)
†H.T.F. Weston	(Northampton)	D.R. Bedell-Sivright	(Cambridge U.)
†B.C. Hartley	(Blackheath)	J.M. Dykes	(Glasgow H.S.F.P.)
A. O'Neill	(Torquay Athletic)	A. Frew	(Edinburgh U.)
N.C. Fletcher	(O.M.Ts.)	R.S. Stronach	(Glasgow Acads.)
†C.S. Edgar	(Birkenhead Park)	A.B. Flett	(Edinburgh U.)
G.R. Gibson	(Northern)	J. Ross	(London Scottish)
H. Alexander	(Birkenhead Park)	J.A. Bell	(Clydesdale)

Try: Robinson

Tries: Fell, Gillespie, Timms, Welsh
Conversions: Gillespie (3)

Referee: Mr R.W. Jeffares (Ireland)

ENGLAND v WALES 1902

Played at Rectory Field, Blackheath, 11 January 1902
Wales won by 1PG, 2T (9) to 1G, 1T (8)

There was little to choose between the two sides on this occasion, and only the antics of the wily Welsh scrum-half, R.M. Owen, allowed Wales to steal a late victory. Five minutes from no-side, Owen tricked his opposite number, Oughtred, into an offside tackle at a scrummage near the English posts and Strand-Jones drop-kicked the resulting penalty.

Before this match there had been much controversy in Wales as to which was the better full-back to replace Bancroft. R.T. Gabe, writing fifty years later, recalled: 'There were eleven selectors at that time. Six voted for Jones and five for Winfield, the names of the voters appearing in the press . . . Strand-Jones played a marvellous game that day. How he got through the game without injury was akin to a miracle. He did not fall on the ball but picked it up and charged through the oncoming forwards with head down. From one of these fearless dashes he ran half the length of the field before passing to me with only Gamlin to beat. I side-stepped the full-back but his hand came into violent contact with my solar-plexus and I was out on my feet, but my momentum carried me over the few yards to the line and then I took the full count!' Thus Wales led by a try after ten minutes, but tries by Dobson and Robinson gave England the lead before the interval.

In the second half, with Wales gaining a slight edge at half-back, Osborne reduced the English lead with a second Welsh try. Then, at the end, Wales pulled the ashes from the fire with that late penalty.

J.J. Robinson became the first international from Headingley club, nine years after winning his first cap as a Cambridge undergraduate. This interval between appearances still remains an England record, although it was equalled by J.E. Williams in 1965. Willcocks was the first England cap from Plymouth Albion.

ENGLAND		WALES	
H.T. Gamlin	(Devonport Albion)	J. Strand-Jones	(Oxford U./Llanelli)
S.F. Coopper	(Blackheath)	W.M. Llewellyn	(Llwynypia/London Welsh)
†J.E. Raphael	(Oxford U.)	*E.G. Nicholls	(Newport)
J.T. Taylor	(West Hartlepool)	R.T. Gabe	(Llanelli/London Welsh)
†P.L. Nicholas	(Exeter)	E. Morgan	(London Welsh)
P.D. Kendall	(Birkenhead Park)	R. Jones	(Swansea)
B. Oughtred	(Hartlepool Rovers)	R.M. Owen	(Swansea)
†S.G. Williams	(Devonport Albion)	J.J. Hodges	(Newport)
†L.R. Tosswill	(Exeter)	A.F. Harding	(Cardiff)
†T.H. Willcocks	(Plymouth Albion)	D. Jones	(Treherbert)
†J. Jewitt	(Hartlepool Rovers)	A. Brice	(Aberavon)
J.J. Robinson	(Headingley)	W.T. Osborne	(Mountain Ash)
†D.D. Dobson	(Newton Abbot/Oxford U.)	G. Boots	(Newport)
†G. Fraser	(Richmond)	W. Joseph	(Swansea)
*H. Alexander	(Birkenhead Park)	N. Walters	(Llanelli)

Tries: Dobson, Robinson
Conversion: Alexander

Tries: Gabe, Osborne   *Penalty:* Strand-Jones

Referee: Mr R.W. Jeffares (Ireland)

ENGLAND v IRELAND 1902

Played at Welford Road, Leicester, 8 February 1902
England won by 2T (6) to 1T (3)

It was reported in the press that the experiment of bringing international matches to the Midlands had proved so successful that plans for further major games in the area were likely to be considered. A crowd of 20,000 watched a fast, even game in which splendid tackling and accurate kicking were the main features.

Oughtred, who had lost them the game at Blackheath with Wales, was retained by the English selection committee, and flourished at the end of Walton's fine service. His fine running enabled the English three-quarters to create many dangerous situations, and after one such break Taylor made a determined run for Coopper to score the first try. Alexander failed to convert but England held their narrow lead at the interval.

In the second half, there were many exciting incidents for the spectators to enjoy, and 15 minutes from no-side Gardiner levelled the scores. Daniell called for a final effort from his men, and Taylor, principal architect of England's first score, produced another run which, together with a remarkable drive by the home forwards, forced a line-out near the Irish line. Williams, gaining possession, then touched down for the deciding score.

ENGLAND		IRELAND	
H.T. Gamlin	(Devonport Albion)	*J. Fulton	(N.I.F.C.)
S.F. Coopper	(Blackheath)	I.G. Davidson	(N.I.F.C.)
J.E. Raphael	(Oxford U.)	J.B. Allison	(Edinburgh U.)
J.T. Taylor	(West Hartlepool)	B.R.W. Doran	(Lansdowne)
R. Forrest	(Blackheath)	C.C. Fitzgerald	(Dungannon/Glasgow U.)
B. Oughtred	(Hartlepool Rovers)	L.M. Magee	(Bective Rangers)
E.J. Walton	(Oxford U./Castleford)	H.H. Corley	(Dublin U.)
S.G. Williams	(Devonport Albion)	J.J. Coffey	(Lansdowne)
L.R. Tosswill	(Exeter)	G.T. Hamlet	(O. Wesley)
*J. Daniell	(Richmond)	F. Gardiner	(N.I.F.C.)
†P.F. Hardwick	(Percy Park)	S.T. Irwin	(Queen's U.)
J.J. Robinson	(Headingley)	A. Tedford	(Malone)
D.D. Dobson	(Oxford U.)	P. Healey	(Limerick)
G. Fraser	(Richmond)	J. Ryan	(Rockwell College)
H. Alexander	(Birkenhead Park)	T.A. Harvey	(Dublin U.)

Tries: Coopper, Williams   *Try:* Gardiner

Referee: Mr R. Welsh (Scotland)

SCOTLAND v ENGLAND 1902

Played at Inverleith, Edinburgh, 15 March 1902
England won by 2T (6) to 1T (3)

Scotland's fall from grace – three successive defeats after the Triple Crown success of the previous season – was one of the most unusual features of the season. For England, victory on a perfect spring day was the first registered over Scotland since 1897 and, as in the Irish game, the English halves and Taylor in the centre were outstanding members of the side which finished second in the Championship.

England made first use of a healthy breeze, but Scotland exerted early pressure and Gamlin, who played a brilliant match, was forced to minor. Useful kicking brought England relief, however, and the scoring opened after 20 minutes when Williams scored his second try of the season. Raphael and Taylor were prominent in several moves following this success, and, at length, Taylor increased the lead to six points at the break.

The second half belonged to Scotland – and the heroic Gamlin. With Welsh in pain on the wing, the Scottish attack was deprived of its full scoring capacity. Nevertheless, early in the half a bout of passing by the Scottish backs resulted in a try by Fell, which Timms just failed to convert with a grand kick. In the last 25 minutes Scotland tried desperately to snatch the game out of the fire. Gamlin, almost single-handed, saved the day for his side and one memorable tackle on Fell prevented a certain try. J.B.G. Thomas, in a memoir on the Somerset full-back, referred to this closing period of the match thus: 'Gamlin stood between them (the Scottish side) and success, and right well he played his vital part. None passed where Gamlin guarded the way. That display epitomized the Gamlin spirit.'

SCOTLAND		ENGLAND	
A.W. Duncan	(Edinburgh U.)	H.T. Gamlin	(Devonport Albion)
A.N. Fell	(Edinburgh U.)	†T. Simpson	(Rockcliff)
A.B. Timms	(Edinburgh U.)	J.T. Taylor	(West Hartlepool)
P. Turnbull	(Edinburgh Acads.)	J.E. Raphael	(Oxford U.)
W.H. Welsh	(Edinburgh U.)	R. Forrest	(Blackheath)
E.D. Simson	(Edinburgh U.)	B. Oughtred	(Hartlepool Rovers)
F.H. Fasson	(Edinburgh U.)	E.J. Walton	(Oxford U./Castleford)
*M.C. Morrison	(Royal H.S.F.P.)	S.G. Williams	(Devonport Albion)
D.R. Bedell-Sivright	(Cambridge U.)	L.R. Tosswill	(Exeter)
J.R.C. Greenlees	(Cambridge U.)	*J. Daniell	(Richmond)
J.M. Dykes	(Glasgow H.S.F.P.)	P.F. Hardwick	(Percy Park)
W.E. Kyle	(Hawick)	J.J. Robinson	(Headingley)
H.O. Smith	(Watsonians)	D.D. Dobson	(Oxford U.)
J.A. Bell	(Clydesdale)	G. Fraser	(Richmond)
W.P. Scott	(West of Scotland)	B.C. Hartley	(Blackheath)

Try: Fell

Tries: Taylor, Williams

Referee: Mr F.M. Hamilton (Ireland)

WALES v ENGLAND 1903

Played at St Helen's, Swansea, 10 January 1903
Wales won by 3G, 2T (21) to 1G (5)

English hopes of securing a first win in the Principality since 1895 were soon scattered and after 20 minutes Wales were ten points clear with only fourteen men on the field. Pearson, recalled to lead the Welsh side after five years of neglect, scored after ten minutes when the Welsh backs passed a slippery ball with amazing speed and accuracy. Five minutes later, however, he was seriously injured in a tackle with Gamlin, the brilliant English full-back. Hodges was withdrawn from the pack and posted to the left wing – and with astounding success, for the Newport forward proceeded to score three tries before the interval. Lloyd had created an opening for Owen to score after 20 minutes before the first of Hodges's efforts. 'Dromio', the noted Welsh Rugby critic, stated that Welsh combination was dominant in smooth-working efficiency and that Hodges had only to take the ball and run for the line. The fact that Hodges was able to cross three times shows the reliability of the player. The second of Hodges's tries was helped by a blunder by Taylor; and Strand-Jones, initiating a counter-attack on half-way, had a share in the third. Conversions of three of the tries hoisted Wales to a 21-points lead at the break.

Wales, cheered on by 30,000 ecstatic followers, had made first use of a strong wind which, perversely, abated in the second half. England held their own after the interval and their forwards, after a rather slovenly performance at the start of the match, produced their best form. After 20 minutes' play in the second half, a cross-kick by Taylor found the Welsh defence in disarray and Dobson scored in a scramble. Taylor's goal gave added respect to England's effort.

Full marks to Wales for playing open attractive Rugby on a bog of a pitch. Their forwards, preferring to hold and heel out in the scrums (as opposed to the push-and-rush-through tactics then in vogue), were the principal architects of a famous victory.

J.H. Miles was the first international player to be capped from the Leicester club.

WALES		ENGLAND	
J. Strand-Jones	(Llanelli)	H.T. Gamlin	(Devonport Albion)
W.F. Jowett	(Swansea)	†J.H. Miles	(Leicester)
D. Rees	(Swansea)	J.T. Taylor	(West Hartlepool)
R.T. Gabe	(Llanelli)	†R.H. Spooner	(Liverpool)
*T.W. Pearson	(Newport)	T. Simpson	(Rockcliff)
G.L. Lloyd	(Newport)	†F.C. Hulme	(Birkenhead Park)
R.M. Owen	(Swansea)	*B. Oughtred	(Hartlepool Rovers)
G. Boots	(Newport)	R.F.A. Hobbs	(Blackheath)
G. Travers	(Pill Harriers)	P.F. Hardwick	(Percy Park)
J.J. Hodges	(Newport)	†R. Bradley	(West Hartlepool)
A.F. Harding	(Cardiff/London Welsh)	R.D. Wood	(Liverpool O.B.)
A. Brice	(Aberavon)	D.D. Dobson	(Newton Abbot)
W. Joseph	(Swansea)	G. Fraser	(Richmond)
D. Jones	(Treherbert)	†J. Duthie	(West Hartlepool)
W.T. Osborne	(Mountain Ash)	†V.H. Cartwright	(Oxford U.)

Tries: Hodges (3), Owen, Pearson   *Try:* Dobson   *Conversion:* Taylor
Conversions: Strand-Jones (3)

Referee: Mr R. Welsh (Scotland)

IRELAND v ENGLAND 1903

Played at Lansdowne Road, Dublin, 14 February 1903
Ireland won by 1PG, 1T (6) to Nil

Ireland deserved their victory in a match of no particular distinction. Conditions were perfect for the handling game, but a tendency by the English backs to hold the ball too long deprived visiting supporters of the spectacle of Simpson and Forrest going for the line. Simpson was the best English back on the field in attack, creating many opportunities from unpromising situations; and Gamlin, as ever, gave an immaculate display behind his team. Fulton, the distinguished Irish back, also produced some match-saving tackles. Hulme and Oughtred, the English halves, were strangely ineffective, and even Magee, the Irish veteran, failed to reproduce his best form.

The Irish captain, Corley, was the best half on the field and scored the first points in the match. A rush by the Irish forwards was repelled by the English pack, but one of the visitors fell off-side and the home skipper landed the penalty goal with a superb kick. Before England had recovered from this setback, another Irish rush, though initially checked by Gamlin, caught the visitors at sixes-and-sevens and Ryan was up to score a try.

Strong tackling by Gamlin and Taylor saved England from further humiliation at the start of the second half. Harvey and D.R. Taylor nearly got in for Ireland before Simpson and Forrest put in strong runs for England. There was no further scoring and a disappointing match resulted in a win for Ireland.

Three of the R.F.U. party which travelled for this match are believed to have contracted typhoid fever whilst in Dublin. Forrest, who played against Scotland later, died of the disease in April, as did R.S. Whalley, a former President of the Union. Oughtred, the captain, made a good recovery and became a successful naval architect.

IRELAND		ENGLAND	
J. Fulton	(N.I.F.C.)	H.T. Gamlin	(Devonport Albion)
C.C. Fitzgerald	(Dungannon)	T. Simpson	(Rockcliff)
G.A.D. Harvey	(Wanderers)	J.T. Taylor	(West Hartlepool)
D.R. Taylor	(Queen's U.)	A.T. Brettargh	(Liverpool O.B.)
H.J. Anderson	(O. Wesley)	R. Forrest	(Blackheath)
L.M. Magee	(Bective Rangers)	*B. Oughtred	(Hartlepool Rovers)
*H.H. Corley	(Dublin U.)	F.C. Hulme	(Birkenhead Park)
J.J. Coffey	(Lansdowne)	S.G. Williams	(Devonport Albion)
F. Gardiner	(N.I.F.C.)	R.D. Wood	(Liverpool O.B.)
T.A. Harvey	(Dublin U.)	†W.G. Heppell	(Devonport Albion)
P. Healey	(Garryowen)	P.F. Hardwick	(Percy Park)
G.T. Hamlet	(O. Wesley)	†B.A. Hill	(Blackheath)
M. Ryan	(Rockwell College)	D.D. Dobson	(Newton Abbot)
A. Tedford	(Malone)	G. Fraser	(Richmond)
R.S. Smyth	(Dublin U.)	V.H. Cartwright	(Oxford U.)

Try: Ryan   *Penalty:* Corley

Referee: Mr J.C. Findlay (Scotland)

ENGLAND v SCOTLAND 1903

Played at Athletic Ground, Richmond, 21 March 1903
Scotland won by 1DG, 2T (10) to 2T (6)

Conditions were perfect and the attendance of 25,000 included Lord Kinnaird and Lord Rosebery. The match itself was not spectacular, though the play and close result made for an exciting and interesting afternoon for the crowd.

Scotland were marginally the better side on the day, and, in Fell, possessed the outstanding back. The passing was generally below the standard expected in international matches, but the tackling was sure and the pace fast.

England made an encouraging start, the halves making an opening for Brettargh to send Forrest dodging over for a try. But England's lead was short-lived, for five minutes later Macdonald made a run and Timms had space to drop a goal, which proved to be the deciding score of the match. A period of even play followed but Scotland increased their lead before half-time when Simson and Knox breached the English threequarter line and Dallas crossed for a try after more good work by Macdonald.

Fell came into his own in the second half, almost scoring twice and halting a fine slashing run by Brettargh after Forrest had been beaten. One minute later, though, there was no-one to prevent Dobson scoring after a scrum, and, with one point between the sides, a frantic period of attack and counter-attack followed. England once looked likely to score, but the visitors forced play back into the English 25. Then Simson, securing possession, made a telling break and beat Gamlin to complete the scoring.

ENGLAND		SCOTLAND	
H.T. Gamlin	(Devonport Albion)	W.T. Forrest	(Hawick)
T. Simpson	(Rockcliff)	A.N. Fell	(Edinburgh U.)
A.T. Brettargh	(Liverpool O.B.)	H.J. Orr	(London Scottish)
†E.I.M. Barrett	(Lennox)	A.B. Timms	(Edinburgh U.)
R. Forrest	(Blackheath)	J.S. Macdonald	(Edinburgh U.)
†W.V. Butcher	(Streatham/Croydon)	E.D. Simson	(Edinburgh U.)
*P.D. Kendall	(Birkenhead Park)	J. Knox	(Kelvinside Acads.)
S.G. Williams	(Devonport Albion)	*J.R.C. Greenlees	(Kelvinside Acads.)
R. Pierce	(Liverpool)	J.D. Dallas	(Watsonians)
N.C. Fletcher	(O.M.Ts.)	L. West	(Edinburgh U.)
P.F. Hardwick	(Percy Park)	W.E. Kyle	(Hawick)
B.A. Hill	(Blackheath)	A.G. Cairns	(Watsonians)
D.D. Dobson	(Newton Abbot)	W.P. Scott	(West of Scotland)
F.M. Stout	(Richmond)	N. Kennedy	(West of Scotland)
V.H. Cartwright	(Oxford U.)	J. Ross	(London Scottish)

Tries: Dobson, Forrest

Tries: Dallas, Simson
Dropped goal: Timms

Referee: Mr W.M. Douglas (Wales)

ENGLAND v WALES 1904

Played at Welford Road, Leicester, 9 January 1904
Drawn: England 1G, 1PG, 2T (14), Wales 2G, 1GM (14)

This was a wonderfully entertaining match with both sides missing opportunities to win the match. Some appalling place-kicking (by Vivyan) robbed England of a rare win over Wales: indeed, the wing missed four kickable penalties in addition to a conversion of a try by Elliot at the posts. Wales, too, felt there were chances to win, laying much blame for their failure on the Scottish referee, Mr Findlay. Owen was penalised for 'feeding' the scrummage so often that he declined to put the ball in, preferring to give the feed to one of the English halves (who, unlike the Welsh, had not yet specialised and continued to select a right-half and left-half).

For once, the English forwards dominated their illustrious Welsh opponents. *The Times* reported that 'they scrummaged skilfully, were quick to break up, and used their feet well in the open'. Cartwright and Stout were outstanding and set a fine example to their fellow forwards; but the passing and kicking of the English halves were wayward and detracted from the overall improvement of the rest of the side. Gamlin, as usual, stood out like a beacon in a stormy sea, saving his side time and again with rock-like tackling and safe line-kicking against the waves of sweeping Welsh threequarter movements.

England led 14–10 with little time remaining. Then Joseph made a mark and Winfield kicked the goal from near the half-way line; and, as Wales finished strongly, a final bout of passing resulted in Morgan crossing for a try on no-side. The referee judged that the final pass had been forward, however, and Wales had to rest content with a draw.

J.G. Milton was the son of W.H. Milton (England 1875); J.G. was the first player to follow his father into an England team. Note, too, that J.G. was capped as a schoolboy.

ENGLAND		WALES	
H.T. Gamlin	(Devonport Albion)	H.B. Winfield	(Cardiff)
E.J. Vivyan	(Devonport Albion)	W.M. Llewellyn	(Newport)
†E.W. Dillon	(Blackheath)	*E.G. Nicholls	(Cardiff)
A.T. Brettargh	(Liverpool O.B.)	R.T. Gabe	(Cardiff)
E.W. Elliot	(Sunderland)	E. Morgan	(London Welsh)
†P.S. Hancock	(Richmond)	R. Jones	(Swansea)
W.V. Butcher	(Bristol)	R.M. Owen	(Swansea)
V.H. Cartwright	(Oxford U.)	G. Boots	(Newport)
†G.H. Keeton	(Richmond)	S.H. Ramsey	(Treorchy)
†C.J. Newbold	(Cambridge U.)	J.J. Hodges	(Newport)
P.F. Hardwick	(Percy Park)	A.F. Harding	(London Welsh)
†J.G. Milton	(Bedford G.S.)	A. Brice	(Cardiff)
†N.H. Moore	(Bristol)	W. Joseph	(Swansea)
*F.M. Stout	(Richmond)	J. Evans	(Blaina)
B.A. Hill	(Blackheath)	D.J. Thomas	(Swansea)

Tries: Elliot (2), Brettargh   *Tries:* Llewellyn, Morgan
Conversion: Stout   *Penalty:* Gamlin   *Conversions:* Winfield (2)
                                              Goal from mark: Winfield

Referee: Mr J.C. Findlay (Scotland)

ENGLAND v IRELAND 1904
Played at Rectory Field, Blackheath, 13 February 1904
England won by 2G, 3T (19) to Nil

John Daniell returned to lead the English side in this big win over the Irish. *The Times* stated that 'for the second time within five weeks they demonstrated that England have the best pack that they have had for many years'. Indeed, the play of the English forwards completely subdued the disruptive type of game preferred by Irish packs of this period. E.J. Vivyan, one of the promising English three-quarters, proved his worth in this match, too, following his indifferent display against Wales. His kicking and running upset the Irish defence so much towards the end of the match that he made a personal contribution of ten points.

For all their superiority, England could only muster one score in the first half – a try by Moore – though Ireland did have a strong wind in their favour. The complete domination by the English forwards prevented the Irish halves from giving their three-quarters any reasonable scoring opportunities, and only the play of Corley, now appearing as a centre, raised any hopes for an Irish try. Gamlin, after an unsure start, finally found good length with his line-kicking and added to the difficulties of the Irish side.

Ten minutes into the second half England increased their lead. Moore was luckily placed on-side after a long kick by Gamlin and scored his second try of the match. Simpson scored the third try – a splendid effort in the corner – before Vivyan added his ten points at the end. His play was described in *The Times* as 'eccentric', but on this occasion he 'came off tremendously; and seemed to be everywhere in the attack'.

ENGLAND		IRELAND	
H.T. Gamlin	(Devonport Albion)	J. Fulton	(N.I.F.C.)
E.J. Vivyan	(Devonport Albion)	C.G. Robb	(Queen's U.)
E.W. Dillon	(Blackheath)	H.H. Corley	(Wanderers)
A.T. Brettargh	(Liverpool O.B.)	J.C. Parke	(Dublin U.)
T. Simpson	(Rockcliff)	G.P. Doran	(Lansdowne)
P.S. Hancock	(Richmond)	T.T.H. Robinson	(Wanderers)
W.V. Butcher	(Bristol)	F.A. Kennedy	(Wanderers)
*J. Daniell	(Richmond)	*C.E. Allen	(Derry)
G.H. Keeton	(Richmond)	F. Gardiner	(N.I.F.C.)
C.J. Newbold	(Cambridge U.)	M. Ryan	(Rockwell College)
P.F. Hardwick	(Percy Park)	J. Ryan	(Rockwell College)
J.G. Milton	(Bedford G.S.)	R.S. Smyth	(Dublin U.)
N.H. Moore	(Bristol)	A. Tedford	(Malone)
F.M. Stout	(Richmond)	Jas. Wallace	(Wanderers)
B.A. Hill	(Blackheath)	Jos. Wallace	(Wanderers)

Tries: Moore (2), Vivyan (2), Simpson *Conversions:* Vivyan (2)

Referee: Mr T. Williams (Wales)

SCOTLAND v ENGLAND 1904
Played at Inverleith, Edinburgh, 19 March 1904
Scotland won by 2T (6) to 1T (3)

Scotland retained the International Championship in a protracted forward battle. The English backs were disappointing by contrast to their opponents, and Scotland's victory was regarded as well-deserved. Indeed, it is surprising that the margin in favour of the Scotsmen was no greater, for the last 20 minutes of the match saw the home pack firmly entrenched along the English goal-line. England had been a little unfortunate early in the match when their leader, Daniell, an inspiration to his men always, suffered a head injury and spent 20 minutes off the field. On his return, he was clearly stunned and did not play up to his usual very high standard.

Playing with the strong south-westerly wind in their favour, Scotland dictated the tactics in the first half and opened the scoring after 15 minutes when Gillespie and MacLeod combined to send Crabbie over in the corner. Despite the injury to Daniell, and an obvious superiority up front, Scotland failed to increase their lead before the interval. Macdonald, Timms, MacLeod and Crabbie made several good efforts to score, but sure tackling – one of the features of England's performance – brought the Scots down close to the line.

Ten minutes after the restart, Vivyan scored a try for England near the posts, but missed the simplest of conversions. Scotland's fluency was upset soon after by an injury to Timms, and the English backs almost penetrated Scotland's reorganised defence (Waters having joined the threequarter line in Timms's place). Some haphazard passing by Vivyan lost England a try-scoring opportunity on one occasion, before Scotland launched their final assault. After a long period of pressure during which the Scots had crossed more than once, only to be recalled, a reckless kick by Vivyan was charged down and, on the point of no-side, Macdonald crossed for the winning try at the corner.

SCOTLAND		ENGLAND	
W.T. Forrest	(Hawick)	H.T. Gamlin	(Blackheath)
J.E. Crabbie	(Edinburgh Acads.)	E.J. Vivyan	(Devonport Albion)
L.M. MacLeod	(Cambridge U.)	A.T. Brettargh	(Liverpool O.B.)
A.B. Timms	(Edinburgh U.)	E.W. Dillon	(Harlequins)
J.S. Macdonald	(Edinburgh U.)	T. Simpson	(Rockcliff)
E.D. Simson	(Edinburgh U.)	P.S. Hancock	(Richmond)
J.I. Gillespie	(Edinburgh Acads.)	W.V. Butcher	(Bristol)
*M.C. Morrison	(Royal H.S.F.P.)	*J. Daniell	(Richmond)
D.R. Bedell-Sivright	(West of Scotland)	G.H. Keeton	(Richmond)
A.G. Cairns	(Watsonians)	C.J. Newbold	(Cambridge U.)
W.E. Kyle	(Hawick)	P.F. Hardwick	(Percy Park)
W.M. Milne	(Glasgow Acads.)	J.G. Milton	(Bedford G.S.)
J.B. Waters	(Cambridge U.)	N.H. Moore	(Bristol)
H.N. Fletcher	(Edinburgh U.)	F.M. Stout	(Richmond)
W.P. Scott	(West of Scotland)	V.H. Cartwright	(Oxford U.)

Tries: Crabbie, Macdonald   *Try:* Vivyan

Referee: Mr S. Lee (Ireland)

WALES v ENGLAND 1905
Played at Cardiff Arms Park, 14 January 1905
Wales won by 2G, 5T (25) to Nil.

The great Revival of 1904–05 had enticed thousands of Welsh Nonconformists to their chapels: now the great Welsh team regularly attracted 30,000 followers to that cathedral of Rugby football, the Cardiff Arms Park. Here, they saw a very weak English team humiliated by the ruthless efficiency of the home pack and the dazzling speed of a famous back division.

England's total failure to apply the rudiments of the four-threequarter game remained a baffling problem for the Rugby Union. Only in defence were any of the Englishmen singled out for praise. Raphael and Coopper showed nerve in their tackling and at right-half Hulme showed 'infinite resource' according to *The Times*, which added that he was the best half-back on the field. Irvin, the new English full-back, had a dismal game and received a terrible review in the press.

Owen and Jones lost no time in getting their backs moving, and Morgan opened the scoring after three minutes. Llewellyn crossed for the next try, after 15 minutes, and just as England were beginning to settle, and Dillon looked as though he would send Palmer away, the Blackheath man blundered and Hodges, intercepting, set off from his own 25. The Newport forward, showing a fine turn of speed, raced past Irvin and Watkins got the simplest of tries. George Davies, previously capped as centre, converted for Wales to lead by 11 points.

Dick Jones opened the second-half scoring with a try in the corner and further points came from Gabe and Morgan before Harding completed the English destruction with the seventh Welsh try of the afternoon.

WALES		**ENGLAND**	
G. Davies	(Swansea)	†S.H. Irvin	(Devonport Albion)
*W.M. Llewellyn	(Newport)	†F.H. Palmer	(Richmond)
D. Rees	(Swansea)	E.W. Dillon	(Blackheath)
R.T. Gabe	(Cardiff)	J.E. Raphael	(Oxford U./O.M.Ts.)
E. Morgan	(London Welsh)	S.F. Coopper	(Blackheath)
R. Jones	(Swansea)	F.C. Hulme	(Birkenhead Park)
R.M. Owen	(Swansea)	W.V. Butcher	(Bristol)
J.J. Hodges	(Newport)	*F.M. Stout	(Richmond)
G. Travers	(Pill Harriers)	C.J. Newbold	(Blackheath)
W. Joseph	(Swansea)	†J.L. Mathias	(Bristol)
A.F. Harding	(London Welsh)	†W.L.Y. Rogers	(Blackheath)
D. Jones	(Treherbert)	B.A. Hill	(Blackheath)
W. O'Neill	(Cardiff)	†T.A. Gibson	(Northern)
C.M. Pritchard	(Newport)	†W.T.C. Cave	(Blackheath)
H.V. Watkins	(Llanelli)	V.H. Cartwright	(Oxford U.)

Tries: Morgan (2), Gabe, Harding, R. Jones, Llewellyn, Watkins
Conversions: Davies (2)

Referee: Mr J. Lefevre (Ireland)

IRELAND v ENGLAND 1905

Played at Mardyke, Cork, 11 February 1905
Ireland won by 1G, 4T (17) to 1T (3)

Basil Maclear, while stationed in Cork, made his debut in this first big match to be played in Cork. Maclear, after being pronounced 'not good enough' to play for England by Rowland Hill, President of the R.F.U., joined Ireland and stamped his class and authority on the match with an excellent debut. He made several scything runs down the centre of the field and created the two Irish tries in the first half: the first scored by Allen and the second, just before half-time, by Moffatt after a bout of passing among the three-quarters.

England held the Irish for a while after the break, but eventually Moffatt gained his second try before the match-winner, Maclear, scored (and goaled) his own try. *The Times* described his play thus: 'He had much to do with Ireland's win. His defence was very fine, and he fitted in well to the passing game. He displayed a fine turn of speed and, making the most of his weight, he was a very difficult man to stop.'

Following Maclear's efforts, Ireland retained the upper hand and Wallace scored after a fine run by Caddell. England's sole reply was a try in the last minute of the match after Brettargh made the running for Coopper to score. E.H.D. Sewell, in a report of this match, describes Coopper's play in this match as 'stern chasing'!

A record crowd of 12,000 paid gate money of £900, and, no doubt, Rowland Hill and the English selection committee made their Channel crossing back to England with very red faces indeed, for their countryman, Maclear, had played the lion's part in England's defeat.

It was noted that the English team travelled from Dublin to Cork in third-class railway compartments for this match, and the R.F.U. were severely criticised for their travel arrangements by the press.

W.M. Grylls was the first England player from Redruth.

IRELAND		ENGLAND	
M.F Landers	(Cork Const.)	†C.F. Stanger-Leathes	(Northern)
J.E. Moffatt	(O. Wesley)	S.F. Coopper	(Blackheath)
B. Maclear	(Cork County/Monkstown)	A.T. Brettargh	(Liverpool O.B.)
G.A.D. Harvey	(Wanderers)	†H.E. Shewring	(Bristol)
H.B. Thrift	(Dublin U.)	T. Simpson	(Rockcliff)
T.T.H. Robinson	(Dublin U.)	F.C. Hulme	(Birkenhead Park)
E.D. Caddell	(Dublin U.)	W.V. Butcher	(Bristol)
*C.E. Allen	(Derry)	*F.M. Stout	(Richmond)
J.J. Coffey	(Lansdowne)	C.J. Newbold	(Blackheath)
A. Tedford	(Malone)	J.L. Mathias	(Bristol)
H.G. Wilson	(Malone)	W.L.Y. Rogers	(Blackheath)
G.T. Hamlet	(O. Wesley)	†W.M. Grylls	(Redruth)
H.J. Knox	(Dublin U.)	†G. Vickery	(Bath/Aberavon)
Jos. Wallace	(Wanderers)	†J. Green	(Skipton)
H.J. Millar	(Monkstown)	V.H. Cartwright	(Oxford U.)

Tries: Moffatt (2), Allen, Maclear, Jos. Wallace   *Try:* Coopper
Conversion: Maclear

Referee: Mr R. Welsh (Scotland)

ENGLAND v SCOTLAND 1905

Played at Athletic Ground, Richmond, 18 March 1905
Scotland won by 1G, 1T (8) to Nil

There were 20,000 present at the Athletic Ground to witness a convincing Scottish victory. The visiting forwards carried all before them and the English halves had a torrid time behind a beaten pack. Stoop, on his debut, showed signs of promise early in the match and created openings for Brettargh; but the latter twice failed to register a score and a dreadful knock-on brought a sigh from the large crowd. Munro and Simson, at the heels of the Scottish pack, had a wonderful afternoon and supplied their three-quarters with a steady stream of quick accurate passes. Schulze, the new Scottish back, acquitted himself well but the selection of Taylor at full-back was a dismal failure by the English selectors – still searching for an adequate replacement for Gamlin. Only Raphael's play earned any praise among the English backs, though Coopper kicked well in defence.

All of the scoring was completed in the first ten minutes of the second half. From a rush, Simson gathered the ball and danced around Taylor for the first try. Then a good round of passing, initiated by the Scottish half-backs and incorporating their three-quarters, resulted in Stronach galloping over for Scott to kick a goal.

England could consider themselves fortunate not to lose by a greater margin, for in the first half Lamond and Ritchie (a last minute replacement for Crabbie) both made dangerous runs to the English line. Thus ended another disappointing season for followers of English Rugby.

ENGLAND		SCOTLAND	
J.T. Taylor	(West Hartlepool)	D.G. Schulze	(London Scottish)
S.F. Coopper	(Blackheath)	W.T. Ritchie	(Cambridge U.)
A.T. Brettargh	(Liverpool O.B.)	*A.B. Timms	(Edinburgh U.)
J.E. Raphael	(Oxford U.)	G.A.W. Lamond	(Bristol)
T. Simpson	(Rockcliff)	T. Elliot	(Gala)
†A.D. Stoop	(Oxford U.)	E.D. Simson	(Edinburgh U.)
W.V. Butcher	(Bristol)	P. Munro	(Oxford U.)
*F.M. Stout	(Richmond)	J.C. MacCallum	(Watsonians)
J.G. Milton	(Camborne S. of Mines)	L. West	(Carlisle)
C.J. Newbold	(Blackheath)	W.E. Kyle	(Hawick)
†C.E.L. Hammond	(Harlequins)	A.G. Cairns	(Watsonians)
J.L. Mathias	(Bristol)	R.S. Stronach	(Glasgow Acads.)
†S.H. Osborne	(Harlequins)	A. Ross	(Royal H.S.F.P.)
T.A. Gibson	(Northern)	H.G. Monteith	(Cambridge U.)
V.H. Cartwright	(Oxford U.)	W.P. Scott	(West of Scotland)

Tries: Simson, Stronach
Conversion: Scott

Referee: Mr D.H. Bowen (Wales)

ENGLAND v NEW ZEALAND 1905
Played at Crystal Palace, London, 2 December 1905
New Zealand won by 5T (15) to Nil

England adopted the back formation of the All Blacks, playing Raphael as rover/extra-three-quarter, and selecting seven forwards. On a dull, cold day, an official attendance of 45,000 saw the visitors beat England on a damp pitch by five tries, with four scored by McGregor.

The home forwards failed to make any headway against the formidable New Zealand combination and play rarely entered the New Zealand half of the pitch. Gillett thus had a quiet day at full-back compared to his opposite number, Jackett. Here, however, the English selectors could gather some cheer in view of the approaching Championship matches, for the West Countryman gave a reliable display at back, and appeared to be the natural successor to Gamlin.

The visitors led by three tries at the interval, scored in the 5th, 15th and 35th minutes of the half by McGregor. Wallace, who landed many goal-points during the tour, was obviously not in his best form with a heavy, wet ball, and failed to convert each time. Roberts and Stead were the attackers-in-chief for New Zealand and had shares in the first three scores.

England managed to hold the All Black forwards a little more effectively in the second half, and no further scoring was registered until ten minutes from no-side when Newton scored from a loose maul near the English line. Finally, a bout of passing initiated by Stead gave McGregor his fourth try. Gillett could not succeed where Wallace had failed and missed the two second-half conversion kicks.

Jackett became the first player capped direct from Falmouth club; while Cartwright was Nottingham R.F.C.'s first England representative, although he had won several caps prior to this match as an Oxford undergraduate.

ENGLAND		NEW ZEALAND	
†E.J. Jackett	(Falmouth)	G.A. Gillett	(Canterbury)
†A.E. Hind	(Leicester)	D. McGregor	(Wellington)
H.E. Shewring	(Bristol)	R.G. Deans	(Canterbury)
†R.E. Godfray	(Richmond)	W.J. Wallace	(Wellington)
†H.M. Imric	(Durham City)		
		J. Hunter	(Taranaki)
J.E. Raphael	(O.M.Ts.)	J.W. Stead	(Southland)
†D.R. Gent	(Gloucester)	F. Roberts	(Wellington)
†J. Braithwaite	(Leicester)	*D. Gallaher	(Auckland)
B.A. Hill	(Blackheath)	S.T. Casey	(Otago)
*V.H. Cartwright	(Nottingham)	G.A. Tyler	(Auckland)
C.E.L. Hammond	(Harlequins)	J.M. O'Sullivan	(Taranaki)
J.L. Mathias	(Bristol)	F. Newton	(Canterbury)
E.W. Roberts	(R.N.E. College)	F.T. Glasgow	(Taranaki)
†R.F. Russell	(Leicester)	A. McDonald	(Otago)
†G.E. Summerscales	(Durham City)	C.E. Seeling	(Auckland)

Tries: McGregor (4), Newton

Referee: Mr G. Evans (England)

ENGLAND v WALES 1906

Played at Athletic Ground, Richmond, 13 January 1906
Wales won by 2G , 2T (16) to 1T (3)

Wales, sole victors over the All Blacks, persisted with their eight backs and seven forwards formation, and defeated England with a controlled and carefully-planned performance. The English selectors were criticised for not fielding the New Zealand formation behind the scrum, though several times Hammond was withdrawn from the pack to stiffen the English defence.

For 35 of the 40 minutes in the first half Wales pressed, and the larger proportion of the time was spent within the English 25. The Welsh forwards had perfected a technique in the scrummage which more than held the eight-man efforts of the English pack. Set positions in the front row of three, and in the second row, allowed the visitors to play with cohesion. Travers was the 'hooker' in this formation and one reporter stated that he heeled out to Owen with 'perfect quickness'.

Wales built an early lead of 13 points with Charles Pritchard and Hodges scoring the first two tries. Then a piece of typically unselfish play by Nicholls – one of the early masters at playing to his wing – created a try for Maddocks. The Cardiff centre, after early-season doubts concerning his ability, beguiled the English three-quarters, Hind and Raphael, with a swerving run and drew the English full-back before sending his right wing clear. Winfield, whose long screw-punts to touch had contributed to Wales's famous win over the New Zealanders, again gave a masterful display of the full-back's art and converted two of these tries. Hudson scored England's points with a try.

England managed to even matters territorially in the second half, but their backs failed to penetrate the Welsh defence and the only score came about 20 minutes into that period when Teddy Morgan scored for Wales.

ENGLAND		WALES	
E.J. Jackett	(Falmouth)	H.B. Winfield	(Cardiff)
†A. Hudson	(Gloucester)	H.T. Maddocks	(London Welsh)
H.E. Shewring	(Bristol)	*E.G. Nicholls	(Cardiff)
J.E. Raphael	(O.M.Ts.)	R.T. Gabe	(Cardiff)
A.E. Hind	(Leicester)	E. Morgan	(London Welsh)
D.R. Gent	(Gloucester)	P.F. Bush	(Cardiff)
†R.A. Jago	(Devonport Albion)	C.C. Pritchard	(Pontypool)
		R.M. Owen	(Swansea)
†H.A. Hodges	(Nottingham)		
†A.L. Kewney	(Rockcliff)	J.J. Hodges	(Newport)
*V.H. Cartwright	(Nottingham)	G. Travers	(Pill Harriers)
C.E.L. Hammond	(Harlequins)	W. Joseph	(Swansea)
†T.S. Kelly	(Exeter)	A.F. Harding	(London Welsh)
E.W. Roberts	(R.N.E. College)	D. Jones	(Treherbert)
†W.A. Mills	(Devonport Albion)	C.M. Pritchard	(Newport)
†G.E.B. Dobbs	(Devonport Albion)	H.V. Watkins	(Llanelli)

Try: Hudson

Tries: Hodges, Maddocks, Morgan, C.M. Pritchard
Conversions: Winfield (2)

Referee: Mr A. Jardine (Scotland)

ENGLAND v IRELAND 1906

Played at Welford Road, Leicester, 10 February 1906
Ireland won by 2G, 2T (16) to 2T (6)

Impressed by the New Zealand system, and the successes of the Welsh XV with an extra back (referred to as a 'flying man' in the press reports), Ireland fielded seven forwards, with Maclear as rover, against the orthodox English line-up. Despite giving England a clear weight advantage, the Irish forwards still managed to hold their own in the tight scrummages and were much sharper on the loose ball. Conditions were heavy, and play was mainly confined to the forwards, though the Irish backs had several chances to show their abilities. England's backs had a miserable afternoon, and even Jackett looked to be well below the form he had shown in his two previous internationals.

England's failure was put down to a devotion to heeling – never wise tactics in heavy conditions – and Cartwright was criticised for not telling his men to adopt the dribbling game. Ireland capitalised upon the errors made by the English halves; and the Irish halves, according to one reporter, 'ran like ghosts'. Purdon was first to swoop, making a fine run for a try which Gardiner converted; then Caddell made a classic break to send Maclear over before half-time. The experiment of playing the Cork man as extra back was judged to be a resounding success, for a criticism of his play was that his enormous pace resulted in the rest of his threequarter line becoming detached so that his play in-formation tended to be unorthodox. The freedom of a roving commission was clearly to his and his fellows' advantage.

In the second half, the Irish threequarter line was again prominent, with the left flank of Casement and Anderson featuring prominently in combined play; but it was Tedford in the pack who scored the two second-half tries (Maclear converting the second).

At 16–0 down, the 10,000 spectators had little to cheer until, by way of a consolation, Mills and Jago added late tries to make England's effort a little more respectable. (Some reports indicate that Milton was a try-scorer instead of Mills.)

ENGLAND		IRELAND	
E.J. Jackett	(Falmouth)	G.J. Henebrey	(Garryowen)
A. Hudson	(Gloucester)	J.C. Parke	(Dublin U.)
†C.H. Milton	(Camborne S. of Mines)	H.B. Thrift	(Dublin U.)
†J.R.P. Sandford	(Marlborough Nomads)	F. Casement	(Dublin U.)
†J.E. Hutchinson	(Durham City)	H.J. Anderson	(O. Wesley)
D.R. Gent	(Gloucester)	B. Maclear	(Cork County/Monkstown)
R.A. Jago	(Devonport Albion)	E.D. Caddell	(Dublin U.)
		W.B. Purdon	(Queen's U.)
C.E.L. Hammond	(Harlequins)		
*V.H. Cartwright	(Nottingham)	F. Gardiner	(N.I.F.C.)
H.A. Hodges	(Nottingham)	*C.E. Allen	(Derry)
T.S. Kelly	(London Devonians/Exeter)	A. Tedford	(Malone)
W.A. Mills	(Devonport Albion)	J.J. Coffey	(Lansdowne)
A.L. Kewney	(Rockcliff)	H.G. Wilson	(Malone)
E.W. Roberts	(R.N.E. College)	H.J. Knox	(Lansdowne)
G.E.B. Dobbs	(Devonport Albion)	M. White	(Queen's College, Cork)

Tries: Jago, Mills

Tries: Tedford (2), Maclear, Purdon
Conversions: Gardiner, Maclear

Referee: Mr A. Llewellyn (Wales)

SCOTLAND v ENGLAND 1906
Played at Inverleith, Edinburgh, 17 March 1906
England won by 3T (9) to 1T (3)

England's first win against the Scots for four years, and their first in any match for two, was as unexpected as it was convincing. Declared *The Times*: 'The success will be particularly appreciated by English Rugby Unionists, coming, as it does, after a very long spell of ill-fortune in international football. Not only was England's victory completely deserved on the day's play, but it came in one of Scotland's great years.'

Scotland's much-vaunted pack executed many dangerous dribbles in the first half but in other aspects of forward play a lively English eight held the edge, enabling the English halves to exercise a hold on the Scottish pair, Simson and Munro. Stoop's quick service from the base of the scrummage gave Peters and the English three-quarters many chances to run the ball. The Scottish backs defended hesitantly and Birkett and Raphael, as a result, were outstanding in attack with their incisive running. Birkett, in fact, had an auspicious debut, for his tackling in defence baulked a number of Scottish raids.

Raphael opened the scoring when he gathered a loose ball to run 40 yards for a try, but Scotland equalised before half-time, thanks to a clever break by Munro to set up a try for Purves. A strong wind and a greasy ball made place-kicking tricky and Cartwright and MacCallum were unable to make their conversions.

Simpson regained the lead for England early in the second half after MacLeod, who had been injured, was slow to cover a ball which Simpson claimed. With the most spectacular run of the match, the wing zig-zagged through feeble tackles to score a try. Stoop and Raphael continued to threaten the Scottish line with strong runs which only timely tackles by Forbes checked; however, slack tackling by the rest of the Scottish backs allowed Birkett to make a break later and a bout of passing was completed by a try from Mills.

M.W. Walter, the Scottish centre, had refused an earlier invitation to represent England against Ireland.

SCOTLAND		ENGLAND	
J.G. Scoular	(Cambridge U.)	E.J. Jackett	(Falmouth)
K.G. MacLeod	(Cambridge U.)	J.E. Raphael	(O.M.Ts.)
J.L. Forbes	(Watsonians)	H.E. Shewring	(Bristol)
M.W. Walter	(London Scottish)	†J.G.G. Birkett	(Harlequins)
A.B.H.L. Purves	(London Scottish)	T. Simpson	(Rockcliff)
E.D. Simson	(Edinburgh U.)	†J. Peters	(Plymouth)
P. Munro	(Oxford U.)	A.D. Stoop	(Harlequins)
D.R. Bedell-Sivright	(Edinburgh U.)	†C.H. Shaw	(Moseley)
A.G. Cairns	(Watsonians)	A.L. Kewney	(Rockcliff)
W.E. Kyle	(Hawick)	*V.H. Cartwright	(Nottingham)
J.C. MacCallum	(Watsonians)	C.E.L. Hammond	(Harlequins)
H.G. Monteith	(London Scottish)	T.S. Kelly	(Exeter)
W.L. Russell	(Glasgow Acads.)	J. Green	(Skipton)
W.P. Scott	(West of Scotland)	W.A. Mills	(Devonport Albion)
*L. West	(London Scottish)	†R. Dibble	(Bridgwater Albion)

Try: Purves   *Tries:* Mills, Raphael, Simpson

Referee: Mr J.W. Allen (Ireland)

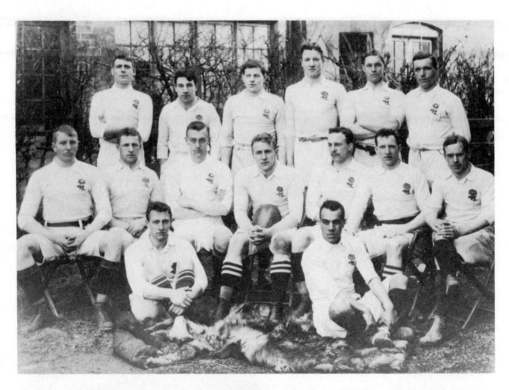

England had a lean time during the 1900s and their unexpected, but convincing, win against Scotland in 1906 marked their first victory for two years: *back* R. Dibble, E. J. Jackett, A. L. Kewney, J. G. G. Birkett, C. H. Shaw, H. E. Shewring; *middle* J. Green, C. E. L. Hammond, J. E. Raphael, V. H. Cartwright, T. S. Kelly, W. A. Mills, T. Simpson; *front* A. D. Stoop, J. Peters. 'Darkie' Peters, who scored against France in the following match, is, to this day, the only coloured gentleman to have won an English Rugby jersey.

A. Hudson, who crossed the line four times during England's first encounter with France.

FRANCE v ENGLAND 1906

Played at Parc des Princes, Paris, 22 March 1906
England won by 4G, 5T (35) to 1G, 1T (8)

England won their first encounter against the French in convincing fashion. The French had entered the international arena earlier in the year with a match against the New Zealand team (losing by a similar score) and a large crowd assembled at Parc des Princes to see the English side. The visitors had selected the same fifteen which had surprised critics a few days earlier by defeating a strong Scottish side – two players were unable to make the journey, however, and their places went to Hudson and Hogarth.

Conditions were not ideal: though the ground was dry, a very strong wind ruined much of the handling and passing. According to one French historian, 'le vent soufflait en ouragan'. And England started like a hurricane, forcing the French to adopt a defensive role. Hudson scored two early tries before Kewney scored in a dash for Cartwright to kick the first goal (his earlier attempts were wrecked by the wind). France recovered momentarily, showing pluck and better organisation, but after a rush by their forwards, Raphael gathered a loose ball and sped the length of the field. Shortly afterwards, Stoop scored and Cartwright kicked his second goal. The replacements, Hudson and Hogarth, scored the fifth and sixth tries and England were 22 points clear at half-time.

France changed sides to play with the wind and immediately scored, Maclos sending Muhr in for a try which Branlat converted into a goal. Ten minutes of French pressure passed before Hudson crossed for his fourth try and Cartwright converted. France countered, and Lesieur, the French 100m and 400m champion, scored his nation's second try. A fine run by Birkett led to England's next try – by Peters – and Cartwright, now having allowed for the wind, was successful with his fourth conversion. Mills completed the scoring soon afterwards.

FRANCE		ENGLAND	
W.H. Crichton	(Le Havre)	E.J. Jackett	(Falmouth)
*G. Lane	(R.C.F.)	J.E. Raphael	(O.M.Ts.)
E.W. Lewis	(Le Havre)	H.E. Shewring	(Bristol)
P. Maclos	(Stade Français)	J.G.G. Birkett	(Harlequins)
E. Lesieur	(Stade Français)	A. Hudson	(Gloucester)
T. Varvier	(R.C.F.)	J. Peters	(Plymouth)
A. Hubert	(A.S.F.)	A.D. Stoop	(Harlequins)
A. Verges	(Stade Français)	†T.B. Hogarth	(Hartlepool Rovers)
Maurin	(A.S.F.)	A.L. Kewney	(Rockcliff)
A. Branlat	(R.C.F.)	*V.H. Cartwright	(Nottingham)
G. Jérôme	(Stade Français)	C.E.L. Hammond	(Harlequins)
A.H. Muhr	(R.C.F.)	T.S. Kelly	(Exeter)
M. Communeau	(Stade Français)	J. Green	(Skipton)
P. Gaudermen	(R.C.F.)	W.A. Mills	(Devonport Albion)
J. Dufourcq	(S.B.U.C.)	R. Dibble	(Bridgwater Albion)

Tries: Lesieur, Muhr
Conversion: Branlat

Tries: Hudson (4), Hogarth, Kewney, Mills, Peters, Stoop   *Conversions:* Cartwright (4)

Referee: Mr L. Dedet (France)

ENGLAND v SOUTH AFRICA 1906

Played at Crystal Palace, London, 8 December 1906
Drawn: England 1T (3), South Africa 1T (3)

There were approximately 40,000 spectators present to see England hold the first Springboks to a draw on a pitch which resembled a morass. A drizzle half an hour before kick-off persisted throughout the match and the game suffered as a result. The ball became impossible to handle after 20 minutes and both sets of backs were reduced to the roles of useless bystanders or, at best, occasional defenders.

The giant South African pack applied enormous pressure in the first half, but only one score resulted. A high kick by Marsburg flustered the usually cool Jackett, and the ball was rushed over the line where Millar scored a try at the corner.

South Africa reorganised their back division after the interval. Joubert began the game at full-back, but later swapped positions with Marsburg; and a spine injury sustained by one of the Morkel brothers prompted further attention to the packing in the tight. England fared better in the second half, as a result, and the presence of two top-flight full-backs was a welcome asset to the Springboks.

Stoop and the English backs were more prominent after the interval and a run by Shewring put the home side in a good position. A formidable rush by the English forwards carried the ball over the South African line after Stoop had restarted play on the narrow side. It seemed that de Melker would surely kick the ball dead, but an unhappy miskick sent it straight into the path of Brooks who thus gained the simplest of tries. The goal kick failed and England earned an honourable draw.

There is an interesting tale in connection with the selection of this England fifteen. Owing to a clerical error, it is believed that Dr A. Alcock won his cap at the expense of L.A.N. Slocock (capped later); but reports do not single out the Guy's doctor for praise or criticism. He was not capped again.

F.G. Brooks was the first England player capped direct from Bedford, though several earlier internationals had made appearances for the club.

ENGLAND		SOUTH AFRICA	
E.J. Jackett	(Falmouth)	S. Joubert	(Western Province)
†F.G. Brooks	(Bedford)	J.A. Loubser	(Western Province)
H.E. Shewring	(Bristol)	S.C. de Melker	(Griqualand West)
J.G.G. Birkett	(Harlequins)	H.A. de Villiers	(Western Province)
T. Simpson	(Rockcliff)	A.W.F. Marsburg	(Griqualand West)
A.D. Stoop	(Harlequins)	F.J. Dobbin	(Griqualand West)
R.A. Jago	(Devonport Albion)	D.C. Jackson	(Western Province)
C.H. Shaw	(Moseley)	P.A. le Roux	(Western Province)
†A. Alcock	(Guy's H.)	D.F.T. Morkel	(Transvaal)
T.S. Kelly	(Exeter)	J.W.E. Raaff	(Griqualand West)
W.A. Mills	(Devonport Albion)	W.S. Morkel	(Transvaal)
J. Green	(Skipton)	H.J. Daneel	(Western Province)
R. Dibble	(Bridgwater Albion)	W.A. Millar	(Western Province)
B.A. Hill	(Blackheath)	D.J. Brink	(Western Province)
*V.H. Cartwright	(Nottingham)	*P. Roos	(Western Province)

Try: Brooks   *Try:* Millar

Referee: Mr J.T. Tulloch (Scotland)

ENGLAND v FRANCE 1907

Played at Athletic Ground, Richmond, 5 January 1907
England won by 5G, 1DG, 4T (41) to 2G, 1PG (13)

Great interest surrounded the first visit of an international side from France to play Rugby football against a British side. *The Times*, with remarkable foresight, predicted that 'within the space of a very few years an international championship, organised on even broader lines than is now the case, will be an accomplished thing. Pure amateurism will, of course, be the essence of that competition, and professional football is never likely to be able to boast so desirable a development. In such a competition France in a short time is likely to play an honourable part. French athletes have all the qualities of good Rugby Union football players, and they only need frequent practice in the company of those who play better than themselves to improve.' Thus was France welcomed into the fold.

There were 6,000 spectators to see the sides take the field – the French an average of one stone per man lighter than the English. The home side were soon 13 points ahead, but France staged a surprising comeback. Vareilles made a rapier-like thrust down the touch-line and sent Muhr over near the corner. Maclos converted with a splendid kick and improved another try, created in similar circumstances to their first with Vareilles, again, the architect and Communeau the scorer. Furthermore, by half-time, France were level as a result of a superb penalty kicked by Maclos.

England ran away with the match after the break, their greater physical presence and superior fitness reducing the French defence to ribbons. Isaac, a tiny full-back, won the admiration of the sporting crowd with several brave tackles, and but for his courage France would have lost by 60 points. Stoop and his fellow Harlequins in the threequarter line, Birkett and Lambert, had a field-day with the giant wing scoring five tries to equal George Lindsay's international record set in 1887. Lee, the English full-back, was badly injured early in the game and forced to leave the field, but one of the features of the match was the sporting manner in which the game was contested.

ENGLAND		FRANCE	
†H. Lee	(Blackheath)	H. Isaac	(R.C.F.)
†T.B. Batchelor	(Oxford U.)	C. Vareilles	(Stade Français)
H.E. Shewring	(Bristol)	P. Maclos	(Stade Français)
J.G.G. Birkett	(Harlequins)	H. Martin	(S.B.U.C.)
†D. Lambert	(Harlequins)	G. Lane	(R.C.F.)
A.D. Stoop	(Harlequins)	A. Hubert	(A.S.F.)
†T.G. Wedge	(St Ives)	A. Lacassagne	(S.B.U.C.)
C.H. Shaw	(Moseley)	A. Verges	(Stade Français)
†L.A.N. Slocock	(Liverpool)	H. Poirier	(S.C.U.F.)
T.S. Kelly	(Exeter)	P. Mauriat	(Lyon)
W.A. Mills	(Devonport Albion)	M. Giaccardy	(S.B.U.C.)
J. Green	(Skipton)	A.H. Muhr	(R.C.F.)
†W.M.B. Nanson	(Carlisle)	*M. Communeau	(Stade Français)
*B.A. Hill	(Blackheath)	C. Beaurin	(Stade Français)
†F.J.V. Hopley	(Blackheath)	J. Dufourcq	(S.B.U.C.)

Tries: Lambert (5), Birkett, Nanson, Shewring, Slocock   *Conversions:* Hill (5),   *Dropped goal:* Birkett

Tries: Communeau, Muhr
Conversions: Maclos (2)
Penalty: Maclos

Referee: Mr W. Williams (England)

WALES v ENGLAND 1907
Played at St Helen's, Swansea, 12 January 1907
Wales won by 2G, 4T (22) to Nil

England, with an experimental pack, were totally eclipsed by a slick Welsh side which played as a unit. Both sides selected their packs with a view to allotting fixed scrummaging places, but the trial was not deemed a resounding success. Wales employed the 2–3–2 diamond scrummage favoured by the New Zealanders, at the recommendation of E.G. Nicholls, and the eight backs gave an interesting demonstration of the new system which it was believed would bring about a revolution on the same scale as the four-threequarter method had in the late 1880s and early 1890s. Wales, with Trew and Gabe outstanding, ran in three tries in each half as England were thoroughly routed. True, England faced a strong wind in the first half, and had the misfortune to see that wind blow itself out before the interval, but the nature of the Welsh win was such that not even the most fervent of England supporters could claim that his side had been unlucky in this turn of conditions.

The Welsh forwards took an early hold on the exchanges up-front, and bad play by the English halves gave the visiting forwards little to hope for as Wales headed, inevitably, to a large score. There was a promising English revival either side of half-time, during which Slocock, Kelly, Mills and occasionally Nanson showed promise; and Jackett, at full-back, despite conceding six tries, gave an encouraging display.

Only 12,000 supporters were present at this match – minute by Welsh norms. A small turn-out was attributed to the recent Welsh failure against the South Africans and dissatisfaction concerning the selection of the home side.

F.S. Scott was the father of E.K. Scott, who captained England in 1948.

WALES		ENGLAND	
D.B. Davies	(Llanelli)	E.J. Jackett	(Falmouth)
J.L. Williams	(Cardiff)	S.F. Coopper	(Blackheath)
R.T. Gabe	(Cardiff)	H.E. Shewring	(Bristol)
J. Evans	(Pontypool)	J.G.G. Birkett	(Harlequins)
H.T. Maddocks	(London Welsh)	†F.S. Scott	(Bristol)
R.A. Gibbs	(Cardiff)	A.D. Stoop	(Harlequins)
W.J. Trew	(Swansea)	R.A. Jago	(Devonport Albion)
*R.M. Owen	(Swansea)		
		C.H. Shaw	(Moseley)
G. Travers	(Pill Harriers)	L.A.N. Slocock	(Liverpool)
W. O'Neill	(Cardiff)	T.S. Kelly	(Exeter)
J. Watts	(Llanelli)	W.A. Mills	(Devonport Albion)
T.H. Evans	(Llanelli)	J. Green	(Skipton)
J. Brown	(Cardiff)	W.M.B. Nanson	(Carlisle)
C.M. Pritchard	(Newport)	*B.A. Hill	(Blackheath)
W.H. Dowell	(Newport)	F.J.V. Hopley	(Blackheath)

Tries: Maddocks (2), Williams (2),
Brown, Gibbs   *Conversions:*
Gibbs (2)

Referee: Mr J.I. Gillespie (Scotland)

IRELAND v ENGLAND 1907

Played at Lansdowne Road, Dublin, 9 February 1907
Ireland won by 1G, 1GM, 3T (17) to 1PG, 2T (9)

England made seven changes from the side defeated heavily by Wales, but poor tackling by their backs in the first half allowed Ireland to build an unassailable 14-points lead by the interval. There was an encouraging second-half display by the English forwards but their new-found vigour appeared too late in the game to alter the final result.

10,000 spectators saw Ireland open the scoring after 15 minutes when Shewring failed to find touch with a free kick. Forbes claimed a mark and Parke used the breeze to land a fine goal. At about this time, the Irish forwards held command up-front and forced England deep into their quarters. Caddell dodged past several would-be tacklers to increase the lead and, from a rush, the new Irish captain, Tedford, crossed for the second try soon after. Parke converted. Another fierce thrust by the Irish pack was supported by some crisp passing amongst their backs and Thrift handed-off Imrie to complete the first-half scoring.

Early English pressure marked the second-half play before a corkscrewing run by Maclear signalled a new Irish offensive, from which Caddell scored his second try. Then, too late in the day by far, came England's reply. Slocock, one of England's best forwards, got over for a try before Pickering (a late replacement for Birkett, who withdrew with a septic toe) landed a penalty. In the later stages, England did have the consolation of scoring the finest try of the match. Peters made a half-break for Shewring to race up to Thompson and send Imrie away for a classic score.

This was Ireland's third consecutive win against the English.
Pickering was the first international from the Harrogate club.

IRELAND		ENGLAND	
C. Thompson	(N.I.F.C.)	E.J. Jackett	(Falmouth)
H.B. Thrift	(Dublin U.)	†W.C. Wilson	(Richmond)
J.C. Parke	(Dublin U.)	H.E. Shewring	(Bristol)
T.J. Greeves	(N.I.F.C.)	†A.S. Pickering	(Harrogate)
B. Maclear	(Cork County/Monkstown)	H.M. Imrie	(Durham City)
E.D. Caddell	(Wanderers)	J. Peters	(Plymouth)
T.T.H. Robinson	(Wanderers)	R.A. Jago	(Devonport Albion)
*A. Tedford	(Malone)	C.H. Shaw	(Moseley)
G.T. Hamlet	(O. Wesley)	L.A.N. Slocock	(Liverpool)
J.J. Coffey	(Lansdowne)	T.S. Kelly	(Exeter)
H.G. Wilson	(Malone)	W.A. Mills	(Devonport Albion)
J.A. Sweeney	(Blackrock College)	*J. Green	(Skipton)
R.E. Forbes	(Malone)	J.G. Milton	(Camborne S. of Mines)
W.St.J. Cogan	(Queen's College, Cork)	†G. Leather	(Liverpool)
M. White	(Queen's College, Cork)	S.G. Williams	(Devonport Albion)

Tries: Caddell (2), Tedford, Thrift   *Tries:* Imrie, Slocock   *Penalty:* Pickering
Conversion: Parke   *Goal from mark:* Parke

Referee: Mr J.T. Tulloch (Scotland)

ENGLAND v SCOTLAND 1907

Played at Rectory Field, Blackheath, 16 March 1907
Scotland won by 1G, 1T (8) to 1T (3)

England's miserable home record against Scotland – one victory since 1884 – was extended in this match which also marked their third defeat of the season. By contrast, the Scots became, incontrovertibly, the team of the season, with a victory over the South Africans to add to the Triple Crown. In addition, the last-minute try by Peters was the only one conceded by the Scots in their four matches.

About 17,000 spectators attended the match and saw Scotland take first advantage of a stiff diagonal breeze. England resisted in an organised fashion in the first half and Scotland's nearest approach to a score came when MacLeod, with a lofty drop-kick from near midfield, tried to land some penalty points. His effort struck an upright and rebounded into play.

The opening of the second half was significant for the way in which the visiting forwards suddenly stamped their authority on the game. Their staying-power compelled *The Scotsman* to record that 'in the end grit and perseverance prevailed. Compared with their opponents, there was no mistaking the superior stamina of the winners, and to this fact Scotland in large measure owed her victory.'

Making full use of the gilt-edged possession gained by his pack, Sloan made a run which MacCallum should have completed with a try but a knock forward prevented a score. Minutes later, J.M.B. Scott put Scotland into a favourable position and, from a scrummage, Simson, with Bedell-Sivright providing an effective screen, dashed over for a splendid try which Geddes narrowly failed to convert. Scotland were now riding high and, five minutes from no-side, a singularly inept piece of English defence following a speculative kick ahead by a Scottish forward enabled Purves to score a try – his fourth in four internationals this season.

England made a belated recovery during which Birkett and Peters made some progress along a touch-line and after a brief interruption Peters continued the attack to score a try. G.D. Roberts failed to convert from a difficult angle.

ENGLAND		SCOTLAND	
E.J. Jackett	(Falmouth)	D.G. Schulze	(London Scottish)
W.C. Wilson	(Richmond)	A.B.H.L. Purves	(London Scottish)
H.E. Shewring	(Bristol)	D.G. Macgregor	(Pontypridd)
J.G.G. Birkett	(Harlequins)	T. Sloan	(Glasgow Acads.)
†A.W. Newton	(Blackheath)	K.G. MacLeod	(Cambridge U.)
J. Peters	(Plymouth)	*P. Munro	(London Scottish)
†S.P. Start	(U.S.)	E.D. Simson	(London Scottish)
C.H. Shaw	(Moseley)	G.M. Frew	(Glasgow H.S.F.P.)
L.A.N. Slocock	(Liverpool)	J.M.B. Scott	(Edinburgh Acads.)
T.S. Kelly	(Exeter)	G.A. Sanderson	(Royal H.S.F.P.)
W.A. Mills	(Devonport Albion)	W.P. Scott	(West of Scotland)
J. Green	(Skipton)	J.C. MacCallum	(Watsonians)
*E.W. Roberts	(R.N.E. College)	I.C. Geddes	(London Scottish)
†G.D. Roberts	(Harlequins/Oxford U.)	L.M. Spiers	(Watsonians)
S.G. Williams	(Devonport Albion)	D.R. Bedell-Sivright	(Edinburgh U.)

Try: Peters

Tries: Purves, Simson   *Conversion:*
Geddes

Referee: Mr T.D. Schofield (Wales)

FRANCE v ENGLAND 1908

Played at Stade Colombes, Paris, 1 January 1908
England won by 2G, 3T (19) to Nil

The match was played in miserable circumstances, a snowstorm during the morning of the match lasting to within an hour of kick-off. When the pitch was cleared, several slippery patches remained and the sodden state of the ground made handling extremely difficult.

England's display was unconvincing, only Lapage of the newcomers gaining any kudos from the critics. It was confirmed that the standard of French play was steadily improving, and it is fair to say that, but for two serious injuries to Mayssonnié and Sagot, the margin of England's victory would have been narrower.

Isaac gave a sure account of himself at full-back and the 4000 supporters were quick to applaud his work in defence. He could not prevent Lapage opening the scoring, however; and soon after, a kick ahead by the Naval man enabled Mills to cross for the second try. Just before the pause, Sagot left the field for attention to a leg injury, and, though he returned later, he was no more than a lame passenger in the French defence.

Playing with no particular distinction, England added further tries in the second half, Portus, Birkett and Lambert (according to the *Times* reporter at the ground) scoring. Roberts kicked two of these into goals. (There are records of this match which credit Hudson with a try, rather than Lambert.)

FRANCE		ENGLAND	
H. Isaac	(R.C.F.)	†A.E. Wood	(Gloucester)
E. Lesieur	(Stade Français)	D. Lambert	(Harlequins)
G. Lane	(R.C.F.)	J.G.G. Birkett	(Harlequins)
R. Sagot	(Stade Français)	†W.N. Lapage	(U.S./R.N.)
C. Vareilles	(Stade Français)	A. Hudson	(Gloucester)
A. Hubert	(A.S.F.)	†G.V. Portus	(Blackheath)
A. Mayssonnié	(Toulouse)	†H.J.H. Sibree	(Harlequins)
P. Mauriat	(Lyon)	†E.L. Chambers	(Bedford)
G. Borchard	(R.C.F.)	†F. Boylen	(Hartlepool Rovers)
P. Guillemin	(R.C.F.)	*T.S. Kelly	(Exeter)
R. Duval	(Stade Français)	G.D. Roberts	(Harlequins)
H. Moure	(S.C.U.F.)	L.A.N. Slocock	(Liverpool)
*M. Communeau	(Stade Français)	R. Dibble	(Bridgwater Albion)
C. Beaurin	(Stade Français)	W.A. Mills	(Devonport Albion)
R.de Malmann	(R.C.F.)	†H. Havelock	(Hartlepool Rovers)

Tries: Birkett, Lambert, Lapage, Mills, Portus   *Conversions:* Roberts (2)

Referee: Mr C.F. Rutherford (Scotland)

ENGLAND v WALES 1908

Played at Ashton Gate, Bristol, 18 January 1908

Wales won by 3G, 1DG, 1PG, 2T (28) to 3G, 1T (18)

Bristol's only international match was staged at the grounds of the Bristol City Association Football Club, and took place on a foggy, damp afternoon. One report asserted that frequently both fifteens disappeared from sight. The play, apparently, followed an entertaining, open pattern so it was a sad disappointment to the crowd to miss the spectacle of nine tries.

The Welsh forwards heeled cleverly in the tight and Vile combined smoothly with Bush who had a hand in most of the Welsh scores 'exhibiting great versatility and resource'. During the first 20 minutes, the Cardiff fly-half dropped a goal and created a try for Gabe, Winfield converting and kicking a penalty to produce a lead of 12 points. A sudden change in the game of the English forwards brought play to Welsh quarters and tries were scored by Williamson and Lapage following fierce rushes. Roberts goaled the first and Bush added a late Welsh try with a dazzling, swerving dash – so at the interval the score was delicately balanced at 15–8.

The ding-dong battle continued in the second half. Play characteristic of Welsh three-quarters during their Golden Era enabled Trew to get in for the first try; but a strong run by Birkett to the Welsh posts resulted in Wood placing an easy conversion to bring England within five points. Finishing supremely, Gabe and Gibbs sealed Wales's success – Winfield stretching his side to 28 points – but Birkett managed another burst to add his second try and Wood converted.

Much experimenting at half-back was taking place in English sides at this time. Adrian Stoop (injured at the time of this match with a broken collar-bone) had shown the way with the Harlequins and, slowly, England was beginning to accept the Welsh convention of playing specialised halves – one to operate the scrummage with the other standing off. The play of Williamson in this match came in for special commendation.

ENGLAND		WALES	
A.E. Wood	(Gloucester)	H.B. Winfield	(Cardiff)
D. Lambert	(Harlequins)	J.L. Williams	(Cardiff)
*J.G.G. Birkett	(Harlequins)	R.T. Gabe	(Cardiff)
W.N. Lapage	(U.S./R.N.)	W.J. Trew	(Swansea)
A. Hudson	(Gloucester)	R.A. Gibbs	(Cardiff)
J. Peters	(Plymouth)	P.F. Bush	(Cardiff)
†R.H. Williamson	(Oxford U.)	T.H. Vile	(Newport)
†R. Gilbert	(Devonport Albion)	W. O'Neill	(Cardiff)
F. Boylen	(Hartlepool Rovers)	G. Travers	(Pill Harriers)
C.E.L. Hammond	(Harlequins)	J. Webb	(Abertillery)
G.D. Roberts	(Harlequins)	*A.F. Harding	(London Welsh)
L.A.N. Slocock	(Liverpool)	J. Brown	(Cardiff)
R. Dibble	(Bridgwater Albion)	C.M. Pritchard	(Newport)
W.A. Mills	(Devonport Albion)	J. Watts	(Llanelli)
H. Havelock	(Hartlepool Rovers)	W.H. Dowell	(Pontypool)

Tries: Birkett (2), Lapage, Williamson
Conversions: Wood (2), Roberts

Tries: Gabe (2), Bush, Gibbs, Trew *Conversions:* Winfield (2), Bush *Dropped goal:* Bush
Penalty: Winfield

Referee: Mr J.T. Tulloch (Scotland)

ENGLAND v IRELAND 1908

Played at Athletic Ground, Richmond, 8 February 1908
England won by 2G, 1T (13) to 1PG (3)

Vassall and Birkett, widely acclaimed as the best centre-pairing in England, made their only appearance together in this match, but there was no dramatic improvement in the standard of the back play. Poor alignment by the home three-quarters resulted in several forward passes and, occasionally, the wings were guilty of overrunning their centres. Portus, the replacement at stand-off, was not a success and at times Birkett was relied on to perform the duties of 'flying man'. Ireland's usual tactics – rush and spoil – were countered by the control of the English pack and the home backs tackled and kicked encouragingly in defence. Realising that their initial plan was failing, the Irish forwards then adopted the Welsh technique of holding and heeling the scrums. But their backs, too, had a disappointing day in attack and many efforts were frustrated by inaccurate handling and staunch English tackling.

Williamson, at scrum-half, was the man of the match and opened the scoring with a fine dash around a scrummage near the Irish line. This was the only score in the first hour of play; then, a series of fine runs by Birkett and Vassall produced two scores by Hudson in the last quarter of the game with Wood kicking two goals. Williamson's judgment in knowing exactly when to release the ball was impeccable, and his falling on the loose ball and defensive play in the first half, more than anything, convinced the Irish pack that their rush-and-harass tactics were to no avail.

Parke kicked Ireland's points with a worthy effort from a wide angle, after England had built an eight-points lead.

ENGLAND		IRELAND	
A.E. Wood	(Gloucester)	W.P. Hinton	(O. Wesley)
A. Hudson	(Gloucester)	*H.B. Thrift	(Dublin U.)
J.G.G. Birkett	(Harlequins)	J.C. Parke	(Monkstown)
†H.H. Vassall	(Oxford U.)	G.C.P. Beckett	(Dublin U.)
W.N. Lapage	(U.S./R.N.)	C. Thompson	(Belfast Collegians)
G.V. Portus	(Blackheath)	H.R. Aston	(Dublin U.)
R.H. Williamson	(Oxford U.)	F.N.B. Smartt	(Dublin U.)
R. Gilbert	(Devonport Albion)	G.T. Hamlet	(O. Wesley)
F. Boylen	(Hartlepool Rovers)	T. Smyth	(Malone)
*C.E.L. Hammond	(Harlequins)	A. Tedford	(Malone)
F.J.V. Hopley	(Blackheath)	E.McG. Morphy	(Dublin U.)
L.A.N. Slocock	(Liverpool)	H.G. Wilson	(Malone)
R. Dibble	(Bridgwater Albion)	B.A. Solomons	(Dublin U.)
T.S. Kelly	(Exeter)	T.G. Harpur	(Dublin U.)
H. Havelock	(Hartlepool Rovers)	C. Adams	(O. Wesley)

Tries: Hudson (2), Williamson   *Penalty:* Parke
Conversions: Wood (2)

Referee: Mr T.D. Schofield (Wales)

SCOTLAND v ENGLAND 1908

Played at Inverleith, Edinburgh, 21 March 1908
Scotland won by 1G, 2DG, 1T (16) to 2G (10)

Fine conditions prevailed and a crowd of 20,000 saw one of the best contests between the two countries for some years. The *Times* correspondent observed: 'The match was in keeping with the modern development of Rugby football. There was almost a complete absence of that hard, close scrummaging which was characteristic of the play of twenty years ago.'

There was disappointment amongst English followers that Vassall had to withdraw through injury, and Lyon, who entered the lists when Wood was unavailable at full-back, was only a moderate substitute. Nevertheless, the visitors had a sensational start when Williamson and Davey engineered an opening for Birkett to run 40 yards, beat Schulze and score at the posts – Lambert converting. MacLeod, playing at his brilliant best, brought Scotland back into the reckoning. He made a fine break to feed Martin outside him, and then took an inside pass to score, but Geddes could not add the goal points. The England forwards pressed home several good attacks – Slocock getting a try – before Dibble, with a spectacular run was foiled just short of the Scottish line by MacLeod. Purves dropped a goal to make the score 10–7 to England at half-time.

Scotland dominated the play at the restart, and only poor handling by the backs prevented an equalising score. At length, England found the energy to launch an attack which nearly brought a score, but Martin and MacLeod, with another delightful passage of play, ripped the English defence to shreds and the latter scored. Geddes's conversion placed Scotland ahead for the first time in the match.

Williamson, definitely the 'find' of the season as far as England were concerned, had another distinguished match 'standing out by himself', but his one error near the end of the game, when he sent a loose kick straight to Schulze, allowed the Scottish full-back to drop a beautiful goal and set the seal on Scotland's victory.

W.L. Oldham was the first player capped for England directly from the Coventry club.

SCOTLAND		**ENGLAND**	
D.G. Schulze	(London Scottish)	†G.H. D'O. Lyon	(U.S./R.N.)
H. Martin	(Oxford U.)	D. Lambert	(Harlequins)
K.G. MacLeod	(Cambridge U.)	J.G.G. Birkett	(Harlequins)
C.M. Gilray	(Oxford U.)	W.N. Lapage	(U.S./R.N.)
A.B.H.L. Purves	(London Scottish)	A. Hudson	(Gloucester)
J. Robertson	(Clydesdale)	†J. Davey	(Redruth)
A.L. Wade	(London Scottish)	R.H. Williamson	(Oxford U.)
H.G. Monteith	(London Scottish)	R. Gilbert	(Devonport Albion)
W.E. Kyle	(Hawick)	F. Boylen	(Hartlepool Rovers)
*I.C. Geddes	(London Scottish)	†W.L. Oldham	(Coventry)
J.M.B. Scott	(Edinburgh Acads.)	†F.B. Watson	(U.S./R.N.)
A.L. Robertson	(London Scottish)	*L.A.N. Slocock	(Liverpool)
J.C. MacCallum	(Watsonians)	R. Dibble	(Bridgwater Albion)
L.M. Spiers	(Watsonians)	T.S. Kelly	(Exeter)
G.M. Frew	(Glasgow H.S.F.P.)	†T. Woods	(Bridgwater Albion)

Tries: MacLeod (2)
Conversion: Geddes
Dropped goals: Purves, Schulze

Tries: Birkett, Slocock
Conversions: Lambert (2)

Referee: Mr H.H. Corley (Ireland)

ENGLAND v AUSTRALIA 1909
Played at Rectory Field, Blackheath, 9 January 1909
Australia won by 3T (9) to 1T (3)

The Australians, lacking the splendour which had accompanied the first tourists from New Zealand and South Africa, met England in the twenty-ninth match of their trip, having succumbed to four Welsh sides and the Midland Counties of England.

Selection problems had compelled the Rugby Union to name ten new caps for this match, and the unavailability of Birkett and Vassall was considered a major setback to England's cause. But, in a dramatic start to the last international match staged by the Blackheath Club, the new-look English threequarter line capitalised on a quick feed by Williamson from a scrummage in midfield, and some intricate passing between Tarr and Mobbs resulted in a try after three minutes. Cooper failed to kick the goal. Unfortunately, a careless lapse by the English defence allowed Row to score, following a kick ahead, and scores were thus even at the changeover.

Russell found the English defence wanting in the second half when another punt up-field was not cleared and the winger seized an opportunity to score a simple try. Williamson left the field five minutes from the end, suffering from a kick on the head, and while the English backs were reorganising themselves a slick round of passing by their opponents finished with Russell scoring again.

ENGLAND		AUSTRALIA	
*G.H.D'O. Lyon	(U.S./R.N.)	P.P. Carmichael	(Queensland)
†E.R. Mobbs	(Northampton)	W. Dix	(N.S.W.)
†F.N. Tarr	(Leicester/Oxford U.)	W.S. Prentice	(N.S.W.)
†E.W. Assinder	(O. Edwardians)	J. Hickey	(N.S.W.)
†B.B. Bennetts	(Penzance)	C.J. Russell	(N.S.W.)
†A.H. Ashcroft	(Cambridge U.)	A.J.M. McCabe	(N.S.W.)
R.H. Williamson	(Oxford U.)	*C.H. McKivat	(N.S.W.)
†J.G. Cooper	(Moseley)	K.A. Gavin	(N.S.W.)
†S.H. Penny	(Leicester)	N.E. Row	(N.S.W.)
†P.J. Down	(Bristol)	J.T. Barnett	(N.S.W.)
A.L. Kewney	(Rockcliff/Leicester)	P.A. McCue	(N.S.W.)
W.L. Oldham	(Coventry)	C.A. Hammand	(N.S.W.)
R. Dibble	(Bridgwater Albion)	M. McArthur	(N.S.W.)
†A.D.W. Morris	(U.S./R.N.)	T.J. Richards	(Queensland)
†F. Knight	(Plymouth)	S.A. Middleton	(N.S.W.)

Try: Mobbs

Tries: Russell (2), Row

Referee: Mr J. Games (Wales)

WALES v ENGLAND 1909

Played at Cardiff Arms Park, 16 January 1909
Wales won by 1G, 1T (8) to Nil

This match had many parallels with the encounter of 1907: again there was a small crowd by Welsh standards (about 25,000) and once more England selected an experimental pack. But there was not the huge defeat for the visitors as there had been in 1907. The new English pack was impressive and helped England to their best performance on Welsh soil since 1895. Wales were unable to adopt their usual forward game of holding the scrummage and heeling out to their backs; and the spoiling tactics of Cooper, the English winger, and Wedge upset the rhythm of the Welsh halves. Consequently, the Welsh backs were hampered in their passing game and, as a spectacle, the game was a disappointment. The English backs also were weak, and the advantage gained by their pack was to no avail as the unimaginative and predictable play of the visiting three-quarters gave the Welsh cover few problems.

Wales won the toss and had no hesitation about making first use of a stiff breeze (which, incidentally, had waned by the time England changed ends). Tries by Hopkins and Williams were registered in the first half, but the play of J.P. Jones was something of a let-down. Poor passing by the Newport centre when the English defence had been already beaten was to rob Williams of two certain scores in the second half. Second-half opportunities fell also to Tarr and Mobbs on the English wing, but they, too, failed to reproduce the skill expected at international level and could not convert their chances into points.

This win stretched Wales's imposing sequence of home victories to fifteen (excluding their matches with Dominion sides).

WALES		ENGLAND	
J. Bancroft	(Swansea)	E.J. Jackett	(Falmouth/Leicester)
P.L. Hopkins	(Swansea)	E.R. Mobbs	(Northampton)
*W.J. Trew	(Swansea)	F.N. Tarr	(Leicester/Oxford U.)
J.P. Jones	(Newport)	E.W. Assinder	(O. Edwardians)
J.L. Williams	(Cardiff)	B.B. Bennetts	(Penzance)
R. Jones	(Swansea)	J. Davey	(Redruth)
R.M. Owen	(Swansea)	T.G. Wedge	(St Ives)
P.D. Waller	(Newport)	A.D.W. Morris	(U.S./R.N.)
G. Travers	(Pill Harriers)	*R. Dibble	(Bridgwater Albion)
T.H. Evans	(Llanelli)	A.L. Kewney	(Rockcliff/Leicester)
J. Webb	(Abertillery)	†W.A. Johns	(Gloucester)
J. Brown	(Cardiff)	†E.D. Ibbitson	(Headingley)
J.H. Blackmore	(Abertillery)	†F.G. Handford	(Manchester)
G. Hayward	(Swansea)	†H. Archer	(Guy's H.)
I. Morgan	(Swansea)	J.G. Cooper	(Moseley)

Tries: Hopkins, Williams
Conversion: Bancroft

Referee: Mr J.D. Dallas (Scotland)

ENGLAND v FRANCE 1909

Played at Welford Road, Leicester, 30 January 1909
England won by 2G, 4T (22) to Nil

England's convincing victory was due to the enterprising play of Mobbs and Tarr, while Laurance Woodhouse in the *Daily Mail* reported: 'Frenchmen do not play "Comic" football nowadays, but their drop-kicking and punting need a lot of improvement.'

Poor handling deprived England of early success and Hutchinson found difficulty in taking Williamson's swift passes from the set-pieces. The French formed several promising threequarter attacks in these early stages too but, at length, Hutchinson found his game and, combining with the irrepressible Poulton, sent Tarr through a gap. Mobbs received the ball on the left and although Lesieur did well to overtake his man, a deft transfer inwards enabled Tarr to score at the posts for Jackett to convert. Minutes later a change of direction by the English midfield backs resulted in another try for Tarr and again Jackett kicked the goal, this time from a considerable angle.

After the restart Tarr featured in a move which produced a try for Mobbs; then Caujolle, a plucky full-back, made a courageous save by diving at the ball with most of the English pack bearing down upon him. Indeed, French full-backs were noted for their daring deeds at this time. Caujolle's brave act inspired his team to launch a series of attacks during which Jackett was injured and forced to retire for 15 minutes – Archer switching to full-back. When the pack was eventually restored, England ran away to a comfortable win. Poulton created a space for Tarr to send Simpson in at the corner; Hutchinson dived over from one of Williamson's bullet-like passes and Johns touched down after good work by Mobbs and Tarr.

ENGLAND		FRANCE	
E.J. Jackett	(Falmouth/Leicester)	J. Caujolle	(Tarbes)
T. Simpson	(Rockcliff)	E. Lesieur	(Stade Français)
F.N. Tarr	(Oxford U./Leicester)	H. Houblain	(S.C.U.F.)
†R.W. Poulton	(Harlequins/Oxford U.)	T. Varvier	(R.C.F.)
E.R. Mobbs	(Northampton)	G. Lane	(R.C.F.)
†F. Hutchinson	(Headingley)	A. Theuriet	(S.C.U.F.)
R.H. Williamson	(Oxford U.)	A. Hubert	(A.S.F.)
A.D.W. Morris	(U.S./R.N.)	R.de Malmann	(R.C.F.)
*R. Dibble	(Bridgwater Albion)	G. Borchard	(R.C.F.)
A.L. Kewney	(Rockcliff/Leicester)	J. Icard	(Stade Français)
W.A. Johns	(Gloucester)	A. Masse	(S.B.U.C.)
E.D. Ibbitson	(Headingley)	*M. Communeau	(Stade Français)
F.G. Handford	(Manchester)	P. Guillemin	(R.C.F.)
H. Archer	(Guy's H.)	R. Duval	(Stade Français)
†C.A. Bolton	(U.S.)	G. Fourcade	(Bordeaux E.C.)

Tries: Tarr (2), Hutchinson, Johns,
Mobbs, Simpson
Conversions: Jackett (2)

Referee: Mr W. Williams (England)

IRELAND v ENGLAND 1909

Played at Lansdowne Road, Dublin, 13 February 1909
England won by 1G, 2T (11) to 1G (5)

England, selecting their fifteen from the far corners of the north, south and south-west, gained a well-earned victory and thus broke a long sequence of disappointments in Dublin, dating back to 1895. Only Jackett of this XV had appeared in a match in Dublin prior to this engagement, though Kewney and Dibble had met the Irish pack in England on another occasion.

The weather was fine, and the pitch immaculate, as the teams took the field before a crowd which had paid a record £1000 for admission to Lansdowne Road. Hamlet kicked off and after a promising burst by Pinion, England relieved the pressure on their goal with a free kick. Play settled in the Irish quarter of the field, and an error by Pinion was quickly turned to good use by the English backs. Palmer crossed to the right of the posts, adding the conversion. Ireland enjoyed a territorial advantage in the following play, but inaccurate place-kicking, first by Parke and later by Pinion, prevented Ireland from gaining a 9–5 lead. Half-time arrived soon after a counter-attack by Palmer had been just thwarted near the Irish goal-line.

Runs by Mobbs and Thrift enlivened the play at the beginning of the second half, and Mobbs stretched the visitors' lead to eight points with a try on the left wing which Palmer failed to goal. Further disaster befell Ireland when, shortly afterwards, Hutchinson gave Palmer the opportunity to score another try. Ireland's hopes half-way through the second session now seemed dashed, but a spirited rush, with Hamlet at the helm, produced a try for Parke which (Irish reports assure) was converted by Pinion. Three minutes from no-side, Mobbs and Palmer executed a thrilling move from their own goal-line and only a desperate tackle in the Irish 25 prevented a certain score.

An encouraging win for England: by this stage in the season the selection committee had enlisted 31 players for four matches!

IRELAND		ENGLAND	
W.P. Hinton	(O. Wesley)	E.J. Jackett	(Falmouth/Leicester)
H.B. Thrift	(Wanderers)	†A.C. Palmer	(London H.)
J.C. Parke	(Monkstown)	†C.C.G. Wright	(Cambridge U.)
C. Thompson	(Collegians)	R.W. Poulton	(Oxford U.)
E.C. Deane	(Monkstown)	E.R. Mobbs	(Northampton)
F.N.B. Smartt	(Dublin U.)	F. Hutchinson	(Headingley)
G. Pinion	(Collegians)	H.J.H. Sibree	(Harlequins)
G.T. Hamlet	(O. Wesley)	†H.J.S. Morton	(Cambridge U.)
T. Smyth	(Malone)	*R. Dibble	(Bridgwater Albion)
O.J.S. Piper	(Cork Const.)	A.L. Kewney	(Rockcliff/Leicester)
*F. Gardiner	(N.I.F.C.)	W.A. Johns	(Gloucester)
C. Adams	(O. Wesley)	E.D. Ibbitson	(Headingley)
B.A. Solomons	(Dublin U.)	F.G. Handford	(Manchester)
H.G. Wilson	(Malone)	H. Archer	(Guy's H.)
M.G. Garry	(Bective Rangers)	†A.J. Wilson	(Camborne S. of Mines)

Try: Parke *Conversion:* Pinion

Tries: Palmer (2), Mobbs
Conversion: Palmer

Referee: Mr J.D. Dallas (Scotland)

ENGLAND v SCOTLAND 1909

Played at Athletic Ground, Richmond, 20 March 1909
Scotland won by 3G, 1T (18) to 1G, 1T (8)

A dispute concerning the payment of expenses (three shillings per day) to the Australian tourists was settled in time for this match to be played, but not without the Scots making their point of view very clear indeed: they refused to play the Australians and regarded the payment as a justification by the R.F.U. of professionalism. Due to a delay in the building of the stands at the newly-acquired ground at Twickenham, the R.F.U. was obliged to stage this match at Richmond.

20,000, including the Prince of Wales, witnessed a thrilling game, though the margin of victory flattered the Scots. It was only at half-back that Scotland outplayed the home side: Cunningham, at the end of an indifferent season for him, and Tennent, playing proficiently behind a sound, hard-scrummaging pack. The English halves, by contrast, were out of their depth, and one critic was moved to lay blame squarely on the shoulders of the selectors, contending that Williamson of Oxford should have been as much a certainty for the English XV as C.B. Fry was for the England cricket XI.

A superb break by Cunningham allowed Simson to score the first try, but, after Mobbs had equalised, a try by Watson, converted by Palmer, gave England a lead at the break. The English forwards had played competently up to this time and England were deservedly ahead.

Scotland's pack began the second half with purpose and zest, and during the first five minutes some rushes, described by the *Times* correspondent as 'stinging attacks', produced tries for Gilray and Tennent which Cunningham gratefully converted. 15 minutes from no-side, Tennent crossed again to pull Scotland clear of any danger. Cunningham converted.

This was the only international match to be refereed by the former Welsh centre Gwyn Nicholls. 'Wasn't I awful?' he commented upon leaving the ground!

ENGLAND		SCOTLAND	
E.J. Jackett	(Falmouth/Leicester)	D.G. Schulze	(London Scottish)
A.C. Palmer	(London H.)	H. Martin	(Oxford U.)
C.C.G. Wright	(Cambridge U.)	C.M. Gilray	(Oxford U.)
R.W. Poulton	(Oxford U.)	J. Pearson	(Watsonians)
E.R. Mobbs	(Northampton)	J.T. Simson	(Watsonians)
F. Hutchinson	(Headingley)	*G. Cunningham	(Oxford U.)
H.J.H. Sibree	(Harlequins)	J.M. Tennent	(West of Scotland)
H.J.S. Morton	(Cambridge U.)	J.M.B. Scott	(Edinburgh Acads.)
*R. Dibble	(Bridgwater Albion)	G.M. Frew	(Glasgow H.S.F.P.)
A.L. Kewney	(Rockcliff/Leicester)	W.E. Kyle	(Hawick)
W.A. Johns	(Gloucester)	J.M. Mackenzie	(Edinburgh U.)
E.D. Ibbitson	(Headingley)	G.C. Gowlland	(London Scottish)
F.G. Handford	(Manchester)	J.C. MacCallum	(Watsonians)
†H.C. Harrison	(Royal Marines)	J. Reid-Kerr	(Greenock Wands.)
F.B. Watson	(U.S./R.N.)	A.R. Moodie	(St Andrew's U.)

Tries: Mobbs, Watson
Conversion: Palmer

Tries: Tennent (2), Gilray, Simson
Conversions: Cunningham (3)

Referee: Mr E.G. Nicholls (Wales)

ENGLAND v WALES,
SATURDAY, JAN. **15**th, 1910. Kick-off 2.45 p.m.

ENGLAND (white)
Back
W. R. JOHNSTON (Bristol)
Three-Quarters
F. E. CHAPMAN   J. G. G. BIRKETT   B. SOLOMON   R. W. POULTON
(Westoe)   (Harlequins)   (Redruth)   (Oxford)
Half-Backs
A. D. STOOP (Harlequins)   D. R. GENT (Gloucester)
Forwards
E. L. CHAMBERS   L. HAIGH   W. JOHNS   H. J. S. MORTON
(Bedford)   (Manchester)   (Gloucester)   (Blackheath)
H. BERRY   L. E. BARRINGTON WARD   D. F. SMITH   C. H. PILLMAN
(Gloucester)   (Edin. Univ)   (Richmond)   (Blackheath)
Touch Judge. T. C. PRING, President, Rugby Union.

RIGHT   LEFT

REFEREE   J. D. DALLAS, Scottish Union.
Touch Judge, H. R. LYNE, President, Welsh Union.
Forwards
J. WEBB   IVOR MORGAN   D. J. THOMAS   C. M. PRITCHARD
(Abertillery)   (Swansea)   (Swansea)   (Newport)
H. JARMAN   J. PUGSLEY   T. EVANS   B. GRONGW
(Newport)   (Cardiff)   (Llanelly)   (Bridgend)
Half-Backs
R. M. OWEN (Swansea)   R. JONES (Swansea)
Three-Quarters
P. HOPKINS   J. P. JONES   W. J. TREW, Capt.   R. A. GIBBS
(Swansea)   (Newport)   (Swansea)   (Cardiff)
Back
J. BANCROFT (Swansea)
WALES

LEFT   RIGHT

The Public are **particularly** requested not to go on the field of play at half time, as at this time of the year it is **essential** that the game should **not be delayed.**

THE RAILWAY TAVERN,   PROPRIETOR,
F. D. GOODMAN
LONDON ROAD,   **TWICKENHAM**
22, 24, 26, P.O. Richmond
Billiard Saloon, 2 Tables.   Well appointed Skittle Saloon.
THE NOTED HOUSE FOR WINES, SPIRITS, &c LUNCHEONS AND TEAS PROVIDED.

Programme of Music.
1 March   "Wein Bleibt, Wien."   Schrammel
2 Selection "The Belle of Brittany."   Talbot
3 Valse   "Remembrance,"   Joyce
4 Romanza   "Nadege,"   Myddleton
5 Selection   "Our Miss Gibbs,"   Caryll
6 Danse   "Des Apaches,"   Clarke
7 Selection "Reminiscences of Wales,"   Godfrey
8 Two-Step "Dreams of Ragtime,"   Thurban
Conductor—Mr. G. KIRKMAN ROBERTS.

The programme for England's first match at Twickenham which had been purchased by the R.F.U. for £5573 in the 1907-08 season.

A page from *The Illustrated Sporting and Dramatic News* depicting England's famous victory over Wales in 1910. England's long-awaited win – they had not beaten Wales since 1898 – was a fitting way to celebrate the first match played on 'Billy Williams's cabbage patch'.

ENGLAND BEATS WALES AT TWICKENHAM.

ENGLAND'S FIRST VICTORY OVER THE WELSHMEN FOR TWELVE YEARS.

A line out.   _Cheering England's first try, gained by Solomon, Chapman, etc., in the first minute._

The first international on the Rugby Union's new ground at Twickenham resulted last Saturday in a great victory for England over Wales by eleven points to six. Between twenty and thirty thousand spectators assembled in wretched weather and saw a match played on heavy ground, of which the result justly represented the ability shown by the respective teams. After Chapman had scored for England in the first minute of the game, his side were always forcing brilliantly or defending tenaciously.

England brought down on the touch-line (upper picture), and heeling out of the scrum.   _A straw heap as a grand stand and foot-warmer._

ENGLAND v WALES 1910

Played at Twickenham, London, 15 January 1910
England won by 1G, 1PG, 1T (11) to 2T (6)

The first international played at Twickenham got off to a sensational start, even though it was delayed 15 minutes by traffic congestion. Gronow kicked off for Wales, but Stoop, instead of playing orthodoxly and punting for touch, veered to his left and sought a passage into Welsh territory. Then according to Solomon, the Cornish centre, 'there was a loose scrum from which D.R. Gent got the ball and passed to Stoop from whom I got it. I passed to Birkett who then gave to Chapman who scored in the right-hand corner.' So England led after one minute. 15 minutes later, Chapman stretched England's lead with a penalty goal, but Wales retaliated with a fine try. The Welsh forwards rushed play into the English 25 and Owen gathered to take the ball up to the full-back. From the ensuing mêlée, Evans dived over, but the conversion failed. England countered with good play and stretched their lead before half-time. From a loose scrum, Gent passed to Solomon, who ran 40 yards, untouched, to score at the Welsh posts after selling Bancroft an outrageous dummy. Chapman's conversion was a formality.

Wales played with more control in the second half, and obtained a try by Gibbs in the right-hand corner early in the half after some clever play by their three-quarters. But England defended stoutly in the later stages, and though Wales had opportunities to win the match, Trew, the Welsh skipper, graciously acknowledged during the after-match exchanges that the English deserved their victory.

The site of the new ground at Twickenham had been purchased for £5573 in the 1907–08 season, with William Cail, Treasurer of the R.F.U., handling the finance, and Billy Williams, one of the R.F.U. committee, taking the credit for the discovery of the site, which had formerly been a cabbage field. 'Billy Williams's cabbage patch' became the Headquarters of the R.F.U., and this first match staged there saw England's long-awaited win over Wales, their first since 1898.

ENGLAND		WALES	
†W.R. Johnston	(Bristol)	J. Bancroft	(Swansea)
†F.E. Chapman	(Westoe)	R.A. Gibbs	(Cardiff)
J.G.G. Birkett	(Harlequins)	J.P. Jones	(Pontypool)
†B. Solomon	(Redruth)	*W.J. Trew	(Swansea)
R.W. Poulton	(Oxford U./Harlequins)	P.L. Hopkins	(Swansea)
*A.D. Stoop	(Harlequins)	R. Jones	(Swansea)
D.R. Gent	(Gloucester)	R.M. Owen	(Swansea)
H.J.S. Morton	(Blackheath)	B. Gronow	(Bridgend)
W.A. Johns	(Gloucester)	J. Pugsley	(Cardiff)
†L. Haigh	(Manchester)	C.M. Pritchard	(Newport)
†D.F. Smith	(Richmond)	D.J. Thomas	(Swansea)
E.L. Chambers	(Bedford)	T.H. Evans	(Llanelli)
†H. Berry	(Gloucester)	H. Jarman	(Newport)
†L.E. Barrington-Ward	(Edinburgh U.)	J. Webb	(Abertillery)
†C.H. Pillman	(Blackheath)	I. Morgan	(Swansea)

Tries: Chapman, Solomon
Conversion: Chapman *Penalty:* Chapman

Tries: Evans, Gibbs

Referee: Mr J.D. Dallas (Scotland)

ENGLAND v IRELAND 1910
Played at Twickenham, London, 12 February 1910
Drawn, neither side scoring

With the euphoria of the win over Wales still evident, a crowd approaching 20,000, and including the Prince of Wales, saw England escape luckily from this match with a pointless draw.

The Irish forwards played with traditional fire, lasting the pace with rare stamina. They held the scrummages with control, wheeled scientifically to rush the ball at the English halves in a series of formidable rushes, and sped about destructively in the loose. Some poor handling and running by the Irish backs – Quinn apart – offset much of the forwards' good work, but there were few who would have protested had Ireland won. Gent and Stoop appeared fragile behind a beaten pack (heroic defence was not a feature of Stoop's otherwise immaculate play) but Johnston dealt bravely with the numerous foot-rushes of the Irish pack, enhancing his reputation earned in the Welsh match to the extent that the *Times* correspondent called him the best back in England since Gamlin.

The sides had their best chances of scoring in the first half. Chapman showed his pace on the right wing and failed narrowly to score once; while Lloyd, the new Irish fly-half, went close with a drop at goal. Mobbs was twice injured in the second half, and left the field 15 minutes from no-side. The seven English forwards did a fine job during this last quarter, for the Irish halves, with their forwards heeling the ball regularly, looked most dangerous while Mobbs was receiving attention. The wing-forward play of Pillman, on the open side of the scrummage, was to become a feature of English forward tactics this season. No doubt his covering and ubiquity in this match helped England to weather the storm of the last 15 minutes.

Old Cheltonians had featured in several of the early England internationals, but in this match L.W. Hayward became the first player capped from Cheltenham R.F.C.

ENGLAND		IRELAND	
W.R. Johnston	(Bristol)	W.P. Hinton	(O. Wesley)
F.E. Chapman	(Westoe)	C. Thompson	(Belfast Collegians)
J.G.G. Birkett	(Harlequins)	A.S. Taylor	(Queen's U.)
†L.W. Hayward	(Cheltenham)	A.R. Foster	(Queen's U.)
E.R. Mobbs	(Northampton)	J.P. Quinn	(Dublin U.)
*A.D. Stoop	(Harlequins)	R.A. Lloyd	(Dublin U.)
D.R. Gent	(Gloucester)	H.M. Read	(Dublin U.)
H.J.S. Morton	(Blackheath)	O.J.S. Piper	(Cork Const.)
W.A. Johns	(Gloucester)	J.C. Blackham	(Queen's College, Cork)
L. Haigh	(Manchester)	*G.T. Hamlet	(O. Wesley)
D.F. Smith	(Richmond)	T. Halpin	(Garryowen)
E.L. Chambers	(Bedford)	T. Smyth	(Malone)
H. Berry	(Gloucester)	W.F. Riordan	(Cork Const.)
L.E. Barrington-Ward	(Edinburgh U.)	B.A. Solomons	(Wanderers)
C.H. Pillman	(Blackheath)	G. McIldowie	(Malone)

Referee: Mr T.D. Schofield (Wales)

FRANCE v ENGLAND 1910

Played at Parc des Princes, Paris, 3 March 1910
England won by 1G, 2T (11) to 1T (3)

A holiday crowd of 8000 saw one of the best French performances in the matches prior to the Great War. Six of England's original side for this match were unable to play, and when the visitors did take the field there were eight new caps in the ranks, but this should not detract from the fact that England were made to struggle for their win.

In excellent conditions, the French backs looked impressive in the early stages. Laterrade played an outstanding game at the heels of a small but lively pack and the tackling of Combe was well received by the crowd. French marking was tight and there was a touch of luck about England's first try – Coverdale managing to send Berry over. Hudson then, with a determined run, scored the second try, to take England to an eight-points lead at the interval.

After half-time France's forwards took a firm grip on the game up-front and the resulting possession enabled the French backs to play an attractive, open game. In addition, the disruptive play of the French forwards prevented the English backs from gaining any rhythm. Reward came after 15 minutes when, following a scramble, Communeau scored for France near the posts. The conversion kick, however, was charged down. Careless handling robbed France of another score and towards the end of a rather disappointing match for England Hudson exploited a disorganised defence, depleted by the retirement of Lane, to complete the scoring with his second try.

FRANCE		ENGLAND	
J. Combe	(Stade Français)	†C.S. Williams	(Manchester)
E. Lesieur	(Stade Français)	F.E. Chapman	(Westoe)
G. Lane	(R.C.F.)	†A.A. Adams	(London H.)
C. Vareilles	(Stade Français)	*E.R. Mobbs	(Northampton)
M. Bruneau	(S.B.U.C.)	A. Hudson	(Gloucester)
J. Dedet	(Stade Français)	†H. Coverdale	(Blackheath)
G. Laterrade	(Tarbes)	†A.L.H. Gotley	(Oxford U.)
R. de Malmann	(R.C.F.)	†N.A. Wodehouse	(U.S.)
P. Mauriat	(Lyon)	W.A. Johns	(Gloucester)
J. Cadenat	(S.C.U.F.)	†R.H.M. Hands	(Oxford U.)
*M. Communeau	(Stade Français)	†E.S. Scorfield	(Percy Park)
P. Guillemin	(R.C.F.)	†J.A.S. Ritson	(Northern)
A. Masse	(Stade Bordelais)	H. Berry	(Gloucester)
M. Hourdebaight	(Stade Bordelais)	L.E. Barrington-Ward	(Edinburgh U.)
G. Thevenot	(S.C.U.F.)	C.H. Pillman	(Blackheath)

Try: Communeau

Tries: Hudson (2), Berry
Conversion: Chapman

Referee: Mr Bowden (Scotland)

SCOTLAND v ENGLAND 1910
Played at Inverleith, Edinburgh, 19 March 1910
England won by 1G, 3T (14) to 1G (5)

This unexpected victory gave England the International Championship for the first time since 1892. 30,000 spectators – quite the largest congregation for a match in Scotland up to this date – saw a fast, open game played in ideal conditions.

The Scottish forwards heeled constantly at the beginning of the match and wheeled several scrummages to maraud into English territory with the ball at their feet. The home backs were disappointing, however, and Pillman's disruption of Tennent's play at the base of the scrum kept England in the game after Macpherson opened the scoring with a try converted by MacCallum. A determined run by Birkett was rewarded by a try at the posts and Chapman's conversion levelled the scores at the interval.

England's forwards got back into the game in the second half and the backs revelled in the conditions, Stoop making several openings for his three-quarters. At length, the outside-half created a try from inside his own half, with Birkett again obtaining the touch-down. Chapman failed to convert. Pillman, who was, according to *The Times*, 'conspicuous and useful in his own peculiar game', inspired a try by Berry and then paved the way for Ritson to complete the scoring.

Sutherland was Scotland's finest back and once beat Chapman and Johnston, only to stumble inches short of the try-line.

The International Board, meeting in Edinburgh on the day of this match, decreed that 'it was desirable . . . where neutral touch-judges were appointed that they should report cases of foul or unfair play to the referee'. It was not until seventy years later that this statement entered the Law Book!

The Stoops were brothers who appeared in the same match.

SCOTLAND		ENGLAND	
D.G. Schulze	(London Scottish)	W.R. Johnston	(Bristol)
J. Pearson	(Watsonians)	F.E. Chapman	(Westoe)
A.W. Angus	(Watsonians)	*J.G.G. Birkett	(Harlequins)
D.G. Macpherson	(London H.)	†F.M. Stoop	(Harlequins)
W.R. Sutherland	(Hawick)	†P.W. Lawrie	(Leicester)
*G. Cunningham	(Oxford U.)	A.D. Stoop	(Harlequins)
J.M. Tennent	(West of Scotland)	A.L.H. Gotley	(Oxford U.)
J.M.B. Scott	(Edinburgh Acads.)	†G.R. Hind	(Guy's H.)
J.C. MacCallum	(Watsonians)	J.A.S. Ritson	(Northern)
L.M. Spiers	(Watsonians)	L. Haigh	(Manchester)
C.D. Stuart	(West of Scotland)	R. Dibble	(Bridgwater Albion)
G.C. Gowlland	(London Scottish)	R.H.M. Hands	(Oxford U.)
C.H. Abercrombie	(U.S.)	H. Berry	(Gloucester)
J.M. Mackenzie	(Edinburgh U.)	L.E. Barrington-Ward	(Edinburgh U.)
R.C. Stevenson	(St Andrew's U.)	C.H. Pillman	(Blackheath)

Try: Macpherson   *Tries:* Birkett (2), Berry, Ritson
Conversion: MacCallum   *Conversion:* Chapman

Referee: Mr G.H.B. Kennedy (Ireland)

WALES v ENGLAND 1911
Played at St Helen's, Swansea, 21 January 1911
Wales won by 1PG, 4T (15) to 1G, 2T (11)

This was one of the finest matches between the two countries to take place before the outbreak of the Great War. England, with the nucleus of the Championship side from 1910 still available, gave the Welsh a thorough examination on their patch, and only a fit home side was capable of holding off England's challenge.

Spalding's Rugby Football Annual summarised the game thus: 'The honours were fairly evenly divided. The visiting forwards were excellent and their three-quarters faster than those of the Welsh.'

Stoop and Birkett created an overlap for Roberts to score the first try, but a typical Welsh try by Gibbs, followed by a splendid penalty goal from Birt, placed Wales in front at the interval. Wales began strongly in the second half, too, with a try by Ivor Morgan before Wales again brought play to the English 25. There, from a scrum, Stoop opened play rather adventurously and passed the ball to Birkett. The Harlequin dropped the pass and Spiller pounced, scooping it up to cross for the decisive score. England retaliated and during a productive period Kewney got over for Lambert to kick the goal. Then, in quite the best move of the match, Scholfield looped around his winger to bring England to within one point of the Welsh.

In an exciting finish, with England striving to gain the winning score, Wales weathered a series of punishing attacks, summoning all of their experience and stamina to assist their defence. At length the pressure was relieved and Owen dribbled the ball over the English line for Pugsley to touch down and put the issue beyond doubt.

WALES		ENGLAND	
J. Bancroft	(Swansea)	†S.H. Williams	(Newport)
R.A. Gibbs	(Cardiff)	D. Lambert	(Harlequins)
F.W. Birt	(Newport)	*J.G.G. Birkett	(Harlequins)
W.J. Spiller	(Cardiff)	†J.A. Scholfield	(Cambridge U.)
J.L. Williams	(Cardiff)	†A.D. Roberts	(Northern)
*W.J. Trew	(Swansea)	A.D. Stoop	(Harlequins)
R.M. Owen	(Swansea)	A.L.H. Gotley	(Blackheath)
H. Jarman	(Pontypool)	†L.G. Brown	(Oxford U.)
A.P. Coldrick	(Newport)	N.A. Wodehouse	(U.S.)
J. Webb	(Abertillery)	R. Dibble	(Bridgwater Albion)
T.H. Evans	(Llanelli)	L. Haigh	(Manchester)
J. Pugsley	(Cardiff)	†W.E. Mann	(U.S.)
D.J. Thomas	(Swansea)	A.L. Kewney	(Leicester)
W. Perry	(Neath)	†J.A. King	(Headingley)
I. Morgan	(Swansea)	C.H. Pillman	(Blackheath)

Tries: Gibbs, Morgan, Pugsley, Spiller
Penalty: Birt

Tries: Kewney, Roberts, Scholfield
Conversion: Lambert

Referee: Mr J.I. Gillespie (Scotland)

ENGLAND v FRANCE 1911

Played at Twickenham, London, 28 January 1911
England won by 5G, 2PG, 2T (37) to Nil

France's first visit to Rugby Union's Headquarters was eagerly awaited, following their sensational victory in Paris against Scotland four weeks earlier. However, England annihilated their visitors in a match principally remembered for Lambert's record contribution of 22 points: five conversions, two tries and two penalty goals.

The French had been forced to make several changes from the fifteen which surprised the Scots, and *Le Figaro*, then, as now, a reliable recorder of Rugby in France, commented: 'Les deux hommes qui furent les artisans de la victoire du 2 janvier, Failliot et Lane, manquaient. Outre que leur absence diminuait nos chances materielles, elles les diminuait plus encore moralement.'

England were restricted to two tries in the first half, but injuries to Dutour, Laterrade and Peyroutou made France's task more difficult and England ran away to a large victory.

ENGLAND		FRANCE	
S.H. Williams	(Newport)	F.X. Dutour	(Toulouse)
D. Lambert	(Harlequins)	E. Lesieur	(Stade Français)
*J.G.G. Birkett	(Harlequins)	M. Burgun	(R.C.F.)
F.M. Stoop	(Harlequins)	T. Varvier	(R.C.F.)
A.D. Roberts	(Northern)	G. Charpentier	(Stade Français)
A.D. Stoop	(Harlequins)	G. Peyroutou	(Périgueux)
A.L.H. Gotley	(Blackheath)	G. Laterrade	(Tarbes)
L.G. Brown	(Oxford U.)	R. Duval	(Stade Français)
N.A. Wodehouse	(U.S.)	J. Bavozet	(Lyon)
R. Dibble	(Bridgwater Albion)	F. Forgues	(Bayonne)
L. Haigh	(Manchester)	*M. Communeau	(Stade Français)
W.E. Mann	(U.S.)	P. Mauriat	(Lyon)
A.L. Kewney	(Leicester)	P. Mounicq	(Toulouse)
J.A. King	(Headingley)	M. Legrain	(Stade Français)
C.H. Pillman	(Blackheath)	P. Guillemin	(R.C.F.)

Tries: Lambert (2), Pillman (2), Mann,
A.D. Stoop, Wodehouse,
Conversions: Lambert (5)
Penalties: Lambert (2)

Referee: Mr E.A. Johns (Wales)

England v France, 1911, forever
remembered as Lambert's match on account
of his record contribution of 22 points:
back F. M. Stoop, W. E. Mann, C. H. Pillman,
A. D. Roberts, L. Haigh, Mr E. A. Johns;
middle N. A. Wodehouse, D. Lambert,
A. D. Stoop, J. G. G. Birkett (captain),
R. Dibble, L. G. Brown, A. L. Kewney;
front J. A. King, A. L. H. Gotley,
S. H. Williams.

Half-time during England's match against
Scotland, 1911: J. G. G. Birkett,
C. H. Pillman, J. A. King, R. O. Lagden,
L. G. Brown.

IRELAND v ENGLAND 1911

Played at Lansdowne Road, Dublin, 11 February 1911
Ireland won by 1T (3) to Nil

Conditions were ideal for England's visit to Dublin, but the thirty-fifth meeting of the countries resulted in a narrow Irish win. This was an exciting match with forwards dominating the play on both sides. The tight tactics of the Irish halves, Lloyd and Read, who kicked with accuracy and tremendous length, meant that the enterprising English three-quarters saw little of the ball and were unable to reproduce the attractive passing game which, at this time, was a feature of Harlequin club football.

England could take consolation in the splendid play of Williams and Gotley in this match. Williams, though of Welsh origin, chose to represent England, and was described as playing 'faultlessly in all four matches' this season, before retiring at an early age. Gotley was brave in the face of many Irish foot-rushes, falling on the ball several times as the Irish pack dribbled away from wheeled scrummages.

The only score in the match came near the end. England were under pressure, deep in their 25, when F.M. Stoop was forced to make a hurried kick. His clearance went astray and Smyth capitalised on the error to score. The angle was too difficult for the place kick.

IRELAND		ENGLAND	
W.P. Hinton	(O. Wesley)	S.H. Williams	(Newport)
C.T. O'Callaghan	(Carlow/O.M.Ts.)	D. Lambert	(Harlequins)
A.R. Foster	(Queen's U.)	*J.G.G. Birkett	(Harlequins)
J.P. Quinn	(Dublin U.)	F.M. Stoop	(Harlequins)
A.R.V. Jackson	(Wanderers)	A.D. Roberts	(Northern)
R.A. Lloyd	(Dublin U.)	A.D. Stoop	(Harlequins)
H.M. Read	(Dublin U.)	A.L.H. Gotley	(Blackheath)
T. Smyth	(Malone)	L.G. Brown	(Oxford U.)
*G.T. Hamlet	(O. Wesley)	N.A. Wodehouse	(U.S.)
M.R. Heffernan	(Cork Const.)	G.R. Hind	(Guy's H.)
S.B.B. Campbell	(Derry)	L. Haigh	(Manchester)
T. Halpin	(Garryowen)	W.E. Mann	(U.S.)
C. Adams	(O. Wesley)	A.L. Kewney	(Leicester)
P.J. Smyth	(Belfast Collegians)	J.A. King	(Headingley)
M.G. Garry	(Bective Rangers)	C.H. Pillman	(Blackheath)

Try: T. Smyth

Referee: Mr J.D. Dallas (Scotland)

ENGLAND v SCOTLAND 1911

Played at Twickenham, London, 18 March 1911
England won by 2G, 1T (13) to 1G, 1T (8)

'A.D. Stoop and his Harlequins were playing great football just now, and had considerable influence on the England side.' Thus wrote F.J. Sellicks in 1925 in the updated version of *Marshall*. But, strange to relate, there were only two 'Quins in this successful English fifteen.

Although the pitch was firm, rain made the greasy ball difficult to control; nevertheless, the 25,000 spectators witnessed a fast match with plenty of scoring. Scotland were first to score when Sutherland, an athletic player with a fine running style, raced over. England countered and Stoop and Birkett – inevitably – combined smoothly to give Wodehouse a try which the new forward, Lagden, kicked into a goal. More running by the Harlequin midfield players resulted in Poulton sending Lawrie over for a try at the left-hand corner before the break.

Soon after half-time, a fine combined move involving most of the English side ended with Birkett planting the ball beside the Scottish posts for a picture-book try. Lagden again converted but Scotland had more to offer. Simson cut through the English defence for a try which Cunningham goaled and Scotland were pressing hard in the closing stages when a singularly embarrassing accident befell Cunningham, the Scottish centre. E.H.D. Sewell takes up the story: 'With only a a few minutes to go ... G. Cunningham broke through the English defence; but in evading England's full back ... he had his breeks almost wholly peeled off him. He was then half-bare and a bare ten yards from the line, fifteen from goal, no opponent near! Rather than anticipate the nudist movement he incontinently sat down – and Scotland lost a try close to, or behind, goal, and with it the chance of drawing the game.'

The last survivor of the Scotland team, Charlie Stuart, recalled shortly before his death in January 1982 that some of the Scottish players were unable to find the entrance to the new R.F.U. ground, and had to walk through allotments to gain access!

ENGLAND		SCOTLAND	
S.H. Williams	(Newport)	C. Ogilvy	(Hawick)
A.D. Roberts	(Northern)	S.S.L. Steyn	(London Scottish)
J.G.G. Birkett	(Harlequins)	G. Cunningham	(London Scottish)
R.W. Poulton	(Oxford U.)	R.F. Simson	(London Scottish)
P.W. Lawrie	(Leicester)	W.R. Sutherland	(Hawick)
A.D. Stoop	(Harlequins)	J.Y.M. Henderson	(Watsonians)
*A.L.H. Gotley	(Blackheath)	E. Milroy	(Watsonians)
L.G. Brown	(Oxford U.)	C.D. Stuart	(West of Scotland)
N.A. Wodehouse	(U.S.)	*J.C. MacCallum	(Watsonians)
R. Dibble	(Bridgwater Albion)	G.M. Frew	(Glasgow H.S.F.P.)
L. Haigh	(Manchester)	F.H. Turner	(Oxford U.)
†R.O. Lagden	(Oxford U.)	W.R. Hutchison	(Glasgow H.S.F.P.)
A.L. Kewney	(Leicester)	D.M. Bain	(Oxford U.)
J.A. King	(Headingley)	R. Fraser	(Cambridge U.)
C.H. Pillman	(Blackheath)	J. Dobson	(Glasgow Acads.)

Tries: Birkett, Lawrie, Wodehouse
Conversions: Lagden (2)

Tries: Simson, Sutherland
Conversion: Cunningham

Referee: Mr T.D. Schofield (Wales)

ENGLAND v WALES 1912

Played at Twickenham, London, 20 January 1912
England won by 1G, 1T (8) to Nil

'An enormous attendance may be expected if only the rain holds off. Every seat in the stands has been taken, and those who wish to secure a good place at the fence will be well-advised to make an early start for the somewhat remote and inaccessible theatre of warfare.' This was the warning issued by *The Times* in a preview of the match. Critics had reservations about the R.F.U.'s new site at Twickenham – it was, they contended, too far from central London to become a popular venue – but on this occasion more than 20,000 descended on the Middlesex village to see England win in the last 15 minutes of the match. *The Times*, with customary attention to detail, noted that a number of Welshmen swelled the crowd and 'sported the honourable leek in their hats and gave pleasant renderings of their national songs'.

The rain held off, though conditions were heavy under foot. The first half saw good Rugby from each side. Wodehouse, and Poulton with one of the corkscrewing runs which were to typify his play, went close to scoring tries for England; while Wales, playing their heeling-out game, won a large share of the possession. Owen, working without the protection of his famous wing-forward, Ivor Morgan, was able to send his backs away time and again, but a tendency to run across field, and particularly accurate English tackling, deprived Wales of a score.

Early in the second half, the Welsh forwards held the upper hand in the tight, but the Welsh three-quarters were unable to breach the English line. Birt and Bancroft maintained the pressure with a series of teasing kicks which forced England into their 25, but at length the English relieved the situation to effect a dramatic recovery in the last quarter of the match.

15 minutes from no-side, Chapman, recalled to the home side after a long absence through injury, drew the defence to feed Pillman. With the grace of a centre three-quarter, the Blackheath forward created an overlap for Brougham to run around and touch down beside the posts. Chapman kicked the goal. Ten minutes later, Pym dodged across the Welsh line from close quarters to complete the scoring: a close but deserved win for England.

Jack Eddison and A.H. MacIlwaine, both alive in early 1982, are the senior English caps.

ENGLAND		WALES	
W.R. Johnston	(Bristol)	J. Bancroft	(Swansea)
F.E. Chapman	(Westoe)	E.G. Davies	(Cardiff)
R.W. Poulton	(Harlequins)	W.J. Spiller	(Cardiff)
J.G.G. Birkett	(Harlequins)	F.W. Birt	(Newport)
†H. Brougham	(Harlequins)	J.P. Jones	(Pontypool)
A.D. Stoop	(Harlequins)	J.M.C. Lewis	(Cardiff)
†J.A. Pym	(Blackheath)	*R.M. Owen	(Swansea)
†A.H. MacIlwaine	(U.S.)	J. Webb	(Abertillery)
†J.H. Eddison	(Headingley)	H. Uzzell	(Newport)
†R.C. Stafford	(Bedford)	L. Trump	(Newport)
J.A. King	(Headingley)	R. Thomas	(Pontypool)
†D. Holland	(Devonport Albion)	A.P. Coldrick	(Newport)
*R. Dibble	(Newport)	G. Stephens	(Neath)
N.A. Wodehouse	(U.S.)	H. Davies	(Neath)
C.H. Pillman	(Blackheath)	D.J. Thomas	(Swansea)

Tries: Brougham, Pym
Conversion: Chapman

Referee: Mr J.T. Tulloch (Scotland)

ENGLAND v IRELAND 1912

Played at Twickenham, London, 10 February 1912
England won by 5T (15) to Nil

An early taste of Spring weather heightened the enjoyment for 25,000 spectators as England romped away to an easy victory. If Coverdale's imagination and distribution as the England pivot had been more inspiring, England's winning margin would have been far greater.

England held a slight advantage at the break, for Roberts, with a brilliant solo effort, in which he capitalised upon a kick ahead to rob Hinton of the ball, had scored at the corner. Lloyd, as usual, had displayed superb kicking ability to keep the Irish in contention. Indeed, shortly after Roberts's effort, the Irish fly-half narrowly failed to capture the lead with a drop at goal.

It was Ireland's pack, running out of steam early in the second period, who were to blame in defeat. Three tries followed in quick succession: Coverdale tidied up some loose play to link with Birkett and Brougham was set free to score in the corner; Birkett scored from a pass by one of the wings; and Roberts maintained his interest in the game by scoring the next try from a scramble near the Irish line. Lloyd then made a memorable kick from his ten-yards line, just failing to convert a penalty, before Poulton wriggled over near the posts. Dibble, before this last score, had crossed but the referee noticed an infringement and the English skipper was recalled.

England's place-kicking was abominable, all five conversion attempts being missed.

ENGLAND		IRELAND	
W.R. Johnston	(Bristol)	W.P. Hinton	(O. Wesley)
A.D. Roberts	(Northern)	C.V. McIvor	(Dublin U.)
R.W. Poulton	(Harlequins)	M. Abraham	(Bective Rangers)
J.G.G. Birkett	(Harlequins)	*A.R. Foster	(Queen's U.)
H. Brougham	(Harlequins)	J.P. Quinn	(Dublin U.)
H. Coverdale	(Blackheath)	R.A. Lloyd	(Dublin U.)
J.A. Pym	(Blackheath)	H.M. Read	(Dublin U.)
A.H. MacIlwaine	(U.S.)	S.B.B. Campbell	(Derry)
J.H. Eddison	(Headingley)	G.V. Killeen	(Garryowen)
R.C. Stafford	(Bedford)	T. Smyth	(Malone)
J.A. King	(Headingley)	W.V. Edwards	(Malone)
D. Holland	(Devonport Albion)	H. Moore	(Queen's U.)
*R. Dibble	(Newport)	T. Halpin	(Garryowen)
N.A. Wodehouse	(U.S.)	R. Hemphill	(Dublin U.)
A.L. Kewney	(Rockcliff)	G. McConnell	(Derry)

Tries: Roberts (2), Birkett, Brougham, Poulton

Referee: Mr T.D. Schofield (Wales)

SCOTLAND v ENGLAND 1912

Played at Inverleith, Edinburgh, 16 March 1912
Scotland won by 1G, 1T (8) to 1T (3)

The teams met before 25,000 spectators in a hard, uncompromising battle. King sustained two broken ribs in the twelfth minute when he was trapped between forwards about to pack down for a scrummage, and retired to take no further part in the game. Johnston, the English full-back, suffered mild concussion as a result of two heavy tackles.

The Scottish forwards, from an early stage, called the tune up-front and there were many fine rounds of passing by the Scottish backs. The English tackling was sound and there was no scoring up to the interval. At the start of the second half, the loss of King made its full impact on the English forwards and Scotland, for the moment, gained unlimited possession in the tight and loose. After five minutes Boyd initiated a passing movement, the culmination of which was a try in the corner by Sutherland. From the restart, Scotland renewed their offensive but, just as another score seemed imminent, a breathtaking dash by Brougham from his 25, and an equally thrilling chase by Will, led to England's sensational equaliser. Will over-hauled Brougham but the ball spilled loose from the Scot's tackle and Birkett, following up like an express train, dribbled the ball over the line for Holland to score.

Inspired by this try, the seven English forwards redoubled their efforts against the Scottish eight and won a good share of the possession from the remaining play. Stoop, usually a reliable handler, had some dreadful moments, however, and much of this hard-earned possession was wasted. Hopes of an English victory finally disappeared late in the game when an execrable pass from an English back, under his goal, let Usher through for a gift try which MacCallum gratefully converted into a five-points victory.

SCOTLAND		ENGLAND	
W.M. Dickson	(Blackheath)	W.R. Johnston	(Bristol)
W.R. Sutherland	(Hawick)	A.D. Roberts	(Northern)
W. Burnet	(Hawick)	R.W. Poulton	(Harlequins)
A.W. Angus	(Watsonians)	J.G.G. Birkett	(Harlequins)
J.G. Will	(Cambridge U.)	H. Brougham	(Harlequins)
J.L. Boyd	(U.S.)	A.D. Stoop	(Harlequins)
E. Milroy	(Watsonians)	J.A. Pym	(Blackheath)
J.M.B. Scott	(Edinburgh Acads.)	A.H. MacIlwaine	(U.S.)
F.H. Turner	(Liverpool)	J.H. Eddison	(Headingley)
C.M. Usher	(U.S./London Scottish)	R.C. Stafford	(Bedford)
D.M. Bain	(Edinburgh Acads.)	J.A. King	(Headingley)
*J.C. MacCallum	(Watsonians)	D. Holland	(Devonport Albion)
L. Robertson	(U.S.)	*R. Dibble	(Newport)
J. Dobson	(Glasgow Acads.)	N.A. Wodehouse	(U.S.)
D.D. Howie	(Kirkcaldy)	A.L. Kewney	(Rockcliff)

Tries: Sutherland, Usher   *Try:* Holland
Conversion: MacCallum

Referee: Mr F. Gardiner (Ireland)

FRANCE v ENGLAND 1912

Played at Parc des Princes, Paris, 8 April 1912
England won by 1G, 1DG, 3T (18) to 1G, 1T (8)

England's victory in Paris on Easter Monday entitled them to share the Championship with Ireland. There were 20,000 present on an overcast afternoon and England, with tries by Birkett, Roberts, Eddison and Brougham – the last converted by Pillman – raced away to a lead of 14–0 by half-time.

Early in the second half, Coverdale put the issue beyond doubt with a well-taken dropped goal. France, though completely outclassed by the faster and more efficient Englishmen, staged a courageous recovery at the end of the game to lend a shade of respectability to the final score. Coverdale was injured during the second half and France exploited England's resulting fragility with tries by Dufau and Failliot.

Dick Stafford died of spinal cancer later in the year, aged only nineteen – the youngest age at which an England international has died.

FRANCE		ENGLAND	
F.X. Dutour	(Toulouse)	W.R. Johnston	(Bristol)
P. Failliot	(R.C.F.)	A.D Roberts	(Northern)
*G. Lane	(R.C.F.)	†M.E. Neale	(Blackheath)
J. Sentilles	(Tarbes)	J.G.G. Birkett	(Harlequins)
J. Dufau	(Biarritz)	H. Brougham	(Harlequins)
G. Charpentier	(Stade Français)	H. Coverdale	(Blackheath)
L. Larribeau	(Périgueux)	J.A. Pym	(Blackheath)
P. Thil	(Nantes)	A.H. MacIlwaine	(U.S.)
J. Pascarel	(T.O.E.C.)	J.H. Eddison	(Headingley)
M. Monniot	(R.C.F.)	R.C. Stafford	(Bedford)
P. Mounicq	(Toulouse)	†W.B. Hynes	(U.S.)
J. Cadenat	(S.C.U.F.)	†J.E. Greenwood	(Cambridge U.)
M. Boyau	(Stade Bordelais)	J.A.S. Ritson	(Northern)
M. Communeau	(Beauvais)	*N.A. Wodehouse	(U.S.)
F. Forgues	(Bayonne)	C.H. Pillman	(Blackheath)

Tries: Dufau, Failliot
Conversion: Boyau

Tries: Birkett, Brougham, Eddison, Roberts   *Conversion:* Pillman
Dropped goal: Coverdale

Referee: Mr T.D. Schofield (Wales)

ENGLAND v SOUTH AFRICA 1913
Played at Twickenham, London, 4 January 1913
South Africa won by 2PG, 1T (9) to 1T (3)

The English selectors nominated five new caps for this match, and included four of the London team which had lowered the Springbok colours on the same ground several weeks earlier.

England began the match strongly and Poulton, with two sensational dashes, gave the visitors a rare fright in the first 25 minutes. O.L. Owen, former critic of *The Times*, wrote in 1955 of Poulton's spectacular runs: 'Poulton's try was one to live in the memory and so for that matter was the "near thing" which followed. The try was the result of an orthodox passing movement, but it required Poulton's genius as an elusive runner to press the attack home. First, he turned in. Then, gathering speed, he brought off two swerves which literally left the defence standing – something seldom seen against a Dominion touring side.

'In its way, however, Poulton's second run was even more astonishing. Few more dramatic efforts have been seen on a Rugby field. Experts argued for months about how it all came about. The ball first emerged from a scrummage near to the right touch-line, well inside the English half of the field. A pass reached Poulton at left centre and again he set off on a swerving run at top speed. The defence in front of him was as beaten as before and the runner's eccentric course carried him like a leaf swept by the wind across to the right-hand corner. There, it seemed to many, he might have linked up with Lowe, but, once fairly on the run, combination was not Poulton's strong point. To the horror of a gasping crowd, McHardy, one of the Springboks' wings, emerged like a bolt out of the blue from his side of the field and tackled his man as he began to slow down a little, a yard or so short of the goal-line.' So, a chance of further glory was lost.

The 30,000 spectators then saw the jumbo Springbok pack claw its way back into the match, slowly but surely gaining dominance over the brave England eight. J.W. Morkel equalised after taking an inside pass from Stegmann, Dick Luyt having made an excellent break. Duggie Morkel, who struck an upright with his attempt to convert the South African try, landed two penalties from difficult positions in the second half, assisted by the wind.

ENGLAND		SOUTH AFRICA	
W.R. Johnston	(Bristol)	P.G. Morkel	(W. Province)
†C.N. Lowe	(Cambridge U.)	E.E. McHardy	(O.F.S.)
F.M. Stoop	(Harlequins)	R.R. Luyt	(W. Province)
R.W. Poulton	(Harlequins)	J.W.H. Morkel	(W. Province)
†V.H.M. Coates	(Bath)	J.A. Stegmann	(Transvaal)
†W.J.A. Davies	(R.N./U.S.)	F.P. Luyt	(W. Province)
†W.I. Cheesman	(O.M.Ts.)	J.D. McCulloch	(Griqualand West)
J.A.S. Ritson	(Northern)	T.F. van Vuuren	(E. Province)
J.A. King	(Headingley)	*D.F.T. Morkel	(Transvaal)
J.E. Greenwood	(Cambridge U.)	J.A.J. Francis	(Transvaal)
A.L. Kewney	(Rockcliff)	S.H. Ledger	(Griqualand West)
L.G. Brown	(Oxford U.)	J.D. Luyt	(E. Province)
*N.A. Wodehouse	(R.N./U.S.)	E.H. Shum	(Transvaal)
†S. Smart	(Gloucester)	A.S. Knight	(Transvaal)
C.H. Pillman	(Blackheath)	W.H. Morkel	(W. Province)

Try: Poulton

Try: J.W.H. Morkel
Penalties: D.F.T. Morkel (2)

Referee: Mr J.T. Tulloch (Scotland)

WALES v ENGLAND 1913

Played at Cardiff Arms Park, 18 January 1913
England won by 1G, 1DG, 1T (12) to Nil

On a pitch which resembled a quagmire, and in front of 20,000 spectators, England registered their first victory at Cardiff. England faced a considerable wind in the first half but did well to prevent Wales gaining a lead. *The Manchester Guardian* reported that the game was in some ways a curious reversal of traditions: 'The usual alertness of the Welshmen, the speed both in deciding on the right thing to do and in doing it were on this occasion lacking; after the first 20 minutes or so the combined advances of the Welsh three-quarters were not very dangerous, and their single-handed efforts were not good enough for a stubborn and a more speedy defence.' Later in the first half, Wales frittered away possession with inept kicks which the competent Johnston dealt with coolly and efficiently for England. Thomas and Vile, the Welsh halves, were heavily criticised by the press after the match, being held responsible for the tactical failure: the circumstances cried out for a close-fought game, with the forwards dribbling instead of heeling out (slowly) to the Welsh backs.

Sensing victory, England seized an opportunity to score during the first five minutes of the second half. Following a rush led by Pillman, Cheesman fed Davies from a scrummage and the naval man threw a long pass to Coates who sped over for a try. Greenwood, with a fine kick, landed the goal. After 20 minutes, an adventurous attack by Johnston down the left touch-line was supported by Coates, but a knock-on by Poulton brought the move to an end. From the ensuing scrum, Poulton atoned for his earlier error by dropping a goal. Wales were a tired and dejected side by this stage and near the end R.F. Williams was beaten, bravely trying to stem an English rush led by Poulton. The ubiquitous Pillman was at hand to complete the scoring in a memorable game for England.

WALES		ENGLAND	
R.F. Williams	(Cardiff)	W.R. Johnston	(Bristol)
R.C.S. Plummer	(Newport)	C.N. Lowe	(Cambridge U.)
F.W. Birt	(Newport)	†F.E. Steinthal	(Ilkley)
W.J. Spiller	(Cardiff)	R.W. Poulton	(Harlequins)
W.P. Geen	(Newport/Oxford U.)	V.H.M. Coates	(Bath)
H.W. Thomas	(Cambridge U.)	W.J.A. Davies	(R.N./U.S.)
*T.H. Vile	(Newport)	W.I. Cheesman	(O.M.Ts.)
G. Stephens	(Neath)	J.A.S. Ritson	(Northern)
R. Thomas	(Pontypool)	J.A. King	(Headingley)
H. Wetter	(Newport)	J.E. Greenwood	(Cambridge U.)
F. Andrews	(Pontypool)	†G. Ward	(Leicester)
P. Jones	(Newport)	L.G. Brown	(Oxford U.)
B. Hollingdale	(Swansea)	*N.A. Wodehouse	(R.N./U.S.)
F.L. Perrett	(Neath)	S. Smart	(Gloucester)
J. Morgan	(Llanelli)	C.H. Pillman	(Blackheath)

Tries: Coates, Pillman
Conversion: Greenwood
Dropped goal: Poulton

Referee: Mr S.H. Crawford (Ireland)

ENGLAND v FRANCE 1913

Played at Twickenham, London, 25 January 1913
England won by 1G, 5T (20) to Nil

French Rugby was under a cloud at the time of this match, for a few weeks earlier in Paris there had been a riot following the international with Scotland, and Mr J. Baxter of the Rugby Union had been assaulted after refereeing the game. As a result, relations between the Scottish Union and the Union des Sociétés Françaises de Sports Athlétique (which then controlled the game in France) were broken. Fortunately there was no repeat of the dreadful demonstration which caused the cessation of French relations with Scotland, and England were able to continue their fixtures with France until war forced an abrupt end in 1914.

France showed several changes from the sides which had earlier lost to the Scots and the South Africans, one of which was forced upon the selectors by the impending marriage of Mauriat, a front-row forward. After a respectable first half, when England scored only two tries, the French side disintegrated and England gained an easy, and expected, victory. That England's margin was not greater was in part due to the plucky tackling of the full-back Caujolle, who saved his side from utter humiliation; it was also due to England's appalling place-kicking. The combined kicking of Cheesman and Greenwood produced only one conversion from seven attempts at goal (including a penalty) and the *Times* correspondent was forced to conclude: 'There is an obvious lesson; if the team does not contain a place-kicker room must be found for one.'

ENGLAND		FRANCE	
W.R. Johnston	(Bristol)	F. Caujolle	(Tarbes)
C.N. Lowe	(Cambridge U.)	G. André	(R.C.F.)
F.E. Steinthal	(Ilkley)	J. Dedet	(Stade Français)
R.W. Poulton	(Harlequins)	M. Burgun	(R.C.F.)
V.H.M. Coates	(Bath)	P. Failliot	(R.C.F.)
W.J.A. Davies	(R.N./U.S.)	M. Bruneau	(Stade Bordelais)
W.I. Cheesman	(O.M.Ts.)	A. Theuriet	(S.C.U.F.)
J.A.S. Ritson	(Northern)	G. Favre	(Lyon)
J.A. King	(Headingley)	J. Pascarel	(T.O.E.C.)
J.E. Greenwood	(Cambridge U.)	P. Thil	(Nantes)
G. Ward	(Leicester)	P. Mounicq	(Toulouse)
L.G. Brown	(Oxford U.)	*M. Leuvielle	(Stade Bordelais)
*N.A. Wodehouse	(R.N./U.S.)	M. Legrain	(R.C.F.)
S. Smart	(Gloucester)	M. Communeau	(Stade Français)
C.H. Pillman	(Blackheath)	J. Sébedio	(Tarbes)

Tries: Coates (3), Pillman (2), Poulton   *Conversion:* Greenwood

Referee: Mr J. Games (Wales)

The England team which, despite the absence of a competent place-kicker, annihilated France in 1913 and went on to win the Grand Slam: *back* W. I. Cheesman, F. E. Steinthal, S. Smart, J. A. S. Ritson, J. E. Greenwood, V. H. M. Coates, G. Ward, W. J. A. Davies; *front* L. G. Brown, C. H. Pillman, R. W. Poulton, N. A. Wodehouse (captain), W. R. Johnston, J. A. King, C. N. Lowe.

The ball leaving a scrum during England's 15-4 victory over Ireland, 1913.

IRELAND v ENGLAND 1913

Played at Lansdowne Road, Dublin, 8 February 1913
England won by 1PG, 4T (15) to 1DG (4)

The match with Ireland saw the England side in action for the fourth time in six weeks. The English forwards were in devastating form and completely overwhelmed the Irish pack. Only some indecisive play by the visiting backs prevented a complete rout of the Irish side.

Conditions were favourable; there was a moderate breeze and 15,000 spectators were there to see England wear down their opponents in the first half and establish a nine-points lead. The scoring opened after 20 minutes when Davies made a superb break, Poulton carried the movement further forward until held, and Ritson was up in support to cross for a try. Greenwood was unable to convert it, but the Cambridge forward made amends later by kicking a penalty goal from an awkward position near touch. Cheesman, a lively and resourceful partner for Davies, made a dash to set up the next points. Young, the Irish full-back, was forced to make a poor clearance and Davies capitalised upon the error to send Coates over for his fifth try of the season.

More combined skill from Davies and Poulton led to Coates beating two Irishmen to increase England's lead after 20 minutes of play in the second half. Lloyd gave his side some encouragement with his customary dropped goal immediately afterwards, but a late try by Pillman, after the English pack had dribbled the ball over the Irish line, made the final winning margin 11 points. Lloyd's dropped goal, from near the half-way line, was the only score conceded by the England XV in the four Championship matches of the season.

Coates made a successful start to his international career, but, amazingly, did not return to the side after this season. F.J. Sellicks wrote of him in 1925: 'Coates . . . proved himself the most determined and dangerous wing in the four countries. His hand-off was devastating, but he proved to be the meteor of a season.'

IRELAND		ENGLAND	
G. Young	(U.C. Cork)	W.R. Johnston	(Bristol)
J.P. Quinn	(Dublin U.)	C.N. Lowe	(Cambridge U.)
G.W. Holmes	(Dublin U.)	†A.J. Dingle	(Hartlepool Rovers)
J.B. Minch	(Bective Rangers)	R.W. Poulton	(Harlequins)
C.V. McIvor	(Dublin U.)	V.H.M. Coates	(Bath)
*R.A. Lloyd	(Dublin U.)	W.J.A. Davies	(R.N./U.S.)
H.M. Read	(Dublin U.)	W.I. Cheesman	(O.M.Ts.)
S.B.B. Campbell	(Derry)	J.A.S. Ritson	(Northern)
E.W. Jeffares	(Wanderers)	J.A. King	(Headingley)
G.V. Killeen	(Garryowen)	J.E. Greenwood	(Cambridge U.)
R.d'A. Patterson	(Wanderers)	†A.E. Kitching	(Blackheath)
W. Tyrrell	(Queen's U.)	L.G. Brown	(Oxford U.)
F.G. Schute	(Dublin U.)	*N.A. Wodehouse	(R.N./U.S.)
J.E. Finlay	(Queen's U.)	S. Smart	(Gloucester)
P. Stokes	(Garryowen)	C.H. Pillman	(Blackheath)

Dropped goal: Lloyd

Tries: Coates (2), Pillman, Ritson
Penalty: Greenwood

Referee: Mr J.R.C. Greenlees (Scotland)

ENGLAND v SCOTLAND 1913

Played at Twickenham, London, 15 March 1913
England won by 1T (3) to Nil

England, inspired by a fast and skilful set of forwards, won their first Grand Slam with a win by a single try in front of the Prince of Wales and 25,000 spectators. This was a fast but disappointing match: given such a vast abundance of possession by their forwards, it was excruciating for the crowd to watch the English backs squander chances with indifferent and unimaginative play. The wings were given occasional opportunities to run in, but resolute defence – by both teams – restricted the scoring. The only try of the match came just before the interval when L.G. Brown directed his thick-set and immensely powerful figure to the corner flag to score in a scramble.

Gaining the vast majority of the play in the second half, the England backs were still unable to penetrate the Scottish line. F.N. Tarr, after a long period in the wilderness, had been recalled to the midfield for this contest, the England selectors hoping that his presence would improve the passing and running of the home attack. But there was no improvement evident and the English threequarter play was described in the press as 'variable as an English summer'.

ENGLAND		SCOTLAND	
W.R. Johnston	(Bristol)	W.M. Wallace	(Cambridge U.)
C.N. Lowe	(Cambridge U.)	W.R. Sutherland	(Hawick)
F.N. Tarr	(Leicester)	E.G. Loudoun-Shand	(Oxford U.)
R.W. Poulton	(Harlequins)	J. Pearson	(Watsonians)
V.H.M. Coates	(Bath)	J.B. Sweet	(Glasgow H.S.F.P.)
W.J.A. Davies	(R.N./U.S.)	T.C. Bowie	(Watsonians)
†F.E. Oakeley	(R.N./U.S.)	E. Milroy	(Watsonians)
J.A.S. Ritson	(Northern)	J.M.B. Scott	(Edinburgh Acads.)
J.A. King	(Headingley)	*F.H. Turner	(Liverpool)
J.E. Greenwood	(Cambridge U.)	C.M. Usher	(London Scottish)
L.G. Brown	(Oxford U.)	P.C.B. Blair	(Cambridge U.)
*N.A. Wodehouse	(R.N./U.S.)	D.M. Bain	(Oxford U.)
S. Smart	(Gloucester)	G.H.H.P. Maxwell	(Edinburgh Acads.)
G. Ward	(Leicester)	W.D.C.L. Purves	(London Scottish)
C.H. Pillman	(Blackheath)	L. Robertson	(London Scottish)

Try: Brown

Referee: Mr T.D. Schofield (Wales)

ENGLAND v WALES 1914

Played at Twickenham, London, 17 January 1914
England won by 2G (10) to 1G, 1DG (9)

England won by the 'small and artistic margin' – *The Times* – of one point in one of the most exciting of the early internationals staged at Twickenham. Once again the match summaries emphasised the reversal of traditions between the teams: Wales looked to a strong and dashing pack for inspiration while England's strength lay in their backs. Wales so completely dominated up-front that it was a wonder that the home side were able to register any points. But the Welsh centres were inexperienced and lacked the quality of judgment needed at international level. Lowe, Watson and Chapman were unable to make much headway against a solid Welsh defence, but Poulton, with his swerving runs, posed several problems for the Welsh to resolve.

Wales faced the wind in the first half but carried the play into English territory immediately. Desperate defence by the English was the early feature of play and after 20 minutes Wales at last took the lead, Lewis passing to Hirst near the touch-line and the Newport wing dropping a fine goal. This score was the stimulus England required and Lowe and Pillman, with some sparkling runs, put pressure on Bancroft and the Welsh backs. An attack initiated by Pillman and Poulton showed up the weakness of the Welsh centres and Brown obtained a try which Chapman goaled, the referee disallowing the charge at the conversion.

The Welsh forwards held a stranglehold on the tight play in the second half but still the backs were unable to score by direct methods. It was an error by Poulton which let Watt, the Llanelli centre, score at the posts for Bancroft to convert. Wales increased the pressure soon after and an unlucky bounce robbed Howell Lewis of a try in the corner. Then, eight minutes from no-side, Watt, who had given Wales the lead, presented Pillman with a 'gift' try when the ball was fumbled near the Welsh line. The try, scored beneath the posts, was converted by Chapman and 'the crowd for the first time in the game really let themselves go'. The closing minutes contained several desperate moments for the English backs, but Wales could not score and retired defeated, most unluckily, by that single point.

ENGLAND		WALES	
W.R. Johnston	(Bristol)	J. Bancroft	(Swansea)
C.N. Lowe	(Cambridge U.)	H. Lewis	(Swansea)
F.E. Chapman	(Hartlepool Rovers)	W.H. Evans	(Llwynypia)
*R.W. Poulton	(Liverpool)	W.J. Watt	(Llanelli)
†J.H.D. Watson	(Blackheath)	G.L. Hirst	(Newport)
†F.M. Taylor	(Leicester)	J.M.C. Lewis	(Cardiff)
†G.W. Wood	(Leicester)	R. Lloyd	(Pontypool)
†A.G. Bull	(Northampton)	H. Uzzell	(Newport)
†A.F. Maynard	(Cambridge U.)	T.C. Lloyd	(Neath)
J.E. Greenwood	(Cambridge U.)	*Rev J. A. Davies	(Llanelli)
L.G. Brown	(London H.)	D. Watts	(Maesteg)
†J. Brunton	(North Durham)	J.B. Jones	(Abertillery)
S. Smart	(Gloucester)	P. Jones	(Pontypool)
G. Ward	(Leicester)	E. Morgan	(Swansea)
C.H. Pillman	(Blackheath)	T. Williams	(Swansea)

Tries: Brown, Pillman
Conversions: Chapman (2)

Try: W.J. Watt
Conversion: Bancroft
Dropped goal: Hirst

Referee: Mr J.R.C. Greenlees (Scotland)

ENGLAND v IRELAND 1914

Played at Twickenham, London, 14 February 1914
England won by 1G, 4T (17) to 1G, 1DG, 1T (12)

The King, on his first visit to Twickenham since his succession in 1910, and Mr Asquith, the Prime Minister, were among the 40,000 spectators. Parliament was discussing the thorny problem of Home Rule for Ireland at this time, but fears about demonstrations marring this match were dismissed and the crowd enjoyed a high-scoring game played in the best of spirits.

Ireland, taking first use of the wind, were kept busy in the opening minutes of the match. The bustling Irish pack swept play into the English quarters and Foster soon crossed, but an infringement deprived him of a score. England failed to clear the ball, however, and after seven minutes Lloyd dropped a goal. Moments later Davies made a rare handling error and the Irish forwards engineered a try for Quinn which went unconverted. England rallied. Oakeley and Davies, recalled after England's narrow shave against Wales, set their centres in motion and the product was a try for Roberts in the corner. A similar move to the right wing enabled Lowe to reduce England's deficit to a single point by the interval.

A winding run by Poulton from his own half was the first item of note in the second half, and Pillman continued his captain's break to score in the corner. Then came a brilliant individualist's try from Davies. A swerve and a couple of dummies took the naval man over near the posts for Chapman to convert, and when Lowe ran in at the corner to make the tally 17–7, England were home and dry.

Near no-side, England conceded a throw-in near their goal-line and a quick feed found Jackson unmarked in front of the English posts. The Irish centre waltzed over and Lloyd kicked the goal.

A.L. Harrison, England's only new cap for this match, won a posthumous V.C. for service during the blocking of Zeebrugge (1918).

ENGLAND		IRELAND	
W.R. Johnston	(Bristol)	F.P. Montgomery	(Queen's U.)
C.N. Lowe	(Cambridge U.)	A.R. Foster	(Derry)
F.E. Chapman	(Hartlepool Rovers)	A.R.V. Jackson	(Wanderers)
*R.W. Poulton	(Liverpool)	J.B. Minch	(Bective Rangers)
A.D. Roberts	(Northern)	J.P. Quinn	(Dublin U.)
W.J.A. Davies	(R.N./U.S.)	*R.A. Lloyd	(Dublin U.)
F.E. Oakeley	(R.N./U.S.)	V. McNamara	(U.C. Cork)
H.C. Harrison	(R.N./U.S.)	W. Tyrrell	(Queen's U.)
A.F. Maynard	(Cambridge U.)	W.P. Collopy	(Bective Rangers)
†A.L. Harrison	(R.N./U.S.)	C. Adams	(O. Wesley)
L.G. Brown	(London H.)	J.J. Clune	(Blackrock College)
J. Brunton	(North Durham)	G.V. Killeen	(Garryowen)
S. Smart	(Gloucester)	P. O'Connell	(Bective Rangers)
G. Ward	(Leicester)	J.S. Parr	(Wanderers)
C.H. Pillman	(Blackheath)	J. Taylor	(Belfast Collegians)

Tries: Lowe (2), Davies, Pillman, Roberts
Conversion: Chapman

Tries: Jackson, Quinn
Conversion: Lloyd
Dropped goal: Lloyd

Referee: Mr T.D. Schofield (Wales)

SCOTLAND v ENGLAND 1914
Played at Inverleith, Edinburgh, 21 March 1914
England won by 2G, 2T (16) to 1G, 1DG, 2T (15)

'Few among the spectators ... could have imagined that in six months time, sport would be thrust out of mind for five full years and that no less than eleven of the men who played in this splendid last encounter would fall in the war.' Thus reflected O.L. Owen many years later, and one can understand that this last home match before the Great War should be well documented.

The game was a 'classic' played at great speed. England gave the crowd a fine exhibition of open, attacking Rugby and seemed to be safely ahead half-way through the second spell when a remarkable Scottish recovery added to a thrilling afternoon.

Poulton had an outstanding game and early on made a slashing break to create an opportunity for Dingle to score. To the horror of the English contingent in the crowd, the latter fumbled the pass and a chance was lost. Scotland too made dangerous runs and the English centres were forced to execute a series of brave and accurate tackles. After 20 minutes Turner sent Will over in the left corner for a try but Lowe equalised to leave the game delicately balanced at half-time.

The Scottish forwards started furiously after the break and Turner was again in action to send Huggan over in the other corner. England answered the pleas and shouts of their supporters with three cracking tries: Lowe crossed at the posts for Harrison to convert; an elegant move involving Davies, Brown, Poulton and Watson brought Lowe his third try of the day; and Poulton scored next to give his side a sound lead.

Scotland's revival began with a dropped goal by Bowie after a strong run by Huggan; and Will, after fluffing an earlier opportunity to score, made adequate reparation with a dazzling sprint to score near the posts. Turner's conversion was followed by a hectic ten minutes to no-side as both sides sought a deciding score. England held on to win the Championship and Triple Crown for the second successive season, though Pillman sustained a broken leg after a nasty kick on the shin.

SCOTLAND		ENGLAND	
W.M. Wallace	(Cambridge U.)	W.R. Johnston	(Bristol)
J.L. Huggan	(London Scottish)	C.N. Lowe	(Cambridge U.)
A.W. Angus	(Watsonians)	J.H.D. Watson	(Blackheath)
R.M. Scobie	(R.M.C./London Scottish)	*R.W. Poulton	(Liverpool)
J.G. Will	(Cambridge U.)	A.J. Dingle	(Hartlepool Rovers)
T.C. Bowie	(Watsonians)	W.J.A. Davies	(R.N./U.S.)
*E. Milroy	(Watsonians)	F.E. Oakeley	(R.N./U.S.)
C.M. Usher	(London Scottish)	H.C. Harrison	(R.N./U.S.)
A.W. Symington	(Cambridge U.)	A.F. Maynard	(Cambridge U.)
A.D. Laing	(Royal H.S.F.P.)	J.E. Greenwood	(Cambridge U.)
G.H.H.P. Maxwell	(Edinburgh Acads.)	L.G. Brown	(London H./Blackheath)
E.T. Young	(Glasgow Acads.)	J. Brunton	(North Durham)
F.H. Turner	(Liverpool)	S. Smart	(Gloucester)
A.R. Ross	(Edinburgh U.)	G. Ward	(Leicester)
I.M. Pender	(London Scottish)	C.H. Pillman	(Blackheath)

Tries: Will (2), Huggan
Conversion: Turner
Dropped goal: Bowie

Tries: Lowe (3), Poulton
Conversions: Harrison (2)

Referee: Mr T.D. Schofield (Wales)

THE RUGBY INTERNATIONAL AT INVERLEITH.—ENGLAND BEATS SCOTLAND BY 16 POINTS TO 15, AND GAINS THE "TRIPLE CROWN."

1. The junior bagpipe band entertains the spectators before the match.   2. Harrison converting for England.   3. Scotland capture the ball in a line out.   4. Harrison converts a try by Lowe.   5. The English forward line at work.—Brown passing out to Lowe, who was thus enabled to score one of his three tries.   6. C. H. Pillman, the Blackheath forward, who had the misfortune to break his leg during the game.

The last international played in Britain before the Great War resulted in the closest of finishes against Scotland, but England held on and went on to win the Championship and Triple Crown for the second successive season. This was how *The Illustrated Sporting and Dramatic News* reported the match.

FRANCE v ENGLAND 1914

Played at Stade Colombes, Paris, 13 April 1914
England won by 6G, 3T (39) to 2G, 1T (13)

In this last international for six seasons, England made two late changes for the match, R.L. Pillman (brother of C.H.) and Stone replacing Ward and Ritson. 20,000 spectators saw France open the scoring in the first five minutes, fine play by the home three-quarters resulting in a try for Capmau. England settled down after 20 minutes and Lowe scored a try, but Besset then put in a high, testing kick which Johnston failed to catch and Forgues sent André skidding over in the corner despite a tackle by Lowe. Clever play by Davies smoothed the way for a couple of tries by Poulton (Poulton-Palmer since becoming a beneficiary of his uncle's will earlier in the month) before the interval and Greenwood's conversions gave England a 13–8 lead.

There were unsavoury scenes, on and off the field, during the second half. Pierrot, with a dangerously high tackle on Johnston, was lucky to remain on the field; and the jeering of the crowd as the English began to play attractive open Rugby was contrary to the traditions of the French. Happily, England were unruffled by these incidents and Lowe completed his hat-trick before Watson scored. Greenwood's conversion placed England out of sight at 24–8, but Forgues, acting as an extra half-back, surprised all by executing a lovely break to send Lubin-Lebrère in for a try, Besset converting.

A run by Dingle from his own half led to a try by Poulton and from the restart H.C. Harrison, Watson and Poulton combined to send Davies in. (Dingle is credited with this try in one report.) Finally, Oakeley got his backs moving again for Poulton to score his fourth try. Greenwood converted each of these last three tries to raise England's points total to 39 and his own contribution to six conversions.

FRANCE		ENGLAND	
J. Caujolle	(Tarbes)	W.R. Johnston	(Bristol)
J. Lacoste	(Tarbes)	C.N. Lowe	(Cambridge U.)
G. Pierrot	(Pau)	J.H.D. Watson	(Blackheath)
A. Besset	(S.C.U.F.)	*R.W. Poulton	(Liverpool)
G. André	(R.C.F.)	A.J. Dingle	(Hartlepool Rovers)
M. Burgun	(Castres)	W.J.A. Davies	(R.N./U.S.)
L. Larribeau	(Biarritz)	F.E. Oakeley	(R.N./U.S.)
E. Iguinitz	(Bayonne)	H.C. Harrison	(R.N./U.S.)
F. Faure	(Tarbes)	†A.R.V. Sykes	(Blackheath)
M.F. Lubin-Lebrère	(Toulouse)	J.E. Greenwood	(Cambridge U.)
*M. Leuvielle	(Stade Bordelais)	L.G. Brown	(London H./Blackheath)
J.C.de Beyssac	(Stade Bordelais)	A.L. Harrison	(R.N./U.S.)
-. Capmau	(Toulouse)	S. Smart	(Gloucester)
P. Bascou	(Bayonne)	†F.le S. Stone	(Blackheath)
F. Forgues	(Bayonne)	†R.L. Pillman	(Blackheath)

Tries: André, Capmau, Lubin-Lebrère
Conversions: Besset (2)

Tries: Poulton (4), Lowe (3), Davies, Watson *Conversions:* Greenwood (6)

Referee: Mr J. Games (Wales)

147

WALES v ENGLAND 1920

Played at St Helen's, Swansea, 17 January 1920
Wales won by 1G, 2DG, 1PG, 1T (19) to 1G (5)

A crowd of 40,000 witnessed a clean match on a wet and muddy pitch. An intelligent, hard-working Welsh pack completely dominated the English forwards and laid the foundation for a well-deserved victory. The English also suffered from a lack of cohesion at half-back where Kershaw was overshadowed by Wetter, and Coverdale was the weakest link in the back line.

Uzzell kicked off for Wales into a drizzling wind and the home forwards forced the English deep into their own territory. A number of promising Welsh passing movements were spoilt by careless passing or selfish play by the centres – Evans on the Welsh left wing rarely seeing the ball all afternoon.

For all the initial Welsh pressure in the tight scrums, the England pack showed up well in the loose. Cumberlege had two opportunities to put his side ahead but failed to land penalty kicks. Then Wales took the lead when Shea drop-kicked a penalty after 30 minutes – an Englishman having fallen off-side. Wales continued to dominate in the tight, but the backs wasted three chances in as many minutes through poor handling. From one loose pass, Hammett intercepted and passed to Day, who ran the length of the pitch for a try which he converted.

Wales regained the lead three minutes after the interval when Shea dropped a goal. From then on, the English defence – Lowe apart – became practically non-existent, and the Welsh backs were able to run amok. Shea converted his own try after poor tackling by Hammett and Day; Beynon made a vintage half-back break to send Powell over in the corner; and Shea completed a hugely successful afternoon for him by adding a late dropped goal.

W.M. Lowry (Birkenhead Park) was photographed with the England fifteen for this game, but was replaced at the last minute by Harold Day. The selectors felt that conditions were more suited to Day's style of Rugby. Lowry won his cap two weeks later, against France.

WALES		ENGLAND	
J. Rees	(Swansea)	†B.S. Cumberlege	(Blackheath)
W.J. Powell	(Cardiff)	C.N. Lowe	(Blackheath)
A. Jenkins	(Llanelli)	†E.D.G. Hammett	(Newport)
J. Shea	(Newport)	†J.A. Krige	(Guy's H.)
B.S. Evans	(Llanelli)	†H.L.V. Day	(Leicester/Army)
B. Beynon	(Swansea)	H. Coverdale	(Blackheath)
J.J. Wetter	(Newport)	†C.A. Kershaw	(U.S./R.N.)
C.W. Jones	(Bridgend)	S. Smart	(Gloucester)
*H. Uzzell	(Newport)	†J.R. Morgan	(Hawick)
J. Williams	(Blaina)	†W.H.G. Wright	(Plymouth Albion)
J. Jones	(Aberavon)	†G. Holford	(Gloucester)
J. Whitfield	(Newport)	†L.P.B. Merriam	(Blackheath)
S. Morris	(Cross Keys)	†F.W. Mellish	(Blackheath)
G. Oliver	(Pontypool)	†W.W. Wakefield	(Harlequins)
T. Parker	(Swansea)	*J.E. Greenwood	(Cambridge U.)

Tries: Powell, Shea   *Try:* Day   *Conversion:* Day
Conversion: Shea
Dropped goals: Shea (2)
Penalty : Shea

Referee: Mr J.T. Tulloch (Scotland)

ENGLAND v FRANCE 1920
Played at Twickenham, London, 31 January 1920
England won by 1G, 1PG (8) to 1T (3)

Without any question of doubt, this was the best performance by France against England since the beginning of matches between the two countries in 1906. The established Rugby centres at Paris, Bayonne, Toulouse and Bordeaux supplied the majority of players for this side, and the forwards showed a scientific approach to their play, heeling the ball quickly and cleanly in the set-scrums.

England made several changes from the side defeated by Wales, the most significant move being the recall of Davies to partner Kershaw at half. In fact, he was to prove the difference between the two sides, bursting through from the French 25 in the middle of the second half with the scores level, to score a try by the posts which Greenwood converted to give England a narrow victory.

The game started quietly with the French forwards holding their own against an English pack in which Wakefield and Greenwood were outstanding. Struxiano moved the ball from the base of the scrum with speed and one round of passing by the French backs nearly resulted in what would have been a spectacular score. A knock forward spoilt the move, but, after 15 minutes, an interception by Lavigne, followed by a dummying run to the line, resulted in a try. England fought back, and chips ahead by Hammett and Davies nearly produced tries – Jauréguy appearing several times in a useful covering role for France. Just before the interval, England equalised when Greenwood landed a fine penalty kick from the touch-line.

England held the upper hand in the second half, but play was generally mediocre and only Lowe, Davies and Kershaw of the backs enhanced their reputations. The only worthwhile move of the half was Davies's solo effort, which won the match for England – but France had certainly proven that they were now a major power in the Rugby world.

F. Taylor was a brother of F.M. Taylor, capped in 1914.

ENGLAND		FRANCE	
†H. Millett	(Guy's H.)	G. Cambre	(Oloron)
C.N. Lowe	(Blackheath)	A. Jauréguy	(R.C.F.)
E.D.G. Hammett	(Newport)	B. Lavigne	(Dax)
†A.M. Smallwood	(Cambridge U.)	R. Crabos	(R.C.F.)
†W.M. Lowry	(Birkenhead Park)	P. Serre	(Perpignan)
W.J.A. Davies	(U.S./R.N.)	E. Billac	(Bayonne)
C.A. Kershaw	(U.S./R.N.)	*P. Struxiano	(Toulouse)
†F. Taylor	(Leicester)	M.F. Lubin-Lebrère	(Toulouse)
†G.S. Conway	(Cambridge U.)	P. Pons	(Toulouse)
W.H.G. Wright	(Plymouth Albion)	E. Soulié	(C.A.S.G.)
G. Holford	(Gloucester)	L. Puech	(Toulouse)
L.P.B. Merriam	(Blackheath)	A. Cassayet	(Tarbes)
F.W. Mellish	(Blackheath)	R. Thierry	(R.C.F.)
W.W. Wakefield	(Harlequins)	A. Guichemerre	(Dax)
*J.E. Greenwood	(Cambridge U.)	J. Laurent	(Bayonne)

Try: Davies *Conversion:* Greenwood   *Try:* Crabos
Penalty: Greenwood

Referee: Mr W.A. Robertson (Scotland)

IRELAND v ENGLAND 1920

Played at Lansdowne Road, Dublin, 14 February 1920
England won by 1G, 3T (14) to 1G, 1PG, 1T (11)

The closeness of the scoreline hides the fact that Ireland were lucky not to lose by about 30 points. Their forwards were comprehensively beaten by a faster, heavier, more skilful English pack which relentlessly provided the visiting backs with 'good ball' from scrums, line-outs and mauls. Yet, unbelievably, England changed ends at half-time trailing by three points – a penalty goal kicked by Lloyd. Their backs had failed miserably to combine effectively and produce a score.

After the interval, Ireland started with a tremendous ten-minute 'purple-patch' in which they increased their lead. Lloyd, playing with all the guile of his pre-war days, was the instigator of the revival: from a scrum inside the English 25, he managed to create an opening and sent Dickson over for a try; two minutes later, he hoisted a high kick to Cumberlege and, when the full-back failed to gather the ball, the Irish fly-half picked up and scored beneath the posts. The conversion meant that England were 11 points behind with 30 minutes to go. To their credit, the English pack regained the initiative and once again their backs were given plenty of scoring opportunities.

England's first try came after a run by Myers which Wakefield completed in fine style. Then, at last, England's good work produced dividends in the form of further tries by Mellish (from a line-out), Myers and Lowe.

IRELAND		ENGLAND	
W.E. Crawford	(Lansdowne)	B.S. Cumberlege	(Blackheath)
J.A.N. Dickson	(Dublin U.)	C.N. Lowe	(Blackheath)
W.J. Cullen	(Manchester)	†E. Myers	(Bradford)
T. Wallace	(Cardiff)	A.M. Smallwood	(Cambridge U.)
C.H. Bryant	(Cardiff)	†S.W. Harris	(Blackheath)
*R.A. Lloyd	(Liverpool)	W.J.A. Davies	(U.S./R.N.)
A.K. Horan	(Blackheath)	C.A. Kershaw	(U.S./R.N.)
N. Butler	(Garryowen)	F. Taylor	(Leicester)
H.H. Coulter	(Queen's U.)	G.S. Conway	(Cambridge U.)
W.S. Smyth	(Belfast Collegians)	S. Smart	(Gloucester)
J.E. Finlay	(Cardiff)	A.H. MacIlwaine	(The Army)
R.Y. Crichton	(Dublin U.)	†A.T. Voyce	(Gloucester)
W.D. Doherty	(Guy's H.)	F.W. Mellish	(Blackheath)
W.J. Roche	(U.C. Cork)	W.W. Wakefield	(Harlequins)
P. Stokes	(Garryowen)	*J.E. Greenwood	(Cambridge U.)

Tries: Dickson, Lloyd
Conversion: Lloyd
Penalty: Lloyd

Tries: Lowe, Mellish, Myers, Wakefield
Conversion: Greenwood

Referee: Mr W.A. Robertson (Scotland)

Edward Myers, who scored a try on his debut for England against Ireland in 1920 and went on to win a further 17 caps.

The England team which dashed Scotland's hopes of winning the Triple Crown in 1920 and thus secured a share of the Championship: *back* T. Woods, E. Myers, E. D. G. Hammett, F. W. Mellish, S. W. Harris, A. T. Voyce, W. W. Wakefield, A. F. Blakiston; *middle* S. Smart, C. N. Lowe, J. E. Greenwood (captain), W. J. A. Davies, B. S. Cumberlege; *front* C. A. Kershaw, G. S. Conway.

ENGLAND v SCOTLAND 1920

Played at Twickenham, London, 20 March 1920
England won by 2G, 1T (13) to 1DG (4)

Scotland came to Twickenham in search of the Triple Crown – but alas, on the day they were outplayed by a faster, more enterprising English team. The visiting pack certainly worked hard for a victory, slightly having the edge over their opponents in the English scrum. But a complete breakdown of understanding between the Scottish halves, and some indifferent running and passing by the centres, spoilt much of the good work put in by Usher and his forwards. The English back play, by comparison, was quite sparkling, and Myers, Hammett and Lowe received a good supply of ball from the brilliant servicemen, Davies and Kershaw. Harris on the wing also had some fine runs, and was unlucky not to score more than one try. Cumberlege, unlike his opposite number Pattullo, was a safe and confident full-back.

In front of a large crowd, England opened the scoring early in the game when Nimmo sent out from one of the first scrums a wild pass which Davies intercepted. The English outside-half made some ground and then cross-kicked to his right where Lowe gathered at full speed to touch down by the posts. Greenwood converted. Both sides then wasted perfect opportunities for scoring. The Scottish backs twice failed to capitalise upon openings in the English defence, electing to kick high over Cumberlege's head instead of passing or kicking along the ground. Each time, the ball rolled dead. England, too, missed a golden chance of a try when Wakefield knocked forward with the Scottish line at his mercy. England did get a try, however, when some clever work by Davies and Hammett created a gap for Harris, and the Blackheath winger ran 20 yards to score. Another Greenwood conversion gave his side a ten-points lead.

Before the interval, Scotland had reduced their points deficit with a dropped goal, and for most of the second half they spent their time in the English 25, desperately trying to get back into the game. Kennedy missed a penalty kick at goal before England managed one of their rare excursions into the Scottish half. Then, Kershaw forced Nimmo to err after a scrum, and the English half raced away to score a fine individual try. Scotland again fought back, but in the end defence triumphed and England won a share in the Championship.

ENGLAND		SCOTLAND	
B.S. Cumberlege	(Blackheath)	G.L. Pattullo	(Panmure)
C.N. Lowe	(Blackheath)	A.T. Sloan	(Edinburgh Acads.)
E. Myers	(Bradford)	A.W. Angus	(Watsonians)
E.D.G. Hammett	(Newport)	J.H. Bruce-Lockhart	(London Scottish)
S.W. Harris	(Blackheath)	G.B. Crole	(Oxford U.)
W.J.A. Davies	(U.S./R.N.)	E.C. Fahmy	(Abertillery)
C.A. Kershaw	(U.S./R.N.)	C.S. Nimmo	(Watsonians)
†T. Woods	(R.N.)	G.H.H.P. Maxwell	(R.A.F.)
G.S. Conway	(Cambridge U.)	A. Wemyss	(Edinburgh Wands.)
S. Smart	(Gloucester)	F. Kennedy	(Stewart's Coll. F.P.)
†A.F. Blakiston	(Northampton)	G. Thom	(Kirkcaldy)
A.T. Voyce	(Gloucester)	*C.M. Usher	(London Scottish)
F.W. Mellish	(Blackheath)	N.C. Macpherson	(Newport)
W.W. Wakefield	(Harlequins)	D.D. Duncan	(Oxford U.)
*J.E. Greenwood	(Cambridge U.)	R.A. Gallie	(Glasgow Acads.)

Tries: Harris, Kershaw, Lowe
Conversions: Greenwood (2)

Dropped goal: Bruce-Lockhart

Referee: Mr T.D. Schofield (Wales)

ENGLAND v WALES 1921

Played at Twickenham, London, 15 January 1921
England won by 1G, 1DG, 3T (18) to 1T (3)

Wales had demolished an experimental English XV in the mud at Swansea in the previous year and the selection of a very heavy Welsh pack gave visiting supporters among the 40,000 spectators high hopes of another victory for the Principality.

The English pack was on trial. Their selectors had discarded the heavier, slower men of the past and turned to faster, looser forwards to support the solid nucleus formed by Edwards, Gardner and Woods. Consequently, they entered this match giving away a huge advantage in weight to the Welshmen. But the result on the field more than justified the trial and by the end of the season this pack, whose contribution to the game was fast forward play, was hailed as one of the finest ever to appear for England. Accurate handling and balanced running also played a significant part in England's win. Davies and his backs were able to get away with some daring experiments while the Welsh outsides were far below international class.

Ring nearly crossed in the first minute when Lowe failed to find touch with a kick but England, gaining in confidence, promptly scored 12 points in as many minutes. Kershaw touched down for a try converted by Hammett; Davies dropped a goal; then Myers tore a huge gap in the Welsh defence and Kershaw sent Lowe over. It seemed as if England were on course for an overwhelming victory, but the Welsh forwards, with Winmill prominent, revealed enormous resources of strength and won ample possession for their backs in the remaining play up to the interval. Atrocious handling by their three-quarters, complications caused by a cartilage injury to Wetter and a broken collar-bone sustained by the veteran centre Jones, combined against the Welsh side and they squandered their chances.

A spark of brilliance from Davies made an opening for Hammett to kick ahead and Smallwood to score at the start of the second half. Wales momentarily rallied with a try by Ring in the corner, but England regained the initiative and a clever switch of direction by Hammett sent Smallwood, from a limited space, over for the final try.

ENGLAND		WALES	
B.S. Cumberlege	(Blackheath)	J. Rees	(Swansea)
C.N. Lowe	(Blackheath)	T. Johnson	(Cardiff)
E.D.G. Hammett	(Newport)	J. Shea	(Newport)
E. Myers	(Bradford)	J.P. Jones	(Pontypool)
A.M. Smallwood	(Leicester)	J. Ring	(Aberavon)
*W.J.A. Davies	(U.S.)	*J.J. Wetter	(Newport)
C.A. Kershaw	(U.S.)	F. Reeves	(Cross Keys)
†R. Edwards	(Newport)	S. Winmill	(Cross Keys)
†E.R. Gardner	(Devonport Services)	L. Attewell	(Newport)
L.G. Brown	(Blackheath)	W. Hodder	(Pontypool)
F.W. Mellish	(Blackheath)	J. Whitfield	(Newport)
T. Woods	(Devonport Services)	T. Parker	(Swansea)
A.F. Blakiston	(Northampton)	D. Edwards	(Glynneath)
W.W. Wakefield	(Harlequins/R.A.F.)	D. Marsden Jones	(Cardiff)
A.T. Voyce	(Gloucester)	E. Morgan	(Llanelli)

Tries: Smallwood (2), Kershaw, Lowe   *Try:* Ring
Conversion: Hammett
Dropped goal: Davies

Referee: Mr J.C. Sturrock (Scotland)

ENGLAND v IRELAND 1921

Played at Twickenham, London, 12 February 1921
England won by 1G, 1DG, 2T (15) to Nil

England took a step closer to winning the Triple Crown and Championship with a convincing victory over Ireland. There were 25–30,000 spectators to see England struggle to a narrow first-half lead. England lost Davies with an injury early in the match and, in a reshuffle, Myers went to the pivot position, with Wakefield leaving the pack to fill the gap in the threequarter line. Kershaw played one of his finest defensive games for England, tidying up the scrappy play at the base of the scrum following Wakefield's secondment to the backs.

The sides were closely matched in the scrums and mauls and it was the fast interpassing of the English pack which was the most attractive feature of the forward play. From a rush led by Edwards, and supported by Wakefield and Mellish, Blakiston scored the only try of the first half.

After the break England won more possession, enabling their backs to execute several dashing movements in attack, despite heavy conditions. At length, Mellish and Smallwood created an opening for Lowe to score, but the conversion attempt by Brown was touched in flight and consequently disallowed. Brown featured at the end of England's next attack. Hammett made a break near half-way which the mercurial Myers supported until held on the Irish line. Brown ambled up to take the pass and score. The conversion gave England an unassailable lead.

Lowe sealed England's victory with a score described as the 'most delightful' of all. Receiving the ball in midfield the wing set off for the right corner. Realising that his path was blocked he turned, balanced on his right foot and swung his left boot through the ball to drop a memorable goal.

ENGLAND		IRELAND	
B.S. Cumberlege	(Blackheath)	W.E. Crawford	(Lansdowne)
C.N. Lowe	(Blackheath)	D.J. Cussen	(Dublin U.)
E.D.G. Hammett	(Newport)	G.V. Stephenson	(Queen's U.)
E. Myers	(Bradford)	A.R. Foster	(Derry)
A.M. Smallwood	(Leicester)	H.S.T. Cormac	(Clontarf)
*W.J.A. Davies	(U.S.)	W. Cunningham	(Lansdowne)
C.A. Kershaw	(U.S.)	T. Mayne	(N.I.F.C.)
R. Edwards	(Newport)	J.J. Bermingham	(Blackrock College)
E.R. Gardner	(Devonport Services)	W.P. Collopy	(Bective Rangers)
L.G. Brown	(Blackheath)	A.W. Courtney	(U.C. Dublin)
F.W. Mellish	(Blackheath)	*W.D. Doherty	(Guy's H.)
T. Woods	(Devonport Services)	P. Stokes	(Garryowen)
A.F. Blakiston	(Northampton)	T.A. McClelland	(Queen's U.)
W.W. Wakefield	(Harlequins/R.A.F.)	N.M. Purcell	(Lansdowne)
A.T. Voyce	(Gloucester)	C.F.G.T. Hallaran	(U.S.)

Tries: Blakiston, Brown, Lowe
Conversion: Cumberlege
Dropped goal: Lowe

Referee: Mr T.D. Schofield (Wales)

SCOTLAND v ENGLAND 1921

Played at Inverleith, Edinburgh, 19 March 1921
England won by 3G, 1T (18) to Nil

England celebrated the fiftieth anniversary of international Rugby with an impressive forward performance which resulted in a decisive win. Myers was not available and Smallwood, not really an effective centre, was moved into the centre with a new man, King, appearing on the wing. The judgment of the English selectors was universally queried on this point for it was generally accepted that Corbett of Bristol was the ideal centre to replace Myers. As a result, Davies seldom ran the ball, preferring to use the kick ahead as the principal weapon of attack. The Scottish backs also showed a reluctance to run with the ball, though an injury to Hume necessitated a rearrangement of personnel and upset the balance of the Scottish team. Likewise, England had to suffer when Gardner – injured in the same incident as Hume – retired.

Cumberlege had an excellent game for his side, inspiring great confidence in the men in front of him as all valuable full-backs should, and it was a well-judged punt of his to the Scottish corner which led to the opening score after 20 minutes. Edwards seized possession and crashed over for an unconverted try, and moments later Woods got over, again from a line-out, after poor Scottish marking. Hammett's goal gave the visitors an eight-points lead at the break.

In the second half, Kershaw and Davies exploited palpable weaknesses in the Scottish centre with a sequence of teasing kicks. Forsayth and Donald covered well, but a cruel rebound from an attempted cross-kick by Davies caught the Scottish defence on the wrong foot and Brown caught the ball off the crossbar to stride over. Hammett again converted.

Scattering their cares to the wind, Scotland finally resorted to all-out attack. Forsayth initiated one move, but a handling error between Thomson and Mackenzie allowed King to scoop up the loose ball and dash over, unchallenged, for the last try, which Hammett converted with ease.

England thus gained possession of the Triple Crown for the sixth time.

SCOTLAND

H.H. Forsayth	(Oxford U.)
A.T. Sloan	(Edinburgh Acads.)
A.E. Thomson	(U.S.)
C.J.G. Mackenzie	(U.S.)
A.L. Gracie	(Harlequins)
R.L.H. Donald	(Glasgow H.S.F.P.)
*J. Hume	(Royal H.S.F.P.)
C.M. Usher	(Edinburgh Wands.)
G.H.H.P. Maxwell	(R.A.F./London Scottish)
N.C. Macpherson	(Newport)
F. Kennedy	(Stewart's College F.P.)
J.C.R. Buchanan	(Stewart's College F.P.)
R.A. Gallie	(Glasgow Acads.)
J.M. Bannerman	(Glasgow H.S.F.P.)
J.B. Macdougall	(Wakefield)

ENGLAND

B.S. Cumberlege	(Blackheath)
C.N. Lowe	(Blackheath)
A.M. Smallwood	(Leicester)
E.D.G. Hammett	(Newport)
†Q.E.M.A. King	(Blackheath/Army)
*W.J.A. Davies	(U.S.)
C.A. Kershaw	(U.S.)
R. Edwards	(Newport)
E.R. Gardner	(Devonport Services)
L.G. Brown	(Blackheath)
T. Woods	(Devonport Services)
†R. Cove-Smith	(Cambridge U.)
A.F. Blakiston	(Northampton)
W. W. Wakefield	(Harlequins/R.A.F.)
A.T. Voyce	(Gloucester)

Tries: Brown, Edwards, (Gardner in some records), King, Woods
Conversions: Hammett (3)

Referee: Mr J.C. Crawford (Ireland)

FRANCE v ENGLAND 1921

Played at Stade Colombes, Paris, 28 March 1921
England won by 2G (10) to 2PG (6)

France gave England a thorough examination in front of a crowd numbering 40,000. Marshall Foch, commander-in-chief of the Allied armies during the First World War, was present to unveil a memorial to French Rugby players who had fallen during the war. The weather was beautiful and an exciting game followed.

The French forwards proved to be England's stiffest opposition of the season and, despite the fact that a feud between the French Rugby controllers and Struxiano, a former captain, prevented the home side from fielding its strongest combination, England were never allowed to gain the secure lead which had been a feature of their earlier matches. The score stood at 10–3 at the break: England scoring two converted tries midway through the half to France's penalty. An elegant movement by the backs yielded a try by Lowe. (Lowe was closely marked afterwards and the remainder of his good work was seen in defence. Twice he raced across to the left wing to execute try-saving tackles on Lobies). Then Conway led a fierce dash into the French 25 and the vigorous Blakiston touched down after the ensuing scramble. Hammett converted both tries.

The second half became increasingly tense. The English forwards had given one penalty to Crabos in the first half and now erred again with only ten minutes remaining. Crabos, with a fine kick, reduced the lead to four points and it was anybody's game. An exciting break by the French fly-half, Bousquet, would have produced a try if instead of recklessly throwing the ball away he had continued forward. Borde, too, had earlier thrown away the chance of a lifetime with the England line at his feet. But England managed to ride the storm and thanks to the unwavering calm of Davies and Cumberlege, with several sound tackles and a number of useful touch kicks, the Grand Slam of beating all four countries in the Championship was achieved for the first time in post-war seasons.

FRANCE		ENGLAND	
J. Clément	(R.C.F.)	B.S. Cumberlege	(Blackheath)
J. Lobies	(R.C.F.)	C.N. Lowe	(Blackheath)
F. Borde	(R.C.F.)	†L.J. Corbett	(Bristol)
*R. Crabos	(R.C.F.)	E.D.G. Hammett	(Newport)
E. Cayrefourcq	(Tarbes)	A.M. Smallwood	(Leicester)
A. Bousquet	(Béziers)	*W.J.A. Davies	(U.S.)
R. Piteu	(Pau)	C.A. Kershaw	(U.S.)
P. Moureu	(Béziers)	R. Edwards	(Newport)
C.A. Gonnet	(Albi)	T. Woods	(Pontypool)
M. Biraben	(Dax)	L.G. Brown	(Blackheath)
A. Cassayet	(St Gaudens)	W.W. Wakefield	(Harlequins/R.A.F.)
L. Puech	(Toulouse)	R. Cove-Smith	(Cambridge U.)
J. Boubée	(Tarbes)	G.S. Conway	(Cambridge U.)
E. Soulié	(C.A.S.G.)	A.T. Blakiston	(Northampton)
A. Guichemerre	(Dax)	A.T. Voyce	(Gloucester)

Penalties: Crabos (2)

Tries: Blakiston, Lowe
Conversions: Hammett (2)

Referee: Mr J.C. Sturrock (Scotland)

WALES v ENGLAND 1922

Played at Cardiff Arms Park, 21 January 1922
Wales won by 2G, 6T (28) to 2T (6)

Torrents of rain during the week rendered the Arms Park playing surface impossible for any sport other than water-polo! And England's failure to adapt to the conditions and copy the close-dribbling tactics employed by the sub-aqua experts in the Welsh pack, coupled with the unavailability of W.J.A. Davies, brought about England's heaviest defeat in Wales since 1907.

Hiddlestone, the Neath veteran, played an excellent game for Wales and destroyed the flow of possession between the English halves. His partner as wing-forward, Jones of Newport, was also successful in bottling-up the English halves, though in their eagerness, the two Welshmen were penalised 13 times. No doubt, in fairer conditions, England would have converted these into useful points.

There were 35,000 present to see the teams take the field, wearing numbers for the first time in a Championship match. Wales opened the scoring after ten minutes when Whitfield scored near the corner. Penalties awarded against the Welsh back row allowed England to make much ground before a sudden counter-attack by Wales, with their forwards and Bowen spearheading the charge, resulted in a try by the Welsh fly-half. England again rallied, but another handling error enabled Wales to counter and Hiddlestone scored. A fine round of passing restored England's pride soon after when Lowe, finding a rare green patch of ground, raced in for a try at the corner. But by the interval, Wales led 17–3, Delahay scoring from a scissors move and Rees converting a try by Parker.

For the second half, England swapped Myers with V.G. Davies, and an immediate improvement was evident in their back play, but the remarkably accurate dribbling of the Welsh forwards produced tries for Palmer and Richards, with a final try by Islwyn Evans. Only the first of these was converted. England had the last say when Cumberlege, running out of defence, linked with Edwards and Wakefield to put Day over.

WALES		**ENGLAND**	
J. Rees	(Swansea)	B.S. Cumberlege	(Blackheath)
C. Richards	(Pontypool)	C.N. Lowe	(Blackheath)
B.S. Evans	(Llanelli)	E.D.G. Hammett	(Blackheath)
I. Evans	(Swansea)	E. Myers	(Bradford)
F. Palmer	(Swansea)	H.L.V. Day	(Leicester)
W. Bowen	(Swansea)	†V.G. Davies	(Harlequins)
W.J. Delahay	(Bridgend)	C.A. Kershaw	(U.S.)
T. Roberts	(Risca)	R. Edwards	(Newport)
J.G. Stephens	(Llanelli)	E.R. Gardner	(Devonport Services)
J. Whitfield	(Newport)	†J.S. Tucker	(Bristol)
S. Morris	(Cross Keys)	W.W. Wakefield	(Harlequins/Cambridge U.)
*T. Parker	(Swansea)	A.F. Blakiston	(Blackheath)
T. Jones	(Newport)	A.T. Voyce	(Gloucester)
W. Cummins	(Treorchy)	*L.G. Brown	(Blackheath)
D.D. Hiddlestone	(Neath)	G.S. Conway	(Cambridge U.)

Tries: Bowen, Delahay, I. Evans, Hiddlestone, Palmer, Parker, Richards, Whitfield
Conversions: Rees (2)

Tries: Day, Lowe

Referee: Mr J.M. Tennent (Scotland)

157

IRELAND v ENGLAND 1922
Played at Lansdowne Road, Dublin, 11 February 1922
England won by 4T (12) to 1T (3)

Several changes prompted by the rout at Cardiff resulted in a reconstituted side gaining a conclusive victory in Dublin. W.J.A. Davies returned to the side, but it was the other half of the famous combination, Kershaw, who won the laurels on this day. Realising that the Irish were marking Davies very closely, the little scrum-half took the opportunity to play a fine individual game, protecting his partner and having a hand in each of the English tries.

The sun shone brilliantly during the afternoon, but a heavy morning frost made the pitch slippery, and the running and handling of the English backs suffered as a result. Much of the blame for the inept threequarter play was due to the weakness of Bradby in the centre, though Myers and Lowe did not enjoy their finest games for England.

Ireland opened the scoring. From a line-out, Kershaw was grabbed by the Irish forwards and Cunningham sent out a quick pass to Wallis who, despite a diving tackle by Pickles, slithered over near the corner for a try. Smallwood was limping at about this time, but soon after, from a slow heel, Kershaw made a break before passing over Voyce's head to the left wing, who managed to limp across the line and equalise. Another clever dash by Kershaw led to a try for Lowe, which made the interval score 6–3 to England.

In the second half, there was no improvement in the English threequarter play. The passing was described as 'showy', but, added the same reporter, 'in sober reality, it was bad'. Play was tedious to follow and apart from England's two tries, there was little to note.

Wakefield, the best of the England forwards, made the break which led to the first score after the interval. Play had been in progress for 15 minutes when the Harlequin forward handed on to Smallwood who made rapid progress to the Irish line. There, a pass inward resulted in a try by Maxwell-Hyslop. An unexpected break by Kershaw produced a try for Gardner, the final score in a tedious second half which saw little improvement in the threequarter play.

IRELAND		ENGLAND	
W.E. Crawford	(Lansdowne)	†R.C.W. Pickles	(Bristol)
T.G. Wallis	(Wanderers)	C.N. Lowe	(Blackheath)
D.B. Sullivan	(U.C. Dublin)	E. Myers	(Bradford)
G.V. Stephenson	(Queen's U.)	†M.S. Bradby	(U.S.)
D.J. Cussen	(Dublin U.)	A.M. Smallwood	(Leicester)
J.R. Wheeler	(Queen's U.)	*W.J.A. Davies	(U.S.)
W. Cunningham	(Lansdowne)	C.A. Kershaw	(U.S.)
*W.P. Collopy	(Bective Rangers)	R. Cove-Smith	(Cambridge U.)
R.H. Owens	(Dublin U.)	E.R. Gardner	(Devonport Services)
T.A. McClelland	(Queens's U.)	†J.E. Maxwell-Hyslop	(Oxford U.)
S. McVicker	(Queen's U.)	†R.F.H. Duncan	(Guy's H.)
M.J. Bradley	(Dolphin)	W.W. Wakefield	(Harlequins/Cambridge U.)
J.K.S. Thompson	(Dublin U.)	†H.L. Price	(Oxford U.)
R.Y. Crichton	(Dublin U.)	G.S. Conway	(Cambridge U.)
C.F.G.T. Hallaran	(U.S.)	A.T. Voyce	(Gloucester)

Try: Wallis

Tries: Gardner, Lowe,
Maxwell-Hyslop, Smallwood

Referee: Mr J.M. Tennent (Scotland)

ENGLAND v FRANCE 1922

Played at Twickenham, London, 25 February 1922
Drawn: England 1G, 2PG (11), France 1G, 2T (11)

Harold Day was England's saviour in this match as France appeared to be heading for their first victory at Twickenham. In addition to landing two first-half penalty goals, Day's conversion in the closing moments of the match gave England the draw and so preserved the Twickenham ground record – England having avoided defeat in all championship matches there since 1910.

The King and 40,000 spectators attended this match which was played in brilliant sunshine. France were unable to field two of their star three-quarters – Jauréguy and Borde – but their replacements, the teenagers Ramis and Laffond, were competent performers and played significant roles in the French attacks. In the line-outs France secured ample possession, but their packing was rather ragged and put the English forwards off their game. The English backs were as ineffective on the dry Twickenham turf as they had been in the bog at Cardiff a month earlier. Piteu contained Kershaw at the base of the scrum and the English backs were scarcely allowed to pose problems for the French defence.

Trailing by six points at the interval, an inspired rally during the first eight minutes of the second half brought France level. Clément made a speculative kick ahead which caused Day some embarrassment and Ramis pounced to send Got over for a try. Moments later, another English fumble (Pickles the offender this time) allowed Cassayet to score following a scrummage. 12 minutes from no-side a well-worked try put France ahead. Got made a cross-kick which bounced remarkably high, deceiving Myers but enabling Lasserre to gather and cross for Crabos to convert.

Few could deny that France deserved to win, but a cruel stroke of luck robbed them of victory two minutes later. Day was called upon to attempt a long penalty kick from the left touch-line. The ball drifted across the face of the goal and Voyce, following up rapidly, was in a position to score. Day converted to save England.

ENGLAND		FRANCE	
R.C.W. Pickles	(Bristol)	J. Clément	(Valence)
C.N. Lowe	(Blackheath)	A. Laffond	(Bayonne)
E. Myers	(Bradford)	R. Ramis	(Perpignan)
M.S. Bradby	(U.S.)	*R. Crabos	(St Sever)
H.L.V. Day	(Leicester)	R. Got	(Perpignan)
*W.J.A. Davies	(U.S.)	J. Pascot	(Perpignan)
C.A. Kershaw	(U.S.)	R. Piteu	(Pau)
R. Cove-Smith	(Cambridge U.)	E. Soulié	(C.A.S.G.)
E.R. Gardner	(R.N.)	C.A. Gonnet	(Albi)
R. Edwards	(Newport)	M. Biraben	(Dax)
R.F.H. Duncan	(Guy's H.)	M.F. Lubin-Lebrère	(Toulouse)
W.W. Wakefield	(Cambridge U./Harlequins)	J. Sébedio	(Carcassonne)
A.T. Voyce	(Gloucester)	J. Boubée	(Biarritz)
G.S. Conway	(Cambridge U.)	A. Cassayet	(St Gaudens)
J.E. Maxwell-Hyslop	(Oxford U.)	R. Lasserre	(Cognac)

Try: Voyce *Conversion:* Day   *Tries:* Cassayet, Got, Lasserre
Penalties: Day (2)   *Conversion:* Crabos

Referee: Mr J.M. Tennent (Scotland)

ENGLAND v SCOTLAND 1922

Played at Twickenham, London, 18 March 1922
England won by 1G, 2T (11) to 1G (5)

At a match filled with incidents, the King was again present, together with 40,000 spectators, to see England put on their most convincing performance of the season. The visitors were unbeaten and possessed a strong pack, but, after an unpromising start, England's pack staged a splendid second-half rally to overpower the Scottish eight and build a platform for victory.

Scotland made first use of a healthy breeze, but only one try was registered despite several promising attacks. This came after 30 minutes. From a line-out on the English 25, the Scottish backs swept the ball along the threequarter line to Mackay who capitalised on some feeble English defence to in-pass for Dykes to score. Bertram converted.

In the second half, England took the game by the scruff of its neck and produced some memorable tries. Davies, after an indifferent match against France and a disappointing first half, finally regained his finest form and one of his spectacular breaks led to a scramble near the corner from which Lowe scored.

Soon after came a try to set before the King. Davies dodged a tackle by Bryce before a round of passing culminated in Myers penetrating the Scottish defence with a powerful burst. Lowe swept up on the right to take the final pass before touching down at the posts. Conway made no mistake with the conversion this time and England thus took the lead.

Several English dashes followed and Gracie twice cleared the danger for Scotland. Foot-up-in-the-scrum against England offered Maxwell the opportunity to tie the scores, but his kick banged against the cross-bar and England again turned to Davies for inspiration. After relieving the pressure with a fine line-kick, the fly-half made a wonderful run from a line-out to swerve past Forsayth for an excellent individual try which marked the close of the match.

ENGLAND		SCOTLAND	
†J.A. Middleton	(Richmond)	H.H. Forsayth	(Oxford U.)
C.N. Lowe	(Blackheath)	E.B. Mackay	(Glasgow Acads.)
E. Myers	(Bradford)	G.P.S. Macpherson	(Oxford U.)
A.M. Smallwood	(Leicester)	A.L. Gracie	(Harlequins)
†I.J. Pitman	(Oxford U.)	J.M. Tolmie	(Glasgow H.S.F.P.)
*W.J.A. Davies	(U.S.)	J.C. Dykes	(Glasgow Acads.)
C.A. Kershaw	(U.S.)	W.E. Bryce	(Selkirk)
†P.B.R.W. William-Powlett	(U.S.)	J.M. Bannerman	(Glasgow H.S.F.P.)
H.L. Price	(Oxford U.)	W.G. Dobson	(Heriot's F.P.)
R.F.H. Duncan	(Guy's H.)	D.M. Bertram	(Watsonians)
R. Cove-Smith	(Cambridge U.)	J.R. Lawrie	(Melrose)
W.W. Wakefield	(Cambridge U./ Harlequins)	J.C.R. Buchanan	(Stewart's College F.P.)
A.T. Voyce	(Gloucester)	G.H.H.P. Maxwell	(London Scottish)
G.S. Conway	(Cambridge U.)	D.S. Davies	(Hawick)
J.E. Maxwell-Hyslop	(Oxford U.)	*C.M. Usher	(Edinburgh Wands.)

Tries: Lowe (2), Davies
Conversion: Conway

Try: Dykes   *Conversion:* Bertram

Referee: Mr R.A. Lloyd (Ireland)

ENGLAND v WALES 1923

Played at Twickenham, London, 20 January 1923
England won by 1DG, 1T (7) to 1T (3)

In a sensational start, England took the lead after ten seconds without a single Welshman touching the ball. Wakefield kicked off into a strong wind, the ball ballooned back into the arms of Price and the Leicester forward attempted to drop a goal. His kick sailed wide of the posts and the Welsh, expecting the ball to roll dead, were surprised to see the wind influence the ball and Price follow up at speed to score a try. Conway missed a simple conversion.

Wales had the better of play up to the interval. The English forwards, with Wakefield at the helm, fought hard against a strong Welsh eight and were to be praised for not squandering the lead. Play was rough at times and several stoppages were necessary while forwards received repairs.

Wales equalised after ten minutes. Johnson obtained possession from a scrum, beat the English halves and danced around Smallwood before handing an inside pass to Michael, who scored. Jenkins could not kick the goal but Wales had several close efforts before half-time. Both Lewis and Cornish got over the English line, but knocks-forward cost them two tries. So England took use of the strong wind with the scores level.

In the first 20 minutes of the second half, Johnson for Wales and Lowe for England figured prominently in threequarter attacks. Davies went near with a drop at goal for England before a truly remarkable score was registered by Smallwood. Kershaw set his backs in motion and, at length, the ball reached Corbett, who was cramped for space. He passed the ball to Smallwood from between his legs and the left wing, standing near half-way and close to touch, dropped one of the most unusual goals ever witnessed in an international match. Wales had an opportunity to create a try immediately afterwards but nothing came of it, and England were content in the closing stages to nurse the touch-line.

Gilbert, the England full-back, is reputed to have been England's oldest player in an international match.

ENGLAND		WALES	
†F. Gilbert	(Devonport Services)	J. Rees	(Swansea)
C.N. Lowe	(Blackheath)	T. Johnson	(Cardiff)
E. Myers	(Bradford)	R.A. Cornish	(Cardiff)
L.J. Corbett	(Bristol)	A. Jenkins	(Llanelli)
A.M. Smallwood	(Leicester)	W.R. Harding	(Swansea)
*W.J.A. Davies	(U.S.)	*J.M.C. Lewis	(Cardiff)
C.A. Kershaw	(U.S.)	W.J. Delahay	(Bridgend)
E.R. Gardner	(Devonport Services)	D.G. Davies	(Cardiff)
R. Edwards	(Newport)	T. Roberts	(Newport)
†W.G.E. Luddington	(Devonport Services)	T. Parker	(Swansea)
W.W. Wakefield	(Cambridge U.)	S.G. Thomas	(Llanelli)
R. Cove-Smith	(O.M.Ts.)	S. Morris	(Cross Keys)
H.L. Price	(Leicester)	G. Michael	(Swansea)
G.S. Conway	(Rugby)	A. Baker	(Neath)
A.T. Voyce	(Gloucester)	J.F. Thompson	(Cross Keys)

Try: Price
Dropped goal: Smallwood

Try: Michael

Referee: Mr J.M.B. Scott (Scotland)

England v Ireland, 1923: *standing* E. R. Gardner, G. S. Conway, A. M. Smallwood, L. J. Corbett, H. L. Price, R. Cove-Smith, F. W. Sanders; *sitting* W. G. E. Luddington, E. Myers, A. T. Voyce, C. N. Lowe, Mr T. H. Vile, W. J. A. Davies (captain), W. W. Wakefield, C. A. Kershaw, F. Gilbert. This match at Leicester was England's last home international played away from Twickenham.

W. J. A. Davies, England's successful captain throughout the Grand Slam years of 1921 and 1923.

ENGLAND v IRELAND 1923
Played at Welford Road, Leicester, 10 February 1923
England won by 2G, 1DG, 3T (23) to 1G (5)

Reports of this game temper their praise for England's convincing win with reservations about the side's ability to exploit openings against teams with sounder defences. Ireland provided little opposition on this occasion, and the result was never in doubt.

Gilbert, a veteran full-back whose selection had been strongly criticised, proved a valuable asset to his side and was in action at an early stage of the match, safely fielding an Irish 'Garryowen' with the Irish pack bearing down upon him. After seven minutes, however, Corbett and Lowe, with an exchange of passes, set up Davies for a left-footed drop at goal. The English pack were well on top throughout the match, but some careless play by the backs detracted from the overall performance of the side. Nevertheless, after 20 minutes Smallwood completed a fine round of passing with a try, and soon after Davies vaulted over an opponent to send Corbett (with the aid of a dummy) in for another try. Before the pause, Gardner secured possession from a line-out and a pass to Price enabled the loose forward to score. Conway's conversion gave England a 15-points lead.

Ireland began the second half with new-found fervour, England slightly relaxing their effort. Gardiner took advantage of this lapse after 15 minutes, stealing away from the defence to send McClelland over for a try which Crawford goaled with a fine kick. After renewed Irish attacks, England tightened their grip again and two glorious tries followed. First, Price led a breakaway and Corbett and Myers continued the move before Lowe appeared out of the blue on the left wing to score. Conway converted before Davies, Myers, Corbett and Smallwood took part in a wonderful sweeping movement towards the touch-line. A pass inward found Myers, but it needed the ubiquitous Voyce to add the finishing touches as the Bradford man was held up on the line. The conversion this time was charged down.

This was the last international in England to be played away from Twickenham. The crowd of 20,000 was considered disappointing and the experiment was never repeated.

ENGLAND		IRELAND	
F. Gilbert	(Devonport Services)	W.E. Crawford	(Lansdowne)
C.N. Lowe	(Blackheath)	D.J. Cussen	(Dublin U.)
E. Myers	(Bradford)	G.V. Stephenson	(Queen's U.)
L.J. Corbett	(Bristol)	F. Jackson	(N.I.F.C.)
A.M. Smallwood	(Leicester)	R.O. McClenahan	(Instonians)
*W.J.A. Davies	(U.S.)	W.H. Hall	(Instonians)
C.A. Kershaw	(U.S.)	J.B. Gardiner	(N.I.F.C.)
E.R. Gardner	(Devonport Services)	R.D. Gray	(O. Wesley)
†F.W. Sanders	(Plymouth Albion)	T.A. McClelland	(Queen's U.)
W.G.E. Luddington	(Devonport Services)	*J.K.S. Thompson	(Dublin U.)
W.W. Wakefield	(Cambridge U.)	M.J. Bradley	(Dolphin)
R. Cove-Smith	(O.M.Ts.)	R. Collopy	(Bective Rangers)
H.L. Price	(Leicester)	D.M. Cunningham	(N.I.F.C.)
G.S. Conway	(Rugby)	J. Mahoney	(Cork Const.)
A.T. Voyce	(Gloucester)	C.F.G.T. Hallaran	(U.S.)

Tries: Corbett, Lowe, Price, Smallwood, Voyce *Conversions:* Conway (2)
Dropped goal: Davies

Try: McClelland
Conversion: Crawford

Referee: Mr T.H. Vile (Wales)

SCOTLAND v ENGLAND 1923
Played at Inverleith, Edinburgh, 17 March 1923
England won by 1G, 1T (8) to 2T (6)

Great interest surrounded England's last visit to Inverleith, for the sides met with the Triple Crown, Championship and Calcutta Cup at stake. In the end it was the directness and stamina of the English pack which laid the foundation of a famous victory. But it was only by the difference of a placed goal that England regained the Crown.

Fine conditions and a large crowd greeted the teams. England had made changes after the Irish match: Holliday replaced Gilbert at the back; Locke was selected in favour of Corbett, and Blakiston and Edwards came into the pack. Gilbert had been incapacitated in the Services' tournament and Edwards, in the end, was unable to take his place in the scrum so Cove-Smith retained his position.

In an evenly contested match both sides went near to scoring in the opening exchanges. Lawrie actually crossed for Scotland but was recalled for a forward pass. Then England went ahead in the 23rd minute. A swift transfer by the English backs found Smallwood in possession but with little room in which to manoeuvre. With a subtle change of pace, he swept past Browning and Drysdale to score. An electrifying run by Liddell brought the Scottish fans to their feet but Holliday, executing a fine tackle, saved England. Scotland maintained the offensive, though, and accurate passing enabled McLaren to equalise before the interval.

A tense struggle followed after half-time, culminating in a try by Scotland after 25 minutes. A mistake by Lowe allowed Gracie to dribble the ball past Holliday and win a close race to touch down just short of the dead-ball line. Drysdale failed to add the goal points. England fought back. Five minutes elapsed before Locke intercepted a loose ball on his 25. Making ground, he then kicked ahead and Voyce, displaying a fine turn of speed, followed up to score near the corner. Luddington and Gardner now came to the rescue, the latter making careful preparations for the former to land a goal from a difficult angle.

In the last ten minutes Scotland desperately strived for a winning score. Gracie and Liddell both gave England frights and on the verge of no-side Stevenson just failed to get over.

SCOTLAND		ENGLAND	
D. Drysdale	(Heriot's F.P.)	†T.E. Holliday	(Aspatria)
A. Browning	(Glasgow H.S.F.P.)	C.N. Lowe	(Blackheath)
E. McLaren	(Royal H.S.F.P.)	E. Myers	(Bradford)
*A.L. Gracie	(Harlequins)	†H.M. Locke	(Birkenhead Park)
E.H. Liddell	(Edinburgh U.)	A.M. Smallwood	(Leicester)
S.B. McQueen	(Waterloo)	*W.J.A. Davies	(U.S.)
W.E. Bryce	(Selkirk)	C.A. Kershaw	(U.S.)
J.M. Bannerman	(Glasgow H.S.F.P.)	E.R. Gardner	(Devonport Services)
J.C.R. Buchanan	(Stewart's College F.P.)	F.W. Sanders	(Plymouth Albion)
L.M. Stuart	(Glasgow H.S.F.P.)	W.G.E. Luddington	(Devonport Services)
D.S. Davies	(Hawick)	W.W. Wakefield	(Cambridge U.)
J.R. Lawrie	(Melrose)	R. Cove-Smith	(O.M.Ts.)
D.M. Bertram	(Watsonians)	A.F. Blakiston	(Northampton)
N.C. Macpherson	(Newport)	G.S. Conway	(Rugby)
A.K. Stevenson	(Glasgow Acads.)	A.T. Voyce	(Gloucester)

Tries: Gracie, McLaren

Tries: Smallwood, Voyce
Conversion: Luddington

Referee: Mr T.H. Vile (Wales)

FRANCE v ENGLAND 1923

Played at Stade Colombes, Paris, 2 April 1923
England won by 1G, 1DG, 1T (12) to 1PG (3)

Victory in Paris on Easter Monday gave England the Grand Slam, and there were over 35,000 spectators there to see them gain it. The match, not a distinguished one, was remarkable for the advance shown in French forward play, and the deplorable handling of the English backs.

France went ahead after only two minutes of play. Davies fumbled a pass from Kershaw and the French forwards rushed play into the English 25. Locke failed to clear and as the ball rolled towards the line, three English forwards were penalised trying to play the ball in offside positions. Béguet kicked the goal.

In the following play, France were on top but the English forwards performed creditably and worked themselves into the ground. Wakefield, leading by example, levelled matters with a try after 20 minutes: Luddington made a hash of a penalty kick, France failed to clear the ball, and Wakefield gathered in full stride to score. The French backs made good use of the breeze in the remaining play until the interval, but a series of rushes by the English pack relieved the situation.

France continued to dominate the second half until Voyce, intercepting a pass from Lousteau near half-way, drew Magnanou and sent Conway on a 40-yards run to the line. Luddington converted and France, now thoroughly demoralised, finally lost by nine points, Davies dropping a goal with his left foot at the end of the match. For England, a flattering margin of victory; for France, according to *Wisden Rugby Football Almanack*, 'the match furnished a notable advance in French football upon anything previously seen in an international contest'.

FRANCE		ENGLAND	
C. Magnanou	(R.C.F.)	T.E. Holliday	(Aspatria)
A. Jauréguy	(Toulouse)	C.N. Lowe	(Blackheath)
A. Behotéguy	(Bayonne)	E. Myers	(Bradford)
R. Salinié	(Perpignan)	H.M. Locke	(Birkenhead Park)
M. Lousteau	(Dax)	A.M. Smallwood	(Leicester)
E. Billac	(Bayonne)	*W.J.A. Davies	(U.S.)
R. Piteu	(Pau)	C.A. Kershaw	(U.S.)
P. Moureu	(Béziers)	E.R. Gardner	(Devonport Services)
J. Bayard	(Toulouse)	F.W. Sanders	(Plymouth Albion)
L. Béguet	(R.C.F.)	W.G.E. Luddington	(Devonport Services)
J. Castets	(Toulon)	W.W. Wakefield	(Cambridge U.)
A. Cassayet	(St Gaudens)	R. Cove-Smith	(O.M.Ts.)
J. Larrieu	(Tarbes)	A.F. Blakiston	(Northampton)
J. Boubée	(Biarritz)	G.S. Conway	(Rugby)
*R. Lasserre	(Cognac)	A.T. Voyce	(Gloucester)

Penalty: Béguet

Tries: Conway, Wakefield
Conversion: Luddington
Dropped goal: Davies

Referee: Mr T.H. Vile (Wales)

WALES v ENGLAND 1924

Played at St Helen's, Swansea, 19 January 1924
England won by 1G, 4T (17) to 3T (9)

This was England's first success in Wales since the War, and their first win at Swansea since 1895. There were 35,000 present to see the visitors gain a most deserved victory. England were quicker, sharper and far more inventive than Wales, and the fears concerning the new back division (Davies, Kershaw and Lowe had retired after the French match in April 1923) were completely dispelled as they ran in five tries.

Conditions were heavy after morning showers – circumstances which had favoured Wales in 1920 and 1922 – but the experienced English pack won good possession for their backs. The Welsh pack, too. had fine moments, but poor defence by the Welsh backs was a weakness fully exploited by the England attack.

Wales took first use of a healthy breeze and opened the scoring after 20 minutes. A kick ahead by Morris led to a forward rush from which Tom Jones scored. England equalised soon after when clever passing between Corbett and Catcheside resulted in Myers crossing. Directly afterwards came the best score of the match. A sweeping movement from the right side of the field, in which Catcheside, Wakefield, Voyce and Locke featured, ended with Jacob swinging over on the left. Conway's conversion stretched the lead and a neat break by Corbett paved the way for Locke to complete the scoring before the interval.

England increased their lead three minutes into the second half. Glorious passing by Young, Myers and Corbett produced a try for Catcheside. Luddington and Voyce were injured shortly after, the latter playing through the half with a broken rib. Wales rallied and tries by Owen and Johnson brought them back into the game. In a tense finish, however, some finely-balanced running by Corbett yielded another opening for Catcheside and the right wing averted Rees's tackle to settle the match.

WALES		ENGLAND	
*J. Rees	(Swansea)	†B.S. Chantrill	(Bristol)
T. Johnson	(Cardiff)	†H.C. Catcheside	(Percy Park)
R.A. Cornish	(Cardiff)	L.J. Corbett	(Bristol)
D.H. Davies	(Aberavon)	H.M. Locke	(Birkenhead Park)
B.M.G. Thomas	(St Bart's H.)	†H.P. Jacob	(Oxford U.)
A. Owen	(Swansea)	E. Myers	(Bradford)
E. Watkins	(Neath)	†A.T. Young	(Cambridge U.)
T. Jones	(Newport)	R. Edwards	(Newport)
I. Thomas	(Bryncethin)	†A. Robson	(Northern)
S. Morris	(Cross Keys)	R. Cove-Smith	(O.M.Ts.)
W.J. Ould	(Cardiff)	W.G.E. Luddington	(Devonport Services)
C.H. Pugh	(Maesteg)	G.S. Conway	(Rugby)
A.C. Evans	(Pontypool)	A.F. Blakiston	(Liverpool)
J.I. Morris	(Swansea)	*W.W. Wakefield	(Leicester)
I. Jones	(Llanelli)	A.T. Voyce	(Gloucester)

Tries: Johnson, T. Jones, Owen

Tries: Catcheside (2), Jacob, Locke, Myers
Conversion: Conway

Referee: Mr A.W. Angus (Scotland)

W. W. Wakefield played in every England international from the resumption of matches after the Great War in 1920 to the end of 1926, his record of 29 consecutive appearances standing until J. V. Pullin overtook it in 1971. He captained England from 1924 to 1926, and this is his Grand Slam side of 1924 prior to England's only match in Belfast: *back* B. S. Chantrill, R. H. Hamilton-Wickes, H. P. Jacob, H. C. Catcheside, R. Cove-Smith, C. K. T. Faithfull; *middle* L. J. Corbett, G. S. Conway, E. Myers, W. W. Wakefield, A. T. Voyce, A. F. Blakiston, W. G. E. Luddington; *front* A. Robson, A. T. Young.

IRELAND v ENGLAND 1924
Played at Ravenhill, Belfast, 9 February 1924
England won by 1G, 3T (14) to 1T (3)

England were the first visitors to Ireland's new international ground in Belfast and this match remains the only one played by England in the North of Ireland. 15,000 spectators had high hopes for Ireland who fielded a strong team with a vigorous pack. One description of the match states that England 'had their most gruelling experience of the season', for the Irish pack played at a hectic pace, controlling matters for three-quarters of the afternoon. Then, in typically Irish fashion, the pack ran out of steam in the last quarter and England's superior fitness saw the visitors safely to victory with 11 points scored in the closing ten minutes.

The English backs were ineffective in attack, the Irish playing a destructive rather than constructive role. However, Hamilton-Wickes made several splendid saving tackles – notably on Harold Stephenson – and Ireland were unable to force a score. Then, after ten minutes, England went ahead. Jacob made an electrifying break to allow Corbett to score the simplest of tries. Moments later, R. Collopy led an Irish dribble which forced a scrum on England's line, and Douglas sneaked over from short range to level the scores.

England were frequently on the defensive in the second half and the loose forwards made a number of try-saving tackles. George Stephenson was criticised for failing to use his brother Harry to full advantage, tending to delay his passes or attempting to break the English defence single-handed on too many occasions. As the half progressed so the stamina of the Irish eight drained, and ten minutes from no-side England reclaimed the lead when Chantrill, who had won his place in the XV without ever figuring in a trial, fielded a misjudged kick by Clarke and set up a movement for Hamilton-Wickes to finish. In the closing minutes Catcheside completed the scoring with a breath-taking try. Fielding the ball on his own line he ran the length of the field, hotly pursued by Harry Stephenson, to stretch England's winning margin to 11 points.

IRELAND		ENGLAND	
*W.E. Crawford	(Lansdowne)	B.S. Chantrill	(Bristol)
H.W.V. Stephenson	(U.S.)	H.C. Catcheside	(Percy Park)
G.V. Stephenson	(Queen's U.)	L.J. Corbett	(Bristol)
J.B. Gardiner	(N.I.F.C.)	H.P. Jacob	(Oxford U.)
A.C. Douglas	(Instonians)	†R.H. Hamilton-Wickes	(Harlequins)
J.R. Wheeler	(Queen's U.)	E. Myers	(Bradford)
J.A.B. Clarke	(Bective Rangers)	A.T. Young	(Cambridge U.)
W.P. Collopy	(Bective Rangers)	†C.K.T. Faithfull	(Harlequins)
R.Y. Crichton	(Dublin U.)	A. Robson	(Northern)
R. Collopy	(Bective Rangers)	R. Cove-Smith	(O.M.Ts.)
J. McVicker	(Belfast Collegians)	W.G.E. Luddington	(Devonport Services)
I.M.B. Stuart	(Dublin U.)	G.S. Conway	(Rugby)
J.D. Clinch	(Dublin U.)	A.F. Blakiston	(Liverpool)
T.A. McClelland	(Queen's U.)	*W.W. Wakefield	(Leicester)
C.F.G.T. Hallaran	(U.S.)	A.T. Voyce	(Gloucester)

Try: Douglas

Tries: Catcheside (2), Corbett, Hamilton-Wickes   *Conversion:* Conway

Referee: Mr T.H. Vile (Wales)

ENGLAND v FRANCE 1924
Played at Twickenham, London, 23 February 1924
England won by 2G, 3T (19) to 1DG, 1T (7)

Agreeable weather attended the King and 40,000 spectators at this match in which England ensured a share in the Championship. Locke and Edwards were fully recovered from the injuries which had prevented their participation in Belfast and England consequently fielded the same side as that which had beaten Wales. France were forced to make three late changes through the unfitness of Dupont, Jauréguy and Lasserre – three leading players.

Jacob came good with three tries, and Young proved an impeccable scrum-half, sending out quick accurate passes to his partner Myers and showing remarkable judgment with his darting runs from the base of the scrum. The whole English side, in fact, played with an assurance and resource rarely shown in the matches with France since 1914.

The home pack were soon on top and the backs, after a hesitant start, put together a well-combined wave of attacks which resulted in Jacob's first try after 18 minutes. A series of passes involving Young, Myers and Locke cleared a path for the wing's second after 30 minutes. From the restart, England should have scored when Myers ripped through, but Voyce dropped the vital pass. Then, just before half-time, Catcheside showed a flash of inspiration when hemmed in with only Pardo to beat: as the French full-back crouched to execute an orthodox tackle, Catcheside nonchalantly hurdled the player to make it 9–0 at half-time.

France started the second half with renewed hopes, the visiting forwards dominating the line-outs. Got, with a cross-kick, nearly penetrated the English defence but Jacob cleared in the nick of time. Behotéguy dropped a goal after 15 minutes but that marked the end of France's hopes: Corbett and Locke delighted the crowd by sending Jacob to the posts where Conway converted; and a forward rush drove France back into their 25 for Young to score from a daring, elusive dash, Conway again converting. A consolation try by Ballarin completed the play.

ENGLAND		FRANCE	
B.S. Chantrill	(Bristol)	L. Pardo	(Stade Hendaye)
H.C. Catcheside	(Percy Park)	J. Ballarin	(Tarbes)
L.J. Corbett	(Bristol)	*F. Borde	(Toulouse)
H.M. Locke	(Birkenhead Park)	A. Behotéguy	(Bayonne)
H. P. Jacob	(Oxford U.)	R. Got	(Perpignan)
E. Myers	(Bradford)	H. Galau	(Toulouse)
A.T. Young	(Cambridge U.)	R. Piteu	(T.O.E.C.)
R. Edwards	(Newport)	L. Béguet	(R.C.F.)
A. Robson	(Northern)	C.A. Gonnet	(R.C.F.)
R. Cove-Smith	(O.M.Ts.)	L. Lepatey	(Mazamet)
W.G.E. Luddington	(Devonport Services)	A. Cassayet	(Narbonne)
G.S. Conway	(Rugby)	P. Moureu	(Béziers)
A.F. Blakiston	(Liverpool)	E. Piquiral	(R.C.F.)
*W.W. Wakefield	(Leicester)	J. Etcheberry	(Cognac)
A.T. Voyce	(Gloucester)	F. Clauzel	(Béziers)

Tries: Jacob (3), Catcheside, Young · *Try:* Ballarin
Conversions: Conway (2) · *Dropped goal:* Behotéguy

Referee: Mr A.E. Freethy (Wales)

ENGLAND v SCOTLAND 1924

Played at Twickenham, London, 15 March 1924
England won by 3G, 1DG (19) to Nil

England's victory gave them the Championship for the sixth time in ten seasons, a period in which 33 of their 40 matches were won. *Wisden* proclaimed that England's supremacy was more pronounced than in 1923, for this season all matches were won by convincing margins.

England's backs were not in such devastating form as they had shown against France, but again the home pack carried all before them and gained a constant stream of possession in the tight. Young, at the heels of this great English eight, had another outstanding game, though it was generally agreed that Chantrill was the principal success among the backs on this occasion. Three times he stopped the speedy Smith from scoring with shattering tackles, and his calm, unflurried manner gave enormous confidence to those in front of him.

In the early exchanges there was little evidence of the scoring spree which was to come after the interval, and England's backs were unable to compose a worthwhile attack until the end of the first half. Then, Young started a passage of play which featured Corbett and Catcheside. Corbett received a return pass from his wing and, finding his path blocked, he kicked high and into the middle of the field where Wakefield gathered to score at the posts. Conway converted to give England an undeserved lead of 5–0.

Scotland's speedy and elusive wingers made several strong runs at the start of the second half but determined tackling by Chantrill and Jacob saved England's line. At length, the English forwards reclaimed forward superiority and forced play to the Scottish 25 where, from a scrum, Myers dropped a superb goal, curling the ball through the posts with his left foot. Moments later, the Yorkshireman ended Scottish aspirations when he gathered the ball in broken play and dashed through a bewildered defence to score at the posts. Conway converted.

England's final score came three minutes from the end when Catcheside picked up a loose ball near half-way and twice handed off Wallace to cover the length of the Scottish half and score. Conway converted, the ball glancing over off the post.

ENGLAND		SCOTLAND	
B.S. Chantrill	(Bristol)	D. Drysdale	(Heriot's F.P.)
H.C. Catcheside	(Percy Park)	I.S. Smith	(Oxford U.)
L.J. Corbett	(Bristol)	G.P.S. Macpherson	(Oxford U.)
H.M. Locke	(Birkenhead Park)	G.G. Aitken	(Oxford U.)
H.P. Jacob	(Oxford U.)	A.C. Wallace	(Oxford U.)
E. Myers	(Bradford)	H. Waddell	(Glasgow Acads.)
A.T. Young	(Cambridge U.)	W.E. Bryce	(Selkirk)
R. Edwards	(Newport)	J.M. Bannerman	(Glasgow H.S.F.P.)
A. Robson	(Northern)	*J.C.R. Buchanan	(Stewart's College F.P.)
R. Cove-Smith	(O.M.Ts.)	D.M. Bertram	(Watsonians)
W.G.E. Luddington	(Devonport Services)	A.C. Gillies	(Watsonians)
G.S. Conway	(Rugby)	R.A. Howie	(Kirkcaldy)
A.F. Blakiston	(Liverpool)	R.G. Henderson	(Northern)
*W.W. Wakefield	(Leicester)	D.S. Davies	(Hawick)
A.T. Voyce	(Gloucester)	J.R. Lawrie	(Leicester)

Tries: Catcheside, Myers, Wakefield
Conversions: Conway (3)
Dropped goal: Myers

Referee: Mr T.H. Vile (Wales)

ENGLAND v NEW ZEALAND 1925
Played at Twickenham, London, 3 January 1925
New Zealand won by 1G, 1PG, 3T (17) to 1G, 1PG, 1T (11)

The All Blacks were at the end of an unbeaten tour, and England were the home champions, so the prospects of an intriguing engagement attracted a record attendance of 60,000. The Rest had defeated an 'England' side containing twelve of the 1924 Grand Slam team a fortnight earlier, but the judgment of the selectors in turning to seven of The Rest was severely questioned. New Zealand still practised the 2–3–2 scrummage, with Parker as rover.

The match started fiercely, with the Welsh referee warning both packs for vigorous play. After ten minutes, Cyril Brownlie was ordered from the field for deliberately kicking an opponent, but the teams settled down to play a classic match. A man short, New Zealand rose to the occasion bravely and two of their tries were the result of sheer forward power. England scored first, however, after 20 minutes. From a wheeled scrum, Voyce slotted the ball past Nepia for Cove-Smith to score. Further English attacks were repelled by Nepia, who played brilliantly, and ten minutes before the interval Cooke sent Svenson over for the equaliser. Five minutes later, Mill fed Steel on the blind-side for a try in the corner. On the stroke of half-time, Hillard was penalised in front of his posts and Nicholls kicked the goal.

England began the second half strongly but New Zealand forward dominance wore the home side down and resulted in a try by M.J. Brownlie which Nicholls converted. Parker then scrambled over near the left corner to give the visitors a 14-points lead with 20 minutes to go. A rally by the English turned the match into a memorable one, with the backs at last finding chinks in the New Zealanders' armour and beginning to handle and run with new-found assurance. Corbett, preferring the drop to the place kick, landed three penalty points before Hamilton-Wickes flashed past Svenson, drew Nepia perfectly, and sent Kittermaster racing 40 yards to the goal for the try of the match. Conway kicked the conversion but no-side was called shortly after with England again attacking.

ENGLAND		NEW ZEALAND	
†J.W. Brough	(Silloth)	G. Nepia	(Hawke's Bay)
R.H. Hamilton-Wickes	(Harlequins)	J. Steel	(West Coast)
V.G. Davies	(Harlequins)	A.E. Cooke	(Auckland)
L.J. Corbett	(Bristol)	K.S. Svenson	(Wellington)
†J.C. Gibbs	(Harlequins)		
		M.F. Nicholls	(Wellington)
†H.J. Kittermaster	(Oxford U.)	N.P. McGregor	(Canterbury)
A.T. Young	(Cambridge U.)	J.J. Mill	(Hawke's Bay)
		J.H. Parker	(Canterbury)
R. Edwards	(Newport)		
J.S. Tucker	(Bristol)	W.R. Irvine	(Hawke's Bay)
†R.J. Hillard	(Oxford U.)	Q. Donald	(Wairarapa)
R. Cove-Smith	(O.M.Ts.)	C.J. Brownlie	(Hawke's Bay)
*W.W. Wakefield	(Harlequins)	R.R. Masters	(Canterbury)
A.F. Blakiston	(Liverpool)	M.J. Brownlie	(Hawke's Bay)
G.S. Conway	(Rugby)	*J. Richardson	(Southland)
A.T. Voyce	(Gloucester)	A. White	(Southland)

Tries: Cove-Smith, Kittermaster
Conversion: Conway
Penalty: Corbett

Tries: M.J. Brownlie, Parker,
Steel, Svenson
Conversion: Nicholls
Penalty: Nicholls

Referee: Mr A.E. Freethy (Wales)

ENGLAND v WALES 1925
Played at Twickenham, London, 17 January 1925
England won by 1PG, 3T (12) to 2T (6)

Right wing Hamilton-Wickes played a major role in England's sixth consecutive victory over Wales at H.Q. He featured prominently in moves which led to two of the English tries and scored the other after a mesmeric run in which he beat three opponents. Generally, however, this was not a memorable match and England failed to show the class or promise of the previous season.

The Prince of Wales was among the 35,000 spectators to see the Welsh forwards combining well. Play settled in the English 25 until three penalty kicks awarded to the home side enabled them to gain a territorial advantage after ten minutes. Then, more Welsh carelessness presented Armstrong with a chance to land the penalty points which opened the scoring. Wales immediately responded, Parker going wide with an effort to kick similar points, and levelled scores after 25 minutes when Delahay, Hopkins, Cornish and Williams figured in a passing movement which produced the opportunity for Thomas to swerve past his marker and beat Brough to score. Kittermaster featured in the next passage of play and nearly dropped a goal before Wales again attacked. While play was in the English quarters, Hamilton-Wickes made an enterprising break which took him to half-way where, faced by Johnson, he passed to Kittermaster. The Oxonian, with a brilliant run, touched down near the posts. Armstrong missed the easy kick at goal.

On the run of the play, Wales deserved to be at least level, and the Welsh forwards, rising to the occasion with rare fervour, forced England back on their heels at the start of the second period. Then another exquisite break by Hamilton-Wickes and Kittermaster created a try for Voyce to score, after play had veered from one corner of the ground to the other. Wales, with a spirited rally, reduced the deficit when a sparkling round of passing finished with James crossing at the corner. In an exciting finish, England guaranteed victory when Hamilton-Wickes scored his much-deserved try.

H.G. Periton, an Irishman, was the first player capped for England from Waterloo.

ENGLAND		WALES	
J.W. Brough	(Silloth)	*T. Johnson	(Cardiff)
R.H. Hamilton-Wickes	(Harlequins)	W.P. James	(Aberavon)
H.M. Locke	(Birkenhead Park)	E. Williams	(Aberavon)
L.J. Corbett	(Bristol)	R.A. Cornish	(Cardiff)
J.C. Gibbs	(Harlequins)	C. Thomas	(Bridgend)
H.J. Kittermaster	(Oxford U.)	W.J. Hopkins	(Aberavon)
†E.J. Massey	(Leicester)	W.J. Delahay	(Cardiff)
W.G.E. Luddington	(Devonport Services)	B. Phillips	(Aberavon)
J.S. Tucker	(Bristol)	C. Williams	(Llanelli)
†R. Armstrong	(Northern)	C.H. Pugh	(Maesteg)
R. Cove-Smith	(O.M.Ts.)	S. Morris	(Cross Keys)
*W.W. Wakefield	(Harlequins)	I. Richards	(Cardiff)
A.F. Blakiston	(Liverpool)	J. Gore	(Blaina)
†H.G. Periton	(Waterloo)	D. Parker	(Swansea)
A.T. Voyce	(Gloucester)	W.I. Jones	(Llanelli/Cambridge U.)

Tries: Hamilton-Wickes, Kittermaster, Voyce
Penalty: Armstrong

Tries: James, Thomas

Referee: Mr A.A. Lawrie (Scotland)

ENGLAND v IRELAND 1925

Played at Twickenham, London, 14 February 1925
Drawn: England 2T (6), Ireland 2T (6)

So ably did the Irish forwards acquit themselves that the English pack found difficulty in heeling the ball in the tight and in handling swiftly in the loose. Critics were unanimous in their praise for this admirable Irish forward performance: England were outplayed for the first 75 minutes of the match. Yet, for all their forward power, Irish back play was sadly disappointing, especially in the first half when George Stephenson found himself playing in the unaccustomed position of left wing. As a result, England led by six points at the break.

England opened the scoring after six minutes. Massey gained some ground with a darting run and from the following scrummage Kittermaster ripped through the defence to feed Locke. The Birkenhead man, drawing his opponent, created the overlap for Smallwood to score. Much against the run of play, Locke and Smallwood exploited a similar opportunity after 30 minutes for the Leicester man to increase England's lead.

The Irish forwards, displaying their natural talent in the loose rushes as well as a new-found ability to heel out from the scrummage, continued to govern the battle up-front, and, on this occasion, even during a torrid last five minutes when England threw everything into all-out attack, they lasted the pace unfalteringly – a far cry from the blood-and-thunder Irish packs of old which ran out of steam early in the second half.

Ireland pulled back three points five minutes after the break. Hamilton-Wickes failed to gather a cross-kick and interpassing between the Irish backs yielded a try for Hewitt. The Irish backs now showed increased confidence and only a desperate piece of defence by Massey prevented a try moments later when George Stephenson punted over Holliday's head. After 20 minutes Ireland drew level when Sugden sold a crafty dummy to enable Harry Stephenson to hurl himself over the English line – brother George just missing the conversion.

The match finished in a flurry of excitement as England repulsed further Irish attacks and, in turn, launched a series of testing moves. No-side arrived with the sides locked in combat and the scores still level.

ENGLAND		IRELAND	
T.E. Holliday	(Aspatria)	*W.E. Crawford	(Lansdowne)
R.H. Hamilton-Wickes	(Harlequins)	H.W.V. Stephenson	(U.S.)
L.J. Corbett	(Bristol)	J.B. Gardiner	(N.I.F.C.)
H.M. Locke	(Birkenhead Park)	T.R. Hewitt	(Queen's U.)
A.M. Smallwood	(Leicester)	G.V. Stephenson	(Queen's U.)
H.J. Kittermaster	(Oxford U.)	F.S. Hewitt	(Instonians)
E.J. Massey	(Leicester)	M. Sugden	(Dublin U.)
W.G.E. Luddington	(Devonport Services)	R.Y. Crichton	(Dublin U.)
J.S. Tucker	(Bristol)	W.R.F. Collis	(Wanderers)
†R.R.F. MacLennan	(O.M.Ts.)	R. Collopy	(Bective Rangers)
R. Cove-Smith	(O.M.Ts.)	J. McVicker	(Belfast Collegians)
*W.W. Wakefield	(Harlequins)	D.M. Cunningham	(N.I.F.C.)
A.F. Blakiston	(Liverpool)	W.F. Browne	(U.S.)
†R.G. Lawson	(Workington)	G.R. Beamish	(Coleraine/R.A.F.)
A.T. Voyce	(Gloucester)	J.D. Clinch	(Dublin U.)

Tries: Smallwood (2) 　　　　　　　*Tries:* T.R. Hewitt, H.W.V. Stephenson

Referee: Mr T.H. Vile (Wales)

SCOTLAND v ENGLAND 1925
Played at Murrayfield, Edinburgh, 21 March 1925
Scotland won by 2G, 1DG (14) to 1G, 1PG, 1T (11)

The S.R.U. celebrated the opening of the new international ground at Murrayfield with a win which secured the Grand Slam, and a record attendance of 80,000 witnessed a match full of incidents in which the lead changed several times. The Scottish captain, G.P.S. Macpherson, wrote of this game several years later: 'England got more of the ball, particularly in the second half, so we could not dictate the play. To some extent they used the touch-line and curiously enough the game moved more along our left-hand side of the field, so that Smith on the left wing ... had no opportunities in attack. The Scottish forwards had some glorious foot-rushes, but somehow these did not fructify with the "good ball" we were looking for.

Macpherson twice broke through in the opening stages, only to lose his shorts in tackles by Corbett. England went ahead after five minutes when Luddington kicked a penalty, but Macpherson's third thrust presented Nelson with a try, the scrum-half bolting 25 yards to score at the posts where Drysdale kicked the goal. England reclaimed the lead on the mark of half-time. Smith dropped an awkward bouncing ball for Hamilton-Wickes and the rapacious Voyce to run from half-way, exchanging passes before the Harlequin scored a gem of a try.

Five minutes into the second half, an adroit kick by Corbett bisected the Scottish cover and Wakefield dived on the ball to score. As the ball was placed for the conversion, the Scottish forwards charged and the referee blew his whistle, whereupon the Scots stood still. When the ball was re-placed, however, the Scots continued charging and kicked the ball away. England were thus denied the chance to kick for goal. Ten minutes later, Wallace bustled over at the corner flag and Gillies's conversion from touch raised an immense cheer.

With only a point in it now, the closing stages were tense. The Scottish forwards advanced with a wave of foot-rushes – one dribble by Aitken rebounding off the posts. Smith almost pierced the defence on the left and then Waddell dropped a fine goal. England countered but Scotland's defence remained secure and they retained their slender lead.

SCOTLAND		ENGLAND	
D. Drysdale	(Heriot's F.P.)	T.E. Holliday	(Aspatria)
A.C. Wallace	(Oxford U.)	R.H. Hamilton-Wickes	(Harlequins)
G.G. Aitken	(Oxford U.)	L.J. Corbett	(Bristol)
*G.P.S. Macpherson	(Oxford U.)	H.M. Locke	(Birkenhead Park)
I.S. Smith	(Oxford U.)	A.M. Smallwood	(Leicester)
H. Waddell	(Glasgow Acads.)	E. Myers	(Bradford)
J.B. Nelson	(Glasgow Acads.)	E.J. Massey	(Leicester)
J.M. Bannerman	(Glasgow H.S.F.P.)	W.G.E. Luddington	(Devonport Services)
J.C.H. Ireland	(Glasgow H.S.F.P.)	J.S. Tucker	(Bristol)
D.S. Davies	(Hawick)	R.R.F. MacLennan	(O.M.Ts.)
A.C. Gillies	(Watsonians)	R. Cove-Smith	(O.M.Ts.)
J.W. Scott	(Stewart's College F.P.)	*W.W. Wakefield	(Harlequins)
D.J. MacMyn	(Cambridge U.)	A.F. Blakiston	(Liverpool)
R.A. Howie	(Kirkcaldy)	†D.C. Cumming	(Cambridge U.)
J.R. Paterson	(Birkenhead Park)	A.T. Voyce	(Gloucester)

Tries: Nelson, Wallace
Conversions: Drysdale, Gillies
Dropped goal: Waddell

Tries: Hamilton-Wickes, Wakefield
Conversion: Luddington
Penalty: Luddington

Referee: Mr A.E. Freethy (Wales)

FRANCE v ENGLAND 1925

Played at Stade Colombes, Paris, 13 April 1925
England won by 2G, 1GM (13) to 1G, 2T (11)

A sporting crowd of about 30,000 spectators attended this Easter Monday match which was played in ideal conditions. The home pack operated in an efficient manner, gaining an equal share of the scrummage possession, acquitting themselves well at the line-out and causing frequent trouble to the visitors with their pace and short passing in the loose. England, with Wakefield playing at the top of his form again, had vast experience up-front, however, and just succeeded in winning an exciting match.

At the beginning of the match there was the rare sight of Luddington placing a goal from a mark on the French 25, but 30 minutes passed before England stretched their lead. A punt by Voyce presented Hamilton-Wickes with an attacking opportunity from which Cumming sent Wakefield over for a try and Luddington converted. Then, in a flurry of activity, both sides scored goals before the interval. Du Manoir, an elegant player, made a handsome break to send Barthe over for a try which Ducousso duly converted; and Cumming instigated a movement which featured Myers and Corbett before Hamilton-Wickes rammed his way over the line at the corner. Luddington, with another good kick, took the half-time score to 13–5.

Increasing French pressure at the restart was transformed into points when, following a rush, Du Manoir penetrated the English defence and passed to Cluchague who crossed at the corner. Although the place kick was too difficult for Ducousso, France replied with further attacks and the English defence was frequently strained, especially when Considine was injured and forced to retire temporarily. Du Manoir took full advantage of England's weakened line and another of his graceful runs produced a try ten minutes from no-side – De Laborderie sending Besson speeding to the corner. Ducousso's conversion failed and only resolute defence by the Englishmen prevented more French points.

FRANCE		ENGLAND	
J. Ducousso	(Tarbes)	T.E. Holliday	(Aspatria)
M. Besson	(C.A.S.G.)	R.H. Hamilton-Wickes	(Harlequins)
C. Magnanou	(Bayonne)	L.J. Corbett	(Bristol)
M. De Laborderie	(R.C.F.)	H.M. Locke	(Birkenhead Park)
L. Cluchague	(Biarritz)	†S.G.U. Considine	(Bath)
Y. Du Manoir	(R.C.F.)	E. Myers	(Bradford)
*R. Piteu	(T.O.E.C.)	A.T. Young	(Cambridge U.)
A. Maury	(Toulouse)	W.G.E. Luddington	(Devonport Services)
J. Marcet	(Albi)	J.S. Tucker	(Bristol)
P. Moureu	(Béziers)	R.R.F. MacLennan	(O.M.Ts.)
A. Laurent	(Biarritz)	R. Cove-Smith	(O.M.Ts.)
R. Levasseur	(Stade Français)	*W.W. Wakefield	(Harlequins)
E. Barthe	(Stade Bordelais)	A.F. Blakiston	(Liverpool)
E. Piquiral	(R.C.F.)	D.C. Cumming	(Cambridge U.)
A. Bioussa	(Toulouse)	A.T. Voyce	(Gloucester)

Tries: Barthe, Besson, Cluchague
Conversion: Ducousso

Tries: Hamilton-Wickes, Wakefield
Conversions: Luddington (2)
Goal from mark: Luddington

Referee: Mr A.E. Freethy (Wales)

WALES v ENGLAND 1926

Played at Cardiff Arms Park, 16 January 1926
Drawn: Wales 1T (3), England 1T (3)

England were the more skilful side in the first half but a failure by the forwards to heel the ball cleanly, compounded by Worton's inability to get his backs moving, resulted in a dismal performance by England's midfield players. Towards the end of the match, Wales's greater stamina put England under such pressure that the visitors were fortunate to emerge from the game with a draw. Wales spent the last 15 minutes of the match encamped on the English line. Only a lack of vision by the Welsh pivot – a rejected English triallist of Oriental origin – and untidy heeling by the forwards, reduced the attacking potential of the home backs. Near the end, Delahay seized the ball from an English heel to pounce for a try which the Irish referee disallowed.

Frost had compelled the groundstaff to protect the ground with a layer of straw and a firm surface was uncovered before the kick-off, promising a fast, open game. There were many attacks by both sides at first, though England looked more likely to score on the evidence of the early play. Hamilton-Wickes actually crossed the Welsh line but was recalled for a forward pass. Just before half-time Francis instigated the move which led to England's try. From broken play the centre weaved inside a couple of Welshmen before veering to his right to link with Wakefield. The England captain then sprinted around the Welsh full-back for a splendid try which Luddington should have converted.

Wales dominated the second half: their forwards constantly threatened the English line with fierce, but organised, rushes. Some of the play was ill-tempered and the referee made several stern warnings to players of both sides. With 15 minutes to go, Wales equalised when Andrews kneed on a pass aimed at his feet. A lucky bounce enabled him to gather and score at the corner. Herrera could not convert.

WALES		ENGLAND	
D.B. Evans	(Swansea)	H.C. Catcheside	(Percy Park)
G.E. Andrews	(Newport)	†H.C. Burton	(Richmond)
A.R. Stock	(Newport)	†A.R. Aslett	(Army/Richmond)
R.A. Cornish	(Cardiff)	†T.E.S. Francis	(Cambridge U.)
*W.R. Harding	(Swansea)	R.H. Hamilton-Wickes	(Harlequins)
R. Jones	(Northampton)	H.J. Kittermaster	(Harlequins)
W.J. Delahay	(Cardiff)	†J.R.B. Worton	(Harlequins)
T.W. Lewis	(Cardiff)	†R.J. Hanvey	(Aspatria)
J.H. John	(Swansea)	J.S. Tucker	(Bristol)
T. Hopkins	(Swansea)	†E. Stanbury	(Plymouth Albion)
D.M. Jenkins	(Treorchy)	A. Robson	(Northern)
R.C. Herrera	(Cross Keys)	W.G.E. Luddington	(Devonport Services)
S. Hinam	(Cardiff)	H.G. Periton	(Waterloo)
D. Jones	(Newport)	*W.W. Wakefield	(Harlequins)
B. Phillips	(Aberavon)	A.T. Voyce	(Gloucester)

Try: Andrews

Try: Wakefield

Referee: Mr W.H. Acton (Ireland)

IRELAND v ENGLAND 1926

Played at Lansdowne Road, Dublin, 13 February 1926
Ireland won by 2G, 1PG, 2T (19) to 3G (15)

A capacity crowd watched Ireland gain their first win against England since 1911. The game was played at a blistering pace, with the vigorous Irish forwards winning plenty of ball for their attractive backs to launch wave after wave of attacks, and the Englishmen defending staunchly.

England repelled a storming start by the Irish pack with intelligent defence and after the sides had settled it was England who opened the scoring after 20 minutes. An England back pierced the Irish defence to send Young in for a try at the posts which was converted. Ten minutes passed before a cunning kick by Sugden defeated Catcheside. Cussen and Stephenson were there to capitalise on the full-back's error, the latter scoring. Five minutes before the interval Young, Kittermaster and Aslett were seen at their best creating a chance for Hamilton-Wickes to cut through. In the follow-up Voyce was at hand to send Periton – an Irishman! – over for a try which Francis, with his second successful kick, made into a goal. A penalty goal landed by Stephenson completed the first-half scoring.

A period of stalemate at the opening of the second half ended abruptly after 20 minutes when the irrepressible Clinch stormed away from a ruck and linked with Sugden, who tricked his way past a few defenders before the muscular Cussen took a pass to dive over in the corner. Stephenson's vital conversion from touch nosed Ireland into the lead. Ten minutes from no-side the impressive Sugden/Cussen combination again worked a try in the corner with Stephenson's goal giving Ireland a useful buffer, but quick thinking by Hamilton-Wickes at a throw-in soon after allowed Haslett to score the simplest of tries. Francis's conversion reduced the Irish lead to 16–15. With the huge crowd willing Ireland towards a narrow victory, there came a final flourish. Cussen gathered a loose ball near the touch-line and drew the English defence before cross-kicking. An English error permitted Frank Hewitt to take the ball and end an epic game with the seventh try of the afternoon.

IRELAND		ENGLAND	
*W.E. Crawford	(Lansdowne)	H.C. Catcheside	(Percy Park)
D.J. Cussen	(Dublin U.)	R.H. Hamilton-Wickes	(Harlequins)
G.V. Stephenson	(N.I.F.C.)	A.R. Aslett	(Richmond)
F.S. Hewitt	(Instonians)	T.E.S. Francis	(Cambridge U.)
T.R. Hewitt	(Queen's U.)	†Sir T.G. Devitt	(Cambridge U.)
E.O'D. Davy	(U.C. Dublin)	H.J. Kittermaster	(Harlequins)
M. Sugden	(Dublin U.)	A.T. Young	(Blackheath)
M.J. Bradley	(Dolphin)	E. Stanbury	(Plymouth Albion)
C.T. Payne	(N.I.F.C.)	J.S. Tucker	(Bristol)
A.McM. Buchanan	(Dublin U.)	R.J. Hanvey	(Aspatria)
J. McVicker	(Collegians)	*W.W. Wakefield	(Harlequins)
J.L. Farrell	(Bective Rangers)	†L.W. Haslett	(Birkenhead Park)
C.F.G.T. Hallaran	(R.N./Wanderers)	H.G. Periton	(Waterloo)
S.J. Cagney	(London Irish)	†W.E. Tucker	(Cambridge U.)
J.D. Clinch	(Wanderers)	A.T. Voyce	(Gloucester)

Tries: Cussen (2), F.S. Hewitt, Stephenson
Conversions: Stephenson (2)
Penalty: Stephenson

Tries: Haslett, Periton, Young
Conversions: Francis (3)

Referee: Mr W.J. Llewellyn (Wales)

ENGLAND v FRANCE 1926

Played at Twickenham, London, 27 February 1926
England won by 1G, 2T (11) to Nil

40,000 watched a dreary match in which England were happy to secure their first win of the season. France played the entertaining football at the beginning of the match and a slow England pack presented the French backs with the scope to make several menacing runs. Indeed, the *Times* correspondent referred to England's pack as 'poor decrepit veterans', for their slowness about the field enabled the opposition to run and handle without constraint.

Graule, displaying slide-rule accuracy with his short punts to the English corner flags and astonishing acceleration through the smallest of gaps, posed many problems at the start of the match. Poor finishing, however, cost France dearly, as witnessed by Cassayet's inability to capitalise on a perfect try-scoring opportunity when he intercepted a reckless pass from Young.

Towards half-time, the English backs began to show some form and Aslett proved to be an influential figure in the centre. He opened the scoring after Young had fed his backs from a scrummage near the French line, and moments later, when Young darted away from a maul, Devitt created the overlap for Aslett to score again. England thus led 6–0 at the break.

The second half revealed lack of basic skills in the players of both sides and there was only one passage of play worthy of mention. This occurred after 20 minutes when a passing movement involving Young, Francis, Devitt, Kittermaster and Periton yielded a try by Kittermaster which Francis converted.

ENGLAND		FRANCE	
T.E. Holliday	(Aspatria)	L. Destarac	(Tarbes)
Sir T.G. Devitt	(Cambridge U.)	J. Revillon	(R.C.F.)
A.R. Aslett	(Richmond/Army)	A. Behotéguy	(Cognac)
T.E.S. Francis	(Blackheath)	F. Borde	(Toulouse)
J.C. Gibbs	(Harlequins)	A. Jauréguy	(Stade Français)
H.J. Kittermaster	(Harlequins)	V. Graule	(Perpignan)
A.T. Young	(Blackheath)	R. Piteu	(T.O.E.C.)
C.K.T. Faithfull	(Harlequins)	A. Maury	(Toulouse)
J.S. Tucker	(Bristol)	C.A. Gonnet	(R.C.F.)
R.J. Hanvey	(Aspatria)	J. Marcet	(Albi)
*W.W. Wakefield	(Harlequins)	*A. Cassayet	(Narbonne)
L.W. Haslett	(Birkenhead Park)	A. Puig	(Perpignan)
H.G. Periton	(Waterloo)	A. Bioussa	(Toulouse)
†J.W.G. Webb	(Northampton)	E. Piquiral	(R.C.F.)
A.T. Voyce	(Gloucester)	J. Etcheberry	(Vienna)

Tries: Aslett (2), Kittermaster
Conversion: Francis

Referee: Mr A.E. Freethy (Wales)

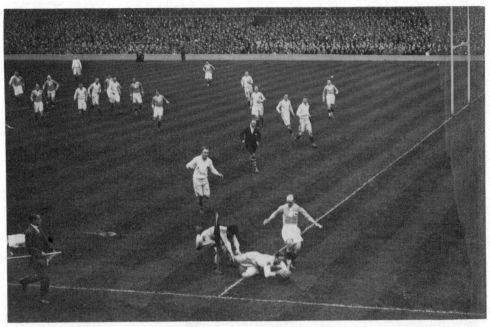

Aslett dives over for one of his two tries against France in 1926. Former England wing, G. C. Robinson, is the touch-judge.

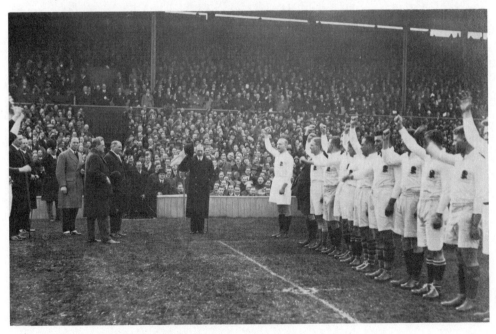

Wakefield, in his last match as captain of England, leads three cheers for HRH King George V before the 1926 Scotland match.

A. R. ASLETT,
RICHMOND, THE ARMY & ENGLAND.

C. K. T. FAITHFULL,
HARLEQUINS, THE ARMY & ENGLAND.

T. E. S. FRANCIS,
BLACKHEATH, CAMBRIDGE & ENGLAND.

R. HAMILTON-WICKES,
HARLEQUINS, CAMBRIDGE & ENGLAND.

R. HANVEY,
ASPATRIA, CUMBERLAND & ENGLAND.

W. W. WAKEFIELD,
CAMBRIDGE, HARLEQUINS & ENGLAND.

T. HOLLIDAY,
ASPATRIA, CUMBERLAND & ENGLAND.

H. J. KITTERMASTER,
OXFORD UNIVERSITY & ENGLAND.

W. E. TUCKER,
BLACKHEATH, CAMBRIDGE & ENGLAND.

A. T. VOYCE,
GLOUCESTER & ENGLAND.

A. T. YOUNG,
BLACKHEATH, CAMBRIDGE & ENGLAND.

Some of Wakefield's men.

ENGLAND v SCOTLAND 1926

Played at Twickenham, London, 20 March 1926
Scotland won by 2G, 1DG, 1T (17) to 3T (9)

The King, by now a regular visitor to Twickenham, and 50,000 of his subjects saw Scotland's first victory at the ground and their first on English soil since 1909.

Scotland were so completely outplayed by England's pack of veterans that it was a minor miracle that the visitors gained enough possession to score three tries. The weakness in the English side lay at full-back and on the wings: lack of speed and a calamitous failure to deal with the high ball allowed Scotland to score three similar tries. Ian Smith's pace in following up good kicks proved to be the crucial factor in Scotland's victory. Scotland's ability to take their chances, and stirring tackling in defence, were the qualities England lacked, for otherwise there was little to choose between the two sides behind the scrum.

A scrummage in front of the English posts provided Dykes with the golden chance to drop a goal and open the scoring. Then an adventurous run out of defence by Drysdale gave Smith his first chance to exploit England's fragile defence. From a kick ahead, the wing regathered the ball to put Waddell over and the fly-half converted to rub salt into the wound. An almost exact replica of this move, with Holliday failing to cover the kick, enabled Smith to score himself and Waddell's conversion stretched the lead to 14 points. The English pack had been playing well up to this point and their reward came when Voyce snapped up the ball near the Scottish line for a try.

Early in the second half, England showed further promise. Aslett sliced through the Scottish shield to force a line-out near the corner from which Sam Tucker scored. But English hopes of a remarkable recovery were dashed when Simmers angled a kick ahead into the path of Smith and the flying winger made Scotland's position safe at 17–6 with his second try.

Voyce, one of the English veterans, was brilliant in the remaining play, very nearly dropping a goal from half way, and Webb got a consolation try to complete the scoring.

ENGLAND		SCOTLAND	
T.E. Holliday	(Aspatria)	*D. Drysdale	(Heriot's F.P.)
R.H. Hamilton-Wickes	(Harlequins)	I.S. Smith	(Edinburgh U.)
A.R. Aslett	(Army/Richmond)	J.C. Dykes	(Glasgow Acads.)
T.E.S. Francis	(Blackheath)	W.M. Simmers	(Glasgow Acads.)
H.L.V. Day	(Leicester)	G.M. Boyd	(Glasgow H.S.F.P.)
H.J. Kittermaster	(Harlequins)	H. Waddell	(Glasgow Acads.)
A.T. Young	(Blackheath)	J.B. Nelson	(Glasgow Acads.)
C.K.T. Faithfull	(Harlequins)	J.M. Bannerman	(Glasgow H.S.F.P.)
J.S. Tucker	(Bristol)	D.S. Davies	(Hawick)
R. J. Hanvey	(Aspatria)	J.C.H. Ireland	(Glasgow H.S.F.P.)
*W.W. Wakefield	(Harlequins)	J. Graham	(Kelso)
E. Stanbury	(Plymouth Albion)	J.W. Scott	(Stewart's College F.P.)
H.G. Periton	(Waterloo)	D.J. MacMyn	(London Scottish)
J.W.G. Webb	(Northampton)	D.S. Kerr	(Heriot's F.P.)
A.T. Voyce	(Gloucester)	J.R. Paterson	(Birkenhead Park)

Tries: Tucker, Voyce, Webb

Tries: Smith (2), Waddell
Conversions: Waddell (2)
Dropped goal: Dykes

Referee: Mr W.H. Acton (Ireland)

ENGLAND v WALES 1927

Played at Twickenham, London, 15 January 1927
England won by 1G, 1GM, 1PG (11) to 1PG, 2T (9)

'There was precious little between the teams' commented *The Sunday News* as Wales again failed to lay the bogy which Twickenham seemed to put on the Principality. The match, as exciting as any played at the ground, was witnessed by 50,000 spectators.

The English backs began well, passing and running at speed to the Welsh 25 and, after seven minutes, Corbett, fielding the ball, claimed a mark and dropped a goal from the free kick. Wales, with Powell superb, rallied and a fierce rush, in which Dai Jones of Newport was prominent, caught Corbett at sixes-and-sevens in defence. Harding crossed at the corner after some slick passing by the Welsh three-quarters, but Male, who played an outstanding attacking game at full-back, failed to convert. Wales were then unlucky to lose Jones with a fractured shoulder bone, although an heroic performance from the rest of the pack kept the visitors in the hunt.

A splendid run from Andrews, crossing the field to score in the left corner, placed Wales in front, but England struck two telling blows before the interval. First, Phillips was guilty of a technical offence at a scrum and Stanbury, with a low kick from the touch-line, landed the penalty; then a dazzling run by Corbett, after Worton had fed Laird, resulted in a try at the Welsh posts which Stanbury converted.

England started the second half with a flourish, Laird slashing through the Welsh defence and handing on to Corbett who was brought down just short of the try-line. But an inhibited referee who refused to let the match flow spoilt the enjoyment of the crowd and there were fewer passing movements. One, instigated by Male, nearly brought a score for Wales; and ten minutes from no-side, the Cardiff back placed a goal when England were guilty of killing the ball. In the dying moments, a desperate ankle-tap by Sellar on Roberts prevented Wales from gaining their first win at Twickenham.

H.C.C. Laird, aged 18 years and 134 days on his debut, became England's youngest international.

ENGLAND

†K.A. Sellar	(R.N./U.S.)
R.H. Hamilton-Wickes	(Harlequins)
*L.J. Corbett	(Bristol)
H.M. Locke	(Birkenhead Park)
J.C. Gibbs	(Harlequins)
†H.C.C. Laird	(Harlequins)
J.R.B. Worton	(Harlequins)
†K.J. Stark	(O. Alleynians)
J.S. Tucker	(Bristol)
†T.J. Coulson	(Coventry)
R. Cove-Smith	(O.M.Ts.)
†J. Hanley	(Plymouth Albion)
E. Stanbury	(Plymouth Albion)
H.G. Periton	(Waterloo)
G.S. Conway	(Hartlepool Rovers)

Try: Corbett
Conversion: Stanbury
Goal from mark: Corbett
Penalty: Stanbury

WALES

B.O. Male	(Cardiff)
G.E. Andrews	(Newport)
*B.R. Turnbull	(Cardiff)
J. Roberts	(Cardiff/Cambridge U.)
W.R. Harding	(Swansea)
W.H. Lewis	(London Welsh/Cambridge U.)
W.C. Powell	(London Welsh)
D. Jones	(Newport)
J.H. John	(Swansea)
R.C. Herrera	(Newport)
S. Lawrence	(Bridgend)
H. Phillips	(Newport)
T.W. Lewis	(Cardiff)
W.G. Thomas	(Llanelli)
W.A. Williams	(Crumlin)

Tries: Andrews, Harding
Penalty: Male

Referee: Mr R.L. Scott (Scotland)

ENGLAND v IRELAND 1927

Played at Twickenham, London, 12 February 1927
England won by 1G, 1T (8) to 1PG, 1T (6)

A covering of straw prevented a heavy frost penetrating the playing surface and 45,000 enthusiastic spectators saw an exciting game on a very cold afternoon with England just managing to win a close match.

Both sides were forced to play below full strength: Wakefield was absent from the English pack with an injured knee and Clinch, Cagney and Bradley were missing from a rather light, but nevertheless lively Irish eight. In fact, England's pack was thoroughly outplayed in the loose, prompting D.R. Gent to write in the *Rugby Football Annual*: 'Much less store should be set upon the discovery of the exact position to which a forward is adapted in the scrummage. The selectors should look for fit men ... who can use their feet, keep their eyes open and go all out. The scrummage places come well behind these qualities in point of importance.'

The only score in the first half was a penalty goal to Ireland placed by Stephenson from near the half-way line, but several near misses were observed at both ends. Stephenson later sustained a knee injury and this upset the attacking balance of the Irish three-quarters. Davy, however, played a splendid game and made many openings for his wings. Ireland's closest approach to a first-half try was just before the pause when Corbett had a kick charged down by the Irish forwards near his own goal. The ball somehow skidded away from the Irishmen.

In the second half, a dreadful error by the usually reliable Crawford allowed Davies to send Laird (who had previously bungled a drop at goal) over for a try which Stanbury converted. A minute later, a dynamic attack by the Irish pack resulted in H. McVicker scoring from a rush despite brave defence by Young: Stephenson failed to convert but Ireland led deservedly by a point. Young retired to receive attention to a head wound but after his return, and with ten minutes to play, the English pack won a scrum ten yards from the Irish line and a swift blind-side feed from the scrum-half enabled Gibbs to race past Cussen and score the winning try.

Pat Davies was the first Sale player to represent England.

ENGLAND		IRELAND	
K.A. Sellar	(R.N./U.S.)	*W.E. Crawford	(Lansdowne)
H.C. Catcheside	(Percy Park)	D.J. Cussen	(St Mary's H.)
*L.J. Corbett	(Bristol)	G.V. Stephenson	(N.I.F.C.)
H.M. Locke	(Birkenhead Park)	F.S. Hewitt	(Instonians)
J.C. Gibbs	(Harlequins)	J.B. Ganly	(Monkstown)
H.C.C. Laird	(Harlequins)	E.O'D. Davy	(Lansdowne)
A.T. Young	(Blackheath)	M. Sugden	(Wanderers)
†D.E. Law	(Birkenhead Park)	C.J. Hanrahan	(Dolphin)
J.S. Tucker	(Bristol)	C.T. Payne	(N.I.F.C.)
K.J. Stark	(Old Alleynians)	J. McVicker	(Collegians)
E. Stanbury	(Plymouth Albion)	J.L. Farrell	(Bective Rangers)
R. Cove-Smith	(O.M.Ts.)	H. McVicker	(Richmond)
H.G. Periton	(Waterloo)	W.F. Browne	(Army)
†W.C.T. Eyres	(R.N./Richmond)	N.G. Ross	(Malone)
†P.H. Davies	(Sale)	T.O. Pike	(Lansdowne)

Tries: Gibbs, Laird   *Try:* H. McVicker
Conversion: Stanbury   *Penalty:* Stephenson

Referee: Mr T.H. Vile (Wales)

SCOTLAND v ENGLAND 1927
Played at Murrayfield, Edinburgh, 19 March 1927
Scotland won by 1G, 1DG, 4T (21) to 2G, 1PG (13)

Scotland's handsome victory before a gathering of 80,000 – a record for an international in Edinburgh – set a new record for points scored by a team in the Calcutta Cup match. The English forwards began feebly and a distinct advantage accrued to the Scotsmen in the tight and loose play. Macpherson, a late inclusion in the Scottish fifteen, gave the threequarter line an attacking edge which, combined with Ian Smith's lethal pace and Waddell's masterly control at half-back, proved enough to dash England's hopes.

Ian Smith made an early cut through the core of the English defence and, though tackled, managed to release the ball for Macpherson to score in the follow-up. Four minutes later, Corbett showed that he could match Macpherson's footballing qualities. Young sent the Bristol centre away and, dodging Dykes, Corbett ran on to feed Locke 15 yards from the Scottish line. Gibbs appeared on the overlap to race over unchallenged and Stanbury converted. Scotland redoubled their efforts and several flowing threequarter movements followed. Waddell, well-placed for a drop at goal, made a hash of his kick but Ian Smith claimed three points from this wayward effort by winning a chase to touch down. Gillies struck the post with his conversion but Scotland were soon to score again when Macpherson floated past the English cover to give Smith a second try. Stark kicked a penalty goal to keep the scores close at half-time.

England, facing the wind in the second half, received a blow when Catcheside was compelled to retire. Waddell dropped a goal and Dykes scored a splendid try which Gillies converted to give Scotland a handsome lead. Then, with 15 minutes to go, England retaliated with renewed pressure by the forwards. Wakefield himself led another raid into the Scottish 25 and Laird kicked a loose ball over the line to score. Stark converted and with England storming back onto the attack a sensational finish appeared possible until the calming influence of Macpherson and Waddell helped Scotland to regain some poise. Near the end Laird fumbled a pass, Macpherson gained possession and opened a passage for Scott, up in support, to score the final try.

SCOTLAND		ENGLAND	
*D. Drysdale	(Heriot's F.P.)	K.A. Sellar	(R.N./U.S.)
I.S. Smith	(Edinburgh U.)	H.C. Catcheside	(Percy Park)
G.P.S. Macpherson	(Edinburgh Acads.)	*L.J. Corbett	(Bristol)
J.C. Dykes	(Glasgow Acads.)	H.M. Locke	(Birkenhead Park)
W.M. Simmers	(Glasgow Acads.)	J.C. Gibbs	(Harlequins)
H. Waddell	(Glasgow Acads.)	H.C.C. Laird	(Harlequins)
J.B. Nelson	(Glasgow Acads.)	A.T. Young	(Blackheath)
J.M. Bannerman	(Glasgow H.S.F.P.)	E. Stanbury	(Plymouth Albion)
J.C.H. Ireland	(Glasgow H.S.F.P.)	J.S. Tucker	(Bristol)
J. Graham	(Kelso)	K.J. Stark	(Old Alleynians)
J.W. Scott	(Stewart's College F.P.)	†W.E. Pratten	(Blackheath)
A.C. Gillies	(Watsonians)	R. Cove-Smith	(O.M.Ts.)
D.J. MacMyn	(London Scottish)	J. Hanley	(Plymouth Albion)
J.R. Paterson	(Birkenhead Park)	W.W. Wakefield	(Harlequins)
D.S. Kerr	(Heriot's F.P.)	H.G. Periton	(Waterloo)

Tries: Smith (2), Dykes, Macpherson, Scott   *Tries:* Gibbs, Laird
Conversion: Gillies   *Conversions:* Stanbury, Stark
Dropped goal: Waddell   *Penalty:* Stark

Referee: Mr N.M. Purcell (Ireland)

FRANCE v ENGLAND 1927

Played at Stade Colombes, Paris, 2 April 1927
France won by 1T (3) to Nil

The seventeenth match between the countries saw France gain their first win – by one try to nil. The French thoroughly deserved victory for the English forwards lacked cohesion and only Tucker, in the front row, played with any fire. Even Wakefield, so often the inspiration to English sides struggling in Paris, had a disappointing game, though a fractured rib and an unpleasant tongue wound no doubt reduced his appetite for the game.

Both sides were forced to make changes from the original selections. Cassayet, the French equivalent of Wakefield, was unable to take his place through illness, and the world of Rugby learnt of his untimely death, a month later, with great sadness. He had often led France on the field, and held the French cap record for more than 25 years.

France began the match determined to avenge the long string of defeats suffered at English hands. In the eleventh minute, Behoteguy thundered through a flat English defence with a glorious run to the English posts. Vellat collected the scoring pass but Gonnet failed to kick the goal. When England restarted, their team moved into the French half for the first time in the match, so intense had been the early French pressure.

Stark was England's best player in the loose and he just failed to gather a bouncing ball on the stroke of half-time when a try seemed likely. There was a greater sense of urgency about the English forward play towards the end of the game, but misguided kicking and ineffective running by a mediocre English back division failed to turn this new-found enthusiasm to advantage. The nearest either side came to scoring was through penalty goals, but attempts by Gonnet, for France, and Stark and Hanley for England, met with no success and Vellat's try sealed the game. No one could begrudge France their victory.

FRANCE		**ENGLAND**	
L. Destarac	(Quillan)	†J.N.S. Wallens	(Waterloo)
E. Vellat	(Grenoble)	†W. Alexander	(Northern)
A. Behotéguy	(Cognac)	*L.J. Corbett	(Bristol)
G. Gérald	(R.C.F.)	†R.A. Buckingham	(Leicester)
*A. Jauréguy	(Stade Français)	J.C. Gibbs	(Harlequins)
A. Verger	(Stade Français)	†C.C. Bishop	(Blackheath)
C. Dupont	(Stade Bordelais)	A.T. Young	(Blackheath)
A. Loury	(R.C.F.)	K.J. Stark	(Old Alleynians)
C.A. Gonnet	(R.C.F.)	J.S. Tucker	(Bristol)
J. Morère	(Toulouse)	E. Stanbury	(Plymouth Albion)
J. Galia	(Quillan)	R. Cove-Smith	(O.M.Ts.)
R. Bousquet	(Albi)	W.E. Pratten	(Blackheath)
E. Ribère	(Quillan)	H.G. Periton	(Waterloo)
E. Piquiral	(Lyon)	W.W. Wakefield	(Harlequins)
A. Cazenave	(Pau)	J. Hanley	(Plymouth Albion)

Try: Vellat

Referee: Mr A.E. Freethy (Wales)

ENGLAND v NEW SOUTH WALES 1928
Played at Twickenham, London, 7 January 1928
England won by 3G, 1T (18) to 1G, 2T (11)

England selected a young back division which was prepared to play open Rugby and the 40,000 spectators saw a fast, exciting game. The Waratahs, as the tourists were named, played in blue jerseys and lived up to their reputation as devotees of flowing football, so the crowd enjoyed a rare treat.

There were four tries before the interval. England began tentatively and N.S.W. nearly scored after ten minutes when Towers pierced a flat defence but chose to kick instead of running to the line. Richardson saved with a relieving kick. Then England broke away and a move involving Young, Aarvold and Taylor led to a cross-kick by Laird. In the follow-up, Tucker was at hand to score (though some reports record that the hooker kicked through for Coulson to claim a score). Richardson converted but the Australians equalised when a combined attack by several of their backs culminated in a try by Towers which Lawton goaled. Laird failed with a drop at goal before Devitt made a useful run, linked with Aarvold, who jinked past an opponent, and Taylor scored. More good work by the English backs resulted in a try for Laird and Richardson's accurate place kicking enabled England to change ends with a 15–5 lead.

Play was entertaining in the second half but no scoring occurred for 25 minutes. Then, the English forwards swarmed around the ball in a rush near the Waratahs' line and Periton touched down. In the closing stages, weak tackling by a brittle English defence permitted Ford to dash over on the right for two tries, but Young and his back row bottled up the main threat from the Waratahs – their halves – and the score at no-side was 18–11 to England.

T.M. Lawson's brother had been capped for England in 1925.

Queensland had withdrawn from the Australian Rugby Union in the 1920s, leaving New South Wales as the only State in which the game was played. Consequently, the R.F.U. awarded caps to the Englishmen and statisticians have come to regard this match as a full international.

ENGLAND		NEW SOUTH WALES	
K.A. Sellar	(U.S./R.N.)	A.W. Ross	(Sydney U.)
†W.J. Taylor	(Blackheath)	E.E. Ford	(Glebe-Balmain)
†C.D. Aarvold	(Cambridge U.)	C.H.T. Towers	(Randwick)
†J.V. Richardson	(Birkenhead Park)	S.C. King	(Western Suburbs)
Sir T.G. Devitt	(Blackheath)	*A.C. Wallace	(Glebe-Balmain)
H.C.C. Laird	(Harlequins)	T. Lawton	(Western Suburbs)
A.T. Young	(Blackheath)	S.J. Malcolm	(Newcastle)
E. Stanbury	(Plymouth Albion)	H.F. Woods	(Y.M.C.A.)
J.S. Tucker	(Bristol)	E.N. Greatorex	(Y.M.C.A.)
*R. Cove-Smith	(O.M.Ts.)	B. Judd	(Randwick)
†D. Turquand-Young	(Richmond)	G.P. Storey	(Western Suburbs)
K.J. Stark	(Old Alleynians)	J.A. Ford	(Glebe-Balmain)
†T.M. Lawson	(Workington)	J.G. Blackwood	(Eastern Suburbs)
T.J. Coulson	(Coventry)	A.N. Finlay	(Sydney U.)
H.G. Periton	(Waterloo)	J.W. Breckenridge	(Glebe-Balmain)

Tries: Laird, Periton, Taylor, Tucker
Conversions: Richardson (3)

Tries: Ford (2), Towers
Conversion: Lawton

Referee: Mr T.H. Vile (Wales)

WALES v ENGLAND 1928

Played at St Helen's, Swansea, 21 January 1928
England won by 2G (10) to 1G, 1T (8)

The press were unanimous: Wales held such a strong advantage in the forward play – they had 32 clean heels to England's 12 – that they should have easily won. However, wretched play by a pedestrian Welsh three-quarter line, combined with heroic defence by Sellar and the English centres, explained a victory England did not deserve.

In driving rain, England made first use of the wind. After eight minutes, Young opened up from a scrum on half-way and Laird and Aarvold quickly transferred the ball to Taylor. Harding, his opponent, slipped on the greasy turf and allowed the wing to waltz past him and up to Rees. Taylor rounded the cover with ease to score at the posts. Richardson converted.

For ten minutes Wales occupied English territory and once crossed the English line, only to be penalised for off-side. Then, an exciting break from Young after a scrum in his own 25 lifted the siege and before the leaden-footed Welsh backs had realised the danger, Aarvold had sent Taylor flying up the field and past Turnbull for the impish Laird to score beneath the goal. Richardson again converted, taking England to a flattering ten-points lead. Soon afterwards the Welsh forwards were rewarded for their industry when, from a fierce rush, Bartlett scrambled over in the right corner for an unconverted try.

Wave after wave of Welsh forward rushes threatened to swamp England in the second half. Sellar, so cool, so calm, kept them out with a series of brave tackles and dives on loose balls, but Wales's superiority in the loose and tight play prevailed. A. John's propensity to take a few steps before delivering the ball to his backs from the scrummage often permitted the English loose forwards to get among the Welsh backs and destroy likely Welsh attacks at their source. Nevertheless, Wales did manage another score. After 13 minutes Turnbull was held up near the English goal after a bout of passing and when the ball was worked clear D. John went over, wide-out on the right. With a superb kick from touch, Ivor Jones converted. Thereafter, the story was one of constant Welsh pressure absorbed by desperate English defence.

WALES		ENGLAND	
T.E. Rees	(London Welsh)	K.A. Sellar	(R.N./U.S.)
J.D. Bartlett	(London Welsh)	W.J. Taylor	(Blackheath)
B.R. Turnbull	(Cardiff)	C.D. Aarvold	(Cambridge U.)
J. Roberts	(Cambridge U.)	J.V. Richardson	(Birkenhead Park)
*W.R. Harding	(Cambridge U.)	Sir T.G. Devitt	(Blackheath)
D.E. John	(Llanelli)	H.C.C. Laird	(Harlequins)
A. John	(Llanelli)	A. T. Young	(Blackheath)
F.A. Bowdler	(Cross Keys)	E. Stanbury	(Plymouth Albion)
C. Pritchard	(Pontypool)	J.S. Tucker	(Bristol)
H. Phillips	(Newport)	*R. Cove-Smith	(O.M.Ts.)
E.M. Jenkins	(Aberavon)	D. Turquand-Young	(Richmond)
A. Skym	(Llanelli)	K.J. Stark	(Old Alleynians)
Y. Jones	(Llanelli)	T.M. Lawson	(Workington)
T. Hollingdale	(Neath)	T.J. Coulson	(Coventry)
I. Jones	(Llanelli)	J. Hanley	(Plymouth Albion)

Tries: Bartlett, D.E. John   *Tries:* Laird, Taylor
Conversion: I. Jones   *Conversions:* Richardson (2)

Referee: Mr R.W. Harland (Ireland)

IRELAND v ENGLAND 1928
Played at Lansdowne Road, Dublin, 11 February 1928
England won by 1DG, 1T (7) to 2T (6)

A howling wind and teeming rain had turned the ground into a morass and the wind prevailed throughout the match. In such atrocious conditions it was not surprising therefore to see England invest in a policy of containment when facing the wind in the first half. The bonus when this policy matured at the interval was that Ireland had rarely managed to penetrate the hard-tackling English defence and the English forwards had gained a distinct advantage up-front. However, Ireland had fashioned a try – albeit fortuitously – in the seventeenth minute when Arigho had charged down a kick and scored in the left corner.

So England approached the second half with well-placed confidence. But this was severely jolted after 15 minutes when Sugden, the scrum-half, produced one of his 'specials' – a blind-side break – from a set scrummage on the English line and scored in the left corner of the ground.

With defeat suddenly staring England in the face, the men in white began to exert more pressure on their opponents. From a controlled rush by the English forwards, Richardson gathered the ball to score a try near the posts three minutes later. Unaccountably, he failed to convert his try but made amends in the dying moments of the game by casually dropping a goal and thus maintained his remarkable record of points scoring.

Ireland had played a restrained, constructive forward game during the second half and it looked certain that England's Championship progress would be halted. Near the end the English pack drew on its enormous resource of stamina and both Hanley and Tucker went close to scoring. Then, with time running out, Prentice won the ball at a line-out and Young fed his backs so smartly that Richardson had sufficient time and space to drop that crucial goal.

IRELAND		ENGLAND	
J.W. Stewart	(Queen's U.)	K.A. Sellar	(R.N./U.S.)
H.W.V. Stephenson	(U.S.)	W.J. Taylor	(Blackheath)
J.B. Ganly	(Monkstown)	C.D. Aarvold	(Cambridge U.)
*G.V. Stephenson	(N.I.F.C.)	J.V. Richardson	(Birkenhead Park)
J.E. Arigho	(Lansdowne)	†G.V. Palmer	(Richmond)
E.O'D. Davy	(Lansdowne)	H.C.C. Laird	(Harlequins)
M. Sugden	(Wanderers)	A.T. Young	(Blackheath)
C.J. Hanrahan	(Dolphin)	E. Stanbury	(Plymouth Albion)
C.T. Payne	(N.I.F.C.)	J.S. Tucker	(Bristol)
T.O. Pike	(Lansdowne)	†R.H.W. Sparks	(Plymouth Albion)
J.L. Farrell	(Bective Rangers)	K.J. Stark	(Old Alleynians)
S.J. Cagney	(London Irish)	*R. Cove-Smith	(O.M.Ts.)
W.F. Browne	(Army)	J. Hanley	(Plymouth Albion)
G.R. Beamish	(R.A.F./Leicester)	†F.D. Prentice	(Leicester)
J.D. Clinch	(Wanderers)	H.G. Periton	(Waterloo)

Tries: Arigho, Sugden

Try: Richardson
Dropped goal: Richardson

Referee: Mr A.E. Freethy (Wales)

ENGLAND v FRANCE 1928

Played at Twickenham, London, 25 February 1928
England won by 3G, 1T (18) to 1G, 1T (8)

England took another step forward on their quest for the Grand Slam with a win over France in an entertaining game. The sun shone after a long bleak fortnight of rain had spoiled many sporting fixtures in the British Isles; but, alas, the back play did not match the occasion until very late in the match and the most promising passages of play were generally confined to the forwards.

France were forced to field a new scrum-half due to an injury to the well-known Dupont and the French backs were unable to play with any cohesion in attack. The English backs were sadly lacking in initiative on this occasion, too, and only Palmer, on the wing, enhanced his reputation.

Galia opened the scoring with a try after good work by Ribère, before the first English try by Palmer was registered in spectacular fashion. Sensing his path to the corner covered by the defence, the English wing veered in towards his centre and took a short pass – less than a foot in length – to speed over. The reliable Richardson added the goal and later converted a try by Periton to give the home side a seven-points lead at the interval.

France began the second half in earnest and a period of pressure lasting some 25 minutes compelled England to defend resolutely. Sellar, the England full-back, was seen at his best, and his fine tackling and kicking made up for minor errors handling the rolling ball. The most attractive Rugby came in the closing quarter of the match. A. Behotéguy was caught by the English forwards on his own 25 and from the mêlée Periton raced away to score. Moments later, Young engaged the French defence with a shrewd run, linked with Richardson and a perfect pass from the centre allowed Palmer to score again. The conversion put England into an unassailable lead but the French, throwing caution to the wind, rallied and a scything run by A. Behotéguy gave Jauréguy a clear run to the line for a try which Verger converted.

ENGLAND		FRANCE	
K.A. Sellar	(U.S./R.N.)	L. Pellissier	(R.C.F.)
W.J. Taylor	(Blackheath)	J. Jardel	(Stade Bordelais)
C.D. Aarvold	(Cambridge U.)	H. Behotéguy	(Cognac)
J.V. Richardson	(Birkenhead Park)	A. Behotéguy	(Cognac)
G.V. Palmer	(Richmond)	*A. Jauréguy	(Stade Français)
H.C.C. Laird	(Harlequins)	A. Verger	(Stade Français)
A.T. Young	(Blackheath)	L. Serin	(Béziers)
E. Stanbury	(Plymouth Albion)	J. Hauc	(Toulon)
J.S. Tucker	(Bristol)	F. Camicas	(Tarbes)
R.H.W. Sparks	(Plymouth Albion)	J. Sayrou	(Perpignan)
K.J. Stark	(Old Alleynians)	J. Galia	(Quillan)
*R. Cove-Smith	(O.M.Ts.)	A. Camel	(Toulouse)
J. Hanley	(Plymouth Albion)	E. Ribère	(Quillan)
F.D. Prentice	(Leicester)	E. Piquiral	(Lyon)
H.G. Periton	(Waterloo)	A. Bioussa	(Toulouse)

Tries: Palmer (2), Periton (2) *Tries:* Galia, Jauréguy
Conversions: Richardson (3) *Conversion:* Verger

Referee: Mr A.E. Freethy (Wales)

A Frenchman being tackled during England's 18-8 win over France in 1928.
Cove-Smith is extreme left; Stanbury is the Englishman with the scrum-cap; and
F. D. Prentice is on the far right.

Cove-Smith's Grand Slam winning side just before the 1928 Scotland match:
back H. G. Periton, C. D. Aarvold, K. J. Stark, J. Hanley, F. D. Prentice,
G. V. Palmer, Mr T. H. Vile; *middle* W. J. Taylor, J. V. Richardson, E. Stanbury,
R. Cove-Smith (captain), J. S. Tucker, T. W. Brown, R. H. W. Sparks;
front H. C. C. Laird, A. T. Young.

ENGLAND v SCOTLAND 1928

Played at Twickenham, London, 17 March 1928
England won by 2T (6) to Nil

To steal Milton's words, England could be said to have used their invincible might to quell the mighty men of Scotland. For their win meant that England had won the Grand Slam and defeated a visiting side in the same season for the only time in their Rugby history.

Twickenham was packed and many spectators spilled over the enclosure boards onto the straw surrounding the by-lines. The King, too, was present to see England's forwards dominate the match and prevent the dangerous Scottish halves running the ball to their adventurous three-quarters.

Scotland began strongly so England's opening score in the twelfth minute came as a surprise. From a scrum within the Scottish half, Young fed Taylor on the narrow side and the wing created some space by slipping past his opposite number. The English back row closely supported the break and Periton and Hanley forced play to the Scottish line where the ball went loose. Laird was at hand, however, to scoop it up and sweep over the line for a corner try.

The second half became a forward tussle with few of the backs accomplishing much in attack. Only Young, the English scrum-half, threatened to pinch the limelight from the forwards. Nelson and Brown, the Scottish half-backs, toiled in vain behind a beaten pack, but on the few occasions when Scotland did win the ball, Macpherson and Simmers looked more enterprising than the English backs and one of Macpherson's typical darting runs should have produced a score for Kelly on the left.

As it was, 30 minutes of second-half stalemate passed before Young fashioned England's second and decisive score. From a scrum in the middle of the field, 30 yards from the Scottish goal, the English forwards heeled cleanly and Young ducked beneath his opponent to pierce a flat defence and race up to Drysdale. Hanley, backing up on the right, took a pass to complete the model try. Richardson had been injured earlier and so Prentice attempted the conversion: he missed!

ENGLAND		SCOTLAND	
†T.W. Brown	(Bristol)	*D. Drysdale	(London Scottish)
W.J. Taylor	(Blackheath)	J. Goodfellow	(Langholm)
C.D. Aarvold	(Cambridge U.)	G.P.S. Macpherson	(Edinburgh Acads.)
J.V. Richardson	(Birkenhead Park)	W.M. Simmers	(Glasgow Acads.)
G.V. Palmer	(Richmond)	R.F. Kelly	(Watsonians)
H.C.C. Laird	(Harlequins)	A.H. Brown	(Heriot's F.P.)
A.T. Young	(Blackheath)	J.B. Nelson	(Glasgow Acads.)
R.H.W. Sparks	(Plymouth Albion)	J.M. Bannerman	(Oxford U.)
J.S. Tucker	(Bristol)	W.G. Ferguson	(Royal H.S.F.P.)
E. Stanbury	(Plymouth Albion)	J. Graham	(Kelso)
K.J. Stark	(Old Alleynians)	D.S. Kerr	(Heriot's F.P.)
*R. Cove-Smith	(O.M.Ts.)	J.R. Paterson	(Birkenhead Park)
J. Hanley	(Plymouth Albion)	W.N. Roughead	(London Scottish)
F.D. Prentice	(Leicester)	J.W. Scott	(Stewart's College F.P.)
H.G. Periton	(Waterloo)	L.M. Stuart	(Glasgow H.S.F.P.)

Tries: Hanley, Laird

Referee: Mr T.H. Vile (Wales)

191

ENGLAND v WALES 1929
Played at Twickenham, London, 19 January 1929
England won by 1G, 1T (8) to 1T (3)

For a number of seasons during the 1920s Welsh backs suffered behind slow-heeling forwards who were selected for size rather than mobility and tactical flair. On this occasion, however, a new Welsh pack played with improved method and, according to *The Times*, 'suggested that the steam-roller idea was dying'.

Conditions were good: a hard frost presented the players with a firm playing surface and there was little wind when Wales kicked off into a bright sun. The Welsh forwards took the larger share of line-out possession, but Tucker won more of the set-scrummages. The English heeling was impressive for its speed and accuracy, and Whitley proved an admirable link between forwards and backs.

After Ivor Jones and Foulds had gone near to kicking penalty points, England demonstrated their edge at three-quarter when, from a quick strike, Laird, moving left, fed Aarvold who careered down the touch-line. The Welsh backs were stretched to deal with Aarvold, and Wilkinson, up in support, collected a pass to score in the thirtieth minute.

Early in the second half another quick heel offered Laird the chance to cut through from half-way and Wilkinson beat a spreadeagled defence to score at the posts. Wilson converted but only five minutes later Powell fed Morley on the left of a scrum on the English 25 and the Welsh wing 'dodged clean through' to touch down with scarcely a finger laid upon him. Ivor Jones failed to convert.

Wales, with their tails high, now scented victory and made every effort to score. The backs showed their finest form in these later stages of the match and only last-ditch tackling by a tight English defence checked the endeavours of the Welshmen. Furthermore, Pritchard missed with an easy penalty and Powell had a dropped goal disallowed in the last minute.

Harry Wilkinson's father had been capped by England against the New Zealand Native team of 1889, and Swayne's brother was in the England XV against Wales in 1931.

ENGLAND		WALES	
T.W. Brown	(Bristol)	J. Bassett	(Penarth)
†R.W. Smeddle	(Cambridge U.)	G. Davies	(Cardiff)
C.D. Aarvold	(Cambridge U.)	J. Roberts	(Cardiff)
†G.M. Sladen	(U.S./R.N.)	W.G. Morgan	(Swansea)
†G.S. Wilson	(Tyldesley)	J.C. Morley	(Newport)
H.C.C. Laird	(Harlequins)	W. Roberts	(Cardiff)
†H. Whitley	(Northern)	W.C. Powell	(London Welsh)
E. Stanbury	(Plymouth Albion)	D. R. Jenkins	(Swansea)
J.S. Tucker	(Bristol)	C. Pritchard	(Pontypool)
†R.T. Foulds	(Waterloo)	F.A. Bowdler	(Cross Keys)
R.H.W. Sparks	(Plymouth Albion)	T. Arthur	(Neath)
*R. Cove-Smith	(K.C.H.)	H. Jones	(Neath)
†H. Wilkinson	(Halifax)	R. Jones	(London Welsh)
†J.W.R. Swayne	(Bridgwater Albion)	W.G. Thomas	(Swansea)
H.G. Periton	(Waterloo)	*I. Jones	(Llanelli)

Tries: Wilkinson (2)   *Try:* Morley
Conversion: Wilson

Referee: Mr R.W. Harland (Ireland)

ENGLAND v IRELAND 1929

Played at Twickenham, 9 February 1929
Ireland won by 2T (6) to 1G (5)

A study of the results of matches played between England and Ireland during the late 1920s and early 1930s shows a remarkable sequence of close scoring. This match, with Ireland gaining their first win at Twickenham, was no exception and the release of emotions at the end is recalled by old-timers to this day.

Ireland's forwards made a storming start, driving play deep into England's territory. Sellar, England's full-back in the 1928 Grand Slam side, was no longer available due to naval service and Brown, his successor, had not inspired confidence in the match with Wales a few weeks earlier. Poor Brown now received a further dent to his standing when, after only three minutes, he failed to gather the ball on his own line and Davy was there to score for Ireland. Despite their furious dashes, the Irish forwards were unable to present their backs with further scoring opportunities in the rest of the first half.

Play resumed with George Stephenson receiving attention for a rib injury. England were fast to exploit Ireland's temporary weakness and a break by Sladen created the space for Smeddle to run in behind the goal. Wilson converted. Stephenson returned and immediately there was a rejuvenation in the Irish side. Browne, a new hooker, gave a good account of himself against his famous opponent, Sam Tucker, and Murray, with some boneshaking tackling, emphatically locked the Irish defence. At length, Ireland attacked and, from a scrum near the English line, Sugden opted for a blind-side run and sold a dummy to score in the corner.

With the tension increasing towards the end of the match, there was high drama when Young found a gap in the Irish defence, darted through and linked with Smeddle. Stephenson miraculously covered the danger by tackling Smeddle just at the instant when he was about to send Wilkinson over. As a result, the wing's pass was misjudged and the Halifax forward knocked forward. Moments later the final whistle was blown and there followed extraordinary scenes as Irish followers threw seat cushions high into the air.

ENGLAND		IRELAND	
T.W. Brown	(Bristol)	J.W. Stewart	(Preston Grasshoppers)
R.W. Smeddle	(Cambridge U.)	R.M. Byers	(N.I.F.C.)
C.D. Aarvold	(Cambridge U.)	P.F. Murray	(Wanderers)
G.M. Sladen	(U.S./R.N.)	*G.V. Stephenson	(N.I.F.C.)
G.S. Wilson	(Tyldesley)	J.E. Arigho	(Lansdowne)
H.C.C. Laird	(Harlequins)	E.O'D. Davy	(Lansdowne)
A.T. Young	(Blackheath)	M. Sugden	(Wanderers)
E. Stanbury	(Plymouth Albion)	C.J. Hanrahan	(Dolphin)
J.S. Tucker	(Bristol)	H.C. Browne	(U.S./R.N.)
R.H.W. Sparks	(Plymouth Albion)	S.J. Cagney	(London Irish)
D. Turquand-Young	(Richmond)	J.L. Farrell	(Bective Rangers)
*R. Cove-Smith	(K.C.H.)	M.J. Dunne	(Lansdowne)
H. Wilkinson	(Halifax)	C.T. Payne	(N.I.F.C.)
R.T. Foulds	(Waterloo)	G.R. Beamish	(R.A.F.)
H.G. Periton	(Waterloo)	J.D. Clinch	(Wanderers)

Try: Smeddle
Conversion: Wilson

Tries: Davy, Sugden

Referee: Mr A.E. Freethy (Wales)

SCOTLAND v ENGLAND 1929
Played at Murrayfield, Edinburgh, 16 March 1929
Scotland won by 4T (12) to 2T (6)

On a cold, grey day more than 80,000 spectators saw Scotland overtake England in the last 15 minutes of the match to win the Championship. England made several changes from the side defeated by Ireland and a further change was enforced when Wilson failed to pass a late fitness test. Aslett was his replacement.

England took the lead after seven minutes when a quick heel from a scrummage gave Novis the freedom to explore a gap in the Scottish defence. He ended a fine dash with a swerve past Aitchison and a try in the corner. Harris could not convert. As the half progressed the handling of the Scottish backs improved. Macpherson began to assert himself in midfield and frequently made openings for Smith on the wing. Only a timely push by Brown prevented Smith from scoring on one occasion and England were lucky to reach half-time holding their narrow lead.

Scotland equalised after 15 minutes in the second half. Richards fed a scrum on his own line when his forwards were clearly off-balance and the ball emerged before the scrum had straightened. Nelson dived on the ball to claim a try but four minutes later an aggressive hand-off and resolute run by Aslett breached the Scottish defence. Although tackled, Aslett managed to kick ahead and Meikle touched down for a try.

Brown equalised with a try on the left for Scotland soon after and in the final 15 minutes, with the Scottish forwards inspired by the storming play of their veteran, Bannerman, and controlling the set-pieces, Ian Smith ran through the tackles of the English full-back to score two winning tries.

Meikle's feat of scoring a try on his debut for England was repeated by his brother in 1934.

SCOTLAND		ENGLAND	
T.G. Aitchison	(Gala)	T.W. Brown	(Bristol)
I.S. Smith	(Edinburgh U.)	R.W. Smeddle	(Cambridge U.)
G.P.S. Macpherson	(Edinburgh Acads.)	A.R. Aslett	(Richmond)
W.M. Simmers	(Glasgow Acads.)	G.M. Sladen	(U.S./R.N.)
C.H.C. Brown	(Dunfermline)	†A.L. Novis	(The Army)
H.D. Greenlees	(Leicester)	†S.S.C. Meikle	(Waterloo)
J.B. Nelson	(Glasgow Acads.)	†E.E. Richards	(Plymouth Albion)
R.T. Smith	(Kelso)	E. Stanbury	(Plymouth Albion)
H.S. Mackintosh	(Glasgow U.)	R.H.W. Sparks	(Plymouth Albion)
J.W. Allan	(Melrose)	J.W.G. Webb	(Northampton)
J.W. Scott	(Bradford)	†T.W. Harris	(Northampton)
*J.M. Bannerman	(Oxford U.)	†H. Rew	(The Army)
J.R. Paterson	(Birkenhead Park)	H. Wilkinson	(Halifax)
K.M. Wright	(London Scottish)	D. Turquand-Young	(Richmond)
W.B. Welsh	(Hawick)	*H.G. Periton	(Waterloo)

Tries: I.S. Smith (2), Brown, Nelson   *Tries:* Meikle, Novis

Referee: Dr J.R. Wheeler (Ireland)

FRANCE v ENGLAND 1929

Played at Stade Colombes, Paris, 1 April 1929
England won by 2G, 2T (16) to 2T (6)

England took a largely experimental fifteen to Paris to fight out the Wooden Spoon decider with France. Sparks was obliged to withdraw from the English side following an ankle injury sustained in a motorcycle accident, but with Tucker substituting at hooker there was no lack of experience for England in the middle of the front row, although five new caps were introduced elsewhere.

France scored first quite early on when Ribère robbed the ball after an English heel near the goal-line and dived over for a try. But the lead was soon lost when Aarvold, making a comeback on the wing, found an opening for Aslett to burst through. An excellent tackle from behind ended his run but Stanbury dribbled the loose ball to the French line where Gummer pounced for a try. Aslett played an outstanding game and his defensive qualities confined Behotéguy, his opposite number, to such an extent that the famous Frenchman could barely raise a trot in attack. Nevertheless, the French wings often had the ball and only unyielding defence by the English backs prevented any further scoring for a long period. Just before half-time, Novis and Reeve escaped wretched tackles to carry play into the French 25 where the latter was grassed by Jauréguy. Gaining the ball from the ensuing maul, Aslett sent Aarvold in for a try which Stanbury converted.

England approached the second half with confidence and Aslett and Reeve made early runs into French ground. After 20 minutes Aarvold evaded Jauréguy to score and again Stanbury converted to place England in the clear, ten points ahead. France kept the match alive, however, when Serin exploited England's blind-side weaknesses to fashion a try for Houdet.

Towards the end of the match Turquand-Young was forced to retire with an injury. England scored the final try after his departure when Periton deflected a kick by Magnol and charged 30 yards for the touch-down.

FRANCE		ENGLAND	
L. Magnol	(Toulouse)	T.W. Brown	(Bristol)
*A. Jauréguy	(Stade Français)	C.D. Aarvold	(Headingley)
A. Behotéguy	(Cognac)	A.R. Aslett	(The Army/Richmond)
G. Gérald	(R.C.F.)	A.L. Novis	(The Army)
R. Houdet	(Stade Français)	†J.S.R. Reeve	(Harlequins)
R. Graciet	(Stade Bordelais)	†R.S. Spong	(Old Millhillians)
L. Serin	(Béziers)	E.E. Richards	(Plymouth Albion)
J. Sayrou	(Perpignan)	E. Stanbury	(Plymouth Albion)
F. Camicas	(Tarbes)	J.S. Tucker	(Bristol)
R. Bousquet	(Albi)	H. Rew	(Blackheath/The Army)
A. Camel	(Toulouse)	†S.A. Martindale	(Kendal)
J. Galia	(Quillan)	D. Turquand-Young	(Richmond)
A. Bioussa	(Toulouse)	*H.G. Periton	(Waterloo)
M. Camel	(Toulouse)	†C.H.A. Gummer	(Plymouth Albion)
E. Ribère	(Quillan)	†E. Coley	(Northampton)

Tries: Houdet, Ribère

Tries: Aarvold (2), Gummer, Periton
Conversions: Stanbury (2)

Referee: Mr A.E. Freethy (Wales)

WALES v ENGLAND 1930
Played at Cardiff Arms Park, 18 January 1930
England won by 1G, 1PG, 1T (11) to 1T (3)

Sam Tucker made a frantic dash by aeroplane across the Bristol Channel on the morning of the match to pack down in the English front row as a late replacement. During the game the English forwards swarmed around the ball in the loose play and scrummaged efficiently in the tight, while the back row earned acclaim from the critics for their speed in disrupting the Welsh backs.

There was a hectic start to the match with play oscillating from goal to goal until Reeve opened the scoring after five minutes, following a swerving run. Black failed to convert but the game already promised victory for England. Roberts, the diminutive Welsh scrum-half, was toiling behind a languid pack and the Welsh backs were unable to spring the shackles cast on them by an eager pair of English centres and a vigorous back row.

The second half began with another English try. As a scrummage unravelled, Reeve popped up in the centre to take a pass from Sobey. Like an express train the Harlequin sped to the Welsh posts and Black converted his try into an eight-points lead. Wales fought back almost immediately. Morley instigated an attack which Bowcott and Williams supported to allow Jones-Davies to nip past an extended defence for a try at the left corner. Parker did not convert, but 30 minutes remained for Wales to get two winning scores, and the huge crowd (the gates had been locked half an hour prior to kick-off) cheered on the Welsh forwards who had begun to play with new-found vigour. Jones-Davies and Hickman made runs after the Welsh halves decided to open up the game, but sure tackling by Askew, the last line of defence, protected England's lead.

Towards the end, Novis, Periton and W.E. Tucker carried an attack to the Welsh 25 where another try nearly resulted. In the last minute Wales were penalised and Black kicked three points to end the scoring.

Malir and Bateson were the first England caps from Otley.

WALES		ENGLAND	
J. Bassett	(Penarth)	†J. G. Askew	(Cambridge U.)
J.C. Morley	(Newport)	A.L. Novis	(Blackheath)
*H.M. Bowcott	(Cardiff)	†F.W.S. Malir	(Otley)
T.E. Jones-Davies	(London Welsh)	†M. Robson	(Oxford U.)
A. Hickman	(Neath)	J.S.R. Reeve	(Harlequins)
F.L. Williams	(Cardiff)	R.S. Spong	(Old Millhillians)
D.E.A. Roberts	(London Welsh)	†W.H. Sobey	(Old Millhillians)
T. Arthur	(Neath)	†D.A. Kendrew	(Woodford)
F.A. Bowdler	(Cross Keys)	J.S. Tucker	(Bristol)
A. Skym	(Cardiff)	†A.H. Bateson	(Otley)
D. Parker	(Swansea)	†B.H. Black	(Oxford U.)
E.M. Jenkins	(Aberavon)	†J.W. Forrest	(U.S./R.N.)
W.T. Thomas	(Abertillery)	W.E. Tucker	(Blackheath)
T. Hollingdale	(Neath)	†P.D. Howard	(O. Millhillians/Oxford U.)
I. Jones	(Llanelli)	*H.G. Periton	(Waterloo)

Try: Jones-Davies

Tries: Reeve (2)
Conversion: Black
Penalty: Black

Referee: Mr R. W. Jeffares (Ireland)

IRELAND v ENGLAND 1930
Played at Lansdowne Road, Dublin, 8 February 1930
Ireland won by 1DG (4) to 1T (3)

Dropped goals had helped France and Scotland to narrow victories in the few weeks before this match; now Ireland, through Paul Murray, jumped on the bandwagon and outpointed England by a dropped goal to a try.

Sobey withdrew from the English fifteen with a heavy cold and his place was taken by Key, who had a splendid match. In the first half there were several sharp breaks by the new English scrum-half and his back row, but a lack of adequate finishing and poor backing-up by the rest of the side deprived England of an early lead. Only after labouring for 30 minutes did the English manage to score. Reeve glided down the left wing drawing the Irish backs towards him. Then the ball was swiftly ferried to the other flank and Novis, with a step inwards, took advantage of an elongated defence to score a try which Black, from a difficult position, failed to convert.

Ireland began the second half as if motivated by some supernatural force. The forwards buzzed around the loose ball in a hive of activity and England were lucky to survive a series of Irish attacks in which forwards collaborated with backs. At length England conceded a scrummage in front of their goal and a quick feed from Sugden permitted Murray to drop his goal.

There were many more opportunities for Ireland to score after this, but a tendency for players to overrun their colleagues, and numerous handling errors, ruined their prospects of lengthening the lead. Reeve was England's most dangerous player and one of his runs took him through the Irish cover, but he was unable to exercise the dashing swerves which had brought him success against Wales at Cardiff and was buried in Williamson's tackle – as were England's hopes of victory.

IRELAND		ENGLAND	
F.W. Williamson	(Dolphin)	J.G. Askew	(Cambridge U.)
*G.V. Stephenson	(London H.)	A.L. Novis	(Blackheath)
E.O'D. Davy	(Lansdowne)	F.W.S. Malir	(Otley)
M.P. Crowe	(Lansdowne)	M. Robson	(Oxford U.)
J.E. Arigho	(Lansdowne)	J.S.R. Reeve	(Harlequins)
P.F. Murray	(Wanderers)	R.S. Spong	(Old Millhillians)
M. Sugden	(Wanderers)	†A. Key	(Old Cranleighans)
H.O'H. O'Neill	(Queen's U.)	D.A. Kendrew	(Woodford)
C.J. Hanrahan	(Dolphin)	J.S. Tucker	(Bristol)
C.T. Payne	(N.I.F.C.)	A.H. Bateson	(Otley)
M.J. Dunne	(Lansdowne)	B.H. Black	(Oxford U.)
J.L. Farrell	(Bective Rangers)	J.W. Forrest	(U.S./R.N.)
N.F. Murphy	(Cork Const.)	W.E. Tucker	(Blackheath)
W.J. McCormick	(Wanderers)	P.D. Howard	(Old Millhillians/Oxford U.)
J.D. Clinch	(Wanderers)	*H.G. Periton	(Waterloo)

Dropped goal: Murray   *Try:* Novis

Referee: Mr A.E. Freethy (Wales)

ENGLAND v FRANCE 1930

Played at Twickenham, London, 22 February 1930
England won by 1G, 2T (11) to 1G (5)

France, with two wins from two matches, were bidding to win the International Championship for the first time. But an improving English pack, described as one of their best for several seasons, foiled the French by controlling the tight and loose play for most of the match. Nevertheless, France scored first. After a brief period of French pressure in the English 25, a wheeled scrummage presented Serin, a burly scrum-half, with the chance to initiate a try. Galia assisted Serin, took a pass and gave a pass back for the scrum-half to bulldoze over like a forward. Ambert converted.

England's early problems were magnified when Askew was injured in a collision with a Frenchman, but he stayed on the field, despite discomfort, and astonished observers with his courageous defence. Black failed to kick an easy penalty goal but England's fortunes changed for the better in the thirty-eighth minute when Sobey escaped from the base of a scrum, drew the French full-back and passed to Reeve, who scored. Play had barely restarted when Robson, receiving the ball from some aimless passing, ran 35 yards for a fine individual try.

After half-time the England pack had to be at its best to cope with the well-organised French forwards. Galia was outstanding in the French scrum but proficient tactical kicking by Sobey countered the advances of the Championship contenders. Later, ten minutes from the end of the match, the indefatigable Sobey dodged away on the blind side of a scrummage backed up by Periton. The Waterloo flanker marked the final try and Black concluded the scoring with a conversion.

ENGLAND		FRANCE	
J.G. Askew	(Cambridge U.)	M. Piquemal	(Tarbes)
J.S.R. Reeve	(Harlequins)	R. Houdet	(Stade Français)
A.L. Novis	(Blackheath)	G. Gérald	(R.C.F.)
M. Robson	(Oxford U.)	M. Baillette	(Quillan)
H.P. Jacob	(Blackheath)	R. Samatan	(Agen)
R.S. Spong	(Old Millhillians)	C. Magnanou	(Bayonne)
W.H. Sobey	(Old Millhillians)	L. Serin	(Béziers)
H. Rew	(The Army/Exeter)	A. Ambert	(Toulouse)
*J.S. Tucker	(Bristol)	C. Bigot	(Quillan)
A.H. Bateson	(Otley)	J. Choy	(Narbonne)
J.W. Forrest	(U.S./R.N.)	R. Majérus	(Stade Français)
B.H. Black	(Oxford U.)	A. Camel	(Toulouse)
H. Wilkinson	(Halifax)	*E. Ribère	(Quillan)
P.D. Howard	(Old Millhillians/Oxford U.)	J. Galia	(Quillan)
H.G. Periton	(Waterloo)	A. Bioussa	(Toulouse)

Tries: Periton, Reeve, Robson
Conversion: Black

Try: Serin
Conversion: Ambert

Referee: Mr A. E. Freethy (Wales)

England v France, 1930. Loose play in the early stages of the match; and the
English team which went on to win the Championship: *back* Mr. A. E. Freethy,
H. P. Jacob, P. D. Howard, J. W. Forrest, B. H. Black, J. G. Askew, H. Rew;
middle J. S. R. Reeve, A. H. Bateson, J. S. Tucker (captain), H. G. Periton,
H. Wilkinson; *front* M. Robson, R. S. Spong, W. H. Sobey, A. L. Novis.

ENGLAND v SCOTLAND 1930

Played at Twickenham, London, 15 March 1930

Drawn, neither side scoring

The back play from both sides left much to be desired and an uninspiring drawn game placed England at the top of the Championship table with five points. Slow heeling by the Scottish forwards impaired the play of their halves and Greenlees's reluctance to run the ball deprived his centres of orthodox handling movements. Aimless kicking by both sides reduced the game to tedium and the only moments for the Duke of York and the large crowd to savour came at the end of the first half.

After 30 minutes, Sobey – the best back on the field – made a superb break from a scrum on the half-way line. He dashed past Nelson, Greenlees and Hutton, swerved away from Macpherson and rounded Warren but, steering towards the Scottish line, he was tackled from behind and fell inches short of a try. Soon after, another run by Sobey enabled Tanner to elude Simmers; however, the Cambridge under-graduate (who was capped before winning his Blue) put a foot into touch and was denied a try. Then, a feinting run by Macpherson, playing in the unaccustomed position of left centre, deceived the English backs and a cross-kick was gathered by an unmarked Waters who, alas for Scotland, was marginally off-side.

Black failed to land a penalty early in the second half and near the end of the game Brook broke through and linked with Tanner. Simmers made an effective tackle and the game petered out to the first scoreless draw between the sides since 1900.

Wales defeated France in the last match of the season a month later and England were left as undisputed Champions.

ENGLAND		**SCOTLAND**	
†J.C. Hubbard	(Harlequins)	R.C. Warren	(Glasgow Acads.)
†C.C. Tanner	(Pembroke C., Cambridge)	D.St.C. Ford	(R.N./U.S.)
M. Robson	(Oxford U.)	J.E. Hutton	(Harlequins)
F.W.S. Malir	(Otley)	*G.P.S. Macpherson	(Edinburgh Acads.)
J.S.R. Reeve	(Harlequins)	W.M. Simmers	(Glasgow Acads.)
R.S. Spong	(Old Millhillians)	H.D. Greenlees	(Leicester)
W.H. Sobey	(Old Millhillians)	J.B. Nelson	(Glasgow Acads.)
H. Rew	(Army/Exeter)	H.S. Mackintosh	(Glasgow U.)
*J.S. Tucker	(Bristol)	W.N. Roughead	(London Scottish)
A.H. Bateson	(Otley)	J.W. Allan	(Melrose)
J.W. Forrest	(R.N./U.S.)	W.B. Welsh	(Hawick)
B.H. Black	(Oxford U.)	L.M. Stuart	(Glasgow H.S.F.P.)
H.G. Periton	(Waterloo)	A.H. Polson	(Gala)
P.D. Howard	(Old Millhillians/Oxford U.)	J. Graham	(Kelso)
†P.W.P. Brook	(Cambridge U.)	F.H. Waters	(London Scottish)

Referee: Mr R.W. Jeffares (Ireland)

ENGLAND v WALES 1931
Played at Twickenham, London, 17 January 1931
Drawn: England 1G, 2PG (11), Wales 1G, 1GM, 1T (11)

Wales found the Twickenham jinx still operating in an exciting match which had an eventful finish. There was a strong wind to help the Welsh make a confident start. Early on, when the English full-back failed to find touch, Powell made a mark and landed a goal with a fine kick, although the English neglected their right to charge. The first try followed Welsh pressure near the left corner on the English line. The ball came back on the Welsh side and their backs started a handling movement to the right, two quick passes presenting Jones-Davies with enough space to dive over wide of the goal. Black kicked a splendid penalty goal from the touch-line immediately after and an error of judgment cost Wales five more points before the interval: a swift Welsh throw-in on their 25 was mistimed and Burland grabbed the ball, sped past a perplexed Bassett and touched down behind the goal. Although the touch-judges disagreed over the conversion, the referee signalled to the scoreboard that the kick was valid.

England used the wind effectively in the second half and Barrington's line-kicking was an inspiration to his tiring pack. There was no further scoring until five minutes from no-side when the Welsh forwards made a final stirring effort. In support of one of their drives, Davey gained possession and Morley took a pass to score. Bassett kicked the goal and many thought that Wales had, at last, laid the Twickenham bogy but Wales were penalised at a scrum seconds later, and Black, with a kick from 50 yards, saved the game for England.

ENGLAND		WALES	
†L.L. Bedford	(Headingley)	*J. Bassett	(Penarth)
J.S.R. Reeve	(Harlequins)	J.C. Morley	(Newport)
†D.W. Burland	(Bristol)	E.C. Davey	(Swansea)
†M.A. McCanlis	(Gloucester)	T.E. Jones-Davies	(London Welsh)
C.D. Aarvold	(Headingley)	R.W. Boon	(Cardiff)
†T.J.M. Barrington	(Bristol)	H.M. Bowcott	(Cardiff)
†E.B. Pope	(Blackheath)	W.C. Powell	(London Welsh)
H. Rew	(Exeter)	T. Arthur	(Neath)
*J.S. Tucker	(Bristol)	H.C. Day	(Newport)
†M.S. Bonaventura	(Blackheath)	A. Skym	(Cardiff)
J.W. Forrest	(U.S./R.N.)	T.B. Day	(Swansea)
B.H. Black	(Blackheath)	E.M. Jenkins	(Aberavon)
†D.H. Swayne	(Oxford U.)	A. Lemon	(Neath)
P. D. Howard	(Old Millhillians/Oxford U.)	W.G. Thomas	(Swansea)
†R.F. Davey	(Leytonstone)	N. Fender	(Cardiff)

Try: Burland *Conversion:* Burland
Penalties: Black (2)

Tries: Jones-Davies, Morley
Conversion: Bassett
Goal from mark: Powell

Referee: Dr J.R. Wheeler (Ireland)

ENGLAND v IRELAND 1931
Played at Twickenham, London, 14 February 1931
Ireland won by 1PG, 1T (6) to 1G (5)

In a close-fought game before 60,000 spectators, lack of penetration in the midfield brought about a disappointing English performance. Their wings looked capable of scoring tries but the mechanical passing of the centres failed to draw an alert Irish defence. As a result, Harrison and Reeve, two elusive runners, had little scope to test the Irish backs.

England had first use of a stiff breeze but failed to score before half-time. The current practice of sending the ball dead from a kick-off, causing the opposition to restart with a drop-out, seems to have been unheard of fifty years ago. When Burland kicked the ball behind the Irish dead-ball line at the start of this match it was regarded as a most unusual incident.

Ireland made a promising start to the second half and courageous tackles by the English wings were required to stop Arigho and Lightfoot when scores seemed imminent. England impressed for a while and went ahead after 25 minutes when Harrison's cross-kick from the left rolled over the Irish line and Black touched down for a try which he converted. England dominated the forward play, but ponderous and unimaginative centre play ruined the attacks which the pack had made possible. A tiring Irish pack found the energy to push play back to the English 25 and they were revived when Murray removed three points from the deficit with a penalty.

The English pack were content to hold the Irish to the end of the match, but an English error in defence gave Ireland a last opportunity to attack and Arigho made a run along the wing. Reeve tackled him but could not prevent McMahon from taking a pass to score the winning try.

G.G. Gregory was the first England player capped direct from Taunton.

ENGLAND		IRELAND	
L.L. Bedford	(Headingley)	J.T. Egan	(Cork Const.)
J.S.R. Reeve	(Harlequins)	E.J. Lightfoot	(Lansdowne)
D.W. Burland	(Bristol)	E.O'D. Davy	(Lansdowne)
M.A. McCanlis	(Gloucester)	L.B. McMahon	(U.C. Dublin)
†A.C. Harrison	(Hartlepool Rovers)	J.E. Arigho	(Lansdowne)
T.J.M. Barrington	(Bristol)	P.F. Murray	(Wanderers)
†G.J. Dean	(Harlequins)	*M. Sugden	(Wanderers)
†P.C. Hordern	(Blackheath)	J.A.E. Siggins	(Collegians)
R.H.W. Sparks	(Plymouth Albion)	H.H.C. Withers	(The Army/N.I.F.C.)
†G.G. Gregory	(Taunton)	V.J. Pike	(Lansdowne)
J.W. Forrest	(U.S./R.N.)	J.L. Farrell	(Bective Rangers)
B.H. Black	(Blackheath)	J. Russell	(U.C. Cork)
*P.D. Howard	(Old Millhillians/Oxford U.)	N.F. Murphy	(Cork Const.)
†E.H. Harding	(Devonport Services)	G.R. Beamish	(R.A.F./London Irish)
†P.E. Dunkley	(Harlequins)	J.D. Clinch	(Wanderers)

Try: Black
Conversion: Black

Try: McMahon
Penalty: Murray

Referee: Mr A.E. Freethy (Wales)

SCOTLAND v ENGLAND 1931

Played at Murrayfield, Edinburgh, 21 March 1931
Scotland won by 5G, 1T (28) to 2G, 1PG, 2T (19)

England's failure to deal with two very fast wings produced a win for Scotland, and loose marking, by both teams, resulted in a high-scoring game. Nevertheless, the crowd of 75,000 were enthralled by an exciting match between two sides anxious to run the ball at all times and from most positions. There was also some sure place kicking, with Allan and Black obtaining eight goals between them.

In the tenth minute, Macpherson, who flitted here, there and everywhere throughout the match, confounded the English cover with a cross-kick. Simmers gathered the ball, ran 35 yards to the English line where he was upended in a tackle and Ford scored in the follow-up. Allan converted and three goals followed in the next five minutes. First, the English defence was confused by Macpherson (again) and Mackintosh scored. Then England struck back. Tallent crossed at the corner, for a beautiful conversion by Black; and scored again after a wide, arcing run to the Scottish posts. With the scores level, Logan, on his debut, stole away from a scrum to beat a static defence and score near the goal in the twentieth minute, Allan converting. Aarvold then ran through some weak tackles to make a try for Reeve, but Black's failure to convert left the Scots two points ahead. Before half-time, Mackintosh scored his second try, following a rush by his colleagues in the pack, and Allan's unerring boot made the score at the interval 20–13.

Smith scored from a delightful break from loose play by Logan early in the second half, then scored again to secure for Scotland a lead of 15 points. Black kicked a penalty from in front of the posts for England and, late in the game, Pope had his finest moment when he made a forceful run to set up a try for Reeve in the corner.

SCOTLAND		ENGLAND	
A.W. Wilson	(Dunfermline)	†E.C.P. Whiteley	(Old Alleynians)
I.S. Smith	(London Scottish)	J.S.R. Reeve	(Harlequins)
*G.P.S. Macpherson	(Edinburgh Acads.)	†J.A. Tallent	(Cambridge U.)
D.St.C. Ford	(R.N.)	*C.D. Aarvold	(Headingley)
W.M. Simmers	(Glasgow Acads.)	A.C. Harrison	(Hartlepool Rovers)
H. Lind	(Dunfermline)	†T.C. Knowles	(Birkenhead Park)
W.R. Logan	(Edinburgh U.)	E.B. Pope	(Blackheath)
J.W. Allan	(Melrose)	H. Rew	(Exeter)
W.N. Roughead	(London Scottish)	R.H.W. Sparks	(Plymouth Albion)
H.S. Mackintosh	(West of Scotland)	G.G. Gregory	(Taunton)
A.W. Walker	(Cambridge U.)	J.W. Forrest	(U.S./R.N.)
J.A. Beattie	(Hawick)	B.H. Black	(Blackheath)
W.B. Welsh	(Hawick)	P.C. Hordern	(Blackheath)
J.S. Wilson	(St Andrew's U.)	P.D. Howard	(Old Millhillians/Oxford U.)
D. Crichton-Miller	(Gloucester)	P. E. Dunkley	(Harlequins)

Tries: Mackintosh (2), Smith (2), Ford, Logan *Conversions:* Allan (5)

Tries: Tallent (2), Reeve (2) *Conversions:* Black (2) *Penalty:* Black

Referee: Dr J.R. Wheeler (Ireland)

FRANCE v ENGLAND 1931

Played at Stade Colombes, Paris, 6 April 1931
France won by 2DG, 2T (14) to 2G, 1T (13)

The recalcitrance of twelve French clubs led to the severance of Rugby Union relations with France. A meeting of the four home Unions on 13 February, 1931, passed a resolution stating that matches would not be resumed with the French until 'the control and conduct of the game (in France) has been placed on a satisfactory basis'. France thus entered this Easter Monday match with everything to prove and they came from behind on three occasions to win in front of a small crowd. England finished the season without a win for the first time since 1905.

England's basic weakness lay in an inexperienced pack which lacked inspiring leadership. The French scrummaging was allowed to improve as the game proceeded and Camo established himself as a line-out specialist who was also conspicuous in the loose.

In the eighteenth minute Smeddle made the running for the only try of the first half. The wing was eventually smothered by a closing defence but a pass to Tallent yielded a try which Black converted. Just before half-time Baillette dropped a goal from 40 yards.

Early in the second half France took the lead when Servole received a reverse pass after supporting a rush by Camo. England's backs were deceived and Galia ended the move with a try. A rearrangement of the English three-quarters saw Burland change places with Aarvold. Immediately, Burland took advantage of the extra space to be found on the wing and he brushed aside tackles by Savy and Samatan to wend his way over the line for a try. England's lead vanished one minute later, however, when Guélorguet instigated an attack which the hard-pressed English backs were unable to contain and the upshot was an easy try for Clady.

England responded with a try by Smeddle, his momentum carrying him through a tackle by Savy, and Forrest converted. Finally, Gérald won the match for France with a low-trajectory dropped goal.

FRANCE		ENGLAND	
M. Savy	(Montferrand)	E.C.P. Whiteley	(Old Alleynians)
R. Samatan	(Agen)	R.W. Smeddle	(Cambridge U.)
G. Gérald	(R.C.F.)	D.W. Burland	(Bristol)
M. Baillette	(Toulon)	J.A. Tallent	(Cambridge U.)
P. Guélorguet	(R.C.F.)	*C.D. Aarvold	(Headingley)
L. Servole	(Toulon)	R.S. Spong	(Old Millhillians)
L. Serin	(Béziers)	E.B. Pope	(Blackheath)
R. Scohy	(Bordeaux E.C.)	H. Rew	(Exeter)
R. Namur	(Toulon)	R.H.W. Sparks	(Plymouth Albion)
H. Buisson	(Béziers)	G.G. Gregory	(Taunton)
E. Camo	(Villeneuve)	J.W. Forrest	(U.S./R.N.)
A. Clady	(Lézignan)	B.H. Black	(Blackheath)
R. Triviaux	(Cognac)	P.W.P. Brook	(Harlequins)
J. Galia	(Villeneuve)	P.D. Howard	(Old Millhillians)
*E. Ribère	(Quillan)	P.C. Hordern	(Blackheath)

Tries: Clady, Galia
Dropped goals: Baillette, Gérald

Tries: Burland, Smeddle, Tallent
Conversions: Black, Forrest
(There are sources which credit Black with both conversions)

Referee: Mr A. E. Freethy (Wales)

ENGLAND v SOUTH AFRICA 1932

Played at Twickenham, London, 2 January 1932
South Africa won by 1DG, 1T (7) to Nil

South Africa possessed a heavy pack which earned a steady supply of ball for the backs to utilise. But a reluctance to open up play by the Springbok backs, a legacy no doubt of the tedious touch-nursing tactics adopted by Osler from the outset of the tour, resulted in a narrow victory for the South Africans; a victory which should have been recorded by a more convincing margin.

The English backs, consequently starved of the ball, gave an excellent defensive performance and Gerrard made an impressive debut. A lucky Springbok try gave the Africans a three-points lead at the interval. In a rush, a visiting forward hacked the ball over the English line where Barr, unluckily for him, succeeded in taking some speed off the ball and thus prevented it from rolling dead. Just as it seemed certain that he would minor the ball, he slipped and two Springboks, Daneel and Bergh, almost simultaneously, pounced for a try.

Gerrard was once prominent in a rare English foray into South African territory, but for the most part play followed the familiar, unimaginative Springbok pattern after the break. Despite their distinct advantage in the tight, South Africa could not outwit England's defence. In the closing minutes, after a period of unremitting Springbok pressure, an English kick failed to find touch and Brand, gathering inside his own half, put over a dropped goal with a prodigious kick, one of the longest dropped goals seen in the history of international Rugby.

The English selectors were criticised for their policy of choosing three hookers for their front row to face the formidable Springbok pack. Many believed that England's big men, Webb and Hobbs, should have been pushed into the front rank: there they would have absorbed the power generated by Mostert, Kipling and Louw more effectively than did Carpenter, Norman and Gregory.

ENGLAND		SOUTH AFRICA	
†R.J. Barr	(Leicester)	G.H. Brand	(Western Province)
C.C. Tanner	(Gloucester)	M. Zimmerman	(Western Province)
J.A. Tallent	(Cambridge U.)	B.G. Gray	(Western Province)
†R.A. Gerrard	(Bath)	F.W. Waring	(Western Province)
*C.D. Aarvold	(Blackheath)	J.H. van der Westhuizen	(Western Province)
R.S. Spong	(Old Millhillians)	*B.L. Osler	(Western Province)
W.H. Sobey	(Old Millhillians)	P. du P. de Villiers	(Western Province)
G.G. Gregory	(Bristol)	P.J. Mostert	(Western Province)
†D.J. Norman	(Leicester)	H.G. Kipling	(Griqualand West)
†A.D. Carpenter	(Gloucester)	M.M. Louw	(Western Province)
†C.S.H. Webb	(Devonport Services)	P.J. Nel	(Natal)
†R.G.S. Hobbs	(The Army/Richmond)	W.F. Bergh	(South West Districts)
†L.E. Saxby	(Gloucester)	L.C. Strachan	(Transvaal)
†A.J. Rowley	(Coventry)	J.A.J. McDonald	(Western Province)
†J.McD. Hodgson	(Northern)	G.M. Daneel	(Western Province)

Try: Bergh   *Dropped goal:* Brand

Referee: Mr W.L. Freeman (Ireland)

WALES v ENGLAND 1932

Played at St Helen's, Swansea, 16 January 1932
Wales won by 1G, 1DG, 1PG (12) to 1G (5)

A lacklustre English side were once again outscrummaged, this time by a heavy, mobile Welsh pack. There was a healthy wind at Swansea and 30,000 spectators watched a pointless first half. Barr and Aarvold kicked shrewdly for the English, but in attack their backs failed lamentably against an unyielding Welsh back division.

Wales, backed by the weather in the second half, surged ahead after only five minutes. The Welsh backs moved the ball to the left and high passes were used to miss out two men. Boon received the ball on the wing but his path to the line was blocked by Tanner. Stepping inwards, Boon threw the English cover off its balance and ran diagonally to score behind the goal. Bassett converted.

A little later Boon found himself cornered again in the English 25, near the posts, and from point-blank range he chipped the ball high over the bar for four more points. Bassett followed this with a penalty from in front of the posts to give his team a comfortable lead.

Towards the end of the match England brought play to the Welsh half for the first time since the interval. Spong, with his only run of the match, covered 30 yards before stumbling near the Welsh line. Many thought that he had knocked the ball forward but the referee awarded a try to Coley, who had followed the ball into the Welsh goal area. Barr converted and soon afterwards the match ended.

It has been widely believed that Saxby, in his last international, was England's oldest-ever player, his age having been estimated at about 40. Public records indicate that a Leslie Eric Saxby was born in the Bradfield area in May 1900, so he may only have been in his early thirties at the time of this match.

WALES		ENGLAND	
*J. Bassett	(Penarth)	R.J. Barr	(Leicester)
J.C. Morley	(Newport)	C.C. Tanner	(Gloucester)
E.C. Davey	(Swansea)	R.A. Gerrard	(Bath)
F.L. Williams	(Cardiff)	J.A. Tallent	(Cambridge U.)
R.W. Boon	(Cardiff)	*C.D. Aarvold	(Blackheath)
A.R. Ralph	(Newport)	R.S. Spong	(Old Millhillians)
W.C. Powell	(London Welsh)	W.H. Sobey	(Old Millhillians)
T.B. Day	(Swansea)	G.G. Gregory	(Bristol)
F.A. Bowdler	(Cross Keys)	D.J. Norman	(Leicester)
A. Skym	(Cardiff)	†N.L. Evans	(R.N.E. College, Keyham)
D. Thomas	(Swansea)	C.S.H. Webb	(Devonport Services)
E.M. Jenkins	(Aberavon)	R.G.S. Hobbs	(Richmond)
W. Davies	(Swansea)	L.E. Saxby	(Gloucester)
W.G. Thomas	(Swansea)	E. Coley	(Northampton)
A. Lemon	(Neath)	J.McD. Hodgson	(Northern)

Try: Boon *Conversion:* Bassett
Dropped goal: Boon
Penalty: Bassett

Try: Coley *Conversion:* Barr

Referee: Mr F.J.C. Moffat (Scotland)

IRELAND v ENGLAND 1932

Played at Lansdowne Road, Dublin, 13 February 1932
England won by 1G, 2PG (11) to 1G, 1PG (8)

This was England's first success for two years and it was achieved with an overhauled side. Burland was recalled and became the man of the match, scoring all of England's points in a game decided by penalties. Murphy drifted off-side at a scrummage early in the match to give Burland his first points, but these were neutralised in the twenty-fifth minute when Murray kicked a goal from 45 yards. Burland landed his second goal before the pause when Waide wandered off-side.

The second half was of the rough-and-tumble kind so common to Lansdowne Road. Elliot nearly dropped a goal, but 30 minutes passed before there was a late burst of scoring. An enterprising run down the touch-line by Aarvold from his own half extended Ireland's defence. Then, an adroit cross-kick fell kindly for Elliot and the ball passed through the hands of Gerrard, moving right, for Burland to cross the line unchallenged and convert his own try.

Ireland replied with their best Rugby of the match. A 'Garryowen' placed Barr under considerable pressure and, although the full-back caught the ball safely, he sliced his kick to touch. Ireland won the line-out, moved the ball orthodoxly to the right but then altered the course of the attack and passed rapidly to the left. Hunt ran intelligently and Waide, on an overlap, took the pass to score. Murray converted, but Ireland's rally came too late to overtake England's 11 points.

IRELAND		ENGLAND	
D.P. Morris	(Bective Rangers)	R.J. Barr	(Leicester)
E.J. Lightfoot	(Lansdowne)	C.C. Tanner	(Gloucester)
P.F. Murray	(Wanderers)	D.W. Burland	(Bristol)
E.W.F.deV. Hunt	(Army)	R.A. Gerrard	(Bath)
S.L. Waide	(N.I.F.C.)	*C.D. Aarvold	(Blackheath)
E.O'D. Davy	(Lansdowne)	†W. Elliot	(U.S.)
M.D. Sheehan	(London Irish)	†B.C. Gadney	(Leicester)
V.J. Pike	(Lansdowne)	G.G. Gregory	(Bristol)
T.C. Casey	(Young Munster)	†R.S. Roberts	(Coventry)
J.L. Farrell	(Bective Rangers)	N.L. Evans	(R.N.E. College, Keyham)
M.J. Dunne	(Lansdowne)	R.G.S. Hobbs	(Richmond)
J.A.E. Siggins	(Collegians)	C.S.H. Webb	(Devonport Services)
N.F. Murphy	(Cork Const.)	†A. Vaughan-Jones	(U.S.)
*G.R. Beamish	(R.A.F./Leicester)	T.W. Harris	(Northampton)
W.McC. Ross	(Queen's U.)	J.McD. Hodgson	(Northern)

Try: Waide
Conversion: Murray
Penalty: Murray

Try: Burland
Conversion: Burland
Penalties: Burland (2)

Referee: Mr W. Burnet (Scotland)

ENGLAND v SCOTLAND 1932
Played at Twickenham, London, 19 March 1932
England won by 2G, 2T (16) to 1T (3)

The Duke of York and 65,000 were present to watch England's best display for a number of seasons. Victory meant a share in the Championship with Wales and Ireland. England were, according to *The Times*, stronger all round 'with the forwards scrummaging low and hard, Gadney at his best at their heels, the threequarter backs refusing to be thrown too much out of their stride by a moderate service from the stand-off player, and, last but not least, Brown, as of old, a model of precision at full-back.'

Nevertheless, Scotland opened the scoring after 17 minutes. Beattie headed a rush, the ball was whipped out to Ian Smith on the wing and a try at the corner followed. England immediately equalised. Burland, who had another good game, capitalised upon a Scottish fumble and ran straight to put Tanner clear. Then, in the thirtieth minute, Aarvold took advantage of a clean English heel from a scrum to score on the left. Lind made a nimble run before the interval but careful marking by Brown and the English centres suppressed the advances of the Scot.

The English forwards overshadowed the Scots in the tight after half-time, and the powerful running of Burland was a constant intimidation to the visiting backs. In the twenty-third minute the Bristol centre made ground from a scrum to send Aarvold over on the left. The conversion gave England an eight-points lead. Later, another strong run by Burland sheared the Scottish defence and Black scored following a scramble under the Scottish goal. Burland converted to complete the scoring.

ENGLAND		SCOTLAND	
T.W. Brown	(Bristol)	A.S. Dykes	(Glasgow Acads.)
C.C. Tanner	(Gloucester)	I.S. Smith	(London Scottish)
D.W. Burland	(Bristol)	*G.P.S. Macpherson	(Edinburgh Acads.)
R.A. Gerrard	(Bath)	G. Wood	(Gala)
*C.D. Aarvold	(Blackheath)	W.M. Simmers	(Glasgow Acads.)
W. Elliot	(U.S.)	H. Lind	(Dunfermline)
B.C. Gadney	(Leicester)	J.P. McArthur	(Waterloo)
†R.J. Longland	(Northampton)	R.A. Foster	(Hawick)
G.G. Gregory	(Bristol)	H.S. Mackintosh	(West of Scotland)
N.L. Evans	(R.N.E. College, Keyham)	R. Rowand	(Glasgow H.S.F.P.)
C.S.H. Webb	(Devonport Services)	F.A. Wright	(Edinburgh Acads.)
R.G.S. Hobbs	(Richmond)	J.A. Beattie	(Hawick)
A. Vaughan-Jones	(U.S.)	W.B. Welsh	(Hawick)
B.H. Black	(Blackheath)	G.F. Ritchie	(Dundee H.S.F.P.)
J. McD. Hodgson	(Northern)	J.S. Wilson	(St Andrew's U.)

Tries: Aarvold (2), Black, Tanner   *Try:* Smith
Conversions: Burland (2)

Referee: Dr J.R. Wheeler (Ireland)

ENGLAND v WALES 1933
Played at Twickenham, London, 21 January 1933
Wales won by 1DG, 1T (7) to 1T (3)

Wales's first victory at Twickenham came at their tenth attempt. The inspiring leadership of Watcyn Thomas and the courageous play of a young Welsh back division which boasted a strong Oxbridge influence were the vital factors in this long-awaited success. Wales awarded seven new caps; England three, with Roncoroni replacing Vallance late in the day.

England made a storming start and Burland broke through the centre several times. Sure tackling by Viv Jenkins, who had entered the match with a high temperature, and accurate kicking by Bowcott protected the Welsh goal at first. Eventually, England scored when Elliot and Burland made an overlap for Booth. When faced with Jenkins, Booth in-passed to Elliot and the fly-half crossed for a try. Many in the crowd believed he had fumbled the ball and failed to score, but the referee awarded the try without hesitation. Black, who had deprived Wales of victory with a late penalty two years earlier, failed to convert.

Wales acquired the lead immediately after the interval when Boon received the ball from a maul and coolly dropped a goal from 20 yards. The Welsh pack now exercised a hold on the English eight and Wooller's side-on tackling reduced the previous danger threatened by Burland. Bowcott nearly dropped a goal, and only a try-saving tackle by Wooller prevented Elliot from racing over after a 30-yards chase.

Gerrard was obliged to retire with an eye injury (Bolton withdrawing from the back row to fill the gap in the threequarter line) but the Welsh tails were high long before this English setback. Bowcott nursed his forwards with a masterly display of touch-finding and near the end Wales laid the Twickenham bogy once and for all. Turnbull fed Davey from a loose scrum in the English 25. Drawing Brown perfectly, Davey then threw a pass to Boon, who galloped over for a try which many of the 64,000 spectators believed Jenkins had converted. However, at the end of the match the Irish referee confirmed that he had disallowed the conversion and Wales were left deserved victors by 7–3.

ENGLAND		WALES	
T.W. Brown	(Bristol)	V.G.J. Jenkins	(Bridgend/Oxford U.)
†L.A. Booth	(Headingley)	R.W. Boon	(Cardiff)
D.W. Burland	(Bristol)	E.C. Davey	(Swansea/Sale)
R.A. Gerrard	(Bath)	W. Wooller	(Rydal School/Sale)
*C.D. Aarvold	(Blackheath)	A.H. Jones	(Cardiff)
W. Elliot	(R.N./U.S.)	H.M. Bowcott	(London Welsh/Cardiff)
A. Key	(Old Cranleighans)	M.J.L. Turnbull	(Cardiff)
R.J. Longland	(Northampton)	E.L. Jones	(Llanelli)
G.G. Gregory	(Bristol)	B. Evans	(Llanelli)
N.L. Evans	(R.N./U.S.)	A. Skym	(Cardiff)
C.S.H. Webb	(R.N./Devonport Services)	D. Thomas	(Swansea)
†A.D.S. Roncoroni	(West Herts/Richmond)	R.B. Jones	(Cambridge U./Waterloo)
†R. Bolton	(Wakefield/U.C.H.)	T. Arthur	(Neath)
B.H. Black	(Blackheath)	*W.G. Thomas	(Swansea/Waterloo)
A. Vaughan-Jones	(U.S.)	I. Isaacs	(Cardiff)

Try: Elliot

Try: Boon *Dropped goal:* Boon

Referee: Mr T. Bell (Ireland)

ENGLAND v IRELAND 1933

Played at Twickenham, London, 11 February 1933
England won by 1G, 4T (17) to 1PG, 1T (6)

England made six changes from the fifteen defeated by Wales in January, and Novis became captain with Kendrew leading the pack. Ireland's pack was 'a rare blend of experienced youth and still more experienced age' – according to *The Times* – but in the first 20 minutes they kept up a rumbustious assault which threatened to sweep the English pack aside. Murray drew first blood with a penalty after five minutes, from in front of the posts, but Ireland had nothing else to show for their exertions when Kendrew pulled his men together, midway through the half, to demand a more organised effort in the tight. Immediately, England improved: the Irish forwards began to fade, and the result was a total rout of the Irish, fore and aft.

An orthodox threequarter movement produced England's first try. Gerrard drew the defence and Novis swerved outside Lightfoot before smashing through the tackle of Pratt on the line. Fortified by this score, England proceeded to play with increased confidence and Gadney, from the cover of a loose scrummage, made a break which Gerrard and Elliot continued. Booth, receiving the ball on the right, made a determined run for the line and touched down in the corner. Gadney scored himself from close range just before the interval.

Ireland made a recovery at the start of the second half but the superior fitness of the Englishmen and the precision of the English scrummaging effectively destroyed Ireland's hopes of regaining a hold on the match. Burland was injured after ten minutes and exchanged places with Novis before Sadler, one of a trio of new loose forwards, crowned a splendid debut with a try from a line-out. Kendrew converted. Novis, who also had an excellent match, completed the English scoring after 30 minutes with an individual effort of the highest class. His sharp eye for an opening and his strength on the break took him clean through the Irish centre for a try. Ireland's only try, by Hunt, followed a scramble near the English line.

ENGLAND		IRELAND	
T.W. Brown	(Bristol)	R.H. Pratt	(Dublin U.)
L.A. Booth	(Headingley)	E.J. Lightfoot	(Lansdowne)
D.W. Burland	(Bristol)	L.B. McMahon	(U.C. Dublin)
R.A. Gerrard	(Bath)	E.W.F.deV. Hunt	(Wanderers/Army)
*A.L. Novis	(Blackheath/Army)	S.L. Waide	(N.I.F.C./Oxford U)
W. Elliot	(R.N./U.S.)	*E.O'D. Davy	(Lansdowne)
B.C. Gadney	(Leicester)	P.F. Murray	(Wanderers)
N.L. Evans	(R.N./U.S.)	M.J. Dunne	(Lansdowne)
G.G. Gregory	(Bristol)	V.J. Pike	(Lansdowne)
D.A. Kendrew	(Leicester)	H.O'H.O'Neill	(U.C. Cork)
A.D.S. Roncoroni	(West Herts/Richmond)	J.A.E. Siggins	(Collegians)
C.S.H. Webb	(R.N./Devonport Services)	J. Russell	(U.C. Cork)
†E.H. Sadler	(Army)	N.F. Murphy	(Cork Const.)
†C.L. Troop	(Army)	G.R. Beamish	(R.A.F./Leicester)
†W.H. Weston	(Northampton)	W.McC. Ross	(Queen's U.)

Tries: Novis (2), Booth, Gadney, Sadler
Conversion: Kendrew

Try: Hunt
Penalty: Murray

Referee: Mr M.A. Allan (Scotland)

Two of the men who contributed tries to England's 17-6 win over Ireland in 1933:
TOP   Novis, England's captain and man of the match, on the burst;
BOTTOM   Lu Booth, with Gerrard in support.

SCOTLAND v ENGLAND 1933
Played at Murrayfield, Edinburgh, 18 March 1933
Scotland won by 1T (3) to Nil

This was only Scotland's second match of the season, poor weather causing the postponement of their match with Ireland until 1 April. A large crowd filled Murrayfield's lofty banks but the fare served up by the two sides was barely worthy of international-class players. Scotland's forwards, through their storming play in the loose, earned the unanimous praise of the press but the backs, especially the three-quarters, were criticised for their aimless passing and running. Burland and Gerrard (with cramp) were unable to function at full throttle and there were few English attacks to stretch a sound Scottish defence. Novis and Lind were the pick of the backs, more for their qualities as individuals than for their abilities in support of colleagues. In defence, Novis startled everyone near the start of the match when Ian Smith had kicked over the English try-line: the England wing managed to outrun the famous Scottish sprinter in a 40-yards chase to touch down.

Scotland's only score crystallised from a touch of genius by Lind. At the receiving end of a low, awkward pass the Scottish centre shrewdly elected to kick the ball forward (not attempting to handle it) and wrong-footed the English backs. Fyfe ran on, used his feet intelligently and foiled Brown's desperate effort to scramble the ball into touch. Fyfe failed to convert his try from a tricky angle, but his three points were enough to take Scotland to a Triple Crown match in Dublin a fortnight later.

In the last 15 minutes of the second half England enjoyed a late and unexpected advantage when the Scottish pack began to tire. Novis, now featuring in the centre, and Booth strived to penetrate Scotland's cover but inexperienced support – a failing of the English backs throughout a disappointing season – and feeble finishing spoiled their good work.

SCOTLAND		ENGLAND	
D.I. Brown	(Cambridge U.)	T.W. Brown	(Bristol)
*I.S. Smith	(London Scottish)	L.A. Booth	(Headingley)
H.D.B. Lorraine	(Oxford U.)	D.W. Burland	(Bristol)
H. Lind	(Dunfermline)	R.A. Gerrard	(Bath)
K.C. Fyfe	(Cambridge U.)	*A.L. Novis	(Blackheath/Army)
K.L.T. Jackson	(Oxford U.)	W. Elliot	(R.N./U.S.)
W.R. Logan	(Edinburgh Wands.)	B.C. Gadney	(Leicester)
J.M. Ritchie	(Watsonians)	D.A. Kendrew	(Leicester)
J.M. Henderson	(Edinburgh Acads.)	G.G. Gregory	(Bristol)
M.S. Stewart	(Stewart's College F.P.)	R.J. Longland	(Northampton)
W.B. Welsh	(Hawick)	C.S.H. Webb	(Devonport Services/R.N.)
J.A. Beattie	(Hawick)	A.D.S. Roncoroni	(West Herts/Richmond)
J.R. Thom	(Watsonians)	W.H. Weston	(Northampton)
R. Rowand	(Glasgow H.S.F.P.)	C.L. Troop	(The Army)
J.A. Waters	(Selkirk)	E.H. Sadler	(The Army)

Try: Fyfe

Referee: Dr J.R. Wheeler (Ireland)

WALES v ENGLAND 1934
Played at Cardiff Arms Park, 20 January 1934
England won by 3T (9) to Nil

England began a successful season with a convincing win against Wales at Cardiff – their third win at the Arms Park. England fielded seven new caps; Wales saw fit to introduce thirteen new players, relying heavily on exiles.

The Welsh forwards were completely outplayed by their English counterparts and Evans and Jones, two tiny halves, were overwhelmed by the lively English pack. Only clumsy handling by the English backs prevented the Welsh defence conceding more than three tries.

The first significant move of a mediocre match occurred after 15 minutes. A speculative kick by Elliot reached Meikle on the left wing and another kick propelled the ball over the line near the Welsh corner flag. Meikle won the chase to touch down but as the referee was about to award a try, the English touch-judge intervened to indicate that the ball had rolled over the dead-ball line. Wales's relief was short-lived, however, for five minutes later Gerrard initiated a round of passing and Meikle slipped past Howells and Cowey for a try near the corner.

England's compact scrummaging and efficient heeling were rewarded in the twenty-fifth minute when Gadney perfectly timed his break from a scrummage, linked with Cranmer who escaped from a weak tackle, and Warr dived over for a try with a Welsh defender clinging to his legs. Wales staged a minor recovery, even in the scrummages where it was felt that their selectors had erred by choosing too many new players. (The *Times* correspondent promised: 'Any good Welsh club pack would have beaten it easily.') Cliff Jones managed to bring his three-quarters into the match just before the break and both Idwal Rees and Cowey made noteworthy runs for the English line.

After the interval, England regained their mastery up-front and six minutes of play passed before Gerrard exploited some poor Welsh tackling to send a low pass to Meikle. The wing took the ball in his stride and galloped over for his second try. For the rest of the match England's superior scrummaging and Elliot's accurate tactical kicking were sufficient to quell the enthusiasm of a crowd of 50,000 Welsh spectators.

WALES		**ENGLAND**	
B. Howells	(Llanelli)	†H.G. Owen-Smith	(Oxford U.)
B.T.V. Cowey	(Army)	†A.L. Warr	(Oxford U.)
E.C. Davey	(Sale)	†P. Cranmer	(Oxford U./Richmond)
J.I. Rees	(Edinburgh Wands.)	R.A. Gerrard	(Bath)
G.R. Rees-Jones	(Oxford U./London Welsh)	†G.W.C. Meikle	(Waterloo)
C.W. Jones	(Cambridge U.)	W. Elliot	(R.N./U.S.)
D.D. Evans	(Cheshire/Cardiff U.)	*B.C. Gadney	(Leicester)
C.R. Davies	(Bedford/R.A.F.)	H. Rew	(Blackheath)
*J.R. Evans	(Newport)	G.G. Gregory	(Bristol)
G. Hughes	(Penarth)	R.J. Longland	(Northampton)
H. Truman	(Llanelli)	†J. C. Wright	(Met. Police)
D. Thomas	(Swansea)	†J. Dicks	(Northampton)
G. Prosser	(Neath)	J.McD. Hodgson	(Northern)
K. W. J. Jones	(London Welsh)	P.C. Hordern	(Gloucester)
A.M. Rees	(Cambridge U.)	†H.A. Fry	(Liverpool)

Tries: Meikle (2), Warr

Referee: Mr F.W. Haslett (Ireland)

IRELAND v ENGLAND 1934

Played at Lansdowne Road, Dublin, 10 February 1934
England won by 2G, 1T (13) to 1T (3)

England took one step closer to winning the Triple Crown with a comfortable victory over an Irish side which promised much in the first 20 minutes but then faded. After an anxious start, England's forwards slowly improved and held a competent and determined grip on the tight play.

Ireland kicked off, supported by a healthy breeze, but their first chance to score – a penalty from in front of goal after two minutes – was fluffed by Siggins. Two minutes later, however, a deafening cheer greeted a splendid try by Morgan following a dash down the right touch-line which was embellished by a couple of dummies.

The Irish maintained a firm grip on the game for the next quarter of an hour: Davy bent the ball around an upright with a drop at goal and Siggins failed to kick a penalty. Then the English backs finally split a determined Irish defence, Cranmer breaking diagonally for the posts before transferring the ball to Elliot. The ball went loose after Elliot was tackled on the goal-line but Fry, an alert wing-forward, claimed the try which levelled the scores.

A few minutes later England moved into the lead. Meikle made a hash of a penalty attempt, but an inaccurate clearance kick by the Irish left wing enabled Owen-Smith to indulge his unorthodox impulses and make a counter-attack from full-back. A reverse pass to Forrest deceived the Irish cover; Forrest handed on to Elliot who drew the Irish full-back; and Fry accepted a pass to score a try which Gregory turned into a goal.

The English pack improved steadily during the second half. The final score came towards the end of the game when Elliot, who had a modest match, drew his opponent and sent a long pass out to the left wing. Meikle, with a side-step, left his marker clutching at thin air, turned inwards and scored at the posts, for Gregory to make an easy conversion.

IRELAND		ENGLAND	
R.H. Pratt	(Dublin U.)	H.G. Owen-Smith	(Oxford U.)
J.J. O'Connor	(U.C. Cork)	A.L. Warr	(Oxford U.)
M.P. Crowe	(Lansdowne/Leicester)	P. Cranmer	(Oxford U./Richmond)
J.V. Reardon	(Cork Const.)	R.A. Gerrard	(Bath)
L.B. McMahon	(U.C. Dublin)	G.W.C. Meikle	(Waterloo)
E.O'D. Davy	(Lansdowne)	W. Elliot	(R.N./U.S.)
G.J. Morgan	(Clontarf)	*B.C. Gadney	(Leicester)
C.R.A. Graves	(Wanderers)	R.J. Longland	(Northampton)
V.J. Pike	(Lansdowne/Army)	G.G. Gregory	(Bristol)
S. Walker	(Instonians)	H. Rew	(Blackheath/Army)
J. Russell	(U.C. Cork)	J.W. Forrest	(R.N./U.S.)
M.J. Dunne	(Lansdowne)	J. Dicks	(Northampton)
W.McC. Ross	(Queen's U.)	W.H. Weston	(Northampton)
*J.A.E. Siggins	(Collegians)	J.McD. Hodgson	(Northern)
M.E. Bardon	(Bohemians)	H.A. Fry	(Liverpool)

Try: Morgan

Tries: Fry (2), Meikle
Conversions: Gregory (2)

Referee: Mr M.A. Allan (Scotland)

ENGLAND v SCOTLAND 1934
Played at Twickenham, London, 17 March 1934
England won by 2T (6) to 1T (3)

England won a fast game to secure the Triple Crown for the first time since 1928 and wrested the Championship title from Scotland in an exciting finish. England made three changes from the side which had won in Dublin five weeks earlier, Lu Booth returning to the right wing after an attack of chicken-pox, Slow replacing Elliot at fly-half, and Kendrew entering the back row.

The English three-quarters were allowed little room in which to manoeuvre and Slow, who was principally a kicking half-back, proved to be negative in attack. The chief virtue of the home backs was defence, consequently, and towards the end of the match, when Lind made several menacing runs, accurate tackling was a valuable English asset.

Scotland began with enthusiasm. The forwards 'showed their mettle and true worth' recorded the *Rugby Football Annual* and only solid defence prevented Scotland scoring early in the match. Owen-Smith, a full-back whose love of the unorthodox made him a popular figure in other sports apart from Rugby, had an 'heroic encounter almost on his own goal-line' very early on when Beattie looked likely to score, but the English defence did prove fallible when Dick made a beautiful break for Lind to send Shaw over in the corner. Fyfe failed to convert but few could begrudge Scotland their lead.

England equalised before the break. Forrest miscued with a penalty kick from the middle of the field but Scotland failed to deal with a loose ball and Fry started an attack which culminated in Gerrard making enough space for Meikle to canter along the touch-line for a try. Meikle, originally selected for his place kicking, had thus scored tries in each of his first three matches: he now failed to convert.

The winning score came ten minutes from no-side when Booth picked up a loose ball and swerved past Marshall for a fine solo try. Scotland tried desperately to regain the lead in the remaining minutes with Lind prominent in the role of chief attacker.

ENGLAND		SCOTLAND	
H.G. Owen-Smith	(St Mary's H.)	K.W. Marshall	(Edinburgh Acads.)
L.A. Booth	(Headingley)	R.W. Shaw	(Glasgow H.S.F.P.)
P. Cranmer	(Oxford U.)	R.C.S. Dick	(Cambridge U.)
R.A. Gerrard	(Bath)	H. Lind	(Dunfermline)
G.W.C. Meikle	(Waterloo)	K.C.Fyfe	(Cambridge U.)
†C.F. Slow	(Leicester)	J.L. Cotter	(Hillhead H.S.F.P.)
*B.C. Gadney	(Leicester)	W.R. Logan	(Edinburgh Wands.)
H. Rew	(Blackheath)	J.W. Allan	(Melrose)
G.G. Gregory	(Bristol)	G.S. Cottington	(Kelso)
R.J. Longland	(Northampton)	J.M. Ritchie	(Watsonians)
J.W. Forrest	(R.N./U.S.)	J.A. Beattie	(Hawick)
J. Dicks	(Northampton)	*M.S. Stewart	(Stewart's College F.P.)
W.H. Weston	(Northampton)	L.B. Lambie	(Glasgow H.S.F.P.)
D.A. Kendrew	(Leicester)	J.A. Waters	(Selkirk)
H.A. Fry	(Liverpool)	J.G. Watherston	(Edinburgh Wands.)

Tries: Booth, Meikle   *Try:* Shaw

Referee: Mr F.W. Haslett (Ireland)

ENGLAND v WALES 1935

Played at Twickenham, London, 19 January 1935
Drawn: England 1PG (3), Wales 1T (3)

A crowd of 72,000 saw a lack-lustre match in which close marking stifled all attempts by the English backs to run the ball and open up the game. Both sides fielded 'jumbo' packs, but the Welsh eight tired rapidly in the last 20 minutes and England were unfortunate not to force a late victory. The Welsh backs, by contrast, looked sharp and enterprising, and Welsh reservations concerning Powell at scrum-half were soon dispelled, for the veteran had a good game, even though it was against an inexperienced opponent who was condemned to operate behind a slow-heeling pack.

An even first half, in which Jones, the Llanelli forward, suffered a cracked rib, ended with neither side scoring; but a dazzling break by Cliff Jones, Wales's quicksilver pivot, led to a try by the powerful Wooller at the beginning of the second half. Cliff Jones in fact was the best player on the field in this match, but his other efforts could not produce further Welsh tries.

During the game, the Irish referee had to deal with several outbreaks of rough play among the packs, and towards the end of the match caught a Welsh forward off-side in a critical position. It fell to Boughton – a remarkable inclusion at full-back for England as he had not appeared in a trial match since 1929 – to save England's bacon with an easy kick.

ENGLAND		WALES	
†H.J. Boughton	(Gloucester)	V.G.J. Jenkins	(Bridgend)
L.A. Booth	(Headingley)	B.T.V. Cowey	(Army/Newport)
P. Cranmer	(Oxford U.)	*E.C. Davey	(Swansea)
†J. Heaton	(Liverpool U.)	W. Wooller	(Cambridge U.)
†R. Leyland	(Waterloo)	A. Bassett	(Aberavon)
†P.L. Candler	(Cambridge U.)	C.W. Jones	(Cambridge U.)
†J.L. Giles	(Coventry)	W.C. Powell	(Northampton)
*D.A. Kendrew	(Army/Leicester)	E.L. Jones	(Llanelli)
†E.S. Nicholson	(Oxford U.)	C.D. Murphy	(Cross Keys)
R.J. Longland	(Northampton)	T.B. Day	(Swansea)
J. Dicks	(Northampton)	D. Thomas	(Swansea)
†A.J. Clarke	(Coventry)	H. Truman	(Llanelli)
†A.G. Cridlan	(Blackheath)	A.M. Rees	(Cambridge U.)
†D.T. Kemp	(Blackheath)	J. Lang	(Llanelli)
W.H. Weston	(Northampton)	A. Skym	(Cardiff)

Penalty: Boughton   *Try:* Wooller

Referee: Mr F.W. Haslett (Ireland)

ENGLAND v IRELAND 1935

Played at Twickenham, London, 9 February 1935
England won by 1G, 3PG (14) to 1T (3)

In a match punctuated by penalty kicks at goal, England ran out winners by 11 points – all kicks by Boughton.

England made three changes from the side held by Wales: Tallent (formerly a centre) was introduced at outside-half and Cranmer exchanged places with Leyland in a positional readjustment to the three-quarters. Payne entered the pack in the middle of the back row. England's midfield problems were not solved, however, for Cranmer switched back to centre at the interval.

Ireland's pack were closely held in the tight and loose, and the backs looked limited in their attacking moves. Nevertheless, a succession of technical infringements around the scrummage allowed Siggins's fifteen to take five kicks at goal in the first half, the skipper entrusting the place kicking to a colleague after a few narrow failures himself. The referee continued to find fault with the scrum-halves and front rows in the second half, and awarded a further ten penalties.

With 18 minutes to no-side, Boughton's conversion of a try by Giles was the difference between the sides. At this critical stage the Gloucester full-back coolly kicked three goals for England when careless Irish forwards fell off-side.

There were few signs in this match, particularly in the last quarter of an hour when Ireland were under severe pressure, that the visitors would progress to their first outright Championship title since 1899.

ENGLAND		IRELAND	
H.J. Boughton	(Gloucester)	D.P.Morris	(Bective Rangers)
L.A. Booth	(Headingley)	D. Lane	(U.C. Cork)
J. Heaton	(Liverpool U.)	P. Crowe	(Blackrock College)
R. Leyland	(Waterloo)	E.C. Ridgeway	(Wanderers)
P. Cranmer	(Oxford U.)	J.J. O'Connor	(U.C. Dublin)
J.A. Tallent	(Blackheath)	A.H. Bailey	(U.C. Dublin)
J.L. Giles	(Coventry)	G.J. Morgan	(Clontarf)
*D.A. Kendrew	(Army/Leicester)	C.E.St.J. Beamish	(R.A.F.)
E.S. Nicholson	(Oxford U.)	C.R.A. Graves	(Wanderers)
R.J. Longland	(Northampton)	S. Walker	(Instonians)
J. Dicks	(Northampton)	S.J. Deering	(Bective Rangers)
A.J. Clarke	(Coventry)	J. Russell	(U.C. Cork)
A.G. Cridlan	(Blackheath)	H.J.M. Sayers	(Aldershot Services)
†A.T. Payne	(Bristol)	*J.A.E. Siggins	(Collegians)
W.H. Weston	(Northampton)	P.J. Lawlor	(Bective Rangers)

Try: Giles
Conversion: Boughton
Penalties: Boughton (3)

Try: O'Connor

Referee: Mr M.A. Allan (Scotland)

SCOTLAND v ENGLAND 1935

Played at Murrayfield, Edinburgh, 16 March 1935
Scotland won by 2G (10) to 1DG, 1T (7)

Fine conditions prevailed and an open game full of incidents was enjoyed by a large crowd. The Scottish halves proved an invaluable asset to the home side and launched their backs into many attacking moves. Heaton and Auty were prominent in the English midfield at the start of the match, but close marking cramped their style later in the afternoon when only Cranmer and Leyland looked likely to overcome an obstinate Scottish defence.

At forward, England held a distinct advantage but failed to utilise a monopoly of scrummage and line-out possession. The Scottish forwards were much sharper in the loose; speed to the point of breakdown often compensating for shortcomings in the tight. Boughton was often required to trap the ball with brave falls at their feet, prompting O.L. Owen to write that 'he revealed a masterly understanding of the full-back position and its peculiar problems'.

Cranmer opened the scoring with a dropped goal, but Fyfe converted his own try after crisp running by Murdoch and Shaw had freed the path to the try-line. Lambie then touched down after Shaw had beaten a couple of opponents in a touchline dash and the ball had broken loose in the English goal area. Fyfe's conversion put Scotland well and truly in the saddle at the interval.

A run by Cranmer in the second half created an opening for Booth and a try followed. Later, Booth crossed when Leyland, whom many believed to be wasted playing on the wing, found a number of loopholes in the Scottish defence. A forward pass spoiled the move and England lost an excellent opportunity to reclaim the lead.

SCOTLAND		ENGLAND	
K.W. Marshall	(Edinburgh Acads.)	H.J. Boughton	(Gloucester)
J.E. Forrest	(Glasgow Acads.)	L.A. Booth	(Headingley)
R.C.S. Dick	(Guy's H.)	P. Cranmer	(Richmond)
W.C.W. Murdoch	(Hillhead H.S.F.P.)	J. Heaton	(Liverpool U.)
K.C. Fyfe	(Cambridge U.)	R. Leyland	(Waterloo)
*R.W. Shaw	(Glasgow H.S.F.P.)	†J.R. Auty	(Headingley)
W.R. Logan	(Edinburgh Wands.)	*B.C. Gadney	(Leicester)
R.O. Murray	(Cambridge U.)	J. Dicks	(Northampton)
P.W. Tait	(Royal H.S.F.P.)	E.S. Nicholson	(Oxford U.)
R.M. Grieve	(Kelso)	R.J. Longland	(Northampton)
J.A. Beattie	(Hawick)	A.J. Clarke	(Coventry)
W.A. Burnet	(West of Scotland)	C.S.H. Webb	(R.N./Devonport Services)
D.A. Thom	(London Scottish)	W.H. Weston	(Northampton)
J.A. Waters	(Selkirk)	A.T. Payne	(Bristol)
L.B. Lambie	(Glasgow H.S.F.P.)	A.G. Cridlan	(Blackheath)

Tries: Fyfe, Lambie
Conversions: Fyfe (2)

Try: Booth
Dropped goal: Cranmer

Referee: Mr R.W. Jeffares (Ireland)

ENGLAND v NEW ZEALAND 1936

Played at Twickenham, London, 4 January 1936
England won by 1DG, 3T (13) to Nil

England's victory was ascribed to the solidity of a heavy pack ably assisted by close-marking midfield backs who showed a fine turn of speed in attack. Gadney gave an impressive display behind his pack and New Zealand, at the end of an arduous, but happy, tour, were a very ordinary side. The attendance, estimated to be in excess of 73,000, included the Prince of Wales – weeks later, King Edward VIII.

The tourists dropped Hart and Sadler for this match, and a partially-fit Caughey (he had missed the Welsh game with a leg injury) regained his place in midfield; but it was a young Russian prince named Obolensky who won eternal fame with two spectacular first-half tries which helped to sink the All Blacks. His first effort, after about 20 minutes, followed pressure by the New Zealanders. Reid and King had each nearly crossed in the corner, before a round of passing sent Obolensky clear with about 40 yards to cover. The blistering pace of the winger took him around Gilbert for a try at the posts which Dunkley failed to convert – his effort striking the cross-bar.

It was the second try, however, which remains the conversation point of this historic game. Just before the interval, Cranmer, backed up by Candler, unleashed the flying prince from outside the New Zealand 25. With the defence converging on the right corner, Obolensky veered to his left and found a passage across the field to the far wing where he outpaced the late cover of Mitchell to complete a magnificent effort. Gerrard, from the left of the posts, failed to convert.

After the break New Zealand made one or two attempts to force a score but England's defence was sound. After ten minutes, the English pack heeled out for Gadney to send Candler away and the fly-half handed on to Cranmer who dropped a beautiful goal with his left foot. New Zealand's rout was complete when Cranmer made the break for Sever to sprint 35 yards and score the third try – again near the posts.

ENGLAND		NEW ZEALAND	
H.G. Owen-Smith	(St Mary's H.)	G.D.M. Gilbert	(West Coast)
†A. Obolensky	(Oxford U.)	N.A. Mitchell	(Southland)
P. Cranmer	(Richmond)	C.J. Oliver	(Canterbury)
R.A. Gerrard	(Bath)	N. Ball	(Wellington)
†H.S. Sever	(Sale)		
		T.H.C. Caughey	(Auckland)
P.L. Candler	(St Bart's H.)	E.W.T. Tindill	(Wellington)
*B.C. Gadney	(Leicester)	M.M.N. Corner	(Auckland)
D.A. Kendrew	(Leicester)	A. Lambourn	(Wellington)
E.S. Nicholson	(Leicester)	W.E. Hadley	(Auckland)
R.J. Longland	(Northampton)	J. Hore	(Otago)
C.S.H. Webb	(Devonport Services)	S.T. Reid	(Hawke's Bay)
A.J. Clarke	(Coventry)	R.R. King	(West Coast)
W.H. Weston	(Northampton)	*J.E. Manchester	(Canterbury)
P.E. Dunkley	(Harlequins)	A. Mahoney	(Bush)
†E.A. Hamilton-Hill	(Harlequins)	H.F. McLean	(Auckland)

Tries: Obolensky (2), Sever
Dropped goal: Cranmer

Referee: Mr J.W. Faull (Wales)

England v New Zealand, 1936.

ABOVE
The team which recorded England's most famous victory over an overseas side: *standing* P. L. Candler, E. S. Nicholson, R. A. Gerrard, E. A. Hamilton-Hill, A. J. Clarke, A. Obolensky, H. S. Sever, P. E. Dunkley, H. G. Owen-Smith, Mr J. W. Faull; *sitting* P. Cranmer, R. J. Longland, D. A. Kendrew, B. C. Gadney (captain), C. S. H. Webb, W. H. Weston.

LEFT
Sever and Obolensky, the England try-scorers, seen here opposing each other in a trial.

WALES v ENGLAND 1936

Played at St Helen's, Swansea, 18 January 1936
Drawn, neither side scoring

The prospect of seeing the two international sides which had lowered the colours of the New Zealanders attracted a crowd of over 50,000 spectators – more, one critic claimed, than those present at the Wales–New Zealand clash. Rumours were rife in Wales at this time that the W.R.U. were planning to close St Helen's as an international match venue and the interest shown by the inhabitants of South Wales for this match was described as 'a fair retort to the Easterners'.

As a spectacle, the match fell far short of its promise and a dour struggle ended in a pointless draw. McCall and Jenkins subdued the attacking flair of Obolensky on the English right and England's nearest approach to a score was a missed penalty by Cranmer – an easy kick hitting a post.

Wales, with Wooller and Cliff Jones showing their paces as finely-balanced runners, threatened to give England a testing in defence near the end of the match, but Gerrard and Cranmer, with their aggressive tackling and safe covering, locked up the middle of the field, as they had against the New Zealand three-quarters.

Wilf Wooller summed up this match, sixteen years later, as follows: 'It was a typical, hard-fought, England–Wales defensive duel of the 'thirties. No quarter asked, none given, and England relying on a defensive back-line, well-supported by a heavy skirmishing pack. With a great attacking spearhead in Haydn Tanner and Cliff Jones, Wales often came near to scoring and once when 'Tuppy' Owen-Smith flicked my ankle in a desperate tackle, I stumbled, only to fall a few feet from the English line. That desperate English defence, cost Wales the Triple Crown!'

WALES		ENGLAND	
V.G.J. Jenkins	(London Welsh)	H.G. Owen-Smith	(St Mary's H.)
G.R. Rees-Jones	(Oxford U.)	A. Obolensky	(Oxford U.)
*J.I. Rees	(Swansea)	R.A. Gerrard	(Bath)
W. Wooller	(Cambridge U.)	P. Cranmer	(Richmond)
B.E.W. McCall	(Welch Regt./Newport)	H.S. Sever	(Sale)
C.W. Jones	(Cambridge U.)	P.L. Candler	(St Bart's H.)
H. Tanner	(Swansea)	*B.C. Gadney	(Leicester)
T.J. Rees	(Newport)	D.A. Kendrew	(Leicester)
B. Evans	(Llanelli)	E.S. Nicholson	(Leicester)
T. Williams	(Cross Keys)	R.J. Longland	(Northampton)
H. Thomas	(Neath)	C.S.H. Webb	(Devonport Services)
G. Williams	(Aberavon)	A.J. Clarke	(Coventry)
A.M. Rees	(London Welsh)	W.H. Weston	(Northampton)
J. Lang	(Llanelli)	P.E. Dunkley	(Harlequins)
E. Long	(Swansea)	E.A. Hamilton-Hill	(Harlequins)

Referee: Mr F.W. Haslett (Ireland)

IRELAND v ENGLAND 1936

Played at Lansdowne Road, Dublin, 8 February 1936
Ireland won by 2T (6) to 1T (3)

A poor but exciting game was watched by a crowd of 36,000 on a cold, crisp and sunny afternoon. The result, an unexpected victory by a faster Irish fifteen, was a disappointment to an English team which had dominated the match in the first half.

The Irish forwards were lively in the loose and, despite conceding a significant weight advantage to England in the scrummaging, tight midfield marking by the Irish centres contained the fitful efforts of the English backs. Slow, ponderous heeling by the English pack did not give Gadney enough time to evade the Irish back row; Candler's tactics were limited; Gerrard and Cranmer were unsure in attack and, of the English backs, only Sever, with his direct running, lived up to his footballing reputation. Sever, in fact, scored England's only try when he picked up a loose ball and ran through a crowd of players midway through the first half. Owen-Smith failed to convert.

Ireland were thus three points behind at the interval, and their cause had been complicated by the loss of Deering with a head injury. The Irish forward required five stitches to a wound received in the first 20 minutes of the match and, although he returned to the fray with a bandaged head, eventually he was compelled to retire.

England's defence became slacker as the game progressed. After 25 minutes in the second half, McMahon led a rush with the ball at his feet. The English cover was disorganised and Boyle followed up for a simple try. Bailey failed to convert but Ireland were inspired by the score and held down England to the end of the match. Three minutes from no-side, Bailey gathered the ball after an English handling movement had broken down and the Dublin student made a diagonal burst for the corner, managing to wriggle through the tackle of Owen-Smith for the winning try.

Both sides wore black arm bands as a sign of respect for the late Patron of the R.F.U., King George V, who had died on 20 January at Sandringham.

IRELAND		ENGLAND	
G.L. Malcolmson	(N.I.F.C.)	H.G. Owen-Smith	(St Mary's H.)
F.G. Moran	(Clontarf)	A. Obolensky	(Oxford U.)
A.H. Bailey	(U.C. Dublin)	R.A. Gerrard	(Bath)
L.B. McMahon	(Blackrock College)	P. Cranmer	(Richmond)
C.V. Boyle	(Dublin U.)	H.S. Sever	(Sale)
V.A. Hewitt	(Instonians)	P.L. Candler	(St Bart's H.)
G.J. Morgan	(Clontarf)	*B.C. Gadney	(Leicester)
S. Walker	(Instonians)	R.J. Longland	(Northampton)
C.R.A. Graves	(Wanderers)	D.A. Kendrew	(Leicester)
C.E.St.J. Beamish	(N.I.F.C./R.A.F.)	†H.F. Wheatley	(Coventry)
S.J. Deering	(Bective Rangers)	A.J. Clarke	(Coventry)
J. Russell	(U.C. Cork)	C.S.H. Webb	(Devonport Services)
H.J.M. Sayers	(Lansdowne)	E.A. Hamilton-Hill	(Harlequins)
*J.A.E. Siggins	(Collegians)	P.E. Dunkley	(Harlequins)
R. Alexander	(N.I.F.C/R.U.C.)	J.McD. Hodgson	(Northern)

Tries: Bailey, Boyle   *Try:* Sever

Referee: Mr M.A. Allan (Scotland)

ENGLAND v SCOTLAND 1936

Played at Twickenham, London, 21 March 1936
England won by 3T (9) to 1G, 1PG (8)

England registered their first success of the Championship with a narrow victory over Scotland. There was little to choose between two ordinary sides though England, in the second half particularly, wasted many scoring opportunities. Obolensky, who had hypnotised the All Blacks with his unorthodox running, was starved for most of the match and closely marked by Fyfe. The introduction of Toft brought much-needed speed to the striking of the English scrum and gave the home side a distinct advantage in this department. Gadney had a regular source of possession but, to the chagrin of a crowd basking in early Spring sunshine, he wasted much of this good ball with an inexplicable inclination to nurse the touch-line and to neglect his backs.

There was a brisk start to the match. Sever flat-footed Shaw in the second minute with a neat piece of footwork and Bolton was at hand to open the scoring. Two minutes later a penalty goal from 40 yards by Fyfe levelled the scores but Scotland were unfortunate to lose Barrie with a broken collar-bone.

Later, from a scrum inside the Scottish half, Candler seduced the defence with a dummy to regain the lead for England with a try. Soon afterwards Cranmer increased it when he dribbled the ball over the try-line, a Scotsman having dropped a pass. Before the interval Shaw ran in at the corner after combining with Fyfe, who kicked the goal from a wide angle.

No points were scored in the second half and Scotland were left holding the Wooden Spoon.

ENGLAND		SCOTLAND	
H.G. Owen-Smith	(St Mary's H.)	J.M. Kerr	(Heriot's F.P.)
A. Obolensky	(Oxford U.)	R.W. Shaw	(Glasgow H.S.F.P.)
R.A. Gerrard	(Bath)	H. Lind	(London Scottish)
P. Cranmer	(Richmond)	R.C.S. Dick	(Guy's H.)
H.S. Sever	(Sale)	K.C. Fyfe	(Sale)
P.L. Candler	(St Bart's H.)	C.F. Grieve	(Oxford U.)
*B.C. Gadney	(Leicester)	W.R. Logan	(Edinburgh Wands.)
R.J. Longland	(Northampton)	R.M. Grieve	(Kelso)
†H.B. Toft	(Waterloo)	G.S. Cottington	(Kelso/Headingley)
J. Dicks	(Northampton)	W.A.H. Druitt	(London Scottish)
C.S.H. Webb	(R.N./Devonport Services)	*J.A. Beattie	(Hawick)
P.E. Dunkley	(Harlequins)	W.A. Burnet	(West of Scotland)
R. Bolton	(Harlequins)	R.W. Barrie	(Hawick)
P.W.P. Brook	(Harlequins)	J.A. Waters	(Selkirk)
W.H. Weston	(Northampton)	V.G. Weston	(Kelvinside Acads.)

Tries: Bolton, Candler, Cranmer

Try: Shaw   *Conversion:* Fyfe
Penalty: Fyfe

Referee: Mr T.H. Phillips (Wales)

ENGLAND v WALES 1937

Played at Twickenham, London, 16 January 1937
England won by 1DG (4) to 1T (3)

England beat Wales 'with the aid of the Welsh selectors', wrote O.L. Owen in his review of the season for the *Rugby Football Annual*; for Wales, without C.W. Jones (badly injured), took the field at Twickenham with a light pack which was more at home scrounging the loose ball than shoving in the scrummages. England's solid forwards thus set the home side on course for a one-point victory in a rather dreary match. The attendance was 65,000.

With the Welshmen outplayed in the scrummages, the English backs enjoyed a limitless supply of ball but, strangely, never looked like scoring a try. The failure of the English line was difficult to explain, for the passing was not particularly wayward, neither was the Welsh tackling unusually fierce: the English backs were simply unable to initiate scoring thrusts.

All of the scoring occurred before the break. Cranmer, with two lively dribbles to the Welsh 25, posed some problems for the Welshmen. D. Thomas cleared the first attack, and the second sortie resulted in a penalty to the visitors near their posts. A Welshman failed to make a safe touch, however, the ball striking Prescott on the shoulder and glancing off to Sever who dropped a goal. Wales soon responded and Tanner, who had momentarily been off the field for repairs after a tackle on Campbell, made a passage on his left to the English line. Owen-Smith ended his progress but Clement was able to continue the move and an inside pass to Wooller produced the only try of the match. Clement gave Wales a glimmer of hope seconds later with a run and chase after a punt ahead, but Sever got back to save England's line.

In an undistinguished second half, both sides were resigned to the fact that tries were impossible to come by, and satisfied their scoring desires with a series of optimistic penalty attempts from near half-way. Cranmer and Jenkins were the chief protagonists in this little scene, but no further scoring resulted and England were content to hold their narrow lead.

ENGLAND		WALES	
*H.G. Owen-Smith	(St Mary's H.)	V.G.J. Jenkins	(London Welsh)
†A.G. Butler	(Harlequins)	J.I. Rees	(Swansea)
P.L. Candler	(St Bart's H.)	*E.C. Davey	(London Welsh)
P. Cranmer	(Richmond)	W. Wooller	(Cardiff)
H.S. Sever	(Sale)	W.H. Clement	(Llanelli)
†T.A. Kemp	(Cambridge U.)	W.T.H. Davies	(Swansea)
J.L. Giles	(Coventry)	H. Tanner	(Swansea)
†R.E. Prescott	(Harlequins)	T.J. Rees	(Newport)
H.B. Toft	(Waterloo)	B. Evans	(Llanelli)
R.J. Longland	(Northampton)	E. Evans	(Llanelli)
†T.F. Huskisson	(O.M.Ts.)	H. Thomas	(Neath)
†A. Wheatley	(Coventry)	D.L. Thomas	(Neath)
†D.A. Campbell	(Cambridge U.)	A.M. Rees	(London Welsh)
†D.L.K. Milman	(Bedford)	J. Lang	(Swansea)
W.H. Weston	(Northampton)	E. Long	(Swansea)

Dropped goal: Sever   *Try:* Wooller

Referee: Mr R.A. Beattie (Scotland)

ENGLAND v IRELAND 1937

Played at Twickenham, London, 13 February 1937
England won by 1PG, 2T (9) to 1G, 1T (8)

In one of the most entertaining, and certainly most exciting international matches played at Twickenham, England scraped home with a memorable late try by Sever – the matchwinner against Wales. The first half had been closely contested with England just about the better side, though the Irish defence showed no signs of cracking. The visiting forwards were, as ever, a handful, but towards the end of the match there was a slight deterioration in their fitness. There was a welcome improvement by the English backs on their rather formless display against Wales, and Malcolmson, the Irish full-back, was often required to show his strengths in defence.

The scoring opened early in the second half when the home forwards dribbled along the right touch-line. Huskisson was prominent at the head of this rush and made a one-handed pick-up which maintained the momentum towards the Irish line. At length, the Irish cover smothered the O.M.T. but Butler was at hand to score near the flag. Cranmer could not convert, and the scores were again level soon after when the Irish forwards enabled Bailey and McMahon to break away. Moran, speeding like an express train, completed the move with a try in the corner. Five minutes later, Moran gave another demonstration of his pace with a second try in the corner after he had kicked ahead and outraced Candler and Sever for the touch-down. Bailey, with a fine kick, stretched Ireland to a five-points lead. Ireland should have won from this vantage point, but foolishly allowed Cranmer to pull back three penalty points and set the scene for a grandstand finish.

Ireland were attacking with about six minutes to go when Morgan managed to find touch inside the English 25. From an ensuing scrum, the English backs ran the ball along the threequarter line to Sever, who set off on a glorious run down the line which took him past several would-be tacklers before he launched himself over the try-line with a tackler on his back. England were home by a point and withstood a last-minute penalty kick at goal.

ENGLAND		IRELAND	
*H.G. Owen-Smith	(St Mary's H.)	G.L. Malcolmson	(N.I.F.C.)
A.G. Butler	(Harlequins)	F.G. Moran	(Clontarf)
P. Cranmer	(Richmond)	L.B. McMahon	(Blackrock College)
P.L. Candler	(St Bart's H.)	A.H. Bailey	(U.C. Dublin)
H.S. Sever	(Sale)	C.V. Boyle	(Dublin U.)
T.A. Kemp	(Cambridge U.)	G.E. Cromey	(Queen's U.)
J.L. Giles	(Coventry)	*G.J. Morgan	(Clontarf)
R.E. Prescott	(Harlequins)	S. Walker	(Instonians)
H.B. Toft	(Waterloo)	T.S. Corken	(Collegians)
R.J. Longland	(Northampton)	C.R.A. Graves	(Wanderers)
T.F. Huskisson	(O.M.Ts.)	J. Russell	(U.C. Cork)
A. Wheatley	(Coventry)	S.J. Deering	(Bective Rangers)
D.A. Campbell	(Cambridge U.)	P.J. Lawlor	(Bective Rangers)
J. Dicks	(Northampton)	J.A.E. Siggins	(Collegians)
W.H. Weston	(Northampton)	R. Alexander	(R.U.C./N.I.F.C.)

Tries: Butler, Sever   *Tries:* Moran (2)   *Conversion:* Bailey
Penalty: Cranmer

Referee: Mr J.W. Faull (Wales)

England v Ireland, 1937. H. G. Owen-Smith leads his Triple Crown winning side on to the pitch, followed by Toft and Sever; and Giles feeds his backs from a scrum.

SCOTLAND v ENGLAND 1937

Played at Murrayfield, Edinburgh, 20 March 1937
England won by 2T (6) to 1PG (3)

England thoroughly deserved their first success at Murrayfield, and victory made them Champions, Triple Crown winners and Calcutta Cup holders. As in the Welsh match, the English forwards carried all before them and fed the English backs with plenty of good ball. The introduction of Reynolds, at half-back to the recalled Gadney, improved the passing along the back line, and Reynolds handled Gadney's long passes with ease and accuracy. Cranmer and Candler were often dangerous but some rock-like defence by Macrae and Shaw, playing in the Scottish centre, thwarted the early advances of the Englishmen.

The only score of the first half came several minutes before the break. The *Yorkshire Post* described the try as follows: 'Once more Candler found a pathway through the shadow of an opening and across the line went the ball to Sever, but this time Johnston refused to be shaken off; England's attacks persisted, though, and if Cook was short with a long penalty kick, there were successive threats by Bolton from Sever's inside pass and Gadney's shrewd kick, so that there was little surprise when quick passing, initiated by Reynolds' invaluable straight-step, sent Unwin swerving away round Marshall to experience the thrill of a lifetime in scoring his first try for England.'

In the remaining minutes of the half, Scotland lost Ross with an injury. After a period of uneventful play in midfield, the game came to life again in the second half when Reynolds executed several lengthy punts down the touch-line which brought England into the Scottish 25. Then, from a set-piece, the ball travelled smoothly out to Sever who neatly side-stepped his opponent to put the ball down beside the Scottish goal. Cook failed to add the conversion, but Scotland's only consolation after this was a penalty kicked by G.D. Shaw.

The Wheatleys were brothers.

SCOTLAND		ENGLAND	
K.W. Marshall	(Edinburgh Acads.)	*H.G. Owen-Smith	(St Mary's H.)
W.G.S. Johnston	(Richmond)	†E.J. Unwin	(Army)
R.W. Shaw	(Glasgow H.S.F.P.)	P.L. Candler	(St Bart's H.)
D.J. Macrae	(St Andrew's U.)	P. Cranmer	(Richmond)
R.H. Dryden	(Watsonians)	H.S. Sever	(Sale)
W.A. Ross	(Hillhead H.S.F.P.)	†F.J. Reynolds	(Army/Old Cranleighans)
*W.R. Logan	(Edinburgh Wands.)	B.C. Gadney	(Leicester)
M.M. Henderson	(Dunfermline)	H.F. Wheatley	(Coventry)
G.L. Gray	(Gala)	H.B. Toft	(Waterloo)
W.M. Inglis	(Cambridge U.)	R.J. Longland	(Northampton)
G.B. Horsburgh	(London Scottish)	T.F. Huskisson	(O.M.Ts.)
C.L. Melville	(The Black Watch)	A. Wheatley	(Coventry)
W.B. Young	(Cambridge U.)	†J.G. Cook	(Bedford)
J.A. Waters	(Selkirk)	R. Bolton	(Harlequins)
G.D. Shaw	(Gala/Sale)	W.H. Weston	(Northampton)

Penalty: G.D. Shaw   *Tries:* Sever, Unwin

Referee: Mr S. Donaldson (Ireland)

WALES v ENGLAND 1938
Played at Cardiff Arms Park, 15 January 1938
Wales won by 1G, 2PG, 1T (14) to 1G, 1T (8)

The fiftieth official international match between the two countries resulted in a good victory for the home side in a match spoiled by gale-force winds. Wales recalled Davey to the threequarter line when Wooller was unfit, but the Welsh backs looked unusually ineffective during the whole afternoon. In fact, it was the forwards who laid the foundation for this win, A.M. Rees calling his men to adopt a 3–4–1 formation mid-way through the first half. As a result, the home forwards were able to counter the strong scrummaging and quick heeling of Toft and his English pack.

Wales had the advantage of the elements in the first half, and opened their scoring after 15 minutes when McCarley dribbled the ball from half-way, and a missed tackle by the English full-back allowed the Neath back-row forward to score near the corner. Jenkins increased the lead eight minutes later with a penalty after the English had offended in a scrum, but fine efforts by the English backs were rewarded just before the interval. Nicholson intercepted a pass in his own 25 and raced down the field to accept a return pass from Unwin, who had made ground along the touch-line before drawing Jenkins. Candler followed up to take the final pass and score. Wales soon went further ahead when Jenkins landed another penalty goal.

Wales faced the gale in the second half with only a six-points lead, and English hopes of victory were high. But Wales obtained the crucial score of the match a few minutes after the restart. From the first scrum of the second half, Jones kicked ahead and Freakes, misjudging the pitch of the ball in the high wind, allowed J.I. Rees to gather the ball in his stride and touch down near the posts. Jenkins converted into the wind to put Wales 11 points up. England stormed back; Cranmer missed two penalties, but, while Watkins was off the field, Sever outpaced the Welsh defence to score a try which Freakes converted into a goal. In the dying moments of the game, Unwin slid over near the corner but touched the corner flag before grounding the ball.

Unwin was the first England player capped while playing for Rosslyn Park R.F.C.

WALES		ENGLAND	
V.G.J. Jenkins	(London Welsh)	†H.D. Freakes	(Oxford U./Harlequins)
W.H. Clement	(Llanelli)	E.J. Unwin	(The Army/Rosslyn Park)
J.I. Rees	(Swansea)	*P. Cranmer	(Moseley)
E.C. Davey	(London Welsh)	†B.E. Nicholson	(Harlequins)
A. Bassett	(Cardiff)	H.S. Sever	(Sale)
*C.W. Jones	(Cardiff)	P.L. Candler	(St Bart's H.)
H. Tanner	(Swansea)	B.C. Gadney	(Headingley)
H. Rees	(Cardiff)	R.J. Longland	(Northampton)
W.H. Travers	(Newport)	H.B. Toft	(Waterloo)
M.E. Morgan	(Swansea)	H.F. Wheatley	(Coventry)
F.L. Morgan	(Llanelli)	T.F. Huskisson	(O.M.Ts.)
E. Watkins	(Cardiff)	A. Wheatley	(Coventry)
A.M. Rees	(London Welsh)	W.H. Weston	(Northampton)
W. Vickery	(Aberavon)	D.L.K. Milman	(Bedford)
A. McCarley	(Neath)	R. Bolton	(Harlequins)

Tries: McCarley, J.I. Rees
Conversion: Jenkins
Penalties: Jenkins (2)

Tries: Candler, Sever
Conversion: Freakes

Referee: Mr R.A. Beattie (Scotland)

IRELAND v ENGLAND 1938

Played at Lansdowne Road, Dublin, 12 February 1938
England won by 6G, 1PG, 1T (36) to 1G, 3T (14)

This was England's highest points-total in an international match since they had scored 39 points against France in the last game played before the 1914–1918 War. Yet, somehow, this was not so convincing a win as it appeared on paper. The Irish were unbelievably weak, and the English performance in the second half, when they conceded 14 points, was rather disorganised. Full marks to Ireland for staging a recovery after trailing by 23 points at the break.

England elected to play with a very strong wind at their backs and were five points ahead in as many minutes – Giles tidying up a heel by his forwards near the Irish line and diving over. Parker, whose place-kicking was very accurate in this match, converted and then landed a penalty. There was no further scoring until the last ten minutes of the half. Then, in an amazing sequence, three tries were obtained, the most spectacular being a 50-yards run by the second-row man from Oxford, Marshall. Parker converted each try.

England were content to sit on their lead in the second half, but the Irish were not going to surrender without a fight. Some good kicks by Morgan put England under pressure, and Cromey scored a try after charging down an attempted clearance by Reynolds. Crowe was unable to match the achievements of Parker. Much of the play in the third quarter was rather poor, but then Giles slipped away to send Bolton over at the posts. Ireland retaliated and Bailey confused Parker with a punt ahead, the ball striking a post and rebounding for the Irish centre to score. Crowe converted the try into a goal before another English try resulted. This time Prescott was the scorer, and, incredibly, Parker failed to convert. Finally, in the closing exchanges of the match, Ireland added tries by Mayne, from a line-out, and Daly; while England had the last say when Nicholson completed a fine individual effort for a try which Parker improved with his seventh successful kick of the day.

IRELAND		ENGLAND	
P. Crowe	(Blackrock College)	†G.W. Parker	(Gloucester)
M.J. Daly	(Harlequins)	E.J. Unwin	(Rosslyn Park)
A.H. Bailey	(U.C. Dublin)	B.E. Nicholson	(Harlequins)
L.B. McMahon	(Blackrock College)	*P. Cranmer	(Moseley)
V.J. Lyttle	(Bedford/Belfast Collegians)	H.S. Sever	(Sale)
G.E. Cromey	(Queen's U.)	F.J. Reynolds	(Old Cranleighans)
*G.J. Morgan	(Old Belvedere)	J.L. Giles	(Coventry)
E. Ryan	(Dolphin)	R.J. Longland	(Northampton)
C.R.A. Graves	(Wanderers)	H.B. Toft	(Waterloo)
D.B. O'Loughlin	(U.C. Cork)	R.E. Prescott	(Harlequins)
R.B. Mayne	(Queen's U.)	†R.M. Marshall	(Oxford U.)
S. Walker	(Instonians)	T.F. Huskisson	(O.M.Ts.)
R. Alexander	(N.I.F.C.)	W.H. Weston	(Northampton)
J.W.S. Irwin	(N.I.F.C.)	D.L.K. Milman	(Bedford)
J. Megaw	(Richmond/Instonians)	R. Bolton	(Harlequins)

Tries: Bailey, Cromey, Daly, Mayne
Conversion: Crowe

Tries: Bolton, Giles, Marshall, Nicholson, Prescott, Reynolds, Unwin   *Conversions:* Parker (6)
Penalty: Parker

Referee: Mr J.C.H. Ireland (Scotland)

ENGLAND v SCOTLAND 1938
Played at Twickenham, London, 19 March 1938
Scotland won by 2PG, 5T (21) to 1DG, 3PG, 1T (16)

Scotland visited Twickenham in the knowledge that victory would again bring the Triple Crown. Both sides were unable to play as originally selected but this match, for ever referred to as Wilson Shaw's match, was one of the most outstanding spectacles of open Rugby since World War 1. The game was played in perfect conditions before 70,000 spectators who saw the lead change hands several times.

England started strongly but Scotland opened the scoring when Parker failed to gather a loose ball. Wilson Shaw kicked diagonally for Renwick to latch on to a lucky bounce and score an unconverted try. Parker made amends for his error, landing two penalties before Renwick got his second try, dashing over from a loose maul on the half-hour. Three further tries were registered before the interval as the pace of the match increased. Dorward robbed Giles of the ball after an English heel and Shaw, Young, Duff, Crawford and Macrae handled before Dick scored a marvellous try. England soon equalised – Reynolds starting a classic threequarter passing movement which sent Unwin diving over in the corner. The third brilliant try in ten minutes put Scotland ahead at half-time. This was a fine opportunist's try in the corner by Shaw, who had beaten Parker with a swerve to make the interval score 12–9.

Reynolds put England back into the lead soon after the restart, dropping a neat goal, though Crawford replied immediately with a penalty goal when England were caught off-side. He landed another, ten minutes later, when Parker failed to play the ball, but England did not give up and a fine goal by Parker from a wide angle and into the breeze brought the score to 18–16. Then, in a final flourish, Shaw put the last nail in England's coffin by setting off on a breathless, swerving run which produced a great individualist's try to end a most memorable match.

ENGLAND		SCOTLAND	
G.W. Parker	(Blackheath)	G. Roberts	(Watsonians)
E.J. Unwin	(Rosslyn Park)	W.N. Renwick	(London Scottish)
P.L. Candler	(St Bart's H.)	R. C. S. Dick	(Guy's H.)
P. Cranmer	(Moseley)	D.J. Macrae	(St Andrew's U.)
H.S. Sever	(Sale)	J.G.S. Forrest	(Cambridge U.)
F.J. Reynolds	(Old Cranleighans)	*R.W. Shaw	(Glasgow H.S.F.P.)
J.L. Giles	(Coventry)	T.F. Dorward	(Gala)
R.J. Longland	(Northampton)	W.F. Blackadder	(West of Scotland)
*H.B. Toft	(Waterloo)	J.D.H. Hastie	(Melrose)
H.F. Wheatley	(Coventry)	W.M. Inglis	(The Army)
R.M. Marshall	(Oxford U.)	G.B. Horsburgh	(London Scottish)
A. Wheatley	(Coventry)	A. Roy	(Waterloo)
W. H. Weston	(Northampton)	W.B. Young	(Cambridge U.)
D.L.K. Milman	(Bedford)	P.L. Duff	(Glasgow Acads.)
†A.A. Brown	(Exeter)	W.H. Crawford	(U.S.)

Try: Unwin *Dropped goal:* Reynolds
Penalties: Parker (3)

Tries: Renwick (2), Shaw (2), Dick
Penalties: Crawford (2)

Referee: Mr I. David (Wales)

ENGLAND v WALES 1939

Played at Twickenham, London, 21 January 1939
England won by 1T (3) to Nil

Conditions at Twickenham for this match resembled a heaving bog and many critics stated that the ground was as bad in wet weather as the infamous Arms Park at Cardiff. In the circumstances, then, it was too much to expect flowing Rugby and the English halves, revelling behind a rampant, all-conquering pack which completely dominated the Welsh eight, played a tight game to their forwards. Wales saw little of the ball in the first 25 minutes, though the defensive play of Wooller and Jenkins kept the English at bay. Then the tide turned slightly and the Welsh began heeling out cleanly at the scrums and the visiting backs were able to show one or two neat moves in attack. The Welsh centres and Williams on the wing revealed flair and determination, while Wooller reminded England of his kicking ability with an enormous drop at goal which just sailed wide of its objective. Soon after, England started their most promising move of the first period. Guest went scrambling down the right wing, beating Wooller with an immaculate side-step and reaching Jenkins with Marshall at his shoulder. It should have been a try-scoring pass, but the back-row man fumbled his take and the 70,000 spectators were quick to air their feelings at his failure.

England looked the tidier and more effective side in the rushes which marked the opening to the second period of play, and, after 15 minutes, Marshall led a dash from which Teden grounded the ball after it had been kicked over the Welsh line. Heaton's conversion attempt struck the far upright. Wales lost Vickery at this stage and Heaton went close with a drop at goal before Davies showed his talent as a neatly-balanced runner in an effort to snatch victory for Wales. There was a gallant attempt by Sid Williams, too, but Wales, in the end, were unable to register their second win at Headquarters.

The Welsh forward, Vickery, was the son of England international G. Vickery, capped in 1905.

ENGLAND		WALES	
H.D. Freakes	(Oxford U./Harlequins)	V.G.J. Jenkins	(London Welsh)
†R.H. Guest	(Liverpool U./Waterloo)	F.J.V. Ford	(Army)
J. Heaton	(Waterloo)	D.I. Davies	(Swansea)
†G.E. Hancock	(Birkenhead Park)	*W. Wooller	(Cardiff)
†R.S.L. Carr	(Old Cranleighans)	S. Williams	(Aberavon)
†G.A. Walker	(R.A.F./Blackheath)	W.T.H. Davies	(Swansea)
†P. Cooke	(Richmond)	H. Tanner	(Swansea)
R.E. Prescott	(Harlequins)	M.E. Morgan	(Swansea)
*H.B. Toft	(Waterloo)	W.H. Travers	(Newport)
†D.E. Teden	(Richmond)	W.E.N. Davis	(Cardiff)
T.F. Huskisson	(O.M.Ts.)	F.L. Morgan	(Llanelli)
H.F. Wheatley	(Coventry)	E. Watkins	(Cardiff)
†J.K. Watkins	(R.N.)	A.R. Taylor	(Cross Keys)
R.M. Marshall	(Oxford U./Harlequins)	W. Vickery	(Aberavon)
†J.T.W. Berry	(Leicester)	C. Challinor	(Neath)

Try: Teden

Referee: Mr J.C.H. Ireland (Scotland)

ENGLAND v IRELAND 1939

Played at Twickenham, London, 11 February 1939
Ireland won by 1G (5) to Nil

England retained the fifteen which had beaten Wales, but, surprisingly, lost to a lively and disruptive Irish team. Morgan, the Irish captain, conducted proceedings skilfully and elected to nurse his pack rather than run the ball out to his backs. In fact, the back play by both teams was most uninspiring: the English halves were guilty of misguided tactical kicking and the three-quarters frittered away attacking opportunities by running across the field and crowding their wings. This was most marked in the last ten minutes of the match when the English forwards were completely on top in the set-pieces and the Irish forwards were showing signs of weakness. Nor was the Irish back play any better: Moran was firmly held by his opposite number, Carr, and the Irish centres were also tending to push their wings too wide, so that the angles in attack were imprecise and unproductive. Lyttle showed some promise, however, and kept Guest on his mettle with some tricky running.

Early in the match Carr made a break which brought him to within a yard of the Irish line, and Teden crossed for a try which was disallowed. Morgan was Ireland's guiding genius, and his little kicks to Moran's wing were a constant threat to England's defence. Infringements constantly interrupted the flow of the game, though, and no score was made before the interval.

Playing against the wind in the second half, Ireland took their scoring chance well after about nine minutes. Good kicking by Torrens and a fine run by Lyttle forced England back into their 25. A rush led by Sayers caught Freakes in a quandary and, before the South African could clear, Irwin snatched the ball from him and crashed over for a try, converted by McKibbin.

Carr and Guest put in runs soon after, and Heaton missed with a penalty before England's great chances in the last ten minutes were squandered by the English backs, who failed miserably to convert the possession won by a grand pack into sorely-needed points.

ENGLAND		IRELAND	
H.D. Freakes	(Oxford U./Harlequins)	C.J. Murphy	(Lansdowne)
R.H. Guest	(Waterloo)	F.G. Moran	(Clontarf)
J. Heaton	(Waterloo)	H.R. McKibbin	(Instonians)
G.E. Hancock	(Birkenhead Park)	J.D. Torrens	(Bohemians)
R.S.L. Carr	(Old Cranleighans)	V.J. Lyttle	(Collegians/Bedford)
G.A. Walker	(R.A.F./Blackheath)	G.E. Cromey	(Collegians)
P. Cooke	(Richmond)	*G.J. Morgan	(O. Belvedere)
R.E. Prescott	(Harlequins)	J.G. Ryan	(U.C. Dublin)
*H.B. Toft	(Waterloo)	C. Teehan	(U.C. Cork)
D.E. Teden	(Richmond)	D. Tierney	(U.C. Cork)
T.F. Huskisson	(O.M.Ts.)	D.B. O'Loughlin	(Garryowen)
H.F. Wheatley	(Coventry)	R.B. Mayne	(Malone)
J.K. Watkins	(R.N.)	H.J.M. Sayers	(Army)
R.M. Marshall	(Oxford U./Harlequins)	J.W.S. Irwin	(N.I.F.C.)
J.T.W. Berry	(Leicester)	R. Alexander	(R.U.C./N.I.F.C.)

Try: Irwin *Conversion:* McKibbin

Referee: Mr J.C.H. Ireland (Scotland)

SCOTLAND v ENGLAND 1939
Played at Murrayfield, Edinburgh, 18 March 1939
England won by 3PG (9) to 2T (6)

This was a thoroughly modern scoreline in which the ability of one side (in the form of Heaton) to kick its goals robbed the other side of a victory. England's forwards gained constant possession in the tight, but it was the same old tale outside the scrum with the backs unable to penetrate the opposition's defence and create tries. Scotland, well beaten up-front, always looked most dangerous when their backs were in flight, and the two tries scored were each the results of clever back play.

After about 12 minutes of play, a cross-kick by Innes was fumbled twice by an unsure English defence, allowing Murdoch to pounce and take the ball in his stride before racing off from near half-way to register a memorable score. Unusually, the place kick which followed was disallowed – the referee ruling that the placer had touched the ball after it had made contact with the ground, thus infringing Law 25.

England were not unduly perturbed by this reverse, and Heaton (with a penalty attempt) and Kemp (with an attempted drop at goal) went near to equalising before Dorward sent his partner away from a loose scrum. Bruce-Lockhart kicked ahead and Shaw followed up at speed, gathered the ball cleanly and outwitted Heaton and Parsons to score wide out to the left. Murdoch succeeded Crawford as place-kicker, but could not add the goal.

The visitors were level before half-time: two enormous kicks from long range and at considerable angles were carefully placed by Heaton – and, as if to rub salt into these wounds, Heaton kicked another long-range goal at the beginning of the second half to complete the scoring. As the second half progressed, so the English forwards continued their total domination of the tiring Scottish pack, and, long before no-side, the Scottish crowd had accepted defeat in a rather dreary match.

SCOTLAND		ENGLAND	
G. Roberts	(Watsonians)	†E.I. Parsons	(R.A.F.)
J.R.S. Innes	(Aberdeen U.)	R.H. Guest	(Waterloo)
D.J. Macrae	(St Andrew's U.)	J. Heaton	(Waterloo)
*R.W. Shaw	(Glasgow H.S.F.P.)	G.E. Hancock	(Birkenhead Park)
W.C.W. Murdoch	(Hillhead H.S.F.P.)	R.S.L. Carr	(Old Cranleighans)
R.B. Bruce-Lockhart	(London Scottish)	T.A. Kemp	(St Mary's H.)
T.F. Dorward	(Gala)	†J. Ellis	(Wakefield)
I.C. Henderson	(Edinburgh Acads.)	D.E. Teden	(Richmond)
I.N. Graham	(Edinburgh Acads.)	*H.B. Toft	(Waterloo)
W. Purdie	(Jedforest)	R.E. Prescott	(Harlequins)
G.B. Horsburgh	(London Scottish)	H.F. Wheatley	(Coventry)
A. Roy	(Waterloo)	T.F. Huskisson	(O.M.Ts.)
W.B. Young	(K.C.H.)	J.K. Watkins	(R.N.)
D.K.A. Mackenzie	(Edinburgh Wands.)	R.M. Marshall	(Oxford U./Harlequins)
W.H. Crawford	(U.S.)	J.T.W. Berry	(Leicester)

Tries: Murdoch, Shaw *Penalties:* Heaton (3)

Referee: Mr I. David (Wales)

England v Ireland, 1939. England's last fifteen at Twickenham before World
War 2, and the side which shared the Championship with Ireland and Wales:
back Mr J. C. H. Ireland, R. S. L. Carr, R. M. Marshall, J. K. Watkins,
J. T. W. Berry, H. D. Freakes, G. E. Hancock, R. H. Guest, D. E. Teden;
middle H. F. Wheatley, J. Heaton, H. B. Toft (captain), T. F. Huskisson,
R. E. Prescott; *front* G. A. Walker, P. Cooke

England v Scotland, 1947. The team which beat Scotland 24-5 in the first
official international at Twickenham for eight years and went on to share the
Championship with Wales: *standing* M. R. Steele-Bodger, N. O. Bennett,
R. H. G. Weighill, A. P. Henderson, D. F. White, C. B. Holmes, J. T. George,
J. O. Newton-Thompson, Mr I. David; *sitting* G. A. Kelly, N. M. Hall, J.
Mycock, J. Heaton (captain), R. H. Guest, A. Gray, H. W. Walker.

WALES v ENGLAND 1947

Played at Cardiff Arms Park, 18 January 1947
England won by 1G, 1DG (9) to 2T (6)

At 2.45 p.m. on the third Saturday of January, Wales and England met each other in an official international match for the first time since 1939. There had, of course, been a series of wartime matches, organised by the armed forces, followed by a popular and successful sequence of games played in 1945–46 and called 'Victory Internationals'; but this day at Cardiff heralded the beginning of another era of Championship encounters between the Home countries. A crowd of 40–45,000 spectators were present – a number well below the pre-war attendance for Cardiff internationals, due to damage caused to the North stand by one of A. Hitler's wayward drops at goal!

Several players took the field on this occasion with many seasons of wartime international-match experience; though only Howard Davies and Tanner of Wales, and Dick Guest of England, had played any pre-war Championship matches.

England received an early setback when Scott was injured after 15 minutes and Steele-Bodger withdrew from the pack to strengthen the threequarter line. The reduced English forwards played brilliantly, however, and the much-fancied Welsh forwards were never allowed to take a grip on the proceedings. England scored first when White capitalised upon an astute punt ahead by his scrum-half. Gray converted, but a try for Wales by Rees Stephens, who had built a reputation for himself in schoolboy internationals before the war, made the score 5–3 to the visitors at the break.

Wales went ahead after the interval – Evans scoring a try – but the lead remained for only a short while. Hall, the excellent St Mary's Hospital pivot, dropped a lovely goal which sealed the match for the Englishmen.

WALES		ENGLAND	
C. H. Davies	(Llanelli)	†A. Gray	(Otley)
K.J. Jones	(Newport)	R.H. Guest	(Waterloo)
J. Matthews	(Cardiff)	†N.O. Bennett	(St Mary's H.)
W.B. Cleaver	(Cardiff)	†E.K. Scott	(St Mary's H.)
L. Williams	(Llanelli)	†D.W. Swarbrick	(Oxford U.)
B.L. Williams	(Cardiff)	†N.M. Hall	(St Mary's H.)
*H. Tanner	(Cardiff)	†W.K.T. Moore	(Devonport Services)
D. Jones	(Swansea)	†G.A. Kelly	(Bedford)
R.E. Blakemore	(Newport)	†A.P. Henderson	(Cambridge U.)
G.W. Bevan	(Llanelli)	†H.W. Walker	(Coventry)
S. Williams	(Llanelli)	*†J. Mycock	(Sale)
G. Parsons	(Newport)	†S.V. Perry	(Cambridge U.)
O. Williams	(Llanelli)	†M.R. Steele-Bodger	(Cambridge U.)
J.R.G. Stephens	(Neath)	†B.H. Travers	(Oxford U.)
G.W. Evans	(Cardiff)	†D.F. White	(Northampton)

Tries: Evans, Stephens

Try: White   *Conversion:* Gray
Dropped goal: Hall

Referee: Mr R.A. Beattie (Scotland)

235

IRELAND v ENGLAND 1947
Played at Lansdowne Road, Dublin, 8 February 1947
Ireland won by 2G, 1PG, 3T (22) to Nil

Cold, icy conditions prevailed in Dublin, but Ireland were inspired to a decisive victory over an English side which lacked initiative and spirit. The Irish success derived from the all-round superiority of their light forwards; while the English backs were inefficient in defence, and unable to create any chances in attack.

Ireland faced a strong, gusty wind in the first half and the scoring commenced when B. Mullen kicked a penalty goal after Moore was caught off-side. O'Hanlon, the new cap on the Irish right wing, made an excellent debut, tackling surely in defence and obtaining the first try of the match after 30 minutes when he dribbled the ball over the goal-line after an Englishman had fumbled an Irish drop at goal. Just before the interval, a rare English attack was initiated by the Waterloo centre, Heaton, and Swarbrick nearly scored.

A feature of the second half was the effective combination of Kyle and Strathdee at half-back, the former continuously making probing breaks which would have resulted in scores if the Irish centres had used the ball more enterprisingly; while the guile and artistry of Strathdee set up a blind-side try for Mullan after 15 minutes of the half. The best try of the match followed this score. O'Hanlon gathered a weak English clearance kick and outpaced Swarbrick before swerving elegantly past the full-back to register his second try of the afternoon. In the closing minutes of the game, when the English defence became practically non-existent, McKay scored a try following a tremendous rush led by Agar; and Mullan obtained his second try when he supported a breakaway by the ebullient McKay. Mullan converted both of the last two tries.

IRELAND		ENGLAND	
*C.J. Murphy	(Lansdowne)	A. Gray	(Otley)
B. O'Hanlon	(Dolphin)	R.H. Guest	(Waterloo)
J.D.E. Monteith	(Queen's U.)	J. Heaton	(Waterloo)
J. Harper	(Instonians)	†M.P. Donnelly	(Oxford U.)
B. Mullan	(Clontarf)	D.W. Swarbrick	(Oxford U.)
J.W. Kyle	(N.I.F.C./Queen's U.)	N.M. Hall	(St Mary's H.)
E. Strathdee	(Queen's U.)	W.K.T. Moore	(Devonport Services)
M.R. Neely	(Belfast Collegians)	H.W. Walker	(Coventry)
K.D. Mullen	(Old Belvedere)	A.P. Henderson	(Cambridge U.)
J.C. Daly	(London Irish)	G.A. Kelly	(Bedford)
C.P. Callan	(Lansdowne)	*J. Mycock	(Sale)
E. Keeffe	(Sunday's Well)	S.V. Perry	(Cambridge U.)
D. Hingerty	(U.C. Dublin)	M.R. Steele-Bodger	(Cambridge U.)
R.D. Agar	(Malone)	B.H. Travers	(Oxford U.)
J.W. McKay	(Queen's U.)	D.F. White	(Northampton)

Tries: O'Hanlon (2), Mullan (2), McKay
Conversions: Mullan (2)
Penalty: Mullan

Referee: Mr M.A. Allan (Scotland)

ENGLAND v SCOTLAND 1947

Played at Twickenham, London, 15 March 1947
England won by 4G, 1DG (24) to 1G (5)

Following one of the severest winters in British history, England and Scotland met on a frozen pitch with both teams clearly short of match practice. Many players were injured during the afternoon and, at times, both sides were reduced to thirteen men. Drummond and Kelly each received injuries which prevented them from completing the game; while Holmes was carried off the field on a stretcher, although he returned later in the match.

Before an attendance of 60,000, the English backs eclipsed their opponents and the home side scored four tries. When Valentine took Drummond's place in the threequarter line, the depleted Scottish pack fared well. However, their English counterparts played well as a unit and much of the Scottish effort was spent in defence. At fly-half, Hall enjoyed a good service from Newton-Thompson and distributed the ball among his backs with great skill, whereas the passing and handling of the Scottish halves was inaccurate and careless.

England opened the scoring in the fifteenth minute while Drummond and Elliot were absent. From a scrummage, Hall dropped a neat goal with his right foot. England extended their lead when Holmes, intercepting a pass from Munro to Jackson on the halfway line, scorched across the ground for a splendid try which Heaton goaled. At half-time, the home side led by 14 points. A short kick ahead by Hall had split the Scottish defence and the fast-running Guest, gathering the ball in full stride, had touched down at the goal-post for Heaton to convert.

Scotland faced a wind which threatened to carry snow in the second half. A foot-rush by the English forwards led to a try by Henderson which the ever-accurate Heaton converted. But with both teams tiring and evidently unfit, play flowed from goal-post to goal-post until Bennett chased a rolling ball to the Scottish line for the fourth try. Then came Scotland's last flourish. A break by Munro sent the large-striding Jackson flying to the English line for a try which even the last-minute tackle of the ubiquitous Steele-Bodger could not prevent.

ENGLAND		SCOTLAND	
A. Gray	(Otley)	K.I. Geddes	(London Scottish)
†C.B. Holmes	(Manchester)	T.G.H. Jackson	(London Scottish)
N.O. Bennett	(St Mary's H.)	C.W. Drummond	(Melrose)
*J. Heaton	(Waterloo)	W.H. Munro	(Glasgow H.S.F.P.)
R.H. Guest	(Waterloo)	D.D. Mackenzie	(Edinburgh U.)
N.M. Hall	(St Mary's H.)	*C.R. Bruce	(Glasgow Acads.)
†J.O. Newton-Thompson	(Oxford U.)	E. Anderson	(Stewart's College F.P.)
H.W. Walker	(Coventry)	T.P.L. McGlashan	(Royal H.S.F.P.)
A.P. Henderson	(Cambridge U.)	A.T. Fisher	(Watsonians)
G.A. Kelly	(Bedford)	H.H. Campbell	(Cambridge U.)
†J.T. George	(Falmouth)	F.H. Coutts	(Melrose)
J. Mycock	(Sale)	I.C. Henderson	(Edinburgh Acads.)
M.R. Steele-Bodger	(Cambridge U.)	D.D. Valentine	(Hawick)
†R.H.G. Weighill	(R.A.F.)	D.I. McLean	(Royal H.S.F.P.)
D.F. White	(Northampton)	W.I.D. Elliot	(Edinburgh Acads.)

Tries: Bennett, Guest, Henderson, Holmes
Conversions: Heaton (4)
Dropped goal: Hall

Try: Jackson *Conversion:* Geddes

Referee: Mr I. David (Wales)

ENGLAND v FRANCE 1947

Played at Twickenham, London, 19 April 1947
England won by 2T (6) to 1PG (3)

A large crowd of 50,000 watched England earn a share of the Championship, but this was a very close affair. Five minutes from no-side the scores were level at 3–3; then a great individual effort by Newton-Thompson, the Oxford captain, ably supported by Vic Roberts, brought a try.

Most of the English possession resulted from Mycock's domination in the line-out, though the French pack provided their backs with a good share of the ball from set-scrums. (England were rarely out of their own half before the interval.) But the French centres lacked penetration and their outsides failed to be a really effective attacking unit.

After holding so little early advantage, England were happy to lead 3–0 at half-time. Guest had chased a punt ahead by Bennett and outpaced the French defence to dive on the ball before it rolled into touch-in-goal. Heaton could not convert. In the second half, Prat equalised after 11 minutes with a splendid dropped penalty goal from a difficult position. This spurred on the English forwards and in a gallant performance they contained the mighty Frenchmen. Roberts was outstanding.

Generally, England had the better of the second half, for the French defence often looked suspect under pressure. Swarbrick had made several dangerous dashes, displaying subtle changes of pace, before Newton-Thompson, breaking clear on the blind-side from a scrum, made 20 yards and passed infield to Roberts, who covered the remaining ten yards to dash over for a try. Heaton failed to convert this winning score.

France tried desperately to save the match in the last ten minutes, but there was no further scoring and England's victory gave them a share of the Championship with Wales.

ENGLAND		FRANCE	
†S.C. Newman	(Oxford U.)	A.J. Alvarez	(Tyrosse)
D.W. Swarbrick	(Oxford U.)	E. Pebeyre	(Brive)
N.O. Bennett	(St Mary's H.)	*L. Junquas	(Bayonne)
*J. Heaton	(Waterloo)	M. Sorondo	(Montauban)
R.H. Guest	(Waterloo)	R. Dutrain	(Toulouse)
N.M. Hall	(St Mary's H.)	M. Terrau	(Bourg)
J.O. Newton-Thompson	(Oxford U.)	Y.R. Bergougnan	(Toulouse)
†G.A. Gibbs	(Bristol)	L. Caron	(Lyon)
A.P. Henderson	(Cambridge U.)	M. Jol	(Biarritz)
H.W. Walker	(Coventry)	E. Buzy	(Lourdes)
J.T. George	(Falmouth)	A. Moga	(Bègles)
J. Mycock	(Sale)	R. Soro	(Romans)
†V.G. Roberts	(Penryn)	J. Matheu	(Castres)
R.H.G. Weighill	(Harlequins/R.A.F.)	G. Basquet	(Agen)
M.R. Steele-Bodger	(Cambridge U.)	J. Prat	(Lourdes)

Tries: Guest, Roberts   *Penalty:* Prat

Referee: Mr T. Jones (Wales)

ENGLAND v AUSTRALIA 1948

Played at Twickenham, London, 3 January 1948
Australia won by 1G, 2T (11) to Nil

A large crowd of 70,000 spectators were entertained to a fast, exciting game. A damp mist and slippery turf made the ball difficult to control but both sides played sensibly and, under the circumstances, errors were rare. England, taking first use of a strong wind, had the better of the opening exchanges with Madge playing steadily at the heels of a pack which was lively in the loose and took much possession in the line-out. England nearly opened the scoring when Bennett put Swarbrick over in the left corner. Only a magnificent covering tackle, which sent the wing into touch-in-goal, prevented a try. Although England continued to dominate the play, there was a general lack of cohesion amongst their backs and they were unable to produce a score.

Shortly before the interval, and against the run of play, Australia went ahead when Newman failed to find touch with a poor kick. Kearney fielded the ball and set up a round of passing between Allan, Emery, Burke, and Windon, and Windon scored in the right corner. In the second half, Newman narrowly missed a penalty kick at goal, the ball striking an upright. Then a short period of intense English pressure followed before Piper relieved the anxious Australians with some accurate catching and steady kicks to touch. Ten minutes before no-side Australia, by far the better team in the second half, launched a final assault on the English goal-line. Walker, playing in his first international of the tour, scored with a remarkable solo effort: receiving the ball from a scrum on the Australian 25, he punted ahead, gathered it on the bounce in his stride and outpaced a converging defence along the left touch-line. Finally, he swerved around Newman to score a sensational try in the corner which Tonkin failed to convert.

England had scarcely recovered from this stunning blow when Windon capitalised upon a knock-on by Kemp and burst through a devastated defence, racing 50 yards to score a try at the posts. Tonkin converted to complete the scoring.

Australia were able to claim the unique distinction that their try-line had remained intact against the four Home Countries.

ENGLAND		AUSTRALIA	
S.C. Newman	(Oxford U.)	B.J.C. Piper	(N.S.W.)
R.H. Guest	(Waterloo)	A.E.J. Tonkin	(N.S.W.)
N.O. Bennett	(U.S.)	*T. Allan	(N.S.W.)
*E.K. Scott	(Redruth)	A.K. Walker	(N.S.W.)
D.W. Swarbrick	(Oxford U.)	J.W.T. MacBride	(N.S.W.)
T.A. Kemp	(Richmond)	N.A. Emery	(N.S.W.)
†R.J.P. Madge	(Exeter)	C.T. Burke	(N.S.W.)
†E. Evans	(Sale)	E. Tweedale	(Queensland)
†J.H. Keeling	(Guy's H.)	K.H. Kearney	(N.S.W.)
H.W. Walker	(Coventry)	N. Shehadie	(N.S.W.)
J. Mycock	(Sale)	G.M. Cooke	(Queensland)
S.V. Perry	(Cambridge U.)	D.F. Kraefft	(N.S.W.)
M.R. Steele-Bodger	(Edinburgh U.)	D.H. Keller	(N.S.W.)
†D.B. Vaughan	(Devonport Services)	A.J. Buchan	(N.S.W.)
B.H. Travers	(Oxford U.)	C.J. Windon	(N.S.W.)

Tries: Windon (2), Walker
Conversion: Tonkin

Referee: Mr N.H. Lambert (Ireland)

ENGLAND v WALES 1948
Played at Twickenham, London, 17 January 1948
Drawn: England 1PG (3), Wales 1T (3)

Wales visited Twickenham in search of their first win since 1933, but against the run of play England were able to deny Wales what certainly would have been a deserved victory. There were 73,000 spectators crammed into the ground to see Newman land a towering 50-yards goal in the opening minutes of the game after the referee had penalised B.L. Williams for handling the ball after a tackle. Wales, however, were unperturbed by this setback and their forwards worked cleverly, dominating their less experienced opponents in the tight and loose. Wales, consequently, held a decided advantage territorially, if not on points, and the large Welsh contingent present must have thought that it was only a matter of time before Wales went ahead. But their hopes were regularly dashed, as careless handling among the Welsh backs and some excellent defensive work by Newman and Kemp spoiled scoring chances.

The finest moves of the first half involved Glyn Davies and Matthews of Wales, and Swarbrick and Guest of England, with Matthews looking the most likely of this quartet to score. On one occasion, following a round of passing among the Welsh backs, the Cardiff man reached the English line with a fine run, but a strong tackle by Newman robbed him of a score. England, on the other hand, had their best chances of scoring with penalty kicks, and both Newman and Vaughan made attempts at goal.

Wales made a more intense effort after the interval and though Tamplin failed to kick a penalty from 30 yards, the equalising score came when Bleddyn Williams kicked ahead for Tanner to gather and send Ken Jones sprinting over. Tamplin failed to convert but the Welsh forwards still won a monopoly of ball for their backs. When Newman left the field with a cracked wrist-bone, Wales threw everything into an all-out attack. Travers, who had withdrawn from the pack to occupy Newman's berth at full-back, defended bravely and Wales could not force a win – though on one occasion, only a pass dropped by Matthews from Cleaver denied Wales glory.

ENGLAND		WALES	
S.C. Newman	(Oxford U.)	R.F. Trott	(Cardiff)
R.H. Guest	(Waterloo)	K.J. Jones	(Newport)
N.O. Bennett	(U.S.)	W.B. Cleaver	(Cardiff)
E.K. Scott	(Redruth)	B.L. Williams	(Cardiff)
D.W. Swarbrick	(Oxford)	J. Matthews	(Cardiff)
*T.A. Kemp	(Richmond)	G. Davies	(Pontypridd)
R.J.P. Madge	(Exeter)	*H. Tanner	(Cardiff)
H.W. Walker	(Coventry)	C. Davies	(Cardiff)
J.H. Keeling	(Guy's H.)	M. James	(Cardiff)
G.A. Kelly	(Bedford)	L. Anthony	(Neath)
S.V. Perry	(Cambridge U.)	W.E. Tamplin	(Cardiff)
†H.F. Luya	(Headingley)	D. Jones	(Llanelli)
M.R. Steele-Bodger	(Edinburgh U.)	O. Williams	(Llanelli)
D.B. Vaughan	(Devonport Services)	L Manfield	(Cardiff)
B.H. Travers	(Oxford U.)	G. Evans	(Cardiff)

Penalty: Newman   *Try:* K.J. Jones

Referee: Mr R.A. Beattie (Scotland)

ENGLAND v IRELAND 1948

Played at Twickenham, London, 14 February 1948
Ireland won by 1G, 2T (11) to 2G (10)

Ireland gained a deserved victory after dominating for most of the match, but not without a scare or two in the dying minutes of an exciting match. With the exception of a few moments of English inspiration, a scientific Irish pack carried the greater guns in this close encounter.

Both sides made several changes from the teams which had figured in the earlier international matches. Ireland had three new caps – one of whom, O'Brien, led the pack – and Karl Mullen was appointed captain. England had two new caps in the backs in Preece and Uren, and both gave creditable performances on their debuts.

Ireland opened with the wind behind them, but were forced to defend staunchly for the first ten minutes as the English pack tore into them. Ireland slowly gained ground from a five-yards-scrum, and Kyle relieved the pressure with a fine jinking run. The superb hooking of Mullen soon brought the visitors a constant stream of quality possession and Uren was given a severe testing by the Irish midfield backs.

England scored first after an Irish attack had petered out. Bennett initiated a thrust which Preece and Vaughan continued before the latter was checked. White followed up to send Guest across for a try in the right corner, and Uren converted with a fine kick. Ireland equalised 20 minutes later when a forward rush resulted in a scrambling try by McKee. Mullan's conversion levelled the scores at half-time.

At the beginning of the second half, Kyle and McKay scored further tries and it appeared that England would be routed. Then Ireland were awarded a penalty. Mullan's attempt at goal rebounded from the post and Walker kicked for touch. Kyle fielded the ball and passed to his left, whereupon Guest intercepted inside his 25 to dash the length of the pitch (beating Mattsson with a dazzling side-step) and score beneath the posts. Uren's goal reduced the Irish lead to a single point, but a performance of great character by Ireland prevented a further English score.

ENGLAND		IRELAND	
†R. Uren	(Waterloo)	J. Mattsson	(Wanderers)
R.H. Guest	(Waterloo)	B. O'Hanlon	(Dolphin)
N.O. Bennett	(U.S.)	W.D. McKee	(N.I.F.C.)
*E.K. Scott	(Redruth)	P.J. Reid	(Garryowen)
C.B. Holmes	(Manchester)	B. Mullan	(Clontarf)
†I. Preece	(Coventry)	J.W. Kyle	(Queen's U.)
R.J.P. Madge	(Exeter)	H.de Lacy	(Harlequins)
H.W. Walker	(Coventry)	A.A. McConnell	(Collegians)
A.P. Henderson	(Cambridge U.)	*K.D. Mullen	(Old Belvedere)
G.A. Gibbs	(Bristol)	J.C. Daly	(London Irish)
S.V. Perry	(Cambridge U.)	C.P. Callan	(Lansdowne)
H.F. Luya	(Headingley)	J.E. Nelson	(Malone)
D.F. White	(Northampton)	J.W. McKay	(Queen's U.)
D.B. Vaughan	(Devonport Services)	D.J. O'Brien	(London Irish)
M.R. Steele-Bodger	(Edinburgh U.)	J.S. McCarthy	(Dolphin)

Tries: Guest (2)
Conversions: Uren (2)

Tries: Kyle, McKay, McKee
Conversion: B. Mullan

Referee: Mr T. Jones (Wales)

SCOTLAND v ENGLAND 1948

Played at Murrayfield, Edinburgh, 20 March 1948
Scotland won by 2T (6) to 1PG (3)

England were unfortunate to lose the services of key players through injury. Madge, the brave little Exeter scrum-half, had to leave the field during the first ten minutes of the game with torn ligaments and England pulled Steele-Bodger from the pack to deputise for him. He, too, found himself in the wars, suffering from concussion after a knock just before half-time, while Scott played throughout the second half with a fractured jaw.

A large crowd of 70,000 saw England, despite their great misfortunes, take the lead after 20 minutes through a penalty goal kicked by Uren from 30 yards and at an angle: he had earlier missed with an attempt from in front of the posts. In fact, the kicking and handling of both sides left much to be desired, though a swirling wind did not help matters in this respect.

England's fourteen more than held their own against the Scots in the first half, with Preece organising the defence effectively. But after the interval, the Scottish advantage in the scrums and line-outs became increasingly obvious, although the Scottish centres lacked imagination in attack. It was out of frustration with the poor play of his insides that Jackson was compelled to initiate an attacking move which saw play sweep across to the left wing – quite unorthodoxly – for Innes to create an overlap and send Drummond over, unchallenged, at the wing's corner flag. Some reports of this score reckoned Jackson's pass to have been forward, but the score stood, and a second Scottish try, 15 minutes from no-side, clinched the match. Young gathered the ball at the back of the line-out and charged directly over the English line, despite the attentions of three English defenders. Apart from one foray led by Bennett, England never really looked like equalising in the closing moments of the match and Scotland registered their second victory of the season.

SCOTLAND		ENGLAND	
W.C.W. Murdoch	(Hillhead H.S.F.P.)	R. Uren	(Waterloo)
T.G.H. Jackson	(London Scottish)	R.H. Guest	(Waterloo)
*J.R.S. Innes	(Aberdeen G.S.F.P.)	N.O. Bennett	(U.S.)
L.Bruce-Lockhart	(London Scottish)	*E.K. Scott	(Redruth)
C.W. Drummond	(Melrose)	†M.F. Turner	(Blackheath)
D.P. Hepburn	(Woodford)	I. Preece	(Coventry)
A.W. Black	(Edinburgh U.)	R.J.P. Madge	(Exeter)
I.C. Henderson	(Edinburgh Acads.)	H.W. Walker	(Coventry)
G.G. Lyall	(Gala)	A.P. Henderson	(Edinburgh Wands.)
H.H. Campbell	(London Scottish)	†T.W. Price	(Gloucester)
W.P. Black	(Glasgow H.S.F.P.)	S.V. Perry	(Cambridge U.)
R. Finlay	(Watsonians)	H.F. Luya	(Headingley)
W.B. Young	(London Scottish)	M.R. Steele-Bodger	(Edinburgh U.)
J.B. Lees	(Gala)	R.H.G. Weighill	(R.A.F.)
W.I.D. Elliot	(Edinburgh Acads.)	D.B. Vaughan	(Devonport Services)

Tries: Drummond, Young   *Penalty:* Uren

Referee: Mr N.H. Lambert (Ireland)

FRANCE v ENGLAND 1948

Played at Stade Colombes, Paris, 29 March 1948
France won by 1G, 1DG, 2T (15) to Nil

The Championship closed on the ground where it had started three months earlier – Stade Colombes in Paris. France's clear victory, in front of about 60,000 people, meant that they had defeated the joint title holders of the previous season, Wales and England, and it was the largest French victory over England since the inception of matches in 1906.

France retained the nucleus of the fifteen which had won at Swansea, though one change brought in a new cap in Siman on the wing, and Dizabo was recalled in place of Junquas at centre. Prat and Uren went close with long penalty attempts in the early moments of the match, and Siman made two fine efforts to score tries – Holmes grassing his man in fine style each time. The French forwards were on top in the tight play at an early stage, but the English pack played a lively and intelligent game.

France led by a try at the interval; Pomathios, who actually changed from right wing against Wales to take the left wing, scoring after a fine run to the left corner in the thirtieth minute. France dominated after the break and were soon further ahead. Uren, who had another hard match, fumbled a ball in front of his own posts early in the second half, but England miraculously cleared the danger. There was no such clearance moments later, however, when a storming run by Soro resulted in a try at the right corner. The French backs now began to show their strengths and the running of Dizabo was a constant worry to the English defence. He made openings for both wingers – only some desperate covering keeping the score at six points. Then, another scything break by Dizabo was supported by Prat who scored at the posts for Alvarez to convert. Finally, Bergougnan dropped a goal to give France an emphatic victory.

FRANCE		ENGLAND	
A.J. Alvarez	(Tyrosse)	R. Uren	(Waterloo)
M. Siman	(Montferrand)	M.F. Turner	(Blackheath)
P. Dizabo	(Tyrosse)	†L.B. Cannell	(Northampton)
M. Terreau	(Bourg)	†A.C. Towell	(Leicester)
M. Pomathios	(Agen)	C.B. Holmes	(Manchester)
L. Bordenave	(Toulon)	I. Preece	(Coventry)
Y.R. Bergougnan	(Toulouse)	†P.W. Sykes	(Wasps)
L. Caron	(Castres)	H.W. Walker	(Coventry)
L. Martin	(Pau)	A.P. Henderson	(Edinburgh Wands.)
E. Buzy	(Lourdes)	T.W. Price	(Gloucester)
R. Soro	(Romans)	S.V. Perry	(Cambridge U.)
A. Moga	(Bègles)	H.F. Luya	(Headingley)
J. Prat	(Lourdes)	M.R. Steele-Bodger	(Edinburgh U.)
*G. Basquet	(Agen)	*R.H.G. Weighill	(R.A.F./Harlequins)
J. Matheu	(Castres)	D.F. White	(Northampton)

Tries: Pomathios, Prat, Soro
Conversion: Alvarez
Dropped goal: Bergougnan

Referee: Mr T. Jones (Wales)

WALES v ENGLAND 1949
Played at Cardiff Arms Park, 15 January 1949
Wales won by 3T (9) to 1DG (3)

Glyn Davies gave a classical display of fly-half skills and Wales, wearing white shorts for the first time, recorded a brilliant victory over England in a fast and open match. England were the better side in the first half and Wales could reflect upon their good fortune to be level at the interval. The home side had many worrying moments, but their defence was sound and with Davies excelling in attack their forwards received the encouragement and stimulus to take charge during the second half.

Wales actually opened the scoring when Glyn Davies glided through the English defence and passed to Les Williams, the left wing, who scored a try. Then Matthews and Bleddyn Williams put in good runs before England deservedly drew level. Hall dropped a fine goal, now valued at three points, to equalise – he had won the corresponding match at Cardiff two years previously with a similar score – and before half-time, Wales had a lucky escape when a gigantic penalty kick by Holmes struck an upright and rebounded away from the goal.

In the second half, the Welsh pack scrummaged assiduously and took control of the forward proceedings. Tanner revelled in the circumstances, giving Glyn Davies a wonderful service and, as a result, Wales were able to score twice. Meredith, in his first international, crossed for a try after Gwilliam had lent sterling support to a forward rush, and Les Williams obtained his second score of the match after another dazzling break by the Welsh fly-half.

WALES		ENGLAND	
R.F. Trott	(Cardiff)	†W.B. Holmes	(Cambridge U.)
K.J. Jones	(Newport)	†J.A. Gregory	(Blackheath)
J. Matthews	(Cardiff)	L.B. Cannell	(Oxford U.)
B.L. Williams	(Cardiff)	†C.B. van Ryneveld	(Oxford U.)
L. Williams	(Cardiff)	†T. Danby	(Harlequins)
G. Davies	(Cambridge U.)	*N.M. Hall	(Huddersfield)
*H. Tanner	(Cardiff)	†G. Rimmer	(Waterloo)
E. Coleman	(Newport)	T.W. Price	(Cheltenham)
W.H. Travers	(Newport)	A.P. Henderson	(Edinburgh Wands.)
D. Jones	(Swansea)	†M.J. Berridge	(Northampton)
D.J. Hayward	(Newbridge)	H.F. Luya	(Headingley)
A. Meredith	(Devonport Services)	†G.R.D'A. Hosking	(Devonport Services)
W.R. Cale	(Newbridge)	†E.L. Horsfall	(Harlequins)
J.A. Gwilliam	(Cambridge U.)	†B. Braithwaite-Exley	(Headingley)
G. Evans	(Cardiff)	V.G. Roberts	(Penryn)

Tries: L. Williams (2), Meredith   *Dropped goal:* Hall

Referee: Mr N.H. Lambert (Ireland)

IRELAND v ENGLAND 1949

Played at Lansdowne Road, Dublin, 12 February 1949
Ireland won by 1G, 2PG, 1T (14) to 1G (5)

England threw away a potential victory in a disastrous five-minutes spell just before half-time. An inspiring try, set up by Rimmer and Hall and completed by van Ryneveld with a graceful swerve and fearsome bolt for the goal-line, had counteracted the early penalty kicked by George Norton. Holmes had converted to give England the lead, and with the English pack initially holding its own against the formidable Irish forwards, hopes of recording the first victory over Ireland since 1938 ran high.

Ireland then struck two blows from which the visitors never recovered. Norton, whose earlier penalty had been awarded in front of the posts, was again presented with an easy kick, this time from 20 yards, and duly accepted the gift of three points to put his side ahead. Even worse followed. An unnecessary quick throw-in by an Englishman was intercepted by Kyle who made an opening for McKay. The wing-forward made some ground before O'Hanlon accelerated on the outside to take a try-scoring pass.

In the second half the Irish forwards took control and, with Strathdee restored as Kyle's partner and a most efficient link, England were outclassed behind the scrummage too. McKee provided the thrust which had previously been missing from the Irish attack and his combination with Kyle in midfield was particularly effective. Indeed, one of the fly-half's bursts led to an exhilarating run by the centre, the culmination of which was a try at the posts. Norton converted to complete the scoring.

For England, Rimmer played courageously behind a pack which, despite the changes made after the failure against Wales, was once more comprehensively beaten, this time by an uncompromising, solid Irish eight which bore ominous resemblance to the invincible unit of the previous season.

IRELAND		ENGLAND	
G.W. Norton	(Bective Rangers)	W.B. Holmes	(Cambridge U.)
M.F. Lane	(U.C. Cork)	D.W. Swarbrick	(Oxford U.)
T.J. Gavin	(London Irish)	L.B. Cannell	(Oxford U.)
W.D. McKee	(N.I.F.C.)	C.B. van Ryneveld	(Oxford U.)
B. O'Hanlon	(Dolphin)	†R.D. Kennedy	(Camborne S. of Mines)
J.W. Kyle	(Queen's U.)	*N.M. Hall	(Huddersfield)
E. Strathdee	(Queen's U.)	G. Rimmer	(Waterloo)
A.A. McConnell	(Collegians)	T.W. Price	(Cheltenham)
*K.D. Mullen	(Old Belvedere)	A.P. Henderson	(Edinburgh Wands.)
T. Clifford	(Young Munster)	M.J. Berridge	(Northampton)
J.E. Nelson	(Malone)	G.R.D'A. Hosking	(Devonport Services)
C.P. Callan	(Lansdowne)	J.T. George	(Falmouth)
J.W. McKay	(Queen's U.)	D.B. Vaughan	(Headingley)
D.J. O'Brien	(London Irish)	†J.M.K. Kendall-Carpenter	(Oxford U.)
J.S. McCarthy	(Dolphin)	V.G. Roberts	(Penryn)

Tries: O'Hanlon, McKee
Conversion: Norton
Penalties: Norton (2)

Try: van Ryneveld
Conversion: Holmes

Referee: Mr R.A. Beattie (Scotland)

ENGLAND v FRANCE 1949

Played at Twickenham, London, 26 February 1949
England won by 1G, 1DG (8) to 1DG (3)

Remembering England's inept performances against Wales and Ireland, and France's rousing forward displays in their matches with Scotland and Ireland, there were few among the 65,000 spectators at Twickenham for this match who expected an English win. However, the six changes which England made after the defeat by Ireland resulted in a glorious revival of English forward play, and for the first time during the season the French pack were outplayed in the tight and loose. With the English pack winning ample possession and their new half-backs combining effectively, the French played only as well as Preece and his men allowed them to.

From the first scrum, Steeds, the new English hooker, heeled the ball and Moore sent Preece away. The fly-half then drew his opposite number before passing to Cannell, who went through a gap in the French defence like a shot out of a gun and scored a try at the posts which Holmes converted.

While the events which followed did not match the quality of this opening move, there was plenty of excitement for the large crowd. Both sides had opportunities to score with penalties but no further scoring came before half-time. In the second half, with England dominating the forward battle against the more experienced French pack, a loose maul won by England enabled Moore to feed Preece who dropped a goal in splendid style.

Not until the last five minutes of the match did France retaliate. Alvarez landed a dropped goal, but it was too late in the game for there to be any chance of changing the overall result – a fine win for England.

ENGLAND		FRANCE	
W.B. Holmes	(Cambridge U.)	A.J. Alvarez	(Tyrosse)
R.H. Guest	(Waterloo)	M. Pomathios	(Lyon)
L.B. Cannell	(Oxford U.)	P. Dizabo	(Tyrosse)
C.B. van Ryneveld	(Oxford U.)	R. Dutrain	(Toulouse)
R.D. Kennedy	(Camborne S. of Mines)	J. Lassègue	(Toulouse)
*I. Preece	(Coventry)	J. Pilon	(Périgueux)
W.K.T. Moore	(Leicester)	Y.R. Bergougnan	(Toulouse)
T.W. Price	(Cheltenham)	L. Caron	(Lyon)
†J.H. Steeds	(Middlesex H.)	M. Jol	(Biarritz)
J.M.K. Kendall-Carpenter	(Oxford U.)	E. Buzy	(Lourdes)
†J.R.C. Matthews	(Harlequins)	A. Moga	(Bègles)
G.R.D'A. Hosking	(Devonport Services)	R. Soro	(Romans)
B.H. Travers	(Harlequins)	J. Prat	(Lourdes)
D.B. Vaughan	(Headingley)	*G. Basquet	(Agen)
V.G. Roberts	(Penryn)	J. Matheu	(Castres)

Try: Cannell *Conversion:* Holmes
Dropped goal: Preece

Dropped goal: Alvarez

Referee: Mr T. Jones (Wales)

ENGLAND v SCOTLAND 1949
Played at Twickenham, London, 19 March 1949
England won by 2G, 3T (19) to 1PG (3)

England and Scotland met for the Calcutta Cup match with much to play for. The visitors, despite losing to Ireland, could still hope for a share in the International Championship; and England needed a draw at least to avoid collecting the Wooden Spoon. England retained the same line-up which had defeated France, while Scotland made three changes from the pack overwhelmed by Ireland at Murrayfield.

In beautiful conditions, there was little to choose between the teams in the first half until Jackson, the Scottish wing, was reduced to the role of a passenger with a leg injury. Then, after Holmes missed a 30-yards penalty kick at goal, Roberts, the liveliest forward on the field, made a break before passing to van Ryneveld who sent Kennedy clear for a try. Prior to this move, Kennedy had been very closely marked by Jackson.

There was only one side in it in the second half as England gave by far their most enterprising display of the season. Much of their new-found success was due to Preece, who controlled the tactics with great authority at fly-half; while the English forwards improved throughout the afternoon. The South African, van Ryneveld, opened the second-half scoring following a counter-attack by Preece; and, after Wilson landed a penalty for Scotland, a similar move resulted in van Ryneveld's second try. Towards the end of the match, as the Scottish tackling and passing became more and more haphazard, further tries were added by Hosking (after a break-away by Vaughan) and the veteran, Guest. This last effort was due to some splendid work by Cannell, who had run half the length of the field to send the Waterloo wing over in the corner.

ENGLAND		SCOTLAND	
W.B. Holmes	(Cambridge U.)	I.J.M. Lumsden	(Bath)
R.H. Guest	(Waterloo)	T.G.H. Jackson	(London Scottish)
L.B. Cannell	(Oxford U.)	L.G. Gloag	(Cambridge U.)
C.B. van Ryneveld	(Oxford U.)	D.P. Hepburn	(Woodford)
R.D. Kennedy	(Camborne S. of Mines)	D.W.C. Smith	(London Scottish)
*I. Preece	(Coventry)	C.R. Bruce	(Glasgow Acads.)
W.K.T. Moore	(Leicester)	W.D. Allardice	(Aberdeen G.S.F.P.)
T.W. Price	(Cheltenham)	S. Coltman	(Hawick)
J.H. Steeds	(Middlesex H.)	J.A.R. MacPhail	(Edinburgh Acads.)
J.M.K. Kendall-Carpenter	(Oxford U.)	S.T.H. Wright	(Stewart's College F.P.)
J.R.C. Matthews	(Harlequins)	L.R. Currie	(Dunfermline)
G.R.D'A. Hosking	(Devonport Services)	G.A. Wilson	(Oxford U.)
B.H. Travers	(Harlequins)	*D.H. Keller	(London Scottish)
D.B. Vaughan	(Headingley)	P.W. Kininmonth	(Oxford U.)
V.G. Roberts	(Penryn)	W.I.D. Elliot	(Edinburgh Acads.)

Tries: van Ryneveld (2), Guest, Hosking, Kennedy   *Penalty:* Wilson
Conversions: Travers (2)

Referee: Mr N.H. Lambert (Ireland)

ENGLAND v WALES 1950

Played at Twickenham, London, 21 January 1950
Wales won by 1G, 1PG, 1T (11) to 1G (5)

This was a glorious day for Wales and the 25,000 Welshmen among the record 75,500 attendance. It was only their second win at Twickenham in forty years. Wales possessed an ace pack, a clever fly-half and a young genius at full-back in Lewis Jones. Once the English forwards had been dominated and subdued, Cleaver dictated the tactics astutely and Wales were able to coast home in the second half. But it was not easy. Wales had been Wooden Spoon holders in the previous season, and on the night before the match Bleddyn Williams, the captain, was forced to withdraw with a thigh injury and there was some reshuffling among the Welsh backs, John Gwilliam becoming skipper. After five minutes of play, Wales were five points down. A lobbed pass had been intercepted by J.V. Smith and the right wing sprinted 40 yards to score in the corner, Hofmeyr converting with a fine kick.

Once the Welsh forwards had assumed the ascendancy, however, it became evident that England would eventually lose. Just before half-time, Lewis Jones gathered a wild kick ahead deep in his own half, but when everyone expected him to find touch, he began a counter-attack with a strong zig-zagging run to the English 25 which caught the opposition defence out of position. A series of short, quick passes ended with Cliff Davies diving over in the corner for a try. There was no conversion, and England held a precarious two-points lead at the interval.

In the second half, there was only one side in it, though Wales could score but one try. The enterprising Lewis Jones kicked a penalty to put Wales ahead; and then converted the try which Ray Cale, the outstanding Welsh forward in the loose, obtained after a well-controlled dribble. This last score settled the match, but England staged a spirited rally in the closing ten minutes and Cannell nearly forced his way though for a try, while Hofmeyr, who made a generally sound debut, went close with penalty kicks. Wales held out and registered their second victory in fifteen visits to Headquarters.

ENGLAND		WALES	
†M.B. Hofmeyr	(Oxford U.)	B.L. Jones	(Devonport Services)
†J.V. Smith	(Cambridge U.)	K.J. Jones	(Newport)
†B. Boobbyer	(Oxford U.)	M.C. Thomas	(Newport)
L.B. Cannell	(Oxford U.)	J. Matthews	(Cardiff)
†I.J. Botting	(Oxford U.)	T.J. Brewer	(Newport)
*I. Preece	(Coventry)	W.B. Cleaver	(Cardiff)
G. Rimmer	(Waterloo)	W.R. Willis	(Cardiff)
J.M.K. Kendall-Carpenter	(Oxford U.)	J.D. Robins	(Birkenhead Park)
E. Evans	(Sale)	D.M. Davies	(Somerset Police)
†W.A. Holmes	(Nuneaton)	C. Davies	(Cardiff)
G.R.D'A. Hosking	(Devonport Services)	D.J. Hayward	(Newbridge)
†H.A. Jones	(Barnstaple)	E.R. John	(Neath)
†H.D. Small	(Oxford U.)	W.R. Cale	(Pontypool)
D.B. Vaughan	(Headingley)	*J.A. Gwilliam	(Edinburgh Wands.)
†J.J. Cain	(Waterloo)	R.T. Evans	(Newport)

Try: Smith
Conversion: Hofmeyr

Tries: Cale, C. Davies
Conversion: B.L. Jones
Penalty: B.L. Jones

Referee: Mr N.H. Lambert (Ireland)

ENGLAND v IRELAND 1950

Played at Twickenham, London, 11 February 1950
England won by 1T (3) to Nil

England were lucky to record their first win over Ireland since 1938, for the visitors lost McKee at half-time and were compelled to play with only seven forwards during the second half – Bill McKay moving into the threequarter line. Ireland were superior in the set pieces but tight marking, heavy conditions and a gusty wind prevented any elaborate passing movements. Consequently, play largely consisted of Irish breakaways followed by English counter-attacks.

England made six changes from the side defeated by Wales, while a series of injuries forced Ireland to alter their threequarter line and introduce two new caps. Preece elected to face the wind in the first half and the gamble paid off, for just before the interval the captain made an opening for Smith, and good support work by Small and Roberts ended with the latter running 20 yards to score a try.

In the second half the Irish were, surprisingly, more dangerous against the wind and Phipps and Crowe made a number of threatening runs. But the new English back row defended admirably and Phipps was twice arrested inches short of the corner flag. For England, Moore and Preece worked effectively together, while Boobbyer was the most enterprising of the backs in attack. Botting and Smith defended safely and Uren gave a sound performance at full-back.

Ireland very nearly snatched a last minute draw when Norton took two late penalty kicks at goal – one from 50 yards; but each attempt failed and the champions of the previous season thus found themselves at the bottom of the table with two matches played.

J.H. Steeds, formerly capped from the Middlesex Hospital R.F.C., became the first man to play for England direct from the Saracens club.

ENGLAND		IRELAND	
R. Uren	(Waterloo)	G.W. Norton	(Bective Rangers)
J.V. Smith	(Cambridge U.)	M.F. Lane	(U.C. Cork)
B. Boobbyer	(Oxford U.)	G.C. Phipps	(Rosslyn Park)
L.B. Cannell	(Oxford U.)	W.D. McKee	(N.I.F.C.)
I.J. Botting	(Oxford U.)	L. Crowe	(Old Belvedere)
*I. Preece	(Coventry)	J.W. Kyle	(Queen's U.)
W.K.T. Moore	(Leicester)	J.H. Burges	(Rosslyn Park)
J.M.K. Kendall-Carpenter	(Oxford U.)	T. Clifford	(Young Munster)
J.H. Steeds	(Saracens)	*K.D. Mullen	(Old Belvedere)
W.A. Holmes	(Nuneaton)	D.R. McKibbin	(Queen's U.)
J.R.C. Matthews	(Harlequins)	J.E. Nelson	(Malone)
H.A. Jones	(Barnstaple)	R.D. Agar	(Malone)
H.D. Small	(Oxford U.)	A.B. Curtis	(Oxford U.)
†S.J. Adkins	(Coventry)	D.J. O'Brien	(London Irish)
V.G. Roberts	(Penryn)	J.W. McKay	(Queen's U.)

Try: Roberts

Referee: Mr R.A. Beattie (Scotland)

FRANCE v ENGLAND 1950
Played at Stade Colombes, Paris, 25 February 1950
France won by 2T (6) to 1T (3)

Heavy morning rain, which had left the pitch sodden, ceased before the match commenced, but the players still had to contend with a greasy ball in the heavy conditions. Neither side played with authority in the tight or loose, but the French attack was marginally better than that of the English and the home side deserved their victory.

Both fly-halves preferred to use the kick ahead rather than move the ball to hand and, consequently, the full-backs had a busy afternoon. Brun, winning his first cap for France, was the man of the match, for his fielding and tackling were safe and his incursions into the threequarter line were perfectly timed and often dangerous. Hofmeyr, too, was reliable and received valuable support from Small and Kendall-Carpenter. Hyde, the young Northampton wing playing in his first international, spent most of his time defending.

The scoring began in the first half. Lauga dropped for goal early in the match (and missed); but soon afterwards, Hofmeyr was caught in possession on his own goal-line by Siman. From the following maul, France won the ball and Pilon crossed for a try in the corner. England soon equalised, and with a similar move. Preece kicked ahead but Brun, faltering for the only time in the entire match, failed to gather and Smith won a race to touch down in the corner.

Both sides failed with penalty shots before the interval but in the second half France were more dominant and only poor handling by the centres prevented any further scoring. Then, after Pilon missed with a long drop at goal, Lauga made amends for earlier mistakes and created an opening for Cazenave to sprint over in the left corner. Prat failed to convert for the second time. Each team made a great effort in the last 15 minutes but weak finishing (particularly on one occasion by Lauga) meant that the score remained at 6–3.

FRANCE		ENGLAND	
G. Brun	(Vienne)	M.B. Hofmeyr	(Oxford U.)
M. Siman	(Castres)	J.V. Smith	(Cambridge U.)
P. Lauga	(Vichy)	B. Boobbyer	(Oxford U.)
J. Merquey	(Toulon)	L.B. Cannell	(Oxford U.)
F. Cazenave	(R.C.F.)	†J.P. Hyde	(Northampton)
J. Pilon	(Périgueux)	*I. Preece	(Coventry)
G. Dufau	(R.C.F.)	W.K.T. Moore	(Leicester)
R. Biénès	(Cognac)	J.M.K. Kendall-Carpenter	(Oxford U.)
P. Pascalin	(Mont-de-Marsan)	J.H. Steeds	(Saracens)
R. Ferrien	(Tarbes)	W.A. Holmes	(Nuneaton)
L. Aristouy	(Pau)	J.R.C. Matthews	(Harlequins)
F. Bonnus	(Toulon)	H.A. Jones	(Barnstaple)
J. Prat	(Lourdes)	H.D. Small	(Oxford U.)
*G. Basquet	(Agen)	S.J. Adkins	(Coventry)
J. Matheu	(Castres)	V.G. Roberts	(Penryn)

Tries: Cazenave, Pilon   *Try:* Smith

Referee: Mr N.H. Lambert (Ireland)

SCOTLAND v ENGLAND 1950
Played at Murrayfield, Edinburgh, 18 March 1950
Scotland won by 2G, 1T (13) to 1G, 1PG, 1T (11)

Scotland relieved England of the Calcutta Cup in an exciting match of fluctuating fortunes. A superb last-minute conversion by Gray gave Scotland victory in wet, muddy conditions.

Despite the dismal conditions, 70,000 spectators were present and five thrilling tries were scored: the first by Scotland when some careless English handling allowed Scott and Sloan to dribble the ball over the line for the latter to touch down. England soon equalised. Gray bravely fell to halt an English forward rush, but the full-back was bundled off the ball, a foot kicked it over the Scottish line and John Smith won the race for the touch-down. A period of forward exchanges followed in which England appeared to dominate, but to the surprise and delight of the crowd Scotland led at half-time. A forward rush with Black in support resulted in Abercrombie diving over near the posts for Gray to kick the goal.

After the interval, England staged a magnificent revival in which full-back Hofmeyr figured prominently. First, he landed a splendid penalty goal from near touch; then, a little later, he converted an opportunist's try by Smith with an excellent kick from wide out, for the ball was heavy and greasy. This made the score 11–8 to England with time running out for Scotland. Not to be outdone, the Scottish forwards found enough energy to stage an astonishing late rally and from a rush which swept play deep into English territory the ball reached Angus Cameron. The fly-half kicked high to the English goal-line and from the ensuing loose maul Sloan crashed over for the match-saving try.

Then followed Gray's kick from midway between the touch-line and the goal, and amid scenes of enthusiasm, the ball slithered over the cross-bar for a narrow Scottish win.

SCOTLAND		ENGLAND	
T. Gray	(Northampton)	M.B. Hofmeyr	(Oxford U.)
D.M. Scott	(Langholm)	J.V. Smith	(Cambridge U.)
D.A. Sloan	(Edinburgh Acads.)	B. Boobbyer	(Oxford U.)
R. Macdonald	(Edinburgh U.)	L.B. Cannell	(Oxford U.)
C.W. Drummond	(Melrose)	J.P. Hyde	(Northampton)
A. Cameron	(Glasgow H.S.F.P.)	*I. Preece	(Coventry)
A.W. Black	(Edinburgh U.)	W.K.T. Moore	(Leicester)
J.C. Dawson	(Glasgow Acads.)	†J.L. Baume	(Northern)
J.G. Abercrombie	(Edinburgh U.)	J.H. Steeds	(Saracens)
G.M. Budge	(Edinburgh Wands.)	W.A. Holmes	(Nuneaton)
D.E. Muir	(Heriot's F.P.)	J.R.C. Matthews	(Harlequins)
R. Gemmill	(Glasgow H.S.F.P.)	S.J. Adkins	(Coventry)
W.I.D. Elliot	(Edinburgh Acads.)	H.D. Small	(Oxford U.)
*P.W. Kininmonth	(Richmond)	J.M.K. Kendall-Carpenter	(Oxford U.)
H. Scott	(St Andrew's U.)	V.G. Roberts	(Penryn)

Tries: Sloan (2), Abercrombie   *Tries:* Smith (2)   *Conversion:* Hofmeyr
Conversions: Gray (2)   *Penalty:* Hofmeyr

Referee: Captain M.J. Dowling (Ireland)

WALES v ENGLAND 1951
Played at St Helen's, Swansea, 20 January 1951
Wales won by 4G, 1T (23) to 1G (5)

Wales fielded eleven members of the 1950 British Lions team and continued in the Grand Slam winning vein of the previous season with a convincing defeat of England. Their star-studded side gave a scintillating display of open Rugby, with the pack dominating all phases of forward play. England had ten new caps in their ranks when Kendall-Carpenter, the chosen captain, was forced to withdraw before the kick-off. Consequently, the visitors were given little chance of producing a winning result when they took the field before a huge crowd of 50,000.

Wales began at a tremendous pace but could only score twice in the first half. From a loose maul, Matthews made a characteristic diagonal run at the English defence, burst through weak tackling and scored a try which Lewis Jones converted. England did well to hold the Welsh until just before the interval. Then Glyn Davies kicked ahead, the Welsh loose-forwards gathered the ball and set up a passing movement which Malcolm Thomas capped with a fine try at the left corner.

The second half was memorable for a show of classical threequarter play by Lewis Jones. He carved an opening for Matthews to break through and score at the posts; then he created a similar move to produce a try for Ken Jones. Later in the half, Lewis Jones intercepted an English pass near his own goal-line and set off on a 60-yards dash which resulted in Malcolm Thomas touching down for Wales's fifth try. Needless to add, Lewis Jones converted all three second-half tries.

During this glorious Welsh scoring spree, England had managed to obtain a consolation try when Rimmer, the bravest and best of the English backs, made a typical scrum-half breakaway to send Rittson-Thomas over for a try with a long pass.

D.T. Wilkins was the first player capped for England direct from Roundhay R.F.C.

WALES		ENGLAND	
G. Williams	(Llanelli)	†E.N. Hewitt	(Coventry)
K.J. Jones	(Newport)	†C.G. Woodruff	(Harlequins)
J. Matthews	(Cardiff)	†L.F.L. Oakley	(Bedford)
B.L. Jones	(Devonport Services)	B. Boobbyer	(Oxford U.)
M.C. Thomas	(Devonport Services)	†V.R. Tindall	(Liverpool U.)
G. Davies	(Cambridge U.)	I. Preece	(Coventry)
W.R. Willis	(Cardiff)	G. Rimmer	(Waterloo)
J.D. Robins	(Birkenhead Park)	†R.V. Stirling	(Leicester)
D.M. Davies	(Somerset Police)	†T. Smith	(Northampton)
C. Davies	(Cardiff)	W. A. Holmes	(Nuneaton)
E.R. John	(Neath)	†D.T. Wilkins	(Roundhay)
D.J. Hayward	(Newbridge)	†J.T. Bartlett	(Waterloo)
P. Evans	(Llanelli)	*V.G. Roberts	(Penryn)
*J.A. Gwilliam	(Edinburgh Wands.)	†P.B.C. Moore	(Blackheath)
R.T. Evans	(Newport)	†G.C. Rittson-Thomas	(Oxford U.)

Tries: Matthews (2), Thomas (2), K.J. Jones
Conversions: B.L. Jones (4)

Try: Rittson-Thomas
Conversion: Hewitt

Referee: Captain M.J. Dowling (Ireland)

IRELAND v ENGLAND 1951

Played at Lansdowne Road, Dublin, 10 February 1951
Ireland won by 1PG (3) to Nil

After their disappointing form against Wales, England's achievement in restricting Ireland, at Lansdowne Road, to a single penalty goal was highly commendable. Ireland owed much to their lively pack and, while the scoreline may look close, the 45,000 crowd had little doubt during the match as to which side would win.

Ireland selected the same fifteen which had beaten France but Lane was forced to withdraw with a broken rib and a new cap, W.H.J. Millar, was introduced. England, not surprisingly, showed several changes from the side routed by Wales. Preece moved to centre to allow Hardy of the Army to partner Rimmer at half-back; while in the pack, Kendall-Carpenter returned, as skipper, and Neale, who had missed the Welsh game through a broken nose, was able to enter the second row and win his first cap.

The game will certainly not be recalled for the quality of play exhibited, but there was plenty of excitement for the crowd. England's display was a considerable improvement on their dismal show against Wales and the new half-back pairing added cohesion and purpose to the back play. One break by Hardy sent the loose forwards, Rittson-Thomas and Roberts, clear and only a fine tackle from behind by Griffin foiled Roberts of a try. Another English attack, in which Roberts and Tindall figured, finished with Rittson-Thomas bound for the Irish line and looking certain to score. On this occasion a covering tackle by Kyle saved Ireland.

The deciding score of the match came in the second half when England were penalised at a scrummage inside their 25: McKibbin landed a goal with a good kick from a wide angle. After this score, a long forward battle followed with honours even. Both sides went close to scoring and Hardy had the misfortune to strike an upright with a magnificent drop-kick from 50 yards. Excitement remained to the closing minutes when an Irish handling movement took the game to the English posts and only an interception by Williams averted a score.

IRELAND		ENGLAND	
G.W. Norton	(Bective Rangers)	E.N. Hewitt	(Coventry)
C.S. Griffin	(London Irish)	C.G. Woodruff	(Harlequins)
N.J. Henderson	(Queen's U.)	I. Preece	(Coventry)
R.R. Chambers	(Instonians)	†J.M. Williams	(Penzance & Newlyn)
W.H.J. Millar	(Queen's U.)	V.R. Tindall	(Liverpool U.)
J.W. Kyle	(Queen's U.)	†E.M.P. Hardy	(Army/Blackheath)
J.A. O'Meara	(U.C. Cork)	G. Rimmer	(Waterloo)
T. Clifford	(Young Munster)	R.V. Stirling	(Leicester)
*K.D. Mullen	(Old Belvedere)	E. Evans	(Sale)
J.H. Smith	(Queen's U.)	W.A. Holmes	(Nuneaton)
J.E. Nelson	(Malone)	D.T. Wilkins	(Roundhay)
D. McKibbin	(Instonians)	†B.A. Neale	(Army/Rosslyn Park)
J.W. McKay	(Queen's U.)	V.G. Roberts	(Penryn)
D.J. O'Brien	(London Irish)	*J.M.K. Kendall-Carpenter	(Oxford U.)
J.S. McCarthy	(Dolphin)	G.C. Rittson-Thomas	(Oxford U.)

Penalty: McKibbin

Referee: Mr T. Jones (Wales)

ENGLAND v FRANCE 1951

Played at Twickenham, London, 24 February 1951
France won by 1G, 1DG, 1T (11) to 1T (3)

For France, victory at last at Rugby Union Headquarters on their eleventh visit since 1911. So often in the past they had been robbed of a deserved win by the luck of the English – notably in 1922 – but on this occasion, in atrocious conditions, they ran out winners by 11–3, placing themselves in firm contention for the Championship.

England made one change from the side which had lost in Dublin. Boobbyer replaced Williams at centre and the Oxford man opened the scoring in the twenty-seventh minute when he supported a breakaway by Rittson-Thomas. England then suffered two demoralising blows from which they never recovered. First, Rittson-Thomas was forced to leave the field injured; then, while he received attention, Pomathios made a break, set up a maul which the French forwards won, and Basquet, the captain, barged over the line for a try. Prat coolly converted from the touch-line with a superb kick.

England could have fought back in the second half, despite losing Hewitt with an eye injury for a period, but chances were squandered through poor team-work and a lack of understanding among the backs. While the English forwards tired and their spirits waned, Prat and Basquet inspired the French pack to perform with tremendous effect in the terrible conditions – rain had fallen incessantly until the Thursday before the match. In the last quarter of the game, France took complete command of the proceedings and with Dufau and Alvarez dictating the tactics, their lead was never in jeopardy. Prat, after missing the Irish match, his first absence from a French side since internationals were restored in 1947, completed an outstanding individual performance with a try and a well-taken dropped goal which put the last nail in the English coffin.

ENGLAND		FRANCE	
E.N. Hewitt	(Coventry)	R. Arcalis	(Brive)
C.G. Woodruff	(Harlequins)	A. Porthault	(R.C.F.)
I. Preece	(Coventry)	G. Brun	(Vienne)
B. Boobbyer	(Oxford U.)	G. Belletante	(Nantes)
V.R. Tindall	(Liverpool U.)	M. Pomathios	(Lyon)
E.M.P. Hardy	(Blackheath)	A.J. Alvarez	(Tyrosse)
G. Rimmer	(Waterloo)	G. Dufau	(R.C.F.)
R.V. Stirling	(Leicester)	R. Bernard	(Bergerac)
E. Evans	(Sale)	P. Pascalin	(Mont-de-Marsan)
W.A. Holmes	(Nuneaton)	P. Bertrand	(Bourg)
D.T. Wilkins	(Roundhay)	L. Mias	(Mazamet)
B.A. Neale	(Army)	H. Fourès	(Toulouse)
V.G. Roberts	(Penryn)	J. Prat	(Lourdes)
*J.M.K. Kendall-Carpenter	(Penzance & Newlyn)	*G. Basquet	(Agen)
G.C. Rittson-Thomas	(Oxford U.)	R. Biénès	(Cognac)

Try: Boobbyer

Tries: Basquet, Prat
Conversion: Prat
Dropped goal: Prat

Referee: Mr V.S. Llewellyn (Wales)

ENGLAND v SCOTLAND 1951
Played at Twickenham, London, 17 March 1951
England won by 1G (5) to 1T (3)

England managed to salvage some respect from a disappointing season by scoring a victory over Scotland to recapture the Calcutta Cup. Despite this belated revival, however, they collected the Wooden Spoon for the second successive season, while Scotland, having failed to fulfil their early promise to develop into a Championship winning team, joined England at the bottom of the table.

England's pack paved the way for this narrow victory, foraging enthusiastically in the loose and scrummaging solidly in the tight. While the heavy going and wet conditions made handling difficult, the new English halves performed effectively as a pair and the three-quarters had, surprisingly, many passing movements. Towell made several exciting bursts and Tindall very nearly scored twice. Only Angus Cameron of the Scottish backs threatened any danger to England.

Don White, recalled to the English ranks for the first time since 1948, gave his side an interval lead when he seized a Scottish scrummage heel, dummied, and ran over for a try which the veteran full-back, Hook, converted into a goal. In the second half, open play was largely restricted by frequent heavy showers which made the ball difficult to pass and kick – both Gray and Hook missed fairly easy opportunities to land penalty points.

Five minutes before no-side, after Roberts had nearly scored for England, Scotland attacked and Cameron crossed for a try near the corner. Gray was unable to convert (he had won the corresponding match the preceding season with virtually the last kick of the game) and England held out during the dying minutes of the match for their first win of the season.

ENGLAND		SCOTLAND	
†W.G. Hook	(Gloucester)	T. Gray	(Heriot's F.P.)
C.G. Woodruff	(Harlequins)	K.J. Dalgleish	(Edinburgh Wands.)
A.C. Towell	(Bedford)	D.A. Sloan	(Edinburgh Acads.)
J.M. Williams	(Penzance & Newlyn)	D.M. Scott	(Langholm)
V.R. Tindall	(Liverpool U.)	D.M. Rose	(Jedforest)
E.M.P. Hardy	(Blackheath/Army)	A. Cameron	(Glasgow H.S.F.P.)
†D.W. Shuttleworth	(Blackheath/Army)	I.A. Ross	(Hillhead H.S.F.P.)
R.V. Stirling	(Leicester)	J.C. Dawson	(Glasgow Acads.)
E. Evans	(Sale)	N.G.R. Mair	(Edinburgh U.)
W.A. Holmes	(Nuneaton)	R.L. Wilson	(Gala)
D.T. Wilkins	(Roundhay)	H.M. Inglis	(Edinburgh Acads.)
B.A. Neale	(Rosslyn Park)	W.P. Black	(Glasgow H.S.F.P.)
D.F. White	(Northampton)	W.I.D. Elliot	(Edinburgh Acads.)
*J.M.K. Kendall-Carpenter	(Penzance & Newlyn)	*P.W. Kininmonth	(Richmond)
V.G. Roberts	(Penryn)	R.C.Taylor	(Kelvinside West)

Try: White   *Conversion:* Hook   *Try:* Cameron

Referee: Captain M.J. Dowling (Ireland)

ENGLAND v SOUTH AFRICA 1952

Played at Twickenham, London, 5 January 1952
South Africa won by 1G, 1PG (8) to 1T (3)

South Africa made two changes from the side which had beaten Wales, recalling Dinkelmann and introducing Bekker in place of Geffin in the front row. Muller assumed the place-kicking duties. England awarded four new caps for this match, three at three-quarter and one in the back row of a fairly experienced scrummage.

As in the game with Wales, the measure of the Springbok victory was due to goal-kicking, each side scoring a try. However, the closeness of the final result slightly flattered England, though they put up a spirited fight. The early scoring opportunities came through penalty kicks at goal, Hook and Muller going close with several attempts. From one of the South African kicks came the first points of the match after 23 minutes. Koch nearly forced his way over and England were compelled to concede a five-yard-scrum from which du Toit, easily the man of the match, beat White to slip round on the open-side and score near the posts. Muller converted. England fought back immediately and secured a controversial try three minutes later. Hook sliced a penalty kick at goal and Brewis failed to gather cleanly in his in-goal area. Winn had followed up in hot pursuit and touched down for a try which the referee awarded, though many spectators and the whole South African team thought that Brewis had recovered and managed to minor the ball. Hook struck the post with his conversion attempt.

England thus changed ends at half-time with their tails high and only two points in arrears. The second half saw the Springbok pack dig in with determination though, and towards the end there was only one side in it. The South Africans so dominated in the tight that Muller was able to withdraw himself from the scrums and strengthen the defence. Woodward gave England some hope with one tremendous dash, but the only further scoring came when Muller landed a penalty goal from 35 yards with the help of a lucky bounce off the goal post. Near the end the visitors twice crossed the English line but were called back for previous infringements.

ENGLAND		SOUTH AFRICA	
W.G. Hook	(Gloucester)	J.U. Buchler	(Transvaal)
†J.E. Woodward	(Wasps)	P. Johnstone	(Western Province)
†A.E. Agar	(Harlequins)	R.A.M. van Schoor	(Rhodesia)
L.B. Cannell	(St Mary's H.)	M.T. Lategan	(Western Province)
†C.E. Winn	(Rosslyn Park)	J.K. Ochse	(Western Province)
*N.M. Hall	(Richmond)	J.D. Brewis	(Northern Transvaal)
G. Rimmer	(Waterloo)	P.A. du Toit	(Northern Transvaal)
R.V. Stirling	(Leicester)	A.C. Koch	(Boland)
E. Evans	(Sale)	W.H. Delport	(Eastern Province)
W.A. Holmes	(Nuneaton)	H.P.J. Bekker	(Northern Transvaal)
J.R.C. Matthews	(Harlequins)	J.A. du Rand	(Rhodesia)
D.T. Wilkins	(R.N./U.S.)	E.E. Dinkelmann	(Northern Transvaal)
D.F. White	(Northampton)	C.J. van Wyk	(Transvaal)
J.M.K. Kendall-Carpenter	(Penzance & Newlyn)	*H.S.V. Muller	(Transvaal)
†A.O. Lewis	(Bath)	S.P. Fry	(Western Province)

Try: Winn

Try: du Toit   *Penalty:* Muller
Conversion: Muller

Referee: Mr W.C.W. Murdoch (Scotland)

ENGLAND v WALES 1952

Played at Twickenham, London, 19 January 1952
Wales won by 1G, 1T (8) to 2T (6)

Both sides selected the fifteens which had done battle in the South African matches, but late changes were enforced by injuries to B.L. Williams and W.A. Holmes. Ground conditions were treacherous after a heavy frost, and handling and running became difficult as the game progressed.

The packs were evenly matched but Wales were superior behind the scrum. The Welsh suffered a serious setback early in the match when Lewis Jones was reduced to the role of a limping passenger after pulling a thigh muscle. Woodward exploited Lewis Jones's weakness, and then his temporary absence, to give England two tries. The first was the result of a kick ahead which the injured Welsh wing could not gather. Woodward followed up and sent Agar over. The next try came while Blyth was deputising on the wing. A fine combined English move involving Kendall-Carpenter, Rimmer, Hall and Cannell ended with Woodward dashing over the line for a grand score. Just before half-time, Willis broke from a line-out to send Morgan clear. The Welsh pivot, having made some ground, gave an inside pass to Ken Jones who raced 40 yards to score a try which Malcolm Thomas converted.

Wales thus began what turned out to be an exciting second half, one point behind. After ten minutes, the most brilliant move of the match evolved and, incredibly, it was Lewis Jones who, by hopping in to make an extra man, was responsible for the winning score. Wales won the ball some 30 yards from the English line and started to move from left to right. Jones's appearance was enough to distract the English defence and Ken Jones was able to take the ball at full pace. The Newport wing weaved his way past Winn and Hook to score in the corner. The rest of the match was a titanic forward struggle and the hearts of many Welshmen were brought to their mouths in the last minute when Rimmer sent Lewis over for a try; but, luckily for Wales, an Englishman had been spotted off-side, and Wales held on to win.

ENGLAND		WALES	
W.G. Hook	(Gloucester)	G. Williams	(Llanelli)
J.E. Woodward	(Wasps)	K.J. Jones	(Newport)
A.E. Agar	(Harlequins)	M.C. Thomas	(Newport)
L.B. Cannell	(St Mary's H.)	A.G. Thomas	(Cardiff)
C.E. Winn	(Rosslyn Park)	B.L. Jones	(Llanelli)
*N.M. Hall	(Richmond)	C.I. Morgan	(Cardiff)
G. Rimmer	(Waterloo)	W.R. Willis	(Cardiff)
†E.E. Woodgate	(Paignton)	W.O. Williams	(Swansea)
E. Evans	(Sale)	D.M. Davies	(Somerset Police)
R. V. Stirling	(Leicester)	D.J. Hayward	(Newbridge)
J.R.C. Matthews	(Harlequins)	E.R. John	(Neath)
D.T. Wilkins	(R.N./U.S.)	J.R.G. Stephens	(Neath)
D.F. White	(Northampton)	L. Blyth	(Swansea)
J.M.K. Kendall-Carpenter	(Penzance & Newlyn)	*J.A. Gwilliam	(Edinburgh Wands.)
A.O. Lewis	(Bath)	A. Forward	(Pontypool)

Tries: Agar, Woodward

Tries: K.J. Jones (2)
Conversion: M.C. Thomas

Referee: Mr N.H. Lambert (Ireland)

SCOTLAND v ENGLAND 1952
Played at Murrayfield, Edinburgh, 15 March 1952
England won by 2G, 1DG, 2T (19) to 1T (3)

England went to Scotland with the team which would have played against Ireland; a team which showed four changes from the side defeated at Twickenham by Wales. Scotland selected a team with five new caps.

The end of a tense first half saw England with a slender lead of five points after a Scottish fumble early in the match had been seized upon by Agar. The Harlequin centre had then kicked ahead for Winn to gather and shake-off the attentions of several would-be tacklers and score a try which Hall turned into a goal. Remarkably, England had been unable to add to this score as the large crowd cheered on their new-look Scottish side.

In the second half, however, the Scottish pack fell away miserably and England gave glimpses of some fine play. Evans scored a try after a run by Boobbyer; and Woodward completed a fine round of passing between Boobbyer, Lewis and Winn by getting over for the third try. Boobbyer, in his first appearance for England this season, was certainly making up for lost time and set up the next try – scored by Kendall-Carpenter – after combining with loose-forward Don White. England thus coasted to a 16-points lead before Johnston crossed for a Scottish try in the dying moments of the match. England then had the final say when Agar dropped an unexpected goal immediately afterwards.

Thus ended Scotland's most miserable international season ever. They lost all of the five matches played; and of the 32 players called upon to do duty for them, only two, Dorward and Davidson, gave any hope for a great revival in the following season.

SCOTLAND		ENGLAND	
N.W. Cameron	(Glasgow U.)	†P.J. Collins	(Camborne)
R.A. Gordon	(Edinburgh Wands.)	J.E. Woodward	(Wasps)
I.F. Cordial	(Edinburgh Wands.)	A.E. Agar	(Harlequins)
I.D.F. Coutts	(Oxford U.)	B. Boobbyer	(Rosslyn Park)
T.G. Weatherstone	(Stewart's College F.P.)	C.E. Winn	(Rosslyn Park)
J.N.G. Davidson	(Edinburgh U.)	*N.M. Hall	(Richmond)
*A.F. Dorward	(Gala)	P.W. Sykes	(Wasps)
J.C. Dawson	(Glasgow Acads.)	W.A. Holmes	(Nuneaton)
J. Fox	(Gala)	E. Evans	(Sale)
J.M. Inglis	(Selkirk)	R.V. Stirling	(Leicester)
J. Johnston	(Melrose)	J.R.C. Matthews	(Harlequins)
D.E. Muir	(Heriot's F.P.)	D.T. Wilkins	(R.N./U.S.)
W.I.D. Elliot	(Edinburgh Acads.)	D.F. White	(Northampton)
J.P. Friebe	(Glasgow H.S.F.P.)	J.M.K. Kendall-Carpenter	(Penzance & Newlyn)
D.S. Gilbert-Smith	(Army/London Scottish)	A.O. Lewis	(Bath)

Try: Johnston

Tries: Evans, Kendall-Carpenter, Winn, Woodward   *Conversions:* Hall (2)
Dropped goal: Agar

Referee: Captain M.J. Dowling (Ireland)

ENGLAND v IRELAND 1952

Played at Twickenham, London, 29 March 1952
England won by 1T (3) to Nil

After being postponed from 9 February through the death of King George VI, this match was eventually played in a blizzard. Conditions were so bad that, but for the previous postponement and the fact that the Irish team was already in London, the match would have been called off. In the circumstances, however, both sides gave a spirited and skilful display, with the English backs attempting, and successfully executing, several exciting runs and moves in the best traditions of good open Rugby.

Ireland, who had possessed the best pack of scrummagers in the Championship for a period of four seasons, made several changes for this match and introduced a new hooker to replace the famous Karl Mullen. The lack of weight and drive in the Irish forwards, however, put the whole side at a disadvantage, and England were able to register a well-deserved, if narrow, victory.

The decisive score of the match came half-way through the first half. An English kick ahead was fumbled by Phipps and Boobbyer followed up, gathered the ball near the Irish line and crossed for a try which Hall failed to convert. England had the better of the remainder of the match and the forwards often threatened to score from rushes with the ball at their feet. The Irish went down bravely on the bone-hard ground to snatch the ball from the toes of the Englishmen, however, and, in so doing, won the admiration of the Twickenham crowd.

ENGLAND		IRELAND	
P.J. Collins	(Camborne)	J.G.M.W. Murphy	(Dublin U.)
C.E. Winn	(Rosslyn Park)	M. Hillary	(U.C. Dublin)
A.E. Agar	(Harlequins)	N.J. Henderson	(Queen's U.)
B. Boobbyer	(Rosslyn Park)	G.C. Phipps	(Rosslyn Park)
†R.C. Bazley	(Waterloo)	N. Bailey	(Northampton)
*N.M. Hall	(Richmond)	J.W. Kyle	(Queen's U.)
P.W. Sykes	(Wasps)	J.A. O'Meara	(U.C. Cork)
W.A. Holmes	(Nuneaton)	W.A. O'Neill	(U.C. Dublin)
E. Evans	(Sale)	R. Roe	(Dublin U.)
R.V. Stirling	(Leicester)	J.H. Smith	(Collegians)
J.R.C. Matthews	(Harlequins)	P.J. Lawler	(Clontarf)
D.T. Wilkins	(R.N./U.S.)	A. O'Leary	(Cork Const.)
D.F. White	(Northampton)	P. Kavanagh	(U.C. Dublin)
J.M.K. Kendall-Carpenter	(Penzance & Newlyn)	*D.J. O'Brien	(Cardiff)
A.O. Lewis	(Bath)	J.S. McCarthy	(Dolphin)

Try: Boobbyer

Referee: Mr I. David (Wales)

FRANCE v ENGLAND 1952

Played at Stade Colombes, Paris, 5 April 1952
England won by 2PG (6) to 1T (3)

Unlucky France! They scored the only try of the match, only to lose by three points – their opponents scoring two penalty goals.

England selected the fifteen which had done duty against Ireland one week earlier – and what a difference in weather conditions that side experienced in just one week! From the freezing blizzard at Twickenham against Ireland, this English side travelled to a Paris basking in lovely spring sunshine.

The spectators, who included Field-Marshal Montgomery, saw France score the only points of the first half when the strong-running Pomathios touched down for a try which Jean Prat could not convert. Then an injury to Pomathios (he was forced to retire with a pulled muscle), and a series of unlucky incidents, prevented France from increasing their lead in the second half.

Hall slowly brought his side back into the game, using the ball heeled by the excellent English forwards to good advantage. His tactical kicking was shrewd and eventually pushed England into positions from which penalty goals could be landed. Hall's first goal, from 55 yards, just after the restart, was a huge drop kick; and his match-winning effort was another fine kick, this time from inside the French 25 after the referee had penalised France for obstruction.

FRANCE		ENGLAND	
G. Brun	(Vienne)	P.J. Collins	(Camborne)
M. Pomathios	(Lyon)	C.E. Winn	(Rosslyn Park)
J. Mauran	(Castres)	B. Boobbyer	(Rosslyn Park)
M. Prat	(Lourdes)	A.E. Agar	(Harlequins)
J. Colombier	(St Junien)	R.C. Bazley	(Waterloo)
J. Carabignac	(Agen)	*N.M. Hall	(Richmond)
P. Lasaosa	(Dax)	P.W. Sykes	(Wasps)
R. Biénès	(Cognac)	W.A. Holmes	(Nuneaton)
P. Labadie	(Bayonne)	E. Evans	(Sale)
R. Bréjassou	(Pau)	R.V. Stirling	(Leicester)
L. Mias	(Mazamet)	J.R.C. Matthews	(Harlequins)
B. Chevallier	(Montferrand)	D.T. Wilkins	(R.N./U.S.)
J. Prat	(Lourdes)	D.F. White	(Northampton)
*G. Basquet	(Agen)	J.M.K. Kendall-Carpenter	(Penzance & Newlyn)
J.R. Bourdeu	(Lourdes)	A.O. Lewis	(Bath)

Try: Pomathios   *Penalties:* Hall (2)

Referee: Mr W.C.W. Murdoch (Scotland)

WALES v ENGLAND 1953

Played at Cardiff Arms Park, 17 January 1953
England won by 1G, 1PG (8) to 1PG (3)

Many of the 56,000 spectators present at this match shrewdly believed that the winners of this fixture would make much of the running towards the International Championship title of 1952–53. Each side retained the nucleii of the packs which had dominated the international matches of the previous season and given the Springboks a close run for their money. England were particularly likely to give a good performance, for they had lost to Wales at Twickenham in 1952 by a single conversion.

The forward exchanges were equally settled: Roy John in the latter stages giving a fine exhibition of line-out skills, and the English heeling and tight scrummaging providing a sound platform for the visiting backs to stretch the Welsh defence to the full. Wales were plagued by injuries to their leading half-back pair prior to the match and, consequently, the Newport pair were selected to represent Wales for the first time. England introduced a new outside-half in Regan.

Wales took the lead early in the match when 19-year-old Terry Davies kicked a penalty goal from 45 yards. England's backs often looked dangerous in attack – Regan was particularly quick off the mark at all times – in contrast to the unusually lethargic Welsh backs. Only the new man, Griffiths, showed any signs of dash and even Ken Jones had an off-day. England took the lead before the interval when a break by Regan, supported by Bazley, brought a try by Cannell which Hall, now appearing at full-back, converted.

After two failures with penalty kicks at goal in the second half, England stretched their lead when Woodward was finally successful. Wales rallied in the last ten minutes of the match and Bleddyn Williams and Malcolm Thomas made some dangerous breaks. But the effort came too late and England hung on to record their fifth victory at Cardiff.

WALES		ENGLAND	
T.J. Davies	(Swansea)	*N.M. Hall	(Richmond)
K.J. Jones	(Newport)	J.E. Woodward	(Wasps)
M.C. Thomas	(Newport)	A.E. Agar	(Harlequins)
B.L. Williams	(Cardiff)	L.B. Cannell	(St Mary's H.)
G.M. Griffiths	(Cardiff)	R.C. Bazley	(Waterloo)
R. Burnett	(Newport)	†M. Regan	(Liverpool)
W.A. Williams	(Newport)	P.W. Sykes	(Wasps)
J.D. Robins	(Bradford)	W.A. Holmes	(Nuneaton)
G. Beckingham	(Cardiff)	†N.A. Labuschagne	(Harlequins)
W.O. Williams	(Swansea)	R.V. Stirling	(Leicester)
E.R. John	(Neath)	S.J. Adkins	(Coventry)
J.R.G. Stephens	(Neath)	D.T. Wilkins	(U.S./R.N.)
S. Judd	(Cardiff)	D.F. White	(Northampton)
*J.A. Gwilliam	(Gloucester)	J.M.K. Kendall-Carpenter	(Bath)
W.D. Johnson	(Swansea)	A.O. Lewis	(Bath)

Penalty: Davies

Try: Cannell   *Conversion:* Hall
Penalty: Woodward

Referee: Captain M.J. Dowling (Ireland)

IRELAND v ENGLAND 1953

Played at Lansdowne Road, Dublin, 14 February 1953
Drawn: Ireland 2PG, 1T (9), England 2PG, 1T (9)

Ireland failed to make the best of their chances on a slippery ground, and with England defending with tremendous resource throughout the afternoon, a drawn game was, on the whole, a fair result. Both sides showed one forward change from their previous winning sides: Evans returned to hook for England and Reid was able to win his cap for Ireland.

Kyle dominated the early part of the game. His probing kicks ahead had the English defence at sixes-and-sevens for a while, and the anxiety caused to the English forced the visitors to wander off-side on one occasion. Henderson nearly landed the penalty points from 40 yards. Regan, the English outside-half, also looked dangerous at times, and it was one of his finest breaks which produced the opening score of the match. Evans supported him intelligently to touch down for a try, slightly against the run of play. Hall failed with a comparatively simple kick at goal. Quinn then went near with a drop at goal before Regan created another scoring chance. This time, however, the final pass, to Woodward, did not quite go to hand and so England changed ends with a narrow lead.

An exciting second half began with Jim McCarthy crossing for a try which was disallowed – the referee having seen a forward pass – but soon after, Henderson equalised with a penalty. The English forwards stormed back and Ireland conceded a penalty to Hall before Mortell rounded-off a lovely bout of passing to score a fine try. An exchange of penalty goals followed, and with only ten minutes of playing time remaining, it still seemed anyone's match. Ireland missed with two kicks at goal, and when the whistle went for no-side both sides were seeking a winning score.

IRELAND		ENGLAND	
R.J. Gregg	(Queen's U.)	*N.M. Hall	(Richmond)
M.F. Lane	(U.C. Cork)	J.E. Woodward	(Wasps)
N.J. Henderson	(N.I.F.C.)	A.E. Agar	(Harlequins)
K. Quinn	(Old Belvedere)	L.B. Cannell	(St Mary's H.)
M. Mortell	(Bective Rangers)	R.C. Bazley	(Waterloo)
*J.W. Kyle	(N.I.F.C.)	M. Regan	(Liverpool)
J.A. O'Meara	(U.C. Cork)	P.W. Sykes	(Wasps)
W.A. O'Neill	(U.C. Dublin)	W.A. Holmes	(Nuneaton)
R. Roe	(Dublin U.)	E. Evans	(Sale)
F.E. Anderson	(Queen's U.)	R.V. Stirling	(Leicester)
J.R. Brady	(C.I.Y.M.S.)	D.T. Wilkins	(U.S./R.N.)
T.E. Reid	(Garryowen)	S.J. Adkins	(Coventry)
J.S. McCarthy	(Dolphin)	D.F. White	(Northampton)
J.R. Kavanagh	(U.C. Dublin)	J.M.K. Kendall-Carpenter	(Bath)
W.E. Bell	(Collegians)	A.O. Lewis	(Bath)

Try: Mortell
Penalties: Henderson (2)

Try: Evans *Penalties:* Hall (2)

Referee: Mr A.W.C. Austin (Scotland)

ENGLAND v FRANCE 1953
Played at Twickenham, London, 28 February 1953
England won by 1G, 2T (11) to Nil

England strengthened their claim to the International Championship title with a convincing win over a depleted French fifteen. It was by no means England's best display of the season, though a new star in Butterfield – chosen to replace Agar in the centre – was discovered. He made a good impression with his attacking running and in the first minute turned an error by Haget, the new French outside-half, to good use. Butterfield intercepted a loose pass and made an opening for Woodward to score a good try. A further three points were added by Evans before half-time when the hooker scored a try after some good combined work by the forwards. In fact, so many of the English pack were at hand that any one of three or four could have scored this try, and one summary of the match later credited Adkins of Coventry with the score.

The French problems in this match began long before their side took the field. Injuries and late withdrawals forced several changes from the original selection. Bréjassou, normally a prop, played in the second row and the Lourdes wing-forward, Bourdeu, had to take the place of Pomathios on the wing. Nor was that the end of their troubles. During the match, Haget was forced to leave the field.

Despite these difficulties, the French gave a spirited effort, especially in the second half, and England were only allowed to score once more. Butterfield crowned an excellent debut by getting a try in the last minute of the match after some good work by Regan, and Hall's successful goal-kick gave England a win by 11 points.

ENGLAND		FRANCE	
*N.M. Hall	(Richmond)	G. Brun	(Vienne)
J.E. Woodward	(Wasps)	J.R. Bourdeu	(Lourdes)
†J. Butterfield	(Northampton)	M. Prat	(Lourdes)
L.B. Cannell	(St Mary's H.)	J. Mauran	(Castres)
R.C. Bazley	(Waterloo)	L. Rogé	(Béziers)
M. Regan	(Liverpool)	A. Haget	(P.U.C.)
P.W. Sykes	(Wasps)	G. Dufau	(R.C.F.)
W.A. Holmes	(Nuneaton)	P. Bertrand	(Bourg)
E. Evans	(Sale)	J. Arrieta	(Stade Français)
R.V. Stirling	(Leicester)	R. Carrère	(Mont-de-Marsan)
D.T. Wilkins	(U.S./R.N.)	R. Bréjassou	(Tarbes)
S.J. Adkins	(Coventry)	B. Chevallier	(Montferrand)
A.O. Lewis	(Bath)	*J. Prat	(Lourdes)
J.M.K. Kendall-Carpenter	(Bath)	M. Celaya	(Biarritz)
†D.S. Wilson	(Harlequins)	R. Biénès	(Cognac)

Tries: Butterfield, Evans, Woodward
Conversion: Hall

Referee: Mr V.J. Parfitt (Wales)

England v Scotland, 1953. The team which won the Championship outright for the first time since 1937: *back* Captain M. J. Dowling, R. C. Bazley, A. O. Lewis, W. P. C. Davies, J. E. Woodward, S. J. Adkins, W. A. Holmes, J. Butterfield, Colonel G. Warden; *middle* E. Evans, D. T. Wilkins, N. M. Hall (captain), J. M. K. Kendall-Carpenter, D. F. White, R. V. Stirling; *front* D. W. Shuttleworth, M. Regan.

J. Butterfield, who scored a try on his international debut against France in 1953, seen here on his way to the try-line during the 1955 Dublin match. J. E. Woodward is in support. A. C. Pedlow and J. W. Kyle are the Irishmen.

ENGLAND v SCOTLAND 1953

Played at Twickenham, London, 21 March 1953
England won by 4G, 2T (26) to 1G, 1T (8)

England gave a fine display of open attacking football to win the International Championship outright for the first time since 1937. Regan played a marvellous game at outside-half – as he had done in all England's previous wins – and formed, with Butterfield and the new man Davies, an exciting midfield division. Scotland failed to take their chances early in the game, missing two kickable penalty attempts. White was prominent in one English break which nearly produced a try by Regan – a perfectly-timed tackle from behind just robbing him of glory. Woodward made a thrilling dash but was crowded into touch, before his colleague on the other flank, Bazley, gathered a cross-kick by Regan and slipped past his opposite number and Scotland's full-back to open the scoring. Hall converted before Weatherstone, Scotland's most enterprising back, initiated an attack with Dorward and the forwards, which he himself completed by scoring a try. England then scored twice in the few minutes before half-time to lead 11–3 at the interval.

The second half was more or less one-way traffic as England enlarged on their forward superiority. Another fine run by Bazley led to some loose play among the forwards near Scotland's goal-line and Stirling scored a try. White and Davies between them presented Butterfield with a gift try, before Henderson replied with a score for Scotland after good support by Dawson. Towards the end of the game, the tackling of the Scots became poorer, and Woodward collected the final try of the afternoon after receiving the ball standing still.

It was a sad end to the season for the hapless Scots and extended their doleful sequence of consecutive defeats to twelve: their last victory in an international match had been against Wales at Murrayfield 25 months earlier.

ENGLAND		SCOTLAND	
*N.M. Hall	(Richmond)	I.H.M. Thomson	(Heriot's F.P.)
J.E. Woodward	(Wasps)	T.G. Weatherstone	(Stewart's College F.P.)
J. Butterfield	(Northampton)	*A. Cameron	(Glasgow H.S.F.P.)
†W.P.C. Davies	(Harlequins)	D. Cameron	(Glasgow H.S.F.P.)
R.C. Bazley	(Waterloo)	J.S. Swan	(St Andrew's U.)
M. Regan	(Liverpool)	L. Bruce-Lockhart	(London Scottish)
D.W. Shuttleworth	(Headingley)	A.F. Dorward	(Gala)
R.V. Stirling	(Leicester)	J.C. Dawson	(Glasgow Acads.)
E. Evans	(Sale)	J.H.F. King	(Selkirk)
W.A. Holmes	(Nuneaton)	R.L. Wilson	(Gala)
D.T. Wilkins	(U.S./R.N.)	J.H. Henderson	(Oxford U.)
S.J. Adkins	(Coventry)	J.J. Hegarty	(Hawick)
A.O. Lewis	(Bath)	W. Kerr	(London Scottish)
J.M.K. Kendall-Carpenter	(Bath)	W.L.K. Cowie	(Edinburgh Wands.)
D.F. White	(Northampton)	K.H.D. McMillan	(Sale)

Tries: Bazley (2), Adkins, Butterfield, Stirling, Woodward
Conversions: Hall (4)

Tries: Henderson, Weatherstone
Conversion: Thomson

Referee: Captain M.J. Dowling (Ireland)

ENGLAND v WALES 1954

Played at Twickenham, London, 16 January 1954
England won by 3T (9) to 1PG, 1T (6)

The Welsh forwards gave a lethargic performance, but this time there was no rousing second-half rally (as there had been in their match against the All Blacks). Wales, it should be added, were a trifle unlucky in the matter of injuries in this match, but the fact remained that they could, and should have beaten England in this first all-ticket Twickenham international.

W.O. Williams was injured early in the game, and Wales did well to open the scoring. A good, controlled dribble by Rowlands after a careless English pass ended with the Cardiff wing winning a race to touch down after the ball had been kicked into the English in-goal area. Woodward equalised soon afterwards after a bullocking run in which the Welsh full-back was badly injured.

Wales lost Willis in the second half and Cliff Morgan became emergency scrum-half. The English backs grasped the opportunity to go ahead at this stage, and Regan, the spearhead of the English attack, started a classic round of passing between Quinn, Wilson and Woodward for the last-named to score his second try. Wales retaliated though, and John made some outstanding jumps in the line-out to enable the Welsh backs to relieve much of the pressure they were under in the later stages of the match. Rowlands levelled matters with a well-taken penalty goal.

Then, in the last minute of the game, England snatched a victory when Winn scored a try. Wales were attacking when Quinn seized on a loose pass and linked with Regan and Wilson. A long run followed and Kendall-Carpenter was up in support to send a pass out to Winn, who dived in at the corner.

ENGLAND		WALES	
†I. King	(Harrogate)	G. Williams	(London Welsh)
J.E. Woodward	(Wasps)	K.J. Jones	(Newport)
†J.P. Quinn	(New Brighton)	A.G. Thomas	(Cardiff)
J. Butterfield	(Northampton)	G. John	(St Luke's College)
C.E. Winn	(Rosslyn Park)	G. Rowlands	(Cardiff)
M. Regan	(Liverpool)	C.I. Morgan	(Cardiff)
G. Rimmer	(Waterloo)	W.R. Willis	(Cardiff)
*R.V. Stirling	(Wasps)	W.O. Williams	(Swansea)
E. Evans	(Sale)	D.M. Davies	(Somerset Police)
†D.L. Sanders	(Harlequins)	C.C. Meredith	(Neath)
†P.D. Young	(Wanderers)	J.A. Gwilliam	(Gloucester)
†P.G. Yarranton	(Wasps)	E.R. John	(Neath)
D.S. Wilson	(Metropolitan Police)	S. Judd	(Cardiff)
J.M.K. Kendall-Carpenter	(Bath)	*J.R.G. Stephens	(Neath)
†R. Higgins	(Liverpool)	R.C.C. Thomas	(Swansea)

Tries: Woodward (2), Winn   *Try:* Rowlands   *Penalty:* Rowlands

Referee: Captain M.J. Dowling (Ireland)

ENGLAND v NEW ZEALAND 1954

Played at Twickenham, London, 30 January 1954
New Zealand won by 1G (5) to Nil

Wales had beaten New Zealand; England had beaten Wales: so England would beat New Zealand! That was the propositional logic which many supporters expected to come true at Twickenham on this bitterly cold day. The weather had been so severe during the week leading up to the match that 17 tons of straw were piled over the turf to keep the ground in a playable condition. All other matches of the day, including the international at Swansea between Wales and Scotland, were postponed.

The ground was firm, but ideal for running Rugby when the match started with 72,000 present. The New Zealand pack soon began to dominate up-front, and only sturdy defence kept them from scoring. England had several promising chances and looked most dangerous when the ball reached their hefty wings. Woodward made one memorable run down his wing and only a desperate late effort by the complete New Zealand back row robbed him of a spectacular score.

Hemi, the All Black hooker, had an outstanding game in the tight and loose, and an early strike of his against the head nearly brought a score when Clark followed a punt ahead by Davis which had King, the English full-back, in great trouble. Clark nearly scored shortly after when he charged down an attempted kick to touch by one of the English backs, but the home side managed to clear in the nick of time. The only score of the match then followed, 20 minutes into the half. White burst away from a line-out and Hemi led a well-controlled dribble from the English 10-yard line. When King went down to kill the ball, Hemi and Clark mauled it clear and sent Dalzell over for a try which Scott converted.

Early in the second half, Woodward had another fine run checked, this time by Jarden; and the New Zealand wing, Dixon, showed one or two surprising turns of speed. But the second half failed to produce another score and New Zealand, as so often happens in Rugby football, confounded the form-books and avenged their 1936 defeat at H.Q. with a good tactical victory.

ENGLAND		NEW ZEALAND	
I. King	(Harrogate)	R.W.H. Scott	(Auckland)
J.E. Woodward	(Wasps)	M.J. Dixon	(Canterbury)
J.P. Quinn	(New Brighton)	C.J. Loader	(Wellington)
J. Butterfield	(Northampton)	R.A. Jarden	(Wellington)
W.P.C. Davies	(Harlequins)		
		D.D. Wilson	(Canterbury)
M. Regan	(Liverpool)	L.S. Haig	(Otago)
G. Rimmer	(Waterloo)	K. Davis	(Auckland)
*R.V. Stirling	(Wasps)	K.L. Skinner	(Otago)
E. Evans	(Sale)	R.C. Hemi	(Waikato)
D.L. Sanders	(Harlequins)	H.L. White	(Auckland)
P.D. Young	(Wanderers)	R.A. White	(Poverty Bay)
P.G. Yarranton	(Wasps)	G.N. Dalzell	(Canterbury)
D.S. Wilson	(Metropolitan Police)	P.F.H. Jones	(North Auckland)
J.M.K. Kendall-Carpenter	(Bath)	*R.C. Stuart	(Canterbury)
R. Higgins	(Liverpool)	W.H. Clark	(Wellington)

Try: Dalzell   *Conversion:* Scott

Referee: Mr I. David (Wales)

ENGLAND v IRELAND 1954

Played at Twickenham, London, 13 February 1954
England won by 1G, 1PG, 2T (14) to 1PG (3)

A rumbustious Irish pack upset the English forwards early in the game, but the English backs showed a refreshing improvement in attack and turned the match in England's favour with two fine tries in the first half. Regan was, once more, an outstanding pivot and was well served by the hardy Rimmer. Ireland, it should be added, took the field without Kyle for the first time since the war in an official international match – the maestro having to withdraw through injury – thus allowing Hewitt, a member of the famous Ulster Rugby family, to win his cap. The new boy could not take advantage of the good ball won by his forwards, however, and many critics thought in their post-match reflections that Ireland could have won this match had Kyle been available to direct operations. Even the loss of new cap, Murphy-O'Connor, in the first half did not prevent the visiting pack from giving a sterling performance.

England led 6–3 at half-time, thanks to fine tries by Regan and Butterfield – Murphy-O'Connor pulling back three points for Ireland with a penalty goal before he was carried off the field. England had an easier task up-front in the second half and increased the lead when King kicked a penalty goal. Wilson, England's loose-forward, played brilliantly in the open and constantly backed up in the broken passages of the game. His tenacity and opportunism were finally rewarded with the last and most decisive score of the afternoon. His try was converted by King, thus extending England's lead to a safe 11 points.

ENGLAND		IRELAND	
I. King	(Harrogate)	R.J. Gregg	(Queen's U.)
J.E. Woodward	(Wasps)	M. Mortell	(Bective Rangers)
J. Butterfield	(Northampton)	N.J. Henderson	(N.I.F.C.)
J.P. Quinn	(New Brighton)	A.C. Pedlow	(Queen's U.)
W.P.C. Davies	(Harlequins)	J.T. Gaston	(Dublin U.)
M. Regan	(Liverpool)	W.J. Hewitt	(Instonians)
G. Rimmer	(Waterloo)	J.A. O'Meara	(Dolphin)
*R.V. Stirling	(Wasps)	F.E. Anderson	(Queen's U.)
E. Evans	(Sale)	R. Roe	(Dublin U.)
D.L. Sanders	(Harlequins)	B.G.M. Wood	(Garryowen)
P.D. Young	(Wanderers)	R.H. Thompson	(Instonians)
P.G. Yarranton	(Wasps)	P.J. Lawler	(Clontarf)
D.S. Wilson	(Met. Police)	G.F. Reidy	(Lansdowne/Dolphin)
J.M.K. Kendall-Carpenter	(Bath)	J. Murphy-O'Connor	(Bective Rangers)
R. Higgins	(Liverpool)	*J.S. McCarthy	(Dolphin)

Tries: Butterfield, Regan, Wilson   *Penalty:* Murphy-O'Connor
Conversion: King   *Penalty:* King

Referee: Mr A.I. Dickie (Scotland)

SCOTLAND v ENGLAND 1954

Played at Murrayfield, Edinburgh, 20 March 1954
England won by 2G, 1T (13) to 1T (3)

England ran out easy winners in this match to secure the Triple Crown for the eleventh time, and Scotland's defeat left them with the Wooden Spoon for the third consecutive season.

The original English side selected for this match showed four changes from the side which defeated Ireland. Then the hooker, Eric Evans, was forced to withdraw through a knee injury, and was replaced by the Coventry player, Robinson. Scotland, too, were forced to make a late change to their front row after selecting 'en bloc' the team beaten in Belfast. A former cap, King of Selkirk, joined the side when MacEwen withdrew.

England had little difficulty inflicting a fifteenth consecutive international defeat on the hapless Scots. Quinn was the outstanding back on the field and paved the way for tries, in the first half by Young and in the second half by Wilson – the first policeman to play for England since J.C. Wright in 1934. Both of these tries were converted by England's new full-back.

Wilson sealed Scotland's fate when he touched down for his second try of the afternoon, though an earlier try by Elgie had made the score a little more respectable as far as the unhappy Scots were concerned.

Nigel Gibbs was the brother of G.A. Gibbs, capped by England in 1947.

SCOTLAND		ENGLAND	
J.C. Marshall	(London Scottish)	†N. Gibbs	(Harlequins)
J.S. Swan	(London Scottish)	J.E. Woodward	(Wasps)
M.K. Elgie	(London Scottish)	J. Butterfield	(Northampton)
D. Cameron	(Glasgow H.S.F.P.)	J.P. Quinn	(New Brighton)
T.G. Weatherstone	(Stewart's College F.P.)	C.E. Winn	(Rosslyn Park)
G.T. Ross	(Watsonians)	M. Regan	(Liverpool)
L.P. MacLachlan	(Oxford U.)	G. Rimmer	(Waterloo)
T.P.L. McGlashan	(Royal H.S.F.P.)	*R.V. Stirling	(Wasps/R.A.F.)
J.H.F. King	(Selkirk)	†E. Robinson	(Coventry)
H.F. McLeod	(Hawick)	D.L. Sanders	(Harlequins)
E.A.J. Fergusson	(Oxford U.)	P.D. Young	(Wanderers)
E.J.S. Michie	(Aberdeen U.)	†J.F. Bance	(Bedford)
*W.I.D. Elliot	(Edinburgh Acads.)	D.S. Wilson	(Metropolitan Police)
P.W. Kininmonth	(Richmond)	†V.H. Leadbetter	(Edinburgh Wands.)
J.H. Henderson	(Richmond)	R. Higgins	(Liverpool)

Try: Elgie

Tries: Wilson (2), Young
Conversions: Gibbs (2)

Referee: Mr O.B. Glasgow (Ireland)

FRANCE v ENGLAND 1954

Played at Stade Colombes, Paris, 10 April 1954
France won by 1G, 1DG, 1T (11) to 1T (3)

This was a historic day for France, for in registering their sixth win over England they also figured at the top of the Championship table for the first time – albeit in a bracket with the Triple Crown winners, England, and Wales, who defeated Scotland on the same day.

France, led ably by the veteran, Prat, took an early advantage up-front where the English forwards looked jaded and unimaginative. The ubiquitous Domec, in the back row, gave the English halves a torrid time. Boniface eventually got his side off the mark after half-an-hour's play when a singularly inept clearance kick by an English defender failed to make touch, and the dashing right wing gathered the ball to glide through several would-be tacklers and score a fine try. Before the interval, England equalised – much against the run of play – when Wilson followed up an attack initiated by Regan.

In the second half, it was the boot of Jean Prat which regained the lead for France. After some scrappy play inside the English half, the Lourdes skipper dropped a fine goal and there was no further scoring until, in the closing minutes of the match, Martine swooped on a careless English pass and sent Maurice Prat over, unopposed, for a try which his brother converted into a goal.

FRANCE		ENGLAND	
P. Albaladejo	(Dax)	N. Gibbs	(Harlequins)
A. Boniface	(Mont-de-Marsan)	J.E. Woodward	(Wasps)
R. Martine	(Lourdes)	J. Butterfield	(Northampton)
M. Prat	(Lourdes)	J.P. Quinn	(New Brighton)
F. Cazenave	(Mont-de-Marsan)	C.E. Winn	(Rosslyn Park)
A. Haget	(P.U.C.)	M. Regan	(Liverpool)
G. Dufau	(R.C.F.)	†J.E. Williams	(Old Millhillians)
R. Biénès	(Cognac)	*R.V. Stirling	(Leicester)
P. Labadie	(Bayonne)	E. Evans	(Sale)
A. Domenech	(Vichy)	D.L. Sanders	(Harlequins)
A. Sanac	(Perpignan)	P.D. Young	(Wanderers)
M. Celaya	(Biarritz)	V.H. Leadbetter	(Edinburgh Wands.)
*J. Prat	(Lourdes)	D.S. Wilson	(Metropolitan Police)
R. Baulon	(Vienne)	J.M.K. Kendall-Carpenter	(Bath)
H. Domec	(Lourdes)	A. O. Lewis	(Bath)

Tries: Boniface, M. Prat   *Try:* Wilson
Conversion: J. Prat
Dropped goal: J. Prat

Referee: Mr I. David (Wales)

WALES v ENGLAND 1955

Played at Cardiff Arms Park, 22 January 1955
Wales won by 1PG (3) to Nil

The English side had the misfortune to travel to Cardiff a week before this date only to return without the match being played, for a particularly heavy snowfall had caused a postponement. Even on the 22nd, following a thaw and some heavy rain, there were doubts that the match would go ahead, and a damp mist added to the discomfort of the 56,000 spectators. A wet and muddy pitch no doubt accounted for the fact that both sides made numerous handling errors, and the back play was of a very low standard. Ken Jones, in his record-breaking 36th appearance for Wales, scarcely received the ball and the play of former stalwarts, Bleddyn Williams and Cliff Morgan (now playing for Bective Rangers in Dublin), was disappointing. Only Phil Davies, the English centre, revealed the sort of play which had earned several of the backs in this match their good reputations, for a strong run of his should have produced a try early in the match – Butterfield just failing to find Woodward when the Welsh defence was stretched. And near the end a typical burst by Davies nearly resulted in a try in the left corner.

England were awarded 13 penalties during the match, and Wales 17 – two of which enabled Edwards to kick at goal in the first half-hour. To his credit, he was able to land his first attempt after ten minutes from a simple position when the Englishmen strayed off-side initiating a rush from in front of their posts. Edwards, who joined the Welsh fifteen after the original selection, G.D. Owen, had cut his knee in practice, thus gained the distinction of winning the match for Wales on his debut.

WALES		ENGLAND	
A.B. Edwards	(London Welsh)	*N.M. Hall	(Richmond)
K.J. Jones	(Newport)	J.E. Woodward	(Wasps)
G.T. Wells	(Cardiff)	J. Butterfield	(Northampton)
*B.L. Williams	(Cardiff)	W.P.C. Davies	(Harlequins)
T.J. Brewer	(London Welsh)	R.C. Bazley	(Waterloo)
C.I. Morgan	(Bective Rangers)	†D.G.S. Baker	(O.M.Ts.)
W.R. Willis	(Cardiff)	J.E. Williams	(Old Millhillians)
W.O. Williams	(Swansea)	†G.W.D. Hastings	(Gloucester)
B.V. Meredith	(Newport)	N.A. Labuschagne	(Guy's H.)
C.C. Meredith	(Neath)	†D.St.G. Hazell	(Leicester)
J.R.G. Stephens	(Neath)	P.D. Young	(Wanderers)
R.J. Robins	(Pontypridd)	†J.H. Hancock	(Newport/Army)
B. Sparks	(Neath)	†P.H. Ryan	(Richmond)
S. Judd	(Cardiff)	†P.J. Taylor	(Northampton)
N.G. Davies	(London Welsh)	R. Higgins	(Liverpool)

Penalty: Edwards

Referee: Mr O.B. Glasgow (Ireland)

IRELAND v ENGLAND 1955
Played at Lansdowne Road, Dublin, 12 February 1955
Drawn: Ireland 1PG, 1T (6), England 2T (6)

Conditions were slippery after a morning hailstorm, but by kick-off the sun had appeared and the 45,000 crowd, in pleasant surroundings, saw the unchanged English side tear away at a phenomenal pace and score two tries within the first ten minutes. The English forwards dominated the early exchanges and the English backs, passing quickly and effectively, constantly stretched the Irish defence. Baker, revelling behind a strong pack, dictated the play at outside-half, and a neatly-placed punt of his allowed Woodward to progress to the Irish line where he was bundled into touch by the burly Cunningham. Soon after, however, the Irish back row could not prevent Williams sending Butterfield clear on the blind-side. Hall's fine conversion attempt, into the wind, just failed. Minutes later, an interception by Baker followed by another kick-on bisected the Irish backs and Davies, Labuschagne and Hastings were first to arrive in the follow-up, and Hastings scored.

England seemed to rest on their laurels after this whirlwind start, and slowly Ireland got back into the game. Henderson missed three kickable penalties, but a misfield by Butterfield to the last attempt allowed Ireland a scrum in a promising position. Despite England's huge superiority up-front, Ireland heeled and Kyle sent O'Reilly over for a try near the left corner.

In an undistinguished second half, Ireland were the more enterprising side and always looked more likely to score. This they did ten minutes from the end of the game: Henderson landing a penalty goal from about 30 yards.

IRELAND		**ENGLAND**	
W.R. Tector	(Wanderers)	*N.M. Hall	(Richmond)
R.E. Roche	(U.C. Galway)	J.E. Woodward	(Wasps)
N.J. Henderson	(N.I.F.C.)	J. Butterfield	(Northampton)
A.J.F. O'Reilly	(Old Belvedere)	W.P.C. Davies	(Harlequins)
A.C. Pedlow	(Queen's U.)	R.C. Bazley	(Waterloo)
J.W. Kyle	(N.I.F.C.)	D.G.S. Baker	(O.M.Ts.)
J.A. O'Meara	(Dolphin)	J.E. Williams	(Old Millhillians)
F.E. Anderson	(N.I.F.C.)	G.W. D. Hastings	(Gloucester)
R. Roe	(Lansdowne)	N.A. Labuschagne	(Guy's H.)
P.J. O'Donoghue	(Bective Rangers)	D.St.G. Hazell	(Leicester)
M.N. Madden	(Sunday's Well)	P.D. Young	(Wanderers)
T.E. Reid	(London Irish)	J.H. Hancock	(Newport/Army)
M.J. Cunningham	(U.C. Cork)	P.H. Ryan	(Richmond)
J.R. Kavanagh	(Wanderers)	P.J. Taylor	(Northampton)
*J.S. McCarthy	(Dolphin)	R. Higgins	(Liverpool)

Try: O'Reilly   *Penalty:* Henderson   *Tries:* Butterfield, Hastings

Referee: Mr A.I. Dickie (Scotland)

ENGLAND v FRANCE 1955
Played at Twickenham, London, 26 February 1955
France won by 2G, 2DG (16) to 2PG, 1T (9)

This was France's second success at Twickenham and gave them three victories out of three matches, with only Wales to dispose of for a Grand Slam. The veteran, Prat, set his men a fine example in all aspects of the game and played no small part in the win, contributing two dropped goals and causing the English backs considerable discomfort.

As in Dublin, England gained a six-points lead in the first half, Sykes and Butterfield paving the way for a try by Higgins. Hazell had added a penalty before Prat dropped his first goal, from about 30 yards, just before half-time.

Hazell missed an early chance to alter scores soon after, failing to land penalty points, but Davies gave England renewed hope with a rousing run which brought the crowd to its feet. Rancoule (a fine name for a wing) initiated a counter-attack from an interception and raced away to the English half where a knock forward deprived the visitors of a try. The French pack viewed the new-found ground with relish and produced their best form when, working in conjunction with Dufau, a kick ahead resulted in a try by Celaya beneath the posts. The goal points gave France the lead for the first time, but a 45-yards penalty goal by Hazell restored England's lead soon after.

Following a passage of uncertain play, France went ahead ten minutes from no-side when Baulon was awarded a try after some neat passing and a punt upfield. Vannier's second conversion, followed by another dropped goal by Prat, completed the scoring.

ENGLAND		FRANCE	
†H. Scott	(Manchester)	M. Vannier	(R.C.F.)
†F.D. Sykes	(Northampton)	H. Rancoule	(Lourdes)
J. Butterfield	(Northampton)	M. Prat	(Lourdes)
W.P.C. Davies	(Harlequins)	J. Bouquet	(Bourgoin)
R.C. Bazley	(Waterloo)	J. Lepatey	(Mazamet)
D.G.S. Baker	(O.M.Ts.)	A. Haget	(P.U.C.)
J.E. Williams	(Old Millhillians)	G. Dufau	(R.C.F.)
G.W.D. Hastings	(Gloucester)	A. Domenech	(Vichy)
N.A. Labuschagne	(Guy's H.)	P. Labadie	(Bayonne)
D.St.G. Hazell	(Leicester)	R. Brejassou	(Tarbes)
*P.D. Young	(Wanderers)	B. Chevallier	(Montferrand)
P.G. Yarranton	(Wasps)	M. Celaya	(Biarritz)
D.S. Wilson	(Metropolitan Police)	*J. Prat	(Lourdes)
†I.D.S. Beer	(Harlequins)	R. Baulon	(Vienne)
R. Higgins	(Liverpool)	H. Domec	(Lourdes)

Try: Higgins *Penalties:* Hazell (2)

Tries: Baulon, Celaya
Conversions: Vannier (2)
Dropped goals: J. Prat (2)

Referee: Mr R. Mitchell (Ireland)

ENGLAND v SCOTLAND 1955

Played at Twickenham, London, 19 March 1955
England won by 1PG, 2T (9) to 1PG, 1T (6)

A brief snowstorm, shortly before the kick-off, did not cool the enthusiasm of the Scottish contingent in the crowd, for they were all set to see their side collect the Triple Crown for the first time since 1938, and possibly claim a share in the Championship title. But, alas, after a long period in the wilderness of international competition, Scotland had to be content with their two home victories over Wales and Ireland: the home internationals ended with England – not without a grim struggle at the end – gaining their first victory of the season.

There was a familiar pattern to England's sequence of scoring: Hazell kicked a penalty from 35 yards and Sykes had a clear run in for a try after Wilson and Butterfield had made a breakaway. England were thus six points ahead at an early stage, as in the previous matches with France and Ireland. Cameron, the strong Scottish fly-half, was not the type to lose heart, and a penalty goal from 45 yards brought his side back into the game. Some enterprising work from England's full-back – their third in three matches – resulted in the three-quarters and the loose forwards combining for a try by Beer. There was no further excitement before the break, though Elgie, who later became a South African Test cricketer, had the opportunity to land a wide-angled penalty from the English 25.

Scotland commenced the second half with great vigour, though their forwards' efforts went unrewarded. At length, the English responded by sending Butterfield on a penetrating run to the Scottish 25. Only a perfectly executed front-on tackle by the slight Scottish full-back, Chisholm, prevented further progress. Cameron, at about this stage, exerted his second grip on the game and, from one of his towering punts, caught the English defence at sixes-and-sevens, and scored in the follow-up. There was no conversion, and after a few scares in the closing stages, England were eventual victors in an entertaining game in which Scotland had been presented with twelve penalty kicks, and England three.

ENGLAND		SCOTLAND	
†N.S.D. Estcourt	(Blackheath)	R.W.T. Chisholm	(Melrose)
F.D. Sykes	(Northampton)	A.R. Smith	(Cambridge U.)
J. Butterfield	(Northampton)	M.K. Elgie	(London Scottish)
W.P.C. Davies	(Harlequins)	R.G. Charters	(Hawick)
R.C. Bazley	(Waterloo)	J.S. Swan	(Coventry)
D.G.S. Baker	(O.M.Ts.)	*A. Cameron	(Glasgow H.S.F.P.)
J.E. Williams	(Old Millhillians)	J.A. Nichol	(Royal H.S.F.P.)
G.W.D. Hastings	(Gloucester)	H.F. McLeod	(Hawick)
N.A. Labuschagne	(Guy's H.)	W.K.L. Relph	(Stewart's College F.P.)
D.St.G. Hazell	(Leicester)	T. Elliot	(Gala)
*P.D. Young	(Wanderers)	E.J.S. Michie	(Aberdeen U.)
P.G. Yarranton	(Wasps)	J.W.Y. Kemp	(Glasgow H.S.F.P.)
D.S. Wilson	(Metropolitan Police)	I.A.A. MacGregor	(Hillhead H.S.F.P.)
I.D.S. Beer	(Harlequins)	J.T. Greenwood	(Dunfermline)
R. Higgins	(Liverpool)	A. Robson	(Hawick)

Tries: Beer, Sykes
Penalty: Hazell

Try: Cameron
Penalty: Cameron

Referee: Mr D.C. Joynson (Wales)

ENGLAND v WALES 1956
Played at Twickenham, London, 21 January 1956
Wales won by 1G, 1T (8) to 1PG (3)

There was a crowd of 75,000 to see ten of the 1955 British Tourists to South Africa in action on this occasion, with the Test halves, Jeeps and Morgan, in opposition – as were the well-known Oxford halves, Smith and Brace. England should have won this match, for their forwards held a distinct advantage over the Welsh pack in the tight and loose, and the Welsh backs were often forced into making errors on the slippery turf. Morgan and Brace did not appear to be an inspired choice as halves, and only some inept play by the English midfield backs prevented Wales from receiving a lesson in confident threequarter play.

The home side had the better of the early exchanges, and thus it was against the run of play that Wales scored in the tenth minute when Clem Thomas and Robins capitalised on some poor English handling to grab a breakaway try. Owen kicked the goal, but England stormed back and Wales were fortunate not to concede tries on a number of occasions – notably after a run by Jackson (who was the best of the English backs) which ended in a penalty to the visitors on their goal-line, when an Englishman failed to play the ball after a tackle.

In the second half, a penalty goal by Allison after ten minutes reduced the Welsh lead, but the English forwards were winning the majority of loose and tight scrummages and it seemed inevitable that the English backs would create an opening for the wings to score. Fate dealt the home side a cruel blow soon afterwards, however, for Smith, looking set to put his side ahead through a dropped goal, had his kick charged down by Sparks. Despite brave attempts to clear, by Allison and Smith himself, Wales obtained their second try against the run of play, for M.C. Thomas had followed up a punt ahead to send C.L. Davies slithering over the line in the corner.

As the match neared its conclusion England still had opportunities to score, but more misjudgement in midfield (after a telling break by Smith), and Allison's failure to land more penalty points, eventually left the men in white unlucky losers.

ENGLAND		WALES	
†D.F. Allison	(Coventry)	G.D. Owen	(Newport)
†P.B. Jackson	(Coventry)	K.J. Jones	(Newport)
J. Butterfield	(Northampton)	H.P. Morgan	(Newport)
W.P.C. Davies	(Harlequins)	M.C. Thomas	(Newport)
†P.H. Thompson	(Headingley)	C.L. Davies	(Cardiff)
†M.J.K. Smith	(Oxford U.)	*C.I. Morgan	(Cardiff)
†R.E.G. Jeeps	(Northampton)	D.O. Brace	(Newport/Oxford U.)
D.L. Sanders	(Harlequins)	W.O. Williams	(Swansea)
*E. Evans	(Sale)	B.V. Meredith	(Newport)
†C.R. Jacobs	(Northampton)	C.C. Meredith	(Neath)
†R.W.D. Marques	(Cambridge U.)	R.H. Williams	(Llanelli)
†J.D. Currie	(Oxford U.)	R.J. Robins	(Pontypridd)
†P.G.D. Robbins	(Oxford U.)	R.C.C. Thomas	(Swansea)
†A. Ashcroft	(Waterloo)	L.H. Jenkins	(Newport)
V.G. Roberts	(Penryn/Harlequins)	B. Sparks	(St Luke's C./Neath)

Penalty: Allison

Tries: Davies, Robins
Conversion: Owen

Referee: Mr R. Mitchell (Ireland)

ENGLAND v IRELAND 1956
Played at Twickenham, London, 11 February 1956
England won by 1G, 3PG, 2T (20) to Nil

The England side, still regarded as 'largely experimental', earned a big victory over an Irish side whose forwards ran out of steam in the second half, after a close-fought affair up to the interval. There was a return of the Regan-Williams combination at half-back for the home side, but it was not until the second half, with the Irish forwards tiring, that the home backs had their finest opportunities.

A protective layer of straw enabled the doubts concerning the state of the pitch to be dispelled, but a blizzard shortly before the kick-off made the ball slippery and several of the players found difficulty maintaining their footing. O'Reilly showed several neat touches in the early exchanges, but the only scoring up to the break came through a penalty goal kicked by Allison when two Irishmen fell off-side in front of their posts.

Jackson opened the scoring in the second period after Butterfield created an opening and thereafter the points came thick and fast. The bustling Evans scored next with the support of several forwards; and a new place-kicker, Currie, landed the conversion before kicking a penalty goal from a difficult position near touch. A brief Irish rally could not produce any points, though a splendid effort by Kyle almost resulted in a memorable try. England's last contribution to the match was a try by Butterfield following a dashing run by Thompson. The veteran Roberts, who had a good match, was also prominent in this move. Currie failed with a relatively easy goal kick but made amends later by landing a penalty to take England to their largest win over Ireland since 1938, and their highest defeat over the men in green at Twickenham.

ENGLAND		IRELAND	
D.F. Allison	(Coventry)	J.M. McKelvey	(Queen's U.)
P.B. Jackson	(Coventry)	S.V.J. Quinlan	(Highfield)
J. Butterfield	(Northampton)	A.J.F. O'Reilly	(Old Belvedere)
L.B. Cannell	(St Mary's H.)	A.C. Pedlow	(Queen's U.)
P.H. Thompson	(Headingley)	J.T. Gaston	(Monkstown/Ballymena)
M. Regan	(Liverpool)	J.W. Kyle	(N.I.F.C.)
J.E. Williams	(Old Millhillians)	A.A. Mulligan	(Cambridge U./L. Irish)
D.L. Sanders	(Harlequins)	C. Fagan	(Moseley/Wanderers)
*E. Evans	(Sale)	R. Roe	(L. Irish/Lansdowne)
C.R. Jacobs	(Northampton)	B.G.M. Wood	(Garryowen)
R.W.D. Marques	(Cambridge U.)	P.J. Lawler	(Clontarf)
J.D. Currie	(Oxford U.)	T.E. Reid	(L. Irish/Garryowen)
P.G.D. Robbins	(Oxford U.)	*J.S. Ritchie	(London Irish)
A. Ashcroft	(Waterloo)	J.R. Kavanagh	(Wanderers)
V.G. Roberts	(Penryn/Harlequins)	N. Feddis	(Lansdowne)

Tries: Butterfield, Evans, Jackson
Conversion: Currie
Penalties: Currie (2), Allison

Referee: Mr A.I. Dickie (Scotland)

SCOTLAND v ENGLAND 1956

Played at Murrayfield, Edinburgh, 17 March 1956
England won by 1G, 2PG (11) to 1PG, 1T (6)

England retained the same pack which had served in the earlier matches with Wales and Ireland, and once again, through these developing forwards, gave a thoroughly sound performance in the tight and loose. The new men, Marques and Currie, dominated the line-outs and Ashcroft and Robbins proved fast and furious foragers in the loose play, but the English backs had little opportunity to shine in attack, and the crowd had to rest content with a forward battle between two fine packs.

The Scottish forwards, led by that great player, Greenwood, gave as good as they received, but suffered from a lack of enterprise at the back. Dorward was as supportive as ever to his forwards, and McClung played a prominent part in the Scottish defence, but neither side possessed a back capable of ripping large holes in the opponent's threequarter line.

All of the scoring occurred in the first half – though Scotland had four penalties from kickable positions in the second half – and England could thank the 15-stone Currie for their victory: the Oxford student kicking the eight points which helped to decide the match. His opening contribution, a penalty goal from the touch-line, was followed by a conversion of a try by Williams which was a typical scrum-half effort on the blind-side. Then, after a period of Scottish pressure, the home side were rewarded with a penalty by Smith (his second attempt at goal) before Currie placed his second penalty from touch. The finest move of the match came in the last quarter of the first half. McClung made a determined run which eventually saw Stevenson take the try-scoring pass at his fingertips while running at full speed ahead, but the conversion, which should have been gained, was fluffed and there the scoring ended.

SCOTLAND		ENGLAND	
R.W.T. Chisholm	(Melrose)	D.F. Allison	(Coventry)
A.R. Smith	(Cambridge U.)	J.E. Woodward	(Wasps)
J.T. Docherty	(Glasgow H.S.F.P.)	J. Butterfield	(Northampton)
G.D. Stevenson	(Hawick)	L.B. Cannell	(St Mary's H.)
J.S. Swan	(Coventry)	P.H. Thompson	(Headingley)
T. McClung	(Edinburgh Acads.)	M. Regan	(Liverpool)
A.F. Dorward	(Gala)	J.E. Williams	(Old Millhillians)
H.F. McLeod	(Hawick)	D.L. Sanders	(Harlequins)
R.K.G. MacEwen	(London Scottish)	*E. Evans	(Sale)
T. Elliot	(Gala)	C.R. Jacobs	(Northampton)
E.J.S. Michie	(Aberdeen G.S.F.P.)	R.W.D. Marques	(Cambridge U.)
J.W.Y. Kemp	(Glasgow H.S.F.P.)	J.D. Currie	(Oxford U.)
I.A.A. MacGregor	(Llanelli)	P.G.D. Robbins	(Oxford U.)
*J.T. Greenwood	(Dunfermline)	A. Ashcroft	(Waterloo)
A. Robson	(Hawick)	V.G. Roberts	(Penryn/Harlequins)

Try: Stevenson
Penalty: Smith

Try: Williams   *Conversion:* Currie
Penalties: Currie (2)

Referee: Captain M.J. Dowling (Ireland)

FRANCE v ENGLAND 1956

Played at Stade Colombes, Paris, 14 April 1956
France won by 1G, 2PG, 1T (14) to 2PG, 1T (9)

A severe frost in Paris on 25 February caused the postponement of this match to April, and on a sunny afternoon, following heavy rainfall in the morning, France completed a hat-trick of victories over England.

Several changes were made to the French side following a defeat in Wales, and the recall of Labuzuy – last capped in 1954 – added considerably to the French scoring power. It was not long after the kick-off that he put his name on the scorecard by kicking a penalty goal, but England soon equalised when Cannell made the running for a try by the Headingley wing, Thompson. Currie failed to convert and missed another scoring opportunity (a penalty kick this time) before Labazuy landed three more points for France. Exchanges were equal by the break, however, for another penalty was presented to England, and Allison was entrusted with the kick and duly scored the goal.

In the second half, England began with promise and Cannell, Butterfield and Williams made encouraging runs. France resisted stoutly, though, and at length their driving forwards forced play into the English quarters, where a quick piece of work by Pauthe in collaring Thompson almost on the Englishman's goal-line resulted in a score which Labazuy subsequently converted into a goal. France stepped up their efforts now, and 15 minutes from no-side a splendid unorthodox run by Rogé from the left touch-line scattered the English cover and finally Dupuy crossed for a try on the other side of the field. Allison, with a late penalty, gave England new-found hope, but the French side finished the stronger and England were fortunate at the end not to concede more points.

Mr Denis Thatcher represented the R.F.U. as the England touch-judge in this match. He was a leading London Society referee in the 1950s.

FRANCE		ENGLAND	
M. Vannier	(R.C.F.)	D.F. Allison	(Coventry)
J. Dupuy	(Tarbes)	P.B. Jackson	(Coventry)
J. Bouquet	(Vienne)	J. Butterfield	(Northampton)
E.G. Stener	(P.U.C.)	L.B. Cannell	(St Mary's H.)
L. Rogé	(Béziers)	P.H. Thompson	(Headingley)
A. Labazuy	(Lourdes)	M. Regan	(Liverpool)
G. Pauthe	(Graulhet)	J.E. Williams	(Old Millhillians)
A. Domenech	(Brive)	D.L. Sanders	(Harlequins)
R. Vigier	(Montferrand)	*E. Evans	(Sale)
R. Biénès	(Cognac)	C.R. Jacobs	(Northampton)
B. Chevallier	(Montferrand)	R.W.D. Marques	(Cambridge U.)
*M. Celaya	(Biarritz)	J.D. Currie	(Oxford U.)
H. Lazies	(Toulouse)	P.G.D. Robbins	(Oxford U.)
J.R. Barthe	(Lourdes)	A. Ashcroft	(Waterloo)
R. Baulon	(Bayonne)	V.G. Roberts	(Penryn/Harlequins)

Tries: Dupuy, Pauthe
Conversion: Labazuy
Penalties: Labazuy (2)

Try: Thompson
Penalties: Allison (2)

Referee: Mr I. David (Wales)

WALES v ENGLAND 1957

Played at Cardiff Arms Park, 19 January 1957
England won by 1PG (3) to Nil

This was England's sixth win at Cardiff since their first visit to the Arms Park ground in 1893. England were good value for their victory, albeit by three points, and there were many critics who tipped them as likely winners of the Championship after this early-season success.

A series of satisfactory trial matches enabled the English selectors to pick a well-balanced fifteen with a fair sprinkling of experience. Eleven of the team had played in the corresponding fixture in 1956, and one of the centres, Cannell, had first played for England in 1948. Wales also had a formidable pack with seven seasoned campaigners; but their selectors were unfortunate in that their trials had given little satisfaction – the Possibles beating the Probables by four tries to nil two weeks before this match. It should be added that Wales took the field in this match without Ken Jones of Newport on the right wing – the first time he had not appeared in an international for his country since World War II.

The backs of neither side created much in this match and the new English fly-half had a nervous afternoon under the close marking of the Welsh back row. Not that Morgan, his famous opposite number, could do much better: he managed only one dangerous break in the whole match, early in the first half, but despite support from Griffiths and Terry Davies, the attack came to naught.

The English back row fared well, although Higgins was badly injured early in the game. Ashcroft was outstanding and a run by him led indirectly to England's winning score in the first half. A fine dash down the left touch-line brought him to within ten yards of the Welsh line before he was forced into touch. At the following line-out, Maddocks was penalised in front of his posts for crossing the off-side line, even though he was some distance from the play. Allison made no mistake with the kick and England, having established a lead, held on firmly throughout the rest of the match.

WALES		ENGLAND	
T.J. Davies	(Llanelli)	D.F. Allison	(Coventry)
G. Howells	(Llanelli)	P.B. Jackson	(Coventry)
G.M. Griffiths	(Cardiff)	J. Butterfield	(Northampton)
*M.C. Thomas	(Newport)	L.B. Cannell	(St Mary's H.)
K. Maddocks	(Neath)	P.H. Thompson	(Headingley)
C.I. Morgan	(Cardiff)	†R.M. Bartlett	(Harlequins)
D.O. Brace	(Newport)	R.E.G. Jeeps	(Northampton)
C.C. Meredith	(Neath)	C.R. Jacobs	(Northampton)
B.V. Meredith	(London Welsh)	*E. Evans	(Sale)
T.R. Prosser	(Pontypool)	G.W.D. Hastings	(Gloucester)
R.H. Williams	(Llanelli)	J.D. Currie	(Oxford U.)
J.R.G. Stephens	(Neath)	R.W.D. Marques	(Cambridge U.)
R. O'Connor	(Aberavon)	P.G.D. Robbins	(Oxford U.)
R.J. Robins	(Pontypridd)	A. Ashcroft	(Waterloo)
R.C.C. Thomas	(Swansea)	R. Higgins	(Liverpool)

Penalty: Allison

Referee: Mr A.I. Dickie (Scotland)

IRELAND v ENGLAND 1957
Played at Lansdowne Road, Dublin, 9 February 1957
England won by 1PG, 1T (6) to Nil

Once again England won away from home by a small margin. But the game itself, a closely fought affair full of hard and accurate tackling, was deservedly won by the visitors who performed tremendous feats in the line-out, despite losing the valuable services of Thompson after 23 minutes with a bruised rib. (Evans was forced to withdraw Ashcroft from his back row to strengthen the defence.) The Irish pack could not hold the seven Englishmen, however, and with Marques dominating in the line-out, the Irish backs were starved of any reasonable possession.

The home three-quarters showed up well in defence – they had done so against France, too – and both sets of half-backs had difficulties getting their outsides moving due to the close attentions of the respective back-row units. Only a brilliant opportunist's try by Jackson penetrated the Irish defence in the first half: a kick ahead by Mulligan failed to reach touch and the Coventry wing fielded the ball, weaved and swerved past several forwards to squeeze over near the corner.

The only score of the second half was a penalty goal kicked for England by Challis, though Henderson for Ireland and Currie had attempted to land penalty points earlier. Challis it should be added had been England's only change from the team which defeated Wales at Cardiff, and he set something of an unusual precedent by taking penalty kicks to touch in this match by means of place kicks.

IRELAND		ENGLAND	
P.J. Berkery	(Lansdowne)	†R. Challis	(Bristol)
A.J.F. O'Reilly	(Old Belvedere)	P.B. Jackson	(Coventry)
*N.J. Henderson	(N.I.F.C.)	L.B. Cannell	(St Mary's H.)
A.C. Pedlow	(Queen's U.)	J. Butterfield	(Northampton)
N.H. Brophy	(U.C. Dublin)	P.H. Thompson	(Headingley)
J.W. Kyle	(N.I.F.C.)	R.M. Bartlett	(Harlequins)
A.A. Mulligan	(Cambridge U.)	R.E.G. Jeeps	(Northampton)
P.J.O'Donoghue	(Bective Rangers)	C.R. Jacobs	(Northampton)
R. Roe	(London Irish)	*E. Evans	(Sale)
B.G.M. Wood	(Garryowen)	G.W.D. Hastings	(Gloucester)
T.E. Reid	(London Irish)	J.D. Currie	(Oxford U.)
J.R. Brady	(C.I.Y.M.S.)	R.W.D. Marques	(Cambridge U.)
H.S. O'Connor	(Dublin U.)	P.G.D. Robbins	(Oxford U.)
P.J.A. O'Sullivan	(Galwegians)	A. Ashcroft	(Waterloo)
J.R. Kavanagh	(Wanderers)	R. Higgins	(Liverpool)

Try: Jackson   *Penalty:* Challis

Referee: Mr A.I. Dickie (Scotland)

ENGLAND v FRANCE 1957

Played at Twickenham, London, 23 February 1957
England won by 3T (9) to 1G (5)

Conditions were wet when England and France met at Twickenham, each side playing its third match of the season. England once again played with assurance and their forwards took control in the tight and loose. But there was a marked improvement in the play of the French, too, despite being without one of their best backs, Prat. The English half-backs, for the first time during the season, had plenty of time to set their threequarter line moving and Bartlett, in particular, was a constant danger to the French defence.

Jackson, at his brilliant best, scored two tries in the first half to give his side a six-points lead. His first effort was initiated by Thompson, who had gathered a loose pass from Jeeps and passed on to Butterfield and Davies. The English centres then made some ground before feeding Jackson who wriggled over near the corner after sending a would-be tackler in the wrong direction with a perfect side-step. The second try came from good line-out possession won by Marques. Jeeps set his back line in motion and a classical break by Davies gave the Coventry wing a clear run in.

England had their lead reduced to a single point soon after the interval. The English seemed to be pressing home a grand attack when Bouquet set up a counter-attack. Dupuy kicked ahead, gathered the ball, and kicked ahead once more for Domenech, following up at speed, to gather and send Darrouy over near the corner. Vannier converted with a fine kick.

The English forwards stormed back immediately and forced a line-out in the French 25. Evans picked up a loose ball and darted between several players to score the important try about ten minutes into the second half. The remainder of the match was a series of rushes from goal to goal as each side tried to improve its score. England held on to win, but not without some brave tackling by the new full-back Challis.

ENGLAND		FRANCE	
R. Challis	(Bristol)	M. Vannier	(R.C.F.)
P.B. Jackson	(Coventry)	C. Darrouy	(Mont-de-Marsan)
J. Butterfield	(Northampton)	J. Bouquet	(Vienne)
W.P.C. Davies	(Harlequins)	R. Monie	(Perpignan)
P.H. Thompson	(Headingley)	J. Dupuy	(Tarbes)
R.M. Bartlett	(Harlequins)	A. Haget	(P.U.C.)
R.E.G. Jeeps	(Northampton)	G. Dufau	(R.C.F.)
C.R. Jacobs	(Northampton)	A. Domenech	(Brive)
*E. Evans	(Sale)	R. Vigier	(Montferrand)
G.W.D. Hastings	(Gloucester)	A. Sanac	(Perpignan)
J.D. Currie	(Oxford U.)	*M. Celaya	(Biarritz)
R.W.D. Marques	(Cambridge U.)	M. Hoche	(P.U.C.)
P.G.D. Robbins	(Oxford U.)	J. Carrère	(Vichy)
A. Ashcroft	(Waterloo)	J.R. Barthe	(Lourdes)
R. Higgins	(Liverpool)	F. Moncla	(R.C.F.)

Tries: Jackson (2), Evans   *Try:* Darrouy *Conversion:* Vannier

Referee: Mr R.C. Williams (Ireland)

The first England team to fly to Paris, 1956.

England v France, 1957. Eric Evans's Grand Slam winning side, the last to win the honour for England until 1980: *back* J. Butterfield, W. P. C. Davies, P. H. Thompson, R. W. D. Marques, J. D. Currie, P. G. D. Robbins, C. R. Jacobs, R. Challis, Dr N. M. Parkes (touch-judge); *middle* P. B. Jackson, G. W. Hastings, E. Evans (captain), A. Ashcroft, R. Higgins; *front* R. M. Bartlett, R. E. G. Jeeps.

ENGLAND v SCOTLAND 1957
Played at Twickenham, London, 16 March 1957
England won by 2G, 1PG, 1T (16) to 1PG (3)

All-round forward superiority helped England to gain the Grand Slam and Triple Crown as they ran out comfortable winners against a spirited Scottish side. A large crowd saw England slowly wear down and then dominate their Scottish opponents, though the score was only 3–0 to the home side at the interval – Butterfield creating space for Davies, on an overlap, to cross at the right corner in the thirty-fifth minute. The nearest Scotland came to scoring in the first half was when a high kick by Ken Scotland forced Challis into making an error. Arthur Smith followed up at speed, only to be beaten by a cruel bounce.

The second-half scoring began with an exchange of penalty points, but England were constantly on the attack and only well-organised defence kept them out on several occasions. Eventually, the Scottish backs were bound to crumble under the immense pressure. Higgins, for whom the second half was a great triumph, broke away in the thirtieth minute to send Thompson flying in for a try which Challis converted. The Liverpool wing-forward then scored himself and Challis's goal kick – the second successful conversion from the touch-line – was followed by the final whistle.

Scotland's defeat was largely due to a failure by the forwards to relieve the backs of the enormous amount of cover-tackling required to hold the English at bay. Behind a beaten pack, Dorward had been unable to give his backs any good possession and consequently the English were able to throw everything into attack, confident that a Scottish breakaway was unlikely. England deserved their success and established themselves as the best champion side since the Welsh of 1952.

It is interesting to note the expression 'grand slam' in the Times *report of England's victory: this may be the first press use of what has become a well-known phrase in international Rugby.*

ENGLAND		SCOTLAND	
R. Challis	(Bristol)	K.J.F. Scotland	(Heriot's F.P.)
P.B. Jackson	(Coventry)	A.R. Smith	(Cambridge U.)
J. Butterfield	(Northampton)	T. McClung	(Edinburgh Acads.)
W.P.C. Davies	(Harlequins)	K.R. Macdonald	(Stewart's College F.P.)
P.H. Thompson	(Headingley)	J.L.F. Allan	(Cambridge U.)
R.M. Bartlett	(Harlequins)	G.H. Waddell	(London Scottish)
R.E.G. Jeeps	(Northampton)	A.F. Dorward	(Gala)
C.R. Jacobs	(Northampton)	H.F. McLeod	(Hawick)
*E. Evans	(Sale)	R.K.G. MacEwen	(London Scottish)
G.W.D. Hastings	(Gloucester)	T. Elliot	(Gala)
J.D. Currie	(Oxford U.)	E.J.S. Michie	(London Scottish)
R.W.D. Marques	(Cambridge U.)	J.W.Y. Kemp	(Glasgow H.S.F.P.)
P.G.D. Robbins	(Oxford U.)	G.K. Smith	(Kelso)
A. Ashcroft	(Waterloo)	*J.T. Greenwood	(Perthshire Acads.)
R. Higgins	(Liverpool)	A. Robson	(Hawick)

Tries: Davies, Higgins, Thompson   *Penalty:* Scotland
Conversions: Challis (2)
Penalty: Challis

Referee: Mr R. Mitchell (Ireland)

ENGLAND v WALES 1958

Played at Twickenham, London, 18 January 1958
Drawn: England 1T (3), Wales 1PG (3)

Wales gave a fine performance to hold the Champions of the previous season. The Welsh forwards took a surprising amount of line-out ball, Evans frequently outjumping the experienced English pair of Currie and Marques; and the urgency of the Welsh mauling and loose play came as a rude shock to the English pack. The home side, as expected, held a distinct advantage in the tight, and the England three-quarters had a good share of the ball.

The Welsh three-quarters looked a limited combination in attack and Cliff Morgan, correctly, decided to play to his forwards. In fact, Morgan's masterly use of the kick to touch and Terry Davies's kicking in defence were key factors in Wales's good performance on a very windy day.

Wales had the tricky wind at their backs in the first half and Terry Davies landed a penalty from 45 yards with a towering kick to open the scoring. The English backs kicked rather ineffectively in attack and Wales were good value for their small lead at the interval.

In the second half, England equalised after 12 minutes when Jeeps sent the Welsh defence on to the wrong foot with a break from a scrummage. Butterfield and Robbins backed him up and Thompson was able to touch down in the left corner. Allison failed to convert.

Both sides came near to scoring in the later stages of the match, Terry Davies giving the large English crowd a considerable fright when he struck a post with a long penalty kick at goal into the wind. There was no further scoring though, and the eighth draw between the countries was recorded.

ENGLAND		WALES	
D.F. Allison	(Coventry)	T.J. Davies	(Llanelli)
P.B. Jackson	(Coventry)	J.R. Collins	(Aberavon)
J. Butterfield	(Northampton)	M.C. Thomas	(Newport)
W.P.C. Davies	(Harlequins)	C.A.H. Davies	(Llanelli)
P.H. Thompson	(Headingley)	G.T. Wells	(Cardiff)
†J.P. Horrocks-Taylor	(Cambridge U.)	C.I. Morgan	(Cardiff)
R.E.G. Jeeps	(Northampton)	L.H. Williams	(Cardiff)
C.R. Jacobs	(Northampton)	T.R. Prosser	(Pontypool)
*E. Evans	(Sale)	B.V. Meredith	(Newport)
G.W.D. Hastings	(Gloucester)	D. Devereux	(Neath)
R.W.D. Marques	(Cambridge U.)	R.H. Williams	(Llanelli)
J.D. Currie	(Oxford U.)	W.R. Evans	(Cardiff)
P.G.D. Robbins	(Oxford U.)	*R.C.C. Thomas	(Swansea)
A. Ashcroft	(Waterloo)	J. Faull	(Swansea)
†R.E. Syrett	(Wasps)	H.J. Morgan	(Abertillery)

Try: Thompson   *Penalty:* T.J. Davies

Referee: Mr R.C. Williams (Ireland)

ENGLAND v AUSTRALIA 1958

Played at Twickenham, London, 1 February 1958
England won by 1PG, 2T (9) to 1PG, 1DG (6)

England provided the third international opposition for the touring Wallabies, in the presence of the Duke of Gloucester. At the start of this match the ground was in perfect condition, and there was little wind to bother the sides in what turned out to be an afternoon packed with incidents and excitement. Apart from Jackson's famous try to win the match, the game will be ever remembered for the large number of English players who were concussed or injured during the course of a bruising 80 minutes. In fact, England played the last ten minutes of the first half and all of the second half with only 14 men: Horrocks-Taylor having to leave the field and Butterfield moving to fly-half with Ashcroft, and later Robbins, filling the vacant midfield position.

The Australians led, deservedly, at half-time by a penalty goal, kicked at the third attempt, by Lenehan. But this was soon equalised when Malcolm Phillips scored a classic centre-threequarter try. Curley put the visitors back into the lead with a splendid dropped goal but it was not until late in the match that England again drew level. Hetherington, who had earlier hit the cross-bar with a kick from 40 yards, landed a penalty while in a state of concussion. Then came Jackson's moment of glory. He received the ball via Robbins and Phillips, near the right touch-line and on the Australian 25. He deceived Phelps with a swerve and hand-off, and set off to face Curley. Feinting inwards, he put the full-back on the wrong foot and evaded him on the outside. But as he reached the goal-line he was again confronted by Phelps, who had made a quick recovery. With the Australian wing on him, Jackson leapt for the line with a desperate do-or-die dive. To the delight of the crowd, he landed just over the Australian line for a memorable try. Hetherington missed the conversion and, after a long period of time added on for stoppages, the final whistle went for no-side as mist and fog thickened over the Twickenham ground.

This was England's first post-war victory over a Dominion side.

ENGLAND		AUSTRALIA	
†J.G.G. Hetherington	(Northampton)	T.G.P. Curley	(N.S.W.)
P.B. Jackson	(Coventry)	K.J. Donald	(Queensland)
J. Butterfield	(Northampton)	J.K. Lenehan	(N.S.W.)
†M.S. Phillips	(Oxford U.)	S.W. White	(N.S.W.)
P.H. Thompson	(Headingley)	R. Phelps	(N.S.W.)
J.P. Horrocks-Taylor	(Cambridge U.)	A.J. Summons	(N.S.W.)
R.E.G. Jeeps	(Northampton)	D.M. Connor	(Queensland)
C.R. Jacobs	(Northampton)	G.N. Vaughan	(Victoria)
*E. Evans	(Sale)	J.V. Brown	(N.S.W.)
G.W.D. Hastings	(Gloucester)	*R.A.L. Davidson	(N.S.W.)
R.W.D. Marques	(Cambridge U.)	A.R. Miller	(N.S.W.)
J.D. Currie	(Oxford U.)	D.M. Emanuel	(N.S.W.)
P.G.D. Robbins	(Oxford U.)	N.M. Hughes	(N.S.W.)
A. Ashcroft	(Waterloo)	K.J. Ryan	(Queensland)
R.E. Syrett	(Wasps)	P.T. Fenwicke	(N.S.W.)

Tries: Jackson, Phillips
Penalty: Hetherington

Penalty: Lenehan
Dropped goal: Curley

Referee: Mr R.C. Williams (Ireland)

ENGLAND v IRELAND 1958

Played at Twickenham, London, 8 February 1958
England won by 1PG, 1T (6) to Nil

Following their unexpected victory over Australia, it was an Irish team full of hope which crossed the Channel to meet England at Twickenham. Ireland fielded the same fifteen which had beaten the Tourists, and Kyle won his 45th cap for his country, thus passing the record of 44 caps created by Ken Jones in the previous season. England originally made one change from the side which beat Australia – bringing Bartlett in at fly-half for Horrocks-Taylor – but an injury to Jackson meant that Young was awarded a first cap on the right wing.

The match itself was affected by the treacherous conditions, there being little accurate passing during the afternoon. In the small quantities of open play seen, Hewitt, for Ireland, and Young, for England, gave good accounts of themselves; but otherwise, most of the match consisted of rushes by the forwards and staunch defence by the backs.

England's points came early in the game when the ball was still dry enough to kick accurately. Hetherington opened the scoring after ten minutes with a good penalty goal, and then narrowly failed to convert a try by Ashcroft, shortly afterwards. The try came after a fly-kick from some broken play, and the conversion attempt struck the woodwork.

In the second half, under pressure from some rumbustious play by the Irish forwards, England were content to allow Jeeps to nurse his pack with some good covering and touch-kicking. In the end, the home side held out for a deserved victory.

ENGLAND		IRELAND	
J.G.G. Hetherington	(Northampton)	P.J. Berkery	(London Irish)
†J.R.C. Young	(Oxford U.)	A.J.F. O'Reilly	(Old Belvedere)
J. Butterfield	(Northampton)	*N.J. Henderson	(N.I.F.C.)
M.S. Phillips	(Oxford U.)	D. Hewitt	(Queen's U.)
P.H. Thompson	(Headingley)	A.C. Pedlow	(C.I.Y.M.S.)
R.M. Bartlett	(Harlequins)	J.W. Kyle	(N.I.F.C.)
R.E.G. Jeeps	(Northampton)	A.A. Mulligan	(Cambridge U.)
C.R. Jacobs	(Northampton)	P.J. O'Donoghue	(Bective Rangers)
*E. Evans	(Sale)	A.R. Dawson	(Wanderers)
G.W.D. Hastings	(Gloucester)	B.G.M. Wood	(Garryowen)
R.W.D. Marques	(Cambridge U.)	J.B. Stevenson	(Instonians)
J.D. Currie	(Oxford U.)	W.A. Mulcahy	(U.C. Dublin)
P.G.D. Robbins	(Oxford U.)	J.A. Donaldson	(Collegians)
A. Ashcroft	(Waterloo)	J.R. Kavanagh	(Wanderers)
R.E. Syrett	(Wasps)	N.A.A. Murphy	(Cork Const.)

Try: Ashcroft
Penalty: Hetherington

Referee: Mr G. Burrell (Scotland)

FRANCE v ENGLAND 1958

Played at Stade Colombes, Paris, 1 March 1958
England won by 1G, 1PG, 2T (14) to Nil

England produced their most impressive performance of the season in fine conditions in Paris. France started the match in a quiet confident manner; Vannier went near to scoring with a drop at goal and Dupuy, almost on the try-line, misjudged his stride in chasing a loose ball. England opened the scoring after 20 minutes when Thompson was able to dash over the line unmarked, after receiving a pass from Butterfield who had gathered a punt ahead by Bartlett. Hastings converted the try, and Thompson was over the line again soon afterwards. This time it was a scything run by Phillips which sent the Headingley wing speeding across the line, despite the tackles of Vannier and one or two other defenders.

Just before the interval came the best try of the match. Jackson, the match-winner against Australia, robbed a French forward of the ball inside the English 25 and set off on a twinkling 75-yards run to the French line for a grand, unconverted try.

One should add that the French difficulties were increased by injuries to Vignes and Danos, and Celaya was forced to remove two men from his pack to strengthen the back division. Strangely though, the second half was a remarkably quiet affair and England seemed happy to sit on their commanding lead. The only score of the half was a penalty goal by Hastings.

This match extended England's run of success in internationals to six wins and one draw in seven games. In contrast, this was France's sixth consecutive defeat in the Championship, and a large section of the crowd, disillusioned by their side's poor performance, called for the resignation of the French selectors.

FRANCE		ENGLAND	
M. Vannier	(R.C.F.)	†J.S.M. Scott	(Oxford U.)
G. Mauduy	(Périgueux)	P.B. Jackson	(Coventry)
A. Boniface	(Mont-de-Marsan)	J. Butterfield	(Northampton)
C. Vignes	(R.C.F.)	M.S. Phillips	(Oxford U.)
J. Dupuy	(Tarbes)	P.H. Thompson	(Headingley)
J. Bouquet	(Vienne)	R.M. Bartlett	(Harlequins)
P. Danos	(Béziers)	R.E.G. Jeeps	(Northampton)
A. Domenech	(Brive)	C.R. Jacobs	(Northampton)
R. Vigier	(Montferrand)	*E. Evans	(Sale)
A. Quaglio	(Mazamet)	G.W.D. Hastings	(Gloucester)
L. Mias	(Mazamet)	R.W.D. Marques	(Cambridge U.)
*M. Celaya	(Biarritz)	J.D. Currie	(Oxford U.)
M. Crauste	(R.C.F.)	†A.J. Herbert	(Wasps)
J.R. Barthe	(Lourdes)	A. Ashcroft	(Waterloo)
H. Domec	(Lourdes)	R.E. Syrett	(Wasps)

Tries: Thompson (2), Jackson
Conversion: Hastings
Penalty: Hastings

Referee: Mr W.J. Evans (Wales)

SCOTLAND v ENGLAND 1958

Played at Murrayfield, Edinburgh, 15 March 1958
Drawn: Scotland 1PG (3), England 1PG (3)

Scotland gave England a rude shock by holding them to a drawn game in Edinburgh. Many critics had expected a heavier, more skilful English combination to win this match quite easily and secure the International Championship. With Wales winning in Dublin, however, it was possible that England could be relieved of their title if Wales won their subsequent match against France at Cardiff. (Wales later lost, so England retained the Championship).

The conditions were suitable for good open Rugby but some tight marking by both defences meant that the crowd of 60,000 had very little to cheer. The early scoring chances were offered in the form of penalty kicks at goal and Currie and Allison, with Ken Scotland who had returned to the Scottish side in place of injured Chisholm, made fair efforts in this respect for their particular sides.

The one exciting move of the first half was initiated by Jackson for England after some Scottish pressure. Running out of defence, Jackson linked up with Thompson to send Bartlett, Herbert, Phillips, Butterfield and Hastings on a lovely sweeping run downfield which almost produced a try.

In the second half, Elliot, the new wing (Arthur Smith was out of the side with an attack of influenza), assumed the place-kicking duties after Ken Scotland had missed with several attempts. He opened the scoring with a good penalty goal from a wide angle and England were forced to defend bravely when Jeeps had to leave the field, temporarily, soon afterwards. Weatherstone and Docherty nearly got over for tries, but England weathered the onslaught and 15 minutes from no-side Hastings equalised for the visitors with a penalty goal.

SCOTLAND		ENGLAND	
K.J.F. Scotland	(Heriot's F.P.)	D.F. Allison	(Coventry)
C. Elliot	(Langholm)	P.B. Jackson	(Coventry)
J.T. Docherty	(Glasgow H.S.F.P.)	J. Butterfield	(Northampton)
G.D. Stevenson	(Hawick)	M.S. Phillips	(Oxford U.)
T.G. Weatherstone	(Stewart's College F.P.)	P.H. Thompson	(Headingley)
G.H. Waddell	(Devonport Services)	R.M. Bartlett	(Harlequins)
J.A.T. Rodd	(U.S./R.N.)	R.E.G. Jeeps	(Northampton)
H.F. McLeod	(Hawick)	C.R. Jacobs	(Northampton)
N.S. Bruce	(Blackheath)	*E. Evans	(Sale)
I.R. Hastie	(Kelso)	G.W.D. Hastings	(Gloucester)
M.W. Swan	(Oxford U./London Scottish)	R.W.D. Marques	(Cambridge U.)
J.W.Y. Kemp	(Glasgow H.S.F.P.)	J.D. Currie	(Oxford U.)
A. Robson	(Hawick)	P.G.D. Robbins	(Oxford U.)
*J.T. Greenwood	(Perthshire Acads.)	A. Ashcroft	(Waterloo)
D.C. Macdonald	(Edinburgh U.)	A.J. Herbert	(Wasps)

Penalty: Elliot   *Penalty:* Hastings

Referee: Mr R.C. Williams (Ireland)

WALES v ENGLAND 1959
Played at Cardiff Arms Park, 17 January 1959
Wales won by 1G (5) to Nil

To describe the conditions at Cardiff Arms Park for this match as wet and muddy would be an understatement! The ground was a quagmire, and a postponement would have satisfied each side. Both threequarter lines were bogged down as a result and a long forward battle ensued.

The two teams played as selected, with thirteen new caps between them. It soon became evident that despite the uselessness of the backs, the Welsh pack were in control of the forward proceedings and Rhys Williams, Faull and Prosser were outstanding. The new Welsh fly-half, Cliff Ashton, successor to the now-retired Cliff Morgan, had few opportunities to prove himself in the mud, but half-back partner Lloyd Williams gave sterling support to his heroic pack.

England, for their part, had new players at half-back and in the front row, but they too were unable to create any impressions, good or bad, in this game. The English pack, without their former captain Eric Evans to inspire them, appeared surprisingly slow and immobile, especially in the loose play where the Welshmen maintained an aggressive dominance.

For one newcomer to international Rugby, however, this was a debut to remember. The Welsh left wing, Dewi Bebb of Carmarthen Training College, had only played five first-class games in Wales before this match. When, about ten minutes before half-time, Rhys Williams tapped the ball to the winger from a line-out, Bebb sidestepped Jackson and accelerated over the 15 yards to the English goal-line, sending Hetherington the wrong way before scoring a try. Terry Davies converted with a fine kick, but this excellent try was the only memorable moment of the afternoon.

WALES		ENGLAND	
T.J. Davies	(Llanelli)	J.G.G. Hetherington	(Northampton)
J.R. Collins	(Aberavon)	P.B. Jackson	(Coventry)
H.J. Davies	(Aberavon/Cambridge U.)	M.S. Phillips	(Oxford U.)
M.J. Price	(Pontypool)	*J. Butterfield	(Northampton)
D.I.E. Bebb	(Carmarthen T.C.)	P.H. Thompson	(Waterloo)
C. Ashton	(Aberavon)	†A.B.W. Risman	(Manchester U.)
L. H. Williams	(Cardiff)	†S.R. Smith	(Cambridge U.)
T.R. Prosser	(Pontypool)	†StL.H. Webb	(Bedford)
B.V. Meredith	(Newport)	†J.A.S. Wackett	(Rosslyn Park)
D.R. Main	(London Welsh)	†G.J. Bendon	(Wasps)
R.H. Williams	(Llanelli)	J.D. Currie	(Harlequins)
I. Ford	(Newport)	R.W.D. Marques	(Harlequins)
*R.C.C. Thomas	(Swansea)	A.J. Herbert	(Wasps)
J. Faull	(Swansea)	†B.J. Wightman	(Moseley)
J. Leleu	(London Welsh)	R. Higgins	(Liverpool)

Try: Bebb   *Conversion:* T.J. Davies

Referee: Mr R.C. Williams (Ireland)

IRELAND v ENGLAND 1959

Played at Lansdowne Road, Dublin, 14 February 1959
England won by 1PG (3) to Nil

Ireland, playing before a crowd of 50,000, were desperately unlucky to lose their opening match of the season. The selection of the Irish team had previously given rise to a number of doubts concerning the balance of the back division: the sagacity of fielding Henderson (a veteran centre) at full-back, and switching the brilliant O'Reilly from his regular wing position to centre-threequarter, were especially questioned. Indeed, in the final analysis, much of the blame for Ireland's defeat lay with the ineffective tactics adopted by their backs. They constantly wasted the good possession earned by the tremendous Irish pack, for the extent of their enterprise was tossing the ball to O'Reilly and expecting the big centre to run straight through the opposition. Excellent English tackling consequently prevented Ireland from penetrating the visitors' defence.

England, too, lacked flair in attack, and only the individual efforts of Jackson represented any danger to the Irish goal-line. The English forwards, showing two changes from the pack which played against Wales, were, once again, quite impotent against a lively opposition, though they showed a considerable improvement in the later stages of the game when the stamina of the Irish was sapped.

Very much against the run of play, England went ahead in the first half when Risman landed a penalty goal from short range. This turned out to be the only score of the match, though Henderson made three attempts to register penalties with efforts from near the half-way line; and a drop at goal by Mick English sailed past the upright to threaten England's undeserved lead.

IRELAND		ENGLAND	
N.J. Henderson	(N.I.F.C.)	J.G.G. Hetherington	(Northampton)
N.H. Brophy	(U.C. Dublin)	P.B. Jackson	(Coventry)
A.J.F. O'Reilly	(Old Belvedere)	M.S. Phillips	(Oxford U.)
J.F. Dooley	(Galwegians)	*J. Butterfield	(Northampton)
A.C. Pedlow	(C.I.Y.M.S.)	P.H. Thompson	(Waterloo)
M.A.F. English	(Bohemians)	A.B.W. Risman	(Manchester U.)
A.A. Mulligan	(London Irish)	R.E.G. Jeeps	(Northampton)
B.G.M. Wood	(Garryowen)	StL.H. Webb	(Bedford)
*A.R. Dawson	(Wanderers)	J.A.S. Wackett	(Rosslyn Park)
S. Millar	(Ballymena)	G.J. Bendon	(Wasps)
W.A. Mulcahy	(U.C. Dublin)	J.D. Currie	(Harlequins)
M.G. Culliton	(Wanderers)	R.W.D. Marques	(Harlequins)
N.A.A. Murphy	(Cork Const.)	A.J. Herbert	(Wasps)
P.J.A. O'Sullivan	(Galwegians)	A. Ashcroft	(Waterloo)
J.R. Kavanagh	(Wanderers)	†J.W. Clements	(Old Cranleighans)

Penalty: Risman

Referee: Mr D.G. Walters (Wales)

ENGLAND v FRANCE 1959

Played at Twickenham, London, 28 February 1959
Drawn: England 1PG (3), France 1PG (3)

A glorious revival of English forward play was apparent in this match, and a fresh solidity and mobility allowed them to hold a French side which clearly missed the inspiring leadership of Mias.

Conditions, on a warm sunny day, were ideal for attractive open Rugby, but the handling of both teams was careless, and the only excitement in the first half was a series of penalty kicks at goal. Shortly before half-time, France opened the scoring when Labazuy landed a goal from 30 yards, but a kick by Hetherington soon after levelled the scores at the interval.

In the second half, the English backs outplayed the French, and Phillips, Thompson and the ever-dangerous Jackson made menacing breaks. Lacaze, however, gave a reliable display at full-back and was the outstanding French player on this occasion. Risman and Smith (who had withdrawn from the Irish fixture through influenza) did not enhance their reputations in this game, for both were unusually slow in passing, and their ineffective kicking towards the end of the afternoon, when the English pack were dominating the forward battle, wasted scoring chances.

The surprising feature of the game for most of the spectators, including a large French contingent, was the mediocrity of the visiting pack which, in the absence of their leader, Mias, lacked the spirit and initiative which had characterised their play against South Africa six months earlier. Barthe, the new French captain, was unable to rouse his team and the general air of complacency which became evident was perfectly illustrated when Dupuy dropped a pass when the English goal-line was at his mercy.

ENGLAND		FRANCE	
J.G.G. Hetherington	(Northampton)	P. Lacaze	(Lourdes)
P.B. Jackson	(Coventry)	C. Darrouy	(Mont-de-Marsan)
M.S. Phillips	(Oxford U.)	A. Boniface	(Mont-de-Marsan)
*J. Butterfield	(Northampton)	A. Marquesuzaa	(R.C.F.)
P.H. Thompson	(Waterloo)	J. Dupuy	(Tarbes)
A.B.W. Risman	(Manchester U.)	A. Labazuy	(Lourdes)
S.R. Smith	(Cambridge U.)	P. Danos	(Béziers)
StL.H. Webb	(Bedford)	A. Quaglio	(Mazamet)
†H.O. Godwin	(Coventry)	R. Vigier	(Montferrand)
G.J. Bendon	(Wasps)	A. Roques	(Cahors)
R.W.D. Marques	(Harlequins)	M. Celaya	(Biarritz)
J.D. Currie	(Harlequins)	B. Mommejat	(Cahors)
A.J. Herbert	(Wasps)	M. Crauste	(R.C.F.)
A. Ashcroft	(Waterloo)	*J. R. Barthe	(Lourdes)
J.W. Clements	(Old Cranleighans)	F. Moncla	(R.C.F.)

Penalty: Hetherington   *Penalty:* Labazuy

Referee: Mr R.C. Williams (Ireland)

ENGLAND v SCOTLAND 1959

Played at Twickenham, London, 21 March 1959
Drawn: England 1PG (3), Scotland 1PG (3)

The features of this match were the poor handling and positioning, and the deadly tackling of both sides. With the Twickenham turf firm and emerald green on a lovely sunny day, Scotland had the early opportunities to open the scoring, but their full-back was unable to land any points with three penalty-goal attempts. Much of the possession from the set-pieces, however, was won by England in the first half with Godwin, the Coventry hooker, proving to be a swift and efficient striker of the ball; and the well-tried partnership of Currie and Marques (playing together in the English second row for the seventeenth time) dominated the line-out. Hence, on the run of play before the interval, England deserved to lead by three points – Risman having kicked a towering penalty goal from 50 yards out near the touch-line.

After half-time, Ken Scotland equalised with a similar score and this inspired a revival in the Scottish forward effort. An attack initiated by A.R. Smith and Scotland completely deceived the English defence, and only a covering tackle by S.R. Smith on Ken Smith saved a certain try. Another dangerous Scottish move was stopped by Jackson, the outstanding English back, when Weatherstone made a determined run down the left wing. But the mastermind behind the visitors' campaign was their fly-half and new captain, Gordon Waddell, who, apart from Ken Smith's run, came nearest to snatching victory with an attempted drop at goal.

For the fifth instance in consecutive international matches, the English team failed to produce a try – a disappointment for the 70,000 spectators at the match.

ENGLAND		**SCOTLAND**	
J.G.G. Hetherington	(Northampton)	K.J.F. Scotland	(Cambridge U.)
P.B. Jackson	(Coventry)	A.R. Smith	(Ebbw Vale)
M.S. Phillips	(Oxford U.)	J.A.P. Shackleton	(London Scottish)
*J. Butterfield	(Northampton)	G.D. Stevenson	(Hawick)
P.H. Thompson	(Waterloo)	T.G. Weatherstone	(Stewart's Coll. F.P.)
A.B.W. Risman	(Manchester U.)	*G.H. Waddell	(Cambridge U.)
S.R. Smith	(Cambridge U.)	S. Coughtrie	(Edinburgh Acads.)
StL.H. Webb	(Bedford)	D.M.D. Rollo	(Howe of Fife)
H.O. Godwin	(Coventry)	N.S. Bruce	(Blackheath)
G.J. Bendon	(Wasps)	H.F. McLeod	(Hawick)
R.W.D. Marques	(Harlequins)	F.H. ten Bos	(Oxford U.)
J.D. Currie	(Harlequins)	J.W.Y. Kemp	(Glasgow H.S.F.P.)
A.J. Herbert	(Wasps)	G.K. Smith	(Kelso)
A. Ashcroft	(Waterloo)	J.A. Davidson	(London Scottish)
J.W. Clements	(Old Cranleighans)	A. Robson	(Hawick)

Penalty: Risman   *Penalty:* Scotland

Referee: Mr D.G. Walters (Wales)

ENGLAND v WALES 1960

Played at Twickenham, London, 16 January 1960
England won by 1G, 2PG, 1T (14) to 2PG (6)

Wales selected a side with plenty of youth and experience. There were seven of the 1959 British Isles Touring team with five new caps in the visiting side, and many of the thousands of Welsh supporters who made the trip to London for the match could be excused for confidently expecting victory. England, for their part, originally selected six new players, but were forced to blood another when Risman, their star fly-half, was forced to withdraw. Jacobs replaced Webb in the front row when the latter had to cry-off.

The new-look English side made a sensational start. Rutherford landed an early penalty before Weston made a classic centre-threequarter break to draw the Welsh defence and send Jim Roberts over for a try. Rutherford converted, then added another penalty goal, and Roberts crossed for his second score of the match to take England to a 14–0 lead at the interval.

Wales were never to recover from this disastrous first half. The chief wrecker for England had been Richard Sharp, the blond Cornishman who had been drafted into the side in place of Risman. He ran rings around the Welsh open-side forward, Haydn Morgan, and constantly had an ordinary Welsh back line at sixes-and-sevens. It was a typical Sharp break from the half-way line which had produced England's most telling score just before the change of ends. After ripping a large hole in the Welsh cover, Sharp had enabled Weston to send Roberts over in the left corner with John Young in support.

In the second half, the out-of-touch Welshmen fared slightly better and Terry Davies reduced Wales's deficit with two very fine penalty kicks. The Welsh three-quarters looked incapable of scoring tries, however, and the outcome of the match was never in doubt, even though England could not add to their earlier efforts.

ENGLAND		WALES	
†D. Rutherford	(Percy Park)	T.J. Davies	(Llanelli)
J.R.C. Young	(Harlequins)	J.R. Collins	(Aberavon)
M.S. Phillips	(Oxford U.)	M.J. Price	(Pontypool)
†M.P. Weston	(Richmond)	G.W. Lewis	(Richmond)
†J. Roberts	(O. Millhillians/Sale)	D.I.E. Bebb	(Swansea)
†R.A.W. Sharp	(Oxford U.)	C. Ashton	(Aberavon)
*R.E.G. Jeeps	(Northampton)	C. Evans	(Pontypool)
C.R. Jacobs	(Northampton)	T.R. Prosser	(Pontypool)
†S.A.M. Hodgson	(Durham City)	B.V. Meredith	(Newport)
†T.P. Wright	(Blackheath)	L.J. Cunningham	(Aberavon)
R.W.D. Marques	(Harlequins)	G.W. Payne	(Pontypridd)
J.D. Currie	(Harlequins)	*R.H. Williams	(Llanelli)
P.G.D. Robbins	(Moseley)	B. Cresswell	(Newport)
†W.G.D. Morgan	(Medicals)	J. Faull	(Swansea)
R.E. Syrett	(Wasps)	H.J. Morgan	(Abertillery)

Tries: Roberts (2)
Conversion: Rutherford
Penalties: Rutherford (2)

Penalties: Davies (2)

Referee: Mr J.A.S. Taylor (Scotland)

England v Wales, 1960. The England team which beat Wales 14-6 at Twickenham and went on to win the Triple Crown: *back* Mr J. A. S. Taylor, J. Roberts, M. P. Weston, R. A. W. Sharp, T. P. Wright, R. W. D. Marques, J. D. Currie, W. G. D. Morgan, R. E. Syrett, Mr R. J. Todd (touch-judge); *middle* S. A. M. Hodgson, M. S. Phillips, R. E. G. Jeeps (captain), P. G. D. Robbins, C. R. Jacobs; *front* J. R. C. Young, D. Rutherford.

ENGLAND v IRELAND 1960

Played at Twickenham, London, 13 February 1960
England won by 1G, 1DG (8) to 1G (5)

It was an unlucky Irish team which left Twickenham after this match, for they had been forced to make a late change to their threequarter line, then O'Reilly was badly injured and became a passenger in the second half. The Irish forwards were in fine form early in the game and Sharp did not enjoy the freedom he had been allowed by the Welsh back row a month before. Culliton in particular enhanced his reputation as an uncompromising all-round forward and it was he who opened the first-half scoring when a kick ahead bounced into the field of play off the English upright. Culliton gathered to score a try which the new full-back, Kiernan, converted into a goal.

Ireland held this lead well into the second half. Then Sharp and Weston led an English revival with some well-judged tactical kicks. Sharp gave the English supporters encouragement with a beautiful dropped goal, and another of his kicks led to the decisive score of the match. A diagonal punt ahead was taken by Roberts on the left, who, seeing his way to the line blocked, attempted to drop a goal. He made a hash of the kick, but succeeded in catching the Irish defence off-balance. Robbins, the complete back-row forward, gathered the ball and fed Phillips, who made ground to the Irish line where he was held and forced to pass to Marques. The giant Harlequins lock took the ball cleanly and powered over for the winning score in superb fashion. Rutherford kicked the goal and England were home by three points – but only just in time.

England retained the side which had beaten Wales for this match, though many of their own most neutral critics could not understand why Jackson, so often in the past a match-winner on the wing, was still overlooked. The Coventry player had been an unqualified success on the Lions tour, and had represented the British Isles in five of the six international matches with Australia and New Zealand.

ENGLAND		IRELAND	
D. Rutherford	(Percy Park)	T.J. Kiernan	(U.C. Cork)
J.R.C. Young	(Harlequins)	W.W. Bornemann	(Wanderers)
M.S. Phillips	(Oxford U.)	A.C. Pedlow	(C.I.Y.M.S.)
M.P. Weston	(Richmond)	D. Hewitt	(Queen's U.)
J. Roberts	(Old Millhillians/Sale)	A.J.F.O'Reilly	(Leicester)
R.A.W. Sharp	(Oxford U.)	M.A.F. English	(Bohemians)
*R.E.G. Jeeps	(Northampton)	*A.A. Mulligan	(London Irish)
C.R. Jacobs	(Northampton)	B.G.M. Wood	(Lansdowne)
S.A.M. Hodgson	(Durham City)	B. McCallan	(Ballymena)
T.P. Wright	(Blackheath)	S. Millar	(Ballymena)
R.W.D. Marques	(Harlequins)	W.A. Mulcahy	(U.C. Dublin)
J.D. Currie	(Harlequins)	M.G. Culliton	(Wanderers)
P.G.D. Robbins	(Moseley)	N.A.A. Murphy	(Cork Const.)
W.G.D. Morgan	(Medicals)	T. McGrath	(Garryowen)
R.E. Syrett	(Wasps)	J.R. Kavanagh	(Wanderers)

Try: Marques *Conversion:* Rutherford   *Try:* Culliton *Conversion:* Kiernan
Dropped goal: Sharp

Referee: Mr D.G. Walters (Wales)

FRANCE v ENGLAND 1960

Played at Stade Colombes, Paris, 27 February 1960
Drawn: France 1PG (3), England 1T (3)

For French supporters, this match was as dull and uninteresting as their previous away game with Scotland had been fast and exciting. The game became an obscure battle between a pair of mighty, well-matched packs, as scrums and line-outs followed one another with growing inevitability. For once, the long throw to the rear of the line-out failed to produce its usual results for the French: the back-row players looked almost bored with proceedings and the French backs were not given the opportunity to link with their forwards in attack. England's ability to hold the French up-front in the tight, and contain the back row in the line-out, meant that the type of game which the French had become used to playing was not possible.

Vannier put France ahead after about 20 minutes of play in the first half with a penalty goal, but England equalised shortly before half-time. The English scrum took one against the head from de Gregorio and Sharp glided through the defence beautifully to send Weston over for a try near the posts. Rutherford made his first error of the season by striking an upright with a simple goal kick.

In the second half, play was rather dour and a long-drawn-out battle amongst the forwards dominated the game. Jeeps led his men by example from the base of the scrum, and frequently disrupted the service of Danos to Martine. England's backs also had some tense moments when a series of high punts were cleverly directed at the visitors' posts, and Rutherford had another anxious second when one of his clearing kicks to touch was charged down on his goal-line. But England managed to hold out, and, in the end, a draw was a fair result.

FRANCE		ENGLAND	
M. Vannier	(R.C.F.)	D. Rutherford	(Percy Park)
L. Rogé	(Béziers)	J.R.C. Young	(Harlequins)
J. Bouquet	(Vienne)	M.S. Phillips	(Oxford U.)
A. Marquesuzaa	(Lourdes)	M.P. Weston	(Richmond)
S. Mericq	(Agen)	J. Roberts	(Old Millhillians/Sale)
R. Martine	(Lourdes)	R.A.W. Sharp	(Oxford U.)
P. Danos	(Béziers)	*R.E.G. Jeeps	(Northampton)
A. Domenech	(Brive)	C.R. Jacobs	(Northampton)
J. de Gregorio	(Grenoble)	S.A.M. Hodgson	(Durham City)
A. Roques	(Cahors)	T.P. Wright	(Blackheath)
B. Mommejat	(Cahors)	R.W.D. Marques	(Harlequins)
M. Celaya	(Bordeaux)	J.D. Currie	(Harlequins)
*F. Moncla	(Pau)	P.G.D. Robbins	(Moseley)
M. Crauste	(Lourdes)	W.G.D. Morgan	(Medicals)
S. Meyer	(Périgueux)	R.E. Syrett	(Wasps)

Penalty: Vannier   *Try:* Weston

Referee: Mr J.A.S. Taylor (Scotland)

SCOTLAND v ENGLAND 1960

Played at Murrayfield, Edinburgh, 19 March 1960
England won by 3G, 1DG, 1PG (21) to 3PG, 1T (12)

Both sides went into this match full of confidence and with teams which were unchanged after their previous games. England started narrow favourites, for their fifteen had been unchanged throughout the season – a record of its kind. There had been some doubt whether Young was fit enough to play – he had been injured in Paris – but he took the field for this match and scored one of the tries.

England made a tremendous start, going 13 points up in as many minutes. Sharp opened the scoring after five minutes with a perfect dropped goal from 30 yards. Soon after, Syrett pounced on a poor pass back by Shillinglaw, charging down a belated kick to touch by Ken Scotland to score a try which Rutherford converted. Within a few more minutes, Rutherford was again converting an English try. This time, a kick ahead by Robbins had been followed up by Roberts, who got his third try of the season. Scotland were clearly not going to get back into a position from which they could win the match and their situation became desperate when the unerring Rutherford kicked a penalty goal.

Scotland (the player) restored a little respect for the Scots with two good penalty kicks before half-time and brought the crowd to its feet with another goal in the second half. Just as the Scots seemed to be grafting their way back into the reckoning, England dealt a hammer-blow which put the issue beyond doubt. Phillips made a break and sent the sprinter, Young, racing away for a try which was again goaled by Rutherford. Scotland's answer to this was a try by the former captain, Arthur Smith, but it was too late to stop England from regaining the Triple Crown they had last won in 1957.

SCOTLAND		ENGLAND	
K.J.F. Scotland	(Cambridge U.)	D. Rutherford	(Percy Park)
A.R. Smith	(Ebbw Vale)	J.R.C. Young	(Harlequins)
G.D. Stevenson	(Hawick)	M.S. Phillips	(Oxford U.)
I.H.P. Laughland	(London Scottish)	M.P. Weston	(Richmond)
R.H. Thomson	(London Scottish)	J. Roberts	(Old Millhillians/Sale)
*G. H. Waddell	(Cambridge U.)	R.A.W. Sharp	(Oxford U.)
R.B. Shillinglaw	(Gala)	*R.E.G. Jeeps	(Northampton)
D.M.D. Rollo	(Howe of Fife)	C.R. Jacobs	(Northampton)
N.S. Bruce	(London Scottish)	S.A.M. Hodgson	(Durham City)
H.F. McLeod	(Hawick)	T.P. Wright	(Blackheath)
T.O. Grant	(Hawick)	R.W.D. Marques	(Harlequins)
J.W.Y. Kemp	(Glasgow H.S.F.P.)	J.D. Currie	(Harlequins)
G.K. Smith	(Kelso)	P.G.D. Robbins	(Moseley)
J.A. Davidson	(Edinburgh Wands.)	W.G.D. Morgan	(Medicals)
D.B. Edwards	(Heriot's F.P.)	R.E. Syrett	(Wasps)

Try: A.R. Smith
Penalties: Scotland (3)

Tries: Roberts, Syrett, Young
Conversions: Rutherford (3)
Penalty: Rutherford
Dropped goal: Sharp

Referee: Mr R.C. Williams (Ireland)

ENGLAND v SOUTH AFRICA 1961

Played at Twickenham, London, 7 January 1961
South Africa won by 1G (5) to Nil

This was the third international of the South Africans' tour, and resulted in a third dour victory. The match, played before 72,000 spectators on a cold day, did little to enhance the reputation of Rugby Football: there were several unsavoury incidents involving vicious use of the boot, and miscellaneous punches were thrown. The tactics of the Springboks inspired few of the critics to warm to South African techniques: in plain language they relied on a huge pack to dominate in the tight while their outsides followed a boring pattern of touch-line nursing completely devoid of enterprise.

The English pack, with Currie and Marques appearing in the second row together for their twenty-second consecutive match, just managed to hold their giant opponents; and Jeeps, as ever, played an encouraging supportive role to his forwards. Risman had few opportunities to open play to his three-quarters, and on the occasions that the English backs were in possession a lack of penetration in midfield was evident and the South African line was rarely threatened.

The only score of an undistinguished game came shortly before the interval. At a scrum the English forwards lost control of the ball while attempting a wheel. Claassen pounced and started an attack along the narrow side with Hopwood in support and the latter, receiving the ball about 15 yards from the English line, powered through a couple of tacklers to score to the left of the goal. Du Preez, a new cap, converted, though later in the afternoon he was to miss several difficult penalty shots. England, too, had their share of penalty awards; however, unlike the South Africans, Rutherford was not offered one effort within his place-kicking compass.

ENGLAND		SOUTH AFRICA	
D. Rutherford	(Percy Park)	L.G. Wilson	(Western Province)
J.R.C. Young	(Harlequins)	J.P. Engelbrecht	(Western Province)
†W.M. Patterson	(Sale)	J.L. Gainsford	(Western Province)
M.P. Weston	(Richmond)	A.I. Kirkpatrick	(O.F.S.)
J. Roberts	(Old Millhillians/Sale)	H.J. van Zyl	(Transvaal)
A.B.W. Risman	(Loughborough College)	D.A. Stewart	(Western Province)
*R.E.G. Jeeps	(Northampton)	P. de W. Uys	(Northern Transvaal)
C.R. Jacobs	(Northampton)	S.P. Kuhn	(Transvaal)
S.A.M. Hodgson	(Durham City)	G.F. Malan	(Western Province)
T.P. Wright	(Blackheath)	P.S. du Toit	(Boland)
R.W.D. Marques	(Harlequins)	*A.S. Malan	(Transvaal)
J.D. Currie	(Harlequins)	J.T. Claassen	(Western Transvaal)
†L.I. Rimmer	(Bath)	G.H. van Zyl	(Western Province)
W.G.D. Morgan	(Medicals)	D.J. Hopwood	(Western Province)
P.G.D. Robbins	(Moseley)	F.C. du Preez	(Northern Transvaal)

Try: Hopwood   *Conversion:* du Preez

Referee: Mr G.J. Treharne (Wales)

WALES v ENGLAND 1961
Played at Cardiff Arms Park, 21 January 1961
Wales won by 2T (6) to 1T (3)

The late 1950s and early 1960s were full of dour international matches, but this match at Cardiff proved an exception to the general rule. 'Wales and England joined in a traditional match of open football, due to the approach of the two captains,' wrote J.B.G. Thomas in *Playfair Rugby Football Annual*, and the crowd enjoyed an exciting match played on a soggy ground.

Wales played well, blending power up-front with speed and invention amongst the backs. The result was two superb tries by Bebb. Richards and O'Connor played major roles in both scores, opening up the play with enterprise and precise judgment. A swift break by Richards and a clever reverse pass to Davies, with co-centre Roberts in support, opened the way for the first try; and another switch of direction led to Bebb's second try before the interval.

A serious leg injury reduced Cyril Davies to a passenger in the second half, and Wales were left to adopt a more defensive stance – particularly when Haydn Morgan was recruited from the pack to act as emergency centre. England now came back into the game a little, and from a charged-down kick the ball was quickly transferred across the threequarter line to Young who, showing remarkable speed, outstripped the Welsh cover to score a grand try. England strived bravely to save the game in the closing stages but heroic Welsh defence, supported by the choral efforts of a partisan crowd, saw the home side to victory.

The withdrawal of Currie, England's second-row player, broke a partnership with Marques which had lasted since 1956 in 22 consecutive matches. Malcolm Phillips, having won his previous caps whilst at Oxford, became the first international capped direct from Fylde R.F.C., the club which he had joined as a schoolboy.

WALES		ENGLAND	
*T.J. Davies	(Llanelli)	†M.N. Gavins	(Leicester)
P.M. Rees	(Newport)	J.R.C. Young	(Harlequins)
C.A.H. Davies	(Cardiff)	M.S. Phillips	(Fylde)
H.M. Roberts	(Cardiff)	M.P. Weston	(Richmond)
D.I.E. Bebb	(Swansea)	J. Roberts	(Old Millhillians/Sale)
K.H.L. Richards	(Bridgend)	A.B.W. Risman	(Loughborough College)
A. O'Connor	(Aberavon)	*R.E.G. Jeeps	(Northampton)
P.E.J. Morgan	(Aberavon)	C.R. Jacobs	(Northampton)
B.V. Meredith	(Newport)	S.A.M. Hodgson	(Durham City)
K.D. Jones	(Cardiff)	T.P. Wright	(Blackheath)
D.J.E. Harris	(Cardiff)	R.W.D. Marques	(Harlequins)
W.R. Evans	(Bridgend)	†R.J. French	(St Helens)
G.D. Davidge	(Newport)	L.I. Rimmer	(Bath)
D. Nash	(Ebbw Vale)	W.G.D. Morgan	(Medicals)
H.J. Morgan	(Abertillery)	P.G.D. Robbins	(Moseley)

Tries: Bebb (2)   *Try:* Young

Referee: Mr K.D. Kelleher (Ireland)

IRELAND v ENGLAND 1961

Played at Lansdowne Road, Dublin, 11 February 1961
Ireland won by 1G, 2PG (11) to 1G, 1T (8)

England made several changes from the side defeated in Cardiff, recalling Ernie Robinson (previously capped in 1954) and shifting Risman into the centre so that Sharp could be accommodated at fly-half. The result was not a success, and it was left to the new men, Willcox and Rogers, to prove their worth as replacements at full-back and flanker. Willcox was a reliable, rather than spectacular back, while Rogers made his mark on the game with a try near the end of the match.

Ireland entered the match without Mulligan, their experienced scrum-half, who was forced out of the side with an attack of measles. However, Moffett, his deputy, proved to be Ireland's match-winner with two first-half penalty goals and a conversion of a second-half try – which came about when Sharp, uncharacteristically, missed his tackle and allowed Kiernan to make the run which led to Kavanagh's try. These scores gave the Irish a comfortable lead of 11 points, but England staged a comeback with Jeeps playing a true captain's part. The scrum-half made a devastating break which was ably supported by Morgan before Roberts touched down. Willcox failed to kick the goal but Risman's conversion of Rogers's try, after the new flanker had charged down a poor Irish clearance, made the final minutes of the match extremely tense.

The Irish defended stoutly and survived a late run by Young to win by three points. England, after an unbeaten run in 1960, now found themselves with three consecutive defeats to their name and little hope of retaining the International Championship which had been shared with France in the previous campaign.

IRELAND		ENGLAND	
T.J. Kiernan	(U.C. Cork)	†J.G. Willcox	(Oxford U.)
R.J. McCarten	(London Irish)	J.R.C. Young	(Harlequins)
D. Hewitt	(Queen's U.)	A.B.W. Risman	(Loughborough College)
J.C. Walsh	(U.C. Cork)	M.P. Weston	(Richmond)
A.J.F. O'Reilly	(Dolphin)	J. Roberts	(Sale/Old Millhillians)
W.K. Armstrong	(N.I.F.C.)	R.A.W. Sharp	(Oxford U.)
J.W. Moffett	(Ballymena)	*R.E.G. Jeeps	(Northampton)
B.G.M. Wood	(Lansdowne)	C.R. Jacobs	(Northampton)
*A.R. Dawson	(Wanderers)	E. Robinson	(Coventry)
S. Millar	(Ballymena)	T.P. Wright	(Blackheath)
W.A. Mulcahy	(U.C. Dublin)	R.J. French	(St Helens)
M.G. Culliton	(Wanderers)	†J. Price	(Coventry)
J.R. Kavanagh	(Wanderers)	L.I. Rimmer	(Bath)
P.J.A. O'Sullivan	(Galwegians)	W.G.D. Morgan	(Medicals)
N.A.A. Murphy	(Garryowen)	†D.P. Rogers	(Bedford)

Try: Kavanagh
Conversion: Moffett
Penalties: Moffett (2)

Tries: Roberts, Rogers
Conversion: Risman

Referee: Mr G.J. Treharne (Wales)

ENGLAND v FRANCE 1961

Played at Twickenham, London, 25 February 1961
Drawn: England 1G (5), France 1G (5)

England and France played their third consecutive drawn game in a match lacking in distinction. France looked jaded and clearly were suffering from the physical demands of their drawn match with the South African tourists (played only one week earlier). England had selected the fifteen which did duty in Dublin, but Price was compelled to withdraw and Harding was awarded his first cap.

A heavy pitch, soaked by rain just prior to the kick-off, did not help the sides to make this an open game to remember. A dour half, full of spoiling and played in fits and starts, not surprisingly ended with neither side scoring.

France were forced to rearrange their back division after the interval when it was realised that Dupuy, who had been injured near the end of the first half, was more severely wounded than first investigations had revealed. But a reduced pack performed ably against an improving English eight, one of whom opened the scoring. Weston gathered a loose ball and evaded several would-be tacklers before confronting Vannier. There, in support, was the new man Harding and he made no mistake in grounding the ball to the left of the posts at the north end of the ground. Willcox converted to give England the lead after an hour of play. However, five minutes later France were level. Moncla and Crauste had figured in several breaks close to the scrum by Lacroix and one such burst by the scrum-half was continued by Moncla who linked with Rancoule on the right wing. Finding his way blocked, the Toulon flyer cross-kicked to the England posts and, though two English defenders appeared to have the ball covered, Crauste pounced for the touch-down. Vannier made no mistake with the goal kick.

ENGLAND		FRANCE	
J.G. Willcox	(Oxford U./Harlequins)	M. Vannier	(Chalon)
J.R.C. Young	(Harlequins)	H. Rancoule	(Toulon)
A.B.W. Risman	(Loughborough College)	G. Boniface	(Mont-de-Marsan)
M.P. Weston	(Richmond)	J. Bouquet	(Vienne)
J. Roberts	(Old Millhillians/Sale)	J. Dupuy	(Tarbes)
R.A.W. Sharp	(Oxford U.)	P. Albaladejo	(Dax)
*R.E.G. Jeeps	(Northampton)	P. Lacroix	(Agen)
C.R. Jacobs	(Northampton)	A. Domenech	(Brive)
E. Robinson	(Coventry)	J. de Gregorio	(Grenoble)
T.P. Wright	(Blackheath)	A. Roques	(Cahors)
R.J. French	(St Helens)	G. Bouguyon	(Grenoble)
†V.S.J. Harding	(Cambridge U./Saracens)	J.P. Saux	(Pau)
L.I. Rimmer	(Bath)	*F. Moncla	(Pau)
W.G.D. Morgan	(Medicals)	M. Celaya	(Bordeaux)
D.P. Rogers	(Bedford)	M. Crauste	(Lourdes)

Try: Harding   *Conversion:* Willcox   *Try:* Crauste   *Conversion:* Vannier

Referee: Mr D.G. Walters (Wales)

ENGLAND v SCOTLAND 1961

Played at Twickenham, London, 18 March 1961
England won by 1PG, 1T (6) to Nil

The English selectors had been ruthlessly criticised during the season for their inability to decide which player, Risman or Sharp, was better equipped to spearhead the English attack from fly-half. The decision to include both men in the earlier sides, with Risman at centre, had not yet proved a success. Well, for this match, the selectors had no such problems: Risman, whose best football was seen in Australasia when touring with the 1959 British Lions, had decided to throw in his lot with the Rugby League, following in his famous father's footsteps. A muscle injury kept Sharp out, so the pivot position went again to Horrocks-Taylor. There was a welcome return to the England fifteen by Jackson, too, though an injury caused him discomfort for much of the match and his best moments were in defence.

England's two scores came before and after half-time. In the first half, an angled kick by Patterson split the Scottish defence and Roberts was there to touch down for a try; and in the second half, Horrocks-Taylor, whose tactical kicking was careful and faultless throughout the match, landed a penalty goal.

Scotland were a disappointing side and could not fulfil their early-season promise: they had beaten both Wales and Ireland. Towards the end of this match they missed a golden opportunity of staging a late recovery. England, after a period of Scottish pressure, won a scrum in front of their posts but a dropped pass gave the visitors a great chance to score. The ground was wet and the ball slippery, however, and a knock-on foiled Scotland's hopes. As this unexciting game limped on to no-side there was a temporary break in the monotony when a drop at goal by Horrocks-Taylor hit the post; otherwise there was little for the crowd to enjoy.

ENGLAND		SCOTLAND	
J.G. Willcox	(Oxford U./Harlequins)	K.J.F. Scotland	(Heriot's F.P.)
P.B. Jackson	(Coventry)	*A.R. Smith	(Edinburgh Wands.)
W.M. Patterson	(Sale)	E. McKeating	(Heriot's F.P.)
M.P. Weston	(Richmond)	G.D. Stevenson	(Hawick)
J. Roberts	(Old Millhillians/Sale)	R.H. Thomson	(London Scottish)
J.P. Horrocks-Taylor	(Leicester)	I.H.P. Laughland	(London Scottish)
*R.E.G. Jeeps	(Northampton)	A.J. Hastie	(Melrose)
C.R. Jacobs	(Northampton)	H.F. McLeod	(Hawick)
E. Robinson	(Coventry)	N.S. Bruce	(London Scottish)
T.P. Wright	(Blackheath)	D.M.D. Rollo	(Howe of Fife)
R.J. French	(St Helens)	F.H. ten Bos	(London Scottish)
V.S.J. Harding	(Cambridge U./Saracens)	J. Douglas	(Stewart's College F.P.)
L.I. Rimmer	(Bath)	K.I. Ross	(Boroughmuir F.P.)
W.G.D. Morgan	(Medicals)	G.K. Smith	(Kelso)
D.P. Rogers	(Bedford)	J.C. Brash	(Cambridge U.)

Try: Roberts   *Penalty:* Horrocks-Taylor

Referee: Mr K.D. Kelleher (Ireland)

ENGLAND v WALES 1962

Played at Twickenham, London, 20 January 1962
Drawn, neither side scoring

A crowd of 72,000 saw England and Wales play a pointless stalemate, with England marginally the better side. Wales, with a seasoned pack and dangerous backs, were the favourites before the match, but the English pack responded to the leadership of Taylor, recalled after an absence of seven seasons, and held the Welsh in the tight. Consequently, the Welsh backs were unable to find the room required to produce any telling breaks, and the much-praised D.K. Jones scarcely had a chance to reveal his ability.

Both sides missed their chances to convert penalties into useful points, and the famous Twickenham swirl robbed Sharp of dropped-goal points on one occasion when a goal seemed certain. Some of Coslett's efforts from long range were commendable attempts, but in all he failed with five kicks at goal.

Wales alone promised to score a try. Close passing between Meredith, K.D. Jones and Cunningham gave Bebb an exciting moment, otherwise the match was an unenterprising affair, much criticised by the press at the inquest.

Near the end, England had just cause to reflect on some bad luck when Rogers punted the ball over the Welsh line and was late-tackled by Coslett. The referee gave Wales the benefit of any doubt, did not award a penalty try, and the visitors took a Championship point from an altogether disappointing match.

ENGLAND		WALES	
J.G. Willcox	(Oxford U.)	K. Coslett	(Aberavon)
†A.M. Underwood	(Northampton)	D.R.R. Morgan	(Llanelli)
†M.R. Wade	(Cambridge U.)	D.K. Jones	(Llanelli)
M.P. Weston	(Richmond)	M.J. Price	(Pontypool)
J. Roberts	(Sale)	D.I.E. Bebb	(Swansea)
R.A.W. Sharp	(Oxford U.)	A. Rees	(Maesteg)
*R.E.G. Jeeps	(Northampton)	*L.H. Williams	(Cardiff)
†P.E. Judd	(Coventry)	K.D. Jones	(Cardiff)
S.A.M. Hodgson	(Durham City)	B.V. Meredith	(Newport)
T.P. Wright	(Blackheath)	L.J. Cunningham	(Aberavon)
V.S.J. Harding	(Sale)	W.R. Evans	(Bridgend)
J.D. Currie	(Bristol)	B. Price	(Newport)
R.E. Syrett	(Wasps)	R.H. Davies	(London Welsh)
P.J. Taylor	(Northampton)	A.E.I. Pask	(Abertillery)
D.P. Rogers	(Bedford)	H.J. Morgan	(Abertillery)

Referee: Mr J.A.S. Taylor (Scotland)

ENGLAND v IRELAND 1962

Played at Twickenham, London, 10 February 1962
England won by 2G, 1PG, 1T (16) to Nil

The same England fifteen which had featured in the drab draw with Wales now faced an inexperienced Irish side which included eight new caps. An entertaining match, with Sharp in excellent form, followed and there were rumours of 'a new England ... pledged to flat-out attack, with, of course, Sharp, as the ideal spearhead'.

In the opening minutes of the game the Cornish fly-half made a scything run through the Irish backs after receiving good service from Jeeps and the English scrummagers. Wade, a large man built like a tank, was up in support to take the pass for a try which Sharp converted into a goal. England appeared confident and purposeful at this stage, and thoughts of a rout were uppermost in the minds of many spectators. But an inability to finish several promising movements, combined with some spirited Irish defence, kept the score to five points at the interval. Kiernan was in fine form and confirmed his reputation as the most accomplished full-back in the northern hemisphere.

Early in the second half, feeble marking by the Irish right flank enabled Roberts to waltz over for a simple try which Sharp failed to convert, though the latter's place kicking was accurate later in the half with a penalty. To cap a splendid performance, Sharp completed the scoring near no-side when, again following efficient service from his scrum and his half-back partner, he broke through the Irish backs to cross the line near the left upright for a classic fly-half try. The conversion was a formality, and raised his tally for the afternoon to ten points.

Johnny Quirke, Ireland's boy-wonder, won his cap in this match at the tender age of seventeen – younger even than the legendary Haydn Tanner on debut. Quirke's passing was long, quick and accurate.

ENGLAND		IRELAND	
J.G. Willcox	(Oxford U.)	T.J. Kiernan	(U.C. Cork)
A.M. Underwood	(Northampton)	L.P.F. L'Estrange	(Dublin U.)
M.R. Wade	(Cambridge U.)	M.K. Flynn	(Wanderers)
M.P. Weston	(Richmond)	W.R. Hunter	(C.I.Y.M.S.)
J. Roberts	(Sale)	N.H. Brophy	(Blackrock College)
R.A.W. Sharp	(Oxford U.)	F.G. Gilpin	(Queen's U.)
*R.E.G. Jeeps	(Northampton)	J.T.M. Quirke	(Blackrock College)
P.E. Judd	(Coventry)	S. Millar	(Ballymena)
S.A.M. Hodgson	(Durham City)	J.S. Dick	(Queen's U.)
T.P. Wright	(Blackheath)	R.J. McLoughlin	(U.C. Dublin)
V.S.J. Harding	(Sale)	*W.A. Mulcahy	(Bohemians)
J.D. Currie	(Bristol)	W.J. McBride	(Ballymena)
R.E. Syrett	(Wasps)	N. Turley	(Blackrock College)
P.J. Taylor	(Northampton)	M.L. Hipwell	(Terenure College)
D.P. Rogers	(Bedford)	N.A.A. Murphy	(Cork Const.)

Tries: Roberts, Sharp, Wade
Conversions: Sharp (2)
Penalty: Sharp

Referee: Mr D.G. Walters (Wales)

FRANCE v ENGLAND 1962

Played at Stade Colombes, Paris, 24 February 1962
France won by 2G, 1T (13) to Nil

The English fifteen which had outclassed Ireland at Twickenham two weeks earlier were selected 'en bloc' for this match with France. The ground at Colombes was hard after a severe frost and favoured the team which was prepared to throw the ball about accurately and constructively. On the day, this was France, and their thoroughly deserved victory brought to an end a series of stalemates between the sides stretching back to 1958.

The English three-quarters, who had looked outstanding against Ireland, now appeared slow and indecisive, though the hard ground caused many stoppages for injuries. Willcox won praise for many brave tackles and his line-kicking was valuable when England came under heavy fire from the French attack early in the match. Indeed, it was to England's credit that the score stood at only 5–0 at the break, for the French always threatened to cut loose and pile up the points. (A dashing move from a line-out in the twenty-third minute had culminated in a try by Crauste which Albaladejo converted.)

Crauste went on in the second half to score two more tries and become the first forward since 1903 to score three tries in an international match. The superb French forwards swarmed around a loose ball, and swift passing from the second phase resulted in a try which went unconverted; and a break and cross-kick by Boniface bisected the English defence for Crauste to complete his hat-trick without an English hand touching him. Albaladejo's goal stretched France to the comfort of a 13-points lead. Reports indicate that France were unlucky to win by only 13!

FRANCE		ENGLAND	
C. Lacaze	(Lourdes)	J.G. Willcox	(Oxford U.)
H. Rancoule	(Tarbes)	A.M. Underwood	(Northampton)
A. Boniface	(Mont-de-Marsan)	M.R. Wade	(Cambridge U.)
J. Bouquet	(Vienne)	M.P. Weston	(Richmond)
J. Dupuy	(Tarbes)	J. Roberts	(Sale)
P. Albaladejo	(Dax)	R.A.W. Sharp	(Oxford U.)
*P. Lacroix	(Agen)	*R.E.G. Jeeps	(Northampton)
A. Domenech	(Brive)	P.E. Judd	(Coventry)
J. de Gregorio	(Grenoble)	S.A.M. Hodgson	(Durham City)
A. Roques	(Cahors)	T.P. Wright	(Blackheath)
J.P. Saux	(Pau)	V.S.J. Harding	(Sale)
B. Mommejat	(Albi)	J.D. Currie	(Bristol)
R. Gensane	(Béziers)	R.E. Syrett	(Wasps)
H. Romero	(Montauban)	P.J. Taylor	(Northampton)
M. Crauste	(Lourdes)	D.P. Rogers	(Bedford)

Tries: Crauste (3)
Conversions: Albaladejo (2)

Referee: Mr D.G. Walters (Wales)

SCOTLAND v ENGLAND 1962
Played at Murrayfield, Edinburgh, 17 March 1962
Drawn: Scotland 1PG (3), England 1PG (3)

Scotland entered the match with the Triple Crown at stake – a trophy the Scots had not claimed since 1938 – and a huge crowd of 82,500 spectators filled the enormous Murrayfield banks and stands. Alas, the game itself did not match the occasion and the result, another dull draw, again drew attention to the boring tactics which the Laws of the Game induced at this time. The problem lay with the definition of the off-side line at the scrummage. Backs were allowed to lie up flat on the advantage line (the gain line of modern coaches) which ran through the tunnel of the scrummage. Defensive sides placed a wing-forward and both centres on this line making attack by the opposition extremely difficult; while a further disappointment was the use of the fly-half as an extra wing-forward on the advantage line at the opponents' put-in, the full-back lining up to cover the fly-half's position and kick for touch should such an opportunity arise.

Scotland began strongly but a tendency to nurse the touch-line by both Waddell and Coughtrie implied that the home side were banking on their forwards to make any decisive breakthroughs. The back play was, to say the least, feeble, and Smith and Cowan were to be congratulated on their initiative, for both succeeded in going within a whisker of scoring tries in their respective corners. Ken Scotland had an off-day with his place kicking, shooting wide from favourable positions on more than one occasion.

England, showing several changes from the fifteen which disappointed in Paris, had fewer scoring chances than the Scots. Nevertheless, the visitors took the lead in the twenty-fifth minute of the first half when Willcox, with textbook correctness, kicked a fine goal from 45 yards and at a tricky angle. Scotland equalised with a similar score just before the interval – and the only event of note in the second half was an early interception by Hodgson which nearly led to a score by Underwood.

SCOTLAND		ENGLAND	
K.J.F. Scotland	(Leicester)	J.G. Willcox	(Oxford U.)
*A.R. Smith	(Edinburgh Wands.)	†A.C.B. Hurst	(Wasps)
J.J. McPartlin	(Oxford U.)	A.M. Underwood	(Northampton)
I.H.P. Laughland	(London Scottish)	†J.M. Dee	(Hartlepool Rovers)
R.C. Cowan	(Selkirk)	J. Roberts	(Sale)
G.H. Waddell	(London Scottish)	J.P. Horrocks-Taylor	(Leicester)
S. Coughtrie	(Edinburgh Acads.)	*R.E.G. Jeeps	(Northampton)
H.F. McLeod	(Hawick)	P.E. Judd	(Coventry)
N.S. Bruce	(London Scottish)	S.A.M. Hodgson	(Durham Ciry)
D.M.D. Rollo	(Howe of Fife)	T.P. Wright	(Blackheath)
F.H.ten Bos	(London Scottish)	†T.A. Pargetter	(Coventry)
M.J. Campbell-Lamerton	(Halifax)	V.S.J. Harding	(Sale)
R.J.C. Glasgow	(Dunfermline)	†S.J. Purdy	(Rugby)
J. Douglas	(Stewart's College F.P.)	P.J. Taylor	(Northampton)
K.I. Ross	(Boroughmuir F.P.)	P.G.D. Robbins	(Coventry)

Penalty: Scotland

Penalty: Willcox

Referee: Mr K.D. Kelleher (Ireland)

WALES v ENGLAND 1963

Played at Cardiff Arms Park, 19 January 1963
England won by 2G, 1DG (13) to 1PG, 1T (6)

Arctic conditions during one of Britain's coldest-ever winters made the ground hard for this opening match of England's campaign. Both teams had a sprinkling of new caps – particularly in the packs – but the young visitors had the better of a game destined to be England's last victory in the Principality to date.

There was no scoring in the early portion of the match, though Wales, with the advantage of the wind, had several near misses. Robert Morgan, Bebb and Watkins, toiling at half-back with Rowlands behind a sluggish scrummage, produced occasional glimpses of creative play, but errors by Morgan and Bebb meant that three scoring chances were lost. England seemed happy to bide their time till a quick, long throw-in from touch by Roberts, on his 25, found Weston in midfield. The centre fed Phillips, and a scissors with Jackson, who committed the Welsh full-back before returning the ball to Phillips, completely bamboozled an inept Welsh defence. Phillips, showing a fine turn of speed – indeed, he had a very good match – outflanked the cover to score a try which Sharp converted.

In the second half, a rush led by Rogers from half-way with Phillips lending support resulted in Owen scoring the second try. Sharp's conversion took England to the comfort of a ten-points lead but a binding offence allowed Hodgson to convert a penalty into three points. Welsh hopes were finally killed when Sharp received from a scrum and dropped England's first goal against Wales since 1949. Ten minutes from the end of the match, Hayward crossed from a line-out to complete the scoring.

WALES		ENGLAND	
G.T.R. Hodgson	(Neath)	J.G. Willcox	(Oxford U.)
D.R.R. Morgan	(Llanelli)	P.B. Jackson	(Coventry)
D.K. Jones	(Llanelli)	M.S. Phillips	(Fylde)
D.B. Davies	(Llanelli)	M.P. Weston	(Durham City)
D.I.E. Bebb	(Swansea)	J. Roberts	(Sale)
D. Watkins	(Newport)	*R.A.W. Sharp	(Wasps)
*D.C.T. Rowlands	(Pontypool)	†S.J.S. Clarke	(Cambridge U.)
K.D. Jones	(Cardiff)	†N.J. Drake-Lee	(Cambridge U.)
N.R. Gale	(Llanelli)	†J.D. Thorne	(Bristol)
D. Williams	(Ebbw Vale)	†B.A. Dovey	(Rosslyn Park)
B.E. Thomas	(Neath/Cambridge U.)	†A.M. Davis	(Torquay Athletic)
B. Price	(Newport)	†J.E. Owen	(Coventry)
A.E.I. Pask	(Abertillery)	†D.C. Manley	(Exeter)
R.C.B. Michaelson	(Aberavon/Cambridge U.)	B.J. Wightman	(Coventry)
D.J. Hayward	(Cardiff)	D.P. Rogers	(Bedford)

Try: Hayward   *Penalty:* Hodgson

Tries: Owen, Phillips
Conversions: Sharp (2)
Dropped goal: Sharp

Referee: Mr K.D. Kelleher (Ireland)

England v Wales, 1963. England's Championship winning side of 1963, which has the destinction of being the last England team to have beaten Wales at Cardiff: *standing* Mr R. A. B. Crowe (touch-judge), D. C. Manley, S. J. S. Clarke, A. M. Davis, B. J. Wightman, J. E. Owen, B. A. Dovey, N. J. Drake-Lee, J. G. Willcox; *sitting* D. P. Rogers, M. S. Phillips, J. Roberts, R. A. W. Sharp (captain), P. B. Jackson, J. D. Thorne, M. P. Weston.

IRELAND v ENGLAND 1963

Played at Lansdowne Road, Dublin, 9 February 1963
Drawn, neither side scoring

A fighting effort by the Irish forwards halted England in their quest for the Triple Crown and the result, a scoreless draw, slightly flattered the visitors. After losing heavily to France two weeks earlier, Ireland had made several changes to their fifteen and recalled English, an adroit tactical kicker who dominated the game behind a lively pack which provided an efficient service from the set-pieces. Dawson hooked with all of his old artistry and precision, and for much of this match the Englishmen were compelled to defend. Willcox showed supreme confidence and reliability at the apex of England's defence. His catching and kicking were unerring and the manner in which he dived at the feet of the Irish forwards during several menacing rushes affirmed his standing as the number-one full-back in Britain.

The frost and snow of Cardiff now gave way to the mud and rain of Dublin and, consequently, there was little more to this game than a forward battle between two uncompromising eights. Not a single threequarter movement materialised in the afternoon and Sharp, receiving the ball behind some slow-heeling forwards, had few opportunities to open up the game. Kelly's quick passing to English allowed the Irish pivot to launch several high punts into England's territory, and four penalties were awarded to the home side in kickable positions as a result. The failure of Marshall, a substitute for Kiernan, to land any penalty points thus denied Ireland a deserved victory.

The performance of a sluggish English eight suggested that, despite victory in Cardiff, this fifteen was not quite ready to carry off a Championship title, and some changes up-front were widely predicted before the English selectors met to choose the team to play France. Only the breakaways, Manley and Rogers, working in close harmony with Clarke at the base of the scrum, enhanced their reputations in this muddy match.

IRELAND		ENGLAND	
B.D.E. Marshall	(Queen's U.)	J.G. Willcox	(Oxford U.)
W.R. Hunter	(C.I.Y.M.S.)	P.B. Jackson	(Coventry)
J.C. Walsh	(U.C. Cork)	M.S. Phillips	(Fylde)
P.J. Casey	(U.C. Dublin)	M.P. Weston	(Durham City)
N.H. Brophy	(Blackrock College)	J. Roberts	(Sale)
M.A.F. English	(Lansdowne)	*R.A.W. Sharp	(Wasps)
J.C. Kelly	(U.C. Dublin)	S.J.S. Clarke	(Cambridge U.)
R.J. McLoughlin	(Blackrock College)	N.J. Drake-Lee	(Cambridge U.)
A.R. Dawson	(Wanderers)	J.D. Thorne	(Bristol)
S. Millar	(Ballymena)	B.A. Dovey	(Rosslyn Park)
*W.A. Mulcahy	(Bective Rangers)	A.M. Davis	(Torquay Athletic)
W.J. McBride	(Ballymena)	J.E. Owen	(Coventry)
E.P. McGuire	(U.C. Galway)	D.C. Manley	(Exeter)
C.J. Dick	(Ballymena)	B.J. Wightman	(Coventry)
M.D. Kiely	(Lansdowne)	D.P. Rogers	(Bedford)

Referee: Mr H.B. Laidlaw (Scotland)

ENGLAND v FRANCE 1963
Played at Twickenham, London, 23 February 1963
England won by 2PG (6) to 1G (5)

The application of hot air – a new concept in protecting turf against penetrating frost in 1963 – meant that Twickenham looked a picture on a sunny, winter's day for this match with France. England had, as expected, tinkered slightly with the pack which played in Ireland. Three changes resulted, one of which led to Pargetter taking the field for his first match in nine weeks due to the cancellations enforced by unsuitable playing surfaces in the country during this severe winter.

The match was undistinguished: England held a small superiority up-front, harassed the French halves incessantly (Rogers and Manley again shone in this aspect of play) and relied on Willcox's goal kicking to win the match. Only when France were in possession and in attacking positions was the game enjoyable to any degree. A good passage of play led to France's try, early in the match, treating the large crowd to one of the few thrills of the afternoon. From a maul, France moved towards the right and exquisitely-timed passes transferred the ball rapidly to Besson, who made ground to the English line. He was checked, but the ball trickled loose and G. Boniface scooped it up and swept over the line for a try converted by Albaladejo.

Albaladejo, usually an infallible place-kicker, missed with a number of penalty kicks – albeit from considerable angles – which should have given France a winning lead. Willcox, on the other hand, was on target and brought about England's narrow victory. Before the interval he narrowed the French lead to 5–3 when he punished the French forwards for collapsing the scrum, and early in the second half he landed another penalty from an angle and into the wind.

With Rogers and Manley bottling up the French threat at its source, the base of the scrum, England held their tenuous lead, and even survived a desperate late challenge from the French. This was England's first win in the series since 1958.

ENGLAND		FRANCE	
J.G. Willcox	(Oxford U.)	P. Dedieu	(Béziers)
P.B. Jackson	(Coventry)	P. Besson	(Brive)
M.S. Phillips	(Fylde)	G. Boniface	(Mont-de-Marsan)
M.P. Weston	(Durham City)	A. Boniface	(Mont-de-Marsan)
J. Roberts	(Sale)	C. Darrouy	(Mont-de-Marsan)
*R.A.W. Sharp	(Wasps)	P. Albaladejo	(Dax)
S.J.S. Clarke	(Cambridge U.)	*P. Lacroix	(Agen)
†K.J. Wilson	(Gloucester)	F. Mas	(Béziers)
J.D. Thorne	(Bristol)	R. Rebujent	(R.C.F.)
N.J. Drake-Lee	(Cambridge U.)	F. Zago	(Montauban)
T.A. Pargetter	(Coventry)	M. Lira	(La Voulte)
J.E. Owen	(Coventry)	J.P. Saux	(Pau)
D.C. Manley	(Exeter)	J. Fabre	(Toulouse)
†D.G. Perry	(Bedford)	H. Romero	(Montauban)
D.P. Rogers	(Bedford)	M. Crauste	(Lourdes)

Penalties: Willcox (2)

Try: G. Boniface
Conversion: Albaladejo

Referee: Mr D.C.J. McMahon (Scotland)

ENGLAND v SCOTLAND 1963

Played at Twickenham, London, 16 March 1963
England won by 2G (10) to 1G, 1DG (8)

In a game for ever referred to as Richard Sharp's match, England stole a narrow victory to gain the International Championship title, outright, for the first time since 1958.

Scotland opened a handsome eight-points lead. Using a stiff breeze to their advantage, they set a lightning pace to a match which turned out to be one of the most entertaining at Twickenham for several years. Even the severe weather of early winter gave way to spring sunshine, so that the conditions were ideal for an open game.

Scotland's first score was the result of storming play by their back-row forwards. From a line-out inside the English 25, a long throw enabled Glasgow to gain possession. Dipping his left shoulder, the loose-forward then drove through a wall of English players and crossed the line buried beneath a pile of bodies. The Welsh referee was in a perfect position to award the try and Coughtrie kicked the goal.

In the fifteenth minute of the half, another storming run by Glasgow, supported by several of his colleagues, placed Willcox under considerable pressure. A scrum followed and Ken Scotland took ample advantage of a quick heel with a neat dropped goal. Before the interval, however, England wiped five points off the lead. The ebullient Jackson combined with Sharp in a move from a line-out, then eluded several defenders and kicked on for Godwin and several other forwards to converge on the ball. Drake-Lee scored and Willcox, with a fine kick from a wide angle, converted.

Sharp's breathtaking effort came quite early in the second half. England's front row, which gained a clear victory in the tight-head count, heeled from a scrum 40 yards out and close to touch. Jackson was standing close to Clarke on the right wing, as if a blind-side ploy was intended. But an orthodox pass to Sharp was given and the fly-half made three audacious dummies, squeezing himself through narrow chinks in the Scottish defence, to score to the left of the goal post. Willcox converted and England held on to their narrow lead until the final whistle.

ENGLAND		**SCOTLAND**	
J.G. Willcox	(Harlequins)	C.F. Blaikie	(Heriot's F.P.)
P.B. Jackson	(Coventry)	C. Elliot	(Langholm)
M.S. Phillips	(Fylde)	B.C. Henderson	(Edinburgh Wands.)
M.P. Weston	(Durham City)	D.M. White	(Kelvinside Acads.)
J. Roberts	(Sale)	R.H. Thomson	(London Scottish)
*R.A.W. Sharp	(Wasps)	*K.J.F. Scotland	(Heriot's F.P.)
S.J.S. Clarke	(Cambridge U.)	S. Coughtrie	(Edinburgh Acads.)
P.E. Judd	(Coventry)	J.B. Neill	(Edinburgh Acads.)
H.O. Godwin	(Coventry)	N.S. Bruce	(London Scottish)
N.J. Drake-Lee	(Cambridge U.)	D.M.D. Rollo	(Howe of Fife)
A.M. Davis	(Torquay Athletic)	F.H. ten Bos	(London Scottish)
J.E. Owen	(Coventry)	M.J. Campbell-Lamerton	(Halifax)
D.C. Manley	(Exeter)	R.J.C. Glasgow	(Dunfermline)
D.G. Perry	(Bedford)	J.P. Fisher	(Royal H.S.F.P.)
D.P. Rogers	(Bedford)	K.I. Ross	(Boroughmuir F.P.)

Tries: Drake-Lee, Sharp
Conversions: Willcox (2)

Try: Glasgow   *Conversion:* Coughtrie
Dropped goal: Scotland

Referee: Mr D.G. Walters (Wales)

NEW ZEALAND v ENGLAND 1963

Played at Eden Park, Auckland, 25 May 1963

New Zealand won by 3G, 1DG, 1PG (21) to 1G, 2PG (11)

England made history by becoming the first home Union to tour New Zealand. Despite arriving as Northern Hemisphere champions, they did not expect to stretch the mighty All Blacks in the two-Test series, for several leading players had been unable to make the trip and an exacting itinerary was arranged. Nevertheless, in this match, before 53,000 spectators, England led 6–0 at the interval before New Zealand's ability to use the ruck as a platform for launching attacking movements allowed the home team to pull clear in the last quarter of the match.

Hosen opened the scoring in the first minute with a penalty for a line-out offence just outside the All Blacks' 25, and added another seven minutes later when Colin Meads fell off-side. Don Clarke, renowned for his place-kicking feats, replied with a penalty for New Zealand at the start of the second half, but England countered with a fine try in the fifth minute. Clarke made a break on the blind side of a ruck some 30 yards from the New Zealand line and Rogers was in support to send Ranson beyond the reach of Don Clarke for a try near the posts. Hosen converted.

From 3–11 down, the New Zealand pack, which had had a quiet first half, gradually steam-rollered England's eight into the ground, dominating both the rucks and the tight scrummages. Watt set up the first try when he chose the short side of a ruck for a kick to the corner. Don Clarke followed up to touch down with one hand but, after failing to convert, the referee ruled 'no-charge' because Ranson had illegally shouted. Clarke succeeded with his second attempt.

As the match entered its final quarter, the All Blacks at last overhauled England when Wolfe and Uttley created a chance for Caulton to run through some ineffective English tackling and score near the posts. Clarke converted. With the English pack tiring, the All Blacks forced the decisive score five minutes from no-side. Watt received from a ruck and burst through on the narrow side before sending Caulton over for a second try behind the posts. Don Clarke converted, then dropped a goal from 40 yards in the dying seconds of the match.

NEW ZEALAND		ENGLAND	
D.B. Clarke	(Waikato)	†R.W. Hosen	(Northampton)
D.W. McKay	(Auckland)	†J.M. Ranson	(Rosslyn Park)
I.N. Uttley	(Wellington)	M.S. Phillips	(Fylde)
R.W. Caulton	(Wellington)	*M.P. Weston	(Durham City)
		J.M. Dee	(Hartlepool Rovers)
T.N. Wolfe	(Taranaki)		
B.A. Watt	(Canterbury)	J.P. Horrocks-Taylor	(Leicester)
D.M. Connor	(Auckland)	S.J.S. Clarke	(Cambridge U.)
I.J. Clarke	(Waikato)	P.E. Judd	(Coventry)
D. Young	(Canterbury)	H.O. Godwin	(Coventry)
*W.J. Whineray	(Auckland)	C.R. Jacobs	(Northampton)
C.E. Meads	(King Country)	T.A. Pargetter	(Coventry)
A.J. Stewart	(Canterbury)	A.M. Davis	(Torquay Athletic)
K.R. Tremain	(Hawke's Bay)	D.P. Rogers	(Bedford)
D.J. Graham	(Canterbury)	D.G. Perry	(Bedford)
W.J. Nathan	(Auckland)	†V.R. Marriott	(Harlequins)

Tries: Caulton (2), D.B. Clarke   *Try:* Ranson   *Conversion:* Hosen
Conversions: D.B. Clarke (3)   *Penalties:* Hosen (2)
Penalty: D.B. Clarke
Dropped goal: D.B. Clarke

Referee: Mr C.F. Robson (New Zealand)

NEW ZEALAND v ENGLAND 1963

Played at Lancaster Park, Christchurch, 1 June 1963
New Zealand won by 1GM, 2T (9) to 1PG, 1T (6)

England made few changes from the side which had lost the first Test: Sykes entered the team on the right wing (Ranson moving to the left to replace Dee) to win his first cap since 1955; and Perry moved to lock for Wightman to return as eighth-man.

The visitors gave their best display of the tour, losing unluckily in the dying moments of the game. The English forwards powered their way into the rucks, held their own in the scrummages, and outjumped the New Zealanders in the line-outs (where Davis, after dislocating a shoulder early in the match, returned from the treatment bench with one arm useless and proceeded to win endless possession with an heroic display of one-handed catching).

England took first use of a stiff wind but there was no scoring for 25 minutes. After Hosen and Clarke had failed to land points from penalty kicks, Connor made a telling break from the middle of the field, linked with Meads and Tremain, and McKay received a pass which sent him flying in at the corner. Hosen equalised five minutes later with a 35-yards penalty from directly in front of the goal.

New Zealand had forged ahead with a try by Walsh just before the end of the first half, but the second half was only five minutes old when England again drew level, this time with a spectacular try. An All Black kick sent the ball into the English 25 and the defending backs enterprisingly chose to attack. The ball reached Ranson who, gaining speed, stretched an already jumbled New Zealand team. At length the wing was forced to pass to Rogers, who kicked long for the goal-line. Phillips, showing a smart turn of pace, streaked upfield, gathered a bouncing ball and touched down in the corner.

England's forwards strove to keep the New Zealanders at a safe distance for the remainder of the match. Then, in the last moments, Don Clarke claimed a mark five yards inside his own half. The referee refused England a charge after a premature rush by several of the visitors, and the full-back landed a goal with, according to the *Christchurch Star*, 'The Daddy of All Kicks'.

NEW ZEALAND		ENGLAND	
D.B. Clarke	(Waikato)	R.W. Hosen	(Northampton)
D.W. McKay	(Auckland)	F.D. Sykes	(Northampton)
I.N. Uttley	(Wellington)	M.S. Phillips	(Fylde)
R.W. Caulton	(Wellington)	*M.P. Weston	(Durham City)
		J.M. Ranson	(Rosslyn Park)
P.T. Walsh	(Counties)		
B.A. Watt	(Canterbury)	J.P. Horrocks-Taylor	(Leicester)
D.M. Connor	(Auckland)	S.J.S. Clarke	(Cambridge U.)
I.J. Clarke	(Waikato)	P.E. Judd	(Coventry)
D. Young	(Canterbury)	H.O. Godwin	(Coventry)
*W.J. Whineray	(Auckland)	C.R. Jacobs	(Northampton)
C.E. Meads	(King Country)	A.M. Davis	(Torquay Athletic)
A.J. Stewart	(Canterbury)	D.G. Perry	(Bedford)
K.R. Tremain	(Hawke's Bay)	D.P. Rogers	(Bedford)
D.J. Graham	(Canterbury)	B.J. Wightman	(Coventry)
W.J. Nathan	(Auckland)	V.R. Marriott	(Harlequins)

Tries: McKay, Walsh
Goal from mark: D.B. Clarke

Try: Phillips
Penalty: Hosen

Referee: Mr J.P. Murphy (New Zealand)

AUSTRALIA v ENGLAND 1963
Played at the Cricket Ground, Sydney, 4 June 1963
Australia won by 3G, 1T (18) to 3T (9)

This was Australia's first victory in an international at home against an I.B. country since 1934. A crowd of 7,864 people watched a young Aussie side, inspired by the leadership of John Thornett, adopt an attractive approach to a match played in awful conditions. The home side played as if conditions were ideal and their commitment to open football brought handsome dividends in the form of four excellent tries. McMullen, at the base of the scrummage, had a perfect match, distributing the ball with efficiency and speed and timing his individual breaks with rare precision. Indeed, the performance of the two halves played a major part in Australia's fine victory. England, too, made a significant contribution to the match, scoring three tries after the Australians had established a winning lead.

At the start the home side bustled England off the ball in the wet conditions. After three minutes, Hawthorne, an exciting player at fly-half, skimmed through an opening to send Marks away and eventually Jones scored beneath the posts for Ryan to convert. Moments later, a kick across by Jones deceived the English defence. Sykes and Hosen failed to gather the ball and Walsham nudged the ball across the line to score at the corner. Ryan's place kick was perfectly executed from a wide angle.

The English defence was split again by a deft kick by Hawthorne, followed by a cross-kick by Boyce which put Heinrich over for the third (unconverted) try. Finally, six minutes from half-time, a move which fused the power of the Australian pack with the slick handling of their fast backs resulted in a try by Davis. Ryan converted to close Australia's account.

England at last found their form and three scores followed. Before the pause, two kicks by McMullen were charged down near his line. From the first, Clarke slipped across on the narrow side of a loose maul; and seconds after Godwin crashed over. Then, three minutes into the second half, a rush led by Sykes paved the way for a try by Phillips. England's retaliatory gestures ended there and a watertight defence stopped the England backs for the remainder of the game.

AUSTRALIA		ENGLAND	
P.F. Ryan	(N.S.W.)	R.W. Hosen	(Northampton)
J.S. Boyce	(N.S.W.)	F.D. Sykes	(Northampton)
R.J.P. Marks	(Queensland)	M.S. Phillips	(Fylde)
P.A. Jones	(N.S.W.)	*M.P. Weston	(Durham City)
K.P. Walsham	(N.S.W.)	J.M. Ranson	(Rosslyn Park)
P.F. Hawthorne	(N.S.W.)	J.P. Horrocks-Taylor	(Leicester)
K.V. McMullen	(N.S.W.)	S.J.S. Clarke	(Cambridge U.)
J.P.L. White	(N.S.W.)	C.R. Jacobs	(Northampton)
P.G. Johnson	(N.S.W.)	H.O. Godwin	(Coventry)
L.R. Austin	(N.S.W.)	P.E. Judd	(Coventry)
J.M. Miller	(N.S.W.)	J.E. Owen	(Coventry)
*J.E. Thornett	(N.S.W.)	D.G. Perry	(Bedford)
E.L. Heinrich	(N.S.W.)	D.P. Rogers	(Bedford)
J.F. O'Gorman	(N.S.W.)	B.J. Wightman	(Coventry)
G.V. Davis	(N.S.W.)	V.R. Marriott	(Harlequins)

Tries: Davis, Heinrich, Jones, Walsham
Conversions: Ryan (3)

Tries: Clarke, Godwin, Phillips

Referee: Mr C.F. Ferguson (Australia)

ENGLAND v NEW ZEALAND 1964

Played at Twickenham, London, 4 January 1964
New Zealand won by 1G, 2PG, 1T (14) to Nil

Many of the players in this match had met twice in the summer of 1963, and following their impressive performance in the Christchurch Test England entered this match with well-placed confidence. However, from the beginning of the match New Zealand outplayed the home side, and at the end registered the largest winning margin at Twickenham since internationals had commenced there in 1910.

65,000 people were present on a foggy day to see a gloomy match. The Laws of the game induced many dull matches at this time, and the definitions of off-side lines, at both scrums and line-outs, did much to destroy Rugby as an attractive, open spectacle. Even Wilson Whineray's competent all-round team adopted a very flat defence at set-pieces and, as a result, England's fitful attempts to launch attacking handling movements were frustrated.

Don Clarke gave New Zealand an early lead with penalty goals from 46 yards and 24 yards after five minutes and 22 minutes, respectively. Then, on the half-hour, a characteristic drive by Tremain and Whineray from a line-out ended with a try by Caulton after the English backs had been tied in to cover the forward threat. For a change, Clarke failed to convert, but New Zealand's nine-points lead at the interval gave them a safe buffer. England began the second half with a rare attack, but a misguided pass by Horrocks-Taylor was intercepted by the dashing Caulton. The Wellington flyer made considerable ground before unloading to Graham, who took play to the English 25. Meads took the next pass and powered through to score beneath the English goal. Clarke converted, to give the All Blacks an unassailable lead, and close marking and safety-first tactics by the visitors kept England at bay for the remainder of the match.

ENGLAND		NEW ZEALAND	
*J.G. Willcox	(Harlequins)	D.B. Clarke	(Waikato)
M.S. Phillips	(Fylde)	M.J. Dick	(Auckland)
M.P. Weston	(Durham City)	P.F. Little	(Auckland)
†R.D. Sangwin	(Hull & E.R.)	R.W. Caulton	(Wellington)
J. Roberts	(Sale)		
		D.A. Arnold	(Canterbury)
J.P. Horrocks-Taylor	(Middlesbrough)	B.A. Watt	(Canterbury)
S.J.S. Clarke	(Cambridge U.)	K.C. Briscoe	(Taranaki)
P.E. Judd	(Coventry)	K.F. Gray	(Wellington)
H.O. Godwin	(Coventry)	D. Young	(Canterbury)
N.J. Drake-Lee	(Cambridge U.)	*W.J. Whineray	(Auckland)
A.M. Davis	(Torquay Athletic)	A.J. Stewart	(Canterbury)
J.E. Owen	(Coventry)	C.E. Meads	(King Country)
V.R. Marriott	(Harlequins)	K.R. Tremain	(Hawke's Bay)
D.G. Perry	(Bedford)	B.J. Lochore	(Wairarapa)
D.P. Rogers	(Bedford)	D.J. Graham	(Canterbury)

Tries: Caulton, Meads
Conversion: Clarke
Penalties: Clarke (2)

Referee: Mr D.C.J. McMahon (Scotland)

ENGLAND v WALES 1964

Played at Twickenham, London, 18 January 1964
Drawn: England 2T (6), Wales 2T (6)

The two sides met with mediocre performances against the All Blacks behind them. Conditions were ideal and critics had the satisfaction of reporting a match free from penalty goals.

The English forwards made a storming start and, after only two minutes, a quick service to Horrocks-Taylor gave the fly-half just enough time to place a teasing kick to the left corner. The Welsh full-back failed to gather the ball cleanly and Ranson was over in a flash for a try. Four minutes later, another Welsh lapse cost the visitors a blind-side try. From a similar position, Horrocks-Taylor gained possession and made some ground on the narrow side before passing inside to Rogers, who had broken swiftly from the set-scrum. Perry was at hand to score, but Willcox failed to convert and then missed a reasonable chance to land penalty points. Wales could thus count themselves fortunate not to be 13 points behind after the first 15 minutes.

Wales slowly sorted our their blind-side difficulties and after Hodgson, with a penalty attempt, and Watkins, with a drop at goal, had given Welsh supporters something to cheer, the nimble fly-half cut out a small opening which Jones and Bradshaw made good use of to send Bebb haring over in the corner. An improving Welsh pack took a hold on the game in the second half and the anticipated equaliser came after only ten minutes. Watkins misdirected a drop at goal, but the kick foxed the English defence and, in the follow-up, Jones snatched the ball which a flustered Phillips had tried to gather in vain. Bebb was there to take the vital pass and score in the corner.

As time ran out for both sides, both Willcox and Grahame Hodgson missed with penalty shots at goal. Poor Hodgson sliced his kick from under the goal posts in the closing seconds of the match – a feat long remembered in the Valleys!

ENGLAND		WALES	
*J.G. Willcox	(Harlequins)	G.T.R. Hodgson	(Neath)
M.S. Phillips	(Fylde)	D. Weaver	(Swansea)
M.P. Weston	(Durham City)	D.K. Jones	(Llanelli/Oxford U.)
R.D. Sangwin	(Hull & E.R.)	K. Bradshaw	(Bridgend)
J.M. Ranson	(Rosslyn Park)	D.I.E. Bebb	(Swansea)
J.P. Horrocks-Taylor	(Middlesbrough)	D. Watkins	(Newport)
S.J.S. Clarke	(Cambridge U.)	*D.C.T. Rowlands	(Pontypool)
C.R. Jacobs	(Northampton)	D. Williams	(Ebbw Vale)
S.A.M. Hodgson	(Durham City)	N.R. Gale	(Llanelli)
N.J. Drake-Lee	(Cambridge U.)	L.J. Cunningham	(Aberavon)
A.M. Davis	(Torquay Athletic)	B. Price	(Newport)
†R.E. Rowell	(Leicester)	B.E. Thomas	(Neath)
†P.J. Ford	(Gloucester)	J.T. Mantle	(Loughborough C./Newport)
D.G. Perry	(Bedford)	A.E.I. Pask	(Abertillery)
D.P. Rogers	(Bedford)	A. Thomas	(Newport)

Tries: Perry, Ranson

Tries: Bebb (2)

Referee: Mr K.D. Kelleher (Ireland)

ENGLAND v IRELAND 1964

Played at Twickenham, London, 8 February 1964
Ireland won by 3G, 1T (18) to 1G (5)

England and Ireland joined in one of the finest matches seen at Twickenham. Five tries were scored, and there were no penalty goals to poison the final scoreline.

The English started furiously, as they had against Wales, and during the first 20 minutes their play in the tight more than held the lively Irish forwards. Brophy made several vivacious breaks for England, but his jinking and darting tended to isolate his centres and much of his enterprise was lost by running back into the forwards. In the line-outs and mauls, Ireland gained swift possession which the new fly-half, Gibson, after a reserved start to the match, utilised with promising imagination. Lacking the flamboyance of Brophy, Gibson preferred to ghost his way through gaps and his exquisite timing made him an 'inconspicuous menace' each time he had the ball. In fact, it was an intricate movement between the Irish halves which opened the path for Murphy to score just before the interval.

Ten minutes into the second half, a zippy run by Brophy gave the England centres an opportunity to contribute to this fast, open game. Weston supported the fly-half to send Rogers speeding over for a try which Willcox converted. The play became more and more intoxicating: players from both sides joined in the spirit of the occasion, with Ireland deriving greater benefits from the second phase. Flynn charged down a punt by Brophy to cross for a try, Kiernan converting; and then inspired running by Gibson from his own 25 created an opening in midfield. Scissors moves between Gibson and Walsh, and then Walsh and Casey, totally beguiled the English defence and Casey completed a memorable try. Ireland, for a while, were reduced to 13 men – Gibson and Fortune departing – but Kelly took over from Gibson as chief magician and one of his runs from deep inside Irish territory, during which he twice deceived gravity to stay on his feet, put Flynn clear. Despite a brave run by Weston, Flynn was able to run around behind the posts. Kiernan's place-kicking augmented Ireland's total to 18 points.

ENGLAND		IRELAND	
*J.G. Willcox	(Harlequins)	T.J. Kiernan	(Cork Const.)
A.M. Underwood	(Exeter)	P.J. Casey	(U.C. Dublin)
M.S. Phillips	(Fylde)	J.C. Walsh	(U.C. Cork)
M.P. Weston	(Durham City)	M.K. Flynn	(Wanderers)
J.M. Ranson	(Rosslyn Park)	J.J. Fortune	(Clontarf)
†T.J. Brophy	(Liverpool)	C.M.H. Gibson	(Cambridge U.)
S.J.S. Clarke	(Blackheath)	J.C. Kelly	(U.C. Dublin)
C.R. Jacobs	(Northampton)	M.P. O'Callaghan	(London Irish)
H.O. Godwin	(Coventry)	A.R. Dawson	(Wanderers)
N.J. Drake-Lee	(Cambridge U.)	R.J. McLoughlin	(Gosforth)
†C.M. Payne	(Harlequins)	W.J. McBride	(Ballymena)
A.M. Davis	(Torquay Athletic)	*W.A. Mulcahy	(Bective Rangers)
P.J. Ford	(Gloucester)	E.P. McGuire	(U.C. Galway)
D.G. Perry	(Bedford)	M.G. Culliton	(Wanderers)
D.P. Rogers	(Bedford)	N.A.A. Murphy	(Cork Const.)

Try: Rogers
Conversion: Willcox

Tries: Flynn (2), Casey, Murphy
Conversions: Kiernan (3)

Referee: Mr D.G. Walters (Wales)

FRANCE v ENGLAND 1964
Played at Stade Colombes, Paris, 22 February 1964
England won by 1PG, 1T (6) to 1T (3)

England made several changes from the fifteen outplayed at Twickenham by Ireland, and Jacobs succeeded Willcox as captain. Thus relieved, Willcox played a prominent part in England's defence, tackling and positioning himself with precision. France, too, had made several changes following a convincing defeat at the hands of the All Blacks, and even Albaladejo, the famous French fly-half, had lost his place to a young 24-year-old from Agen.

Hosen, playing in the unaccustomed position of right wing, scared the French crowd with two 50-yards penalty goal attempts early in the match, and eventually put his side into the lead with a kick from the French 25, ten yards in from touch. The English forwards played soundly in the tight and loose, with Godwin winning the tight-head competition by 6–0. Smith nursed his pack with intelligent tactical kicking and Brophy kicked well in defence, although he was more diffident in attack than he had been at Twickenham a fortnight earlier.

France equalised before half-time, but a forceful break by the new man, Peart, put Hosen clear down the wing. A pass to Phillips was perfectly timed and the Fylde centre crossed for the deciding score of the match. As the French effort waned towards the end of the game, their supporters, disillusioned with the selectors, jeered loudly and clamoured for the resignation of Mr Lerou, the chairman of the selection panel.

FRANCE		ENGLAND	
C. Lacaze	(Angoulême)	J.G. Willcox	(Harlequins)
J. Gachassin	(Lourdes)	R.W. Hosen	(Northampton)
A. Boniface	(Mont-de-Marsan)	M.S. Phillips	(Fylde)
J. Piqué	(Pau)	M.P. Weston	(Durham City)
C. Darrouy	(Mont-de-Marsan)	J.M. Ranson	(Rosslyn Park)
J.C. Hiquet	(Agen)	T.J. Brophy	(Liverpool)
J.C. Lasserre	(Dax)	S.R. Smith	(Richmond)
J.B. Amestoy	(Mont-de-Marsan)	*C.R. Jacobs	(Northampton)
J. de Gregorio	(Grenoble)	H.O. Godwin	(Coventry)
J. Bayardon	(Chalon)	†D.F.B. Wrench	(Harlequins)
J. le Droff	(Auch)	C.M. Payne	(Harlequins)
B. Dauga	(Mont-de-Marsan)	A.M. Davis	(Torquay Athletic)
M. Crauste	(Lourdes)	P.J. Ford	(Gloucester)
*J. Fabre	(Toulouse)	†T.G.A.H. Peart	(Hartlepool Rovers)
A. Herrero	(Toulon)	D.P. Rogers	(Bedford)

Try: Darrouy

Try: Phillips   *Penalty:* Hosen

Referee: Mr D.G. Walters (Wales)

SCOTLAND v ENGLAND 1964
Played at Murrayfield, Edinburgh, 21 March 1964
Scotland won by 3G (15) to 1PG, 1T (6)

Scotland thoroughly deserved a victory which gave them the Calcutta Cup for the first time since 1950. A drawn match at Cardiff between Wales and France, on the same day, allowed the Scots to feature at the top of the Championship (with Wales) for the first time in 26 years.

Scotland's memorable victory was due to a committed forward effort which enabled the backs to create scoring opportunities. In addition, a fine performance by the back row of Telfer, Fisher and Glasgow placed the English halves under extreme pressure, and as a result England had few chances to move the ball among the three-quarters.

There was no scoring for 30 minutes. Then, in a move from the base of the scrum, Glasgow swooped to register a try which Wilson converted into a goal. Just before the interval another forward effort, this time from a line-out, produced a try by Bruce, a break by Brown paving the way for this score with Telfer making the important pass. Hosen landed penalty points at the beginning of the second half, but England never threatened Scotland's forward supremacy. Telfer capped a good all-round display with a try near the end of the match, and England's only reply was a push-over try in the dying seconds of the game.

SCOTLAND		ENGLAND	
S. Wilson	(Oxford U.)	J.G. Willcox	(Harlequins)
C. Elliot	(Langholm)	R.W. Hosen	(Northampton)
B.C. Henderson	(Edinburgh Wands.)	M.S. Phillips	(Fylde)
I.H.P. Laughland	(London Scottish)	M.P. Weston	(Durham City)
G.D. Stevenson	(Hawick)	J.M. Ranson	(Rosslyn Park)
D.H. Chisholm	(Melrose)	T.J. Brophy	(Liverpool)
A.J. Hastie	(Melrose)	S.R. Smith	(Blackheath)
D.M.D. Rollo	(Howe of Fife)	*C.R. Jacobs	(Northampton)
N.S. Bruce	(London Scottish)	H.O. Godwin	(Coventry)
*J.B. Neill	(Edinburgh Acads.)	D.F.B. Wrench	(Harlequins)
P.C. Brown	(West of Scotland)	C.M. Payne	(Harlequins)
M.J. Campbell-Lamerton	(London Scottish)	A.M. Davis	(Torquay Athletic)
J.P. Fisher	(Royal H.S.F.P.)	P.J. Ford	(Gloucester)
J.W. Telfer	(Melrose)	T.G.A.H. Peart	(Hartlepool Rovers)
R.J.C. Glasgow	(Dunfermline)	D.P. Rogers	(Bedford)

Tries: Bruce, Glasgow, Telfer
Conversions: Wilson (3)

Try: Rogers
Penalty: Hosen

Referee: Mr R.C. Williams (Ireland)

WALES v ENGLAND 1965
Played at Cardiff Arms Park, 16 January 1965
Wales won by 1G, 1DG, 2T (14) to 1PG (3)

Changes in the Laws (including the definitions of new off-side lines at mauls and scrummages, and the introduction of the ten-yards-back rule at line-outs) designed to give backs the time and space to play a more expansive style of Rugby were introduced this season. The advantages of these changes had little opportunity for expression at Cardiff as Wales, adopting kick-and-chase tactics, overwhelmed an inexperienced England unit. The abominable conditions again drew attention to the inadequacy of the Arms Park ground for football in wet January matches, and prompted critics to clamour for a rotation of international fixtures in future arrangements.

Wales, relying on a nucleus of experienced forwards, had first use of a gusty wind, but, despite a superiority up-front, only a dropped goal from 30 yards, after 17 minutes, appeared on the scoreboard at half-time. English aspirations were frustrated immediately after half-time, though, when, from the kick-off, a rush down the left touch-line by the Welsh forwards took play to the English 25. A quick service to Rowlands and some efficient passing by the Welsh three-quarters saw the ball travel across the field for S. Watkins to score at the Taff end. Terry Price, a 19-year-old Llanelli full-back who played like a veteran, converted.

Rutherford kicked a 35-yards penalty after 20 minutes, but Wales ran in two further tries to settle the match. First, Pask picked up from the rear of a scrum in the right corner and deftly tapped the ball over the line for Morgan to claim a try in the twenty-sixth minute; then, a kick ahead by one of the loose-forwards caught the English cover out of position and the Newport wing touched down for a second time.

Frankcom, one of the new English centres, was the victim of a particularly vicious and totally unnecessary attack by one of the Welsh forwards, and displayed prominent bite marks in the dressing room after the match.

WALES		ENGLAND	
T.G. Price	(Llanelli)	D. Rutherford	(Gloucester)
S.J. Watkins	(Newport)	†E.L. Rudd	(Oxford U.)
J.R. Uzzell	(Newport)	†D.W.A. Rosser	(Cambridge U.)
S.J. Dawes	(London Welsh)	†G.P. Frankcom	(Cambridge U.)
D.I.E. Bebb	(Swansea)	†C.P. Simpson	(Harlequins)
D. Watkins	(Newport)	T.J. Brophy	(Liverpool)
*D.C.T. Rowlands	(Pontypool)	J.E. Williams	(Sale)
D. Williams	(Ebbw Vale)	†A.L. Horton	(Blackheath)
N.R. Gale	(Llanelli)	†S.B. Richards	(Richmond)
R. Waldron	(Neath)	N.J. Drake-Lee	(Leicester)
B. Price	(Newport)	J.E. Owen	(Coventry)
B.E. Thomas	(Neath)	R.E. Rowell	(Leicester)
G.J. Prothero	(Bridgend)	†N. Silk	(Harlequins)
A.E.I. Pask	(Abertillery)	*D.G. Perry	(Bedford)
H.J. Morgan	(Abertillery)	D.P. Rogers	(Bedford)

Tries: S.J. Watkins (2), Morgan
Conversion: Price
Dropped goal: D. Watkins

Penalty: Rutherford

Referee: Mr K.D. Kelleher (Ireland)

IRELAND v ENGLAND 1965

Played at Lansdowne Road, Dublin, 13 February 1965
Ireland won by 1G (5) to Nil

This was a disappointing match for the large crowd which attended. Many hoped that, with Brophy and Gibson again at the spearhead of their respective attacks, there would be a repetition of the spectacular open game seen at Twickenham the season before. But lightning does not strike in the same place more than once and, with the wind destroying play, neither side was able to get into its stride. On the day, Ireland were just worth their victory by one goal.

The Irish forwards gained a slender hold in the tight scrummages and line-outs, and the new Irish pairing of Young and Gibson, after a promising 'first night' against the French three weeks earlier, again gave a polished act at half-back. Young's tactical kicking and service were immaculate but Gibson tended to over-kick and neglect his three-quarters. Brophy, too, had an indifferent match and the English outsides had few privileges granted them in attack. Only Rosser, with occasional breaks in midfield, brightened England's performance.

The only score of an undistinguished match came 15 minutes from the end. Young broke rapidly from a scrum, stretching the English shield to the open side. Then a change of direction with a pass to Doyle deceived the English back row and Lamont gathered the final pass to score near the corner. Kiernan, with an excellent effort against an unpredictable wind, added two points from the side-line; but seconds later, he missed a sitter when Ireland were awarded a penalty. Nevertheless, Ireland held out to win by five points and the Irish full-back, despite this late place-kicking lapse, could look back on one of his best defensive matches for his country – his positional play was perfect.

IRELAND		ENGLAND	
T.J. Kiernan	(Cork Const.)	D. Rutherford	(Gloucester)
P.J. Casey	(Lansdowne)	E.L. Rudd	(Oxford U.)
M.K. Flynn	(Wanderers)	D.W.A. Rosser	(Cambridge U.)
K.J. Houston	(Oxford U.)	G.P. Frankcom	(Cambridge U.)
P.J. McGrath	(U.C. Cork)	†P.W. Cook	(Richmond)
C.M.H. Gibson	(Cambridge U./N.I.F.C.)	T.J. Brophy	(Liverpool)
R.M. Young	(Queen's U.)	S.J.S. Clarke	(Blackheath)
S. MacHale	(Lansdowne)	A.L. Horton	(Blackheath)
K.W. Kennedy	(Queen's U.)	S.B. Richards	(Richmond)
*R.J. McLoughlin	(Gosforth)	P.E. Judd	(Coventry)
W.J. McBride	(Ballymena)	J.E. Owen	(Coventry)
W.A. Mulcahy	(Bective Rangers)	C.M. Payne	(Harlequins)
M.G. Doyle	(U.C. Dublin)	N. Silk	(Harlequins)
R.A. Lamont	(Instonians)	*D.G. Perry	(Bedford)
N.A.A. Murphy	(Cork Const.)	D.P. Rogers	(Bedford)

Try: Lamont   *Conversion:* Kiernan

Referee: Mr H.B. Laidlaw (Scotland)

ENGLAND v FRANCE 1965

Played at Twickenham, London, 27 February 1965
England won by 2PG, 1T (9) to 1PG, 1T (6)

The French had led the Northern Hemisphere in Rugby tactics from the late fifties into the early sixties, and their reward had been several Championship titles. Now, their line-out ploys involving fast back-row men who ran and handled like three-quarters became part of the British game and in this match England showed that Britain had at last caught up with the French developments. Perry, the England number-eight, had a brilliant match, setting up many attacking moves from the base of the scrum and leading his pack by example. Richards gave ample support in the loose and, according to the *Rugby World* reporter, took ten strikes against the head. Weston, now at fly-half, gave an impeccable display of tactical kicking, exploiting the high kick into 'the box' most effectively.

There was an exchange of penalty goals in the first half: Rutherford opened the England account with an effort from a simple position in the nineteenth minute; and Dedieu, from 45 yards, levelled the scores after 32 minutes. France had entered the match as clear favourites but England's performance showed that such prejudice was misplaced. However, when Darrouy put France into the lead after 20 minutes of play in the second half, following an orthodox threequarter move, it looked as if England were about to face a defeat. Then, four minutes later, a 20-yards dash by Payne brought England on equal terms, and, in the thirty-sixth minute, Rutherford, as cool as a cucumber, kicked the winning penalty goal from the French 25 and 15 yards in from touch.

ENGLAND		FRANCE	
D. Rutherford	(Gloucester)	P. Dedieu	(Béziers)
†A.W. Hancock	(Northampton)	J. Gachassin	(Lourdes)
D.W.A. Rosser	(Cambridge U.)	G. Boniface	(Mont-de-Marsan)
G.P. Frankcom	(Cambridge U.)	J. Piqué	(Pau)
P.W. Cook	(Richmond)	C. Darrouy	(Mont-de-Marsan)
M.P. Weston	(Durham City)	J.P. Capdouze	(Pau)
S.J.S. Clarke	(Blackheath)	C. Laborde	(R.C.F.)
A.L. Horton	(Blackheath)	A. Gruarin	(Toulon)
S.B. Richards	(Richmond)	Y. Menthiller	(Romans)
P.E. Judd	(Coventry)	J.C. Berejnoi	(Tulle)
J.E. Owen	(Coventry)	W. Spanghero	(Narbonne)
C.M. Payne	(Harlequins)	B. Dauga	(Mont-de-Marsan)
N. Silk	(Harlequins)	J.J. Rupert	(Tyrosse)
*D.G. Perry	(Bedford)	A. Herrero	(Toulon)
D.P. Rogers	(Bedford)	*M. Crauste	(Lourdes)

Try: Payne
Penalties: Rutherford (2)

Try: Darrouy
Penalty: Dedieu

Referee: Mr R.W. Gilliland (Ireland)

ENGLAND v SCOTLAND 1965
Played at Twickenham, London, 20 March 1965
Drawn: England 1T (3), Scotland 1DG (3)

The Queen was present to watch England seize victory from Scotland's grasp with a sensational last-minute try by Hancock, the Northampton wing.

Heavy rain during the morning of the match had left the pitch soggy and after ten minutes the turf cut up so badly that runners found difficulty gaining any grip in the muddy conditions. Scotland adapted to the elements with greater ease than England, dominating the line-outs (where Stagg was literally head and shoulders above all else) and possessing more authority at half-back, where Chisholm and Hastie played with confidence if little adventure.

There was no scoring until shortly after the break, when Chisholm took his chance to drop an admirable goal. Hastie actually crossed for a try but the referee had spotted an earlier infringement. Scotland's hopes of recording a first win at Twickenham since 1938 were thus pinned on a small lead. Then, in the dying moments of the match, came one of Twickenham's famous moments. Richards pinched a heel against the head 15 yards from his own line and Weston kicked for touch. Whyte, who prevented Weston's kick finding touch, fielded the ball and set off towards the English line, seeking some support. At length he was held in the English 25; England won the ball and Weston passed to Hancock on the left. The wing then swerved round the Scottish loose-forwards, evaded an ineffective tackle by Wilson and raced 90 yards, hotly pursued by Laughland, to lunge over at the north end of the ground, just as a despairing Laughland completed his tackle. It was the longest run for a try ever seen in international Rugby and saved England's bacon.

Official cameramen were anticipating another Scottish score and grouped in the English half at the time of Hancock's run. As a result, few press photographs of one of the game's finest tries are available.

ENGLAND		SCOTLAND	
D. Rutherford	(Gloucester)	*S. Wilson	(London Scottish)
E.L. Rudd	(Oxford U.)	D.J. Whyte	(Edinburgh Wands.)
D.W.A. Rosser	(Cambridge U.)	B.C. Henderson	(Edinburgh Wands.)
G.P. Frankcom	(Cambridge U.)	I.H.P. Laughland	(London Scottish)
A.W. Hancock	(Northampton)	W.D. Jackson	(Hawick)
M.P. Weston	(Durham City)	D.H. Chisholm	(Melrose)
S.J.S. Clarke	(Blackheath)	A.J. Hastie	(Melrose)
A.L. Horton	(Blackheath)	N. Suddon	(Hawick)
S.B. Richards	(Richmond)	F.A.L. Laidlaw	(Melrose)
P.E. Judd	(Coventry)	D.M.D. Rollo	(Howe of Fife)
J.E. Owen	(Coventry)	P.K. Stagg	(Sale)
C.M. Payne	(Harlequins)	M.J. Campbell-Lamerton	(London Scottish)
N. Silk	(Harlequins)	J.P. Fisher	(London Scottish)
*D.G. Perry	(Bedford)	P.C. Brown	(West of Scotland)
D.P. Rogers	(Bedford)	D. Grant	(Hawick)

Try: Hancock   *Dropped goal:* Chisholm

Referee: Mr D.G. Walters (Wales)

ENGLAND v WALES 1966
Played at Twickenham, London, 15 January 1966
Wales won by 1G, 2PG (11) to 1PG, 1T (6)

This was not a match for the connoisseur: play was often indecisive and accurate place kicking proved the vital factor in a rather disappointing game. Wales had the match-winner in full-back Terry Price. His three successful kicks only served to emphasise Rutherford's miserable failures in this department – the Gloucester man having an off-day, missing with two kickable penalties, and a drop at goal, in the first 15 minutes of the game. It would be fair to credit Wales with a deserved victory, for their pack heeled the ball more quickly in the tight than a somewhat sluggish English eight. Lewis, the new Welsh scrum-half, played competently and gave his outsides a stream of fast passes. By contrast, the slowness of the English heeling restricted the home backs to fitful attacks which the Welsh back row were eager to suppress.

A large contingent of Welshmen were in the crowd to see Price open the scoring after 30 minutes with a penalty goal from in front of the posts, but a similar score by Rutherford, in the thirty-fifth minute, brought the sides level at the interval. Price regained the lead for Wales with his second penalty, this time from an angle, before a wily run by Ken Jones bisected England's defence and Pask appeared on the left flank to hurl himself over near the corner for a try. Price, with another beauty, placed Wales eight points clear. There was a plucky rearguard action by England in the last quarter. Poor Rutherford missed another penalty kick at goal and then Perry enlivened the proceedings by going over for a try from a set-scrummage. Again, Rutherford failed to add goal points and the match petered out with Wales holding on to a five-points lead.

ENGLAND		WALES	
D. Rutherford	(Gloucester)	T.G. Price	(Llanelli)
E.L. Rudd	(Liverpool)	S.J. Watkins	(Newport)
†T.G. Arthur	(Wasps)	D.K. Jones	(Cardiff)
D.W.A. Rosser	(Wasps)	K. Bradshaw	(Bridgend)
†K.F. Savage	(Northampton)	L. Davies	(Bridgend)
T.J. Brophy	(Liverpool)	D. Watkins	(Newport)
†J. Spencer	(Harlequins)	R.A. Lewis	(Abertillery)
P.E. Judd	(Coventry)	D. Williams	(Ebbw Vale)
†J.V. Pullin	(Bristol)	N.R. Gale	(Llanelli)
†D.L. Powell	(Northampton)	D.J. Lloyd	(Bridgend)
C.M. Payne	(Harlequins)	B. Price	(Newport)
A.M. Davis	(Devonport Services)	B.E. Thomas	(Neath)
†R.B. Taylor	(Northampton)	G.J. Prothero	(Bridgend)
D.G. Perry	(Bedford)	*A.E.I. Pask	(Abertillery)
*D.P. Rogers	(Bedford)	H.J. Morgan	(Abertillery)

Try: Perry
Penalty: Rutherford

Try: Pask
Conversion: T.G. Price
Penalties: T.G. Price (2)

Referee: Mr R.W. Gilliland (Ireland)

ENGLAND v IRELAND 1966

Played at Twickenham, London, 12 February 1966
Drawn: England 1PG, 1T (6), Ireland 1PG, 1T (6)

History was made in this match as Mr B. Marie became the first Frenchman to referee a Five Nations match. During the France–Wales match in Paris in 1965, the Irish referee had been injured and Marie, acting as touch-judge, substituted for the remainder of the game. As a result of his scrupulous fairness and obvious flair for the handling of international matches – qualities later shown by a long list of excellent French arbiters – he was invited to take charge of this match at Twickenham.

Unfortunately, the quality of play did not live up to the happy occasion. A prolonged forward struggle was aggravated by unimaginative punting by the two pivots and the back play was totally uninspired. The English forwards held a slight advantage at the line-outs, with Ireland having the edge in the scrummages.

Starting well, England were unlucky when Savage crossed the line and grounded the ball, only to see the referee signalling for a penalty to England. However, justice was done when Brophy's high kick caused Kiernan and McGrath some difficulty and new-cap Greenwood gathered the ball to dive in one foot from the flag in the fifteenth minute. Kiernan made amends in the twenty-third minute by punishing Greenwood for falling off-side 40 yards from the posts; but a good kick by Rutherford, from a similar distance, recaptured the lead for England two minutes later. These were the only scores of the half, though one of the Irish backs had misjudged a situation earlier when, with the English defence spreadeagled, a kick ahead might have been preferred to an attempt to pick up a loose ball.

Ireland attacked for most of the second half but 25 minutes passed before the equaliser was scored. Gibson, who had constantly tried to outwit the English backs with largely ineffective kicks, at last forced an error. Rudd failed to dispatch the ball to touch, Gibson held him and the ball spilled loose for McGrath to kick on and claim a try.

ENGLAND		IRELAND	
D. Rutherford	(Gloucester)	T.J. Kiernan	(Cork Const.)
E.L. Rudd	(Liverpool)	W.R. Hunter	(C.I.Y.M.S.)
T.G. Arthur	(Wasps)	M.K. Flynn	(Wanderers)
†C.W. McFadyean	(Moseley)	F.P.K. Bresnihan	(U.C. Dublin)
K.F. Savage	(Northampton)	P.J. McGrath	(U.C. Cork)
T.J. Brophy	(Liverpool)	C.M.H. Gibson	(N.I.F.C.)
†R.C. Ashby	(Wasps)	R.M. Young	(Queen's U.)
P.E. Judd	(Coventry)	S. MacHale	(Lansdowne)
†W.T. Treadwell	(Wasps)	K.W. Kennedy	(C.I.Y.M.S.)
D.L. Powell	(Northampton)	*R.J. McLoughlin	(Gosforth)
C.M. Payne	(Harlequins)	W.J. McBride	(Ballymena)
J.E. Owen	(Coventry)	M.G. Molloy	(U.C. Galway)
†J.R.H. Greenwood	(Waterloo)	N.A.A. Murphy	(Cork Const.)
D.G. Perry	(Bedford)	R.A. Lamont	(Instonians)
*D.P. Rogers	(Bedford)	M.G. Doyle	(Cambridge U.)

Try: Greenwood
Penalty: Rutherford

Try: McGrath
Penalty: Kiernan

Referee: Mr B. Marie (France)

FRANCE v ENGLAND 1966

Played at Stade Colombes, Paris, 26 February 1966
France won by 2G, 1T (13) to Nil

England were hopelessly outclassed. France gave a breathless display of fast, open Rugby with all the backs participating in a lively and interesting match. It was a stroke of genius which inspired the French selectors to play Gachassin at outside-half – all of his previous caps had been won on the wing – for the will-o'-the-wisp flyer from Lourdes gave a dynamic performance which energised the entire French fifteen.

Admittedly, England had severe problems. Perry tore a cartilage after 16 minutes and Hancock tore a hamstring just before the break; both continued but operated well below par. Further injuries to Rogers (a broken bone in the nose) and Horton reduced the efficiency of the English pack. But for all this, there could be no denying that France thoroughly deserved to win and would certainly have done so had England played at full strength for 80 minutes.

There was a fresh wind to contend with at the start of the match and England's aim was clearly to gain a winning lead by half-time. However, in the twenty-seventh minute, a drop at goal by the effervescent Gachassin struck the cross-bar and rebounded into the little fly-half's arms as he followed up speedily. He dived over for a try and Lacaze converted.

The English defence had been found wanting at the first try; another lapse, after 30 minutes in the second half, allowed Gruarin to pounce from short range and cross on the blind side for an unconverted try. In the final minutes, France moved into overdrive and Gachassin, with an arcing run, created an overlap for André Boniface to score one of the finest tries of the season. Lacaze completed the scoring with a conversion.

FRANCE		ENGLAND	
C. Lacaze	(Angoulême)	D. Rutherford	(Gloucester)
B. Duprat	(Bayonne)	A.W. Hancock	(Northampton)
G. Boniface	(Mont-de-Marsan)	†R.D. Hearn	(Bedford)
A. Boniface	(Mont-de-Marsan)	C.W. McFadyean	(Moseley)
C. Darrouy	(Mont-de-Marsan)	K.F. Savage	(Northampton)
J. Gachassin	(Lourdes)	T.J. Brophy	(Liverpool)
L. Camberabero	(La Voulte)	R.C. Ashby	(Wasps)
A. Gruarin	(Toulon)	P.E. Judd	(Coventry)
J.M. Cabanier	(Montauban)	W.T. Treadwell	(Wasps)
J.C. Berejnoi	(Tulle)	A.L. Horton	(Blackheath)
W. Spanghero	(Narbonne)	C.M. Payne	(Harlequins)
E. Cester	(T.O.E.C.)	J.E. Owen	(Coventry)
J.J. Rupert	(Tyrosse)	J.R.H. Greenwood	(Waterloo)
B. Dauga	(Mont-de-Marsan)	D.G. Perry	(Bedford)
*M. Crauste	(Lourdes)	*D.P. Rogers	(Bedford)

Tries: A. Boniface, Gachassin, Gruarin
Conversions: Lacaze (2)

Referee: Mr D.G. Walters (Wales)

SCOTLAND v ENGLAND 1966

Played at Murrayfield, Edinburgh, 19 March 1966
Scotland won by 1PG, 1T (6) to 1DG (3)

Defeat left England floundering at the bottom of the International Championship with only one point from four matches – their worst return in the competition since 1948.

The Scottish forwards were the architects of a sound victory. Stagg, Telfer and Campbell-Lamerton dominated at the line-outs; and in the loose, the verve and versatility of their back-row trio helped the home side to a large supply of second-phase possession. Blaikie was an accomplished full-back – an ample deputy for the injured Stewart Wilson – and his fielding and tackling upset English ideas that here may be the weak link in the Scottish defence. Weston, recalled at fly-half, had clearly been given strict instructions to test the replacement, for his incessant use of the high kick ahead overlooked the fact that England had, in Savage, one of the most powerful wings in the British Isles. The Northampton man was given just one run in the first half.

It was fitting that Blaikie should open the scoring after 29 minutes. His penalty goal from wide out on the left rebounded off the far post to give Scotland a lead at half-time. McFadyean brought the scores level after 12 minutes in the second half with a dropped goal, but the decisive try came four minutes later. Chisholm split the tight English defence with an exquisite run – the best of the afternoon – and the three-quarters handled swiftly to give Whyte a half chance. Somehow the wing wriggled through and the crowd greeted his try in the corner with rapturous applause.

SCOTLAND		ENGLAND	
C.F. Blaikie	(Heriot's F.P.)	D. Rutherford	(Gloucester)
A.J.W. Hinshelwood	(London Scottish)	E.L. Rudd	(Liverpool)
B.C. Henderson	(Edinburgh Wands.)	R.D. Hearn	(Bedford)
*I.H.P. Laughland	(London Scottish)	C.W. McFadyean	(Moseley)
D.J. Whyte	(Edinburgh Wands.)	K.F. Savage	(Northampton)
D.H. Chisholm	(Melrose)	M.P. Weston	(Durham City)
A.J. Hastie	(Melrose)	†T.C. Wintle	(Northampton)
J.D. Macdonald	(London Scottish)	A.L. Horton	(Blackheath)
F.A.L. Laidlaw	(Melrose)	W.T. Treadwell	(Wasps)
D.M.D. Rollo	(Howe of Fife)	P.E. Judd	(Coventry)
P.K. Stagg	(Sale)	J.E. Owen	(Coventry)
M.J. Campbell-Lamerton	(London Scottish)	C.M. Payne	(Harlequins)
J.P. Fisher	(London Scottish)	J.R.H. Greenwood	(Waterloo)
J.W. Telfer	(Melrose)	†G.A. Sherriff	(Saracens)
D. Grant	(Hawick)	*D.P. Rogers	(Bedford)

Try: Whyte *Penalty:* Blaikie   *Dropped goal:* McFadyean

Referee: Mr K.D. Kelleher (Ireland)

ENGLAND v AUSTRALIA 1967
Played at Twickenham, London, 7 January 1967
Australia won by 1G, 3DG, 2PG, 1T (23) to 1G, 2PG (11)

Australia, on a long visit, reserved their best tour performance for this match with England in which they created a new record by scoring 23 points at Twickenham: the most conceded by England at the ground since the first international there in 1910.

The Australians ran and handled with aplomb and their halves, Catchpole and Hawthorne, were a joy to watch. The manner with which they worked the ball quickly out to the wings was to influence coaching for the next decade. Analysts were quick to note that Catchpole rarely employed the dive pass, staying on his feet at all times. The long half-back passing which pushed attacking back divisions halfway across the field – an obsession with British scrum-halves in the following years – was not part of Catchpole's repertoire. The success of the Wallabies' game relied on short, sharp passing which stretched defences until overlaps appeared.

For this match, Catchpole captained the visitors in John Thornett's absence, and the instructions to the pack were to ruck and maul the ball swiftly back to the outsides. After Hosen had given England an early lead with two penalties, a clean heel from a set-scrum gave Hawthorne enough time to drop a goal. More penalties, by Hawthorne and Lenehan, put Australia 9–6 in front before the sides changed ends.

Two more perfect heels early in the second half allowed Hawthorne to push his team nine points clear with two dropped goals, making him only the second player (following Pierre Albaladejo) to drop three goals in an international match. In the twenty-fifth minute he split the English defence with an astute cross-kick for Brass to hack the ball over the line for a try. England made a late effort and produced a try on the blind side of a scrum by Ashby, but the Aussies had the last word when Hawthorne sent Catchpole over for a try which Lenehan converted.

ENGLAND		AUSTRALIA	
R.W. Hosen	(Bristol)	J.K. Lenehan	(N.S.W.)
†P.B. Glover	(R.A.F.)	E.S. Boyce	(N.S.W.)
C.W. McFadyean	(Moseley)	R.J.P. Marks	(Queensland)
†C.R. Jennins	(Waterloo)	J.E. Brass	(N.S.W.)
K.F. Savage	(Northampton)	A.M. Cardy	(N.S.W.)
*R.A.W. Sharp	(Bristol)	P.F. Hawthorne	(N.S.W.)
R.C. Ashby	(Wasps)	*K.W. Catchpole	(N.S.W.)
P.E. Judd	(Coventry)	J.M. Miller	(N.S.W.)
S.B. Richards	(Richmond)	P.G. Johnson	(N.S.W.)
†M.J. Coulman	(Moseley)	R.B. Prosser	(N.S.W.)
A.M. Davis	(U.S.)	R.G. Teitzel	(Queensland)
†P.J. Larter	(Northampton)	P.C. Crittle	(N.S.W.)
J.R.H. Greenwood	(Waterloo)	J. Guerassimoff	(Queensland)
G.A. Sherriff	(Saracens)	J.F. O'Gorman	(N.S.W.)
D.P. Rogers	(Bedford)	G.V. Davis	(N.S.W.)

Try: Ashby *Conversion:* Hosen
Penalties: Hosen (2)

Tries: Brass, Catchpole
Conversion: Lenehan
Penalties: Hawthorne, Lenehan
Dropped goals: Hawthorne (3)

Referee: Mr K.D. Kelleher (Ireland)

IRELAND v ENGLAND 1967
Played at Lansdowne Road, Dublin, 11 February 1967
England won by 1G, 1PG (8) to 1PG (3)

The English selectors responded to the defeat against Australia with wholesale changes for the match with Ireland. New half-backs and completely fresh middle and back rows in the scrum were introduced, with Judd taking over as captain.

Ireland were most unfortunate to lose this match, for they had done more attacking than England during the first 80 minutes, only to lose by a run-away try in injury time at the end of the match. Gibson made several useful breaks for Ireland and nearly dropped two goals; and Kiernan, still one of the most respected citizens in international Rugby, crossed the line for a try which the referee refused, ruling that an Irishman had strayed off-side. England's opportunities were few and far between, though a penalty goal struck by Hosen was sufficient to give them the lead at the end of the first 40 minutes.

As ever, the Irish forwards were playing with great gusto and McBride was a dominant figure at the line-outs. In the tight, England managed to hold their own and Richards hooked with precision to supply his backs with some good possession. Finlan, the new pivot from Moseley, had a sound, if unspectacular, debut.

Ireland were awarded a penalty in the second minute of the second half and Kiernan placidly converted it into three points. As the game reached its conclusion, it was almost certain that the outcome would be a draw. At length, Ireland gained a promising attacking position near the English 25 only to be pushed back to half-way by a relieving kick from Finlan. Launching an attack from the ensuing line-out, a poor Irish pass was kneed on by McFadyean, and with Kiernan having joined the three-quarters the Irish line lay at England's mercy. A fortunate bounce presented the Moseley man with the gift of the afternoon and his pace took him at full tilt to the posts where Hosen made short work of an easy conversion.

IRELAND		ENGLAND	
T.J. Kiernan	(Cork Const.)	R.W. Hosen	(Bristol)
R.D. Scott	(Queen's U.)	K.F. Savage	(Northampton)
F.P.K. Bresnihan	(U.C. Dublin)	R.D. Hearn	(Bedford)
J.C. Walsh	(Sunday's Well)	C.R. Jennins	(Waterloo)
N.H. Brophy	(Blackrock College)	C.W. McFadyean	(Moseley)
C.M.H. Gibson	(N.I.F.C.)	†J.F. Finlan	(Moseley)
B.F. Sherry	(Terenure College)	†R.D.A. Pickering	(Bradford)
T.A. Moroney	(U.C. Dublin)	*P.E. Judd	(Coventry)
K.W. Kennedy	(C.I.Y.M.S.)	S.B. Richards	(Richmond)
P. O'Callaghan	(Dolphin)	M.J. Coulman	(Moseley)
W.J. McBride	(Ballymena)	†J. Barton	(Coventry)
M.G. Molloy	(U.C. Galway)	†D.E.J. Watt	(Bristol)
*N.A.A. Murphy	(Cork Const.)	†D.M. Rollitt	(Bristol)
K.G. Goodall	(Newcastle U.)	†J.N. Pallant	(Notts.)
M.G. Doyle	(Edinburgh Wands.)	R.B. Taylor	(Northampton)

Penalty: Kiernan

Try: McFadyean
Conversion: Hosen
Penalty: Hosen

Referee: Mr D.M. Hughes (Wales)

ENGLAND v FRANCE 1967

Played at Twickenham, London, 25 February 1967
France won by 2G, 1DG, 1PG (16) to 3PG, 1DG (12)

This was a thrilling contest with France gaining their third victory at Twickenham. From the start, when Dourthe ripped through with a glorious burst to score under the posts, this match kept the large crowd on tenter-hooks, both sides contributing to a classic encounter full of imaginative Rugby. A penalty by Hosen in the ninth minute and a dropped goal from Finlan after 15 minutes pushed England ahead but the lead was short-lived, for exhilarating play by the French backs culminated in a try by Duprat. Guy Camberabero, master of the kicking arts, converted gracefully, though a howitzer from Hosen, three yards from touch, reminded France that England, too, had an effective kicking machine ready to punish any offences within 55 yards of goal. A lovely dropped goal by Camberabero meant that France led by 13–9 at half-time.

The main talking point at half-time, however, concerned neither the kicking styles of the respective goal scorers nor the subtle strategies of the French backs. Judd, the rugged English captain, had been involved in a dubious incident in the first half when he crossed the French line after a tackle. The referee, who was in an ideal position to judge, ruled that Judd was held in the field of play before wriggling over the line. Since he had failed to play the ball, the referee awarded a penalty kick to France, but there were many who disputed the decision, and its bearing on the final score could have been crucial.

Facing a considerable wind in the second half, Hosen gave England heart with a 48-yards penalty before the main protagonist, Camberabero, made his bow with a 25-yarder when Finlan fell off-side.

The critics were delighted by the match and *Playfair* commented: 'Rugby football … gained enormously in prestige by the standard of the entertainment provided by both sides.'

ENGLAND		FRANCE	
R.W. Hosen	(Bristol)	C. Lacaze	(Angoulême)
K.F. Savage	(Northampton)	B. Duprat	(Bayonne)
R.D. Hearn	(Bedford)	C. Dourthe	(Dax)
C.R. Jennins	(Waterloo)	J.P. Lux	(Tyrosse)
C.W. McFadyean	(Moseley)	*C. Darrouy	(Mont-de-Marsan)
J.F. Finlan	(Moseley)	G. Camberabero	(La Voulte)
R.D.A. Pickering	(Bradford)	L. Camberabero	(La Voulte)
*P.E. Judd	(Coventry)	A. Gruarin	(Toulon)
S.B. Richards	(Richmond)	J.M. Cabanier	(Montauban)
M. J. Coulman	(Moseley)	J.C. Berejnoi	(Tulle)
J. Barton	(Coventry)	W. Spanghero	(Narbonne)
D.E.J. Watt	(Bristol)	B. Dauga	(Mont-de-Marsan)
D.M. Rollitt	(Bristol)	M. Sitjar	(Agen)
J.N. Pallant	(Notts.)	A. Herrero	(Toulon)
R.B. Taylor	(Northampton)	C. Carrère	(Toulon)

Penalties: Hosen (3)
Dropped goal: Finlan

Tries: Dourthe, Duprat
Conversions: G. Camberabero (2)
Dropped goal: G. Camberabero
Penalty: G. Camberabero

Referee: Mr D.P. d'Arcy (Ireland)

ENGLAND v SCOTLAND 1967

Played at Twickenham, London, 18 March 1967
England won by 3G, 2PG, 1DG, 1T (27) to 1G, 2PG, 1T (14)

The two sides played inventive Rugby and the result was one of the best matches seen at Twickenham for a long time. Scotland were only overwhelmed in the dying moments of the game, for with six minutes remaining the score stood at 14–13 in their favour. A flurry of scoring then permitted England to gain a comfortable winning margin.

Hosen had played second fiddle in the place-kicking stakes to Camberabero against France, but on this occasion his boot was the main difference between the fifteens. Not a particularly mobile player about the field, Hosen's kicking skills more than out-weighed any positional weaknesses. The scoring in a see-saw match went as follows: Hosen, penalty (3–0); Turner, try (3–3); Hinshelwood, try converted by Wilson from the corner (3–8); McFadyean, try from a break by Pickering, converted by Hosen (8–8); and Wilson a penalty to give the Scots an interval lead, 8–11.

In the second half England claimed the lead when, from a scrum, Pickering and Hearn worked a passage for Taylor to score and Hosen kicked the important goal. Wilson nudged the men in blue back in front with his second penalty goal and play remained tense until, with six minutes to go, Hosen kicked a penalty and the powerful Webb scored a try to pull England clear. The best move of the afternoon followed shortly after. Finlan intercepted the ball near half-way and ran 35 yards before passing to Hearn. As the centre was tackled he returned the ball to Finlan who, realising that McFadyean was only half covered, whipped one of those quick, simple passes which crowds love to see and which invariably clear the way for a try. Sure enough, McFadyean held the pass to touch down, virtually unchallenged, beneath the Scottish goal. Hosen converted and Finlan ended an excellent match with a dropped goal.

Webb, who made his debut in this match, had just said farewell to his brother, a member of the Australian touring team!

ENGLAND		SCOTLAND	
R.W. Hosen	(Bristol)	S. Wilson	(London Scottish)
K.F. Savage	(Northampton)	A.J.W. Hinshelwood	(London Scottish)
R.D. Hearn	(Bedford)	J.W.C. Turner	(Gala)
C.W. McFadyean	(Moseley)	R.B. Welsh	(Hawick)
†R.E. Webb	(Coventry)	D.J. Whyte	(Edinburgh Wands.)
J.F. Finlan	(Moseley)	I.H.P. Laughland	(London Scottish)
R.D.A. Pickering	(Bradford)	I.G. McCrae	(Gordonians)
*P.E. Judd	(Coventry)	J.D. Macdonald	(London Scottish)
S.B. Richards	(Richmond)	F.A.L. Laidlaw	(Melrose)
M.J. Coulman	(Moseley)	D.M.D. Rollo	(Howe of Fife)
J.N. Pallant	(Notts.)	P.K. Stagg	(Sale)
D.E.J. Watt	(Bristol)	W.J. Hunter	(Hawick)
D.P. Rogers	(Bedford)	*J.P. Fisher	(London Scottish)
D.M. Rollitt	(Bristol)	J.W. Telfer	(Melrose)
R.B. Taylor	(Northampton)	D. Grant	(Hawick)

Tries: McFadyean (2), Taylor, Webb *Conversions:* Hosen (3) *Penalties:* Hosen (2) *Dropped goal:* Finlan

Tries: Hinshelwood, Turner *Conversion:* Wilson *Penalties:* Wilson (2)

Referee: Mr D.P. d'Arcy (Ireland)

WALES v ENGLAND 1967
Played at Cardiff Arms Park, 15 April 1967
Wales won by 5G, 2PG, 1DG (34) to 4PG, 3T (21)

England journeyed to Cardiff in search of a Triple Crown, but departed with the name of Keith Jarrett ringing in their ears after the 18-year old Newport centre, playing as a full-back, had equalled a Welsh individual scoring record (set as far back as 1910) by totalling 19 points. The match was played in beautiful conditions, a sharp contrast to the wind and mud which usually greeted the sides at Cardiff in January. (The Australian tour had pushed the Wales–England game back to the end of the season.)

In a fascinating match, Wales threw away the inhibitions which had cost them four defeats earlier in the season and, despite accurate goal kicking by Hosen which kept England in the hunt for a long time, ran away to a golden victory. After opening the scoring in the ninth minute with a penalty which cannoned off the upright, Jarrett did not put a foot wrong. His kicking, the opportunism of Dai Morris, and a surprise dropped goal by Raybould from 35 yards, helped Wales to a 14–6 lead at the break.

Hosen landed a penalty at the start of the next half before Gerald Davies went through the English defence like a rapier for Jarrett to convert his try. England countered this with a try by Savage and a Hosen penalty: 19–15, and anybody's match. But there was to be only one hero in this drama and his moment came soon after. England won a line-out inside their 25 and McFadyean sought touch with a long punt towards the North stand. He had been England's champion against Ireland: at Cardiff he was to wear the badge of infamy, for his kick failed to reach touch. The ball bounced kindly for Jarrett to gather and run 50 yards along the touch-line for a try which brought the house down. To add insult to injury, the youngster converted to push Wales clear. These five points heralded another ten: Bebb scrambled over in the corner, four minutes later Gerald Davies scored again and Jarrett converted both. Hosen kicked a penalty before Barton ran over for the last score of the afternoon.

Hosen's four penalties brought his points tally for the season to 46, a new English record.

WALES		ENGLAND	
K.S. Jarrett	(Newport)	R.W. Hosen	(Bristol)
S.J. Watkins	(Newport)	K.F. Savage	(Northampton)
W.H. Raybould	(London Welsh)	R.D. Hearn	(Bedford)
T.G.R. Davies	(Cardiff)	C.W. McFadyean	(Moseley)
D.I.E. Bebb	(Swansea)	R.E. Webb	(Coventry)
*D. Watkins	(Newport)	J.F. Finlan	(Moseley)
G.O. Edwards	(Cardiff T.C.)	R.D.A. Pickering	(Bradford)
D. Williams	(Ebbw Vale)	*P.E. Judd	(Coventry)
N.R. Gale	(Llanelli)	S.B. Richards	(Richmond)
D.J. Lloyd	(Bridgend)	M.J. Coulman	(Moseley)
B. Price	(Newport)	J. Barton	(Coventry)
W.T. Mainwaring	(Aberavon)	D.E.J. Watt	(Bristol)
R.E. Jones	(Coventry)	D.P. Rogers	(Bedford)
W.D. Morris	(Neath)	D.M. Rollitt	(Bristol)
J. Taylor	(London Welsh)	R.B. Taylor	(Northampton)

Tries: Davies (2), Bebb, Jarrett, Morris
Conversions: Jarrett (5)   *Penalties:*
Jarrett (2)   *Dropped goal:* Raybould

Tries: Barton (2), Savage
Penalties: Hosen (4)

Referee: Mr D.C.J. McMahon (Scotland)

ENGLAND v NEW ZEALAND 1967
Played at Twickenham, London, 4 November 1967
New Zealand won by 4G, 1T (23) to 1G, 1PG, 1T (11)

Coaching was to become an important facet in international Rugby from the mid-sixties, and the 1967 All Blacks had, in Fred Allen, one of the first influential coaches in the modern game. He showed that it was possible to blend individual flair with an appreciation of the basic skills to produce Rugby played to a pattern without necessarily being stereotyped. This touring side, the first to undertake a shorter tour of Britain, was one of the most attractive and popular sides to come from New Zealand.

The staggering forward power of the New Zealand pack, allied to a refreshing commitment to fifteen-man Rugby, carried them to a secure lead of 18 points in the first 35 minutes.

A wayward pass by Gittings presented the All Blacks with an advantage after six minutes and Davis, making ground to his left, timed a perfect pass to send Kirton over beneath the posts. Birtwistle scored in the corner from a scramble in the twenty-fifth minute, and England's humiliation continued in the thirty-second minute when Laidlaw pounced at a scrum on the home line for another try. Then, from the restart, came the memory of the match. Lochore, standing off at a scrum, was fed by Laidlaw and drove purposefully towards the English 25 where a ruck developed. The ball emerged quickly and Kirton, with a shake of the hips and a burst of speed, deceived the English backs on the narrow side to score in the corner. With a fine kick, McCormick converted his third goal of the match.

Rutherford missed a sitter, but England took some consolation in entering the second half 5–18 down after a smashing try by Lloyd. A classic break through the centre by Davis set up a try for Dick in the third minute of the second spell and McCormick's fourth conversion restored New Zealand's 18-points lead. England came more into the match now, with the All Blacks easing up a little, and Larter kicked a penalty after 30 minutes before Lloyd completed a pleasing debut with his second try at the end of the match.

ENGLAND		NEW ZEALAND	
D. Rutherford	(Gloucester)	W.F. McCormick	(Canterbury)
K.F. Savage	(Northampton)	M.J. Dick	(Auckland)
C.W. McFadyean	(Moseley)	W.L. Davis	(Hawke's Bay)
†R.H. Lloyd	(Harlequins)	W.M. Birtwistle	(Waikato)
R.E. Webb	(Coventry)		
		I.R. MacRae	(Hawke's Bay)
J.F. Finlan	(Moseley)	E.W. Kirton	(Otago)
†W.J. Gittings	(Coventry)	C.R. Laidlaw	(Otago)
A.L. Horton	(Blackheath)	E.J. Hazlett	(Southland)
H.O. Godwin	(Coventry)	B.E. McLeod	(Counties)
*P.E. Judd	(Coventry)	B.L. Muller	(Taranaki)
P.J. Larter	(Northampton)	S.C. Strahan	(Manawatu)
J.E. Owen	(Coventry)	C.E. Meads	(King Country)
D.P. Rogers	(Bedford)	G.C. Williams	(Wellington)
G.A. Sherriff	(Saracens)	*B.J. Lochore	(Wairarapa)
R.B. Taylor	(Northampton)	K.R. Tremain	(Hawke's Bay)

Tries: Lloyd (2)   *Tries:* Kirton (2), Birtwistle, Dick,
Conversion: Rutherford   Laidlaw
Penalty: Larter   *Conversions:* McCormick (4)

Referee: Mr D.C.J. McMahon (Scotland)

ENGLAND v WALES 1968
Played at Twickenham, London, 20 January 1968
Drawn: England 1G, 1PG, 1T (11), Wales 1G, 1DG, 1T (11)

Keith Jarrett had sunk England at Cardiff in 1967; curiously it was his failure to place goals which contributed to their demise on this occasion. Twice his long kicks at goal were knocked-on by English fielders and Wales capitalised on these errors to score two tries and gain eight points.

The English forwards played admirably: they outjumped the Welsh at the line-outs and Gale was outhooked by Pullin in the set-pieces. But unimaginative tactics in the English midfield off-set the advantage gained up-front, and Wales were allowed to get away from this match with a draw they did not deserve. Finlan was England's villain, for his kicking not only deprived the backs of attacking opportunities but lacked the probing accuracy required to place the Welsh defence under any pressure.

England opened the scoring after seven minutes when a kick ahead by Lloyd caught the Welsh defence by surprise and McFadyean dived on the loose ball for a try. Then McFadyean dropped a kick at goal from Jarrett and Edwards dived over from the ensuing scrum. Next, a splendid run by the other scrum-half, Redwood, resulted in a try which Hiller, a recognised expert at place-kicking in the swirling Twickenham winds, converted into a goal. England changed ends nursing an 8–3 lead and looked set for a handsome win after Hiller again demonstrated his ability to land goals – a penalty this time – to extend the lead to 11–3.

Jarrett stepped up to take a 60-yards kick at goal with the game approaching its last quarter. His soaring kick missed the goal but Hiller blotted his copybook by failing to gather the ball. From a scrum, Wanbon picked up and crashed over for Jarrett to convert. Barry John added a dropped goal to level the scores and, despite England's abundance of possession from the set-pieces, there were no further opportunities for either side to win an exciting match.

ENGLAND		WALES	
†R. Hiller	(Harlequins)	P.J. Wheeler	(Aberavon)
†D.H. Prout	(Northampton)	S.J. Watkins	(Newport)
*C.W. McFadyean	(Moseley)	K.S. Jarrett	(Newport)
R.H. Lloyd	(Harlequins)	T.G.R. Davies	(Cardiff)
K.F. Savage	(Northampton)	W.K. Jones	(Cardiff)
J.F. Finlan	(Moseley)	B. John	(Cardiff)
†B.W. Redwood	(Bristol)	G.O. Edwards	(Cardiff)
†B.W. Keen	(Newcastle U.)	D. Williams	(Ebbw Vale)
J.V. Pullin	(Bristol)	*N.R. Gale	(Llanelli)
M.J. Coulman	(Moseley)	B.J. James	(Bridgend)
†M.J. Parsons	(Northampton)	M. Wiltshire	(Aberavon)
P.J. Larter	(Northampton)	W.T. Mainwaring	(Aberavon)
†P.J. Bell	(Blackheath)	W.D. Morris	(Neath)
†D.J. Gay	(Bath)	R. Wanbon	(Aberavon)
†B.R. West	(Loughborough C./Northampton)	A.J. Gray	(London Welsh)

Tries: McFadyean, Redwood
Conversion: Hiller
Penalty: Hiller

Tries: Edwards, Wanbon
Conversion: Jarrett
Dropped goal: John

Referee: Mr D.P. d'Arcy (Ireland)

ENGLAND v IRELAND 1968

Played at Twickenham, London, 10 February 1968
Drawn: England 2PG, 1DG (9), Ireland 3PG (9)

This match had little to commend it. Neither side managed to score a try, nor was there a constructive movement likely to produce one in the entire match. It was a scrappy engagement made worse by the loss of Redwood after 30 minutes with concussion. Bell disengaged himself from the pack – a curious decision for he had been the best forward on the field until that moment – and the resulting loss of weight caused the scrummages to slew and slide to such an extent that putting the ball into the tunnel became one of the most difficult jobs of the afternoon. Bell, in particular, was frequently penalised for putting the ball in crookedly; and on the few occasions that the English pack did win the heel legally, Sherry was around to hamper Bell's service with smothering tackles.

Kiernan was the outstanding personality in this dull game. His positioning and line-kicking were impeccable, and his place-kicking promised to win the match for Ireland. The first of his three penalty goals gave Ireland the lead in the first half before Finlan dropped a lovely goal. Kiernan and Hiller exchanged penalties before the interval, and Kiernan regained the lead with his third successful kick from 30–40 yards.

England did not save the match until the dying moments when a most unusual incident occurred. Sherry, under pressure in his own 25, deliberately threw the ball into touch in front of the spectators in the West enclosure. The referee awarded the penalty to England (Law 26) and Hiller collected the points with a grand kick.

ENGLAND		IRELAND	
R. Hiller	(Harlequins)	*T.J. Kiernan	(Cork Const.)
D.H. Prout	(Northampton)	A.T.A. Duggan	(Lansdowne)
*C.W. McFadyean	(Moseley)	B.A.P. O'Brien	(Shannon)
R.H. Lloyd	(Harlequins)	F.P.K. Bresnihan	(U.C.Dublin)
R.E. Webb	(Coventry)	R.D. Scott	(Queen's U.)
J.F. Finlan	(Moseley)	C.M.H. Gibson	(N.I.F.C.)
B.W. Redwood	(Bristol)	B.F. Sherry	(Terenure College)
B.W. Keen	(Newcastle U.)	S. Millar	(Ballymena)
J.V. Pullin	(Bristol)	A.M. Brady	(Malone)
M.J. Coulman	(Moseley)	P.O'Callaghan	(Dolphin)
M.J. Parsons	(Northampton)	M.G. Molloy	(U.C. Galway)
P.J. Larter	(Northampton)	W.J. McBride	(Ballymena)
P.J. Bell	(Blackheath)	M.G. Doyle	(Blackrock College)
D.J. Gay	(Bath)	K.G. Goodall	(Newcastle U.)
B.R. West	(Loughborough C./Northampton)	T.J. Doyle	(Wanderers)

Penalties: Hiller (2)   *Dropped goal:* Finlan   *Penalties:* Kiernan (3)

Referee: Mr M. Joseph (Wales)

335

FRANCE v ENGLAND 1968

Played at Stade Colombes, Paris, 24 February 1968
France won by 1G, 2DG, 1PG (14) to 1DG, 2PG (9)

France's victory put them three-quarters of the way towards a first Grand Slam, with Wales at Cardiff the final hurdle. But England gave the champions a run for their money on a sure ground in Paris. Weston, restored as pivot, gave England a much-needed incentive early in the match with a towering dropped goal; and the visitors, gaining a fair share of possession in the tight and loose, turned round at half time 6–3 ahead after Hiller and Camberabero had added penalty points.

Five minutes into the second half, Hiller coolly landed another penalty and England, now six points clear, seemed to be heading for a controlled and well-earned success. Up to that point the French backs had appeared rather sterile in their play, but at length a typically unpredictable move changed the whole complexion of the match. A bout of passing involving most of the French backs created a little space for Campaes to put in a tantalising kick ahead which bounced into the English in-goal area. Gachassin buzzed over to claim the try and Camberabero's conversion left England with a precarious one-point lead. The French, inspired by this score, now launched several more attacks but the English backs tackled like demons and two late dropped goals, by Camberabero and Lacaze, were necessary before France could enjoy victory.

England could reflect on a satisfactory performance, despite defeat, and if the bounce of the ball had been kinder at times France would have been a defeated side. On one occasion, too, England were extremely unlucky when Savage crossed for an apparently valid try, only to be recalled by the unsatisfied referee.

FRANCE		ENGLAND	
C. Lacaze	(Angoulême)	R. Hiller	(Harlequins)
J.M. Bonal	(Toulouse)	K.F. Savage	(Northampton)
J. Gachassin	(Lourdes)	†T.J. Brooke	(Richmond)
J.P. Lux	(Tyrosse)	R.H. Lloyd	(Harlequins)
A. Campaes	(Lourdes)	R.E. Webb	(Coventry)
G. Camberabero	(La Voulte)	*M.P. Weston	(Durham City)
L. Camberabero	(La Voulte)	R.D.A. Pickering	(Bradford)
M. Lasserre	(Agen)	B.W. Keen	(Newcastle U.)
M. Yachvili	(Tulle)	J.V. Pullin	(Bristol)
J.C. Noble	(La Voulte)	M.J. Coulman	(Moseley)
E. Cester	(T.O.E.C.)	M.J. Parsons	(Northampton)
A. Plantefol	(Agen)	P.J. Larter	(Northampton)
J.P. Salut	(T.O.E.C.)	P.J. Bell	(Blackheath)
W. Spanghero	(Narbonne)	D.J. Gay	(Bath)
*C. Carrère	(Toulon)	B.R. West	(Loughborough C./ Northampton)

Try: Gachassin
Conversion: G. Camberabero
Penalty: G. Camberabero
Dropped goals: G. Camberabero, Lacaze

Dropped goal: Weston
Penalties: Hiller (2)

Referee: Mr H.B. Laidlaw (Scotland)

SCOTLAND v ENGLAND 1968

Played at Murrayfield, Edinburgh, 16 March 1968
England won by 1G, 1PG (8) to 1PG, 1DG (6)

This match was the Wooden Spoon decider and Scotland, after leading by six points at half-time, collected Rugby's most unwanted prize in a second-rate match. The conditions were unhelpful and the tactics adopted by both sides were extremely dull. Weston persisted with high kicks to the Scottish 25 which were easily dealt with by Wilson; and the Scottish backs, by their fruitless crossfield running, wasted the line-out advantage gained by the enormous Stagg.

Wilson opened the scoring in the fourteenth minute with a penalty goal and Scotland extended the lead after a further 18 minutes when Connell, despite being held, dropped a most unusual goal from virtually beneath the English cross-bar. If Wilson had been able to convert any one of a succession of penalty kicks at goal, Scotland would have won the match before the interval.

The shortened line-out had been a common sight in the internationals of 1968 and with Stagg the principal threat to England in this department it was natural that England should rely on the long throw over the players participating in the line-out as a source of possession. In the eleventh minute of the second half England gave the text-book example of this as an attacking ploy. With Coulman standing off, about 30 yards from the Scottish line, a long throw was accurately placed for him to run onto and gather. A powerful, straight burst carried the burly prop to the line where, although tackled, he crashed over for a try which Hiller converted. Hiller completed a successful performance by landing the winning penalty goal.

SCOTLAND		ENGLAND	
S. Wilson	(London Scottish)	R. Hiller	(Harlequins)
A.J.W. Hinshelwood	(London Scottish)	K.F. Savage	(Northampton)
J.W.C. Turner	(Gala)	T.J. Brooke	(Richmond)
J.N.M. Frame	(Edinburgh U.)	R.H. Lloyd	(Harlequins)
C.G. Hodgson	(London Scottish)	R.E. Webb	(Coventry)
I. Robertson	(London Scottish)	*M.P. Weston	(Durham City)
G.C. Connell	(Trinity Acads.)	R.D.A. Pickering	(Bradford)
N. Suddon	(Hawick)	B.W. Keen	(Newcastle U.)
D.T. Deans	(Hawick)	J.V. Pullin	(Bristol)
A.B. Carmichael	(West of Scotland)	M.J. Coulman	(Moseley)
P.K. Stagg	(Sale)	P.J. Larter	(Northampton)
A.F. McHarg	(West of Scotland)	M.J. Parsons	(Northampton)
J.P. Fisher	(London Scottish)	P.J. Bell	(Blackheath)
*J.W. Telfer	(Melrose)	D.J. Gay	(Bath)
R.J. Arneil	(Edinburgh Acads.)	B.R. West	(Loughborough C./ Northampton)

Dropped goal: Connell *Penalty:* Wilson

Try: Coulman *Conversion:* Hiller
Penalty: Hiller

Referee: Mr D.P. d'Arcy (Ireland)

IRELAND v ENGLAND 1969

Played at Lansdowne Road, Dublin, 8 February 1969
Ireland won by 1G, 1DG, 2PG, 1T (17) to 4PG, 1T (15)

This was England's first match played under the new Australian dispensation law which restricted direct kicking to touch from outside the kicker's 25. In addition, the permission granted for replacements was first exercised in this season's Championship, and Ireland were grateful for the new law in the first half when Young was injured and Grimshaw substituted.

England blooded five new caps and showed eleven changes from the side which had played at Murrayfield the previous March. The match turned out to be a close, entertaining conflict with neither side deserving to lose. Ireland held a slight superiority in the line-outs, but England scrummaged solidly in the tight, so that both sets of backs were given ample opportunity to exploit the new law regarding kicking. Gibson spearheaded the Irish attacks, constantly probing for openings which the English defence were reluctant to present. And there was a welcome infusion of enterprise in the English ranks, with Duckham and Fielding looking particularly dangerous when given the ball on the run.

Hiller opened the scoring with a penalty from 30 yards but Bresnihan equalised with a fine try. Hiller and Kiernan took turns to kick penalties and moved the score to 9–9 at half-time. England regained the lead in the second half with a superb try. Finlan made an adventurous break from his own 25 and the ball reached Webb at half-way. Duckham popped up outside the wing and made a breathtaking dash for the corner.

McGann dropped a vital goal to bring Ireland level and in the seventeenth minute Murphy drove over, wide out, to give the home side the lead for the first time in the match. Kiernan kicked the goal. In the closing stages Hiller landed another penalty and, with English pressure mounting, Ireland were fortunate five minutes from the end when the England full-back just failed to put over a kick from 50 yards into a considerable wind.

IRELAND		ENGLAND	
*T.J. Kiernan	(Cork Const.)	R. Hiller	(Harlequins)
A.T.A. Duggan	(Lansdowne)	†K.J. Fielding	(Loughborough College)
C.M.H. Gibson	(N.I.F.C.)	†D.J. Duckham	(Coventry)
F.P.K. Bresnihan	(U.C. Dublin)	†J.S. Spencer	(Cambridge U.)
J.C.M. Moroney	(London Irish)	R.E. Webb	(Coventry)
B.J. McGann	(Lansdowne)	J.F. Finlan	(Moseley)
¹R.M. Young	(Queen's U.)	T.C. Wintle	(Northampton)
S. Millar	(Ballymena)	D.L. Powell	(Northampton)
K. W. Kennedy	(London Irish)	J.V. Pullin	(Bristol)
P. O'Callaghan	(Dolphin)	†K.E. Fairbrother	(Coventry)
W.J. McBride	(Ballymena)	P.J. Larter	(Northampton)
M.G. Molloy	(London Irish)	†N.E. Horton	(Moseley)
N.A.A. Murphy	(Cork Const.)	*J.R.H. Greenwood	(Waterloo)
K.G. Goodall	(City of Derry)	D.M. Rollitt	(Bristol)
J.C. Davidson	(Dungannon)	D.P. Rogers	(Bedford)

¹Replaced by C. Grimshaw (Queen's U.)

Tries: Bresnihan, Murphy
Conversion: Kiernan
Dropped goal: McGann
Penalties: Kiernan (2)

Try: Duckham   *Penalties:* Hiller (4)

Referee: Mr R.P. Burrell (Scotland)

ENGLAND v FRANCE 1969

Played at Twickenham, London, 22 February 1969
England won by 2G, 3PG, 1T (22) to 1G, 1DG (8)

One of the peculiarities of this season was the demise of France from Grand Slammers to Wooden Spoonists. A long string of defeats during a summer tour, and poor performances in the Championship against Scotland and Ireland, led the French selectors to despair, and the fifteen was completely reconstructed about four new caps and a fly-half whose chief experience at international level was at full-back. England took full advantage of a disorganised side and held the lead throughout the match to finish winners by their biggest margin over France since 1914.

Greenwood was injured playing squash the night before the match and so Rogers was given the captaincy. In addition, he surpassed W.W. Wakefield's 42-year-old record of appearances for England.

Despite their inexperience, France still won a share of the line-out ball and Dauga was outstanding in this department. The backs, too, began well with Lacaze looking comfortable at pivot. A typical French move produced a wonderful try by Bonal, after a 50-yards run, when the visitors were two penalty goals behind. Lacaze converted and even though Fielding made a jinking run to send Rollitt in at the corner before half-time, the French only trailed 5–11 when the sides changed ends.

In the second half Fielding created and scored a try from a punt ahead, and when Webb bullocked his way to the corner to make the score 19–5, it was all over bar the shouting. Lacaze dropped a goal but then wandered off-side on the French 25 for Hiller to kick his third penalty and score his 13th point of the game.

ENGLAND		FRANCE	
R. Hiller	(Harlequins)	P. Villepreux	(Toulouse)
K.J. Fielding	(Moseley/Loughborough C.)	B. Moraitis	(Toulon)
J.S. Spencer	(Headingley/Cambridge U.)	J.P. Lux	(Tyrosse)
D.J. Duckham	(Coventry)	J. Trillo	(Bègles)
R.E. Webb	(Coventry)	J.M. Bonal	(Toulouse)
J.F. Finlan	(Moseley)	C. Lacaze	(Angoulême)
T.C. Wintle	(Northampton)	*M. Puget	(Brive)
D.L. Powell	(Northampton)	M. Lasserre	(Agen)
J.V. Pullin	(Bristol)	C. Swierczinski	(Bègles)
K.E. Fairbrother	(Coventry)	J.M. Esponda	(Perpignan)
N.E. Horton	(Moseley)	E. Cester	(T.O.E.C.)
P.J. Larter	(Northampton)	A. Plantefol	(Agen)
R.B. Taylor	(Northampton)	P. Biémouret	(Agen)
D.M. Rollitt	(Bristol)	B. Dauga	(Mont-de-Marsan)
*D.P. Rogers	(Bedford)	M. Hauser	(Lourdes)

Tries: Fielding, Rollitt, Webb
Conversions: Hiller (2)
Penalties: Hiller (3)

Try: Bonal
Conversion: Lacaze
Dropped goal: Lacaze

Referee: Mr D.P. d'Arcy (Ireland)

ENGLAND v SCOTLAND 1969

Played at Twickenham, London, 15 March 1969
England won by 1G, 1T (8) to 1PG (3)

England started as hot favourites, for it was thought that their strong pack and attacking backs would be too powerful for an undistinguished Scottish fifteen. However, the visiting forwards, despite giving away much weight in the scrummage, had a good afternoon and supplied their halves with sufficient ball for the Scottish backs to make a tactical impression on the match. Lack of penetration in the centre limited the Scottish back play though, and penalty kicks at goal were their principal chances to gain points. In this department Blaikie and later Lauder missed easy kicks, and only Peter Brown, five minutes from the end of the match, with an almost careless style, succeeded in landing three points.

England retained the same fifteen which had defeated France, but an ankle injury to Fielding after 30 minutes compelled the wing to retire and Dalton came on as the first replacement used in an English team. The only score of the first half followed shortly afterwards when Finlan kicked high into the Scottish 25. Blaikie was unable to field the ball and Duckham picked it up to flash over the line near the posts. Hiller converted.

The speedy Duckham scored England's other try 12 minutes after the interval. Rollitt, a hard-working loose-forward, started a move which Spencer continued with a break through on the right to extend the Scottish defence. Dalton took a pass but his path appeared to be blocked until Duckham, on a loop, popped up on the outside and sidestepped Blaikie to score near the corner. The place kick was too difficult for Hiller.

ENGLAND		SCOTLAND	
R. Hiller	(Harlequins)	C.F. Blaikie	(Heriot's F.P.)
[1]K.J. Fielding	(Moseley)	W.C.C. Steele	(Langholm)
J.S. Spencer	(Headingley)	J.N.M. Frame	(Gala)
D.J. Duckham	(Coventry)	I. Robertson	(Watsonians)
R.E. Webb	(Coventry)	W.D. Jackson	(Hawick)
J.F. Finlan	(Moseley)	C.M. Telfer	(Hawick)
T.C. Wintle	(Northampton)	G.C. Connell	(London Scottish)
D.L. Powell	(Northampton)	J. McLauchlan	(Jordanhill College)
J.V. Pullin	(Bristol)	F.A.L. Laidlaw	(Melrose)
K.E. Fairbrother	(Coventry)	A.B. Carmichael	(West of Scotland)
N.E. Horton	(Moseley)	P.C. Brown	(Gala)
P.J. Larter	(Northampton)	A.F. McHarg	(London Scottish)
R.B. Taylor	(Northampton)	W. Lauder	(Neath)
D.M. Rollitt	(Bristol)	*J.W. Telfer	(Melrose)
*D.P. Rogers	(Bedford)	R.J. Arneil	(Edinburgh Acads.)

[1]Replaced by †T.J. Dalton (Coventry)

Tries: Duckham (2) *Penalty:* Brown
Conversion: Hiller

Referee: Mr C. Durand (France)

WALES v ENGLAND 1969

Played at Cardiff Arms Park, 12 April 1969
Wales won by 3G, 2PG, 1DG, 2T (30) to 3PG (9)

England were overwhelmed in the second half by a Welsh side setting out at the beginning of a glorious era of unparalleled success. The much-vaunted English pack was taken to pieces by the Welsh eight and the English backs spent most of the match dealing with wave after wave of Welsh attacks. J.P.R. Williams, the young full-back, showed how the new laws offered players in his position the opportunity to join in threequarter attacks, and Maurice Richards on the wing had a memorable afternoon scoring four tries.

There was a strong wind in England's favour at the start of the match and Hiller judged it well to give the visitors the lead with a penalty, but Richards' first try made the half-time score level at 3–3. Two penalties by Jarrett, and a try by John after a weaving run to the line, extended Wales to a 14–3 lead – the sure-footed Jarrett converting. Then, in the last 15 minutes, Richards completed staggering Welsh back moves to sink England without trace and Barry John added a dropped goal for good measure. Two touchline conversions by Jarrett and two penalty goals by Hiller completed the scoring in a match which few Englishmen will want to remember.

Wales thus gained the Triple Crown for the eleventh time and the first time since 1965.

WALES		**ENGLAND**	
J.P.R. Williams	(London Welsh)	R. Hiller	(Harlequins)
S.J. Watkins	(Newport)	†K.C. Plummer	(Bristol)
K.S. Jarrett	(Newport)	J.S. Spencer	(Headingley)
S.J. Dawes	(London Welsh)	D.J. Duckham	(Coventry)
M.C.R. Richards	(Cardiff)	R.E. Webb	(Coventry)
B. John	(Cardiff)	J.F. Finlan	(Moseley)
*G.O. Edwards	(Cardiff)	T.C. Wintle	(Northampton)
D. Williams	(Ebbw Vale)	D.L. Powell	(Northampton)
J. Young	(Harrogate)	J.V. Pullin	(Bristol)
D.J. Lloyd	(Bridgend)	K.E. Fairbrother	(Coventry)
W.D. Thomas	(Llanelli)	N.E. Horton	(Moseley)
B.E. Thomas	(Neath)	P.J. Larter	(Northampton)
W.D. Morris	(Neath)	R.B. Taylor	(Northampton)
T.M. Davies	(London Welsh)	D.M. Rollitt	(Bristol)
J. Taylor	(London Welsh)	*D.P. Rogers	(Bedford)

Tries: Richards (4), John   *Penalties:* Hiller (3)
Conversions: Jarrett (3)
Penalties: Jarrett (2)
Dropped goal: John

Referee: Mr D.P. d'Arcy (Ireland)

ENGLAND v SOUTH AFRICA 1969
Played at Twickenham, London, 20 December 1969
England won by 1G, 1T, 1PG (11) to 1G, 1PG (8)

For the first time England adopted a squad system, naming thirty players for this match four months before the game took place. The group met monthly under the direction of former international, Don White, and the team which was to gain England's first victory over South Africa included five new caps. From the South African angle this was not a happy tour, for they were constantly harassed by demonstrators protesting about the apartheid laws which operate in the sub-continent.

Visagie opened the scoring after six minutes when England were penalised near their 25 for a line-out offence, and six minutes before the interval Starmer-Smith made a frightful error of judgment near his line when trying to pass to Hiller under pressure. His pass was intercepted by Walton and Greyling scored at the corner for Visagie to convert. However, the Harlequin scrum-half made suitable amends for his mistake a few moments later. Breaking from a scrum, he linked with Shackleton and took a return pass before making a determined dash for the Springbok line. Despite aggressive defence by the South Africans, the strength of the English support was sufficient for Larter to score in the corner.

England were inspired by this try and played with renewed spirit after the break. Hiller landed a penalty in the twentieth minute of the second half, and as the excitement increased so did the power of the English pack. Eight minutes from no-side there was a line-out on the South African line and from an ensuing maul the ball trickled over the line for Pullin to claim the touch-down. Hiller, who left the field injured minutes before the end, converted to complete the scoring.

ENGLAND		SOUTH AFRICA	
*R. Hiller[1]	(Harlequins)	H.O. de Villiers	(Western Province)
K.J. Fielding	(Moseley)	S.H. Nomis	(Transvaal)
J.S. Spencer	(Headingley/Cambridge U.)	O.A. Roux	(Northern Transvaal)
D.J. Duckham	(Coventry)	[1]E. Olivier	(Western Province)
†P.M. Hale	(Moseley)	A.E. van der Watt	(Western Province)
†I.R. Shackleton	(Harrogate/Cambridge U.)	P.J. Visagie	(Griqualand West)
†N.C. Starmer-Smith	(Harlequins)	*D.J. de Villiers	(Boland)
†C.B. Stevens	(Penzance & Newlyn)	J.L. Myburgh	(Northern Transvaal)
J.V. Pullin	(Bristol)	D.C. Walton	(Natal)
K.E. Fairbrother	(Coventry)	J.F.K. Marais	(North East Cape)
A.M. Davis	(Harlequins)	A.E. de Wet	(Western Province)
P.J. Larter	(Northampton)	I.J. de Klerk	(Transvaal)
†A.L. Bucknall	(Richmond)	P.J.F. Greyling	(Transvaal)
R.B. Taylor	(Northampton)	T.P. Bedford	(Natal)
B.R. West	(Northampton)	A.J. Bates	(Western Transvaal)

[1]Replaced by †C.S. Wardlow (Carlisle)   [1]Replaced by M.J. Lawless (W. Province)

Tries: Larter, Pullin   *Conversion:* Hiller   *Try:* Greyling   *Conversion:* Visagie
Penalty: Hiller   *Penalty:* Visagie

Referee: Mr K.D. Kelleher (Ireland)

ENGLAND v IRELAND 1970
Played at Twickenham, London, 14 February 1970
England won by 2DG, 1T (9) to 1PG (3)

The abiding memory from this match is not of the quality of the football but the remarkable recall to the Irish side of Tony O'Reilly. The big Irishman had not played in an international since 1963 and was called into the side on the day before the match when Brown was declared unfit. O'Reilly, in fact, contributed the principal article to the official match programme – surely no other player can claim the distinction of introducing and playing in the same match? – but he had little to do during the game.

England retained the same fifteen which had defeated the South Africans but the Irish forwards played with such spirit and expertise in the first half that England were fortunate not to concede more than three points before the break – Kiernan landing a penalty. Stout defence by the English backs thwarted several promising Irish breaks, and intensive spoiling by the home pack prevented the visitors gaining clean ball for much of the time.

It was more than midway through the second half when Hiller frustrated Ireland with two dropped goals. The first was almost an act of desperation, for England had never looked like manufacturing a try. From loose play near touch and 45 yards from the goal, Hiller picked up the ball and took a hopeful swing at it with his right boot. The ball just reached the goal to level the scores, and two minutes later another pot from the same position proved a matchwinner. Near the end Shackleton weaved past some would-be tacklers to score in the right corner.

ENGLAND		IRELAND	
*R. Hiller	(Harlequins)	*T.J. Kiernan	(Cork Const.)
K.J. Fielding	(Moseley)	A.T.A. Duggan	(Lansdowne)
J.S. Spencer	(Headingley)	F.P.K. Bresnihan	(London Irish)
D.J. Duckham	(Coventry)	C.M.H. Gibson	(N.I.F.C.)
P.M. Hale	(Moseley)	A.J.F. O'Reilly	(London Irish)
I.R. Shackleton	(Harrogate)	B.J. McGann	(Lansdowne)
N.C. Starmer-Smith	(Harlequins)	R.M. Young	(Collegians)
C.B. Stevens	(Penzance & Newlyn)	S. Millar	(Ballymena)
J.V. Pullin	(Bristol)	K.W. Kennedy	(London Irish)
K.E. Fairbrother	(Coventry)	P. O'Callaghan	(Dolphin)
A.M. Davis	(Harlequins)	W.J. McBride	(Ballymena)
P.J. Larter	(Northampton)	M.G. Molloy	(London Irish)
A.L. Bucknall	(Richmond)	R.A. Lamont	(Instonians)
R.B. Taylor	(Northampton)	K.G. Goodall	(City of Derry)
B.R. West	(Northampton)	J.F. Slattery	(U.C. Dublin)

Try: Shackleton   *Penalty:* Kiernan
Dropped goals: Hiller (2)

Referee: Mr R. Lewis (Wales)

ENGLAND v WALES 1970
Played at Twickenham, London, 28 February 1970
Wales won by 1G, 1DG, 3T (17) to 2G, 1PG (13)

England, buoyed up by wins over South Africa and Ireland, approached the match with confidence and began at a terrific rate, playing fluent, open football. Shackleton judged the healthy breeze perfectly to put J.P.R. Williams under pressure with a kick in the ninth minute and Novak, a late replacement for Fielding, tackled the full-back deep in the Welsh half. England won the following maul smartly, Taylor appeared in the back line and Duckham, on the overlap, waltzed over with another man spare outside him. Hiller converted; Mervyn Davies flopped over for a try from the back of a line-out; Novak scored a try; and the sure-footed Hiller added a conversion and penalty goal. In all, England looked good value for a 13–3 lead at the interval.

Wales started the second half with an all-out attack on the English line. A careless lapse by the English defence allowed John to ghost past several players and claim a try from loose play, but disaster seemingly befell Wales after 20 minutes when their captain, Gareth Edwards, was injured and replaced by Hopkins, the man from Maesteg. Suddenly the large Welsh following on the South terrace came to life as, from a scrum ten yards from the English line, Hopkins broke to the blind side to send J.P.R. Williams through a brittle defence for a crucial try. Then, from a line-out near the English line, Hopkins gathered the ball to dart over for a try: a try scored by a substitute and awarded by a substitute referee. (In the commotion of a ruck just prior to the interval the French referee was unfortunately injured and at half-time retired to be replaced by the English touch-judge.) J.P.R. Williams, after careful preparations, kicked the vital conversion to place Wales one point ahead at 14–13. In the dying moments of the match Barry John sealed Wales's victory with a casually dropped goal from 35 yards.

ENGLAND		WALES	
*R. Hiller	(Harlequins)	J.P.R. Williams	(London Welsh)
†M.J. Novak	(Harlequins)	S.J. Watkins	(Cardiff)
J.S. Spencer	(Headingley)	S.J. Dawes	(London Welsh)
D.J. Duckham	(Coventry)	W.H. Raybould	(Newport)
P.M. Hale	(Moseley)	I. Hall	(Aberavon)
I.R. Shackleton	(Harrogate)	B. John	(Cardiff)
N.C. Starmer-Smith	(Harlequins)	*G.O. Edwards[1]	(Cardiff)
C.B. Stevens	(Penzance & Newlyn)	D.B. Llewellyn	(Newport)
J.V. Pullin	(Bristol)	J. Young	(Harrogate)
K.E. Fairbrother	(Coventry)	D. Williams	(Ebbw Vale)
A.M. Davis	(Harlequins)	W.D. Thomas	(Llanelli)
P.J. Larter	(Northampton)	T.G. Evans	(London Welsh)
A.L. Bucknall	(Richmond)	W.D. Morris	(Neath)
R.B. Taylor	(Northampton)	T.M. Davies	(London Welsh)
B.R. West	(Northampton)	W.D. Hughes	(Newbridge)

[1] Replaced by R. Hopkins (Maesteg)

Tries: Duckham, Novak
Conversions: Hiller (2)
Penalty: Hiller

Tries: Davies, Hopkins, John, J.P.R. Williams
Conversion: J.P.R. Williams
Dropped goal: John

Referee: Mr R. Calmet (France)/Mr R.F. Johnson (England)

SCOTLAND v ENGLAND 1970
Played at Murrayfield, Edinburgh, 21 March 1970
Scotland won by 1G, 2PG, 1T (14) to 1G (5)

England's forwards were unexpectedly outplayed by a lively and efficient Scottish pack, and the home backs prospered against an English side which spent most of the match on the defensive. Robertson was the spearhead of the Scottish attack and varied his tactics shrewdly, distributing the ball carefully to his centres and making his individual breaks with elegance.

Scotland led from the start. Peter Brown kicked a penalty goal from long range after three minutes, and in the ninth minute Robertson made an exhilarating run down the middle of the field to link with Frame, who sent Biggar, a powerful runner, over in the corner. Hiller, with four colossal place kicks, went near to landing penalty points, but Scotland were comfortably in control at half-time, leading by six points.

15 minutes passed in the second half before Brown stretched the lead to nine points with a penalty goal kicked with insouciance. What a contrast there was in the kicking styles of Brown and Hiller! England cast away the fetters of defence in the closing stages in an effort to save the match and they were rewarded with a spectacular try – the try of the season in fact – seven minutes from no-side. A short penalty near half-way resulted in Shackleton sending Spencer on a 60-yards dash to the corner and Hiller converted from a difficult angle. England's joy was short-lived, however, for West had to retire with a leg injury, and in the final moments of the match the irrepressible Robertson performed a scissors with Turner and the latter scored. Brown converted.

Replacement B.S. Jackson was the first England player capped direct from Broughton Park R.F.C.

SCOTLAND		ENGLAND	
I.S.G. Smith	(London Scottish)	*R. Hiller	(Harlequins)
M.A. Smith	(London Scottish)	M.J. Novak	(Harlequins)
J.N.M. Frame	(Gala)	J.S. Spencer	(Headingley)
J.W.C. Turner	(Gala)	D.J. Duckham	(Coventry)
A.G. Biggar	(London Scottish)	†M.P. Bulpitt	(Blackheath)
I. Robertson	(Watsonians)	I.R. Shackleton	(Harrogate)
D.S. Paterson	(Gala)	N.C. Starmer-Smith	(Harlequins)
N. Suddon	(Hawick)	C.B. Stevens	(Penzance & Newlyn)
*F.A.L. Laidlaw	(Melrose)	J.V. Pullin	(Bristol)
A.B. Carmichael	(West of Scotland)	K.E. Fairbrother	(Coventry)
P.K. Stagg	(Sale)	A.M. Davis	(Harlequins)
G.L. Brown	(West of Scotland)	P.J. Larter	(Northampton)
T.G. Elliot	(Langholm)	A.L. Bucknall	(Richmond)
P.C. Brown	(Gala)	R.B. Taylor	(Northampton)
R.J. Arneil	(Leicester)	¹B.R. West	(Northampton)

¹Replaced by †B.S. Jackson (Broughton Park)

Tries: Biggar, Turner	*Try:* Spencer
Conversion: P.C. Brown	*Conversion:* Hiller
Penalties: P.C. Brown (2)	

Referee: Mr M. Joseph (Wales)

FRANCE v ENGLAND 1970
Played at Stade Colombes, Paris, 18 April 1970
France won by 4G, 2DG, 1PG, 2T (35) to 2G, 1PG (13)

After a promising start to the season, England's hopes were submerged by a French side in such devastating form that they scored more points against England than any team in nearly 100 years of matches. The English selectors had reacted with a capriciousness often suspected of French selectors, naming six changes from the side beaten at Murrayfield. Most remarkable of all was the dropping of Hiller, the captain, for young Jorden, who had a baptism of fire; while the demotion of Davis from second row to the substitutes' bench was difficult to fathom.

The French backs and forwards passed irresistibly in combination and the incredible speed with which they performed their manoeuvres was wonderful to watch. The English backs had a torrid time trying to staunch the continuous flow of French attacks. England were overwhelmingly beaten in the line-out, and the recall of le Droff – previously capped in 1964 – increased the attacking opportunities available to the French in this department of the game.

Conditions were ideal; the weather warm. France led by 14 points at the break and a try by Dauga, converted by Villepreux, extended the margin between the teams to 19 points before England made a minor recovery. Taylor scored a try after an interception and Spencer crossed for Jorden, with his second conversion, to make the score 19–10. A Jorden penalty increased England's respectability but France found their second wind and romped away to that record score of 35 points.

FRANCE		ENGLAND	
P. Villepreux	(Toulouse)	†A.M. Jorden	(Cambridge U.)
R. Bourgarel	(Toulouse)	K.J. Fielding	(Moseley)
J. Trillo	(Bègles)	J.S. Spencer	(Headingley)
J.P. Lux	(Tyrosse)	D.J. Duckham	(Coventry)
J.M. Bonal	(Toulouse)	M.J. Novak	(Harlequins)
J.L. Bérot	(Toulouse)	J.F. Finlan	(Moseley)
M. Pebeyre	(Vichy)	N.C. Starmer-Smith	(Harlequins)
M. Lasserre	(Agen)	B.S. Jackson	(Broughton Park)
R. Bénésis	(Narbonne)	J.V. Pullin	(Bristol)
J. Iraçabal	(Bayonne)	K.E. Fairbrother	(Coventry)
J. le Droff	(Auch)	†M.M. Leadbetter	(Broughton Park)
E. Cester	(T.O.E.C.)	P.J. Larter	(Northampton)
P. Biémouret	(Agen)	A.L. Bucknall	(Richmond)
B. Dauga	(Mont-de-Marsan)	†G.F. Redmond	(Cambridge U.)
*C. Carrère	(Toulon)	*R.B. Taylor	(Northampton)

Tries: Bérot, Bonal, Bourgarel, Dauga, Lux, Trillo
Conversions: Villepreux (4)
Dropped goals: Bérot, Villepreux
Penalty: Villepreux

Tries: Spencer, Taylor
Conversions: Jorden (2)
Penalty: Jorden

Referee: Mr W.K.M. Jones (Wales)

WALES v ENGLAND 1971

Played at Cardiff Arms Park, 16 January 1971
Wales won by 2G, 2DG, 1PG, 1T (22) to 1PG, 1T (6)

Welsh Rugby was in its prime and an efficient system of coaching and squad training brought together a team of all the talents. The Welsh pack overwhelmed an inexperienced English eight and those devilish halves, John and Edwards, exercised such a tight tactical control that the English outsides had scant opportunity to show their prowess in attack. The Welsh three-quarters, revelling in the first-class service provided by their forwards and halves, scored all of the Welsh tries.

John started the ball rolling in the eighth minute with a lovely dropped goal, but a loss of concentration by the Welsh defence allowed Hannaford to pick up a loose ball and score a try to the left of the goal, two minutes later. Splendid back play created a chance for Gerald Davies, now playing on the right wing, and the brilliant wing slithered over at the corner for John Taylor to convert. Bevan scored the next try, before Gerald of Wales went over in the corner again, and Taylor, with another splendid left-footed place kick, added the conversion. Janion failed to gather a pass with the Welsh line at his mercy just on the interval, and England had no such easy chances later. Wales were more subdued in the second half. J.P.R. Williams and Rossborough swapped penalty goals before John, the man of the match, completed the scoring with his second dropped goal.

This was not an auspicious start for England's Centenary season, and their selectors were strongly criticised. Nevertheless, in the view of many eminent observers, this was the finest fifteen Wales ever fielded.

WALES		ENGLAND	
J.P.R. Williams	(London Welsh)	†P.A. Rossborough	(Coventry)
T.G.R. Davies	(London Welsh)	†J.P.A.G. Janion	(Bedford)
*S.J. Dawes	(London Welsh)	C.S. Wardlow	(Northampton)
A.J.L. Lewis	(Ebbw Vale)	J.S. Spencer	(Headingley)
J.C. Bevan	(Cardiff)	D.J. Duckham	(Coventry)
B. John	(Cardiff)	†I.D. Wright	(Northampton)
G.O. Edwards	(Cardiff)	†J.J. Page	(Bedford)
D.B. Llewellyn	(Llanelli)	D.L. Powell	(Northampton)
J. Young	(Harrogate)	J.V. Pullin	(Bristol)
D. Williams	(Ebbw Vale)	K.E. Fairbrother	(Coventry)
W.D. Thomas	(Llanelli)	P.J. Larter	(Northampton)
M.G. Roberts	(London Welsh)	†B.F. Ninnes	(Coventry)
W.D. Morris	(Neath)	*A.L. Bucknall	(Richmond)
T.M. Davies	(London Welsh)	†R.C. Hannaford	(Bristol)
J. Taylor	(London Welsh)	†A. Neary	(Broughton Park)

Tries: T.G.R. Davies (2), Bevan
Conversions: Taylor (2)
Penalty: J.P.R. Williams
Dropped goals: John (2)

Try: Hannaford
Penalty: Rossborough

Referee: Mr D.P. d'Arcy (Ireland)

IRELAND v ENGLAND 1971

Played at Lansdowne Road, Dublin, 13 February 1971
England won by 3PG (9) to 2T (6)

England made two changes from the fifteen defeated in Cardiff and, most significantly, recalled Bob Hiller at full-back. The big Harlequin turned this game in England's favour, his three first-half penalty goals sinking two Irish tries. Ireland had good reason to fear Hiller, for in the matches since 1968 the Englishman had landed nine penalties and two dropped goals.

The Irish forwards played well and won enough ball to give their backs plenty of chances to win the match. But sound defence by the English backs and a failure to land goals prevented Ireland from gaining victory.

Hiller's first penalty came after ten minutes and was a gigantic effort from 50 yards. Then, from an English attack, Ireland equalised. A promising English move midway between the Irish 25 and half-way featured Wright. The fly-half was moving to his right with two men outside him and only Grant to beat, but his pass to Hiller was intercepted by the Irish wing, who dashed 75 yards to score despite a frantic chase by Duckham. Many observers thought that the referee's interpretation of the readjustment law was charitable to the Irish cause, but few could deny that Ireland deserved this score. Hiller's two other penalties, one from in front of the posts and the other from a long distance, gave England a 9–3 lead at the break.

In the second half Duggan just beat the English defence for a try after the best passing movement of the game.

IRELAND		ENGLAND	
B.J. O'Driscoll	(Manchester)	R. Hiller	(Harlequins)
A.T.A. Duggan	(Lansdowne)	J.P.A.G. Janion	(Bedford)
F.P.K. Bresnihan	(London Irish)	*J.S. Spencer	(Headingley)
*C.M.H. Gibson	(N.I.F.C.)	C.S. Wardlow	(Northampton)
E.L. Grant	(C.I.Y.M.S.)	D.J. Duckham	(Coventry)
B.J. McGann	(Cork Const.)	I.D. Wright	(Northampton)
R.M. Young	(Collegians)	J.J. Page	(Bedford)
R.J. McLoughlin	(Blackrock College)	D.L. Powell	(Northampton)
K.W. Kennedy	(London Irish)	J.V. Pullin	(Bristol)
J.F. Lynch	(St Mary's College)	K.E. Fairbrother	(Coventry)
W.J. McBride	(Ballymena)	N.E. Horton	(Moseley)
M.G. Molloy	(London Irish)	P.J. Larter	(Northampton)
M.L. Hipwell	(Terenure College)	A.L. Bucknall	(Richmond)
D.J. Hickie	(St Mary's College)	R.C. Hannaford	(Bristol)
J.F. Slattery	(U.C. Dublin)	A. Neary	(Broughton Park)

Tries: Duggan, Grant

Penalties: Hiller (3)

Referee: Mr M. Joseph (Wales)

ENGLAND v FRANCE 1971
Played at Twickenham, London, 27 February 1971
Drawn: England 1G, 3PG (14), France 1G, 1PG, 1DG, 1T (14)

Bob Hiller was England's saviour again, scoring all of his side's points in an exciting match full of incidents. Most of the enterprise came from the French and Cantoni, an unorthodox wing, tantalised the English defence with his sorcerous running. Bertranne, in his debut, looked an accomplished centre and crowned a beautiful performance with a try. Honours were shared between the packs but unimaginative kicking by Wright wasted much of the good possession won in the set pieces, while the impetuous French forwards often lost promising situations by incurring penalties.

Hiller kicked a penalty from 30 yards after two minutes but Villepreux equalised soon after with a similar score. Hiller's second penalty was followed by a fine try by Bertranne before England's best move of the match. Duckham, moving left, found Hiller up as extra man and accurate passing enabled Glover to swerve round Sillières. The Bath wing, who had come into the England side when Spencer was injured in practice, kicked ahead and Hiller beat Yachvili and Sillières to score a try. Hiller – who else? – converted and later kicked a penalty to place England 14–6 in the lead when half-time arrived.

France, who had started the match quietly, adopted a different attitude at the start of the second half. Bérot dropped a goal after four minutes and England relied on the aggressive tackling of Janion and Wardlow to hold the lively French backs. Only Cantoni managed to jink past the English defence and his try behind the posts, converted by Villepreux, tied the scores. This was Villepreux's second successful kick in eight attempts; Hiller, on the other hand, had four successes in six efforts at goal.

ENGLAND		**FRANCE**	
*R. Hiller	(Harlequins)	P. Villepreux	(Toulouse)
J.P.A.G. Janion	(Bedford)	J. Sillières	(Tarbes)
C.S. Wardlow	(Northampton)	R. Bertranne	(Bagnères)
D.J. Duckham	(Coventry)	J.P. Lux	(Tyrosse)
P.B. Glover	(Bath)	J. Cantoni	(Béziers)
I.D. Wright	(Northampton)	J.L. Bérot	(Toulouse)
J.J. Page	(Bedford)	M. Barrau	(Beaumont)
D.L. Powell	(Northampton)	M. Lasserre	(Agen)
J.V. Pullin	(Bristol)	R. Bénésis	(Narbonne)
K.E. Fairbrother	(Coventry)	J.L. Azarète	(St Jean-de-Luz)
P.J. Larter	(Northampton)	W. Spanghero	(Narbonne)
N.E. Horton	(Moseley)	C. Spanghero	(Narbonne)
A.L. Bucknall	(Richmond)	M. Yachvili	(Brive)
R.C. Hannaford	(Bristol)	B. Dauga	(Mont-de-Marsan)
A. Neary	(Broughton Park)	*C. Carrère	(Toulon)

Try: Hiller
Conversion: Hiller
Penalties: Hiller (3)

Tries: Bertranne, Cantoni
Conversion: Villepreux
Penalty: Villepreux
Dropped goal: Bérot

Referee: Mr R. Lewis (Wales)

ENGLAND v SCOTLAND 1971

Played at Twickenham, London, 20 March 1971
Scotland won by 2G, 1DG, 1T (16) to 3PG, 2T (15)

Scotland celebrated England's Centenary with their first post-war win at Twickenham. Conditions were ideal and a large crowd, basking in early-Spring sunshine, enjoyed an exciting game.

England opened the scoring after 15 minutes with a gem of a try. Janion fielded a kick ahead and set off on a side-stepping run which took him past several defenders. The ball then passed through the hands of Cowman, Taylor, Wardlow and Spencer, and Hiller popped up on the overlap to score in the right corner. An electrifying run by Rea, supported by Biggar and MacEwan, led to Scotland's equaliser soon after, and Peter Brown's conversion of his own try put the Scots in front. Hiller kicked two penalties before the pause.

Early in the second half Paterson was given possession by his pack deep in England's half, and, finding his options limited, he swivelled his body to drop a sweet goal. England edged further ahead when a slow Scottish heel permitted Page to snatch a loose ball and open the door for Neary to score. After 32 minutes, Hiller kicked another penalty and England, it seemed, were certain to win.

Scotland produced a remarkable recovery. England could not control a loose ball near their line and Paterson was presented with a gift try. Then, in a final flourish, Rea made a telling break to score to the left of the goal at the North end of the ground. Brown, with the minimum of fuss, kicked the conversion to win the match.

At the break England brought on Wright as a replacement for Wardlow. This was a perplexing move as the Northampton fly-half had already failed in earlier matches; furthermore, Glover, a wing of proven ability, was also on the replacements' bench!

ENGLAND		SCOTLAND	
R. Hiller	(Harlequins)	A.R. Brown	(Gala)
J.P.A.G. Janion	(Bedford)	W.C.C. Steele	(Bedford)
[1]C.S. Wardlow	(Northampton)	[1]J.N.M. Frame	(Gala)
*J.S. Spencer	(Headingley)	C.W.W. Rea	(Headingley)
D.J. Duckham	(Coventry)	A.G. Biggar	(London Scottish)
†A.R. Cowman	(Loughborough College)	J.W.C. Turner	(Gala)
J.J. Page	(Bedford)	D.S. Paterson	(Gala)
D.L. Powell	(Northampton)	J. McLauchlan	(Jordanhill College)
J.V. Pullin	(Bristol)	Q. Dunlop	(West of Scotland)
†F.E. Cotton	(Loughborough College)	A.B. Carmichael	(West of Scotland)
P.J. Larter	(Northampton)	A.F. McHarg	(London Scottish)
N.E. Horton	(Moseley)	G.L. Brown	(West of Scotland)
A.L. Bucknall	(Richmond)	N.A. MacEwan	(Gala)
R.B. Taylor	(Northampton)	*P.C. Brown	(Gala)
A. Neary	(Broughton Park)	R.J. Arneil	(Leicester)
[1]Replaced by I.D. Wright (Northampton)		[1]Replaced by A.S. Turk (Langholm)	

Tries: Hiller, Neary
Penalties: Hiller (3)

Tries: P.C. Brown, Paterson, Rea
Conversions: P.C. Brown (2)
Dropped goal: Paterson

Referee: Mr C. Durand (France)

SCOTLAND v ENGLAND 1971
Played at Murrayfield, Edinburgh, 27 March 1971
Scotland won by 4G, 1PG, 1T (26) to 1DG, 1PG (6)

This was a special match, outside the Championship, staged to commemorate the first international exactly 100 years earlier. The Prince of Wales and Mr Heath, the Prime Minister, were guests of honour.

Scotland made an auspicious start, scoring from the kick-off. Turner aimed for a deep touch to his left and Hiller gathered the ball. To optimise the angle for a kick to touch, the English full-back passed infield to Janion who, for some curious reason, did not kick the ball but whipped a hurried pass to Cowman. The English backs appeared to be playing pass-the-parcel, for Cowman handed on to his captain Spencer. Meanwhile, Frame had sped towards the English posts and, to his amazement, Spencer dropped the ball and he was able to sweep it over the line for a try. (The television recording of the incident showed that the score came in the thirteenth second of the match.) Arthur Brown converted and minutes later Peter Brown kicked a penalty. Cowman dropped a goal for England but a try by Peter Brown stretched Scotland to an 11–3 lead at the break.

The Scottish forwards dominated the match in the second half and Gordon Brown gave a fine display in the line-out. The home backs revealed their best form of the season and Frame increased the lead with his second try, Arthur Brown converting. England were completely bereft of attacking ideas, and, although Hiller landed three penalty points, further Scottish tries were obtained by Steele and Rea.

SCOTLAND		ENGLAND	
A.R. Brown	(Gala)	R. Hiller	(Harlequins)
W.C.C. Steele	(Bedford)	J.P.A.G. Janion	(Bedford)
J.N.M. Frame	(Gala)	C.S. Wardlow	(Northampton)
C.W.W. Rea	(Headingley)	*J.S. Spencer	(Headingley)
A.G. Biggar	(London Scottish)	D.J. Duckham	(Coventry)
J.W.C. Turner	(Gala)	A.R. Cowman	(Loughborough College)
D.S. Paterson	(Gala)	N.C. Starmer-Smith	(Harlequins)
J. McLauchlan	(Jordanhill College)	D.L. Powell	(Northampton)
Q. Dunlop	(West of Scotland)	J.V. Pullin	(Bristol)
A.B. Carmichael	(West of Scotland)	F.E. Cotton	(Loughborough College)
A.F. McHarg	(London Scottish)	P.J. Larter	(Northampton)
¹G.L. Brown	(West of Scotland)	†C.W. Ralston	(Richmond)
N.A. MacEwan	(Gala)	A.L. Bucknall	(Richmond)
*P.C. Brown	(Gala)	R.B. Taylor	(Northampton)
R.J. Arneil	(Leicester)	A. Neary	(Broughton Park)

¹Replaced by G.M. Strachan (Jordanhill C.)

Tries: Frame (2), P.C. Brown, Rea, Steele
Conversions: A.R. Brown (4)
Penalty: P.C. Brown

Dropped goal: Cowman
Penalty: Hiller

Referee: Mr M. Joseph (Wales)

ENGLAND v R.F.U. PRESIDENT'S XV 1971

Played at Twickenham, London, 17 April 1971

President's XV won by 5G, 1T (28) to 1G, 2PG (11)

To celebrate its Centenary, the R.F.U. invited a team of gifted overseas players to undertake a short, four-match tour during the spring of 1971. The highlight of the tour was the match against England, a match for which the R.F.U. awarded caps: hence its inclusion in the international record.

The English front row proved a strong unit and many critics were surprised by the large amount of good possession earned by the home pack. Their backs, however, were up against formidable opponents and there were few English breaks which penetrated the cast-iron defence of the President's men.

Conditions were bright and sunny at the start and 50,000, including the Queen, were present to see an entertaining match. Marais scored first, but a Hiller penalty from 40 yards tied the scores at 3–3 until the interval. Kirkpatrick capitalised on an English mix-up after a line-out to score at the posts early in the second half, Villepreux converting, but another Hiller penalty from 40 yards kept the English in contention. Next, de Villiers started a move which opened the way for the first of Williams's three tries, but England retaliated with their most constructive attacks of the afternoon. Spencer, with the help of a dummy, created some space for himself and placed a grub-kick to the right corner where Hiller, following up, scored a try which he then converted. Soon afterwards, Duckham made a sparkling counter-attack from his 25, collected the ball after kicking ahead and whipped it out to Janion, who was held up at the corner flag following a determined dash.

The overseas XV were now stimulated to produce their best form and at the end of an extended second half the lead was widened by 15 points from three goals. De Villiers created a try for Kirkpatrick, and Williams completed his hat-trick with two elegant runs. Villepreux added the conversions.

ENGLAND		R.F.U. PRESIDENT'S XV	
R. Hiller	(Harlequins)	P. Villepreux	(France)
J.P.A.G. Janion	(Bedford)	S.O. Knight	(Australia)
*J.S. Spencer	(Headingley)	J.J. Maso	(France)
D.J. Duckham	(Coventry)	J.S. Jansen	(South Africa)
P.B. Glover	(Bath)	B.G. Williams	(New Zealand)
A.R. Cowman	(Loughborough College)	W.D. Cottrell	(New Zealand)
N.C. Starmer-Smith	(Harlequins)	D.J. de Villiers	(South Africa)
C.B. Stevens	(Harlequins)	R.B. Prosser	(Australia)
J.V. Pullin	(Bristol)	P.G. Johnson	(Australia)
F.E. Cotton	(Loughborough College)	J.F.K. Marais	(South Africa)
P.J. Larter	(Northampton)	C.E. Meads	(New Zealand)
C.W. Ralston	(Richmond)	F.C. du Preez	(South Africa)
†R.N. Creed	(Coventry)	G.V. Davis	(Australia)
†P.J. Dixon	(Harlequins)	*B.J. Lochore	(New Zealand)
A. Neary	(Broughton Park)	I.A. Kirkpatrick	(New Zealand)

Try: Hiller

Conversion: Hiller

Penalties: Hiller (2)

Tries: Williams (3), Kirkpatrick (2), Marais

Conversions: Villepreux (5)

Referee: Mr M.H. Titcomb (England)

England v R.F.U. President's XV, 1971:
back C. B. Stevens, A. Neary, J. P. A. G. Janion, P. J. Larter, C. W. Ralston,
P. J. Dixon, F. E. Cotton, P. B. Glover; *front* A. R. Cowman, J. V. Pullin,
D. J. Duckham, J. S. Spencer (captain), R. Hiller, N. C. Starmer-Smith,
R. N. Creed.

Two record-breaking England full-backs: LEFT R. Hiller, who scored 138 points
in his 19 appearances for England and thus became England's most prolific
scorer to date; RIGHT R. W. Hosen, who scored 38 points in 1966-67 to become
England's highest points-scorer in a Championship season. (Hosen also scored
eight points against Australia, giving him 46 for the international season.)

ENGLAND v WALES 1972

Played at Twickenham, London, 15 January 1972
Wales won by 1G, 2PG (12) to 1PG (3)

Wales, fielding ten of the successful 1971 British Lions touring party, withstood a mighty first-half English onslaught to win their sixth consecutive international match and register their seventh victory at Twickenham. For the first 40 minutes, the new English forwards gave a sterling performance in the loose and line-outs with Burton, Brinn and Ripley frequently catching the eye. At their heels, another new player, Webster, gave a good account of himself against his illustrious opponent, Gareth Edwards. But for all their early promise, England's failure in the end was due to a lack of stamina against a team of greater experience and superior basic skill.

English hopes soared when Hiller put the home side ahead in the first half with a carefully prepared penalty kick at goal which sailed over the bar; but within the five minutes before the interval, Wales sneaked ahead through two penalties by Barry John and thereafter looked to be safe.

The only score of the second half resulted from a Welsh heel at a five-yards-scrum midway between the English goal and left wing. A well-planned blind-side move in which John feinted to the open side, drawing the English defence with him, allowed Williams to take a pass from Edwards and crash over for a try. John converted. In the final stages, Wales had little to fear in defence apart from one promising dash by Duckham.

ENGLAND		WALES	
*R. Hiller	(Harlequins)	J.P.R. Williams	(London Welsh)
J.P.A.G. Janion	(Bedford)	T.G.R. Davies	(London Welsh)
†M.C. Beese	(Liverpool)	R.T.E. Bergiers	(Llanelli)
D.J. Duckham	(Coventry)	A.J.L. Lewis	(Ebbw Vale)
K.J. Fielding	(Moseley)	J.C. Bevan	(Cardiff)
†A.G.B. Old	(Middlesbrough)	B. John	(Cardiff)
†J.G. Webster	(Moseley)	G.O. Edwards	(Cardiff)
C.B. Stevens	(Harlequins)	*D.J. Lloyd	(Bridgend)
J.V. Pullin	(Bristol)	J. Young	(R.A.F.)
†M.A. Burton	(Gloucester)	D.B. Llewellyn	(Llanelli)
†A. Brinn	(Gloucester)	W.D. Thomas	(Llanelli)
C.W. Ralston	(Richmond)	T.G. Evans	(London Welsh)
P.J. Dixon	(Harlequins)	W.D. Morris	(Neath)
†A.G. Ripley	(Rosslyn Park)	T.M. Davies	(London Welsh)
A. Neary	(Broughton Park)	J. Taylor	(London Welsh)

Penalty: Hiller

Try: Williams
Conversion: John
Penalties: John (2)

Referee: Mr J. Young (Scotland)

ENGLAND v IRELAND 1972
Played at Twickenham, London, 12 February 1972
Ireland won by 1G, 1PG, 1DG, 1T (16) to 1G, 2PG (12)

This was to be one of the most memorable occasions in the long and illustrious career of the Irish skipper, Tom Kiernan. Not only was it Ireland's third post-war win at Headquarters, but it was also the old master's fiftieth international appearance. There was a short stoppage during the first half when a demonstrator strayed on to the pitch, but fortunately the incident did not last long and an exciting game was allowed to run its natural course.

Kiernan put his team ahead in the first half with a penalty goal. Hiller equalised with a similar score and converted a try by Ralston to complete the scoring before the break. Early in the second half, right wing Tom Grace received the ball on the English 25, punted the ball over the English defence and raced outside the field of play before veering inwards to touch down for a good try. Hiller then pushed England five points ahead with his second penalty goal and this deficit remained for Ireland until three minutes from no-side.

Gibson missed a penalty goal but from this apparently harmless situation an Englishman fumbled the ball in-goal and, following the resulting five-yards-scrum, McGann dropped a perfect goal. With one minute to go, Ireland came storming back and, from a heel near the right touch-line on the English 25, the Irish backs started an orthodox passing movement. Flynn was about to continue the move to the left when he suddenly sliced through a narrow chink in the English defence and won the game for Ireland with a classic try. Kiernan, fittingly, had the last word, converting the try into a goal.

ENGLAND		IRELAND	
*R. Hiller	(Harlequins)	*T.J. Kiernan	(Cork Const.)
K.J. Fielding	(Moseley)	T.O. Grace	(U.C. Dublin)
M.C. Beese	(Liverpool)	C.M.H. Gibson	(N.I.F.C.)
D.J. Duckham	(Coventry)	M.K. Flynn	(Wanderers)
R.E. Webb	(Coventry)	A.W. McMaster	(Ballymena)
A.G.B. Old	(Middlesbrough)	B.J. McGann	(Cork Const.)
J.G. Webster	(Moseley)	J.J. Moloney	(St Mary's College)
C.B. Stevens	(Harlequins)	J.F. Lynch	(St Mary's College)
J.V. Pullin	(Bristol)	K.W. Kennedy	(London Irish)
M.A. Burton	(Gloucester)	R.J. McLoughlin	(Blackrock College)
A. Brinn	(Gloucester)	W.J. McBride	(Ballymena)
C.W. Ralston	(Richmond)	C.F.P. Feighery	(Lansdowne)
P.J. Dixon	(Harlequins)	J.F. Slattery	(Blackrock College)
A.G. Ripley	(Rosslyn Park)	D.J. Hickie	(St Mary's College)
A. Neary	(Broughton Park)	S.A. McKinney	(Dungannon)

Try: Ralston
Conversion: Hiller
Penalties: Hiller (2)

Tries: Flynn, Grace
Conversion: Kiernan
Penalty: Kiernan
Dropped goal: McGann

Referee: Mr R. Austry (France)

355

FRANCE v ENGLAND 1972

Played at Stade Colombes, Paris, 26 February 1972
France won by 5G, 1PG, 1T (37) to 1G, 2PG (12)

Following the defeats against Scotland and Ireland, the French selectors, not surprisingly, made ten changes in their side after one Paris critic had written, 'Our rugby is at the gates of hell.' Interestingly, the French experiment of fielding the members of the strong Béziers club – they were holders of the French club championship and confident of retaining the title at the time of this match – was abandoned, and only Estève of the seven who had done duty against Ireland was retained. England, too, were not without selection problems after defeats at home against Wales and Ireland. In the end, their selectors were more conservative than the French and only three changes were made, the most notable alteration being the introduction of Knight for the former captain and full-back, Bob Hiller.

The match itself, the last international to take place at Stade Colombes, was one of the greatest played on that famous ground. No other international side had scored 37 points against England before and the margin of victory, 25 points, was the largest recorded by France in matches with the English. (Wales defeated them by the same margin in 1905.)

France played spectacular fifteen-man Rugby and completely mastered the Englishmen. They were leading by 15 points after only 23 minutes, but strangely allowed England to get back into the game. Beese scored a try after Duckham had hacked ahead, Old converted and then landed a penalty soon after the interval to make the score 15–9. Any chances of an English victory were rudely crushed after this, as the French turned on a dazzling handling display which resulted in four tries – Villepreux converting three of them. England's only reply to this avalanche of scoring was another penalty by Old.

FRANCE		ENGLAND	
P. Villepreux	(Toulouse)	†P.M. Knight	(Bristol)
B. Duprat	(Bayonne)	K.J. Fielding	(Moseley)
J. Maso	(Narbonne)	M.C. Beese	(Liverpool)
J.P. Lux	(Dax)	D.J. Duckham	(Coventry)
J. Sillières	(Tarbes)	R.E. Webb	(Coventry)
J.L. Bérot	(Toulouse)	A.G.B. Old	(Middlesbrough)
M. Barrau	(Beaumont)	†L.E. Weston	(West of Scotland)
J. Iraçabal	(Bayonne)	C.B. Stevens	(Harlequins)
R. Bénésis	(Agen)	J.V. Pullin	(Bristol)
J.L. Azarète	(St Jean-de-Luz)	M.A. Burton	(Gloucester)
A. Estève	(Béziers)	J. Barton	(Coventry)
C. Spanghero	(Narbonne)	C.W. Ralston	(Richmond)
J.C. Skrela	(Toulouse)	*P.J. Dixon	(Harlequins)
*W. Spanghero	(Narbonne)	A.G. Ripley	(Rosslyn Park)
P. Biémouret	(Agen)	¹A. Neary	(Broughton Park)

¹Replaced by †N.O. Martin (Harlequins)

Tries: Duprat (2), Biémouret,
Lux, Sillières, W. Spanghero
Conversions: Villepreux (5)
Penalty: Villepreux

Try: Beese
Conversion: Old
Penalties: Old (2)

Referee: Mr T.F.E. Grierson (Scotland)

SCOTLAND v ENGLAND 1972

Played at Murrayfield, Edinburgh, 18 March 1972
Scotland won by 1DG, 4PG, 2T (23) to 3PG (9)

Defeat for England meant that they had lost all four of their matches in the International Championship for the first time ever. In addition, Scotland's victory was their fourth successive win over England, a feat they had last achieved in 1896.

The Scottish forwards, with four of the 1971 British Lions' pack, dominated this match, and their skipper Peter Brown had a particularly good day, scoring 13 of his side's points. His pack rucked and mauled skilfully and the loose-forwards were a constant thorn in the side of the English backs. Indeed, one of them, MacEwan, opened the scoring in the third minute when he crossed for a try after some lax play by the English defence. In the line-out, Brown varied his tactics intelligently, employing the throw to the back of the line with good effect; and his positioning – he placed himself at various times during the afternoon at five, six, seven and eight in the line-up – constantly upset the English forwards.

Old reduced Scotland's lead to a point when he landed a penalty, but a similar score by Peter Brown, from 55 yards, increased his team's lead before he drove over for a try from a line-out on the English line. The visitors had clearly expected him to feed his backs, leaving a wide gap for the Scottish skipper to dash over. Telfer then dropped a goal to give Scotland a commanding lead at half-time.

The second half was rather a dull affair, five penalty goals resulting. Old kicked two of these for England, bringing them back into the game at 14–9 down, but the other three goals fell to the Scots later on and the Browns, first Arthur and then Peter, were clearly in good kicking form.

SCOTLAND		ENGLAND	
A.R. Brown	(Gala)	P.M. Knight	(Bristol)
W.C.C. Steele	(Bedford)	K.J. Fielding	(Moseley)
J.N.M. Frame	(Gala)	J.P.A.G. Janion	(Bedford)
J.M. Renwick	(Hawick)	†G.W. Evans	(Coventry)
L.G. Dick	(Loughborough College)	D.J. Duckham	(Coventry)
C.M. Telfer	(Hawick)	A.G.B. Old	(Middlesbrough)
A.J.M. Lawson	(Edinburgh Wands.)	L.E. Weston	(West of Scotland)
J. McLauchlan	(Jordanhill College)	C.B. Stevens	(Harlequins)
R.L. Clark	(Edinburgh Wands.)	J.V. Pullin	(Bristol)
A.B. Carmichael	(West of Scotland)	M.A. Burton	(Gloucester)
A.F. McHarg	(London Scottish)	A. Brinn	(Gloucester)
G.L. Brown	(West of Scotland)	C.W. Ralston	(Richmond)
N.A. MacEwan	(Gala)	*P.J. Dixon	(Harlequins)
*P.C. Brown	(Gala)	A.G. Ripley	(Rosslyn Park)
R.J. Arneil	(Northampton)	A. Neary	(Broughton Park)

Tries: P.C. Brown, MacEwan   *Penalties:* Old (3)
Dropped goal: Telfer
Penalties: P.C. Brown (3), A.R. Brown

Referee: Mr M. Joseph (Wales)

SOUTH AFRICA v ENGLAND 1972
Played at Ellis Park, Johannesburg, 3 June 1972
England won by 1G, 4PG (18) to 3PG (9)

England, after their worst-ever season in the International Championship, surprised the Rugby world by completing an invincible tour of South Africa. Victory in the international was due to a competent performance by the whole team. The forwards held and then mastered the Springbok eight; Webster exercised a strong hold on the tactical development of the match; Doble kicked some fine goals; and the backs, particularly the centres, tackled like demons to preserve the lead established early in the second half.

The conditions were good and a crowd of 77,400 saw a tense first half in which five penalty goals were kicked. The sequence of scoring was Snyman, Doble, Snyman, Doble and Doble again, just on the break.

The English halves used the ball to good advantage and, after Williams had governed the early line-outs, Ripley, Ralston and Larter won ample possession later in the game. Pullin won the tight-head duel 2–1 against van Wyk. The dynamic little Webster caused many problems for the Springbok back row with his darting breaks from the base of the scrum, and a high kick of his, two minutes into the second half, preceded the only try of the match. Carlson could not hold the ball and the English scrum-half pounced to send Morley through a tackle for a try in the corner. Doble converted and kicked another penalty before Snyman landed his third goal.

South Africa had started the match as firm favourites, having won eight of their nine previous internationals. Reg Sweet, doyen of South African reporters, criticised the Springboks for a lack of midfield cohesion and added that Snyman and Viljoen were an incompatible pair at half-back.

Peter Preece was the son of Ivor Preece, the England and British Isles stand-off of the immediate post-war era.

SOUTH AFRICA		ENGLAND	
R.A. Carlson	(Western Province)	†S.A. Doble	(Moseley)
S.H. Nomis	(Transvaal)	†A.J. Morley	(Bristol)
J.S. Jansen	(O.F.S.)	J.P.A.G. Janion	(Bedford)
O.A. Roux	(Northern Transvaal)	†P.S. Preece	(Coventry)
G.H. Muller	(Transvaal)	P.M. Knight	(Bristol)
D.S.L. Snyman	(Western Province)	A.G.B. Old	(Middlesbrough)
J.F. Viljoen	(Eastern Province)	J.G. Webster	(Moseley)
N.S.E. Bezuidenhoudt	(Northern Transvaal)	C.B. Stevens	(Penzance & Newlyn)
J.F.B. van Wyk	(Northern Transvaal)	*J.V. Pullin	(Bristol)
J.T. Sauermann	(Transvaal)	M.A. Burton	(Gloucester)
J.G. Williams	(Northern Transvaal)	P.J. Larter	(Northampton)
P.G. du Plessis	(Northern Transvaal)	C.W. Ralston	(Richmond)
*P.J.F. Greyling	(Transvaal)	†J.A. Watkins	(Gloucester)
A.J. Bates	(Northern Transvaal)	A.G. Ripley	(Rosslyn Park)
J.H. Ellis	(South West Africa)	A. Neary	(Broughton Park)

Penalties: Snyman (3)

Try: Morley   *Conversion:* Doble
Penalties: Doble (4)

Referee: Dr J. Moolman (South Africa)

ENGLAND v NEW ZEALAND 1973

Played at Twickenham, London, 6 January 1973

New Zealand won by 1G, 1DG (9) to Nil

The New Zealanders were too strong for a spirited England side. The masterly control of the All Blacks' forwards, the strategic brilliance of Going at their heels, and the tight defensive net thrown over the English backs by the New Zealand backs were the features of a match watched by a capacity crowd of 72,000.

The weather was overcast and cold when the sides took the field. In the eighth minute of the match, Batty's long throw into a line-out on the English 25 was gathered by Going who shook off a couple of tackles to stride towards the English line. Going linked with his back row and Wyllie and Sutherland increased the momentum of the move to create a ruck beneath the English goal. Kirkpatrick gathered the ball, beguiled the defence with a dummy and touched down between the posts for a try which Karam converted.

There was no further scoring in this period, although Doble missed three penalty kicks and Karam failed with a kick at goal five minutes before half-time. Another miss by Doble, after 12 minutes in the second half and from 45 yards, was followed by England's best chance of the afternoon. From a ruck on the New Zealand 25, Warfield passed the ball to Preece who flashed through a gap for a try, only to be called back for a forward pass. England's moment of glory had passed, and hopes for an English victory vanished after 18 minutes when Finlan, who had entered the side as a replacement for Alan Old, failed to clear the ball to touch. Williams collected it and dropped a fine goal from nearly 40 yards to end the scoring.

Fran Cotton withdrew from the English side at the last minute and was replaced by Frank Anderson of Orrell, who thus became the first capped player from the Lancashire club.

ENGLAND		NEW ZEALAND	
S.A. Doble	(Moseley)	J.F. Karam	(Wellington)
A.J. Morley	(Bristol)	B.G. Williams	(Auckland)
†P.J. Warfield	(Rosslyn Park)	B.J. Robertson	(Counties)
P.S. Preece	(Coventry)	G.B. Batty	(Wellington)
D.J. Duckham	(Coventry)		
		R.M. Parkinson	(Poverty Bay)
J.F. Finlan	(Moseley)	I.N. Stevens	(Wellington)
J.G. Webster	(Moseley)	S.M. Going	(North Auckland)
C.B. Stevens	(Penzance & Newlyn)	G.J. Whiting	(King Country)
*J.V. Pullin	(Bristol)	R.W. Norton	(Canterbury)
†W.F. Anderson	(Orrell)	K.K. Lambert	(Manawatu)
P.J. Larter	(Northampton)	H.H. Macdonald	(Canterbury)
C.W. Ralston	(Richmond)	P.J. Whiting	(Auckland)
J.A. Watkins	(Gloucester)	A.J. Wyllie	(Canterbury)
A.G. Ripley	(Rosslyn Park)	A.R. Sutherland	(Marlborough)
A. Neary	(Broughton Park)	*I.A. Kirkpatrick	(Poverty Bay)

Try: Kirkpatrick
Conversion: Karam
Dropped goal: Williams

Referee: Mr J. Young (Scotland)

WALES v ENGLAND 1973
Played at Cardiff Arms Park, 20 January 1973
Wales won by 1G, 4T, 1PG (25) to 2PG, 1DG (9)

Wales, with a team of overwhelming talent, defeated England for the fifth year in succession. With Cardiff R.F.C. now occupying the ground adjacent to the international pitch, the wear and tear on the Arms Park surface was considerably reduced. Consequently, the turf was in excellent condition for this match and remained so throughout a wet afternoon.

Wales were well organised up-front and Bennett and Edwards kept a tight tactical grip on the match for the first 60 minutes. Then, in a final flourish, Wales underlined their immense all-round strength with two elegant tries in four minutes.

England elected to face a strong wind in the first half and opened the scoring after 15 minutes. From a line-out near the Welsh line, Larter and Cotton peeled-off to carry the ball towards the Welsh posts. England won a ruck and Cowman dropped a goal from 12 yards. Wales countered this with a spendid try by Bevan after Edwards and Bergiers had moved left from a ruck, and England's problems were magnified when Warfield retired with a shoulder injury. Before Evans could replace him, Bennett kicked diagonally for Gerald Davies to score. Doble kicked a simple penalty goal when Quinnell was caught off-side in the loose, but another Welsh try, this time by Edwards after Morris and Lloyd had driven play into the corner, gave Wales a 12–6 lead at half-time.

Taylor kicked a penalty after 13 minutes in the second half and Doble kept England in the hunt with an excellent kick from 42 yards when Young was penalised for crouching in a scrum. Then the English front row buckled and Wales began to play a more expansive and entertaining game. A lateral break by Edwards from a scrum lured the defence onto the wrong foot and Lewis, from a scissors move, scored beneath the posts for Bennett to convert. In the last minute, the ball passed through the hands of each Welsh back and Bevan crossed after the best move of the match.

WALES		ENGLAND	
J.P.R. Williams	(London Welsh)	S.A. Doble	(Moseley)
T.G.R. Davies	(London Welsh)	A.J. Morley	(Bristol)
R.T.E. Bergiers	(Llanelli)	[1]P.J. Warfield	(Rosslyn Park)
*A.J.L. Lewis	(Ebbw Vale)	P.S. Preece	(Coventry)
J.C. Bevan	(Cardiff)	D.J. Duckham	(Coventry)
P. Bennett	(Llanelli)	A.R. Cowman	(Coventry)
G.O. Edwards	(Cardiff)	J.G. Webster	(Moseley)
D.J. Lloyd	(Bridgend)	C.B. Stevens	(Penzance & Newlyn)
J. Young	(London Welsh)	*J.V. Pullin	(Bristol)
G. Shaw	(Neath)	F.E. Cotton	(Loughborough College)
D.L. Quinnell	(Llanelli)	P.J. Larter	(Northampton)
W.D. Thomas	(Llanelli)	C.W. Ralston	(Richmond)
W.D. Morris	(Neath)	A. Neary	(Broughton Park)
T.M. Davies	(Swansea)	A.G. Ripley	(Rosslyn Park)
J. Taylor	(London Welsh)	J.A. Watkins	(Gloucester)

[1]Replaced by G.W. Evans (Coventry)

Tries: Bevan (2), T.G.R. Davies, Edwards, Lewis *Conversion:* Bennett *Penalty:* Taylor

Dropped goal: Cowman *Penalties:* Doble (2)

Referee: Mr G. Domercq (France)

IRELAND v ENGLAND 1973

Played at Lansdowne Road, Dublin, 10 February 1973
Ireland won by 2G, 1PG, 1DG (18) to 1G, 1PG (9)

Ireland's political troubles had forced Scotland and Wales to cancel visits to Dublin in 1972. Consequently, the English fifteen received a warm welcome when they entered the field for this match, 50,000 spectators greeting John Pullin's team with an ovation which lasted many minutes. Irish hospitality ceased during the match, of course, and England, in a disappointing performance, were overrun in the loose by an eager Irish pack, and Kennedy took the strikes 2–0 against the head in the tight.

England made a promising start when Jorden kicked a penalty from 45 yards, downwind, after only five minutes, but Ireland went ahead in the fourteenth minute when Moloney carved a huge gap in the English defence to send Grace over near the right corner. McGann converted with an excellent kick and converted again, just before half-time, when the finesse of Moloney and Gibson made an overlap for Milliken to bolt over.

England, 3–12 down at the break, had to face a strong wind in the second half and did well to restrict Ireland to a further six points. The Irish forwards relaxed as the game progressed and McGann's dropped goal from a scrum, early in the second half, made their position secure. England's best period of the match came after 22 minutes, when Ripley hounded Moloney, gathered the ball and smuggled it to Neary who charged through three Irish players for a try. Jorden converted from a difficult angle.

McGann, a prolific scorer of points (like many of the fly-halves who succeeded him in the Irish fifteen) completed the scoring with a penalty, after 32 minutes, from an easy position.

Peter Dixon and Roger Uttley became Gosforth's first England internationals.

IRELAND		ENGLAND	
*T.J. Kiernan	(Cork Const.)	A.M. Jorden	(Blackheath)
T.O. Grace	(St Mary's College)	A.J. Morley	(Bristol)
R.A. Milliken	(Bangor)	P.J. Warfield	(Rosslyn Park)
C.M.H. Gibson	(N.I.F.C.)	P.S. Preece	(Coventry)
A.W. McMaster	(Ballymena)	D.J. Duckham	(Coventry)
B.J. McGann	(Cork Const.)	A.R. Cowman	(Coventry)
J.J. Moloney	(St Mary's College)	†S.J. Smith	(Sale)
R.J. McLoughlin	(Blackrock College)	C.B. Stevens	(Penzance & Newlyn)
K.W. Kennedy	(London Irish)	*J.V. Pullin	(Bristol)
J.F. Lynch	(St Mary's College)	F.E. Cotton	(Loughborough College)
K.M.A. Mays	(U.C. Dublin)	†R.M. Uttley	(Gosforth)
W.J. McBride	(Ballymena)	C.W. Ralston	(Richmond)
J.F. Slattery	(Blackrock College)	P.J. Dixon	(Gosforth)
T.A.P. Moore	(Highfield)	A.G. Ripley	(Rosslyn Park)
J.H. Buckley	(Sunday's Well)	A. Neary	(Broughton Park)

Tries: Grace, Milliken
Conversions: McGann (2)
Penalty: McGann
Dropped goal: McGann

Try: Neary
Conversion: Jorden
Penalty: Jorden

Referee: Mr A.M. Hosie (Scotland)

ENGLAND v FRANCE 1973

Played at Twickenham, London, 24 February 1973
England won by 2PG, 2T (14) to 1G (6)

England's first Championship win for two seasons was fabricated by a swift and determined pack which outplayed a much-vaunted French eight. Jorden kicked a splendid goal from 45 yards to open the scoring and France's problems began soon after when Barrau was compelled to withdraw with a back injury. Astre replaced him but proved to be an inadequate substitute for the lively Barrau. Just before half-time Preece sped through an opening in the French threequarter line, drew Droitecourt perfectly, and whipped the ball out to Duckham, who romped over in the corner.

After the resumption Evans took advantage of slack French marking and found a gap in the French defence. Valuable support was lent by Stevens who gave a pass to Duckham. The Coventry wing, after several miserable matches for the English backs, received it gratefully and crossed in the corner for his second try. Although Jorden failed to convert, his penalty goal from 25 yards, a little later, was a crucial score which virtually assured England of a comfortable victory.

Near the end, Romeu brought his backs into action and a lovely flowing move, in which the ball was elegantly transferred from left to right, culminated in a try by Bertranne which Romeu made into a goal.

ENGLAND		FRANCE	
A.M. Jorden	(Blackheath)	M. Droitecourt	(Montferrand)
†P.J. Squires	(Harrogate)	R. Bertranne	(Toulon)
G.W. Evans	(Coventry)	C. Dourthe	(Dax)
P.S. Preece	(Coventry)	J. Trillo	(Bègles)
D.J. Duckham	(Coventry)	J.P. Lux	(Dax)
†M.J. Cooper	(Moseley)	J.P. Romeu	(Montferrand)
S.J. Smith	(Sale)	¹M. Barrau	(Toulouse)
C.B. Stevens	(Penzance & Newlyn)	A. Darrieussecq	(Biarritz)
*J.V. Pullin	(Bristol)	R. Bénésis	(Agen)
F.E. Cotton	(Loughborough College)	J. Iraçabal	(Bayonne)
R.M. Uttley	(Gosforth)	A. Estève	(Béziers)
C.W. Ralston	(Richmond)	J.P. Bastiat	(Dax)
P.J. Dixon	(Gosforth)	O. Saisset	(Béziers)
A.G. Ripley	(Rosslyn Park)	*W. Spanghero	(Narbonne)
A. Neary	(Broughton Park)	P. Biémouret	(Agen)

¹Replaced by R. Astre (Béziers)

Tries: Duckham (2)   *Try:* Bertranne
Penalties: Jorden (2)   *Conversion:* Romeu

Referee: Mr K.H. Clark (Ireland)

ENGLAND v SCOTLAND 1973

Played at Twickenham, London, 17 March 1973
England won by 2G, 2T (20) to 1G, 1PG, 1T (13)

Scotland were deprived of the Triple Crown by an impressive English pack which totally subdued their Scottish counterparts. In the tight, Pullin took the strikes against the head by 2–0; Ralston and Ripley (in the middle and at the tail, respectively) dominated the line-outs; and in the loose the Scottish forwards were unable to cope with the enthusiastic raids of Ripley, Neary, Uttley and Dixon. Cooper, playing under instructions, relied rigidly on his boot as the chief attacking weapon, otherwise the English backs would have been able to play a more fluent, open game.

The first-half scoring came in a three-minutes spell, midway through the half. Smith slipped away from a scrum in the twenty-first minute, Cooper continued the move and threw a pass to Squires, who scored in the corner. From the restart, the English centres worked the ball out to Duckham who made a run for the Scottish line. Although McHarg collared Duckham, Dixon drove over after the ball had emerged from the ensuing maul.

After three minutes in the second half, an accurate palm from the back of a line-out by Ripley set up a try for Dixon, and Jorden converted to give England a secure lead. Scotland made a spirited rally and after Morgan had kicked a 50-yards penalty Steele, with a fine individual effort, raced over for a try. Then, in the thirty-third minute, Peter Brown made the extra man in the Scottish line, sent an overhead pass to Steele, and the winger touched down for his second try. Irvine's conversion from the touch-line brought Scotland to within one point.

It was anybody's match, now, but two minutes later a diagonal kick by Preece bounced unkindly for Steele and Evans dived on the ball for a try. Jorden converted to complete a deserved English victory.

ENGLAND		SCOTLAND	
A.M. Jorden	(Blackheath)	A.R. Irvine	(Heriot's F.P.)
P.J. Squires	(Harrogate)	W.C.C. Steele	(Bedford)
G.W. Evans	(Coventry)	I.R. McGeechan	(Headingley)
P.S. Preece	(Coventry)	I.W. Forsyth	(Stewart's College F.P.)
D.J. Duckham	(Coventry)	D. Shedden	(West of Scotland)
M.J. Cooper	(Moseley)	C.M. Telfer	(Hawick)
S.J. Smith	(Sale)	D.W. Morgan	(Melville College F.P.)
C.B. Stevens	(Penzance & Newlyn)	*J. McLauchlan	(Jordanhill College)
*J.V. Pullin	(Bristol)	R.L. Clark	(Edinburgh Wands.)
F.E. Cotton	(Loughborough College)	A.B. Carmichael	(West of Scotland)
R.M. Uttley	(Gosforth)	P.C. Brown	(Gala)
C.W. Ralston	(Richmond)	A.F. McHarg	(London Scottish)
P.J. Dixon	(Gosforth)	N.A. MacEwan	(Gala).
A.G. Ripley	(Rosslyn Park)	G.M. Strachan	(Jordanhill College)
A. Neary	(Broughton Park)	¹J.G. Millican	(Edinburgh U.)

¹Replaced by G.L. Brown (West of Scotland)

Tries: Dixon (2), Evans, Squires
Conversions: Jorden (2)

Tries: Steele (2) *Conversion:* Irvine
Penalty: Morgan

Referee: Mr J.C. Kelleher (Wales)

1973 was England's best year in an otherwise undistinguished decade. J. V. Pullin, who had begun his captaincy in fine style in June 1972 by leading his side to victory in England's only international in South Africa, secured four consecutive victories for England against France, Scotland, New Zealand, and Australia. This was the line-up for England v Scotland, 1973: *standing* F. E. Cotton, R. M. Uttley, C. W. Ralston, A. G. Ripley, P. J. Dixon, A. M. Jorden, P. S. Preece, S. J. Smith, D. J. Duckham; *sitting* A. Neary, M. J. Cooper, J. V. Pullin (captain), C. B. Stevens, G. W. Evans, P. J. Squires.

P. J. Squires, who made his debut against France in 1973 and scored tries in the matches against Scotland and New Zealand, went on to score a further four tries in his record 29 appearances on the wing for England.

NEW ZEALAND v ENGLAND 1973
Played at Eden Park, Auckland, 15 September 1973
England won by 2G, 1T (16) to 1G, 1T (10)

England had planned to tour Argentina in the Summer of 1973, but, following cancellation, arranged a short tour to Fiji and New Zealand instead. After losing three provincial matches, the tourists stunned the Rugby world. John Brooks, writing in *Rothmans Rugby Yearbook*, stated: 'The outcome ... numbed most New Zealand Rugby followers. England played with admirable efficiency, while New Zealand showed a great lack of tactical appreciation and serious flaws in technique. It was the All Blacks' poorest display in an international for years ... but the team's many shortcomings did not detract from the merit of England's achievement.'

Old kicked off into a stiff westerly wind and the New Zealanders were rewarded with a try after several minutes of intense forward pressure inside the English 25, Wyllie and Going working a blind-side ploy from a scrummage for Batty to score. Three minutes later, Webster, who was the mainspring of the English attack, broke from a scrum in Going-fashion and Squires went over in the corner for Rossborough to convert from a wide angle. The English forwards played a disciplined game and the back row contained Going, New Zealand's most dangerous player. However, in the twenty-seventh minute New Zealand regained the lead when a cross-kick by Williams led to a ruck beneath the English goal. A quick pass from Going gave Hurst the simplest of tries near the posts and Lendrum converted.

England, playing controlled, ten-man Rugby in the second half, scored twice from mistakes by Lendrum. In the eighth minute, Lendrum missed a clearance to touch and Webster caught the ball before linking with his forwards. Fast, accurate passing led to a try by Stevens which tied the scores. Then, in the thirty-fifth minute, Lendrum muffed his catch of a kick ahead. The ubiquitous Webster gathered the ball and Old sent Neary across for a try which Rossborough goaled.

The English withstood late New Zealand pressure to gain a memorable win.

NEW ZEALAND		ENGLAND	
R.N. Lendrum	(Counties)	P.A. Rossborough	(Coventry)
G.B. Batty	(Wellington)	P. J. Squires	(Harrogate)
I.A. Hurst	(Canterbury)	P.S. Preece	(Coventry)
B.G. Williams	(Auckland)	[1]G.W. Evans	(Coventry)
		D.J. Duckham	(Coventry)
[1]R.M. Parkinson	(Poverty Bay)		
J.P. Dougan	(Wellington)	A.G.B. Old	(Leicester)
S.M. Going	(North Auckland)	J.G. Webster	(Moseley)
K.K. Lambert	(Manawatu)	C.B. Stevens	(Penzance & Newlyn)
R.W. Norton	(Canterbury)	*J.V. Pullin	(Bristol)
M.G. Jones	(North Auckland)	F.E. Cotton	(Coventry)
H.H. Macdonald	(Canterbury)	R.M. Uttley	(Gosforth)
S.C. Strahan	(Manawatu)	C.W. Ralston	(Richmond)
K.W. Stewart	(Southland)	J.A. Watkins	(Gloucester)
A.J. Wyllie	(Canterbury)	A.G. Ripley	(Rosslyn Park)
*I.A. Kirkpatrick	(Poverty Bay)	A. Neary	(Broughton Park)
[1]Replaced by T.G. Morrison (Otago)		[1]Replaced by M.J. Cooper (Moseley)	

Tries: Batty, Hurst
Conversion: Lendrum

Tries: Neary, Squires, Stevens
Conversions: Rossborough (2)

Referee: Mr R.F. McMullen (New Zealand)

ENGLAND v AUSTRALIA 1973

Played at Twickenham, London, 17 November 1973
England won by 1G, 2T, 2PG (20) to 1PG (3)

Australia made a short tour to England and Wales during the Autumn of 1973, but two heavy defeats in the internationals and a mediocre record in the provincial games left the Wallabies with the unenviable record of two wins from eight matches. This was the last match of the tour and Sullivan, who had been injured in the international at Cardiff a week earlier, handed over the captaincy to Hipwell.

England's comfortable win in an undistinguished match completed an unusual treble: three wins over South Africa, New Zealand and Australia in 18 months. Furthermore, John Pullin was the successful captain on each occasion.

Neary scored the only try of the first half (with a move from the tail of a line-out) and a penalty goal kicked by Rossborough produced a seven-points lead at the interval. The English pack were powerful in the set-scrummages and dominated the tight play, although Fay won a good share of possession for Australia in the line-outs. Both back divisions lacked penetration and there were few passages of play for the purists to enjoy. Fairfax was the most exciting of the backs, his timely runs from full-back occasionally upsetting the equilibrium of the English defence.

England's first try of the second half was from a pushover. Ripley, who made the touch-down, had been the outstanding loose-forward of the match and impressed the crowd with his lively contributions in broken play. Rossborough converted the try and kicked a penalty goal. Old took advantage of some ragged marking near the end of the match to score a good individualist's try.

The Australian place kicking was disappointing with McLean and Fairfax missing eight kicks at goal (out of nine attempts).

ENGLAND		AUSTRALIA	
P.A. Rossborough	(Coventry)	R.L. Fairfax	(N.S.W.)
P.J. Squires	(Harrogate)	L.E. Monaghan	(N.S.W.)
J.P.A.G. Janion	(Richmond)	R.D. L'Estrange	(Queensland)
†D.F.K. Roughley	(Liverpool)	G.A. Shaw	(N.S.W.)
D.J. Duckham	(Coventry)	J.J. McLean	(N.S.W.)
A.G.B. Old	(Leicester)	P.G. Rowles	(N.S.W.)
S.J. Smith	(Sale)	*J.N.B. Hipwell	(N.S.W.)
C.B. Stevens	(Penzance & Newlyn)	R. Graham	(N.S.W.)
*J.V. Pullin	(Bristol)	[1]C.M. Carberry	(N.S.W.)
F.E. Cotton	(Coventry)	S.G. Macdougall	(N.S.W.)
R.M. Uttley	(Gosforth)	S.C. Gregory	(N.S.W.)
C.W. Ralston	(Richmond)	G. Fay	(N.S.W.)
J.A. Watkins	(Gloucester)	M.R. Cocks	(Queensland)
A.G. Ripley	(Rosslyn Park)	A.A. Shaw	(Queensland)
A. Neary	(Broughton Park)	B.R. Battishall	(N.S.W.)

[1]Replaced by M.E. Freney (Q'land)

Tries: Neary, Old, Ripley
Conversion: Rossborough
Penalties: Rossborough (2)

Penalty: Fairfax

Referee: Mr R. Lewis (Wales)

SCOTLAND v ENGLAND 1974
Played at Murrayfield, Edinburgh, 2 February 1974
Scotland won by 1G, 2PG, 1T (16) to 1DG, 1PG, 2T (14)

In one of the most talked-of matches of the 1970s, Scotland deprived England of victory with a late penalty from 45 yards kicked by Andy Irvine.

Scotland promised to run-up a huge total at the start of the game: Irvine opened the scoring with a penalty goal from about 40 yards; Webster had to juggle with a ball received at a line-out on his own line, and Madsen swiftly intervened to send Lauder over in the corner; and Irvine's fine conversion in the twelfth minute extended Scotland's lead to nine points. By this stage the Scottish pack had established a firm grip in the tight play, but as the interval approached England's forwards successfully restored the equilibrium up-front. Squires initiated a passage of play which featured close-passing by the forwards and Cotton finished the move by battering his way over the line. Near half-time Old landed a penalty from 40 yards and England, now just two points behind, made several dangerous attacks in the opening 20 minutes of the second half. Only brave defence, particularly by McGeechan, frustrated England's attempts to win. (They had not won at Murrayfield since 1968.)

A pulsating last quarter, during which the lead switched four times, transformed this match into a really memorable one. From a short penalty near half-way, Webster sent Ripley striding down the middle of an unprepared defence. He was eventually smothered but managed to find Neary with a pass to his left and the flanker's try placed England ahead for the first time. Irvine, the man of the match, scored next with a brilliant individual effort, but in the thirty-seventh minute a poor clearance to Rossborough presented the English full-back with an opportunity to drop a goal from 40 yards. He took his chance beautifully. Then, three minutes into injury time, an English back was caught off-side in front of a kick ahead and Irvine, with the last kick of the match and from the right touch-line, won the game for Scotland.

SCOTLAND		ENGLAND	
A.R. Irvine	(Heriot's F.P.)	P.A. Rossborough	(Coventry)
A.D. Gill	(Gala)	P.J. Squires	(Harrogate)
J.M. Renwick	(Hawick)	D.F.K. Roughley	(Liverpool)
I.R. McGeechan	(Headingley)	G.W. Evans	(Coventry)
L.G. Dick	(Jordanhill College)	D.J. Duckham	(Coventry)
C.M. Telfer	(Hawick)	A.G.B. Old	(Leicester)
A.J.M. Lawson	(Edinburgh Wands.)	J.G. Webster	(Moseley)
*J. McLauchlan	(Jordanhill College)	C.B. Stevens	(Penzance & Newlyn)
D.F. Madsen	(Gosforth)	*J.V. Pullin	(Bristol)
A.B. Carmichael	(West of Scotland)	F.E. Cotton	(Coventry)
G.L. Brown	(West of Scotland)	N.E. Horton	(Moseley)
A.F. McHarg	(London Scottish)	C.W. Ralston	(Richmond)
N.A. MacEwan	(Highland)	P.J. Dixon	(Gosforth)
W.S. Watson	(Boroughmuir)	A.G. Ripley	(Rosslyn Park)
W. Lauder	(Neath)	A. Neary	(Broughton Park)

Tries: Irvine, Lauder
Conversion: Irvine
Penalties: Irvine (2)

Tries: Cotton, Neary
Dropped goal: Rossborough
Penalty: Old

Referee: Mr J. St. Guilhem (France)

ENGLAND v IRELAND 1974

Played at Twickenham, London, 16 February 1974
Ireland won by 2G, 2T, 1PG, 1DG (26) to 1G, 5PG (21)

England's rally towards the end of a match full of incidents was not sufficient to overtake a big Irish lead established early in the second half. The packs were evenly matched but the inspiring play of Mike Gibson gave an edge to the Irish backs which proved to be the vital difference between the sides. The English mid-field play was sterile by comparison and Squires's try – England's only one of the match – derived from a burst by Ripley near the end of the game.

England were in a miserable position at half-time. After making poor use of a stiff breeze they found themselves 6–10 in arrears (a penalty by Ensor, a try by Moore from a short line-out and a dropped goal by Quinn answering two penalties by Old). Ireland, playing attractive, open Rugby added a further 16 points in the first 20 minutes of the second half. In an 'inspired spell', wrote Paul MacWeeney, 'their attacks were as incisive and exciting as any seen throughout the season.' During the purple patch Moloney took advantage of a fumble by Old and ran to the line for a try; and Gibson, first with a dummy and then on the overlap after a long, diagonal run by Ensor, scored twice. Gibson converted each of his tries, giving Ireland a safe 26–9 lead, Old having kicked another penalty goal.

There was the consolation of two more Old penalties for England in the last 20 minutes, and when Old converted the try by Squires the Leicester pivot raised to 17 points his individual contribution to the game.

Bill McBride won his 56th cap in this international, surpassing the world record total held previously by Colin Meads. For England, John Pullin equalled 'Budge' Rogers's record of 34 appearances.

ENGLAND		IRELAND	
P.A. Rossborough	(Coventry)	A.H. Ensor	(Lansdowne)
P.J. Squires	(Harrogate)	T.O. Grace	(U.C. Dublin)
G.W. Evans	(Coventry)	R.A. Milliken	(Bangor)
D.F.K. Roughley	(Liverpool)	C.M.H. Gibson	(N.I.F.C.)
D.J. Duckham	(Coventry)	A.W. McMaster	(Ballymena)
A.G.B. Old	(Leicester)	M.A.M. Quinn	(Lansdowne)
S.J. Smith	(Sale)	J.J. Moloney	(St Mary's College)
C.B. Stevens	(Penzance & Newlyn)	R.J. McLoughlin	(Blackrock College)
*J.V. Pullin	(Bristol)	K.W. Kennedy	(London Irish)
F.E. Cotton	(Coventry)	J.F. Lynch	(St Mary's College)
R.M. Uttley	(Gosforth)	*W.J. McBride	(Ballymena)
C.W. Ralston	(Richmond)	M.I. Keane	(Lansdowne)
P.J. Dixon	(Gosforth)	J.F. Slattery	(Blackrock College)
A.G. Ripley	(Rosslyn Park)	T.A.P. Moore	(Highfield)
A. Neary	(Broughton Park)	S.A. McKinney	(Dungannon)

Try: Squires
Conversion: Old
Penalties: Old (5)

Tries: Gibson (2), Moloney, Moore
Conversions: Gibson (2) *Penalty:* Ensor
Dropped goal: Quinn

Referee: Mr M. Joseph (Wales)

FRANCE v ENGLAND 1974

Played at Parc des Princes, Paris, 2 March 1974

Drawn: France 1G, 1PG, 1DG (12), England 1G, 1PG, 1DG (12)

England confounded the Rugby critics by gaining a draw on this first visit to the new Parc des Princes ground in Paris. After a series of humiliating defeats in the French capital, and two lacklustre performances earlier in the season, few gave England a chance of holding an undefeated French side.

England's forwards excelled in the tight, winning a large share of possession. But an inability to function at speed and a tendency to practise too complicated moves amongst the backs reduced the efficiency of the visiting side. As a result, the French defence was rarely stretched and England never really threatened to win a match which, on forward power alone, they were quite capable of doing.

Romeu, the leading French player of 1973, scored all of his side's points. His precision with the boot produced a six-points lead through a dropped goal (from 30 yards) and a penalty (from 50 yards) early in the match; the only scores before half-time.

Evans dropped a goal from 25 yards in the second half, but English hopes of victory faded when Romeu made a run from deep inside his own half and collected a return pass from Claude Spanghero to score near the posts. Romeu converted his try, then Old, with a perfectly-judged kick from 40 yards and close to the touch-line, reduced the margin after France were penalised.

Duckham showed the French a clean pair of heels towards the end, completing the only successful English back move of the afternoon with a try. The English backs started passing inside their 25 before Smith and Evans created the overlap for Duckham to run the last 30 yards for the try which, after a conversion by Old, saved the game for England.

On the morning after this match, numerous England supporters lost their lives in an air-crash in northern France. England and France met in a charity match later in the season, proceeds going to the dependants of those who had died in the crash.

FRANCE		ENGLAND	
M. Droitecourt	(Montferrand)	A.M. Jorden	(Blackheath)
R. Bertranne	(Bagnères)	P.J. Squires	(Harrogate)
J. Pécune	(Tarbes)	G.W. Evans	(Coventry)
J.P. Lux	(Dax)	†K. Smith	(Roundhay)
A. Dubertrand	(Montferrand)	D.J. Duckham	(Coventry)
J.P. Romeu	(Montferrand)	A.G.B. Old	(Leicester)
J. Fouroux	(La Voulte)	S.J. Smith	(Sale)
J. Iraçabal	(Bayonne)	C.B. Stevens	(Penzance & Newlyn)
R. Bénésis	(Agen)	*J.V. Pullin	(Bristol)
A. Vaquerin	(Béziers)	M.A. Burton	(Gloucester)
*E. Cester	(Valence)	R.M. Uttley	(Gosforth)
A. Estève	(Béziers)	C.W. Ralston	(Richmond)
J.C. Skrela	(Toulouse)	P.J. Dixon	(Gosforth)
C. Spanghero	(Narbonne)	A.G. Ripley	(Rosslyn Park)
V. Boffelli	(Aurillac)	A. Neary	(Broughton Park)

Try: Romeu   *Try:* Duckham
Conversion: Romeu   *Conversion:* Old
Penalty: Romeu   *Penalty:* Old
Dropped goal: Romeu   *Dropped goal:* Evans

Referee: Mr J.C. Kelleher (Wales)

369

ENGLAND v WALES 1974
Played at Twickenham, London, 16 March 1974
England won by 1G, 2PG, 1T (16) to 1G, 2PG (12)

England's forwards strengthened their claim to being the strongest pack in the Championship with a masterly display in the line-outs and mauls and a competent approach in the tight (although a strong Welsh front row stole the strikes against the head by 5–2). Ripley was outstanding and crowned a memorable individual game with a decisive try from a five-yards-scrum shortly after the interval.

England faced a gusty breeze in the first half but the hopes of their supporters soared when the Welsh eight were clearly disrupted at the first scrum. After ten minutes Evans and Old, with perfect timing, worked a scissors from a line-out on the Welsh 25 and the Coventry centre ran back to his forwards. Ralston and Uttley were quick to support the move, before Duckham received the ball and sidestepped past a defender to score on the left. Old landed a penalty after 22 minutes, but Wales responded with a try by Mervyn Davies after careless English defence at the tail of a line-out. Phil Bennett's trusty right boot banged over the conversion and later added a penalty to push Wales ahead at half-time.

Ripley's important try, converted by Old, regained the lead for England, a lead they were never to relinquish, despite another penalty by Bennett and Welsh claims that J.J. Williams had scored in a race for the ball against the English wingers. England also had a try disallowed, and when Old kicked his second penalty, 15 minutes from no-side, England's defence was tight enough to hold out for a thoroughly well-earned victory which deprived Wales of the Championship. England's win was their first against Wales for eleven years.

ENGLAND		WALES	
†W.H. Hare	(Nottingham)	W.R. Blyth	(Swansea)
P.J. Squires	(Harrogate)	T.G.R. Davies	(London Welsh)
G.W. Evans	(Coventry)	R.T.E. Bergiers	(Llanelli)
K. Smith	(Roundhay)	A.A.J. Finlayson	(Cardiff)
D.J. Duckham	(Coventry)	J.J. Williams	(Llanelli)
A.G.B. Old	(Leicester)	P. Bennett	(Llanelli)
J.G. Webster	(Moseley)	*G.O. Edwards	(Cardiff)
C.B. Stevens	(Penzance & Newlyn)	G. Shaw	(Neath)
*J.V. Pullin	(Bristol)	R.W. Windsor	(Pontypool)
M.A. Burton	(Gloucester)	P.D. Llewellyn	(Swansea)
R.M. Uttley	(Gosforth)	W.D. Thomas	(Llanelli)
C.W. Ralston	(Richmond)	¹I.R. Robinson	(Cardiff)
P.J. Dixon	(Gosforth)	W.D. Morris	(Neath)
A.G. Ripley	(Rosslyn Park)	T.M. Davies	(Swansea)
A. Neary	(Broughton Park)	T.J. Cobner	(Pontypool)
		¹Replaced by G.A.D. Wheel (Swansea)	

Tries: Duckham, Ripley
Conversion: Old
Penalties: Old (2)

Try: T.M. Davies
Conversion: Bennett
Penalties: Bennett (2)

Referee: Mr J.R. West (Ireland)

IRELAND v ENGLAND 1975
Played at Lansdowne Road, Dublin, 18 January 1975
Ireland won by 2G (12) to 1G, 1DG (9)

Mike Gibson, playing in his twelfth successive international against England, was the outstanding influence in a match which Ireland won in the last ten minutes. His first-half try and steadiness in defence were of priceless value to an Irish fifteen which registered a fourth consecutive win over the English. For England's new coach, John Burgess, this was a disappointing result, for his team began with promise, building a 9–6 lead against the wind in the first half, only to lose the match in a moment of carelessness seven minutes from no-side.

England selected a side with no new caps, but two changes were enforced: Burton, the Gloucestershire prop, was sent off in a county match and was withdrawn from the national side as a disciplinary measure; and Uttley pulled out through injury to admit Bill Beaumont, a new cap, at lock.

Against the run of play, England were first to score. In the twenty-eighth minute, Squires, England's best back, made a dazzling run down the right, sending several defenders astray with his sidesteps before passing to Stevens, who strided over for Old to convert. Ireland soon equalised when Gibson popped up outside Dennison and ran 40 yards to score wide out to the left. McCombe, with a superb kick, converted from the sideline. Old dropped a goal from just outside the Irish 25 to give England a three-points lead at half-time.

England, playing with the wind in the second half, dominated the match for the next 20 minutes. Ralston took control of the line-outs and the English backs carved several openings in a moderate Irish defence. Gibson's covering was splendid and this, together with hesitant English finishing, kept Ireland in the game. The Irish forwards were as lively as ever in the loose and their new hooker did well against Pullin in the scrummages. At length, Irish pressure pushed England deep into defence and, from a scrum-five, Webster was hounded into making a rash pass. Gibson disrupted Preece as he was about to gather the ball and the result was a gift try for McCombe. McCombe completed a tidy return to the Irish fifteen by converting his try.

IRELAND		ENGLAND	
A.H. Ensor	(Wanderers)	P.A. Rossborough	(Coventry)
T.O. Grace	(St Mary's College)	P.J. Squires	(Harrogate)
R.A. Milliken	(Bangor)	P.J. Warfield	(Cambridge U.)
C.M.H. Gibson	(N.I.F.C.)	P.S. Preece	(Coventry)
J.P. Dennison	(Garryowen)	D.J. Duckham	(Coventry)
W.M. McCombe	(Bangor)	A.G.B. Old	(Middlesbrough)
J.J. Moloney	(St Mary's College)	J.G. Webster	(Moseley)
R.J. McLoughlin	(Blackrock College)	C.B. Stevens	(Penzance & Newlyn)
P.C. Whelan	(Garryowen)	J.V. Pullin	(Bristol)
R.J. Clegg	(Bangor)	*F.E. Cotton	(Coventry)
*W.J. McBride	(Ballymena)	†W.B. Beaumont	(Fylde)
M.I. Keane	(Lansdowne)	C.W. Ralston	(Richmond)
J.F. Slattery	(Blackrock College)	P.J. Dixon	(Gosforth)
W.P. Duggan	(Blackrock College)	A.G. Ripley	(Rosslyn Park)
S.A. McKinney	(Dungannon)	A. Neary	(Broughton Park)

Tries: Gibson, McCombe
Conversions: McCombe (2)

Try: Stevens *Conversion:* Old
Dropped goal: Old

Referee: Mr F. Palmade (France)

ENGLAND v FRANCE 1975

Played at Twickenham, London, 1 February 1975
France won by 4G, 1PG (27) to 4PG, 2T (20)

French flair and artistry defeated the robot-like working of an English side anxious to please but unable to create fast attacks with the spontaneity of their opponents. France, with nine changes from the team beaten a fortnight earlier by Wales in Paris, opened up a 12-points lead in the first 17 minutes. Guilbert started the scoring in support of runs by Skrela and Estève; then a spectacular 30-yards run by Gourdon brought the large French contingent in the crowd to their feet. Gourdon's try, the result of an adventurous break by Taffary, was converted by Pariès (who had also improved Guilbert's try). Rossborough led the English rally and two penalties and a try – the product of a glorious round of English passing from right to left – brought England back to 10–12 at half-time.

England's failure to cope with a drop at goal by Pariès permitted Spanghero to score the next try, duly converted by Pariès, and Etchenique ended a series of conjuring tricks performed by the French backs to register France's fourth try. Pariès converted again and later kicked a penalty goal. Poor England could only muster two more sets of penalty goals, courtesy of Rossborough (who thus brought his tally for the match to 16 points), and a try by Duckham after a chip ahead by Preece and a chase against a couple of Frenchmen.

This was France's fourth win at Twickenham and their total of 27 points was a new record for them in England.

ENGLAND		FRANCE	
P.A. Rossborough	(Coventry)	M. Taffary	(R.C.F.)
P.J. Squires	(Harrogate)	J.F. Gourdon	(R.C.F.)
P.J. Warfield	(Cambridge U.)	J.M. Etchenique	(Biarritz)
P.S. Preece	(Coventry)	*C. Dourthe	(Dax)
D.J. Duckham	(Coventry)	R. Bertranne	(Bagnères)
M.J. Cooper	(Moseley)	L. Pariès	(Narbonne)
J.G. Webster	(Moseley)	R. Astre	(Béziers)
C.B. Stevens	(Penzance & Newlyn)	A. Vaquerin	(Béziers)
†P.J. Wheeler	(Leicester)	A. Paco	(Béziers)
*F.E. Cotton	(Coventry)	G. Cholley	(Castres)
R.M. Uttley	(Gosforth)	A. Estève	(Béziers)
C.W. Ralston	(Richmond)	A. Guilbert	(Toulon)
J.A. Watkins	(Gloucester)	J.P. Rives	(Toulouse)
A.G. Ripley	(Rosslyn Park)	C. Spanghero	(Narbonne)
A. Neary	(Broughton Park)	J.C. Skrela	(Toulouse)

Tries: Duckham, Rossborough
Penalties: Rossborough (4)

Tries: Etchenique, Gourdon, Guilbert, Spanghero
Conversions: Pariès (4)
Penalty: Pariès

Referee: Mr T.F.E. Grierson (Scotland)

WALES v ENGLAND 1975
Played at Cardiff Arms Park, 15 February 1975
Wales won by 1G, 2PG, 2T (20) to 1T (4)

The English backs were unable to make constructive use of the ball provided by their forwards at the beginning of the match, and the result, an easy victory for Wales, was never in doubt. The English pack did well to win the decisive line-outs, but the strong Welsh scrummaging and competent back-row play by Cobner, Mervyn Davies and Trevor Evans allowed Gareth Edwards to dominate the match from the base of the set-pieces.

Allan Martin opened the scoring after three minutes with a penalty from 50 yards and a scissors between Bevan and Gravell set up the first try. Fenwick drew Squires before sending an overhead pass to an unmarked J.J. Williams who scored wide out to the left. Martin kicked another penalty, from 40 yards this time, and Fenwick and Gravell created enough space for Gerald Davies to zip over for the next try. Martin converted from a difficult angle to place Wales 16 points ahead by half-time.

Wales relaxed in the second half and the match lost much of its appeal as a spectacle. Edwards's tactical kicking was a pleasure to watch and the strength of the Welsh rucking won praise from the purists.

Five minutes from the end, Horton enlivened the game when he crashed over the Welsh line following a line-out. Wales, as if insulted by this try, were catapulted out of their second-half lethargy and in the final minute Fenwick completed a fine individual match with a try. Quinnell, who had come on as replacement for Wheel, deflected a poor English kick and several Welsh players handled before Fenwick's last flourish.

WALES		**ENGLAND**	
J.P.R. Williams	(London Welsh)	A.M. Jorden	(Bedford)
T.G.R. Davies	(Cardiff)	P.J. Squires	(Harrogate)
S.P. Fenwick	(Bridgend)	K. Smith	(Roundhay)
R.W.R. Gravell	(Llanelli)	P.S. Preece	(Coventry)
J.J. Williams	(Llanelli)	D.J. Duckham	(Coventry)
J.D. Bevan	(Aberavon)	M.J. Cooper	(Moseley)
G.O. Edwards	(Cardiff)	[1]J.G. Webster	(Moseley)
A.G. Faulkner	(Pontypool)	C.B. Stevens	(Penzance & Newlyn)
R.W. Windsor	(Pontypool)	[2]P.J. Wheeler	(Leicester)
G. Price	(Pontypool)	*F.E. Cotton	(Coventry)
A.J. Martin	(Aberavon)	N.E. Horton	(Moseley)
[1]G.A.D. Wheel	(Swansea)	C.W. Ralston	(Richmond)
T.J. Cobner	(Pontypool)	J.A. Watkins	(Gloucester)
*T.M. Davies	(Swansea)	R.M. Uttley	(Gosforth)
T.P. Evans	(Swansea)	A. Neary	(Broughton Park)

[1]Replaced by D.L. Quinnell (Llanelli)

[1]Replaced by S.J. Smith (Sale)
[2]Replaced by J.V. Pullin (Bristol)

Tries: T.G.R. Davies, Fenwick, J.J. Williams
Conversion: Martin
Penalties: Martin (2)

Try: Horton

Referee: Mr A.M. Hosie (Scotland)

ENGLAND v SCOTLAND 1975

Played at Twickenham, London, 15 March 1975
England won by 1PG, 1T (7) to 2PG (6)

England's first win of the season deprived Scotland of the Triple Crown, but a dreary match was witnessed by the large crowd. Conditions were wet and gloomy, accurately matching the football.

The English selectors recalled two veterans, J.J. Page and Dave Rollitt. Both were prominent in England's win: Rollitt forming part of a back row which harried the Scottish halves out of the game and Page exercising a calming influence over the backs from his position at the heels of the pack. The fifteen Englishmen tackled steadfastly, smothering Scottish attempts to run the ball in attack.

Scotland were the better side in the first half but the courageous English defence and poor finishing by the Scottish backs resulted in stalemate at the break, penalties by Morgan and Bennett producing the points. Scotland continued to have the better of the play in the second half and an early penalty by Morgan regained the lead. It was, therefore, against the run of play that England went ahead. Warfield made a harmless kick ahead from midfield which Irvine looked certain to gather; however, a spiteful bounce resulted in the ball flying over Irvine's shoulder and Morley sped up to score a try near the left corner. Bennett failed to convert.

In the last quarter of an hour, Scotland had a couple of chances to win the match. Morgan's failure to land penalty points from a reasonable position and a narrow miss from a drop at goal by McGeechan enabled England to gain international respect at last, despite finishing as holders of the Wooden Spoon.

ENGLAND		SCOTLAND	
A.M. Jorden	(Bedford)	A.R. Irvine	(Heriot's F.P.)
P.J. Squires	(Harrogate)	W.C.C. Steele	(London Scottish)
P.J. Warfield	(Cambridge U.)	J.M. Renwick	(Hawick)
K. Smith	(Roundhay)	D.L. Bell	(Watsonians)
A.J. Morley	(Bristol)	L.G. Dick	(Jordanhill College)
†W.N. Bennett	(Bedford)	I.R. McGeechan	(Headingley)
J.J. Page	(Northampton)	D.W. Morgan	(Stewart's Melville F.P.)
C.B. Stevens	(Penzance & Newlyn)	*J. McLauchlan	(Jordanhill College)
J.V. Pullin	(Bristol)	D.F. Madsen	(Gosforth)
M.A. Burton	(Gloucester)	A.B. Carmichael	(West of Scotland)
R.M. Uttley	(Gosforth)	A.F. McHarg	(London Scottish)
C.W. Ralston	(Richmond)	G.L. Brown	(West of Scotland)
D.M. Rollitt	(Bristol)	M.A. Biggar	(London Scottish)
A.G. Ripley	(Rosslyn Park)	D.G. Leslie	(Dundee H.S.F.P.)
*A. Neary	(Broughton Park)	[1]N.A. MacEwan	(Highland)

[1]Replaced by I.A. Barnes (Hawick)

Try: Morley   *Penalty:* Bennett   *Penalties:* Morgan (2)

Referee: Mr D.P. d'Arcy (Ireland)

AUSTRALIA v ENGLAND 1975
Played at Sydney Cricket Ground, 24 May 1975
Australia won by 2DG, 2PG, 1T (16) to 1G, 1PG (9)

England's short tour of Australia was an unmitigated failure. The selectors adopted the brave policy of sending a party full of youth and promise, but a cruel sequence of injuries reduced the touring team's morale very early in the trip. Cotton, Keith Smith, Ashton and Preece were eliminated before the first test; and the problems multiplied when Bennett (with a back injury) and Neary (with damaged cartilages) retired in the first half of this match. (Neary handed over the captaincy to John Pullin.) Furthermore, the tour was marred by several outbursts of violence on the field of play.

It was the handling of the young Australian players which thrilled the 40,000 spectators who watched this match, and the 1–1 try tally rather flattered England. Several times the English defence was torn apart by the exciting play of the Australian backs and only good fortune kept England in contention at half-time. Loane scored Australia's try after supporting a break by Osborne, and Brown landed a penalty. For England, Squires made the most of some disorganised play by the Australian backs. He ran from the Aussie 25 for a try converted by Butler. In the second half, teenager Wright (the star of the match) and Brown, with a kick of 45 yards, dropped goals for Australia and Butler and Brown each kicked penalties.

The English backs were offered few opportunities to make use of the ball in attack. On the few occasions that chances were presented, possession was wasted with a tendency to overdo the kicking.

AUSTRALIA		ENGLAND	
R.C. Brown	(N.S.W.)	†P.E. Butler	(Gloucester)
L.E. Monaghan	(N.S.W.)	P.J. Squires	(Harrogate)
L.J. Weatherstone	(A.C.T.)	J.P.A.G. Janion	(Richmond)
G.A. Shaw	(N.S.W.)	†A.W. Maxwell	(New Brighton)
D.H. Osborne	(Victoria)	A.J. Morley	(Bristol)
K.J. Wright	(N.S.W.)	[1]W.N. Bennett	(Bedford)
*J.N.B. Hipwell	(N.S.W.)	†P. Kingston	(Gloucester)
S.G. Macdougall	(A.C.T.)	M.A. Burton	(Gloucester)
P.A. Horton	(N.S.W.)	J.V. Pullin	(Bristol)
S.C. Finnane	(N.S.W.)	†B.G. Nelmes	(Cardiff)
R.A. Smith	(N.S.W.)	R.M. Uttley	(Gosforth)
G. Fay	(N.S.W.)	†N.D. Mantell	(Rosslyn Park)
A.A. Shaw	(Queensland)	D.M. Rollitt	(Bristol)
M.E. Loane	(Queensland)	A.G. Ripley	(Rosslyn Park)
R.A. Price	(N.S.W.)	*A. Neary[2]	(Broughton Park)

[1]Replaced by †A.J. Wordsworth (Cambridge U.)
[2]Replaced by W.B. Beaumont (Fylde)

Try: Loane
Dropped goals: Brown, Wright
Penalties: Brown (2)

Try: Squires
Conversion: Butler   *Penalty:* Butler

Referee: Mr W.M. Cooney (Australia)

AUSTRALIA v ENGLAND 1975
Played at Ballymore, Brisbane, 31 May 1975
Australia won by 2G, 2PG, 3T (30) to 2G, 3PG (21)

Australia began the match with an unprecedented outburst of thuggery: fists and feet were brutally used at the first ruck of the match and a further fracas took place after the first line-out. England's Mike Burton was reprimanded for butting an opponent and moments later, when he late-tackled Osborne, the referee gave Burton his marching orders. The prop thus became the first England player to be ordered off in an international match.

Not surprisingly, England's fourteen were eventually overwhelmed by the weight advantage gained by the Australian pack. However, with Old playing his first tour match (after arriving five days earlier as a replacement) and kicking four goals, England managed to hold a 15–9 lead at the pause. Squires's try after 30 minutes was the best feature of the first half and resulted from crisp passing and direct running by England's backs. Old converted the try and kicked three penalties, the last, near to half-time, from inside his own half. Brown kicked a penalty for Australia and converted a try which Price scored from the tail of a line-out.

England's pack had dominated in the rucks and line-outs up to half-time but Australia took charge in the second half. In a ten-minutes spell, Wright created two splendid tries to place his side 17–15 ahead. Then, an ill-judged English clearance kick presented Monaghan with a chance to jink past several English defenders. Smith scored and England's misery was complete when a flowing movement by the Australians, virtually the length of the pitch, finished in a try for Monaghan. Wright converted one try and kicked a penalty.

Ripley, England's leading forward, made one of his typical swashbuckling runs near the end and Uttley scored a try which Old converted.

AUSTRALIA		ENGLAND	
R.C. Brown	(N.S.W.)	†A.J. Hignell	(Cambridge U.)
L.E. Monaghan	(N.S.W.)	P.J. Squires	(Harrogate)
L.J. Weatherstone	(A.C.T.)	J.P.A.G. Janion	(Richmond)
G.A. Shaw	(N.S.W.)	P.S. Preece	(Coventry)
D.H. Osborne	(Victoria)	A.J. Morley	(Bristol)
K.J. Wright	(N.S.W.)	A.G.B. Old	(Middlesbrough)
*J.N.B. Hipwell	(N.S.W.)	P. Kingston	(Gloucester)
S.G. Macdougall	(A.C.T.)	M.A. Burton	(Gloucester)
P.A. Horton	(N.S.W.)	*J.V. Pullin	(Bristol)
R. Graham	(N.S.W.)	B.G. Nelmes	(Cardiff)
R.A. Smith	(N.S.W.)	†R.M. Wilkinson	(Bedford)
G. Fay	(N.S.W.)	W.B. Beaumont	(Fylde)
A.A. Shaw	(Queensland)	D.M. Rollitt	(Bristol)
M.E. Loane	(Queensland)	A.G. Ripley	(Rosslyn Park)
R.A. Price	(N.S.W.)	R.M. Uttley	(Gosforth)

Tries: Fay, Monaghan, Price, Smith, Weatherstone
Conversions: Brown, Wright
Penalties: Brown, Wright

Tries: Squires, Uttley
Conversions: Old (2)
Penalties: Old (3)

Referee: Mr R.T. Burnett (Australia)

ENGLAND v AUSTRALIA 1976

Played at Twickenham, London, 3 January 1976
England won by 1G, 3PG, 2T (23) to 2PG (6)

England's team for their third successive match against Australia was prepared by a new coach, Peter Colston of Bristol. He had a sturdy pack at his disposal and they were to fashion a convincing English win by 17 points. The industry of Peter Wheeler gained England four strikes against the head, while the catching and jumping of Ripley was an advantage in the line-outs. Unfortunately, England's backs were still unable to use possession with any imagination and the contentment which followed this victory concealed the fact that the selectors did not have the right mix behind their forwards.

The first half produced few notable passages of play. Hignell, kicking into the wind, landed two penalty goals, against one by McLean, for England to lead 6–3 at half-time. In the second half, the English forward strength was too great for the Australians and, in the twenty-seventh minute, Corless made use of the narrow side to score a try and enliven the match. Lampkowski went over from a scrummage soon after and Duckham ended a spirited move by the English backs with a try on the left. Hignell converted the last try and added a penalty late in the match. Australia, who had been unable to field their best side for the match, could only respond with another penalty goal by McLean.

ENGLAND		AUSTRALIA	
A.J. Hignell	(Cambridge U.)	P.E. McLean	(Queensland)
P.J. Squires	(Harrogate)	P.G. Batch	(Queensland)
A.W. Maxwell	(Headingley)	W.A. McKid	(N.S.W.)
†B.J. Corless	(Coventry)	*G.A. Shaw	(N.S.W.)
D.J. Duckham	(Coventry)	L.E. Monaghan	(N.S.W.)
M.J. Cooper	(Moseley)	L.J. Weatherstone	(A.C.T.)
†M.S. Lampkowski	(Headingley)	R.G. Hauser	(Queensland)
F.E. Cotton	(Sale)	S.C. Finnane	(N.S.W.)
P.J. Wheeler	(Leicester)	P.A. Horton	(N.S.W)
M.A. Burton	(Gloucester)	S.G. Macdougall	(A.C.T.)
W.B. Beaumont	(Fylde)	R.A. Smith	(N.S.W.)
R.M. Wilkinson	(Bedford)	D.W. Hillhouse	(Queensland)
†M. Keyworth	(Swansea)	G. Cornelsen	(N.S.W.)
A.G. Ripley	(Rosslyn Park)	M.E. Loane	(Queensland)
*A. Neary	(Broughton Park)	A.A. Shaw	(Queensland)

Tries: Corless, Duckham, Lampkowski   *Penalties:* McLean (2)
Conversion: Hignell
Penalties: Hignell (3)

Referee: Mr M. Joseph (Wales)

ENGLAND v WALES 1976

Played at Twickenham, London, 17 January 1976
Wales won by 3G, 1PG (21) to 3PG (9)

Wales began their four 'Crowning Years' with a 12-points win at Twickenham, their largest winning margin there to date. However, their greedy supporters were not entirely satisfied with the result, for Wales, after holding a 15–6 interval lead, relaxed in the second half and managed just one late try.

England's forwards were again the mainstay of the home side. They held the Welsh in all aspects of tight and loose play – rucks excepted – but lacked a tactical coordinator to support them. Wales, of course, had Gareth Edwards to run the show and his long raking kicks to touch provided inspiration to his pack and attacking opportunities for his backs.

Wales had several uncomfortable moments in the first quarter of an hour. Once Hignell was through and only one of J.P.R. Williams's finest tackles prevented a score. But, as so often with Wales at Twickenham in the 1970s, a quick try, followed by a couple of accurate goal kicks, pulled them clear and left England with little hope of victory. Edwards was the try-scorer after 17 minutes. England heeled the ball from a scrummage on their line but Lampkowski failed to pick it up and Edwards touched down. Fenwick converted. Martin landed a penalty (which Hignell cancelled with another) and just before half-time J.P.R. Williams received an inside pass from J.J. Williams to power over in the left corner. Fenwick converted from a difficult angle.

Hignell, with penalties just before and shortly after half-time, kept England's deficit to six points. Then, near the end, J.P.R. Williams made an arcing run inside Phil Bennett, took a short pass, and scored his second try of the match. Fenwick converted from an easy position.

ENGLAND		WALES	
A.J. Hignell	(Cambridge U.)	J.P.R. Williams	(London Welsh)
[1]P.J. Squires	(Harrogate)	T.G.R. Davies	(Cardiff)
A.W. Maxwell	(Headingley)	R.W.R. Gravell	(Llanelli)
†D.A. Cooke	(Harlequins)	S.P. Fenwick	(Bridgend)
D.J. Duckham	(Coventry)	J.J. Williams	(Llanelli)
M.J. Cooper	(Moseley)	P. Bennett	(Llanelli)
M.S. Lampkowski	(Headingley)	G.O. Edwards	(Cardiff)
F.E. Cotton	(Sale)	A.G. Faulkner	(Pontypool)
P.J. Wheeler	(Leicester)	R.W. Windsor	(Pontypool)
M.A. Burton	(Gloucester)	G. Price	(Pontypool)
W.B. Beaumont	(Fylde)	A.J. Martin	(Aberavon)
R.M. Wilkinson	(Bedford)	G.A.D. Wheel	(Swansea)
M. Keyworth	(Swansea)	T.J. Cobner	(Pontypool)
A.G. Ripley	(Rosslyn Park)	*T.M. Davies	(Swansea)
*A. Neary	(Broughton Park)	T.P. Evans	(Swansea)

[1]Replaced by P.S. Preece (Coventry)

Penalties: Hignell (3)

Tries: J.P.R. Williams (2),
Edwards
Conversions: Fenwick (3)
Penalty: Martin

Referee: Mr G. Domercq (France)

SCOTLAND v ENGLAND 1976

Played at Murrayfield, Edinburgh, 21 February 1976
Scotland won by 2G, 2PG, 1T (22) to 1G, 2PG (12)

The Queen and Prince Philip were among the 70,000 spectators who saw an exciting game. The packs were evenly matched but the Scottish backs were sharper than their leaden-footed opponents and England flopped to their fifth successive defeat at Murrayfield.

England scored first after six minutes, Old sending Maxwell in for a try to the left of the goal and converting his side into a six-points lead. Penalties by Irvine and Old came next before fluent, cohesive work by the Scots carried play 70 yards and Lawson scored a try which Irvine converted. Old, with another penalty, put England in front before half-time, but Irvine equalised early in the second half and the stage was set for a grandstand finish.

The decisive score, just as the match was entering its final quarter, came from an English error. A rash pass by Burton put Old under pressure on the English 25 and Leslie smothered Old's attempt to clear the ball to touch. Leslie took advantage of a kind bounce and raced 20 yards for a try. Lawson made Scotland's victory secure when he nipped across the English line after sustained pressure by his forwards. Irvine converted this try from near the posts.

The game was played in an excellent spirit throughout, but the pace of the play and the vigour of the tackling took their toll on the players. Duckham and Shedden were injured in tackles during the first half and Maxwell had to be replaced in the second half.

SCOTLAND		ENGLAND	
A.R. Irvine	(Heriot's F.P.)	A.J. Hignell	(Cambridge U.)
W.C.C. Steele	(London Scottish)	K.C. Plummer	(Bristol)
A.G. Cranston	(Hawick)	[2]A.W. Maxwell	(Headingley)
I.R. McGeechan	(Headingley)	D.A. Cooke	(Harlequins)
[1]D. Shedden	(West of Scotland)	[1]D.J. Duckham	(Coventry)
R. Wilson	(London Scottish)	A.G.B. Old	(Middlesbrough)
A.J.M. Lawson	(London Scottish)	M.S. Lampkowski	(Headingley)
*J. McLauchlan	(Jordanhill)	F.E. Cotton	(Sale)
C.D. Fisher	(Waterloo)	P.J. Wheeler	(Leicester)
A.B. Carmichael	(West of Scotland)	M.A. Burton	(Gloucester)
A.J. Tomes	(Hawick)	W.B. Beaumont	(Fylde)
G.L. Brown	(West of Scotland)	R.M. Wilkinson	(Bedford)
M.A. Biggar	(London Scottish)	M. Keyworth	(Swansea)
A.F. McHarg	(London Scottish)	A.G. Ripley	(Rosslyn Park)
D.G. Leslie	(West of Scotland)	*A. Neary	(Broughton Park)

[1]Replaced by J.M. Renwick (Hawick)

[1]Replaced by †D.M. Wyatt (Bedford)
[2]Replaced by W.N. Bennett (Bedford)

Tries: Lawson (2), Leslie
Conversions: Irvine (2)
Penalties: Irvine (2)

Try: Maxwell
Conversion: Old
Penalties: Old (2)

Referee: Mr D.M. Lloyd (Wales)

ENGLAND v IRELAND 1976

Played at Twickenham, London, 6 March 1976
Ireland won by 2PG, 1DG, 1T (13) to 4PG (12)

England's downhearted supporters saw their side make a confident start and build a comfortable lead before McGann led a timely Irish recovery which finished in Ireland's third consecutive victory at Twickenham.

In the first half the English forwards controlled the tight play and Ireland were restricted to sporadic attacks which caused little disturbance to the home defence. One notable raid, after only five minutes, nearly created a try for Grace, but he was checked five yards from the English line. Otherwise, Ireland's principal weapon was the tactical kicking of McGann: he had a good match and helped Ireland to ride the storm brewed up by England's pack in the opening half. England's backs disappointed again and penalties were the only source of points up to the interval. Old landed goals from 50 and 45 yards with grand kicks and another penalty put the English 9–0 ahead at half-time.

Ireland attacked at the beginning of the second half and Gibson was tackled without the ball. Some argued that there was a case for awarding a penalty try, but McGann kicked three penalty points instead and Ireland were now a rejuvenated side. Next, Ensor started an attack which McGann continued and Grace, cutting inside from the wing, took a short pass to score wide of the posts. Although McGann failed to convert, he later placed his side in the lead with a penalty and then dropped a superb goal from 30 yards.

England were offered a penalty in the last minute of the match and Old kicked a goal from 35 yards when most people expected some kind of set-move aimed at producing a try.

ENGLAND		IRELAND	
[1]A.J. Hignell	(Cambridge U.)	A.H. Ensor	(Lansdowne)
K.C. Plummer	(Bristol)	*T.O. Grace	(St Mary's College)
A.W. Maxwell	(Headingley)	J.A. Brady	(Wanderers)
D.A. Cooke	(Harlequins)	C.M.H. Gibson	(N.I.F.C.)
†M.A.C. Slemen	(Liverpool)	S.E.F. Blake-Knox	(N.I.F.C.)
A.G.B. Old	(Middlesbrough)	B.J. McGann	(Cork Const.)
M.S. Lampkowski	(Headingley)	D.M. Canniffe	(Lansdowne)
F.E. Cotton	(Sale)	P.A. Orr	(Old Wesley)
P.J. Wheeler	(Leicester)	J.L. Cantrell	(U.C. Dublin)
M.A. Burton	(Gloucester)	P. O'Callaghan	(Dolphin)
W.B. Beaumont	(Fylde)	M.I. Keane	(Lansdowne)
R.M. Wilkinson	(Bedford)	B.O. Foley	(Shannon)
M. Keyworth	(Swansea)	S.M. Deering	(Garryowen)
†G.J. Adey	(Leicester)	H.W. Steele	(Ballymena)
*A. Neary	(Broughton Park)	S.A. McKinney	(Dungannon)

[1]Replaced by B.J. Corless (Coventry)

Penalties: Old (4)

Try: Grace   *Dropped goal:* McGann
Penalties: McGann (2)

Referee: Mr A.M. Hosie (Scotland)

FRANCE v ENGLAND 1976

Played at Parc des Princes, Paris, 20 March 1976
France won by 3G, 3T (30) to 1G, 1PG (9)

England introduced a new half-back pair and recalled Peter Butler (previously capped in Australia) and another old hand, Peter Dixon, for this last match of the season, against the French. The result, a humiliating defeat by 21 points, meant that England had been whitewashed for only the second time in the Five Nations Tournament.

England took the lead in the third minute when Butler kicked a penalty, but a try by Romeu put France ahead soon after and England were never in the game after that. Romeu converted his try and Paparemborde bulldozed a path through a maul for another try to give France a 10–3 advantage at half-time.

The English pack buckled in the second half and the defence of the team was pathetic against a succession of impressive French thrusts. Bastiat, and Paparemborde again, scored after intense French forward pressure; Gourdon's try was the result of a move involving Fouroux and Bertranne; while a cheeky piece of robbery by Fouroux, when he pinched the ball from the back of an English scrum early in the second half, exposed the lack of commitment of a very weak English side.

Dixon, England's best forward, scored his side's only try when Williams opened the French lines with a couple of side-steps and a deceptive change of pace. Butler converted.

FRANCE		ENGLAND	
[1]J.M. Aguirre	(Bagnères)	P.E. Butler	(Gloucester)
J.F. Gourdon	(R.C.F.)	K.C. Plummer	(Bristol)
R. Bertranne	(Bagnères)	A.W. Maxwell	(Headingley)
J. Pécune	(Tarbes)	D.A. Cooke	(Harlequins)
J.L. Averous	(La Voulte)	M.A.C. Slemen	(Liverpool)
J.P. Romeu	(Montferrand)	†C.G. Williams	(Gloucester)
*J. Fouroux	(La Voulte)	S.J. Smith	(Sale)
G. Cholley	(Castres)	F.E. Cotton	(Sale)
A. Paco	(Béziers)	J.V. Pullin	(Bristol)
R. Paparemborde	(Pau)	M.A. Burton	(Gloucester)
J.F. Imbernon	(Perpignan)	W.B. Beaumont	(Fylde)
M. Palmié	(Béziers)	R.M. Wilkinson	(Bedford)
J.P. Rives	(Toulouse)	P.J. Dixon	(Gosforth)
J.P. Bastiat	(Dax)	G.J. Adey	(Leicester)
J.C. Skrela	(Toulouse)	*A. Neary	(Broughton Park)

[1]Replaced by R. Berges-Cau (Lourdes)

Tries: Paparemborde (2), Bastiat, Fouroux, Gourdon, Romeu
Conversions: Romeu (3)

Try: Dixon   *Conversion:* Butler
Penalty: Butler

Referee: Mr K.H. Clark (Ireland)

ENGLAND v SCOTLAND 1977
Played at Twickenham, London, 8 January 1977
England won by 2G, 2PG, 2T (26) to 2PG (6)

England forgot the traumas of 1976 and produced a superb performance in front of 68,000 spectators. Total dominance by the English forwards in the rucks, mauls and scrums disrupted the Scottish eight and the much-praised Scottish backs were deprived of the ball for most of the game. Cooper and Young controlled the match from half-back: both kicked shrewdly and Cooper's use of Kent on the crash-ball was most effective and led to two tries.

Irvine had opened the scoring with a penalty before Kent's first sortie set up a ruck in the Scottish 25. The English forwards laid the ball back swiftly and Cooper moved to the narrow side, putting Slemen over in the corner. Hignell and Irvine kicked penalties and Young scored a try from a five-yards-scrum just before half-time. Hignell converted and opened the second-half scoring with another penalty.

The crowd, sensing a famous victory, inspired England with their vocal support after half-time and two more tries followed. England's forwards won a maul after a line-out and Kent charged through a mass of bodies after taking a short pass from Cooper. One minute from no-side, Uttley gathered the ball at a five-yards-scrum and scored near the posts, Hignell converting.

This was England's biggest-ever win against Scotland and if Hignell had not failed with several of his attempts at goal, the English winning margin would have been nearer to 40.

ENGLAND		SCOTLAND	
A.J. Hignell	(Bristol)	A.R. Irvine	(Heriot's F.P.)
P.J. Squires	(Harrogate)	W.C.C. Steele	(London Scottish)
B.J. Corless	(Moseley)	*I.R. McGeechan	(Headingley)
†C.P. Kent	(Rosslyn Park)	A.G. Cranston	(Hawick)
M.A.C. Slemen	(Liverpool)	L.G. Dick	(Swansea)
M.J. Cooper	(Moseley)	R. Wilson	(London Scottish)
†M. Young	(Gosforth)	A.J.M. Lawson	(London Scottish)
†R.J. Cowling	(Leicester)	J. Aitken	(Gala)
P.J. Wheeler	(Leicester)	D.F. Madsen	(Gosforth)
F.E. Cotton	(Sale)	A.B. Carmichael	(West of Scotland)
W.B. Beaumont	(Fylde)	A.J. Tomes	(Hawick)
N.E. Horton	(Moseley)	A.F. McHarg	(London Scottish)
P.J. Dixon	(Gosforth)	W. Lauder	(Neath)
*R.M. Uttley	(Gosforth)	D.S.M. Macdonald	(Oxford U.)
†M. Rafter	(Bristol)	A.K. Brewster	(Stewart's Melville F.P.)

Tries: Kent, Slemen, Uttley, Young
Conversions: Hignell (2)
Penalties: Hignell (2)

Penalties: Irvine (2)

Referee: Mr M. Joseph (Wales)

IRELAND v ENGLAND 1977

Played at Lansdowne Road, Dublin, 5 February 1977
England won by 1T (4) to Nil

The result, England's second success of the season, was their first win over Ireland since 1971 and ended a six-year run without an away Championship victory.

Uttley and his forwards, once again, showed outstanding qualities and provided perfect possession for their backs. However, a persistent drizzle, which hampered the handling of the backs, began soon after the start of the match and prevented Cooper from making extensive use of his three-quarters. Nevertheless, the Moseley pivot had one of his best matches for England and scored the only try of the afternoon. Kent again figured in crash-ball ploys but this time he was carefully marked by his young opponent, McKibbin. Indeed, one of the Irishman's unforgettable tackles on Kent elicited considerable vocal approval from the crowd.

The Irish backs could not achieve much in attack: McGrath often had to collect the ball while his forwards were on the retreat and he was under constant pressure from the English back row. Consequently, the service to Gibson, who was playing in his sixtieth match for Ireland, was mediocre.

The only try was scored in the twenty-second minute of the second half. England's forwards squeezed the ball out of a ruck on the left of the field and Young fed Cooper before Slemen, who had cut in from the blind-side wing, passed to Hignell. An angled kick by the full-back deceived an Irish defender, Horton hacked the ball towards the right and Cooper followed up to score at the corner flag. Hignell failed to convert from a wide angle; he also missed two penalties, one from 35 yards, but made amends for these lapses with a faultless technical display in defence.

IRELAND		ENGLAND	
F. Wilson	(C.I.Y.M.S.)	A.J. Hignell	(Bristol)
*T.O. Grace	(St Mary's College)	P.J. Squires	(Harrogate)
A.R. McKibbin	(Instonians)	B.J. Corless	(Moseley)
J.A. McIlrath	(Ballymena)	C.P. Kent	(Rosslyn Park)
D. St. J. Bowen	(Cork Const.)	M.A.C. Slemen	(Liverpool)
C.M.H. Gibson	(N.I.F.C.)	M.J. Cooper	(Moseley)
R.J.M. McGrath	(Wanderers)	M. Young	(Gosforth)
P.A. Orr	(Old Wesley)	R.J. Cowling	(Leicester)
P.C. Whelan	(Garryowen)	P.J. Wheeler	(Leicester)
T.A.O. Feighery	(St Mary's College)	F.E. Cotton	(Sale)
M.I. Keane	(Lansdowne)	W.B. Beaumont	(Fylde)
R.F. Hakin	(C.I.Y.M.S.)	N.E. Horton	(Moseley)
S.A. McKinney	(Dungannon)	P.J. Dixon	(Gosforth)
W.P. Duggan	(Blackrock College)	*R.M. Uttley	(Gosforth)
S.M. Deering	(Garryowen)	A. Neary	(Broughton Park)

Try: Cooper

Referee: Mr F. Palmade (France)

ENGLAND v FRANCE 1977

Played at Twickenham, London, 19 February 1977
France won by 1T (4) to 1PG (3)

This was a match which England would have won, handsomely too, if Hignell had landed his goal kicks. The full back, indomitable as always as the last line of defence, had a miserable afternoon with his boot and only succeeded with one penalty attempt out of six.

The French forwards, fresh from their victory over the Welsh in Paris, set the sternest test yet to the new, steadily improving English pack. But, with Uttley and Horton holding their own in the line-outs and the English pack effectively disrupting France's eight-man-shove by quick wheels in the scrummages, it was soon evident that France would find England their most difficult obstacle on the road to the Grand Slam.

England, with the advantage of a gusty wind, should have scored two tries in the first half. Both Corless and Slemen were guilty of poor judgment when unmarked players appeared on overlaps. Corless weaved past Bastiat before coming to grief five yards from the French line with Squires free beyond him and Slemen, who had Dixon isolated on his left, was smothered by three Frenchmen when going solo in the visitors' 25.

Just before half-time Young suffered a broken nose when tackling Bastiat. Smith, his replacement, played soundly but could not prevent France scoring the first try of the match, nine minutes after the restart. Aguirre looped around Averous on a blind-side attack from a ruck and Sangalli took the final pass to slip past Smith for a try to the left of the posts. Nine minutes later, Hignell kicked a goal when France infringed at a line-out on their 25, but his inability to convert two subsequent penalties deprived England of a deserved win.

ENGLAND		FRANCE	
A.J. Hignell	(Bristol)	J.M. Aguirre	(Bagnères)
P.J. Squires	(Harrogate)	D. Harize	(Toulouse)
B.J. Corless	(Moseley)	R. Bertranne	(Bagnères)
C.P. Kent	(Rosslyn Park)	F. Sangalli	(Narbonne)
M.A.C. Slemen	(Liverpool)	J.L. Averous	(La Voulte)
M.J. Cooper	(Moseley)	J.P. Romeu	(Montferrand)
[1]M. Young	(Gosforth)	*J. Fouroux	(La Voulte)
R.J. Cowling	(Leicester)	G. Cholley	(Castres)
P.J. Wheeler	(Leicester)	A. Paco	(Béziers)
F.E. Cotton	(Sale)	R. Paparemborde	(Pau)
W.B. Beaumont	(Fylde)	J.F. Imbernon	(Perpignan)
N.E. Horton	(Moseley)	M. Palmié	(Béziers)
P.J. Dixon	(Gosforth)	J.P. Rives	(Toulouse)
*R.M. Uttley	(Gosforth)	J.P. Bastiat	(Dax)
M. Rafter	(Bristol)	J.C. Skrela	(Toulouse)

[1]Replaced by S.J. Smith (Sale)

Penalty: Hignell   *Try:* Sangalli

Referee: Mr J.C. Kelleher (Wales)

WALES v ENGLAND 1977

Played at Cardiff Arms Park, 5 March 1977
Wales won by 2PG, 2T (14) to 3PG (9)

For once, England approached Cardiff with justifiable optimism. Their pack had conquered the French eight which, earlier, had mastered the Welsh. Surely nothing could stop England gaining the Triple Crown now? But Wales rose to the occasion and England were beaten, although the final losing margin of five points was the best return at the Arms Park since 1963 for the wearers of the rose.

Hignell was his side's outstanding player, kicking with polish and length in difficult conditions. His place-kicking, much maligned after the French match, improved vastly too, and a couple of penalties (one from 45 yards) supported a confident start by England. It was noticeable, however, that the Welsh pack were holding their efficient opponents and, after 20 minutes, superb Welsh control at a scrum-five enabled Edwards to gather the ball and charge through Slemen for an unconverted try. Fenwick, with a kick of 40 yards, gave Wales the lead before half-time, but Hignell kept England's hopes alive with another penalty, early in the second half, when Martin was caught pushing at a line-out.

England's problems were increasing when Fenwick regained the lead for Wales with a penalty from 45 yards, midway through the second half. Uttley had bruised his back at the end of the first half and Wales now had a distinct advantage up-front. Wheel wrested the ball out of the mauls with ease and the quality of the possession won by the Welsh forwards in the scrums and line-outs allowed Edwards to push his side into the English half with several long, raking kicks designed to demoralise the most optimistic of sides.

From one of his kicks, ten minutes from no-side, Wales launched the move which brought about the decisive try of the match. Edwards found touch in the English 25 and flicked an immaculate reverse-pass to Bennett from the ensuing line-out. Burcher made a break, moving right, and J.P.R. Williams slipped in as the extra man for his fifth try against England.

WALES		ENGLAND	
J.P.R. Williams	(Bridgend)	A.J. Hignell	(Bristol)
T.G.R. Davies	(Cardiff)	P.J. Squires	(Harrogate)
S.P. Fenwick	(Bridgend)	B.J. Corless	(Moseley)
D.H. Burcher	(Newport)	C.P. Kent	(Rosslyn Park)
J.J. Williams	(Llanelli)	M.A.C. Slemen	(Liverpool)
*P. Bennett	(Llanelli)	M.J. Cooper	(Moseley)
G.O. Edwards	(Cardiff)	M. Young	(Gosforth)
C. Williams	(Aberavon)	R.J. Cowling	(Leicester)
R.W. Windsor	(Pontypool)	P.J. Wheeler	(Leicester)
G. Price	(Pontypool)	F.E. Cotton	(Sale)
A.J. Martin	(Aberavon)	W.B. Beaumont	(Fylde)
G.A.D. Wheel	(Swansea)	N.E. Horton	(Moseley)
T.J. Cobner	(Pontypool)	P.J. Dixon	(Gosforth)
D.L. Quinnell	(Llanelli)	*R.M. Uttley	(Gosforth)
R.C. Burgess	(Ebbw Vale)	M. Rafter	(Bristol)

Tries: Edwards, J.P.R. Williams

Penalties: Fenwick (2)

Penalties: Hignell (3)

Referee: Mr D.I.H. Burnett (Ireland)

FRANCE v ENGLAND 1978
Played at Parc des Princes, Paris, 21 January 1978
France won by 2G, 1PG (15) to 2DG (6)

France, playing adventurous and disciplined Rugby, ran away to a convincing win in the second half. England lacked pace and flair behind the scrum but their forwards applied firm control to win the decisive line-outs and rucks, despite the fact that Cowling had to prop for half of the game with a dislocated shoulder (England having used their quota of replacements when Maxwell and Dixon were injured in an earlier incident, ten minutes before half-time).

England went ahead after three minutes. Old received the ball from a ruck to drop a neat goal, and shortly before the interval his second dropped goal gave England a 6–3 lead which, on the evidence of the half, they just deserved. France, it should be added, had been awarded several kickable penalties but only three points accrued, Aguirre landing a goal from in front of the posts when England were penalised for handling the ball in a ruck.

In the second half the French frequently criss-crossed the field with crisp handling movements carried out at top speed. 15 minutes passed before the outstanding attack of the match, involving Gallion, Viviès and a scissors by Bertranne and Aguirre, gave Averous the space to score a try at the posts. Aguirre converted. Eight minutes later, Bastiat collected the ball from the tail of a line-out and Cholley fed Gallion, who raced through flimsy English covering for a try in his first international. Aguirre, again, kicked the goal.

FRANCE		ENGLAND	
J.M. Aguirre	(Bagnères)	W.H. Hare	(Leicester)
J.F. Gourdon	(Bagnères)	P.J. Squires	(Harrogate)
R. Bertranne	(Bagnères)	B.J. Corless	(Moseley)
C. Belascain	(Bayonne)	[1]A.W. Maxwell	(Headingley)
J.L. Averous	(La Voulte)	M.A.C. Slemen	(Liverpool)
B. Viviès	(Agen)	A.G.B. Old	(Sheffield)
J. Gallion	(Toulon)	M. Young	(Gosforth)
G. Cholley	(Castres)	R.J. Cowling	(Leicester)
A. Paco	(Béziers)	P.J. Wheeler	(Leicester)
R. Paparemborde	(Pau)	M.A. Burton	(Gloucester)
J.F. Imbernon	(Perpignan)	*W.B. Beaumont	(Fylde)
M. Palmié	(Béziers)	N.E. Horton	(Toulouse)
J.P. Rives	(Toulouse)	[2]P.J. Dixon	(Gosforth)
*J.P. Bastiat	(Dax)	†J.P. Scott	(Rosslyn Park)
J.C. Skrela	(Toulouse)	M. Rafter	(Bristol)

[1]Replaced by C.P. Kent (Rosslyn P.)
[2]Replaced by A. Neary (Broughton P.)

Tries: Averous, Gallion   *Dropped goals:* Old (2)
Conversions: Aguirre (2)
Penalty: Aguirre

Referee: Mr N.R. Sanson (Scotland)

ENGLAND v WALES 1978

Played at Twickenham, London, 4 February 1978
Wales won by 3PG (9) to 2PG (6)

This was a match for which the R.F.U. could have sold sufficient tickets to fill Twickenham ten more times. Demand for admission to the stadium was so great for this game that stories unfolded later of spectators paying up to £200 on the black market for stand seats originally valued at £8. Many believed the game would decide the Championship, yet the occasion never matched its promise, mainly because conditions were so wet and heavy that running Rugby was impossible. It teemed with rain throughout the morning and afternoon and, not surprisingly, the game developed into a war of attrition between two powerful packs.

The only difference between the sides at the end was a penalty by Phil Bennett kicked eight minutes from no-side when Mordell handled the ball in a ruck on the English 22. Penalties punctuated the match. The English forwards were on top in the first half and at the interval Hignell's two goals, in the eighth and twenty-fifth minutes, outpointed Bennett's penalty in the tenth minute. The Welsh captain hit his second goal to level the scores two minutes after the restart, but even after Bennett's winning kick there was a chance for Hignell to square the match with a penalty from 40 yards. Alas for England, his shot passed outside the left upright.

Gareth Edwards, playing his fiftieth game for Wales, stamped his personality on the contest with a collection of impressive kicks of all varieties which invariably found touch to relieve the pressure on the Welsh defence. In the second half he provided the lasting memory of this dour match when he found touch 70 yards upfield with an extraordinary kick made from the touch-line near his own 22.

ENGLAND		WALES	
A.J. Hignell	(Bristol)	J.P.R. Williams	(Bridgend)
P.J. Squires	(Harrogate)	T.G.R. Davies	(Cardiff)
B.J. Corless	(Moseley)	R.W.R. Gravell	(Llanelli)
†P.W. Dodge	(Leicester)	S.P. Fenwick	(Bridgend)
M.A.C. Slemen	(Liverpool)	J.J. Williams	(Llanelli)
†J.P. Horton	(Bath)	*P. Bennett	(Llanelli)
M. Young	(Gosforth)	G.O. Edwards	(Cardiff)
B.G. Nelmes	(Cardiff)	A.G. Faulkner	(Pontypool)
P.J. Wheeler	(Leicester)	R.W. Windsor	(Pontypool)
M.A. Burton	(Gloucester)	G. Price	(Pontypool)
*W.B. Beaumont	(Fylde)	A.J. Martin	(Aberavon)
N.E. Horton	(Toulouse)	G.A.D. Wheel	(Swansea)
†R.J. Mordell	(Rosslyn Park)	J. Squire	(Newport)
J.P. Scott	(Rosslyn Park)	D.L. Quinnell	(Llanelli)
M. Rafter	(Bristol)	T.J. Cobner	(Pontypool)

Penalties: Hignell (2)   *Penalties:* Bennett (3)

Referee: Mr N.R. Sanson (Scotland)

SCOTLAND v ENGLAND 1978

Played at Murrayfield, Edinburgh, 4 March 1978
England won by 2G, 1PG (15) to Nil

Despite the fact that both sides were without a win in the Championship, a crowd of 70,000 assembled in perfect conditions to see the English forwards dominate the match. Cotton and Dixon, returning to the English pack, considerably strengthened the visitors' scrum and England's win was their first in Scotland for ten years.

Both sides were forced to make late changes: Breakey entered the Scottish fifteen when McGeechan was injured and Caplan won his cap when Hignell damaged a hamstring on the eve of the match. Caplan in fact nearly scored in the second minute of the match. A burst by Colclough from a line-out, supported by Horton, allowed Caplan to make ground on the short side until the Scottish forwards managed to suppress the danger near the Scottish line. Indeed, the Scots spent most of the first half defending their line as massive English pressure constantly threatened to produce a score, and English supporters were beginning to worry when the half-hour was reached with no points on the board. Then, from near half-way, Young and Slemen instigated the move of the match and Wheeler, Nelmes, Dixon and Beaumont were involved in an attack which left Squires in possession on the right. The Harrogate wing swivelled inwards, deceived a few defenders and scored near the posts for Young to convert. Three minutes before the interval Dodge kicked a penalty goal from 58 metres.

Scotland were supported by a healthy breeze in the second half but a tendency to kick away hard-earned possession prevented the Scottish backs from making the most of their opportunities. When they did run the ball, Irvine and Renwick were the danger men and Slemen's defensive qualities were invaluable to England on a couple of occasions when Irvine looked set to score.

Ten minutes from no-side England made victory certain when Dodge cut back to his forwards inside the Scottish 22 and Nelmes crashed through for a try which Young converted.

SCOTLAND		**ENGLAND**	
A.R. Irvine	(Heriot's F.P.)	†D.W.N. Caplan	(Headingley)
W.B.B. Gammell	(Edinburgh Wands.)	P.J. Squires	(Harrogate)
J.M. Renwick	(Hawick)	B.J. Corless	(Moseley)
A.G. Cranston	(Hawick)	P.W. Dodge	(Leicester)
B.H. Hay	(Boroughmuir)	M.A.C. Slemen	(Liverpool)
R.W. Breakey	(Gosforth)	J.P. Horton	(Bath)
*D.W. Morgan	(Stewart's Melville F.P.)	M. Young	(Gosforth)
J. McLauchlan	(Jordanhill)	B.G. Nelmes	(Cardiff)
C.T. Deans	(Hawick)	P.J. Wheeler	(Leicester)
N.E.K. Pender	(Hawick)	F.E. Cotton	(Sale)
A.J. Tomes	(Hawick)	*W.B. Beaumont	(Fylde)
D. Gray	(West of Scotland)	†M.J. Colclough	(Angoulême)
M.A. Biggar	(London Scottish)	P.J. Dixon	(Gosforth)
D.S.M. Macdonald	(West of Scotland)	J.P. Scott	(Rosslyn Park)
C.B. Hegarty	(Hawick)	M. Rafter	(Bristol)

Tries: Nelmes, Squires
Conversions: Young (2)
Penalty: Dodge

Referee: Mr J.R. West (Ireland)

ENGLAND v IRELAND 1978

Played at Twickenham, London, 18 March 1978
England won by 2G, 1PG (15) to 1DG, 2PG (9)

Michael Green, writing in *The Sunday Times*, summed up this match perfectly: 'For England a gratifying and important win which proves that the momentum of the resurgence begun last season is still there. The victory was built on the foundations of their forwards' superiority in the loose.'

In an entertaining game England faced a strong wind in the first half and defended skilfully to prevent Ireland scoring. The English forwards completely controlled the line-outs and rucks in the first half and the only try of the session came after 20 minutes. Ward was caught in possession on his 22, Young put Horton away on the narrow side and Colclough, playing a supportive role, sent Dixon storming over for a try which Young converted.

Ireland staged a comeback at the start of the second half. Ward kicked a penalty and dropped a goal from near the English posts to level the scores, but dangerous play by the Irish forwards was punished by Young who kicked three penalty points for England. Moments later Ward equalled a Championship record with his 38th point of the season, a penalty falling to Ireland when Gibson was tackled without the ball.

15 minutes from the end England moved the ball with style and produced the best score of the afternoon. Dodge received the ball from a scrum on the Irish 22 and made a lovely break before sending a long pass out to Squires on the right. Slemen had 'ghosted' across from the blind-side and he now appeared outside Squires to take the final pass and speed over in the corner. A superb kick by Young converted the try into a goal.

ENGLAND		IRELAND	
D.W.N. Caplan	(Headingley)	A.H. Ensor	(Wanderers)
P.J. Squires	(Harrogate)	C.M.H. Gibson	(N.I.F.C.)
B.J. Corless	(Moseley)	A.R. McKibbin	(London Irish)
P.W. Dodge	(Leicester)	P.P. McNaughton	(Greystones)
M.A.C. Slemen	(Liverpool)	A.C. McLennan	(Wanderers)
J.P. Horton	(Bath)	A.J.P. Ward	(Garryowen)
M. Young	(Gosforth)	*J.J. Moloney	(St Mary's College)
B.G. Nelmes	(Cardiff)	P.A. Orr	(Old Wesley)
P.J. Wheeler	(Leicester)	P.C. Whelan	(Garryowen)
F.E. Cotton	(Sale)	E.M.J. Byrne	(Blackrock College)
*W.B. Beaumont	(Fylde)	M.I. Keane	(Lansdowne)
M.J. Colclough	(Angoulême)	H.W. Steele	(Ballymena)
P.J. Dixon	(Gosforth)	S.A. McKinney	(Dungannon)
J.P. Scott	(Rosslyn Park)	W.P. Duggan	(Blackrock College)
M. Rafter	(Bristol)	J.F. Slattery	(Blackrock College)

Tries: Dixon, Slemen
Conversions: Young (2)
Penalty: Young

Dropped goal: Ward
Penalties: Ward (2)

Referee: Mr F. Palmade (France)

ENGLAND v NEW ZEALAND 1978

Played at Twickenham, London, 25 November 1978
New Zealand won by 1G, 2PG, 1T (16) to 1DG, 1PG (6)

This was a match which had little to commend it. The All Blacks were on an 18-match tour of the British Isles, during which they won each of the four international matches – something no other touring side from New Zealand had achieved. The strengths of the side were a solid pack inspiringly led by Mourie and a well-organised defence which conceded only one try in four internationals. These features, appreciated by the purist perhaps, and a ragged liaison between Horton and the English three-quarters, spoiled the game as a spectacle for the majority of a capacity crowd. Had they taken full use of their opportunities in attack, the New Zealanders would surely have won by 20 rather than 10 points: indeed, in the first half Osborne twice chose the wrong option when the try-line beckoned.

For all that, New Zealand's win was still conclusive, despite the fact that Hare opened the scoring with a splendid dropped goal from 40 metres after a short penalty. England, however, then gave away a simple try to Oliver. Wheeler threw in to a line-out 15 metres from the English line, the big Otago lock caught the ball and, unchallenged, sidled over for a try. Hare regained the lead for England with a penalty goal after 26 minutes, but more poor marking by the home forwards in the line-out presented the All Blacks with their second gift try, just before half-time. Johnstone claimed the score this time (from an English throw-in a metre from the corner flag) and McKechnie, after one or two earlier failures, at last kicked a goal.

Penalty goals by McKechnie in the thirteenth and thirty-fifth minutes of the second half completed the scoring.

ENGLAND		NEW ZEALAND	
W.H. Hare	(Leicester)	B.J. McKechnie	(Southland)
P.J. Squires	(Harrogate)	S.S. Wilson	(Wellington)
†A.M. Bond	(Sale)	B.J. Robertson	(Counties)
P.W. Dodge	(Leicester)	B.G. Williams	(Auckland)
M.A.C. Slemen	(Liverpool)		
		W.M. Osborne	(Wanganui)
J.P. Horton	(Bath)	O.D. Bruce	(Canterbury)
M. Young	(Gosforth)	M.W. Donaldson	(Manawatu)
R.J. Cowling	(Leicester)	B.R. Johnstone	(Auckland)
P.J. Wheeler	(Leicester)	A.G. Dalton	(Counties)
B.G. Nelmes	(Cardiff)	G.A. Knight	(Manawatu)
*W.B. Beaumont	(Fylde)	A.M. Haden	(Auckland)
J.P. Scott	(Cardiff)	F.J. Oliver	(Otago)
P.J. Dixon	(Gosforth)	L.M. Rutledge	(Southland)
R.M. Uttley	(Gosforth)	G.A. Seear	(Otago)
M. Rafter	(Bristol)	*G.N.K. Mourie	(Taranaki)

Dropped goal: Hare
Penalty: Hare

Tries: Johnstone, Oliver
Conversion: McKechnie
Penalties: McKechnie (2)

Referee: Mr N.R. Sanson (Scotland)

ENGLAND v SCOTLAND 1979
Played at Twickenham, London, 3 February 1979
Drawn: England 1PG, 1T (7), Scotland 1PG, 1T (7)

'Good possession gone to waste' led the scholarly David Frost in his report of this match for *The Guardian*. Here was a match in which England failed to capitalise on a wealth of ruck and line-out possession, when, after a promising start, the fine work of the home forwards was degraded by unimaginative back play. The English centres were preoccupied with cutting back to the forwards and, as a result, two skilful wings such as Squires and Slemen were not seen in attack as often as a large, patriotic crowd would have wished. At half-back, the new pairing of Bennett and Young did no better than any previous combination: Bennett tended to overdo the kicking and Young was constantly harassed by an energetic Scottish back row. Scotland, for their part, were better in defence. Renwick and McGeechan bottled-up the threat posed by the crash-ball ploys of the English centres and Lawson did his bit at the base of the scrum to aid his loose forwards in their disruption of Young.

England had a marvellous start. Horton plucked the ball out of the air at a line-out in the second minute and Bond created an opening for Hignell to enter the threequarter line and send Slemen gliding over in the corner. Bennett failed to convert but kicked a splendid penalty from touch after 15 minutes to put England seven points ahead. Scotland had been unable to make any telling attacks up to this moment but shortly afterwards a swift transfer from a set-scrum enabled Irvine to appear on an overlap with Hay. Irvine kicked ahead and was impeded before Rutherford, up in support, touched down for a try. Many argued that a penalty try should have been awarded.

In the second half Irvine equalised with a penalty after 23 minutes. His kick, from 35 metres, followed a transgression by Beaumont at a shortened line-out. Had Irvine been offered the earlier conversion from in front of the posts, as the penalty-try law permits, Scotland could have won a match they deserved to lose.

ENGLAND		SCOTLAND	
A.J. Hignell	(Bristol)	A.R. Irvine	(Heriot's F.P.)
P.J. Squires	(Harrogate)	K.W. Robertson	(Melrose)
A.M. Bond	(Sale)	J.M. Renwick	(Hawick)
P.W. Dodge	(Leicester)	*I.R. McGeechan	(Headingley)
M.A.C. Slemen	(Liverpool)	B.H. Hay	(Boroughmuir)
W.N. Bennett	(London Welsh)	J.Y. Rutherford	(Selkirk)
M. Young	(Gosforth)	A.J.M. Lawson	(London Scottish)
R.J. Cowling	(Leicester)	J. McLauchlan	(Jordanhill)
P.J. Wheeler	(Leicester)	C.T. Deans	(Hawick)
†G.S. Pearce	(Northampton)	R.F. Cunningham	(Gala)
W.B. Beaumont	(Fylde)	A.J. Tomes	(Hawick)
N.E. Horton	(Toulouse)	A.F. McHarg	(London Scottish)
A. Neary	(Broughton Park)	M.A. Biggar	(London Scottish)
*R.M. Uttley[1]	(Gosforth)	I.K. Lambie	(Watsonians)
M. Rafter	(Bristol)	G. Dickson	(Gala)

[1]Replaced by J.P. Scott (Cardiff)

Try: Slemen   *Penalty:* Bennett   *Try:* Rutherford   *Penalty:* Irvine

Referee: Mr C. Norling (Wales)

IRELAND v ENGLAND 1979
Played at Lansdowne Road, Dublin, 17 February 1979
Ireland won by 1G, 1DG, 1PG (12) to 1PG, 1T (7)

Ireland won an ill-mannered and undistinguished match with the aid of Ward's boot. The Irish pivot took every kicking opportunity that came his way to contribute eight of Ireland's 12 points. Bennett, by sharp contrast, managed only one successful kick at goal from five attempts.

The first score came after eight minutes. Ward was felled by a blatant late-tackle after chipping ahead from near half-way but the referee allowed play to continue. Hignell launched a counter-attack and when his final pass to Squires out on the wing was intercepted by McLennan, the Irish left winger had a clear run of 35 metres to the English line for a try which Ward converted. Bennett kicked a penalty from 30 metres just prior to the break but these three points were all that England had to show after 40 minutes with a strong wind blowing to their advantage.

Indeed, the wind wrecked a couple of efforts by Bennett, early in the second half: these were penalty attempts which, under normal conditions, the fly-half would have converted with ease. The English forwards were playing well in the tight and Hignell, on his return to the English fifteen, marshalled his defences with aplomb. In the line-outs, however, Gibson was causing several problems to England's jumpers and a fine catch of his at a shortened line on the English 22 gave Ward sufficient space to drop a goal from 35 metres. A subsequent penalty by Ward made Ireland's lead impregnable but England did manage a final attack, launched by Bennett and Slemen on the short side, which found the Irish defence in disarray. Spring failed to deal with Slemen's kick on and Steele hastily threw the ball back over his own line for Bennett to dash forward and score.

IRELAND		ENGLAND	
R.M. Spring	(Lansdowne)	A.J. Hignell	(Bristol)
[1]M.C. Finn	(U.C. Cork)	P.J. Squires	(Harrogate)
A.R. McKibbin	(London Irish)	A.M. Bond	(Sale)
P.P. McNaughton	(Greystones)	P.W. Dodge	(Leicester)
A.C. McLennan	(Wanderers)	M.A.C. Slemen	(Liverpool)
A.J.P. Ward	(Garryowen)	W.N. Bennett	(London Welsh)
C.S. Patterson	(Instonians)	P. Kingston	(Gloucester)
P.A. Orr	(Old Wesley)	R.J. Cowling	(Leicester)
P.C. Whelan	(Garryowen)	P.J. Wheeler	(Leicester)
G.A.J. McLoughlin	(Shannon)	G.S. Pearce	(Northampton)
M.I. Keane	(Lansdowne)	*W.B. Beaumont	(Fylde)
H.W. Steele	(Ballymena)	N.E. Horton	(Toulouse)
W.P. Duggan	(Blackrock College)	A. Neary	(Broughton Park)
M.E. Gibson	(Lansdowne)	J.P. Scott	(Cardiff)
*J.F. Slattery	(Blackrock College)	M. Rafter	(Bristol)

[1]Replaced by T.J. Kennedy (St Mary's C.)

Try: McLennan   *Try:* Bennett
Conversion: Ward   *Penalty:* Bennett
Dropped goal: Ward
Penalty: Ward

Referee: Mr A.M. Hosie (Scotland)

ENGLAND v FRANCE 1979
Played at Twickenham, London, 3 March 1979
England won by 1PG, 1T (7) to 1G (6)

Roger Uttley could not regain his place in the English fifteen, so Beaumont retained the captaincy and it was his inspiring leadership more than any other factor which helped England to raise their game and claim a famous victory. The English pack ruled the line-outs; their halves forged a fluent link between forwards and backs; Dodge and Cardus tackled with urgency and, at the back, Hignell was the corner-stone of an efficient defence.

In front of 70,000 spectators, and on a grey day, England faced a strong wind in the first half. Imagine their joy, then, when half-time arrived and the unbeaten French were 3–0 down. England, playing with confidence and style, deserved this narrow interval lead, the points coming from a penalty goal by Bennett after 30 minutes when Joinel fell off-side at a scrum. The kick, from 40 metres and into the wind, was a beauty.

France played attractive attacking football in the second half but could not penetrate England's determined tackling. Somewhat against the run of play, England increased their lead midway through the second period: Scott went on the rampage from the tail of a line-out and Kingston supplied Cardus with the ball from the ensuing ruck. The centre, moving left on the narrow side, took play close to the French line and from a scramble Bennett touched down for a try. France now abandoned all caution and, seven minutes from no-side, Aguirre split the English defence with a clever kick ahead which enabled Costes to gather the ball, untroubled, and score near the posts. Aguirre converted but England held on desperately to a one-point lead.

ENGLAND		FRANCE	
A.J. Hignell	(Bristol)	J.M. Aguirre	(Bagnères)
P.J. Squires	(Harrogate)	J.F. Gourdon	(Bagnères)
†R.M. Cardus	(Roundhay)	R. Bertranne	(Bagnères)
P.W. Dodge	(Leicester)	C. Belascain	(Bayonne)
M.A.C. Slemen	(Liverpool)	F. Costes	(Montferrand)
W.N. Bennett	(London Welsh)	A. Caussade	(Lourdes)
P. Kingston	(Gloucester)	J. Gallion	(Toulon)
†C.E. Smart	(Newport)	A. Vaquerin	(Béziers)
P.J. Wheeler	(Leicester)	A. Paco	(Béziers)
G.S. Pearce	(Northampton)	R. Paparemborde	(Pau)
*W.B. Beaumont	(Fylde)	F. Haget	(Biarritz)
N.E. Horton	(Toulouse)	A. Maleig	(Oloron)
A. Neary	(Broughton Park)	*J.P. Rives	(Toulouse)
J.P. Scott	(Cardiff)	A. Guilbert	(Toulon)
M. Rafter	(Bristol)	J.L. Joinel	(Brive)

Try: Bennett   *Try:* Costes
Penalty: Bennett   *Conversion:* Aguirre

Referee: Mr J.R. West (Ireland)

WALES v ENGLAND 1979

Played at Cardiff Arms Park, 17 March 1979
Wales won by 2G, 1DG, 3T (27) to 1PG (3)

England's recent success against France, and the selection of an experimental Welsh fifteen, gave English supporters just cause to believe that the Championship title was to be claimed at Cardiff in this final match of the season. But composure at half-back, implacable defence and total dominance up-front were the qualities which benefited Wales most in what was believed to be J.P.R. Williams's final international. The result was Wales's largest winning margin over England since 1905.

It was some time, however, before Wales established a clear lead. Gareth Davies opened the scoring after 13 minutes with a dropped goal and Richards capitalised on a spirited run by Quinnell in the thirty-third minute. Quinnell had been stopped near the English 22 but the efficient Welsh forwards served the ball back and the Swansea centre pierced the stretched English cover to run in for a fine try. Neil Bennett kicked a penalty from 30 yards soon after, when a player was off-side in a ruck, and that completed the scoring before the interval.

England had their best moments of the match in the first 20 minutes of the second half. Scott was outstanding in the back row and Cardus made one memorable break, before J.P.R. Williams was forced to leave the field with a calf injury. The departure of the Welsh captain inspired his men and England, curiously, surrendered just when their moment of success seemed imminent. A run by Hignell was England's last attacking gesture, but he was smothered by Fenwick and Ringer in a heavy (but perfectly legal) tackle. Wales lifted the siege and set about scoring 20 points in the final 20 minutes. Roberts, from a line-out, and Ringer and J.J. Williams after clever play by the Welsh centres, added tries, Martin converting J.J.'s from the touch-line. Finally, substitute Clive Griffiths made a run of 35 yards before kicking ahead for Elgan Rees to score. Fenwick converted.

WALES		ENGLAND	
*J.P.R. Williams[1]	(Bridgend)	A.J. Hignell	(Bristol)
H.E. Rees	(Neath)	P.J. Squires	(Harrogate)
D.S. Richards	(Swansea)	R.M. Cardus	(Roundhay)
S.P. Fenwick	(Bridgend)	P.W. Dodge	(Leicester)
J.J. Williams	(Llanelli)	M.A.C. Slemen	(Liverpool)
W.G. Davies	(Cardiff)	W.N. Bennett	(London Welsh)
T.D. Holmes	(Cardiff)	P. Kingston	(Gloucester)
S.J. Richardson	(Aberavon)	C.E. Smart	(Newport)
A.J. Phillips	(Cardiff)	P.J. Wheeler	(Leicester)
G. Price	(Pontypool)	G.S. Pearce	(Northampton)
A.J. Martin	(Aberavon)	*W.B. Beaumont	(Fylde)
M.G. Roberts	(London Welsh)	N.E. Horton	(Toulouse)
P. Ringer	(Llanelli)	A. Neary	(Broughton Park)
D.L. Quinnell	(Llanelli)	J.P. Scott	(Cardiff)
J. Squire	(Pontypool)	M. Rafter	(Bristol)

[1]Replaced by C. Griffiths (Llanelli)

Tries: Rees, Richards, Ringer, Roberts, J.J. Williams
Conversions: Martin, Fenwick
Dropped goal: Davies

Penalty: Bennett

Referee: Mr J.P. Bonnet (France)

ENGLAND v NEW ZEALAND 1979
Played at Twickenham, London, 24 November 1979
New Zealand won by 2PG, 1T (10) to 3PG (9)

This was the last match of a short tour to Scotland and England for Mourie's All Blacks. The tourists lacked the all-round strengths of their 1978 predecessors, but meticulous defence, good goal-kicking (by Richard Wilson) and the thoughtful captaincy of Mourie helped the New Zealanders to win nine of their ten matches in Britain. Their only defeat, against the Northern Division at Otley, took place one week before the English international.

Conditions were good and a large crowd anticipated a fast, exciting match. Alas, their expectations were not realised and the game, one of the poorest seen at Twickenham for many years, was matched only by the dreary, grey sky of this late-Autumn afternoon. England could not decide whether to play ten- or fifteen-man Rugby. The intricate back-row moves which had disrupted the New Zealanders at Otley were not so successful second time round – Mourie saw to that – and Cusworth, on his debut, failed to bring out the best in an English back division which, on paper, looked very strong. In the second half England certainly won enough possession to threaten a slim All Black lead, but Cusworth tended to overdo the kicking and several attacking opportunities were missed.

Wilson opened the scoring after three minutes when England were off-side at the second line-out. Then, after Fraser had knocked-on with the English line at his mercy, Loveridge kicked ahead minutes later and Fleming followed up to gather and score. Hare kicked a penalty after 35 minutes but Wilson restored New Zealand's seven-points lead with his second penalty, just before half-time.

In a boring second half, Hare landed two more penalties: the first, in the second minute, was kicked from 22 metres; his second, after 20 minutes, brought England one point behind. Late in the game Hare had the chance to win the match for England but his penalty kick, from 40 metres, was a failure and New Zealand thus gained their second win in twelve months over England.

ENGLAND		NEW ZEALAND	
W.H. Hare	(Leicester)	R.G. Wilson	(Canterbury)
†J. Carleton	(Orrell)	B.R. Ford	(Marlborough)
A.M. Bond	(Sale)	S.S. Wilson	(Wellington)
†N.J. Preston	(Richmond)	B.G. Fraser	(Wellington)
M.A.C. Slemen	(Liverpool)		
		G.R. Cunningham	(Auckland)
†L. Cusworth	(Leicester)	M.B. Taylor	(Waikato)
S.J. Smith	(Sale)	D.S. Loveridge	(Taranaki)
C.E. Smart	(Newport)	B.R. Johnstone	(Auckland)
P.J. Wheeler	(Leicester)	P.H. Sloane	(North Auckland)
F.E. Cotton	(Sale)	J.E. Spiers	(Counties)
*W.B. Beaumont	(Fylde)	A.M. Haden	(Auckland)
M.J. Colclough	(Angoulême)	J.K. Fleming	(Wellington)
A. Neary	(Broughton Park)	K.W. Stewart	(Southland)
J.P. Scott	(Cardiff)	M.G. Mexted	(Wellington)
M. Rafter	(Bristol)	*G.N.K. Mourie	(Taranaki)

Penalties: Hare (3)

Try: Fleming
Penalties: R.G. Wilson (2)

Referee: Mr N.R. Sanson (Scotland)

ENGLAND v IRELAND 1980

Played at Twickenham, London, 19 January 1980
England won by 3G, 2PG (24) to 3PG (9)

England, casting aside the unhappy memories of the 1970s, started the new decade with a resounding triumph over Ireland. The home pack were brilliant, winning the decisive line-outs, the rucks and the mauls and even taking the only strike against the head. Beaumont set a high personal example to his men; Blakeway made an impressive debut in the front row; and the English halves played with a composure rarely seen since the heady days of 1960 when Jeeps and Sharp guided England to the Triple Crown.

Hare kicked an early penalty, but three quick goals by Campbell gave Ireland an unconvincing lead after 20 minutes, before the English pack saw their dominance turned to good effect by the backs. English forward pressure near the Irish line gave Smith the chance to nip across for a try from a ruck, and not long afterwards the same player, working on the blind-side this time, created a try for Slemen. Hare converted both of these tries, giving England an interval lead of 15–9.

England stormed into the Irish 22 at the start of the second period and Smith was unlucky to have a try disallowed when the Irish forwards were shoved into their in-goal area at a scrummage. Hare, soon after, turned the territorial gain into points, kicking a penalty goal; but England suffered a setback after 20 minutes when Bond broke his leg and was replaced by Woodward.

Scott completed the scoring near the end when he romped over for a try after picking the ball up at the base of a scrum, ten metres from the Irish line. Hare's conversion was the finishing touch to a most emphatic English victory.

ENGLAND		IRELAND	
W.H. Hare	(Leicester)	K.A. O'Brien	(Broughton Park)
J. Carleton	(Orrell)	T.J. Kennedy	(St Mary's College)
[1]A.M. Bond	(Sale)	A.R. McKibbin	(London Irish)
N.J. Preston	(Richmond)	[1]P.P. McNaughton	(Greystones)
M.A.C. Slemen	(Liverpool)	A.C. McLennan	(Wanderers)
J.P. Horton	(Bath)	S.O. Campbell	(Old Belvedere)
S.J. Smith	(Sale)	C.S. Patterson	(Instonians)
F.E. Cotton	(Sale)	P.A. Orr	(Old Wesley)
P.J. Wheeler	(Leicester)	C.F. Fitzgerald	(St Mary's College)
†P.J. Blakeway	(Gloucester)	G.A.J. McLoughlin	(Shannon)
*W.B. Beaumont	(Fylde)	M.I. Keane	(Lansdowne)
N.E. Horton	(Moseley)	J.J. Glennon	(Skerries)
R.M. Uttley	(Wasps)	J.B. O'Driscoll	(London Irish)
J.P. Scott	(Cardiff)	W.P. Duggan	(Blackrock College)
A. Neary	(Broughton Park)	*J.F. Slattery	(Blackrock College)

[1]Replaced by †C.R. Woodward (Leicester)

[1]Replaced by I.J. Burns (Wanderers)

Tries: Scott, Slemen, Smith
Conversions: Hare (3)
Penalties: Hare (2)

Penalties: Campbell (3)

Referee: Mr C. Thomas (Wales)

FRANCE v ENGLAND 1980

Played at Parc des Princes, Paris, 2 February 1980
England won by 1PG, 2DG, 2T (17) to 1G, 1PG, 1T (13)

Remorseless pressure by the English forwards during the middle half of the match created the platform for victory – England's first in Paris since 1964. The pack controlled the tight play to such an extent in this vital period that England were able to force their way back into the game, transforming a 3–7 deficit into a convincing 17–7 lead. Beaumont, again, was an inspiring leader and much of England's success was due to his mobility in the loose and strength in the tight.

France began with a try in the second minute, Rives completing an attack in which Bertranne and Gallion were the principal invaders. Hare and Caussade landed penalty goals in the following events and then came England's purple patch. From a ruck, the English backs moved the ball quickly into the French 22 and Preston escaped from two tacklers to level the scores; Carleton scored next, after a blind-side break by Scott; Horton dropped a goal, just before half-time, when Uttley was temporarily out of action; and early in the second half, Horton added another dropped goal, taking his cue on the French 22 after the English forwards had wrested the ball out of a maul.

In the last quarter of the match, France stormed back in an adventurous attempt to win. Jérôme Gallion was checked on the English line after a tap penalty and Salas knocked-on in front of the English posts. Then, from the following scrum, France took the head and the ball was transferred to Averous who handed off Carleton to score a try which Caussade converted into a goal. Moments later Averous was in full-flight again, this time in an attack from deep inside the French half. The English defence managed to shepherd him into touch and Horton ended the match after the line-out by gratefully thumping the ball back into the crowd.

FRANCE		ENGLAND	
S. Gabernet	(Toulouse)	W.H. Hare	(Leicester)
D. Bustaffa	(Carcassonne)	J. Carleton	(Orrell)
R. Bertranne	(Bagnères)	C.R. Woodward	(Leicester)
D. Codorniou	(Narbonne)	N.J. Preston	(Richmond)
J.L. Averous	(La Voulte)	M.A.C. Slemen	(Liverpool)
A. Caussade	(Lourdes)	J.P. Horton	(Bath)
J. Gallion	(Toulon)	S.J. Smith	(Sale)
P. Salas	(Narbonne)	F.E. Cotton	(Sale)
P. Dintrans	(Tarbes)	P.J. Wheeler	(Leicester)
R. Paparemborde	(Pau)	P.J. Blakeway	(Gloucester)
Y. Duhard	(Bagnères)	*W.B. Beaumont	(Fylde)
A. Maleig	(Oloron)	M.J. Colclough	(Angoulême)
*J.P. Rives	(Toulouse)	R.M. Uttley	(Wasps)
M. Carpentier	(Lourdes)	J.P. Scott	(Cardiff)
J.L. Joinel	(Brive)	A. Neary	(Broughton Park)

Tries: Averous, Rives
Conversion: Caussade
Penalty: Caussade

Tries: Carleton, Preston
Penalty: Hare
Dropped goals: Horton (2)

Referee: Mr C. Norling (Wales)

ENGLAND v WALES 1980
Played at Twickenham, London, 16 February 1980
England won by 3PG (9) to 2T (8)

The expulsion of Paul Ringer – the first man to be sent off at Twickenham since Cyril Brownlie received his marching orders in 1925 – remains the permanent memory of England's first win against Wales for six years. Both sides were unbeaten and the game was built up as the key to the Championship. Consequently, some of the players allowed their undisciplined emotions to overshadow their skills, and after the referee had quite early on requested the captains to pacify their teams, Mr Burnett had no alternative but to send Ringer off when the Llanelli flanker late-tackled Horton in the fifteenth minute of the first half. Hare kicked the penalty from 30 metres to rub salt into Wales's considerable wound.

The Welsh scrummage was frequently wheeled on their own put-in in the subsequent play, but the strength of Holmes and the exquisite line-kicking of Gareth Davies kept Welsh hopes of victory alive throughout the game. In fact, soon after Ringer's departure, Wales went ahead. England heeled from a scrum near their line but Squire stole a try after Smith had lost control of the ball. Davies failed to convert, but Wales retained the lead until 28 minutes into the second half, when Hare landed his second penalty, the Welsh forwards handling the ball in a ruck.

Three minutes from no-side Wales regained the lead through Elgan Rees. Phillips charged down a kick by Smith and darted along the right touch-line before drawing the English cover to send Rees sprinting over for the try which many believed would win the match. In injury time, however, Hare, from the right touch-line, landed his third goal and seconds after England were celebrating a fortunate victory.

ENGLAND		WALES	
W.H. Hare	(Leicester)	W.R. Blyth	(Swansea)
J. Carleton	(Orrell)	H.E. Rees	(Neath)
C.R. Woodward	(Leicester)	D.S. Richards	(Swansea)
P.W. Dodge	(Leicester)	S.P. Fenwick	(Bridgend)
M.A.C. Slemen	(Liverpool)	L. Keen	(Aberavon)
J.P. Horton	(Bath)	W.G. Davies	(Cardiff)
S.J. Smith	(Sale)	T.D. Holmes	(Cardiff)
F.E. Cotton	(Sale)	C. Williams	(Swansea)
P.J. Wheeler	(Leicester)	A.J. Phillips	(Cardiff)
P.J. Blakeway	(Gloucester)	G. Price	(Pontypool)
*W.B. Beaumont	(Fylde)	A.J. Martin	(Aberavon)
M.J. Colclough	(Angoulême)	G.A.D. Wheel	(Swansea)
[1]R.M. Uttley	(Wasps)	P. Ringer	(Llanelli)
J.P. Scott	(Cardiff)	E.T. Butler	(Pontypool)
A. Neary	(Broughton Park)	*J. Squire	(Pontypool)

[1]Replaced by M. Rafter (Bristol)

Penalties: Hare (3)   *Tries:* Rees, Squire

Referee: Mr D.I.H. Burnett (Ireland)

SCOTLAND v ENGLAND 1980

Played at Murrayfield, Edinburgh, 15 March 1980
England won by 2G, 2PG, 3T (30) to 2G, 2PG (18)

England gained the Triple Crown and Grand Slam in an entertaining match watched by a crowd of 75,000. Scotland were overwhelmed by the scrummaging power of the English pack, and the purposeful running of Woodward in the centre frequently embarrassed a rather brittle Scottish defence. However, towards the end of the game, the Scottish three-quarters came into their own and moved the ball in a series of fast, creative attacks designed to unsettle England's backs.

England led by 16 points after 30 minutes. Woodward paved the way for tries by Carleton and Slemen in the fifteenth and twenty-fifth minutes respectively, and Hare converted both into goals. Scott and Smith, driving forward on the blind side of a five-metres-scrum, presented Carleton with a try in the thirtieth minute, before Irvine opened Scotland's account with a penalty goal – a fine kick which cannoned off the upright. England led 19–3 at half-time, Hare kicking a penalty just before the break.

Irvine landed a penalty early in the second half, but England's answer to this was the try of the season. Uttley won a line-out and the ball was handled by more than a dozen English players before Smith scored. With the crowd warming to an excellent match now, a thrust by Renwick resulted in a splendid try by Tomes, which Irvine converted; but England immediately wrecked Scotland's hopes of a recovery. Hare added his second penalty, before a high kick by Dodge was misjudged by Irvine and the ball bounced kindly for Carleton to gather it and sprint 40 metres, unchallenged, to complete his hat-trick – the first by an Englishman in an international since 1924.

Then came Scotland's rally and Rutherford, with a classic fly-half break, darted through to dot the ball down beneath the English posts for a try which Irvine converted. Robertson, Johnston and Irvine were prominent in Scottish attacks during the last ten minutes, but England somehow managed to hold out and hang on to a 12-points lead.

Neary, by playing in his forty-third match, became his nation's most-capped player.

SCOTLAND		ENGLAND	
*A.R. Irvine	(Heriot's F.P.)	W.H. Hare	(Leicester)
K.W. Robertson	(Melrose)	J. Carleton	(Orrell)
J.M. Renwick	(Hawick)	C.R. Woodward	(Leicester)
D.I. Johnston	(Watsonians)	P.W. Dodge	(Leicester)
¹B.H. Hay	(Boroughmuir)	M.A.C. Slemen	(Liverpool)
J.Y. Rutherford	(Selkirk)	J.P. Horton	(Bath)
R.J. Laidlaw	(Jedforest)	S.J. Smith	(Sale)
J.N. Burnett	(Heriot's F.P.)	F.E. Cotton	(Sale)
K.G. Lawrie	(Gala)	P.J. Wheeler	(Leicester)
N.A. Rowan	(Boroughmuir)	P.J. Blakeway	(Gloucester)
A.J. Tomes	(Hawick)	*W.B. Beaumont	(Fylde)
D. Gray	(West of Scotland)	M.J. Colclough	(Angoulême)
D.G. Leslie	(Gala)	R.M. Uttley	(Wasps)
J.R. Beattie	(Glasgow Acads.)	J.P. Scott	(Cardiff)
M.A. Biggar	(London Scottish)	A. Neary	(Broughton Park)

¹Replaced by J.S. Gossman (W. of Scotland)

Tries: Rutherford, Tomes
Conversions: Irvine (2)
Penalties: Irvine (2)

Tries: Carleton (3), Slemen, Smith
Conversions: Hare (2)
Penalties: Hare (2)

Referee: Mr J.P. Bonnet (France)

W. B. Beaumont's 1980 Grand Slam side against Scotland: *back (team only)*
W. H. Hare, P. W. Dodge, R. M. Uttley, M. J. Colclough, J. P. Scott,
F. E. Cotton, A. Neary; *middle* P. J. Wheeler, C. R. Woodward, M. A. C. Slemen,
W. B. Beaumont (captain), S. J. Smith, J. Carleton, P. J. Blakeway;
front J. P. Horton.

LEFT   W. B. Beaumont, who led England on more occasions than any other
captain, on the burst against Ireland in 1980.
RIGHT   M. A. C. Slemen, who is almost certainly going to become England's
most-capped wing, in action against Scotland.

WALES v ENGLAND 1981

Played at Cardiff Arms Park, 17 January 1981
Wales won by 1G, 4PG, 1DG (21) to 5PG, 1T (19)

This was a game that the Welsh, celebrating their Centenary, desperately wanted to win. That they did was a tribute to their pack, which just won the battle for possession against an excellent English eight. Davis, Wheel and Williams were prominent in the line-outs, and the Welsh front row stabilised in the scrums after Cotton was injured in the fifteenth minute. Behind the scrum, Gareth Davies was the outstanding personality, excelling with long, teasing kicks.

What the match lacked in spectacle it made up for in excitement. For Wales did not gain their winning points until injury time, when Brynmor Williams and the Welsh back row conspired to lure Woodward off-side at a scrummage, and Fenwick, from 20 metres and in front of the posts, landed the penalty goal. Even then, Hare had a further kick at goal from 40 metres, but with the last kick of the afternoon he sent the ball across the face of the Welsh posts.

The only tries of the match were scored in the first half. One of Gareth Davies's kicks placed Hare under pressure near his line and Ackerman was quickly up to snatch the ball and send Davis over for a try. Fenwick converted to add to an earlier penalty and Wales led 9–0. Hare, then Fenwick, then Hare again, kicked penalties, before England produced the best move of the match. Beaumont ripped the ball from a maul and Smith sent his backs away to the right. Carleton, on a dummy run, confused the Welsh backs and Dodge sent Hare over for a try to reduce Wales's lead at the interval to 12–10.

Hare put England ahead early in the second half but Gareth Davies dropped a beautiful goal from 40 metres soon afterwards. Another penalty by Fenwick stretched Wales to a five-points lead, then Hare took his personal contribution to the match up to 19 points with a brace of penalties before Fenwick kicked the winning score in the dying moments of the match.

Beaumont, who captained England for the fourteenth time in this match, thus passed the previous captaincy record held by Wakefield, Hall, Evans, Jeeps and Pullin.

WALES		ENGLAND	
J.P.R. Williams	(Bridgend)	W.H. Hare	(Leicester)
R.A. Ackerman	(Newport)	J. Carleton	(Orrell)
D.S. Richards	(Swansea)	C.R. Woodward	(Leicester)
*S.P. Fenwick	(Bridgend)	P.W. Dodge	(Leicester)
D.L. Nicholas	(Llanelli)	M.A.C. Slemen	(Liverpool)
W.G. Davies	(Cardiff)	J.P. Horton	(Bath)
D.B. Williams	(Swansea)	S.J. Smith	(Sale)
I. Stephens	(Bridgend)	[1]F.E. Cotton	(Sale)
A.J. Phillips	(Cardiff)	P.J. Wheeler	(Leicester)
G. Price	(Pontypool)	P.J. Blakeway	(Gloucester)
C.E. Davis	(Newbridge)	*W.B. Beaumont	(Fylde)
G.A.D. Wheel	(Swansea)	M.J. Colclough	(Angoulême)
J.R. Lewis	(Cardiff)	M. Rafter	(Bristol)
G.P. Williams	(Bridgend)	J.P. Scott	(Cardiff)
J. Squire	(Pontypool)	†D.H. Cooke	(Harlequins)

[1]Replaced by †A. Sheppard (Bristol)

Try: Davis   *Conversion:* Fenwick   *Try:* Hare
Penalties: Fenwick (4)   *Penalties:* Hare (5)
Dropped goal: Davies

Referee: Mr J.B. Anderson (Scotland)

ENGLAND v SCOTLAND 1981
Played at Twickenham, London, 21 February 1981
England won by 1G, 3PG, 2T (23) to 1G, 1PG, 2T (17)

There were six tries in this match and a large crowd enjoyed one of the finest games of the season. The firm and dependable English forwards held an overwhelming advantage in the tight and foraged eagerly in the loose; while in the backs, the incisive running of Woodward and the solidity of Dodge were important factors in England's success. Huw Davies, a late replacement for John Horton, made an impressive debut, scoring the winning try of the match just before no-side.

Despite their obvious all-round superiority, England were forced to work very hard for victory by a plucky Scottish side. The lead altered five times during the game as the Scots, spearheaded by Rutherford, refused to surrender to the might of the English pack. Irvine and Hare opened their sides' accounts with penalty goals before Munro capitalised upon Hare's failure to deal with a kick by Renwick. Irvine failed to convert Munro's try, but Woodward, weaving past several Scottish defenders, scored next for Hare to kick the goal which gave England the lead at the pause.

Precise Scottish passing helped Munro to claim his second try and open the scoring in the second half, Irvine's conversion taking the score to 9–13 in Scotland's favour. And the Scots still led when Hare collected three more points with another penalty goal. Later, thoughtful play by Slemen brought the Liverpool wing his sixth try for England, but again Scotland took the lead, Calder crossing for a try. Then, a brilliant run by Slemen from broken play, and an accurate pass from Carleton to Davies, deceived the Scottish defence and the new English pivot ran 40 metres for a try which thrilled the crowd and won the match for his side. Hare concluded the scoring with his third penalty goal.

ENGLAND		SCOTLAND	
W.H. Hare	(Leicester)	*A.R. Irvine	(Heriot's F.P.)
J. Carleton	(Orrell)	S. Munro	(Ayr)
C.R. Woodward	(Leicester)	J.M. Renwick	(Hawick)
P.W. Dodge	(Leicester)	K.W. Robertson	(Melrose)
M.A.C. Slemen	(Liverpool)	B.H. Hay	(Boroughmuir)
†G.H. Davies	(Cambridge U.)	J.Y. Rutherford	(Selkirk)
S.J. Smith	(Sale)	R.J. Laidlaw	(Jedforest)
C.E. Smart	(Newport)	J. Aitken	(Gala)
P.J. Wheeler	(Leicester)	C.T. Deans	(Hawick)
P.J. Blakeway	(Gloucester)	N.A. Rowan	(Boroughmuir)
*W.B. Beaumont	(Fylde)	W. Cuthbertson	(Kilmarnock)
M.J. Colclough	(Angoulême)	A.J. Tomes	(Hawick)
†N.C. Jeavons[1]	(Moseley)	J.H. Calder	(Stewart's Melville F.P.)
J.P. Scott	(Cardiff)	J.R. Beattie	(Heriot's F.P.)
D.H. Cooke	(Harlequins)	D.G. Leslie	(Gala)

[1]Replaced by †R. Hesford (Bristol)

Tries: Davies, Slemen, Woodward *Conversion:* Hare
Penalties: Hare (3)

Tries: Munro (2), Calder
Conversion: Irvine
Penalty: Irvine

Referee: Mr D.I.H. Burnett (Ireland)

IRELAND v ENGLAND 1981

Played at Lansdowne Road, Dublin, 7 March 1981
England won by 1G, 1T (10) to 2DG (6)

For the second time during the season, the strength of the English pack, the front row, was disrupted by an injury early in the match. On this occasion it was Blakeway, with a neck injury, who was obliged to retire. Thus England, without the two props who had played such a key role in the Grand Slam wins of 1980, had to rely on the invaluable support of Steve Smith at the heels of the pack and the inspiration of Rose, at full-back, to triumph over a spirited Irish side.

Sargent, a loose head, replaced Blakeway on the tight head after 22 minutes and the Irish scrummagers immediately concentrated on upsetting the balance of the English striking unit. At length, Smart went over to the other side of the scrum to relieve Sargent from some of the pressure. Fortunately for England, Smith, who still had plenty of untidy ball to contend with from the scrums, played admirably and had one of his best matches.

Ireland opened the scoring after 13 minutes. Jeavons fed the ball back cleanly from a maul near the English 22, but Slemen's clearance kick glanced off the side of his boot straight to MacNeill, who calmly dropped a goal from 40 metres. Campbell dropped another goal a couple of minutes later, from 35 metres this time, after Orr had pounded his way up to the English 22. Quinn nearly put Ireland further ahead when he charged down a poor kick by Rose near the English line. Then just before the interval, the English three-quarters moved the ball out to the left from a scrum near half-way and Rose, on the overlap, took a pass from Slemen to race 50 metres for a corner try.

Half-way through the second half Rose's vision, when Campbell hastily sent the ball into the English half from a 22 metres drop-out, enabled Dodge to win the match from an excellent counter-attack along the left side of the field. Slemen and Woodward played their parts in a capital try, re-aligning quickly from the drop-out to transfer the ball to Dodge, who ran 40 metres before touching down. Fittingly, Rose kicked the goal.

IRELAND		ENGLAND	
H.P. MacNeill	(Dublin U.)	†W.M.H. Rose	(Cambridge U.)
F.P. Quinn	(Old Belvedere)	J. Carleton	(Orrell)
D.G. Irwin	(Queen's U.)	C.R. Woodward	(Leicester)
S.O. Campbell	(Old Belvedere)	P.W. Dodge	(Leicester)
A.C. McLennan	(Wanderers)	M.A.C. Slemen	(Liverpool)
A.J.P. Ward	(Garryowen)	G.H. Davies	(Cambridge U.)
J.C. Robbie	(Greystones)	S.J. Smith	(Sale)
P.A. Orr	(Old Wesley)	C.E. Smart	(Newport)
P.C. Whelan	(Garryowen)	P.J. Wheeler	(Leicester)
M.P. Fitzpatrick	(Wanderers)	¹P.J. Blakeway	(Gloucester)
M.I. Keane	(Lansdowne)	*W.B. Beaumont	(Fylde)
B.O. Foley	(Shannon)	M.J. Colclough	(Angoulême)
J.B. O'Driscoll	(London Irish)	N.C. Jeavons	(Moseley)
W.P. Duggan	(Blackrock College)	J.P. Scott	(Cardiff)
*J.F. Slattery	(Blackrock College)	D.H. Cooke	(Harlequins)

¹Replaced by †G.A.F. Sargent (Gloucester)

Dropped goals: Campbell, MacNeill

Tries: Dodge, Rose
Conversion: Rose

Referee: Mr J.P. Bonnet (France)

ENGLAND v FRANCE 1981

Played at Twickenham, London, 21 March 1981
France won by 1G, 2DG, 1T (16) to 4PG (12)

England were deprived of a share in the Championship by a French fifteen for whom victory meant a third Grand Slam. The English scrummaging was considerably disrupted by an aggressive, efficient French eight, and their only source of possession was the line-out, where Colclough helped England to win 23 of the 35 decisive line-outs.

France were fortunate to have the first benefit of a gale-force wind, and opened a 16-points gap by half-time. Laporte, a colossal kicker, was the first to score, dropping a long goal, and shortly afterwards Rives put Lacans over on the left from a quick throw-in near the English 22. This try was awarded in error because the ball which Berbizier had thrown from touch to Rives was supplied by a bystander, while Law 23 B (10) prescribes that 'the ball that went into touch is used, it has been handled only by the players and it is thrown in correctly'. Nevertheless, France deserved their points and Laporte converted with a fine kick. Three minutes before the pause France increased their lead with an impressive try. Rives was the active agent in a move which saw the ball transferred to the left for Pardo to score in the corner. Laporte concluded the French scoring with his second dropped goal.

Rose kicked four penalties in the second half but France retained their lead. The match, which had been built up as the show-down of the season, was conducted in a sporting manner under the quiet authority of the shrewd Mr Hosie.

ENGLAND		**FRANCE**	
W.M.H. Rose	(Cambridge U.)	S. Gabernet	(Toulouse)
J. Carleton	(Orrell)	S. Blanco	(Biarritz)
C.R. Woodward	(Leicester)	R. Bertranne	(Bagnères)
P.W. Dodge	(Leicester)	D. Codorniou	(Narbonne)
M.A.C. Slemen	(Liverpool)	L. Pardo	(Bayonne)
G.H. Davies	(Cambridge U.)	G. Laporte	(Graulhet)
S.J. Smith	(Sale)	P. Berbizier	(Lourdes)
C.E. Smart	(Newport)	P. Dospital	(Bayonne)
P.J. Wheeler	(Leicester)	P. Dintrans	(Tarbes)
P.J. Blakeway	(Gloucester)	R. Paparemborde	(Pau)
*W.B. Beaumont	(Fylde)	D. Revallier	(Graulhet)
M.J. Colclough	(Angoulême)	J.F. Imbernon	(Perpignan)
N.C. Jeavons	(Moseley)	*J.P. Rives	(Toulouse)
J.P. Scott	(Cardiff)	J.L. Joinel	(Brive)
D.H. Cooke	(Harlequins)	P. Lacans	(Béziers)

Penalties: Rose (4)

Tries: Lacans, Pardo
Conversion: Laporte
Dropped goals: Laporte (2)

Referee: Mr A.M. Hosie (Scotland)

ARGENTINA v ENGLAND 1981
Played at Ferrocarril Oeste Stadium, Buenos Aires, 30 May 1981
Drawn: Argentina 1G, 2DG, 1PG, 1T (19), England 2G, 1PG, 1T (19)

During a successful tour to Argentina, England became the first country to take advantage of the new ruling that caps may be awarded for matches played against non-I.B. countries. England won six of their seven tour games and Beaumont's men attracted a crowd of 28,000, on an overcast day, to this first international of the two-match series.

The English pack influenced the game from the start, winning most of the ball from the set-pieces and disrupting the play of the brilliant South American halves, Porta and Landajo. Rafter had an outstanding game and was singled out for high praise by his captain at the after-match inquest. Nevertheless, England were behind at half-time and were grateful for a late try by Woodward (converted by Hare) to save the game.

Huw Davies, with a handsome outside break, opened the Argentine defence in the seventh minute to score a try which Hare, nine times out of ten, would have converted. Alas, for England, he failed: a critical miss in view of the final score. Porta dropped a goal from a penalty given against the English front row, and a try by Campo, following an exciting run from half-way by Baetti (and on the stroke of half-time), saw the home side take a 7–4 lead.

Porta landed a penalty goal early in the second half but a high, teasing kick by Davies deceived Baetti and Woodward cashed in on the full-back's error for a try at the posts. Hare's conversion tied the scores. Sustained English pressure was the feature of the play which followed this score, but Campo intercepted a loose pass and ran 50 metres for a try at the posts which Porta converted. Unperturbed, England continued to press and Hare succeeded with a penalty when the Argentine forwards were caught going over the top at a ruck. Landajo dropped a goal from 20 metres but Dodge made a timely break to open the way for Woodward to score. Hare's conversion squared the points.

ARGENTINA		ENGLAND	
D. Baetti	(Rosario)	W.H. Hare	(Leicester)
M. Campo	(Pueyrredon)	J. Carleton	(Orrell)
M.H. Loffreda	(San Isidro)	P.W. Dodge	(Leicester)
R. Madero	(San Isidro)	C.R. Woodward	(Leicester)
A. Cappelletti	(Banco Nacion)	†A.H. Swift	(Swansea)
*H. Porta	(Banco Nacion)	G.H. Davies	(Cambridge U.)
T.R. Landajo	(Pueyrredon)	S.J. Smith	(Sale)
E.E. Rodriguez	(El Tala, Cordoba)	C.E. Smart	(Newport)
J. Perez-Cobo	(San Isidro)	†S.G.F. Mills	(Gloucester)
F. Morel	(San Isidro)	G.S. Pearce	(Northampton)
A. Iachetti	(Hindu)	*W.B. Beaumont	(Fylde)
E. Branca	(San Isidro)	†J.H. Fidler	(Gloucester)
T. Petersen	(San Isidro)	N.C. Jeavons	(Moseley)
G. Travaglini	(San Isidro)	J.P. Scott	(Cardiff)
E. Ure	(Buenos Aires U.)	M. Rafter	(Bristol)

Tries: Campo (2)
Conversion: Porta
Penalty: Porta
Dropped goals: Porta, Landajo

Tries: Woodward (2), Davies
Conversions: Hare (2)
Penalty: Hare

Referee: Mr J.P. Bonnet (France)

ARGENTINA v ENGLAND 1981

Played at Ferrocarril Oeste Stadium, Buenos Aires, 6 June 1981
England won by 1G, 2PG (12) to 1G (6)

In a hard, uncompromising match which occasionally became brutal, England showed the strength of character that had typified their Grand Slam victories twelve months earlier. 'Resolution and application were happily married' wrote John Mason in the *Daily Telegraph* after Beaumont's eight (containing only two survivors from the 1980 pack) had dominated the line-outs and shown the Pumas a thing or two in the rucks and mauls. Rafter, once again, had an excellent match as chief spoiler, giving Porta, the Argentine fly-half and captain, a torrid time.

England went into the lead after 15 minutes with a penalty by Hare, Ure failing to release the ball in a tackle. 15 minutes later Hare landed his second penalty when Landajo assaulted Carleton at a maul near the Argentine line. So England led 6–0 at half-time.

A powerful drive by the English forwards kept Argentina under pressure at the start of the second half and after three minutes England gained the first try of the match. Carleton was the key man in a well-planned crash-ball move, entering the threequarter line between the centres to take a pass at speed and launch the first offensive. The ball was swiftly transferred to Hare, who made the second telling run until he was tackled 20 metres from the line. Smith gained possession on the open side, broke through and drew Baetti before sending Huw Davies under the posts for a try which Hare converted.

The Pumas had the better of the last quarter of the match, although Porta failed with a couple of kicks at goal. Travaglini scored a try in a pushover scrum, Porta converting; and near the end England had a fright when Cappelletti popped up on the right wing to chase a kick by Porta. The ball skidded away beneath the winger's body and England held on to win the series.

ARGENTINA		ENGLAND	
D. Baetti	(Rosario)	W.H. Hare	(Leicester)
M. Campo	(Pueyrredon)	J. Carleton	(Orrell)
M.H. Loffreda	(San Isidro)	P.W. Dodge	(Leicester)
[1]R. Madero	(San Isidro)	C.R. Woodward	(Leicester)
A. Cappelletti	(Banco Nacion)	A.H. Swift	(Swansea)
*H. Porta	(Banco Nacion)	G.H. Davies	(Cambridge U.)
T.R. Landajo	(Pueyrredon)	S.J. Smith	(Sale)
E.E. Rodriguez	(El Tala, Cordoba)	C.E. Smart	(Newport)
J. Perez-Cobo	(San Isidro)	S.G.F. Mills	(Gloucester)
F. Morel	(San Isidro)	G.S. Pearce	(Northampton)
A. Iachetti	(Hindu)	*W.B. Beaumont	(Fylde)
E. Branca	(San Isidro)	J.H. Fidler	(Gloucester)
T. Petersen	(San Isidro)	N.C. Jeavons	(Moseley)
G. Travaglini	(San Isidro)	J.P. Scott	(Cardiff)
E. Ure	(Buenos Aires U.)	M. Rafter	(Bristol)

[1]Replaced by J.P. Piccardo (Hindu)

Try: Travaglini
Conversion: Porta

Try: Davies
Conversion: Hare
Penalties: Hare (2)

Referee: Mr J.P. Bonnet (France)

ENGLAND v AUSTRALIA 1982
Played at Twickenham, London, 2 January 1982
England won by 1G, 3PG (15) to 1PG, 2T (11)

Beaumont won the toss and Rose managed two penalties with the wind in the first half. In the tenth minute Australia were guilty of killing the ball at a ruck on their 22, in front of goal, presenting Rose with his first penalty points; but McLean equalised after 30 minutes from 26 metres, when England transgressed at a line-out. Just before half-time Australia were fortunate to survive a poor clearance by Paul McLean from inside his in-goal area. A kick to touch was gathered by Carleton just a few metres from the try-line, but tackles by Loane and Moon, from blatantly off-side positions, deprived England of a try. Seconds later, however, Australia were penalised from a drop-out and Rose, with a fine kick, landed his second goal.

Australia swept into the lead very early in the second half. Davies dropped a pass on the Australian 22 and Hawker, showing remarkable control, twice hacked the loose ball down the right touch-line before Moon, crossing from the left wing, took advantage of a sketchy English defence to score a try. In the next 20 minutes England had two good chances to score: Dodge hit an upright with a penalty attempt, and Winterbottom just missed a try on his debut when he charged down an Australian kick to touch. Then, in the twenty-eighth minute, a sweeping England attack was stopped by a heavy tackle on Slemen in the left corner. Slemen was concussed and forced to leave the field; but before Stringer stepped on to replace him, England went ahead. Ella ran into trouble near his own goal and a maul developed. Jeavons rolled off the left of the maul to score, Dodge converting from 15 metres in from touch.

Rose increased England's lead in the thirty-eighth minute with a penalty from 30 metres and at an angle; but Australia scored the last try, four minutes into injury time. A high up-and-under by McLean forced Rose to make an error on his goal-line, Australia heeled from the following scrum and Hipwell sent Moon in at the corner.

ENGLAND		AUSTRALIA	
W.M.H. Rose	(Cambridge U.)	P.E. McLean	(Queensland)
J. Carleton	(Orrell)	M.D. O'Connor	(Queensland)
C.R. Woodward	(Leicester)	A.G. Slack	(Queensland)
P.W. Dodge	(Leicester)	M.J. Hawker	(N.S.W.)
¹M.A.C. Slemen	(Liverpool)	B.J. Moon	(Queensland)
G.H. Davies	(Cambridge U.)	M.G. Ella	(N.S.W.)
S.J. Smith	(Sale)	J.N.B. Hipwell	(N.S.W.)
C.E. Smart	(Newport)	J.E.C. Meadows	(Victoria)
P.J. Wheeler	(Leicester)	C.M. Carberry	(Queensland)
G.S. Pearce	(Northampton)	A.M. d'Arcy	(Queensland)
*W.B. Beaumont	(Fylde)	S.A. Williams	(N.S.W.)
M.J. Colclough	(Angoulême)	P.W. McLean	(Queensland)
N.C. Jeavons	(Moseley)	S.P. Poidevin	(N.S.W.)
R. Hesford	(Bristol)	*M.E. Loane	(Queensland)
†P.J. Winterbottom	(Headingley)	G. Cornelsen	(N.S.W.)

¹Replaced by †N.C. Stringer (Wasps)

Try: Jeavons   *Tries:* Moon (2)
Conversion: Dodge   *Penalty:* P.E. McLean
Penalties: Rose (3)

Referee: Mr A. Richards (Wales)

SCOTLAND v ENGLAND 1982

Played at Murrayfield, Edinburgh, 16 January 1982

Drawn: Scotland 1DG, 2PG (9), England 3PG (9)

Scotland and England retained fifteens which had defeated Australia by similar scores, so it was no surprise, perhaps, that the sides should then play a draw in this opening match of the Championship. Severe weather had curtailed Rugby football in Britain since just before Christmas, and both teams entered the match with anxieties about the fitness of their players.

The game was not particularly memorable for the quality of play, but there was an exciting finish – Irvine landing a penalty kick from two metres inside his own half, four minutes into injury time, when Smart obstructed Paxton in an incident off the ball. The goal balanced the scores, leaving the large crowd to reflect on the first drawn match between the teams in Scotland for twenty years.

Scotland made a confident start against a healthy wind. Clever kicking by Rutherford pushed the Scottish forwards into a handy position and from a clean heel near the English 22 the Selkirk pivot dropped a splendid goal after five minutes. Dodge equalised with a penalty in the twenty-third minute, Rose having failed with two earlier kicks at goal; and Irvine landed a penalty from 30 metres when England were penalised for obstruction in the twenty-sixth minute. Further penalties – by Dodge and Rose – gave England a slender interval lead.

The only score of a nondescript second half was Irvine's timely goal. Colclough, who had an outstanding first half, suffered a leg strain early in the second half, and his discomfort greatly reduced the efficiency of the English pack, particularly in the line-out. In addition, Hesford did not appear to have recovered from an ankle injury.

England's finest chance to score a try passed midway through the half. Rose made a lovely break in the threequarter line and carried play to the Scottish 22 where he tried to bulldoze through a solid opponent. To the frustration of his colleagues and the English followers in the crowd, Rose had overlooked Woodward, free on an overlap, and they had wasted an excellent opportunity to score the winning points.

SCOTLAND		ENGLAND	
*A.R. Irvine	(Heriot's F.P.)	W.M.H. Rose	(Cambridge U.)
K.W. Robertson	(Melrose)	J. Carleton	(Orrell)
J.M. Renwick	(Hawick)	C.R. Woodward	(Leicester)
D.I. Johnston	(Watsonians)	P.W. Dodge	(Leicester)
G.R.T. Baird	(Kelso)	M.A.C. Slemen	(Liverpool)
J.Y. Rutherford	(Selkirk)	G.H. Davies	(Cambridge U.)
R.J. Laidlaw	(Jedforest)	S.J. Smith	(Sale)
J. Aitken	(Gala)	C.E. Smart	(Newport)
C.T. Deans	(Hawick)	P.J. Wheeler	(Leicester)
I.G. Milne	(Heriot's F.P.)	G.S. Pearce	(Northampton)
W. Cuthbertson	(Kilmarnock)	*W.B. Beaumont	(Fylde)
A.J. Tomes	(Hawick)	M.J. Colclough	(Angoulême)
J.H. Calder	(Stewart's Melville F.P.)	N.C. Jeavons	(Moseley)
I.A.M. Paxton	(Selkirk)	R. Hesford	(Bristol)
D.G. Leslie	(Gala)	P.J. Winterbottom	(Headingley)

Dropped Goal: Rutherford
Penalties: Irvine (2)

Penalties: Dodge (2), Rose

Referee: Mr K. Rowlands (Wales)

ENGLAND v IRELAND 1982

Played at Twickenham, London, 6 February 1982
Ireland won by 1G, 2PG, 1T (16) to 1G, 3PG (15)

Bill Beaumont, injured leading Lancashire to the County Championship one week earlier, was advised to stand down from this match, ending a sequence of 33 consecutive matches for England. Paul Dodge was also absent through injury, but Scott and Blakeway were recalled by the selectors in place of Hesford and Pearce.

Ireland, on course for their first Triple Crown since 1949, were easy winners, despite the one-point difference between the sides. The Irish pack, through their loose forwards, disrupted the English forwards and bustled the English backs off the ball in the open play. Fitzgerald was an inspiring captain, reminding the critics of two distinguished predecessors – Ron Dawson and Karl Mullen – who had led Ireland with success from the middle of the front row.

The Irish went ahead in the twelfth minute when Campbell kicked a penalty downwind for off-side; and in the twenty-second minute, poor defence by the English backs at a scrum, five metres from their goal-line, enabled McGrath, a splendid scrum-half, to send MacNeill over in the right corner for a try. Ollie Campbell struck the upright with his conversion attempt. Rose, and then Campbell, added penalties before the changeover.

Soon after the restart, Rose landed a penalty when Lenihan was caught receiving a lift in the line-out, but hopes of an English victory were rocked 15 minutes later. An Irish drop at goal was charged down by Smith, Fitzgerald wrenched the ball from the ensuing maul, and accurate Irish handling on the narrow side led to a rousing try by McLoughlin in the south-west corner of the ground. Campbell converted from the touch-line.

Rose punished an indiscretion by Duggan four minutes later, kicking England's third penalty, and the best move of the match came in the closing minutes when Winterbottom charged forward from the tail of a line-out. Eventually he was held five metres from Ireland's line before the ball was worked out to Davies. Then, a well-judged pass allowed Slemen to glide around the Irish cover for a try converted by Rose.

ENGLAND		IRELAND	
W.M.H. Rose	(Cambridge U.)	H.P. MacNeill	(Dublin U.)
J. Carleton	(Orrell)	T.M. Ringland	(Queen's U.)
C.R. Woodward	(Leicester)	M.J. Kiernan	(Dolphin)
A.M. Bond	(Sale)	P.M. Dean	(St Mary's College)
M.A.C. Slemen	(Liverpool)	M.C. Finn	(Cork Const.)
G.H. Davies	(Cambridge U.)	S.O. Campbell	(Old Belvedere)
*S.J. Smith	(Sale)	R.J.M. McGrath	(Wanderers)
C.E. Smart	(Newport)	P.A. Orr	(Old Wesley)
P.J. Wheeler	(Leicester)	*C.F. Fitzgerald	(St Mary's College)
P.J. Blakeway	(Gloucester)	G.A.J. McLoughlin	(Shannon)
†J.P. Syddall	(Waterloo)	M.I. Keane	(Lansdowne)
M.J. Colclough	(Angoulême)	D.G. Lenihan	(U.C. Cork)
N.C. Jeavons	(Moseley)	J.F. Slattery	(Blackrock College)
J.P. Scott	(Cardiff)	W.P. Duggan	(Blackrock College)
P.J. Winterbottom	(Headingley)	J.B.O'Driscoll	(London Irish)

Try: Slemen
Conversion: Rose
Penalties: Rose (3)

Tries: MacNeill, McLoughlin
Conversion: Campbell
Penalties: Campbell (2)

Referee: Mr A.M. Hosie (Scotland)

FRANCE v ENGLAND 1982

Played at Parc des Princes, Paris, 20 February 1982
England won by 2G, 5PG (27) to 1G, 1DG, 2PG (15)

Several days before the game, Bill Beaumont, having been reappointed England captain, accepted medical advice to retire from Rugby football. England thus lost the man whose leadership had had so much to do with the revival of English Rugby during the late 1970s, a revival which had culminated in the Grand Slam of 1980.

Smith led the team in Beaumont's absence and Hare was recalled when Stringer, the original selection at full-back, damaged a hamstring playing for his club one week before this match. The experienced Leicester kicker contributed 19 points to England's second consecutive victory in Paris, and the opening penalty goals in the fifth and thirteenth minutes brought his tally of points in internationals to a century.

The French had selected an experimental fifteen with an exciting back division and a weaving run by Blanco, midway through the half, caused havoc amongst the English backs. But when Carleton minored the ball for a drop-out, few expected England to launch a remarkable counter-attack. Slemen took a quick drop-kick and Woodward exploited a hopelessly disorganised French defence to dribble the ball the length of the field and over the line for a try beneath the posts. Hare kicked the goal. 14 minutes from half-time, Sallefranque made an open-side break from a scrum near half-way and Pardo took a pass to score the finest try of the season. Sallefranque converted.

The second half was dominated by the kickers: Hare placed three penalties; Lescarboura dropped a goal from 45 metres; and Sallefranque landed two penalties before England made success certain with a try in the corner in the last minute of the game. Smith broke on the narrow side of a ruck and Smart was up to give a perfect pass to Carleton, who scored. Hare converted with a grand kick from near touch.

FRANCE		ENGLAND	
M. Sallefranque	(Dax)	W.H. Hare	(Leicester)
S. Blanco	(Biarritz)	J. Carleton	(Orrell)
P. Perrier	(Bayonne)	C.R. Woodward	(Leicester)
C. Belascain	(Bayonne)	P.W. Dodge	(Leicester)
L. Pardo	(Bayonne)	M.A.C. Slemen	(Liverpool)
J.P. Lescarboura	(Dax)	L. Cusworth	(Leicester)
G. Martinez	(Toulouse)	*S.J. Smith	(Sale)
D. Dubroca	(Agen)	C.E. Smart	(Newport)
P. Dintrans	(Tarbes)	P.J. Wheeler	(Leicester)
J.P. Wolff	(Béziers)	P.J. Blakeway	(Gloucester)
M. Carpentier	(Lourdes)	†S.J. Bainbridge	(Gosforth)
L. Rodriguez	(Mont-de-Marsan)	M.J. Colclough	(Angoulême)
*J.P. Rives	(Toulouse)	¹N.C. Jeavons	(Moseley)
J.L. Joinel	(Brive)	J.P. Scott	(Cardiff)
E. Buchet	(Nice)	P.J. Winterbottom	(Headingley)

¹Replaced by R. Hesford (Bristol)

Try: Pardo
Conversion: Sallefranque
Penalties: Sallefranque (2)
Dropped goal: Lescarboura

Tries: Woodward, Carleton
Conversions: Hare (2)
Penalties: Hare (5)

Referee: Mr M.D.M. Rea (Ireland)

ENGLAND v WALES 1982

Played at Twickenham, London, 6 March 1982
England won by 3PG, 2T (17) to 1DG, 1T (7)

England played with zest and enterprise, entertaining a capacity crowd to a thoroughly enjoyable match. There was an unusually diffident display by the Welsh in the first half, and England took advantage of a stiff, swirling breeze to run up an 11-points lead in the opening 26 minutes. Many expected Wales to recover in the second half, but the early loss of Terry Holmes removed Wales's principal attacking force and England's win by ten points was their best against the Welsh since 1921.

Smith, an inspiring leader, had an excellent match and sent Slemen over on the narrow side of a maul for the first try after 12 minutes. A late tackle by Rees on Hare, in the seventeenth minute, resulted in a penalty which Hare gratefully converted into points. Next came England's decisive score. Their alert, mobile forwards created a ruck from a Welsh drop-out. Smith became engulfed by the two packs but Carleton, showing great presence of mind, swiftly moved up to the heels of his pack, grabbed the ball as it popped out from the ruck and dashed 30 metres through a flimsy defence to score a try.

Donovan, the best of a mediocre Welsh division, evaded a tackle by Dodge to make a fine break three minutes later. Lewis steamed up inside the centre to cross in the left corner, but before Wales could gain in confidence, Hare landed a penalty when Moriarty was caught wrestling with Winterbottom. Three minutes before half-time Davies dropped a goal from a free kick for foot-up.

Holmes left the field after six minutes in the second half nursing a shoulder injury, and Hare's third penalty, in the thirteenth minute, made England's victory sure.

ENGLAND		WALES	
W.H. Hare	(Leicester)	G. Evans	(Maesteg)
J. Carleton	(Orrell)	R.A. Ackerman	(Newport)
C.R. Woodward	(Leicester)	R.W.R. Gravell	(Llanelli)
P.W. Dodge	(Leicester)	A.J. Donovan	(Swansea)
M.A.C. Slemen	(Liverpool)	C.F.W. Rees	(London Welsh)
L. Cusworth	(Leicester)	*W.G. Davies	(Cardiff)
*S.J. Smith	(Sale)	[1]T.D. Holmes	(Cardiff)
C.E. Smart	(Newport)	I. Stephens	(Bridgend)
P.J. Wheeler	(Leicester)	A.J. Phillips	(Cardiff)
P.J. Blakeway	(Gloucester)	G. Price	(Pontypool)
M.J. Colclough	(Angoulême)	S. Sutton	(Pontypool)
S.J. Bainbridge	(Gosforth)	R.D. Moriarty	(Swansea)
N.C. Jeavons	(Moseley)	R.C. Burgess	(Ebbw Vale)
J.P. Scott	(Cardiff)	J. Squire	(Pontypool)
P.J. Winterbottom	(Headingley)	J.R. Lewis	(Cardiff)

[1]Replaced by G. Williams (Bridgend)

Tries: Carleton, Slemen   *Try:* Lewis
Penalties: Hare (3)   *Dropped goal:* Davies

Referee: Mr F. Palmade (France)

English International Rugby Records
1871–1982

MATCH RECORDS

SCORING

Until 1875 international matches were decided by a majority of goals, but from 1876 the majority of tries could decide a match if teams were level on goals. The scoring of points was not formally introduced until the late 1880s, a try scoring one point, a conversion two and a dropped goal three. Various experiments were tried up to 1890–91, when the International Board system was adopted to make points-scoring uniform in international matches. (In 1889–90, for example, England's two tries against Scotland in Edinburgh were worth two points each according to the S.R.U. system; two weeks later, at Blackheath against Ireland, England's three tries were worth one point each in accordance with R.F.U. laws.)

The table below sets out the scoring values since the 1890–91 season. Note that the penalty goal did not become a device for scoring until 1891, and the goal from a mark ceased to exist when the Free Kick clause was introduced in 1977–78.

	Try (T)	Conversion (C)	Dropped goal (D)	Penalty goal (P)	Goal from a mark (★)
1890–91	1	2	3	2	3
1891–92 to 1892–93	2	3	4	3	4
1893–94 to 1904–05	3	2	4	3	4
1905–06 to 1947–48	3	2	4	3	3
1948–49 to 1970–71	3	2	3	3	3
1971–72 to 1976–77	4	2	3	3	3
1977–78 to date	4	2	3	3	Void

VENUES

Where there is more than one ground in a town or city, the following key has been used to identify different venues:

Blackheath[1]	Richardson's Field	Glasgow[1]	West of Scotland Club
Blackheath[2]	Rectory Field	Glasgow[2]	Old Hampden Park
Dublin[1]	Rathmines	Leeds[1]	Cardigan Fields
Dublin[2]	Lansdowne Road	Leeds[2]	Headingley
Edinburgh[1]	Raeburn Place	Leeds[3]	Meanwood Road
Edinburgh[2]	Powderhall	Manchester[1]	Whalley Range
Edinburgh[3]	Inverleith	Manchester[2]	Fallowfield
Edinburgh[4]	Murrayfield	Paris[1]	Parc des Princes
		Paris[2]	Stade Colombes

MATCH RESULTS 1871 to 1982

England have played 370 international matches, winning 178, drawing 43 and losing 149. There have been 666 tries; 283 conversions; 48 dropped goals; 238 penalty goals and four goals from marks scored by England in these matches, giving a points total of 3172 (using the points-values at the start of this section).

Match	Date	Opponents	For					Against					Result	Venue	Captain
			T	C	D	P	Pts	T	C	D	P	Pts			
1	27.3.1871	Scotland	—	1	—	—	—	2	1	—	—		Lost	Edinburgh[1]	F. Stokes
2	5.2.1872	Scotland	3	1	1	—		—	—	1	—		Won	The Oval	F. Stokes
3	3.3.1873	Scotland	—	—	—	—		—	—	—	—		Drawn	Glasgow[1]	F. Stokes
4	23.2.1874	Scotland	—	—	1	—		1	—	—	—		Won	The Oval	A.St.G.Hamersley
5	15.2.1875	Ireland	2	1	1	—		—	—	—	—		Won	The Oval	Hon. H. A. Lawrence
6	8.3.1875	Scotland	—	—	—	—		—	—	—	—		Drawn	Edinburgh[1]	Hon. H. A. Lawrence
7	13.12.1875	Ireland	2	1	—	—		—	—	—	—		Won	Dublin[1]	F. Luscombe
8	6.3.1876	Scotland	2	1	—	—		—	—	—	—		Won	The Oval	F. Luscombe
9	5.2.1877	Ireland	4	2	—	—		—	—	—	—		Won	The Oval	E. Kewley
10	5.3.1877	Scotland	—	—	—	—		—	—	1	—		Lost	Edinburgh[1]	E. Kewley
11	4.3.1878	Scotland	—	—	—	—		—	—	—	—		Drawn	The Oval	E. Kewley
12	11.3.1878	Ireland	3	2	—	—		—	—	—	—		Won	Dublin[1]	M. W. Marshall
13	10.3.1879	Scotland	1	1	—	—		—	—	1	—		Drawn	Edinburgh[1]	F. R. Adams
14	24.3.1879	Ireland	4	2	1	—		—	—	—	—		Won	The Oval	F. R. Adams
15	30.1.1880	Ireland	2	1	—	—		1	—	—	—		Won	Dublin[2]	L. Stokes
16	28.2.1880	Scotland	5	2	—	—		1	1	—	—		Won	Manchester[1]	L. Stokes
17	5.2.1881	Ireland	4	2	—	—		—	—	—	—		Won	Manchester[1]	L. Stokes
18	19.2.1881	Wales	13	7	1	—		—	—	—	—		Won	Blackheath[1]	L. Stokes
19	19.3.1881	Scotland	1	—	1	—		2	1	—	—		Drawn	Edinburgh[1]	L. Stokes
20	6.2.1882	Ireland	2	—	—	—		2	—	—	—		Drawn	Dublin[2]	C. Gurdon
21	4.3.1882	Scotland	—	—	—	—		2	—	—	—		Lost	Manchester[1]	A. N. Hornby
22	16.12.1882	Wales	6	2	—	—		—	—	—	—		Won	Swansea	E. T. Gurdon
23	5.2.1883	Ireland	4	1	—	—		1	—	—	—		Won	Manchester[1]	E. T. Gurdon
24	3.3.1883	Scotland	2	—	—	—		1	—	—	—		Won	Edinburgh[1]	E. T. Gurdon
25	5.1.1884	Wales	3	1	—	—		1	1	—	—		Won	Leeds[1]	E. T. Gurdon
26	4.2.1884	Ireland	1	1	—	—		—	—	—	—		Won	Dublin[2]	E. T. Gurdon
27	1.3.1884	Scotland	1	1	—	—		1	—	—	—		Won	Blackheath[2]	E. T. Gurdon
28	3.1.1885	Wales	5	1	—	—		2	1	—	—		Won	Swansea	E. T. Gurdon
29	7.2.1885	Ireland	2	—	—	—		1	—	—	—		Won	Manchester[1]	E. T. Gurdon
30	2.1.1886	Wales	2	—	★	—		1	1	—	—		Won	Blackheath[2]	C. J. B. Marriott
31	6.2.1886	Ireland	1	—	—	—		—	—	—	—		Won	Dublin[2]	C. J. B. Marriott
32	13.3.1886	Scotland	—	—	—	—		—	—	—	—		Drawn	Edinburgh[1]	E. T. Gurdon
33	8.1.1887	Wales	—	—	—	—		—	—	—	—		Drawn	Llanelli	A. Rotherham
34	5.2.1887	Ireland	—	—	—	—		2	2	—	—		Lost	Dublin[2]	A. Rotherham
35	5.3.1887	Scotland	1	—	—	—		1	—	—	—		Drawn	Manchester[1]	A. Rotherham
36	16.2.1889	NZ Natives	5	1	—	—	7	—	—	—	—	0	Won	Blackheath[2]	F. Bonsor
37	15.2.1890	Wales	—	—	—	—	0	1	—	—	—	1	Lost	Dewsbury	A. E. Stoddart
38	1.3.1890	Scotland	2	1	—	—	6	—	—	—	—	0	Won	Edinburgh[1]	J. L. Hickson
39	15.3.1890	Ireland	3	—	—	—	3	—	—	—	—	0	Won	Blackheath[2]	A. E. Stoddart
40	3.1.1891	Wales	3	2	—	—	7	1	1	—	—	3	Won	Newport	F. H. R. Alderson
41	7.2.1891	Ireland	5	2	—	—	9	—	—	—	—	0	Won	Dublin[2]	F. H. R. Alderson
42	7.3.1891	Scotland	1	1	—	—	3	2	2	1	—	9	Lost	Richmond	F. H. R. Alderson
43	2.1.1892	Wales	4	3	—	—	17	—	—	—	—	0	Won	Blackheath[2]	F. H. R. Alderson

★ in the drop-goal column denotes a goal from a mark

continued

Match	Date	Opponents	For					Against					Result	Venue	Captain
			T	C	D	P	Pts	T	C	D	P	Pts			
44	6.2.1892	Ireland	2	1	—	—	7	—	—	—	—	0	Won	Manchester[1]	S. M. J. Woods
45	5.3.1892	Scotland	1	1	—	—	5	—	—	—	—	0	Won	Edinburgh[1]	F. H. R. Alderson
46	7.1.1893	Wales	4	1	—	—	11	3	1	—	1	12	Lost	Cardiff	A. E. Stoddart
47	4.2.1893	Ireland	2	—	—	—	4	—	—	—	—	0	Won	Dublin[2]	S. M. J. Woods
48	4.3.1893	Scotland	—	—	—	—	0	—	—	2	—	8	Lost	Leeds[2]	A. E. Stoddart
49	6.1.1894	Wales	4	4	★	—	24	1	—	—	—	3	Won	Birkenhead	R. E. Lockwood
50	3.2.1894	Ireland	1	1	—	—	5	1	—	1	—	7	Lost	Blackheath[2]	R. E. Lockwood
51	17.3.1894	Scotland	—	—	—	—	0	2	—	—	—	6	Lost	Edinburgh[1]	E. W. Taylor
52	5.1.1895	Wales	4	1	—	—	14	2	—	—	—	6	Won	Swansea	S. M. J. Woods
53	2.2.1895	Ireland	2	—	—	—	6	1	—	—	—	3	Won	Dublin[2]	S. M. J. Woods
54	9.3.1895	Scotland	—	—	—	1	3	1	—	—	1	6	Lost	Richmond	S. M. J. Woods
55	4.1.1896	Wales	7	2	—	—	25	—	—	—	—	0	Won	Blackheath[2]	E. W. Taylor
56	1.2.1896	Ireland	—	—	1	—	4	2	2	—	—	10	Lost	Leeds[3]	E. W. Taylor
57	14.3.1896	Scotland	—	—	—	—	0	3	1	—	—	11	Lost	Glasgow[2]	F. Mitchell
58	9.1.1897	Wales	—	—	—	—	0	3	1	—	—	11	Lost	Newport	E. W. Taylor
59	6.2.1897	Ireland	1	—	—	2	9	3	—	★	—	13	Lost	Dublin[2]	E. W. Taylor
60	13.3.1897	Scotland	2	1	1	—	12	1	—	—	—	3	Won	Manchester[2]	E. W. Taylor
61	5.2.1898	Ireland	1	—	—	1	6	2	—	—	1	9	Lost	Richmond	J. F. Byrne
62	12.3.1898	Scotland	1	—	—	—	3	1	—	—	—	3	Drawn	Edinburgh[2]	J. F. Byrne
63	2.4.1898	Wales	4	1	—	—	14	1	—	1	—	7	Won	Blackheath[2]	J. F. Byrne
64	7.1.1899	Wales	1	—	—	—	3	6	4	—	—	26	Lost	Swansea	A. Rotherham
65	4.2.1899	Ireland	—	—	—	—	0	1	—	—	1	6	Lost	Dublin[2]	A. Rotherham
66	11.3.1899	Scotland	—	—	—	—	0	1	1	—	—	5	Lost	Blackheath[2]	A. Rotherham
67	6.1.1900	Wales	1	—	—	—	3	2	2	—	1	13	Lost	Gloucester	R. H. B. Cattell
68	3.2.1900	Ireland	3	1	1	—	15	—	—	1	—	4	Won	Richmond	J. Daniell
69	10.3.1900	Scotland	—	—	—	—	0	—	—	—	—	0	Drawn	Edinburgh[3]	J. Daniell
70	5.1.1901	Wales	—	—	—	—	0	3	2	—	—	13	Lost	Cardiff	J. T. Taylor
71	9.2.1901	Ireland	1	—	—	1	6	2	2	—	—	10	Lost	Dublin[2]	W. L. Bunting
72	9.3.1901	Scotland	1	—	—	—	3	4	3	—	—	18	Lost	Blackheath[2]	W. L. Bunting
73	11.1.1902	Wales	2	1	—	—	8	2	—	—	1	9	Lost	Blackheath[2]	H. Alexander
74	8.2.1902	Ireland	2	—	—	—	6	1	—	—	—	3	Won	Leicester	J. Daniell
75	15.3.1902	Scotland	2	—	—	—	6	1	—	—	—	3	Won	Edinburgh[3]	J. Daniell
76	10.1.1903	Wales	1	1	—	—	5	5	3	—	—	21	Lost	Swansea	B. Oughtred
77	14.2.1903	Ireland	—	—	—	—	0	1	—	—	1	6	Lost	Dublin[2]	B. Oughtred
78	21.3.1903	Scotland	2	—	—	—	6	2	—	1	—	10	Lost	Richmond	P. D. Kendall
79	9.1.1904	Wales	3	1	—	1	14	2	2	★	—	14	Drawn	Leicester	F. M. Stout
80	13.2.1904	Ireland	5	2	—	—	19	—	—	—	—	0	Won	Blackheath[2]	J. Daniell
81	19.3.1904	Scotland	1	—	—	—	3	2	—	—	—	6	Lost	Edinburgh[3]	J. Daniell
82	14.1.1905	Wales	—	—	—	—	0	7	2	—	—	25	Lost	Cardiff	F. M. Stout
83	11.2.1905	Ireland	1	—	—	—	3	5	1	—	—	17	Lost	Cork	F. M. Stout
84	18.3.1905	Scotland	—	—	—	—	0	2	1	—	—	8	Lost	Richmond	F. M. Stout
85	2.12.1905	New Zealand	—	—	—	—	0	5	—	—	—	15	Lost	Crystal Palace	V. H. Cartwright
86	13.1.1906	Wales	1	—	—	—	3	4	2	—	—	16	Lost	Richmond	V. H. Cartwright
87	10.2.1906	Ireland	2	—	—	—	6	4	2	—	—	16	Lost	Leicester	V. H. Cartwright
88	17.3.1906	Scotland	3	—	—	—	9	1	—	—	—	3	Won	Edinburgh[3]	V. H. Cartwright
89	22.3.1906	France	9	4	—	—	35	2	1	—	—	8	Won	Paris[1]	V. H. Cartwright
90	8.12.1906	South Africa	1	—	—	—	3	1	—	—	—	3	Drawn	Crystal Palace	V. H. Cartwright
91	5.1.1907	France	9	5	1	—	41	2	2	—	1	13	Won	Richmond	B. A. Hill
92	12.1.1907	Wales	—	—	—	—	0	6	2	—	—	22	Lost	Swansea	B. A. Hill
93	9.2.1907	Ireland	2	—	—	1	9	4	1	★	—	17	Lost	Dublin[2]	J. Green
94	16.3.1907	Scotland	1	—	—	—	3	2	1	—	—	8	Lost	Blackheath[2]	E. W. Roberts
95	1.1.1908	France	5	2	—	—	19	—	—	—	—	0	Won	Paris[2]	T. S. Kelly

★ *in the drop-goal column denotes a goal from a mark*

continued

Match	Date	Opponents	For T	C	D	P	Pts	Against T	C	D	P	Pts	Result	Venue	Captain
96	18.1.1908	Wales	4	3	—	—	18	5	3	1	1	28	Lost	Bristol	J. G. G. Birkett
97	8.2.1908	Ireland	3	2	—	—	13	—	—	—	1	3	Won	Richmond	C. E. L. Hammond
98	21.3.1908	Scotland	2	2	—	—	10	2	1	2	—	16	Lost	Edinburgh[3]	L. A. N. Slocock
99	9.1.1909	Australia	1	—	—	—	3	3	—	—	—	9	Lost	Blackheath[2]	G. H. D'O. Lyon
100	16.1.1909	Wales	—	—	—	—	0	2	1	—	—	8	Lost	Cardiff	R. Dibble
101	30.1.1909	France	6	2	—	—	22	—	—	—	—	0	Won	Leicester	R. Dibble
102	13.2.1909	Ireland	3	1	—	—	11	1	1	—	—	5	Won	Dublin[2]	R. Dibble
103	20.3.1909	Scotland	2	1	—	—	8	4	3	—	—	18	Lost	Richmond	R. Dibble
104	15.1.1910	Wales	2	1	—	1	11	2	—	—	—	6	Won	Twickenham	A. D. Stoop
105	12.2.1910	Ireland	—	—	—	—	0	—	—	—	—	0	Drawn	Twickenham	A. D. Stoop
106	3.3.1910	France	3	1	—	—	11	1	—	—	—	3	Won	Paris[1]	E. R. Mobbs
107	19.3.1910	Scotland	4	1	—	—	14	1	1	—	—	5	Won	Edinburgh[3]	J. G. G. Birkett
108	21.1.1911	Wales	3	1	—	—	11	4	—	—	1	15	Lost	Swansea	J. G. G. Birkett
109	28.1.1911	France	7	5	—	2	37	—	—	—	—	0	Won	Twickenham	J. G. G. Birkett
110	11.2.1911	Ireland	—	—	—	—	0	1	—	—	—	3	Lost	Dublin[2]	J. G. G. Birkett
111	18.3.1911	Scotland	3	2	—	—	13	2	1	—	—	8	Won	Twickenham	A. L. H. Gotley
112	20.1.1912	Wales	2	1	—	—	8	—	—	—	—	0	Won	Twickenham	R. Dibble
113	10.2.1912	Ireland	5	—	—	—	15	—	—	—	—	0	Won	Twickenham	R. Dibble
114	16.3.1912	Scotland	1	—	—	—	3	2	1	—	—	8	Lost	Edinburgh[3]	R. Dibble
115	8.4.1912	France	4	1	1	—	18	2	1	—	—	8	Won	Paris[1]	N. A. Wodehouse
116	4.1.1913	South Africa	1	—	—	—	3	1	—	—	2	9	Lost	Twickenham	N. A. Wodehouse
117	18.1.1913	Wales	2	1	1	—	12	—	—	—	—	0	Won	Cardiff	N. A. Wodehouse
118	25.1.1913	France	6	1	—	—	20	—	—	—	—	0	Won	Twickenham	N. A. Wodehouse
119	8.2.1913	Ireland	4	—	—	1	15	—	—	1	—	4	Won	Dublin[2]	N. A. Wodehouse
120	15.3.1913	Scotland	1	—	—	—	3	—	—	—	—	0	Won	Twickenham	N. A. Wodehouse
121	17.1.1914	Wales	2	2	—	—	10	1	1	1	—	9	Won	Twickenham	R. W. Poulton
122	14.2.1914	Ireland	5	1	—	—	17	2	1	—	1	12	Won	Twickenham	R. W. Poulton
123	21.3.1914	Scotland	4	2	—	—	16	3	1	1	—	15	Won	Edinburgh[3]	R. W. Poulton
124	13.4.1914	France	9	6	—	—	39	3	2	—	—	13	Won	Paris[2]	R. W. Poulton
125	17.1.1920	Wales	1	1	—	—	5	2	1	2	1	19	Lost	Swansea	J. E. Greenwood
126	31.1.1920	France	1	1	—	1	8	1	—	—	—	3	Won	Twickenham	J. E. Greenwood
127	14.2.1920	Ireland	4	1	—	—	14	2	1	—	1	11	Won	Dublin[2]	J. E. Greenwood
128	20.3.1920	Scotland	3	2	—	—	13	—	—	1	—	4	Won	Twickenham	J. E. Greenwood
129	15.1.1921	Wales	4	1	1	—	18	1	—	—	—	3	Won	Twickenham	W. J. A. Davies
130	12.2.1921	Ireland	3	1	1	—	15	—	—	—	—	0	Won	Twickenham	W. J. A. Davies
131	19.3.1921	Scotland	4	3	—	—	18	—	—	—	—	0	Won	Edinburgh[3]	W. J. A. Davies
132	28.3.1921	France	2	2	—	—	10	—	—	—	2	6	Won	Paris[2]	W. J. A. Davies
133	21.1.1922	Wales	2	—	—	—	6	8	2	—	—	28	Lost	Cardiff	L. G. Brown
134	11.2.1922	Ireland	4	—	—	—	12	1	—	—	—	3	Won	Dublin[2]	W. J. A. Davies
135	25.2.1922	France	1	1	—	2	11	3	1	—	—	11	Drawn	Twickenham	W. J. A. Davies
136	18.3.1922	Scotland	3	1	—	—	11	1	1	—	—	5	Won	Twickenham	W. J. A. Davies
137	20.1.1923	Wales	1	—	1	—	7	1	—	—	—	3	Won	Twickenham	W. J. A. Davies
138	10.2.1923	Ireland	5	2	1	—	23	1	1	—	—	5	Won	Leicester	W. J. A. Davies
139	17.3.1923	Scotland	2	1	—	—	8	2	—	—	—	6	Won	Edinburgh[3]	W. J. A. Davies
140	2.4.1923	France	2	1	1	—	12	—	—	—	1	3	Won	Paris[2]	W. J. A. Davies
141	19.1.1924	Wales	5	1	—	—	17	3	—	—	—	9	Won	Swansea	W. W. Wakefield
142	9.2.1924	Ireland	4	1	—	—	14	1	—	—	—	3	Won	Belfast	W. W. Wakefield
143	23.2.1924	France	5	2	—	—	19	1	—	1	—	7	Won	Twickenham	W. W. Wakefield
144	15.3.1924	Scotland	3	3	1	—	19	—	—	—	—	0	Won	Twickenham	W. W. Wakefield
145	3.1.1925	New Zealand	2	1	—	1	11	4	1	—	1	17	Lost	Twickenham	W. W. Wakefield
146	17.1.1925	Wales	3	—	—	1	12	2	—	—	—	6	Won	Twickenham	W. W. Wakefield
147	14.2.1925	Ireland	2	—	—	—	6	2	—	—	—	6	Drawn	Twickenham	W. W. Wakefield
148	21.3.1925	Scotland	2	1	—	1	11	2	2	1	—	14	Lost	Edinburgh[4]	W. W. Wakefield

continued

Match	Date	Opponents	For T	C	D	P	Pts	Against T	C	D	P	Pts	Result	Venue	Captain
149	13.4.1925	France	2	2	★	—	*13*	3	1	—	—	*11*	Won	Paris[2]	W. W. Wakefield
150	16.1.1926	Wales	1	—	—	—	*3*	1	—	—	—	*3*	Drawn	Cardiff	W. W. Wakefield
151	13.2.1926	Ireland	3	3	—	—	*15*	4	2	—	1	*19*	Lost	Dublin[2]	W. W. Wakefield
152	27.2.1926	France	3	1	—	—	*11*	—	—	—	—	*0*	Won	Twickenham	W. W. Wakefield
153	20.3.1926	Scotland	3	—	—	—	*9*	3	2	1	—	*17*	Lost	Twickenham	W. W. Wakefield
154	15.1.1927	Wales	1	1	★	1	*11*	2	—	—	1	*9*	Won	Twickenham	L. J. Corbett
155	12.2.1927	Ireland	2	1	—	—	*8*	1	—	—	1	*6*	Won	Twickenham	L. J. Corbett
156	19.3.1927	Scotland	2	2	—	1	*13*	5	1	1	—	*21*	Lost	Edinburgh[4]	L. J. Corbett
157	2.4.1927	France	—	—	—	—	*0*	1	—	—	—	*3*	Lost	Paris[2]	L. J. Corbett
158	7.1.1928	NSW	4	3	—	—	*18*	3	1	—	—	*11*	Won	Twickenham	R. Cove-Smith
159	21.1.1928	Wales	2	2	—	—	*10*	2	1	—	—	*8*	Won	Swansea	R. Cove-Smith
160	11.2.1928	Ireland	1	—	1	—	*7*	2	—	—	—	*6*	Won	Dublin[2]	R. Cove-Smith
161	25.2.1928	France	4	3	—	—	*18*	2	1	—	—	*8*	Won	Twickenham	R. Cove-Smith
162	17.3.1928	Scotland	2	—	—	—	*6*	—	—	—	—	*0*	Won	Twickenham	R. Cove-Smith
163	19.1.1929	Wales	2	1	—	—	*8*	1	—	—	—	*3*	Won	Twickenham	R. Cove-Smith
164	9.2.1929	Ireland	1	1	—	—	*5*	2	—	—	—	*6*	Lost	Twickenham	R. Cove-Smith
165	16.3.1929	Scotland	2	—	—	—	*6*	4	—	—	—	*12*	Lost	Edinburgh[4]	H. G. Periton
166	1.4.1929	France	4	2	—	—	*16*	2	—	—	—	*6*	Won	Paris[2]	H. G. Periton
167	18.1.1930	Wales	2	1	—	1	*11*	1	—	—	—	*3*	Won	Cardiff	H. G. Periton
168	8.2.1930	Ireland	1	—	—	—	*3*	—	—	1	—	*4*	Lost	Dublin[2]	H. G. Periton
169	22.2.1930	France	3	1	—	—	*11*	1	1	—	—	*5*	Won	Twickenham	J. S. Tucker
170	15.3.1930	Scotland	—	—	—	—	*0*	—	—	—	—	*0*	Drawn	Twickenham	J. S. Tucker
171	17.1.1931	Wales	1	1	—	2	*11*	2	1	★	—	*11*	Drawn	Twickenham	J. S. Tucker
172	14.2.1931	Ireland	1	1	—	—	*5*	1	—	—	1	*6*	Lost	Twickenham	P. D. Howard
173	21.3.1931	Scotland	4	2	—	1	*19*	6	5	—	—	*28*	Lost	Edinburgh[4]	C. D. Aarvold
174	6.4.1931	France	3	2	—	—	*13*	2	—	2	—	*14*	Lost	Paris[2]	C. D. Aarvold
175	2.1.1932	South Africa	—	—	—	—	*0*	1	—	1	—	*7*	Lost	Twickenham	C. D. Aarvold
176	16.1.1932	Wales	1	1	—	—	*5*	1	1	1	1	*12*	Lost	Swansea	C. D. Aarvold
177	13.2.1932	Ireland	1	1	—	2	*11*	1	1	—	1	*8*	Won	Dublin[2]	C. D. Aarvold
178	19.3.1932	Scotland	4	2	—	—	*16*	1	—	—	—	*3*	Won	Twickenham	C. D. Aarvold
179	21.1.1933	Wales	1	—	—	—	*3*	1	—	1	—	*7*	Lost	Twickenham	C. D. Aarvold
180	11.2.1933	Ireland	5	1	—	—	*17*	1	—	—	1	*6*	Won	Twickenham	A. L. Novis
181	18.3.1933	Scotland	—	—	—	—	*0*	1	—	—	—	*3*	Lost	Edinburgh[4]	A. L. Novis
182	20.1.1934	Wales	3	—	—	—	*9*	—	—	—	—	*0*	Won	Cardiff	B. C. Gadney
183	10.2.1934	Ireland	3	2	—	—	*13*	1	—	—	—	*3*	Won	Dublin[2]	B. C. Gadney
184	17.3.1934	Scotland	2	—	—	—	*6*	1	—	—	—	*3*	Won	Twickenham	B. C. Gadney
185	19.1.1935	Wales	—	—	—	1	*3*	1	—	—	—	*3*	Drawn	Twickenham	D. A. Kendrew
186	9.2.1935	Ireland	1	1	—	3	*14*	1	—	—	—	*3*	Won	Twickenham	D. A. Kendrew
187	16.3.1935	Scotland	1	—	1	—	*7*	2	2	—	—	*10*	Lost	Edinburgh[4]	B. C. Gadney
188	4.1.1936	New Zealand	3	—	1	—	*13*	—	—	—	—	*0*	Won	Twickenham	B. C. Gadney
189	18.1.1936	Wales	—	—	—	—	*0*	—	—	—	—	*0*	Drawn	Swansea	B. C. Gadney
190	8.2.1936	Ireland	1	—	—	—	*3*	2	—	—	—	*6*	Lost	Dublin[2]	B. C. Gadney
191	21.3.1936	Scotland	3	—	—	—	*9*	1	1	—	1	*8*	Won	Twickenham	B. C. Gadney
192	16.1.1937	Wales	—	—	1	—	*4*	1	—	—	—	*3*	Won	Twickenham	H. G. Owen-Smith
193	13.2.1937	Ireland	2	—	—	1	*9*	2	1	—	—	*8*	Won	Twickenham	H. G. Owen-Smith
194	20.3.1937	Scotland	2	—	—	—	*6*	—	—	—	1	*3*	Won	Edinburgh[4]	H. G. Owen-Smith
195	15.1.1938	Wales	2	1	—	—	*8*	2	1	—	2	*14*	Lost	Cardiff	P. Cranmer
196	12.2.1938	Ireland	7	6	—	1	*36*	4	1	—	—	*14*	Won	Dublin[2]	P. Cranmer
197	19.3.1938	Scotland	1	—	1	3	*16*	5	—	—	2	*21*	Lost	Twickenham	H. B. Toft

★ *in the drop-goal column denotes a goal from a mark*

continued

Match	Date	Opponents	For T	C	D	P	Pts	Against T	C	D	P	Pts	Result	Venue	Captain
198	21.1.1939	Wales	1	—	—	—	*3*	—	—	—	—	*0*	Won	Twickenham	H. B. Toft
199	11.2.1939	Ireland	—	—	—	—	*0*	1	1	—	—	*5*	Lost	Twickenham	H. B. Toft
200	18.3.1939	Scotland	—	—	—	3	*9*	2	—	—	—	*6*	Won	Edinburgh[4]	H. B. Toft
201	18.1.1947	Wales	1	1	1	—	*9*	2	—	—	—	*6*	Won	Cardiff	J. Mycock
202	8.2.1947	Ireland	—	—	—	—	*0*	5	2	—	1	*22*	Lost	Dublin[2]	J. Mycock
203	15.3.1947	Scotland	4	4	1	—	*24*	1	1	—	—	*5*	Won	Twickenham	J. Heaton
204	19.4.1947	France	2	—	—	—	*6*	—	—	—	1	*3*	Won	Twickenham	J. Heaton
205	3.1.1948	Australia	—	—	—	—	*0*	3	1	—	—	*11*	Lost	Twickenham	E. K. Scott
206	17.1.1948	Wales	—	—	1	—	*3*	1	—	—	—	*3*	Drawn	Twickenham	T. A. Kemp
207	14.2.1948	Ireland	2	2	—	—	*10*	3	1	—	—	*11*	Lost	Twickenham	E. K. Scott
208	20.3.1948	Scotland	—	—	—	1	*3*	2	—	—	—	*6*	Lost	Edinburgh[4]	E. K. Scott
209	29.3.1948	France	—	—	—	—	*0*	3	1	1	—	*15*	Lost	Paris[2]	R. H. G. Weighill
210	15.1.1949	Wales	—	—	1	—	*3*	3	—	—	—	*9*	Lost	Cardiff	N. M. Hall
211	12.2.1949	Ireland	1	1	—	—	*5*	2	1	—	2	*14*	Lost	Dublin[2]	N. M. Hall
212	26.2.1949	France	1	1	1	—	*8*	—	—	1	—	*3*	Won	Twickenham	I. Preece
213	19.3.1949	Scotland	5	2	—	—	*19*	—	—	—	1	*3*	Won	Twickenham	I. Preece
214	21.1.1950	Wales	1	1	—	—	*5*	2	1	—	1	*11*	Lost	Twickenham	I. Preece
215	11.2.1950	Ireland	1	—	—	—	*3*	—	—	—	—	*0*	Won	Twickenham	I. Preece
216	25.2.1950	France	1	—	—	—	*3*	2	—	—	—	*6*	Lost	Paris[2]	I. Preece
217	18.3.1950	Scotland	2	1	—	1	*11*	3	2	—	—	*13*	Lost	Edinburgh[4]	I. Preece
218	20.1.1951	Wales	1	1	—	—	*5*	5	4	—	—	*23*	Lost	Swansea	V. G. Roberts
219	10.2.1951	Ireland	—	—	—	—	*0*	—	—	—	1	*3*	Lost	Dublin[2]	J. M. K. Kendall-Carpenter
220	24.2.1951	France	1	—	—	—	*3*	2	1	1	—	*11*	Lost	Twickenham	J. M. K. Kendall-Carpenter
221	17.3.1951	Scotland	1	1	—	—	*5*	1	—	—	—	*3*	Won	Twickenham	J. M. K. Kendall-Carpenter
222	5.1.1952	South Africa	1	—	—	—	*3*	1	1	—	1	*8*	Lost	Twickenham	N. M. Hall
223	19.1.1952	Wales	2	—	—	—	*6*	2	1	—	—	*8*	Lost	Twickenham	N. M. Hall
224	15.3.1952	Scotland	4	2	1	—	*19*	1	—	—	—	*3*	Won	Edinburgh[4]	N. M. Hall
225	29.3.1952	Ireland	1	—	—	—	*3*	—	—	—	—	*0*	Won	Twickenham	N. M. Hall
226	5.4.1952	France	—	—	—	2	*6*	1	—	—	—	*3*	Won	Paris[2]	N. M. Hall
227	17.1.1953	Wales	1	1	—	1	*8*	—	—	—	1	*3*	Won	Cardiff	N. M. Hall
228	14.2.1953	Ireland	1	—	—	2	*9*	1	—	—	2	*9*	Drawn	Dublin[2]	N. M. Hall
229	28.2.1953	France	3	1	—	—	*11*	—	—	—	—	*0*	Won	Twickenham	N. M. Hall
230	21.3.1953	Scotland	6	4	—	—	*26*	2	1	—	—	*8*	Won	Twickenham	N. M. Hall
231	16.1.1954	Wales	3	—	—	—	*9*	1	—	—	1	*6*	Won	Twickenham	R. V. Stirling
232	30.1.1954	New Zealand	—	—	—	—	*0*	1	1	—	—	*5*	Lost	Twickenham	R. V. Stirling
233	13.2.1954	Ireland	3	1	—	1	*14*	—	—	—	1	*3*	Won	Twickenham	R. V. Stirling
234	20.3.1954	Scotland	3	2	—	—	*13*	1	—	—	—	*3*	Won	Edinburgh[4]	R. V. Stirling
235	10.4.1954	France	1	—	—	—	*3*	2	1	1	—	*11*	Lost	Paris[2]	R. V. Stirling
236	22.1.1955	Wales	—	—	—	—	*0*	—	—	—	1	*3*	Lost	Cardiff	N. M. Hall
237	12.2.1955	Ireland	2	—	—	—	*6*	1	—	—	1	*6*	Drawn	Dublin[2]	N. M. Hall
238	26.2.1955	France	1	—	—	2	*9*	2	2	2	—	*16*	Lost	Twickenham	P. D. Young
239	19.3.1955	Scotland	2	—	—	1	*9*	1	—	—	1	*6*	Won	Twickenham	P. D. Young
240	21.1.1956	Wales	—	—	—	1	*3*	2	1	—	—	*8*	Lost	Twickenham	E. Evans
241	11.2.1956	Ireland	3	1	—	3	*20*	—	—	—	—	*0*	Won	Twickenham	E. Evans
242	17.3.1956	Scotland	1	1	—	2	*11*	1	—	—	1	*6*	Won	Edinburgh[4]	E. Evans
243	14.4.1956	France	1	—	—	2	*9*	2	1	—	2	*14*	Lost	Paris[2]	E. Evans
244	19.1.1957	Wales	—	—	—	1	*3*	—	—	—	—	*0*	Won	Cardiff	E. Evans
245	9.2.1957	Ireland	1	—	—	1	*6*	—	—	—	—	*0*	Won	Dublin[2]	E. Evans
246	23.2.1957	France	3	—	—	—	*9*	1	1	—	—	*5*	Won	Twickenham	E. Evans
247	16.3.1957	Scotland	3	2	—	1	*16*	—	—	1	—	*3*	Won	Twickenham	E. Evans

continued

Match	Date	Opponents	For T	C	D	P	Pts	Against T	C	D	P	Pts	Result	Venue	Captain
248	18.1.1958	Wales	1	—	—	—	3	—	—	—	1	3	Drawn	Twickenham	E. Evans
249	1.2.1958	Australia	2	—	—	1	9	—	—	1	1	6	Won	Twickenham	E. Evans
250	8.2.1958	Ireland	1	—	—	1	6	—	—	—	—	0	Won	Twickenham	E. Evans
251	1.3.1958	France	3	1	—	1	14	—	—	—	—	0	Won	Paris[2]	E. Evans
252	15.3.1958	Scotland	—	—	—	1	3	—	—	—	1	3	Drawn	Edinburgh[4]	E. Evans
253	17.1.1959	Wales	—	—	—	—	0	1	1	—	—	5	Lost	Cardiff	J. Butterfield
254	14.2.1959	Ireland	—	—	—	1	3	—	—	—	—	0	Won	Dublin[2]	J. Butterfield
255	28.2.1959	France	—	—	—	1	3	—	—	—	1	3	Drawn	Twickenham	J. Butterfield
256	21.3.1959	Scotland	—	—	—	1	3	—	—	—	1	3	Drawn	Twickenham	J. Butterfield
257	16.1.1960	Wales	2	1	—	2	14	—	—	—	2	6	Won	Twickenham	R. E. G. Jeeps
258	13.2.1960	Ireland	1	1	1	—	8	1	1	—	—	5	Won	Twickenham	R. E. G. Jeeps
259	27.2.1960	France	1	—	—	—	3	—	—	—	1	3	Drawn	Paris[2]	R. E. G. Jeeps
260	19.3.1960	Scotland	3	3	1	1	21	1	—	—	3	12	Won	Edinburgh[4]	R. E. G. Jeeps
261	7.1.1961	South Africa	—	—	—	—	0	1	1	—	—	5	Lost	Twickenham	R. E. G. Jeeps
262	21.1.1961	Wales	1	—	—	—	3	2	—	—	—	6	Lost	Cardiff	R. E. G. Jeeps
263	11.2.1961	Ireland	2	1	—	—	8	1	1	—	2	11	Lost	Dublin[2]	R. E. G. Jeeps
264	25.2.1961	France	1	1	—	—	5	1	1	—	—	5	Drawn	Twickenham	R. E. G. Jeeps
265	18.3.1961	Scotland	1	—	—	1	6	—	—	—	—	0	Won	Twickenham	R. E. G. Jeeps
266	20.1.1962	Wales	—	—	—	—	0	—	—	—	—	0	Drawn	Twickenham	R. E. G. Jeeps
267	10.2.1962	Ireland	3	2	—	1	16	—	—	—	—	0	Won	Twickenham	R. E. G. Jeeps
268	24.2.1962	France	—	—	—	—	0	3	2	—	—	13	Lost	Paris[2]	R. E. G. Jeeps
269	17.3.1962	Scotland	—	—	—	1	3	—	—	—	1	3	Drawn	Edinburgh[4]	R. E. G. Jeeps
270	19.1.1963	Wales	2	2	1	—	13	1	—	—	1	6	Won	Cardiff	R. A. W. Sharp
271	9.2.1963	Ireland	—	—	—	—	0	—	—	—	—	0	Drawn	Dublin[2]	R. A. W. Sharp
272	23.2.1963	France	—	—	—	2	6	1	1	—	—	5	Won	Twickenham	R. A. W. Sharp
273	16.3.1963	Scotland	2	2	—	—	10	1	1	1	—	8	Won	Twickenham	R. A. W. Sharp
274	25.5.1963	New Zealand	1	1	—	2	11	3	3	1	1	21	Lost	Auckland	M. P. Weston
275	1.6.1963	New Zealand	1	—	—	1	6	2	—	★	—	9	Lost	Christchurch	M. P. Weston
276	4.6.1963	Australia	3	—	—	—	9	4	3	—	—	18	Lost	Sydney	M. P. Weston
277	4.1.1964	New Zealand	—	—	—	—	0	2	1	—	2	14	Lost	Twickenham	J. G. Willcox
278	18.1.1964	Wales	2	—	—	—	6	2	—	—	—	6	Drawn	Twickenham	J. G. Willcox
279	8.2.1964	Ireland	1	1	—	—	5	4	3	—	—	18	Lost	Twickenham	J. G. Willcox
280	22.2.1964	France	1	—	—	1	6	1	—	—	—	3	Won	Paris[2]	C. R. Jacobs
281	21.3.1964	Scotland	1	—	—	1	6	3	3	—	—	15	Lost	Edinburgh[4]	C. R. Jacobs
282	16.1.1965	Wales	—	—	—	1	3	3	1	1	—	14	Lost	Cardiff	D. G. Perry
283	13.2.1965	Ireland	—	—	—	—	0	1	1	—	—	5	Lost	Dublin[2]	D. G. Perry
284	27.2.1965	France	1	—	—	2	9	1	—	—	1	6	Won	Twickenham	D. G. Perry
285	20.3.1965	Scotland	1	—	—	—	3	—	—	1	—	3	Drawn	Twickenham	D. G. Perry
286	15.1.1966	Wales	1	—	—	1	6	1	1	—	2	11	Lost	Twickenham	D. P. Rogers
287	12.2.1966	Ireland	1	—	—	1	6	1	—	—	1	6	Drawn	Twickenham	D. P. Rogers
288	26.2.1966	France	—	—	—	—	0	3	2	—	—	13	Lost	Paris[2]	D. P. Rogers
289	19.3.1966	Scotland	—	—	1	—	3	1	—	—	1	6	Lost	Edinburgh[4]	D. P. Rogers
290	7.1.1967	Australia	1	1	—	2	11	2	1	3	2	23	Lost	Twickenham	R. A. W. Sharp
291	11.2.1967	Ireland	1	1	—	1	8	—	—	—	1	3	Won	Dublin[2]	P. E. Judd
292	25.2.1967	France	—	—	1	3	12	2	2	1	1	16	Lost	Twickenham	P. E. Judd
293	18.3.1967	Scotland	4	3	1	2	27	2	1	—	2	14	Won	Twickenham	P. E. Judd
294	15.4.1967	Wales	3	—	—	4	21	5	5	1	2	34	Lost	Cardiff	P. E. Judd
295	4.11.1967	New Zealand	2	1	—	1	11	5	4	—	—	23	Lost	Twickenham	P. E. Judd
296	20.1.1968	Wales	2	1	—	1	11	2	1	1	—	11	Drawn	Twickenham	C. W. McFadyean

★ *in the drop-goal column denotes a goal from a mark*

continued

Match	Date	Opponents	For					Against					Result	Venue	Captain
			T	C	D	P	Pts	T	C	D	P	Pts			
297	10.2.1968	Ireland	—	—	1	2	9	—	—	—	3	9	Drawn	Twickenham	C. W. McFadyean
298	24.2.1968	France	—	—	1	2	9	1	1	2	1	14	Lost	Paris²	M. P. Weston
299	16.3.1968	Scotland	1	1	—	1	8	—	—	1	1	6	Won	Edinburgh⁴	M. P. Weston
300	8.2.1969	Ireland	1	—	—	4	15	2	1	1	2	17	Lost	Dublin²	J. R. H. Greenwood
301	22.2.1969	France	3	2	—	3	22	1	1	1	—	8	Won	Twickenham	D. P. Rogers
302	15.3.1969	Scotland	2	1	—	—	8	—	—	—	1	3	Won	Twickenham	D. P. Rogers
303	12.4.1969	Wales	—	—	—	3	9	5	3	1	2	30	Lost	Cardiff	D. P. Rogers
304	20.12.1969	South Africa	2	1	—	1	11	1	1	—	1	8	Won	Twickenham	R. Hiller
305	14.2.1970	Ireland	1	—	2	—	9	—	—	—	1	3	Won	Twickenham	R. Hiller
306	28.2.1970	Wales	2	2	—	1	13	4	1	1	—	17	Lost	Twickenham	R. Hiller
307	21.3.1970	Scotland	1	1	—	—	5	2	1	—	2	14	Lost	Edinburgh⁴	R. Hiller
308	18.4.1970	France	2	2	—	1	13	6	4	2	1	35	Lost	Paris²	R. B. Taylor
309	16.1.1971	Wales	1	—	—	1	6	3	2	2	1	22	Lost	Cardiff	A. L. Bucknall
310	13.2.1971	Ireland	—	—	—	3	9	2	—	—	—	6	Won	Dublin²	J. S. Spencer
311	27.2.1971	France	1	1	—	3	14	2	1	1	1	14	Drawn	Twickenham	R. Hiller
312	20.3.1971	Scotland	2	—	—	3	15	3	2	1	—	16	Lost	Twickenham	J. S. Spencer
313	27.3.1971	Scotland	—	—	1	1	6	5	4	—	1	26	Lost	Edinburgh⁴	J. S. Spencer
314	17.4.1971	R.F.U. President's XV	1	1	—	2	11	6	5	—	—	28	Lost	Twickenham	J. S. Spencer
315	15.1.1972	Wales	—	—	—	1	3	1	1	—	2	12	Lost	Twickenham	R. Hiller
316	12.2.1972	Ireland	1	1	—	2	12	2	1	1	1	16	Lost	Twickenham	R. Hiller
317	26.2.1972	France	1	1	—	2	12	6	5	—	1	37	Lost	Paris²	P. J. Dixon
318	18.3.1972	Scotland	—	—	—	3	9	2	—	1	4	23	Lost	Edinburgh⁴	P. J. Dixon
319	3.6.1972	South Africa	1	1	—	4	18	—	—	—	3	9	Won	Johannesb'g	J. V. Pullin
320	6.1.1973	New Zealand	—	—	—	—	0	1	1	1	—	9	Lost	Twickenham	J. V. Pullin
321	20.1.1973	Wales	—	—	1	2	9	5	1	—	1	25	Lost	Cardiff	J. V. Pullin
322	10.2.1973	Ireland	1	1	—	1	9	2	2	1	1	18	Lost	Dublin²	J. V. Pullin
323	24.2.1973	France	2	—	—	2	14	1	1	—	—	6	Won	Twickenham	J. V. Pullin
324	17.3.1973	Scotland	4	2	—	—	20	2	1	—	1	13	Won	Twickenham	J. V. Pullin
325	15.9.1973	New Zealand	3	2	—	—	16	2	1	—	—	10	Won	Auckland	J. V. Pullin
326	17.11.1973	Australia	3	1	—	2	20	—	—	—	1	3	Won	Twickenham	J. V. Pullin
327	2.2.1974	Scotland	2	—	1	1	14	2	1	—	2	16	Lost	Edinburgh⁴	J. V. Pullin
328	16.2.1974	Ireland	1	1	—	5	21	4	2	1	1	26	Lost	Twickenham	J. V. Pullin
329	2.3.1974	France	1	1	1	1	12	1	1	1	1	12	Drawn	Paris¹	J. V. Pullin
330	16.3.1974	Wales	2	1	—	2	16	1	1	—	2	12	Won	Twickenham	J. V. Pullin
331	18.1.1975	Ireland	1	1	1	—	9	2	2	—	—	12	Lost	Dublin²	F. E. Cotton
332	1.2.1975	France	2	—	—	4	20	4	4	—	1	27	Lost	Twickenham	F. E. Cotton
333	15.2.1975	Wales	1	—	—	—	4	3	1	—	2	20	Lost	Cardiff	F. E. Cotton
334	15.3.1975	Scotland	1	—	—	1	7	—	—	—	2	6	Won	Twickenham	A. Neary
335	24.5.1975	Australia	1	1	—	1	9	1	—	2	2	16	Lost	Sydney	A. Neary
336	31.5.1975	Australia	2	2	—	3	21	5	2	—	2	30	Lost	Brisbane	J. V. Pullin
337	3.1.1976	Australia	3	1	—	3	23	—	—	—	2	6	Won	Twickenham	A. Neary
338	17.1.1976	Wales	—	—	—	3	9	3	3	—	1	21	Lost	Twickenham	A. Neary
339	21.2.1976	Scotland	1	1	—	2	12	3	2	—	2	22	Lost	Edinburgh⁴	A. Neary
340	6.3.1976	Ireland	—	—	—	4	12	1	—	1	2	13	Lost	Twickenham	A. Neary
341	20.3.1976	France	1	1	—	1	9	6	3	—	—	30	Lost	Paris¹	A. Neary
342	8.1.1977	Scotland	4	2	—	2	26	—	—	—	2	6	Won	Twickenham	R. M. Uttley
343	5.2.1977	Ireland	1	—	—	—	4	—	—	—	—	0	Won	Dublin²	R. M. Uttley
344	19.2.1977	France	—	—	—	1	3	1	—	—	—	4	Lost	Twickenham	R. M. Uttley

continued

Match	Date	Opponents	For T	C	D	P	Pts	Against T	C	D	P	Pts	Result	Venue	Captain
345	5.3.1977	Wales	—	—	—	3	9	2	—	—	2	14	Lost	Cardiff	R. M. Uttley
346	21.1.1978	France	—	—	2	—	6	2	2	—	1	15	Lost	Paris[1]	W. B. Beaumont
347	4.2.1978	Wales	—	—	—	2	6	—	—	—	3	9	Lost	Twickenham	W. B. Beaumont
348	4.3.1978	Scotland	2	2	—	1	15	—	—	—	—	0	Won	Edinburgh[4]	W. B. Beaumont
349	18.3.1978	Ireland	2	2	—	1	15	—	—	1	2	9	Won	Twickenham	W. B. Beaumont
350	25.11.1978	New Zealand	—	—	1	1	6	2	1	—	2	16	Lost	Twickenham	W. B. Beaumont
351	3.2.1979	Scotland	1	—	—	1	7	1	—	—	1	7	Drawn	Twickenham	R. M. Uttley
352	17.2.1979	Ireland	1	—	—	1	7	1	1	1	1	12	Lost	Dublin[2]	W. B. Beaumont
353	3.3.1979	France	1	—	—	1	7	1	1	—	—	6	Won	Twickenham	W. B. Beaumont
354	17.3.1979	Wales	—	—	—	1	3	5	2	1	—	27	Lost	Cardiff	W. B. Beaumont
355	24.11.1979	New Zealand	—	—	—	3	9	1	—	—	2	10	Lost	Twickenham	W. B. Beaumont
356	19.1.1980	Ireland	3	3	—	2	24	—	—	—	3	9	Won	Twickenham	W. B. Beaumont
357	2.2.1980	France	2	—	2	1	17	2	1	—	1	13	Won	Paris[1]	W. B. Beaumont
358	16.2.1980	Wales	—	—	—	3	9	2	—	—	—	8	Won	Twickenham	W. B. Beaumont
359	15.3.1980	Scotland	5	2	—	2	30	2	2	—	2	18	Won	Edinburgh[4]	W. B. Beaumont
360	17.1.1981	Wales	1	—	—	5	19	1	1	1	4	21	Lost	Cardiff	W. B. Beaumont
361	21.2.1981	Scotland	3	1	—	3	23	3	1	—	1	17	Won	Twickenham	W. B. Beaumont
362	7.3.1981	Ireland	2	1	—	—	10	—	—	2	—	6	Won	Dublin[2]	W. B. Beaumont
363	21.3.1981	France	—	—	—	4	12	2	1	2	—	16	Lost	Twickenham	W. B. Beaumont
364	30.5.1981	Argentina	3	2	—	1	19	2	1	2	1	19	Drawn	Buenos Aires	W. B. Beaumont
365	6.6.1981	Argentina	1	1	—	2	12	1	1	—	—	6	Won	Buenos Aires	W. B. Beaumont
366	2.1.1982	Australia	1	1	—	3	15	2	—	—	1	11	Won	Twickenham	W. B. Beaumont
367	16.1.1982	Scotland	—	—	—	3	9	—	—	1	2	9	Drawn	Edinburgh[4]	W. B. Beaumont
368	6.2.1982	Ireland	1	1	—	3	15	2	1	—	2	16	Lost	Twickenham	S. J. Smith
369	20.2.1982	France	2	2	—	5	27	1	1	1	2	15	Won	Paris[1]	S. J. Smith
370	6.3.1982	Wales	2	—	—	3	17	1	—	1	—	7	Won	Twickenham	S. J. Smith

SUMMARY OF ENGLISH INTERNATIONAL MATCHES

Opponents	P	W	D	L	For T	C	D	GM	P	Pts*	Against T	C	D	GM	P	Pts*
Argentina	2	1	1	0	4	3	0	0	3	31	3	2	2	0	1	25
Australia	10	4	0	6	17	7	0	0	15	120	20	7	6	0	11	133
France	57	32	6	19	127	59	11	1	52	706	90	52	20	0	21	528
Ireland	94	53	8	33	176	68	12	0	53	734	106	40	14	2	41	564
New South Wales	1	1	0	0	4	3	0	0	0	18	3	1	0	0	0	11
New Zealand	12	2	0	10	12	5	2	0	9	83	28	13	2	1	8	149
New Zealand Natives	1	1	0	0	5	1	0	0	0	7	0	0	0	0	0	0
R.F.U. President's XV	1	0	0	1	1	1	0	0	2	11	6	5	0	0	0	28
Scotland	98	47	16	35	166	75	14	0	48	786	132	57	20	0	42	669
South Africa	7	2	1	4	6	2	0	0	5	38	6	3	1	0	7	49
Wales	87	35	11	41	148	59	9	3	51	638	170	69	17	2	42	839
TOTALS	370	178	43	149	666	283	48	4	238	3172	564	249	82	5	173	2995

* Points are actual points scored since scoring values were adopted (1889).

420

MOST CONSECUTIVE MATCHES WON

10	*1883* W,I,S *1884* W,I,S *1885* W,I *1886* W,I
9	*1922* S, *1923* W,I,S,F *1924* W,I,F,S
8	*1913* W,F,I,S *1914* W,I,S,F
7	*1920* F,I,S *1921* W,I,S,F
6	*1928* NSW,W,I,F,S *1929* W
5	*1879* I *1880* I,S *1881* I,W

MOST CONSECUTIVE MATCHES WITHOUT DEFEAT

Matches	Wins	Draws	Period
12	10	2	1882–83 to 1886–87
11	10	1	1921–22 to 1923–24
10	6	4	1877–78 to 1881–82
9	7	2	1956–57 to 1957–58
8	6	2	1871–72 to 1876–77
8	8		1912–13 to 1913–14
8	7	1	1951–52 to 1953–54
7	7		1919–20 to 1920–21
7	4	3	1958–59 to 1959–60
6	6		1927–28 to 1928–29
5	4	1	1933–34 to 1934–35
5	3	2	1961–62 to 1962–63

MOST CONSECUTIVE MATCHES WITHOUT CONCEDING A TRY

10	between 1874–75 and 1878–79
6	between 1956–57 and 1957–58
4	in 1912–13
4	between 1958–59 and 1959–60

MOST CONSECUTIVE MATCHES WITHOUT CONCEDING A SCORE

5	between 1874–75 and 1876–77

MOST POINTS IN A MATCH

By the team

Pts	Opponents	Venue	Season	Pts	Opponents	Venue	Season
41	France	Richmond	1906–07	23	Ireland	Leicester	1922–23
39	France	Paris[2]	1913–14	23	Australia	Twickenham	1975–76
37	France	Twickenham	1910–11	23	Scotland	Twickenham	1980–81
36	Ireland	Dublin[2]	1937–38	22	France	Leicester	1908–09
35	France	Paris[1]	1905–06	22	France	Twickenham	1968–69
30	Scotland	Edinburgh[4]	1979–80	21	Scotland	Edinburgh[4]	1959–60
27	Scotland	Twickenham	1966–67	21	Wales	Cardiff	1966–67
27	France	Paris[1]	1981–82	21	Ireland	Twickenham	1973–74
26	Scotland	Twickenham	1952–53	21	Australia	Brisbane	1975
26	Scotland	Twickenham	1976–77	20	France	Twickenham	1912–13
25	Wales	Blackheath[2]	1895–96	20	Ireland	Twickenham	1955–56
24	Wales	Birkenhead	1893–94	20	Scotland	Twickenham	1972–73
24	Scotland	Twickenham	1946–47	20	Australia	Twickenham	1973–74
24	Ireland	Twickenham	1979–80	20	France	Twickenham	1974–75

NB England scored heavily in several matches before scoring by points was adopted

By a player

Pts	Player	Opponents	Venue	Season
22	D. Lambert	France	Twickenham	1910–11
19	W. H. Hare	Wales	Cardiff	1980–81
19	W. H. Hare	France	Paris[1]	1981–82
17	A. G. B. Old	Ireland	Twickenham	1973–74
16	P. A. Rossborough	France	Twickenham	1974–75
15	D. Lambert	France	Richmond	1906–07
15	G. W. Parker	Ireland	Dublin[2]	1937–38
14	R. Hiller	France	Twickenham	1970–71
14	S. A. Doble	South Africa	Johannesburg	1972
13	R. Hiller	France	Twickenham	1968–69
13	A. G. B. Old	Australia	Brisbane	1975
12	A. Hudson	France	Paris[1]	1905–06
12	J. E. Greenwood	France	Paris[2]	1913–14
12	R. W. Poulton	France	Paris[2]	1913–14
12	R. W. Hosen	Scotland	Twickenham	1966–67
12	R. W. Hosen	Wales	Cardiff	1966–67
12	R. Hiller	Ireland	Dublin[2]	1968–69
12	R. Hiller	Scotland	Twickenham	1970–71
12	A. G. B. Old	Ireland	Twickenham	1975–76
12	W. H. Hare	Ireland	Twickenham	1979–80
12	J. Carleton	Scotland	Edinburgh[4]	1979–80
12	W. M. H. Rose	France	Twickenham	1980–81
11	D. W. Burland	Ireland	Dublin[2]	1931–32
11	H. J. Boughton	Ireland	Twickenham	1934–35
11	R. Hiller	RFU President's XV	Twickenham	1970–71

Pts	Player	Opponents	Venue	Season
11	A. J. Hignell	Australia	Twickenham	1975–76
11	W. H. Hare	Scotland	Twickenham	1980–81
11	W. M. H. Rose	Ireland	Twickenham	1981–82
10	E. J. Vivyan	Ireland	Blackheath[2]	1903–04
10	B. A. Hill	France	Richmond	1906–07
10	R. A. W. Sharp	Ireland	Twickenham	1961–62
10	A. J. Hignell	Scotland	Twickenham	1976–77
10	W. H. Hare	Scotland	Edinburgh[4]	1979–80
9	R. E. Lockwood	Wales	Birkenhead	1893–94
9	E. W. Taylor	Wales	Birkenhead	1893–94
9	V. H. M. Coates	France	Twickenham	1912–13
9	C. N. Lowe	Scotland	Edinburgh[3]	1913–14
9	C. N. Lowe	France	Paris[2]	1913–14
9	H. P. Jacob	France	Twickenham	1923–24
9	G. W. Parker	Scotland	Twickenham	1937–38
9	J. Heaton	Scotland	Edinburgh[4]	1938–39
9	D. Rutherford	Scotland	Edinburgh[4]	1959–60
9	R. W. Hosen	France	Twickenham	1966–67
9	R. Hiller	Wales	Cardiff	1968–69
9	R. Hiller	Ireland	Dublin[2]	1970–71
9	A. G. B. Old	Scotland	Edinburgh[4]	1971–72
9	A. J. Hignell	Wales	Twickenham	1975–76
9	A. J. Hignell	Wales	Cardiff	1976–77
9	W. H. Hare	New Zealand	Twickenham	1979–80
9	W. H. Hare	Wales	Twickenham	1979–80
9	W. M. H. Rose	Australia	Twickenham	1981–82
9	W. H. Hare	Wales	Twickenham	1981–82
8	V. H. Cartwright	France	Paris[1]	1905–06
8	A. C. Palmer	Ireland	Dublin[2]	1908–09
8	F. E. Chapman	Wales	Twickenham	1909–10
8	H. L. V. Day	France	Twickenham	1921–22
8	J. Heaton	Scotland	Twickenham	1946–47
8	N. M. Hall	Scotland	Twickenham	1952–53
8	J. D. Currie	Ireland	Twickenham	1955–56
8	J. D. Currie	Scotland	Edinburgh[4]	1955–56
8	D. Rutherford	Wales	Twickenham	1959–60
8	R. W. Hosen	New Zealand	Auckland	1963
8	R. W. Hosen	Australia	Twickenham	1966–67
8	R. Hiller	Ireland	Twickenham	1971–72
8	A. G. B. Old	France	Paris[2]	1971–72
8	D. J. Duckham	France	Twickenham	1972–73
8	P. J. Dixon	Scotland	Twickenham	1972–73
8	P. A. Rossborough	Australia	Twickenham	1973–74
8	A. G. B. Old	Wales	Twickenham	1973–74
8	A. G. B. Old	Scotland	Edinburgh[4]	1975–76
8	C. R. Woodward	Argentina	Buenos Aires (1st Test)	1981
8	W. H. Hare	Argentina	Buenos Aires (2nd Test)	1981

NB Several players scored heavily in matches played before scoring by points was adopted

MOST TRIES IN A MATCH

By the team

T	Opponents	Venue	Season	T	Opponents	Venue	Season
13	Wales	Blackheath[1]	1880–81	5	N. Z. Natives	Blackheath[2]	1888–89
9	France	Paris[1]	1905–06	5	Ireland	Dublin[2]	1890–91
9	France	Richmond	1906–07	5	Ireland	Blackheath[2]	1903–04
9	France	Paris[2]	1913–14	5	France	Paris[2]	1907–08
7	Wales	Blackheath[2]	1895–96	5	Ireland	Twickenham	1911–12
7	France	Twickenham	1910–11	5	Ireland	Twickenham	1913–14
7	Ireland	Dublin[2]	1937–38	5	Ireland	Leicester	1922–23
6	Wales	Swansea	1882–83	5	Wales	Swansea	1923–24
6	France	Leicester	1908–09	5	France	Twickenham	1923–24
6	France	Twickenham	1912–13	5	Ireland	Twickenham	1932–33
6	Scotland	Twickenham	1952–53	5	Scotland	Twickenham	1948–49
5	Scotland	Manchester[1]	1879–80	5	Scotland	Edinburgh[4]	1979–80
5	Wales	Swansea	1884–85				

By a player

T	Player	Opponents	Venue	Season
5	D. Lambert	France	Richmond	1906–07
4	G. W. Burton	Wales	Blackheath[1]	1880–81
4	A. Hudson	France	Paris[1]	1905–06
4	R. W. Poulton	France	Paris[2]	1913–14
3	H. H. Taylor	Ireland	Manchester[1]	1880–81
3	H. Vassall	Wales	Blackheath[1]	1880–81
3	C. G. Wade	Wales	Swansea	1882–83
3	H. Marshall	Wales	Cardiff	1892–93
3	V. H. M. Coates	France	Twickenham	1912–13
3	C. N. Lowe	Scotland	Edinburgh[3]	1913–14
3	C. N. Lowe	France	Paris[2]	1913–14
3	H. P. Jacob	France	Twickenham	1923–24
3	J. Carleton	Scotland	Edinburgh[4]	1979–80
2	W. C. Hutchinson	Ireland	The Oval	1876–77
2	H. H. Taylor	Scotland	Manchester[1]	1879–80
2	H. Bedford	New Zealand Natives	Blackheath[2]	1888–89
2	P. Christopherson	Wales	Newport	1890–91
2	R. E. Lockwood	Ireland	Dublin[2]	1890–91
2	R. P. Wilson	Ireland	Dublin[2]	1890–91
2	S. Morfitt	Wales	Blackheath[2]	1895–96
2	R. H. B. Cattell	Wales	Blackheath[2]	1895–96

T	Player	Opponents	Venue	Season
2	E. F. Fookes	Wales	Blackheath[2]	1895–96
2	E. F. Fookes	Wales	Blackheath[2]	1897–98
2	G. C. Robinson	Ireland	Richmond	1899–1900
2	E. W. Elliot	Wales	Leicester	1903–04
2	E. J. Vivyan	Ireland	Blackheath[2]	1903–04
2	N. H. Moore	Ireland	Blackheath[2]	1903–04
2	J. G. G. Birkett	Wales	Bristol	1907–08
2	A. Hudson	Ireland	Richmond	1907–08
2	F. N. Tarr	France	Leicester	1908–09
2	A. C. Palmer	Ireland	Dublin[2]	1908–09
2	A. Hudson	France	Paris[1]	1909–10
2	J. G. G. Birkett	Scotland	Edinburgh[3]	1909–10
2	D. Lambert	France	Twickenham	1910–11
2	C. H. Pillman	France	Twickenham	1910–11
2	A. D. Roberts	Ireland	Twickenham	1911–12
2	C. H. Pillman	France	Twickenham	1912–13
2	V. H. M. Coates	Ireland	Dublin[2]	1912–13
2	C. N. Lowe	Ireland	Twickenham	1913–14
2	A. M. Smallwood	Wales	Twickenham	1920–21
2	C. N. Lowe	Scotland	Twickenham	1921–22
2	H. C. Catcheside	Wales	Swansea	1923–24
2	H. C. Catcheside	Ireland	Belfast	1923–24
2	A. M. Smallwood	Ireland	Twickenham	1924–25
2	A. R. Aslett	France	Twickenham	1925–26
2	G. V. Palmer	France	Twickenham	1927–28
2	H. G. Periton	France	Twickenham	1927–28
2	H. Wilkinson	Wales	Twickenham	1928–29
2	C. D. Aarvold	France	Paris[2]	1928–29
2	J. S. R. Reeve	Wales	Cardiff	1929–30
2	J. S. R. Reeve	Scotland	Edinburgh[4]	1930–31
2	J. A. Tallent	Scotland	Edinburgh[4]	1930–31
2	C. D. Aarvold	Scotland	Twickenham	1931–32
2	A. L. Novis	Ireland	Twickenham	1932–33
2	G. W. C. Meikle	Wales	Cardiff	1933–34
2	H. A. Fry	Ireland	Dublin[2]	1933–34
2	A. Obolensky	New Zealand	Twickenham	1935–36
2	R. H. Guest	Ireland	Twickenham	1947–48
2	C. B. van Ryneveld	Scotland	Twickenham	1948–49
2	J. V. Smith	Scotland	Edinburgh[4]	1949–50
2	R. C. Bazley	Scotland	Twickenham	1952–53
2	J. E. Woodward	Wales	Twickenham	1953–54
2	D. S. Wilson	Scotland	Edinburgh[4]	1953–54
2	P. B. Jackson	France	Twickenham	1956–57
2	P. H. Thompson	France	Paris[2]	1957–58
2	J. Roberts	Wales	Twickenham	1959–60
2	C. W. McFadyean	Scotland	Twickenham	1966–67
2	J. Barton	Wales	Cardiff	1966–67
2	R. H. Lloyd	New Zealand	Twickenham	1967–68
2	D. J. Duckham	Scotland	Twickenham	1968–69
2	D. J. Duckham	France	Twickenham	1972–73
2	P. J. Dixon	Scotland	Twickenham	1972–73
2	C. R. Woodward	Argentina	Buenos Aires (1st Test)	1981

MOST CONVERSIONS IN A MATCH

By the team

C	Opponents	Venue	Season	C	Opponents	Venue	Season
7	Wales	Blackheath[1]	1880–81	4	Wales	Birkenhead	1893–94
6	France	Paris[2]	1913–14	4	France	Paris[1]	1905–06
6	Ireland	Dublin[2]	1937–38	4	Scotland	Twickenham	1946–47
5	France	Richmond	1906–07	4	Scotland	Twickenham	1952–53
5	France	Twickenham	1910–11				

By a player

C	Player	Opponents	Venue	Season
6	L. Stokes	Wales	Blackheath[1]	1880–81
6	J. E. Greenwood	France	Paris[2]	1913–14
6	G. W. Parker	Ireland	Dublin[2]	1937–38
5	B. A. Hill	France	Richmond	1906–07
5	D. Lambert	France	Twickenham	1910–11
4	V. H. Cartwright	France	Paris[1]	1905–06
4	J. Heaton	Scotland	Twickenham	1946–47
4	N. M. Hall	Scotland	Twickenham	1952–53
3	R. E. Lockwood	Wales	Birkenhead	1893–94
3	E. D. G. Hammett	Scotland	Edinburgh[3]	1920–21
3	G. S. Conway	Scotland	Twickenham	1923–24
3	T. E. S. Francis	Ireland	Dublin[2]	1925–26
3	J. V. Richardson	New South Wales	Twickenham	1927–28
3	J. V. Richardson	France	Twickenham	1927–28
3	D. Rutherford	Scotland	Edinburgh[4]	1959–60
3	R. W. Hosen	Scotland	Twickenham	1966–67
3	W. H. Hare	Ireland	Twickenham	1979–80
2	L. Stokes	Ireland	The Oval	1876–77
2	A. W. Pearson	Ireland	Dublin[2]	1877–78
2	L. Stokes	Ireland	The Oval	1878–79
2	L. Stokes	Scotland	Dublin[2]	1879–80
2	L. Stokes	Ireland	Manchester[1]	1880–81
2	A. M. Evanson	Wales	Swansea	1882–83
2	F. H. R. Alderson	Wales	Newport	1890–91
2	R. E. Lockwood	Ireland	Dublin[2]	1890–91
2	R. E. Lockwood	Wales	Blackheath[2]	1891–92
2	E. J. Vivyan	Ireland	Blackheath[2]	1903–04
2	G. D. Roberts	France	Paris[2]	1907–08
2	A. E. Wood	Wales	Bristol	1907–08
2	A. E. Wood	Ireland	Richmond	1907–08
2	D. Lambert	Scotland	Edinbugh[3]	1907–08
2	E. J. Jackett	France	Leicester	1908–09
2	R. O. Lagden	Scotland	Twickenham	1910–11
2	F. E. Chapman	Wales	Twickenham	1913–14
2	H. C. Harrison	Scotland	Edinburgh[3]	1913–14
2	J. E. Greenwood	Scotland	Twickenham	1919–20
2	E. D. G. Hammett	France	Paris[2]	1920–21

C	Player	Opponents	Venue	Season
2	G. S. Conway	Ireland	Leicester	1922–23
2	G. S. Conway	France	Twickenham	1923–24
2	W. G. E. Luddington	France	Paris[2]	1924–25
2	J. V. Richardson	Wales	Swansea	1927–28
2	E. Stanbury	France	Paris[2]	1928–29
2	B. H. Black	Scotland	Edinburgh[4]	1930–31
2	D. W. Burland	Scotland	Twickenham	1931–32
2	G. G. Gregory	Ireland	Dublin[2]	1933–34
2	R. Uren	Ireland	Twickenham	1947–48
2	B. H. Travers	Scotland	Twickenham	1948–49
2	N. M. Hall	Scotland	Edinburgh[4]	1951–52
2	N. Gibbs	Scotland	Edinburgh[4]	1953–54
2	R. Challis	Scotland	Twickenham	1956–57
2	R. A. W. Sharp	Ireland	Twickenham	1961–62
2	R. A. W. Sharp	Wales	Cardiff	1962–63
2	J. G. Willcox	Scotland	Twickenham	1962–63
2	R. Hiller	France	Twickenham	1968–69
2	R. Hiller	Wales	Twickenham	1969–70
2	A. M. Jorden	France	Paris[2]	1969–70
2	A. M. Jorden	Scotland	Twickenham	1972–73
2	P. A. Rossborough	New Zealand	Auckland	1973
2	A. G. B. Old	Australia	Brisbane	1975
2	A. J. Hignell	Scotland	Twickenham	1976–77
2	M. Young	Scotland	Edinburgh[4]	1977–78
2	M. Young	Ireland	Twickenham	1977–78
2	W. H. Hare	Scotland	Edinburgh[4]	1979–80
2	W. H. Hare	Argentina	Buenos Aires (1st Test)	1981
2	W. H. Hare	France	Paris[1]	1981–82

MOST DROPPED GOALS IN A MATCH

By the team

DG	Opponents	Venue	Season
2	Ireland	Twickenham	1969–70
2	France	Paris[1]	1977–78
2	France	Paris[1]	1979–80

By a player

DG	Player	Opponents	Venue	Season
2	R. Hiller	Ireland	Twickenham	1969–70
2	A. G. B. Old	France	Paris[1]	1977–78
2	J. P. Horton	France	Paris[1]	1979–80

MOST PENALTY GOALS IN A MATCH

By the team

PG	Opponents	Venue	Season	PG	Opponents	Venue	Season
5	Ireland	Twickenham	1973–74	4	South Africa	Johannesburg	1972
5	Wales	Cardiff	1980–81	4	France	Twickenham	1974–75
5	France	Paris[1]	1981–82	4	Ireland	Twickenham	1975–76
4	Wales	Cardiff	1966–67	4	France	Twickenham	1980–81
4	Ireland	Dublin[2]	1968–69				

By a player

PG	Player	Opponents	Venue	Season
5	A. G. B. Old	Ireland	Twickenham	1973–74
5	W. H. Hare	Wales	Cardiff	1980–81
5	W. H. Hare	France	Paris[1]	1981–82
4	R. W. Hosen	Wales	Cardiff	1966–67
4	R. Hiller	Ireland	Dublin[2]	1968–69
4	S. A. Doble	South Africa	Johannesburg	1972
4	P. A. Rossborough	France	Twickenham	1974–75
4	A. G. B. Old	Ireland	Twickenham	1975–76
4	W. M. H. Rose	France	Twickenham	1980–81
3	H. J. Boughton	Ireland	Twickenham	1934–35
3	G. W. Parker	Scotland	Twickenham	1937–38
3	J. Heaton	Scotland	Edinburgh[4]	1938–39
3	R. W. Hosen	France	Twickenham	1966–67
3	R. Hiller	France	Twickenham	1968–69
3	R. Hiller	Wales	Cardiff	1968–69
3	R. Hiller	Ireland	Dublin[2]	1970–71
3	R. Hiller	France	Twickenham	1970–71
3	R. Hiller	Scotland	Twickenham	1970–71
3	A. G. B. Old	Scotland	Edinburgh[4]	1971–72
3	A. G. B. Old	Australia	Brisbane	1975
3	A. J. Hignell	Australia	Twickenham	1975–76
3	A. J. Hignell	Wales	Twickenham	1975–76
3	A. J. Hignell	Wales	Cardiff	1976–77
3	W. H. Hare	New Zealand	Twickenham	1979–80
3	W. H. Hare	Wales	Twickenham	1979–80
3	W. H. Hare	Scotland	Twickenham	1980–81
3	W. M. H. Rose	Australia	Twickenham	1981–82
3	W. M. H. Rose	Ireland	Twickenham	1981–82
3	W. H. Hare	Wales	Twickenham	1981–82
2	J. F. Byrne	Ireland	Dublin[2]	1896–97
2	D. Lambert	France	Twickenham	1910–11
2	H. L. V. Day	France	Twickenham	1921–22
2	B. H. Black	Wales	Twickenham	1930–31
2	D. W. Burland	Ireland	Dublin[2]	1931–32
2	N. M. Hall	France	Paris[2]	1951–52
2	N. M. Hall	Ireland	Dublin[2]	1952–53
2	D. St. G. Hazell	France	Twickenham	1954–55

PG	Player	Opponents	Venue	Season
2	J. D. Currie	Ireland	Twickenham	1955–56
2	J. D. Currie	Scotland	Edinburgh[4]	1955–56
2	D. F. Allison	France	Paris[2]	1955–56
2	D. Rutherford	Wales	Twickenham	1959–60
2	J. G. Willcox	France	Twickenham	1962–63
2	R. W. Hosen	New Zealand	Auckland	1963
2	D. Rutherford	France	Twickenham	1964–65
2	R. W. Hosen	Australia	Twickenham	1966–67
2	R. W. Hosen	Scotland	Twickenham	1966–67
2	R. Hiller	Ireland	Twickenham	1967–68
2	R. Hiller	France	Paris[2]	1967–68
2	R. Hiller	RFU President's XV	Twickenham	1970–71
2	R. Hiller	Ireland	Twickenham	1971–72
2	A. G. B. Old	France	Paris[2]	1971–72
2	S. A. Doble	Wales	Cardiff	1972–73
2	A. M. Jorden	France	Twickenham	1972–73
2	P. A. Rossborough	Australia	Twickenham	1973–74
2	A. G. B. Old	Wales	Twickenham	1973–74
2	A. G. B. Old	Scotland	Edinburgh[4]	1975–76
2	A. J. Hignell	Scotland	Twickenham	1976–77
2	A. J. Hignell	Wales	Twickenham	1977–78
2	W. H. Hare	Ireland	Twickenham	1979–80
2	W. H. Hare	Scotland	Edinburgh[4]	1979–80
2	W. H. Hare	Argentina	Buenos Aires (2nd Test)	1981
2	P. W. Dodge	Scotland	Edinburgh[4]	1981–82

GOALS FROM MARKS

★	Player	Opponents	Venue	Season
1	A. E. Stoddart	Wales	Blackheath[2]	1885–86
1	E. W. Taylor	Wales	Birkenhead	1893–94
1	W. G. E. Luddington	France	Paris[2]	1924–25
1	L. J. Corbett	Wales	Twickenham	1926–27

MOST MATCHES AS CAPTAIN

21	W. B. Beaumont	(11 victories)		6	E. W. Taylor	(2 victories)
13	W. W. Wakefield	(7 victories)		6	J. Daniell	(4 victories)
13	N. M. Hall	(6 victories)		6	V. H. Cartwright	(2 victories)
13	E. Evans	(9 victories)		6	N. A. Wodehouse	(5 victories)
13	R. E. G. Jeeps	(5 victories)		6	I. Preece	(3 victories)
13	J. V. Pullin	(6 victories)		5	L. Stokes	(4 victories)
11	W. J. A. Davies	(10 victories)		5	F. H. R. Alderson	(4 victories)
9	E. T. Gurdon	(8 victories)		5	S. M. J. Woods	(4 victories)
8	B. C. Gadney	(5 victories)		5	J. G. G. Birkett	(2 victories)
7	R. Dibble	(4 victories)		5	R. V. Stirling	(3 victories)
7	R. Cove-Smith	(6 victories)		5	R. A. W. Sharp	(3 victories)
7	C. D. Aarvold	(2 victories)		5	M. P. Weston	(1 victory)
7	D. P. Rogers	(2 victories)		5	P. E. Judd	(2 victories)
7	R. Hiller	(2 victories)		5	R. M. Uttley	(2 victories)
7	A. Neary	(2 victories)				

CAPTAIN ON INTERNATIONAL DEBUT

Player	Opponents	Venue	Season
F. Stokes	Scotland	Edinburgh[1]	1870–71
F. H. R. Alderson	Wales	Newport	1890–91
J. Mycock	Wales	Cardiff	1946–47

TRIES ON DEBUT AND FOLLOWING MATCHES

Player	Matches	Season	Player	Matches	Season
G. C. Robinson	5	1897–1900	R. H. Williamson	2	1908
H. C. Catcheside	4	1924	H. Brougham	2	1912
G. W. C. Meikle	3	1934	H. L. V. Day	2	1920–1922
C. G. Wade	2	1883	H. J. Kittermaster	2	1925
J. J. Hawcridge	2	1885	W. J. Taylor	2	1928
E. Wilkinson	2	1886	J. A. Tallent	2	1931
D. Lambert	2	1907–1908	J. Butterfield	2	1953
W. N. Lapage	2	1908			

TRY ON DEBUT

Player	Opponents	Venue	Season
R. H. Birkett	Scotland	Edinburgh[1]	1870–71
S. Finney	Scotland	The Oval	1871–72
F. B. G. d'Aguilar	Scotland	The Oval	1871–72
A. T. Michell	Ireland	The Oval	1874–75
C. W. H. Clark	Ireland	Dublin[1]	1875–76
F. H. Lee	Scotland	The Oval	1875–76
A. N. Hornby	Ireland	The Oval	1876–77
H. P. Gardner	Ireland	Dublin[2]	1877–78
W. J. Penny	Ireland	Dublin[2]	1877–78
G. W. Burton	Scotland	Edinburgh[1]	1878–79
H. T. Twynam	Ireland	The Oval	1878–79
S. S. Ellis	Ireland	Dublin[2]	1879–80
E. T. Markendale	Ireland	Dublin[2]	1879–80
H. Vassall	Wales	Blackheath[1]	1880–81
W. N. Bolton	Ireland	Dublin[2]	1881–82
C. G. Wade	Wales	Swansea	1882–83
R. S. F. Henderson	Wales	Swansea	1882–83
J. J. Hawcridge	Wales	Swansea	1884–85
H. J. Ryalls	Wales	Swansea	1884–85
E. Wilkinson	Wales	Blackheath[2]	1885–86
J. W. Sutcliffe	NZ Natives	Blackheath[2]	1888–89
F. Evershed	NZ Natives	Blackheath[2]	1888–89
H. Bedford	NZ Natives	Blackheath[2]	1888–89
J. W. Dyson	Scotland	Edinburgh[1]	1889–90
P. Christopherson	Wales	Newport	1890–91
G. C. Hubbard	Wales	Blackheath[2]	1891–92
W. Nichol	Wales	Blackheath[2]	1891–92
H. Marshall	Wales	Cardiff	1892–93
F. C. Lohden	Wales	Cardiff	1892–93
S. Morfitt	Wales	Birkenhead	1893–94
F. A. Leslie-Jones	Wales	Swansea	1894–95
G. M. Carey	Wales	Swansea	1894–95
E. F. Fookes	Wales	Blackheath[2]	1895–96
G. C. Robinson	Ireland	Dublin[2]	1896–97
P. M. R. Royds	Scotland	Edinburgh[2]	1897–98
E. T. Nicholson	Wales	Gloucester	1899–1900
D. D. Dobson	Wales	Blackheath[2]	1901–02
A. Hudson	Wales	Richmond	1905–06
T. B. Hogarth	France	Paris[1]	1905–06
F. G. Brooks	South Africa	Crystal Palace	1906–07
D. Lambert	France	Richmond	1906–07
W. M. B. Nanson	France	Richmond	1906–07
L. A. N. Slocock	France	Richmond	1906–07
W. N. Lapage	France	Paris[2]	1907–08
G. V. Portus	France	Paris[2]	1907–08
R. H. Williamson	Wales	Bristol	1907–08
E. R. Mobbs	Australia	Blackheath[2]	1908–09
F. Hutchinson	France	Leicester	1908–09
A. C. Palmer	Ireland	Dublin[2]	1908–09
F. E. Chapman	Wales	Twickenham	1909–10
B. Solomon	Wales	Twickenham	1909–10
A. D. Roberts	Wales	Swansea	1910–11

Player	Opponents	Venue	Season
J. A. Scholfield	Wales	Swansea	1910–11
H. Brougham	Wales	Twickenham	1911–12
J. A. Pym	Wales	Twickenham	1911–12
H. L. V. Day	Wales	Swansea	1919–20
E. Myers	Ireland	Dublin[2]	1919–20
Q. E. M. A. King	Scotland	Edinburgh[3]	1920–21
J. E. Maxwell-Hyslop	Ireland	Dublin[2]	1921–22
H. C. Catcheside	Wales	Swansea	1923–24
H. P. Jacob	Wales	Swansea	1923–24
R. H. Hamilton-Wickes	Ireland	Belfast	1923–24
H. J. Kittermaster	New Zealand	Twickenham	1924–25
L. W. Haslett	Ireland	Dublin[2]	1925–26
W. J. Taylor	New South Wales	Twickenham	1927–28
H. Wilkinson	Wales	Twickenham	1928–29
A. L. Novis	Scotland	Edinburgh[4]	1928–29
S. S. C. Meikle	Scotland	Edinburgh[4]	1928–29
C. H. A. Gummer	France	Paris[2]	1928–29
D. W. Burland	Wales	Twickenham	1930–31
J. A. Tallent	Scotland	Edinburgh[4]	1930–31
E. H. Sadler	Ireland	Twickenham	1932–33
A. L. Warr	Wales	Cardiff	1933–34
G. W. C. Meikle	Wales	Cardiff	1933–34
A. Obolensky	New Zealand	Twickenham	1935–36
H. S. Sever	New Zealand	Twickenham	1935–36
E. J. Unwin	Scotland	Edinburgh[4]	1936–37
R. M. Marshall	Ireland	Dublin[4]	1937–38
D. E. Teden	Wales	Twickenham	1938–39
D. F. White	Wales	Cardiff	1946–47
C. B. Holmes	Scotland	Twickenham	1946–47
V. G. Roberts	France	Twickenham	1946–47
J. V. Smith	Wales	Twickenham	1949–50
G. C. Rittson-Thomas	Wales	Swansea	1950–51
C. E. Winn	South Africa	Twickenham	1951–52
J. Butterfield	France	Twickenham	1952–53
M. S. Phillips	Australia	Twickenham	1957–58
J. Roberts	Wales	Twickenham	1959–60
D. P. Rogers	Ireland	Dublin[2]	1960–61
V. S. J. Harding	France	Twickenham	1960–61
J. E. Owen	Wales	Cardiff	1962–63
J. M. Ranson	New Zealand	Auckland	1963
J. R. H. Greenwood	Ireland	Twickenham	1965–66
R. E. Webb	Scotland	Twickenham	1966–67
R. H. Lloyd	New Zealand	Twickenham	1967–68
B. W. Redwood	Wales	Twickenham	1967–68
D. J. Duckham	Ireland	Dublin[2]	1968–69
M. J. Novak	Wales	Twickenham	1969–70
R. C. Hannaford	Wales	Cardiff	1970–71
A. J. Morley	South Africa	Johannesburg	1972
B. J. Corless	Australia	Twickenham	1975–76
M. S. Lampkowski	Australia	Twickenham	1975–76
C. P. Kent	Scotland	Twickenham	1976–77
M. Young	Scotland	Twickenham	1976–77
G. H. Davies	Scotland	Twickenham	1980–81
W. M. H. Rose	Ireland	Dublin[2]	1980–81

ALL THE POINTS FOR ENGLAND IN A MATCH

(where more than one scoring action is involved)

Pts	Player	Opponents	Venue	Season
19	W. H. Hare	Wales	Cardiff	1980–81
14	R. Hiller	France	Twickenham	1970–71
12	A. G. B. Old	Ireland	Twickenham	1975–76
12	W. M. H. Rose	France	Twickenham	1980–81
11	D. W. Burland	Ireland	Dublin[2]	1931–32
11	R. Hiller	RFU President's XV	Twickenham	1970–71
9	J. Heaton	Scotland	Edinburgh[4]	1938–39
9	R. Hiller	Wales	Cardiff	1968–69
9	R. Hiller	Ireland	Dublin[2]	1970–71
9	A. G. B. Old	Scotland	Edinburgh[4]	1971–72
9	A. J. Hignell	Wales	Twickenham	1975–76
9	A. J. Hignell	Wales	Cardiff	1976–77
9	W. H. Hare	New Zealand	Twickenham	1979–80
9	W. H. Hare	Wales	Twickenham	1979–80
7	J. V. Richardson	Ireland	Dublin[2]	1927–28
7	W. N. Bennett	Ireland	Dublin[2]	1978–79
7	W. N. Bennett	France	Twickenham	1978–79
6	A. M. Smallwood	Ireland	Twickenham	1924–25
6	N. M. Hall	France	Paris[2]	1951–52
6	J. G. Willcox	France	Twickenham	1962–63
6	A. G. B. Old	France	Paris[1]	1977–78
6	A. J. Hignell	Wales	Twickenham	1977–78
6	W. H. Hare	New Zealand	Twickenham	1978–79
5	H. L. V. Day	Wales	Swansea	1919–20
5	B. H. Black	Ireland	Twickenham	1930–31

TRIES BY FULL BACKS

Player	Opponents	Venue	Season
W. J. Penny	Ireland	Dublin[2]	1877–78
T. W. Fry	Scotland	Manchester[1]	1879–80
R. Hiller	France	Twickenham	1970–71
R. Hiller	Scotland	Twickenham	1970–71
R. Hiller	RFU President's XV	Twickenham	1970–71
P. A. Rossborough	France	Twickenham	1974–75
W. H. Hare	Wales	Cardiff	1980–81
W. M. H. Rose	Ireland	Dublin[2]	1980–81

NB   There is an account of the 1880–81 match against Ireland which credits A. N. Hornby, the full-back, with a try

433

MOST NEW CAPS IN A MATCH

New Caps	Opponents	Venue	Season	New Caps	Opponents	Venue	Season
20	Scotland	Edinburgh[1]	1870–71	11	Wales	Swansea	1919–20
14	Scotland	The Oval	1871–72	10	Scotland	Glasgow[1]	1872–73
14	Wales	Cardiff	1946–47	10	Wales	Swansea	1894–95
13	Wales	Gloucester	1899–1900	10	Wales	Cardiff	1900–01
12	Scotland	The Oval	1873–74	10	Australia	Blackheath[2]	1908–09
12	NZ Natives	Blackheath[2]	1888–89	10	Wales	Swansea	1950–51
11	Ireland	Dublin[1]	1875–76	10	Wales	Twickenham	1955–56

REPLACEMENTS

(The International Board decided to allow replacements in international matches in March 1968)

Replacement	Player replaced	Opponents	Venue	Season
T. J. Dalton	K. J. Fielding	Scotland	Twickenham	1968–69
C. S. Wardlow	R. Hiller	South Africa	Twickenham	1969–70
B. S. Jackson	B. R. West	Scotland	Edinburgh[4]	1969–70
I. D. Wright	C. S. Wardlow	Scotland	Twickenham	1970–71
N. O. Martin	A. Neary	France	Paris[2]	1971–72
G. W. Evans	P. J. Warfield	Wales	Cardiff	1972–73
M. J. Cooper	G. W. Evans	New Zealand	Auckland	1973
S. J. Smith	J. G. Webster	Wales	Cardiff	1974–75
J. V. Pullin	P. J. Wheeler	Wales	Cardiff	1974–75
A. J. Wordsworth	W. N. Bennett	Australia	Sydney	1975
W. B. Beaumont	A. Neary	Australia	Sydney	1975
P. S. Preece	P. J. Squires	Wales	Twickenham	1975–76
W. N. Bennett	A. W. Maxwell	Scotland	Edinburgh[4]	1975–76
D. M. Wyatt	D. J. Duckham	Scotland	Edinburgh[4]	1975–76
B. J. Corless	A. J. Hignell	Ireland	Twickenham	1975–76
S. J. Smith	M. Young	France	Twickenham	1976–77
C. P. Kent	A. W. Maxwell	France	Paris[1]	1977–78
A. Neary	P. J. Dixon	France	Paris[1]	1977–78
J. P. Scott	R. M. Uttley	Scotland	Twickenham	1978–79
C. R. Woodward	A. M. Bond	Ireland	Twickenham	1979–80
M. Rafter	R. M. Uttley	Wales	Twickenham	1979–80
A. Sheppard	F. E. Cotton	Wales	Cardiff	1980–81
R. Hesford	N. C. Jeavons	Scotland	Twickenham	1980–81
G. A. F. Sargent	P. J. Blakeway	Ireland	Dublin[2]	1980–81
N. C. Stringer	M. A. C. Slemen	Australia	Twickenham	1981–82
R. Hesford	N. C. Jeavons	France	Paris[1]	1981–82

SEASON RECORDS

CHAMPIONSHIP HONOURS

Outright Winners	Triple Crown	Grand Slam
1882–83	1882–83	—
1883–84	1883–84	—
1891–92	1891–92	—
1909–10	—	—
1912–13	1912–13	1912–13
1913–14	1913–14	1913–14
1920–21	1920–21	1920–21
1922–23	1922–23	1922–23
1923–24	1923–24	1923–24
1927–28	1927–28	1927–28
1929–30	—	—
1933–34	1933–34	—
1936–37	1936–37	—
1952–53	—	—
—	1953–54	—
1956–57	1956–57	1956–57
1957–58	—	—
—	1959–60	—
1962–63	—	—
1979–80	1979–80	1979–80

England were also joint winners of the Championship in 1885–86, 1889–90, 1911–12, 1919–20, 1931–32, 1938–39, 1946–47, 1953–54, 1959–60, and 1972–73.

RESULTS FOR THE SEASONS 1870–71 to 1981–82

1870–71   Played 1 Won 1
Tries (1): R. H. Birkett

1871–72   Played 1 Won 1
Tries (3): F. B. G. D'Aguilar, S. Finney, A. St G. Hamersley
Conversions (1): F. W. Isherwood
Drop goals (1): H. Freeman

1872–73   Played 1 Drawn 1
England failed to score

1873–74   Played 1 Won 1
Drop goals (1): H. Freeman

1874–75   Played 2 Won 1 Drawn 1
Tries (2): A. T. Michell, E. C. Cheston
Conversions (1): A. W. Pearson
Drop goals (1): E. H. Nash

1875–76   Played 2 Won 2
Tries (4): C. W. H. Clark, E. Kewley, W. E. Collins, F. H. Lee
Conversions (2): A. W. Pearson, L. Stokes

1876–77   Played 2 Won 1 Lost 1
Tries (4): W. C. Hutchinson (2); A. N. Hornby, F. R. Adams
Conversions (2): L. Stokes

1877–78   Played 2 Won 1 Drawn 1
Tries (3): H. P. Gardner, E. B. Turner, W. J. Penny
Conversions (2): A. W. Pearson

1878–79   Played 2 Won 1 Drawn 1
Tries (5): G. W. Burton, W. A. D. Evanson, H. T. Twynam,
F. R. Adams, H. C. Rowley
Conversions (3): L. Stokes
Drop goals (1): L. Stokes

1879–80   Played 2 Won 2
Tries (7): H. H. Taylor (2); S. S. Ellis, E. T. Markendale,
T. W. Fry, G. W. Burton, E. T. Gurdon
Conversions (3): L. Stokes

1880–81   Played 3 Won 2 Drawn 1
Tries (18): H. H. Taylor, G. W. Burton (4); H. Vassall (3);
H. C. Rowley (2); C. M. Sawyer, C. W. L. Fernandes, A. Budd,
H. T. Twynam, R. Hunt
Conversions (9): L. Stokes (8); R. Hunt
Drop goals (2): L. Stokes, R. Hunt

1881–82   Played 2 Drawn 1 Lost 1
Tries (2): W. N. Bolton, R. Hunt

1882–83 Triple Crown Championship	Played 3 Won 3 *Tries (12):* C. G. Wade (4); W. N. Bolton (3); R. S. F. Henderson, G. T. Thomson, W. M. Tatham, H. T. Twynam, A. Rotherham *Conversions (3):* A. M. Evanson

1883–84
Triple Crown
Championship

Played 3 Won 3
Tries (5): C. G. Wade, H. T. Twynam, A. Rotherham,
W. N. Bolton, R. S. Kindersley
Conversions (3): W. N. Bolton (2); C. H. Sample

1884–85

Played 2 Won 2
Tries (7): J. J. Hawcridge (2); C. G. Wade, R. S. Kindersley,
A. Teggin, H. J. Ryalls, W. N. Bolton
Conversions (1): J. H. Payne

1885–86
Championship
Shared

Played 3 Won 2 Drawn 1
Tries (3): E. Wilkinson (2); C. G. Wade
Goals from mark (1): A. E. Stoddart

1886–87

Played 3 Drawn 2 Lost 1
Tries (1): G. L. Jeffery

1888–89

Played 1 Won 1   For 7 Against 0
Tries (5): H. Bedford (2); J. W. Sutcliffe, A. E. Stoddart,
F. Evershed
Conversions (1): J. W. Sutcliffe
Points (7): J. W. Sutcliffe (3); H. Bedford (2); A. E. Stoddart,
F. Evershed (1)

1889–90
Championship
Shared

Played 3 Won 2 Lost 1   For 9 Against 1
Tries (5): J. W. Dyson, F. Evershed, P. H. Morrison,
A. E. Stoddart, J. H. Rogers
Conversions (1): D. Jowett
Points (9): D. Jowett, J. W. Dyson, F. Evershed (2); J. H. Rogers,
P. H. Morrison, A. E. Stoddart (1)

1890–91

Played 3 Won 2 Lost 1   For 19 Against 12
Tries (9): R. E. Lockwood (3); P. Christopherson,
R. P. Wilson (2); R. T. D. Budworth, J. T. Toothill
Conversions (5): F. H. R. Alderson (3); R. E. Lockwood (2)
Points (19): R. E. Lockwood (7); F. H. R. Alderson (6);
P. Christopherson, R. P. Wilson (2); R. T. D. Budworth,
J. T. Toothill (1)

1891–92
Triple Crown
Championship

Played 3 Won 3   For 29 Against 0
Tries (7): F. Evershed (2); G. C. Hubbard, F. H. R. Alderson,
W. Nichol, L. J. Percival, W. E. Bromet
Conversions (5): R. E. Lockwood (3); F. H. R. Alderson,
S. M. J. Woods
Points (29): R. E. Lockwood (9); F. H. R. Alderson (5);
F. Evershed (4); S. M. J. Woods (3); G. C. Hubbard, W. Nichol,
W. E. Bromet, L. J. Percival (2)

1892–93	Played 3 Won 1 Lost 2 For 15 Against 20

1892–93   Played 3 Won 1 Lost 2   For 15 Against 20
Tries (6): H. Marshall (3); F. C. Lohden, H. Bradshaw,
E. W. Taylor
Conversions (1): A. E. Stoddart
Points (15): H. Marshall (6); A. E. Stoddart (3); F. C. Lohden,
H. Bradshaw, E. W. Taylor (2)

1893–94   Played 3 Won 1 Lost 2   For 29 Against 16
Tries (5): R. E. Lockwood (2); S. Morfitt, E. W. Taylor,
H. Bradshaw
Conversions (5): R. E. Lockwood (3); E. W. Taylor (2)
Goals from mark (1): E. W. Taylor
Points (29): R. E. Lockwood (12); E. W. Taylor (11);
S. Morfitt, H. Bradshaw (3)

1894–95   Played 3 Won 2 Lost 1   For 23 Against 15
Tries (6): W. B. Thomson, F. A. Leslie-Jones, G. M. Carey
S. M. J. Woods, J. H. C. Fegan, C. Thomas
Conversions (1): F. Mitchell
Penalties (1): J. F. Byrne
Points (23): W. B. Thomson, F. A. Leslie-Jones, G. M. Carey,
S. M. J. Woods, J. H. C. Fegan, C. Thomas, J. F. Byrne (3);
F. Mitchell (2)

1895–96   Played 3 Won 1 Lost 2   For 29 Against 21
Tries (7): E. F. Fookes, R. H. B. Cattell, S. Morfitt (2);
F. Mitchell
Conversions (2): J. Valentine, E. W. Taylor
Drop goals (1): J. F. Byrne
Points (29): S. Morfitt, R. H. B. Cattell, E. F. Fookes (6);
J. F. Byrne (4); F. Mitchell (3); J. Valentine, E. W. Taylor (2)

1896–97   Played 3 Won 1 Lost 2   For 21 Against 27
Tries (3): G. C. Robinson (2); E. F. Fookes
Conversions (1): J. F. Byrne
Drop goals (1): J. F. Byrne
Penalties (2): J. F. Byrne
Points (21): J. F. Byrne (12); G. C. Robinson (6); E. F. Fookes (3)

1897–98   Played 3 Won 1 Drawn 1 Lost 1   For 23 Against 19
Tries (6): E. F. Fookes (2); G. C. Robinson, P. M. R. Royds,
P. W. Stout, F. M. Stout
Conversions (1): J. F. Byrne
Penalties (1): J. F. Byrne
Points (23): E. F. Fookes (6); J. F. Byrne (5); G. C. Robinson,
P. M. R. Royds, P. W. Stout, F. M. Stout (3)

1898–99   Played 3 Lost 3   For 3 Against 37
Tries (1): G. C. Robinson
Points (3): G. C. Robinson

1899–1900   Played 3 Won 1 Drawn 1 Lost 1   For 18 Against 17
Tries (4): G. C. Robinson (2); G. W. Gordon-Smith,
E. T. Nicholson
Conversions (1): H. Alexander

Drop goals (1): G. W. Gordon-Smith
Points (18): G. W. Gordon-Smith (7); G. C. Robinson (6);
E. T. Nicholson (3); H. Alexander (2)

1900–01	Played 3 Lost 3	For 9 Against 41

Tries (2): G. C. Robinson (2)
Penalties (1): H. Alexander
Points (9): G. C. Robinson (6); H. Alexander (3)

1901–02	Played 3 Won 2 Lost 1	For 20 Against 15

Tries (6): S. G. Williams (2); J. J. Robinson, D. D. Dobson,
S. F. Coopper, J. T. Taylor
Conversions (1): H. Alexander
Points (20): S. G. Williams (6); J. J. Robinson, D. D. Dobson,
S. F. Coopper, J. T. Taylor (3); H. Alexander (2)

1902–03	Played 3 Lost 3	For 11 Against 37

Tries (3): D. D. Dobson (2); R. Forrest
Conversions (1): J. T. Taylor
Points (11): D. D. Dobson (6); R. Forrest (3); J. T. Taylor (2)

1903–04	Played 3 Won 1 Drawn 1 Lost 1	For 36 Against 20

Tries (9): E. J. Vivyan (3); E. W. Elliot, N. H. Moore (2);
A. T. Brettargh, T. Simpson
Conversions (3): E. J. Vivyan (2); F. M. Stout (1)
Penalties (1): H. T. Gamlin
Points (36): E. J. Vivyan (13); E. W. Elliot, N. H. Moore (6);
A. T. Brettargh, T. Simpson, H. T. Gamlin (3); F. M. Stout (2)

1904–05	Played 3 Lost 3	For 3 Against 50

Tries (1): S. F. Coopper
Points (3): S. F. Coopper

1905–06	Played 5 Won 2 Lost 3	For 53 Against 58

Tries (15): A. Hudson (5); W. A. Mills (3); R. A. Jago,
J. E. Raphael, T. Simpson, J. Peters, A. D. Stoop,
A. L. Kewney, T. B. Hogarth
Conversions (4): V. H. Cartwright
Points (53): A. Hudson (15); W. A. Mills (9); V. H. Cartwright
(8); R. A. Jago, J. E. Raphael, T. Simpson, J. Peters,
A. D. Stoop, A. L. Kewney, T. B. Hogarth (3)

1906–07	Played 5 Won 1 Drawn 1 Lost 3	For 56 Against 63

Tries (13): D. Lambert (5); L. A. N. Slocock (2);
F. G. Brooks, H. E. Shewring, J. G. G. Birkett,
W. M. B. Nanson, H. M. Imrie, J. Peters
Conversions (5): B. A. Hill
Drop goals (1): J. G. G. Birkett
Penalties (1): A. S. Pickering
Points (56): D. Lambert (15); B. A. Hill (10); J. G. G. Birkett
(7); L. A. N. Slocock (6); F. G. Brooks, H. E. Shewring,
W. M. B. Nanson, H. M. Imrie, J. Peters, A. S. Pickering (3)

1907–08   Played 4 Won 2 Lost 2   For 60 Against 47
Tries (14): J. G. G. Birkett (4); W. N. Lapage,
R. H. Williamson, A. Hudson (2); D. Lambert, G. V. Portus,
W. A. Mills, L. A. N. Slocock
Conversions (9): A. E. Wood (4); G. D. Roberts (3);
D. Lambert (2)
Points (60): J. G. G. Birkett (12); A. E. Wood (8); D. Lambert
(7); W. N. Lapage, R. H. Williamson, A. Hudson,
G. D. Roberts (6); G. V. Portus, W. A. Mills, L. A. N. Slocock
(3)

1908–09   Played 5 Won 2 Lost 3   For 44 Against 40
Tries (12): E. R. Mobbs (4); F. N. Tarr, A. C. Palmer (2);
T. Simpson, F. Hutchinson, W. A. Johns, F. B. Watson
Conversions (4): E. J. Jackett, A. C. Palmer (2)
Points (44): E. R. Mobbs (12); A. C. Palmer (10); F. N. Tarr
(6); E. J. Jackett (4); T. Simpson, F. Hutchinson, W. A. Johns,
F. B. Watson (3)

1909–10   Played 4 Won 3 Drawn 1   For 36 Against 14
Championship   *Tries (9):* A. Hudson, H. Berry, J. G. G. Birkett (2);
F. E. Chapman, B. Solomon, J. A. S. Ritson
Conversions (3): F. E. Chapman
Penalties (1): F. E. Chapman
Points (36): F. E. Chapman (12); A. Hudson, H. Berry,
J. G. G. Birkett (6); B. Solomon, J. A. S. Ritson (3)

1910–11   Played 4 Won 2 Lost 2   For 61 Against 26
Tries (13): D. Lambert, N. A. Wodehouse, C. H. Pillman (2);
A. D. Roberts, J. A. Scholfield, A. L. Kewney, A. D. Stoop,
W. E. Mann, P. W. Lawrie, J. G. G. Birkett
Conversions (8): D. Lambert (6); R. O. Lagden (2)
Penalties (2): D. Lambert
Points (61): D. Lambert (24); N. A. Wodehouse, C. H. Pillman
(6); R. O. Lagden (4); A. D. Roberts, J. A. Scholfield,
A. L. Kewney, A. D. Stoop, W. E. Mann, P. W. Lawrie,
J. G. G. Birkett (3)

1911–12   Played 4 Won 3 Lost 1   For 44 Against 16
Championship   *Tries (12):* H. Brougham, A. D. Roberts (3); J. G. G. Birkett
Shared   (2); J. A. Pym, R. W. Poulton, D. Holland, J. H. Eddison
Conversions (2): F. E. Chapman, C. H. Pillman
Drop goals (1): H. Coverdale
Points (44): H. Brougham, A. D. Roberts (9); J. G. G. Birkett
(6); H. Coverdale (4); J. A. Pym, R. W. Poulton, D. Holland,
J. H. Eddison (3); F. E. Chapman, C. H. Pillman (2)

1912–13   Played 5 Won 4 Lost 1   For 53 Against 13
Grand Slam   *Tries (14):* V. H. M. Coates (6); C. H. Pillman (4);
Triple Crown   R. W. Poulton (2); J. A. S. Ritson, L. G. Brown
Championship   *Conversions (2):* J. E. Greenwood
Drop goals (1): R. W. Poulton
Penalties (1): J. E. Greenwood
Points (53): V. H. M. Coates (18); C. H. Pillman (12);

R. W. Poulton (10); J. E. Greenwood (7); J. A. S. Ritson,
L. G. Brown (3)

1913–14 Grand Slam Triple Crown Championship	Played 4 Won 4	For 82 Against 49

Tries (20); C. N. Lowe (8); R. W. Poulton (5); C. H. Pillman,
W. J. A. Davies (2); L. G. Brown, A. D. Roberts,
J. H. D. Watson
Conversions (11): J. E. Greenwood (6); F. E. Chapman (3);
H. C. Harrison (2)
Points (82): C. N. Lowe (24); R. W. Poulton (15);
J. E. Greenwood (12); C. H. Pillman, W. J. A. Davies,
F. E. Chapman (6); H. C. Harrison (4); L. G. Brown,
A. D. Roberts, J. H. D. Watson (3)

1919–20 Championship Shared	Played 4 Won 3 Lost 1	For 40 Against 37

Tries (9): C. N. Lowe (2); H. L. V. Day, W. J. A. Davies,
E. Myers, F. W. Mellish, W. W. Wakefield, S. W. Harris,
C. A. Kershaw
Conversions (5): J. E. Greenwood (4); H. L. V. Day (1)
Penalties (1): J. E. Greenwood
Points (40): J. E. Greenwood (11); C. N. Lowe (6);
H. L. V. Day (5); E. Myers, W. J. A. Davies, F. W. Mellish,
W. W. Wakefield, S. W. Harris, C. A. Kershaw (3)

1920–21 Grand Slam Triple Crown Championship	Played 4 Won 4	For 61 Against 9

Tries (13): C. N. Lowe (3); A. M. Smallwood, A. F. Blakiston,
L. G. Brown (2); C. A. Kershaw, Q. E. M. A. King, T. Woods,
R. Edwards
Conversions (7): E. D. G. Hammett (6); B. S. Cumberlege
Drop goals (2): W. J. A. Davies, C. N. Lowe
Points (61): C. N. Lowe (13); E. D. G. Hammett (12);
A. M. Smallwood, L. G. Brown, A. F. Blakiston (6);
W. J. A. Davies (4); C. A. Kershaw, T. Woods,
Q. E. M. A. King, R. Edwards (3); B. S. Cumberlege (2)

1921–22	Played 4 Won 2 Drawn 1 Lost 1	For 40 Against 47

Tries (10): C. N. Lowe (4); H. L. V. Day, A. M. Smallwood,
A. T. Voyce, E. R. Gardner, W. J. A. Davies, J. E. Maxwell-
Hyslop
Conversions (2): H. L. V. Day, G. S. Conway
Penalties (2): H. L. V. Day
Points (40): C. N. Lowe (12); H. L. V. Day (11);
A. M. Smallwood, A. T. Voyce, E. R. Gardner,
W. J. A. Davies, J. E. Maxwell-Hyslop (3); G. S. Conway (2)

1922–23 Grand Slam Triple Crown Championship	Played 4 Won 4	For 50 Against 17

Tries (10): H. L. Price, A. M. Smallwood, A. T. Voyce (2);
W. W. Wakefield, C. N. Lowe, L. J. Corbett, G. S. Conway
Conversions (4): G. S. Conway, W. G. E. Luddington (2)
Drop goals (3): W. J. A. Davies (2); A. M. Smallwood
Points (50): A. M. Smallwood (10); W. J. A. Davies (8);
G. S. Conway (7); H. L. Price, A. T. Voyce (6);
W. G. E. Luddington (4); W. W. Wakefield, C. N. Lowe,
L. J. Corbett (3)

1923–24
Grand Slam
Triple Crown
Championship

Played 4 Won 4   For 69 Against 19
Tries (17): H. C. Catcheside (6); H. P. Jacob (4); E. Myers (2);
H. M. Locke, L. J. Corbett, R. H. Hamilton-Wickes,
A. T. Young, W. W. Wakefield
Conversions (7): G. S. Conway
Drop goals (1): E. Myers
Points (69): H. C. Catcheside (18); G. S. Conway (14);
H. P. Jacob (12); E. Myers (10); H. M. Locke, L. J. Corbett,
R. H. Hamilton-Wickes, A. T. Young, W. W. Wakefield (3)

1924–25

Played 5 Won 2 Drawn 1 Lost 2   For 53 Against 54
Tries (11): R. H. Hamilton-Wickes (3); H. J. Kittermaster,
A. M. Smallwood, W. W. Wakefield (2); R. Cove-Smith,
A. T. Voyce
Conversions (4): W. G. E. Luddington (3); G. S. Conway
Penalties (3): L. J. Corbett, R. Armstrong,
W. G. E. Luddington
Goals from mark (1): W. G. E. Luddington
Points (53): W. G. E. Luddington (12); R. H. Hamilton-
Wickes (9); H. J. Kittermaster, A. M. Smallwood,
W. W. Wakefield (6); R. Cove-Smith, A. T. Voyce,
L. J. Corbett, R. Armstrong (3); G. S. Conway (2)

1925–26

Played 4 Won 1 Drawn 1 Lost 2   For 38 Against 39
Tries (10): A. R. Aslett (2); W. W. Wakefield, H. G. Periton,
A. T. Young, L. W. Haslett, H. J. Kittermaster,
J. W. G. Webb, J. S. Tucker, A. T. Voyce
Conversions (4): T. E. S. Francis
Points (38): T. E. S. Francis (8); A. R. Aslett (6);
W. W. Wakefield, H. G. Periton, A. T. Young, L. W. Haslett,
H. J. Kittermaster, J. W. G. Webb, J. S. Tucker, A. T. Voyce
(3)

1926–27

Played 4 Won 2 Lost 2   For 32 Against 39
Tries (5): J. C. Gibbs, H. C. C. Laird (2); L. J. Corbett
Conversions (4): E. Stanbury (3); K. J. Stark
Penalties (2): E. Stanbury, K. J. Stark
Goals from mark (1): L. J. Corbett
Points (32): E. Stanbury (9); J. C. Gibbs, H. C. C. Laird,
L. J. Corbett (6); K. J. Stark (5)

1927–28
Grand Slam
Triple Crown
Championship

Played 5 Won 5   For 59 Against 33
Tries (13): H. C. C. Laird, H. G. Periton (3); W. J. Taylor,
G. V. Palmer (2); J. S. Tucker, J. V. Richardson, J. Hanley
Conversions (8): J. V. Richardson
Drop goals (1): J. V. Richardson
Points (59): J. V. Richardson (23); H. C. C. Laird,
H. G. Periton (9); W. J. Taylor, G. V. Palmer (6); J. S. Tucker,
J. Hanley (3)

1928–29

Played 4 Won 2 Lost 2   For 35 Against 27
Tries (9): H. Wilkinson, C. D. Aarvold (2); R. W. Smeddle,
A. L. Novis, S. S. C. Meikle, H. G. Periton, C. H. A. Gummer
Conversions (4): G. S. Wilson, E. Stanbury (2)
Points (35): H. Wilkinson, C. D. Aarvold (6); G. S. Wilson,

E. Stanbury (4); R. W. Smeddle, A. L. Novis, S. S. C. Meikle,
H. G. Periton, C. H. A. Gummer (3)

1929–30 Championship	Played 4 Won 2 Drawn 1 Lost 1　　　　For 25 Against 12 *Tries (6):* J. S. R. Reeve (3); A. L. Novis, M. Robson, H. G. Periton *Conversions (2):* B. H. Black *Penalties (1):* B. H. Black *Points (25):* J. S. R. Reeve (9); B. H. Black (7); A. L. Novis, M. Robson, H. G. Periton (3)
1930–31	Played 4 Drawn 1 Lost 3　　　　For 48 Against 59 *Tries (9):* J. A. Tallent (3); D. W. Burland, J. S. R. Reeve (2); B. H. Black, R. W. Smeddle *Conversions (6):* B. H. Black (4); D. W. Burland, J. W. Forrest *Penalties (3):* B. H. Black *Points (48):* B. H. Black (20); J. A. Tallent (9); D. W. Burland (8); J. S. R. Reeve (6); R. W. Smeddle (3); J. W. Forrest (2)
1931–32 Championship Shared	Played 4 Won 2 Lost 2　　　　For 32 Against 30 *Tries (6):* C. D. Aarvold (2); E. Coley, D. W. Burland, C. C. Tanner, B. H. Black *Conversions (4):* D. W. Burland (3); R. J. Barr *Penalties (2):* D. W. Burland *Points (32):* D. W. Burland (15); C. D. Aarvold (6); E. Coley, C. C. Tanner, B. H. Black (3); R. J. Barr (2)
1932–33	Played 3 Won 1 Lost 2　　　　For 20 Against 16 *Tries (6):* A. L. Novis (2); W. Elliot, L. A. Booth, B. C. Gadney, E. H. Sadler *Conversions (1):* D. A. Kendrew *Points (20):* A. L. Novis (6); W. Elliot, L. A. Booth, B. C. Gadney, E. H. Sadler (3); D. A. Kendrew (2)
1933–34 Triple Crown Championship	Played 3 Won 3　　　　For 28 Against 6 *Tries (8):* G. W. C. Meikle (4); H. A. Fry (2); A. L. Warr, L. A. Booth *Conversions (2):* G. G. Gregory *Points (28):* G. W. C. Meikle (12); H. A. Fry (6); G. G. Gregory (4); A. L. Warr, L. A. Booth (3)
1934–35	Played 3 Won 1 Drawn 1 Lost 1　　　　For 24 Against 16 *Tries (2):* J. L. Giles, L. A. Booth *Conversions (1):* H. J. Boughton *Drop goals (1):* P. Cranmer *Penalties (4):* H. J. Boughton *Points (24):* H. J. Boughton (14); P. Cranmer (4); J. L. Giles, L. A. Booth (3)
1935–36	Played 4 Won 2 Drawn 1 Lost 1　　　　For 25 Against 14 *Tries (7):* A. Obolensky, H. S. Sever (2); P. Cranmer, P. L. Candler, R. Bolton *Drop goals (1):* P. Cranmer *Points (25):* P. Cranmer (7); A. Obolensky, H. S. Sever (6); P. L. Candler, R. Bolton (3)

1936–37
Triple Crown
Championship

Played 3 Won 3   For 19 Against 14
Tries (4): H. S. Sever (2); E. J. Unwin, A. G. Butler
Drop goals (1): H. S. Sever
Penalties (1): P. Cranmer
Points (19): H. S. Sever (10); E. J. Unwin, A. G. Butler,
P. Cranmer (3)

1937–38

Played 3 Won 1 Lost 2   For 60 Against 49
Tries (10): E. J. Unwin (2); H. S. Sever, P. L. Candler,
B. E. Nicholson, J. L. Giles, F. J. Reynolds, R. E. Prescott,
R. M. Marshall, R. Bolton
Conversions (7): G. W. Parker (6); H. D. Freakes
Penalties (4): G. W. Parker
Drop goals (1): F. J. Reynolds
Points (60): G. W. Parker (24); F. J. Reynolds (7);
E. J. Unwin (6); H. S. Sever, P. L. Candler, B. E. Nicholson,
J. L. Giles, R. E. Prescott, R. Bolton, R. M. Marshall (3);
H. D. Freakes (2)

1938–39
Championship
Shared

Played 3 Won 2 Lost 1   For 12 Against 11
Tries (1): D. E. Teden
Penalties (3): J. Heaton
Points (12): J. Heaton (9); D. E. Teden (3)

1946–47
Championship
Shared

Played 4 Won 3 Lost 1   For 39 Against 36
Tries (7): R. H. Guest (2); D. F. White, C. B. Holmes,
N. O. Bennett, A. P. Henderson, V. G. Roberts
Conversions (5): J. Heaton (4); A. Gray
Drop goals (2): N. M. Hall
Points (39): J. Heaton, N. M. Hall (8); R. H. Guest (6);
D. F. White, C. B. Holmes, N. O. Bennett, A. P. Henderson,
V. G. Roberts (3); A. Gray (2)

1947–48

Played 5 Drawn 1 Lost 4   For 16 Against 46
Tries (2): R. H. Guest
Conversions (2): R. Uren
Penalties (2): S. C. Newman, R. Uren
Points (16): R. Uren (7); R. H. Guest (6); S. C. Newman (3)

1948–49

Played 4 Won 2 Lost 2   For 35 Against 29
Tries (7): C. B. van Ryneveld (3); L. B. Cannell, R. H. Guest,
R. D. Kennedy, G. R. d'A. Hosking
Conversions (4): W. B. Holmes, B. H. Travers (2)
Drop goals (2): N. M. Hall, I. Preece
Points (35): C. B. van Ryneveld (9); W. B. Holmes,
B. H. Travers (4); L. B. Cannell, R. H. Guest, R. D. Kennedy,
G. R. d'A. Hosking, N. M. Hall, I. Preece (3)

1949–50

Played 4 Won 1 Lost 3   For 22 Against 30
Tries (5): J. V. Smith (4); V. G. Roberts
Conversions (2): M. B. Hofmeyr
Penalties (1): M. B. Hofmeyr
Points (22): J. V. Smith (12); M. B. Hofmeyr (7);
V. G. Roberts (3)

1950–51	Played 4 Won 1 Lost 3 For 13 Against 40

1950–51
Played 4 Won 1 Lost 3   For 13 Against 40
Tries (3): G. C. Rittson-Thomas, B. Boobbyer, D. F. White
Conversions (2): E. N. Hewitt, W. G. Hook
Points (13): G. C. Rittson-Thomas, B. Boobbyer, D. F. White
(3); E. N. Hewitt, W. G. Hook (2)

1951–52
Played 5 Won 3 Lost 2   For 37 Against 22
Tries (8): C. E. Winn, J. E. Woodward (2); A. E. Agar,
E. Evans, B. Boobbyer, J. M. K. Kendall-Carpenter
Conversions (2): N. M. Hall
Drop goals (1): A. E. Agar
Penalties (2): N. M. Hall
Points (37): N. M. Hall (10); C. E. Winn, J. E. Woodward,
A. E. Agar (6); E. Evans, B. Boobbyer,
J. M. K. Kendall-Carpenter (3)

1952–53
Championship
Played 4 Won 3 Drawn 1   For 54 Against 20
Tries (11): E. Evans, J. E. Woodward, J. Butterfield,
R. C. Bazley (2); L. B. Cannell, R. V. Stirling, S. J. Adkins
Conversions (6): N. M. Hall
Penalties (3): N. M. Hall (2); J. E. Woodward
Points (54): N. M. Hall (18); J. E. Woodward (9); E. Evans,
J. Butterfield, R. C. Bazley (6); L. B. Cannell, R. V. Stirling,
S. J. Adkins (3)

1953–54
Triple Crown
Championship
Shared
Played 5 Won 3 Lost 2   For 39 Against 28
Tries (10): D. S. Wilson (4); J. E. Woodward (2); C. E. Winn,
J. Butterfield, M. Regan, P. D. Young
Conversions (3): N. Gibbs (2); I. King
Penalties (1): I. King
Points (39): D. S. Wilson (12); J. E. Woodward (6); I. King
(5); N. Gibbs (4); C. E. Winn, J. Butterfield, M. Regan,
P. D. Young (3)

1954–55
Played 4 Won 1 Drawn 1 Lost 2   For 24 Against 31
Tries (5): J. Butterfield, G. W. D. Hastings, R. Higgins,
F. D. Sykes, I. D. S. Beer
Penalties (3): D. St G. Hazell
Points (24): D. St G. Hazell (9); J. Butterfield,
G. W. D. Hastings, R. Higgins, F. D. Sykes, I. D. S. Beer (3)

1955–56
Played 4 Won 2 Lost 2   For 43 Against 28
Tries (5): P. B. Jackson, J. Butterfield, E. Evans, J. E. Williams,
P. H. Thompson
Conversions (2): J. D. Currie
Penalties (8): D. F. Allison, J. D. Currie (4)
Points (43): J. D. Currie (16); D. F. Allison (12); P. B. Jackson,
J. Butterfield, E. Evans, J. E. Williams, P. H. Thompson (3)

1956–57
Grand Slam
Triple Crown
Championship
Played 4 Won 4   For 34 Against 8
Tries (7): P. B. Jackson (3); E. Evans, W. P. C. Davies,
P. H. Thompson, R. Higgins
Conversions (2): R. Challis
Penalties (3): R. Challis (2); D. F. Allison
Points (34): R. Challis (10); P. B. Jackson (9); E. Evans,
W. P. C. Davies, R. Higgins, P. H. Thompson, D. F. Allison (3)

| 1957–58 | Played 5 Won 3 Drawn 2 | For 35 Against 12 |

Championship *Tries (7):* P. H. Thompson (3); P. B. Jackson (2); M. S. Phillips, A. Ashcroft
Conversions (1): G. W. D. Hastings
Penalties (4): J. G. G. Hetherington, G. W. D. Hastings (2)
Points (35): P. H. Thompson (9); G. W. D. Hastings (8); P. B. Jackson, J. G. G. Hetherington (6); M. S. Phillips, A. Ashcroft (3)

| 1958–59 | Played 4 Won 1 Drawn 2 Lost 1 | For 9 Against 11 |

Penalties (3): A. B. W. Risman (2); J. G. G. Hetherington
Points (9): A. B. W. Risman (6); J. G. G. Hetherington (3)

| 1959–60 | Played 4 Won 3 Drawn 1 | For 46 Against 26 |

Triple Crown *Tries (7):* J. Roberts (3); R. W. D. Marques, M. P. Weston,
Championship J. R. C. Young, R. E. Syrett
Shared *Conversions (5):* D. Rutherford
Drop goals (2): R. A. W. Sharp
Penalties (3): D. Rutherford
Points (46): D. Rutherford (19); J. Roberts (9); R. A. W. Sharp (6); R. W. D. Marques, M. P. Weston, J. R. C. Young, R. E. Syrett (3)

| 1960–61 | Played 5 Won 1 Drawn 1 Lost 3 | For 22 Against 27 |

Tries (5): J. Roberts (2); J. R. C. Young, D. P. Rogers, V. S. J Harding
Conversions (2): A. B. W. Risman, J. G. Willcox
Penalties (1): J. P. Horrocks-Taylor
Points (22): J. Roberts (6); J. R. C. Young, D. P. Rogers, V. S. J. Harding, J. P. Horrocks-Taylor (3); A. B. W. Risman, J. G. Willcox (2)

| 1961–62 | Played 4 Won 1 Drawn 2 Lost 1 | For 19 Against 16 |

Tries (3): M. R. Wade, J. Roberts, R. A. W. Sharp
Conversions (2): R. A. W. Sharp
Penalties (2): R. A. W. Sharp, J. G. Willcox
Points (19): R. A. W. Sharp (10); M. R. Wade, J. Roberts, J. G. Willcox (3)

| 1962–63 | Played 4 Won 3 Drawn 1 | For 29 Against 19 |

Championship *Tries (4):* M. S. Phillips, J. E. Owen, R. A. W. Sharp, N. J. Drake-Lee
Conversions (4): R. A. W. Sharp, J. G. Willcox (2)
Drop goals (1): R. A. W. Sharp
Penalties (2): J. G. Willcox
Points (29): R. A. W. Sharp, J. G. Willcox (10); M. S. Phillips, N. J. Drake-Lee, J. E. Owen (3)

| 1963 | Played 3 Lost 3 | For 26 Against 48 |

Tries (5): M. S. Phillips (2); J. M. Ranson, S. J. S. Clarke, H. O. Godwin
Conversions (1): R. W. Hosen
Penalties (3): R. W. Hosen
Points (26): R. W. Hosen (11); M. S. Phillips (6); J. M. Ranson, S. J. S. Clarke, H. O. Godwin (3)

1963–64   Played 5 Won 1 Drawn 1 Lost 3   For 23 Against 56
           Tries (5): D. P. Rogers (2); J. M. Ranson, D. G. Perry,
           M. S. Phillips
           Conversions (1): J. G. Willcox
           Penalties (2): R. W. Hosen
           Points (23): D. P. Rogers, R. W. Hosen (6); J. M. Ranson,
           D. G. Perry, M. S. Phillips (3); J. G. Willcox (2)

1964–65   Played 4 Won 1 Drawn 1 Lost 2   For 15 Against 28
           Tries (2): C. M. Payne, A. W. Hancock
           Penalties (3): D. Rutherford
           Points (15): D. Rutherford (9); C. M. Payne, A. W. Hancock (3)

1965–66   Played 4 Drawn 1 Lost 3   For 15 Against 36
           Tries (2): D. G. Perry, J. R. H. Greenwood
           Drop goals (1): C. W. McFadyean
           Penalties (2): D. Rutherford
           Points (15): D. Rutherford (6); D. G. Perry,
           J. R. H. Greenwood, C. W. McFadyean (3)

1966–67   Played 5 Won 2 Lost 3   For 79 Against 90
           Tries (9): C. W. McFadyean (3); J. Barton (2); R. C. Ashby,
           R. E. Webb, R. B. Taylor, K. F. Savage
           Conversions (5): R. W. Hosen
           Drop goals (2): J. F. Finlan
           Penalties (12): R. W. Hosen
           Points (79): R. W. Hosen (46); C. W. McFadyean (9); J. Barton
           J. F. Finlan (6); R. C. Ashby, R. E. Webb, R. B. Taylor,
           K. F. Savage (3)

1967–68   Played 5 Won 1 Drawn 2 Lost 2   For 48 Against 63
           Tries (5): R. H. Lloyd (2); B. W. Redwood, M. J. Coulman,
           C. W. McFadyean
           Conversions (3): R. Hiller (2); D. Rutherford
           Drop goals (2): J. F. Finlan, M. P. Weston
           Penalties (7): R. Hiller (6); P. J. Larter
           Points (48): R. Hiller (22); R. H. Lloyd (6); B. W. Redwood,
           M. J. Coulman, C. W. McFadyean, J. F. Finlan,
           M. P. Weston, P. J. Larter (3); D. Rutherford (2)

1968–69   Played 4 Won 2 Lost 2   For 54 Against 58
           Tries (6): D. J. Duckham (3); K. J. Fielding, R. E. Webb,
           D. M. Rollitt
           Conversions (3): R. Hiller
           Penalties (10): R. Hiller
           Points (54): R. Hiller (36); D. J. Duckham (9); K. J. Fielding,
           R. E. Webb, D. M. Rollitt (3)

1969–70   Played 5 Won 2 Lost 3   For 51 Against 77
           Tries (8): J. S. Spencer (2); J. V. Pullin, P. J. Larter,
           I. R. Shackleton, M. J. Novak, D. J. Duckham, R. B. Taylor
           Conversions (6): R. Hiller (4); A. M. Jorden (2)
           Drop goals (2): R. Hiller
           Penalties (3): R. Hiller (2); A. M. Jorden

Points (51): R. Hiller (20); A. M. Jorden (7); J. S. Spencer (6); J. V. Pullin, P. J. Larter, J. R. Shackleton, M. J. Novak, D. J. Duckham, R. B. Taylor (3)

1970–71 Played 6 Won 1 Drawn 1 Lost 4 For 61 Against 112
Tries (5): R. Hiller (3); R. C. Hannaford, A. Neary
Conversions (2): R. Hiller
Drop goals (1): A. R. Cowman
Penalties (13): R. Hiller (12); P. A. Rossborough
Points (61): R. Hiller (49); R. C. Hannaford, A. Neary,
A. R. Cowman, P. A. Rossborough (3)

1971–72 Played 4 Lost 4 For 36 Against 88
Tries (2): C. W. Ralston, M. C. Beese
Conversions (2): R. Hiller, A. G. B. Old
Penalties (8): A. G. B. Old (5); R. Hiller (3)
Points (36): A. G. B. Old (17); R. Hiller (11); C. W. Ralston,
M. C. Beese (4)

1972 Played 1 Won 1 For 18 Against 9
Tries (1): A. J. Morley
Conversions (1): S. A. Doble
Penalties (4): S. A. Doble
Points (18): S. A. Doble (14); A. J. Morley (4)

1972–73
Championship
Shared
Played 5 Won 2 Lost 3 For 52 Against 71
Tries (7): D. J. Duckham, P. J. Dixon (2); A. Neary,
P. J. Squires, G. W. Evans
Conversions (3): A. M. Jorden
Drop goals (1): A. R. Cowman
Penalties (5): A. M. Jorden (3); S. A. Doble (2)
Points (52): A. M. Jorden (15); D. J. Duckham, P. J. Dixon (8);
S. A. Doble (6); A. Neary, P. J. Squires, G. W. Evans (4);
A. R. Cowman (3)

1973 Played 1 Won 1 For 16 Against 10
Tries (3): P. J. Squires, C. B. Stevens, A. Neary
Conversions (2): P. A. Rossborough
Points (16): P. J. Squires, C. B. Stevens, A. Neary,
P. A. Rossborough (4)

1973–74 Played 5 Won 2 Drawn 1 Lost 2 For 83 Against 69
Tries (9): A. G. Ripley, A. Neary, D. J. Duckham (2);
A. G. B. Old, F. E. Cotton, P. J. Squires
Conversions (4): A. G. B. Old (3); P. A. Rossborough
Drop goals (2): P. A. Rossborough, G. W. Evans
Penalties (11): A. G. B. Old (9); P. A. Rossborough (2)
Points (83): A. G. B. Old (37); P. A. Rossborough (11);
A. G. Ripley, D. J. Duckham, A. Neary (8); F. E. Cotton,
P. J. Squires (4); G. W. Evans (3)

1974–75 Played 4 Won 1 Lost 3 For 40 Against 65
Tries (5): C. B. Stevens, P. A. Rossborough, D. J. Duckham,
N. E. Horton, A. J. Morley

Conversions (1): A. G. B. Old
Drop goals (1): A. G. B. Old
Penalties (5): P. A. Rossborough (4); W. N. Bennett
Points (40): P. A. Rossborough (16); A. G. B. Old (5);
C. B. Stevens, N. E. Horton, D. J. Duckham, A. J. Morley (4);
W. N. Bennett (3)

1975	Played 2 Lost 2	For 30 Against 46

Tries (3): P. J. Squires (2); R. M. Uttley
Conversions (3): A. G. B. Old (2); P. E. Butler
Penalties (4): A. G. B. Old (3); P. E. Butler
Points (30): A. G. B. Old (13); P. J. Squires (8); P. E. Butler
(5); R. M. Uttley (4)

1975–76	Played 5 Won 1 Lost 4	For 65 Against 92

Tries (5): B. J. Corless, D. J. Duckham, A. W. Maxwell,
M. S. Lampkowski, P. J. Dixon
Conversions (3): A. J. Hignell, A. G. B. Old, P. E. Butler
Penalties (13): A. J. Hignell, A. G. B. Old (6); P. E. Butler
Points (65): A. J. Hignell A. G. B. Old (20); P. E. Butler (5);
B. J. Corless, D. J. Duckham, A. W. Maxwell,
M. S. Lampkowski, P. J. Dixon (4)

1976–77	Played 4 Won 2 Lost 2	For 42 Against 24

Tries (5): C. P. Kent, M. A. C. Slemen, M. Young, R. M. Uttley,
M. J. Cooper
Conversions (2): A. J. Hignell
Penalties (6): A. J. Hignell
Points (42): A. J. Hignell (22); C. P. Kent, M. A. C. Slemen,
M. Young, R. M. Uttley, M. J. Cooper (4)

1977–78	Played 4 Won 2 Lost 2	For 42 Against 33

Tries (4): P. J. Squires, B. G. Nelmes, M. A. C. Slemen,
P. J. Dixon
Conversions (4): M. Young
Drop goals (2): A. G. B. Old
Penalties (4): A. J. Hignell (2); P. W. Dodge, M. Young
Points (42): M. Young (11); A. J. Hignell, A. G. B. Old (6);
P. J. Squires, B. G. Nelmes, M. A. C. Slemen, P. J. Dixon (4);
P. W. Dodge (3)

1978–79	Played 5 Won 1 Drawn 1 Lost 3	For 30 Against 68

Tries (3): W. N. Bennett (2); M. A. C. Slemen
Drop goals (1): W. H. Hare
Penalties (5): W. N. Bennett (4); W. H. Hare
Points (30): W. N. Bennett (20); W. H. Hare (6);
M. A. C. Slemen (4)

1979–80	Played 5 Won 4 Lost 1	For 89 Against 58
Grand Slam		
Triple Crown		
Championship		

Tries (10): J. Carleton (4); M. A. C. Slemen, S. J. Smith (2);
J. P. Scott, N. J. Preston
Conversions (5): W. H. Hare
Drop goals (2): J. P. Horton
Penalties (11): W. H. Hare

449

Points (89): W. H. Hare (43); J. Carleton (16);
M. A. C. Slemen, S. J. Smith (8); J. P. Horton (6); J. P. Scott,
N. J. Preston (4)

1980–81
Played 4 Won 2 Lost 2   For 64 Against 60
Tries (6): W. H. Hare, C. R. Woodward, M. A. C. Slemen,
G. H. Davies, W. M. H. Rose, P. W. Dodge
Conversions (2): W. H. Hare, W. M. H. Rose
Penalties (12): W. H. Hare (8); W. M. H. Rose (4)
Points (64): W. H. Hare (30); W. M. H. Rose (18);
C. R. Woodward, M. A. C. Slemen, G. H. Davies,
P. W. Dodge (4)

1981
Played 2 Won 1 Drawn 1   For 31 Against 25
Tries (4): C. R. Woodward, G. H. Davies (2)
Conversions (3): W. H. Hare
Penalties (3): W. H. Hare
Points (31): W. H. Hare (15); C. R. Woodward, G. H. Davies (8)

1981–82
Played 5 Won 3 Drawn 1 Lost 1   For 83 Against 58
Tries (6): J. Carleton, M. A. C. Slemen (2); N. C. Jeavons,
C. R. Woodward
Conversions (4): W. H. Hare (2); W. M. H. Rose, P. W. Dodge
Penalties (17): W. H. Hare (8); W. M. H. Rose (7);
P. W. Dodge (2)
Points (83): W. H. Hare (28); W. M. H. Rose (23); J. Carleton,
M. A. C. Slemen, P. W. Dodge (8); N. C. Jeavons,
C. R. Woodward (4)

MOST POINTS IN A SEASON

By the team

Pts	T	C	DG	PG	Matches	Season	Pts	T	C	DG	PG	Matches	Season
89	10	5	2	11	5	1979–80	60	10	7	1	4	3	1937–38
83	9	4	2	11	5	1973–74	59	13	8	1	–	5	1927–28
83	6	4	–	17	5	1981–82	56	13	5	1	1	5	1906–07
82	20	11	–	–	4	1913–14	54	11	6	–	3	4	1952–53
79	9	5	2	12	5	1966–67	54	6	3	–	10	4	1968–69
69	17	7	1	–	4	1923–24	53	15	4	–	–	5	1905–06
65	5	3	–	13	5	1975–76	53	14	2	1	1	5	1912–13
64	6	2	–	12	4	1980–81	53	11	4	★	3	5	1924–25
61	13	8	–	2	4	1910–11	52	7	3	1	5	5	1972–73
61	13	7	2	–	4	1920–21	51	8	6	2	3	5	1969–70
61	5	2	1	13	6	1970–71	50	10	4	3	–	4	1922–23
60	14	9	–	–	4	1907–08							

By a player

Pts	Player	T	C	DG	PG	Season	Pts	Player	T	C	DG	PG	Season
49	R. Hiller	3	2	–	12	1970–71	15	A. Hudson	5	–	–	–	1905–06
46	R. W. Hosen	–	5	–	12	1966–67	15	D. Lambert	5	–	–	–	1906–07
43	W. H. Hare	–	5	–	11	1979–80	15	R. W. Poulton	5	–	–	–	1913–14
37	A. G. B. Old	1	3	–	9	1973–74	15	D. W. Burland	1	3	–	2	1931–32
36	R. Hiller	–	3	–	10	1968–69	15	A. M. Jorden	–	3	–	3	1972–73
30	W. H. Hare	1	1	–	8	1980–81	15	W. H. Hare	–	3	–	3	1981
28	W. H. Hare	–	2	–	8	1981–82	14	G. S. Conway	–	7	–	–	1923–24
24	D. Lambert	2	6	–	2	1910–11	14	H. J. Boughton	–	1	–	4	1934–35
24	C. N. Lowe	8	–	–	–	1913–14	14	S. A. Doble	–	1	–	4	1972
24	G. W. Parker	–	6	–	4	1937–38	13	E. J. Vivyan	3	2	–	–	1903–04
23	J. V. Richardson	1	8	1	–	1927–28	13	C. N. Lowe	3	–	1	–	1920–21
23	W. M. H. Rose	–	1	–	7	1981–82	13	A. G. B. Old	–	2	–	3	1975
22	R. Hiller	–	2	–	6	1967–68	12	R. E. Lockwood	2	3	–	–	1893–94
22	A. J. Hignell	–	2	–	6	1976–77	12	J. F. Byrne	–	1	1	2	1896–97
20	B. H. Black	1	4	–	3	1930–31	12	J. G. G. Birkett	4	–	–	–	1907–08
20	R. Hiller	–	4	2	2	1969–70	12	E. R. Mobbs	4	–	–	–	1908–09
20	A. J. Hignell	–	1	–	6	1975–76	12	F. E. Chapman	1	3	–	1	1909–10
20	A. G. B. Old	–	1	–	6	1975–76	12	C. H. Pillman	4	–	–	–	1912–13
20	W. N. Bennett	2	–	–	4	1978–79	12	J. E. Greenwood	–	6	–	–	1913–14
19	D. Rutherford	–	5	–	3	1959–60	12	E. D. G. Hammett	–	6	–	–	1920–21
18	V. H. M. Coates	6	–	–	–	1912–13	12	C. N. Lowe	4	–	–	–	1921–22
18	H. C. Catcheside	6	–	–	–	1923–24	12	H. P. Jacob	4	–	–	–	1923–24
18	N. M. Hall	–	6	–	2	1952–53	12	W. G. E. Luddington	–	3	★	1	1924–25
18	W. M. H. Rose	1	1	–	4	1980–81	12	G. W. C. Meikle	4	–	–	–	1933–34
17	A. G. B. Old	–	1	–	5	1971–72	12	J. V. Smith	4	–	–	–	1949–50
16	J. D. Currie	–	2	–	4	1955–56	12	D. S. Wilson	4	–	–	–	1953–54
16	P. A. Rossborough	1	–	–	4	1974–75	12	D. F. Allison	–	–	–	4	1955–56
16	J. Carleton	4	–	–	–	1979–80							

★ *in the drop-goal column denotes a goal from a mark*

MOST TRIES IN A SEASON

By the team

T	Matches	Season	T	Matches	Season
20	4	1913–14	10	4	1921–22
18	3	1880–81	10	4	1922–23
17	4	1923–24	10	4	1925–26
15	5	1905–06	10	3	1937–38
14	4	1907–08	10	5	1953–54
14	5	1912–13	10	5	1979–80
13	5	1906–07	9	3	1890–91
13	4	1910–11	9	3	1903–04
13	4	1920–21	9	4	1909–10
13	5	1927–28	9	4	1919–20
12	3	1882–83	9	4	1928–29
12	5	1908–09	9	4	1930–31
12	4	1911–12	9	5	1966–67
11	5	1924–25	9	5	1973–74
11	4	1952–53			

By a player

T	Player	Opponents	Season
8	C. N. Lowe	I(2), S(3), F(3)	1913–14
6	V. H. M. Coates	W(1), F(3), I(2)	1912–13
6	H. C. Catcheside	W(2), I(2), F(1), S(1)	1923–24
5	A. Hudson	W(1), F(4)	1905–06
5	D. Lambert	F(5)	1906–07
5	R. W. Poulton	S(1), F(4)	1913–14
4	H. H. Taylor	I(3), W(1)	1880–81
4	G. W. Burton	W(4)	1880–81
4	C. G. Wade	W(3), I(1)	1882–83
4	J. G. G. Birkett	F(1), W(2), S(1)	1907–08
4	E. R. Mobbs	A(1), F(1), I(1), S(1)	1908–09
4	C. H. Pillman	W(1), F(2), I(1)	1912–13
4	C. N. Lowe	W(1), I(1), S(2)	1921–22
4	H. P. Jacob	W(1), F(3)	1923–24
4	G. W. C. Meikle	W(2), I(1), S(1)	1933–34
4	J. V. Smith	W(1), F(1), S(2)	1949–50
4	D. S. Wilson	I(1), S(2), F(1)	1953–54
4	J. Carleton	F(1), S(3)	1979–80
3	H. Vassall	W(3)	1880–81
3	W. N. Bolton	W(1), I(1), S(1)	1882–83
3	R. E. Lockwood	I(2), S(1)	1890–91
3	H. Marshall	W(3)	1892–93
3	E. J. Vivyan	I(2), S(1)	1903–04
3	W. A. Mills	I(1), S(1), F(1)	1905–06
3	H. Brougham	W(1), I(1), F(1)	1911–12
3	A. D. Roberts	I(2), F(1)	1911–12

T	Player	Opponents	Season
3	C. N. Lowe	W(1), I(1), F(1)	1920–21
3	R. H. Hamilton-Wickes	W(1), S(1), F(1)	1924–25
3	H. C. C. Laird	NSW(1), W(1), S(1)	1927–28
3	H. G. Periton	NSW(1), F(2)	1927–28
3	J. S. R. Reeve	W(2), F(1)	1929–30
3	J. A. Tallent	S(2), F(1)	1930–31
3	C. B. van Ryneveld	I(1), S(2)	1948–49
3	P. B. Jackson	I(1), F(2)	1956–57
3	P. H. Thompson	W(1), F(2)	1957–58
3	J. Roberts	W(2), S(1)	1959–60
3	C. W. McFadyean	I(1), S(2)	1966–67
3	D. J. Duckham	I(1), S(2)	1968–69
3	R. Hiller	F(1), S(1), P(1)	1970–71

MOST CONVERSIONS IN A SEASON

By the team

C	Matches	Season	C	Matches	Season
11	4	1913–14	6	5	1969–70
9	3	1880–81	5	3	1890–91
9	4	1907–08	5	3	1891–92
8	4	1910–11	5	3	1893–94
8	5	1927–28	5	5	1906–07
7	4	1920–21	5	4	1919–20
7	4	1923–24	5	4	1946–47
7	3	1937–38	5	4	1959–60
6	4	1930–31	5	5	1966–67
6	4	1952–53	5	5	1979–80

By a player

C	Player	Opponents	Season
8	L. Stokes	I(2), W(6)	1880–81
8	J. V. Richardson	NSW(3), W(2), F(3)	1927–28
7	G. S. Conway	W(1), I(1), F(2), S(3)	1923–24
6	D. Lambert	W(1), F(5)	1910–11
6	J. E. Greenwood	F(6)	1913–14
6	E. D. G. Hammett	W(1), S(3), F(2)	1920–21
6	G. W. Parker	I(6)	1937–38
6	N. M. Hall	W(1), F(1), S(4)	1952–53
5	B. A. Hill	F(5)	1906–07
5	D. Rutherford	W(1), I(1), S(3)	1959–60
5	R. W. Hosen	A(1), I(1), S(3)	1966–67
5	W. H. Hare	I(3), S(2)	1979–80
4	V. H. Cartwright	F(4)	1905–06

C	Player	Opponents	Season
4	A. E. Wood	W(2), I(2)	1907–08
4	J. E. Greenwood	F(1), I(1), S(2)	1919–20
4	T. E. S. Francis	I(3), F(1)	1925–26
4	B. H. Black	I(1), S(2), F(1)	1930–31
4	J. Heaton	S(4)	1946–47
4	R. Hiller	SA(1), W(2), S(1)	1969–70
4	M. Young	S(2), I(2)	1977–78
3	L. Stokes	S(1), I(2)	1878–79
3	L. Stokes	I(1), S(2)	1879–80
3	A. M. Evanson	W(2), I(1)	1882–83
3	F. H. R. Alderson	W(2), S(1)	1890–91
3	R. E. Lockwood	W(2), S(1)	1891–92
3	R. E. Lockwood	W(3)	1893–94
3	G. D. Roberts	F(2), W(1)	1907–08
3	F. E. Chapman	W(1), F(1), S(1)	1909–10
3	F. E. Chapman	W(2), I(1)	1913–14
3	W. G. E. Luddington	S(1), F(2)	1924–25
3	E. Stanbury	W(1), I(1), S(1)	1926–27
3	D. W. Burland	I(1), S(2)	1931–32
3	R. Hiller	F(2), S(1)	1968–69
3	A. M. Jorden	I(1), S(2)	1972–73
3	A. G. B. Old	I(1), F(1), W(1)	1973–74
3	W. H. Hare	Arg 1st(2), Arg 2nd(1)	1981

MOST DROPPED GOALS IN A SEASON

By the team

DG	Matches	Season	DG	Matches	Season
3	4	1922–23	2	5	1966–67
2	3	1880–81	2	5	1967–68
2	4	1920–21	2	5	1969–70
2	4	1946–47	2	5	1973–74
2	4	1948–49	2	4	1977–78
2	4	1959–60	2	5	1979–80

By a player

DG	Player	Opponents	Season
2	W. J. A. Davies	I(1), F(1)	1922–23
2	N. M. Hall	W(1), S(1)	1946–47
2	R. A. W. Sharp	I(1), S(1)	1959–60
2	J. F. Finlan	F(1), S(1)	1966–67
2	R. Hiller	I(2)	1969–70
2	A. G. B. Old	F(2)	1977–78
2	J. P. Horton	F(2)	1979–80

MOST PENALTY GOALS IN A SEASON

By the team

PG	Matches	Season	PG	Matches	Season
17	5	1981–82	8	4	1955–56
13	6	1970–71	8	4	1971–72
13	5	1975–76	7	5	1967–68
12	5	1966–67	6	4	1976–77
12	4	1980–81	5	5	1972–73
11	5	1973–74	5	4	1974–75
11	5	1979–80	5	5	1978–79
10	4	1968–69			

By a player

PG	Player	Opponents	Season
12	R. W. Hosen	A(2), I(1), F(3), S(2), W(4)	1966–67
12	R. Hiller	I(3), F(3), S 1st(3), S 2nd(1), P(2)	1970–71
11	W. H. Hare	NZ(3), I(2), F(1), W(3), S(2)	1979–80
10	R. Hiller	I(4), F(3), W(3)	1968–69
9	A. G. B. Old	S(1), I(5), F(1), W(2)	1973–74
8	W. H. Hare	W(5), S(3)	1980–81
8	W. H. Hare	F(5), W(3)	1981–82
7	W. M. H. Rose	A(3), S(1), I(3)	1981–82
6	R. Hiller	W(1), I(2), F(2), S(1)	1967–68
6	A. G. B. Old	S(2), I(4)	1975–76
6	A. J. Hignell	A(3), W(3)	1975–76
6	A. J. Hignell	S(2), F(1), W(3)	1976–77
5	A. G. B. Old	F(2), S(3)	1971–72
4	H. J. Boughton	W(1), I(3)	1934–35
4	G. W. Parker	I(1), S(3)	1937–38
4	D. F. Allison	W(1), I(1), F(2)	1955–56
4	J. D. Currie	I(2), S(2)	1955–56
4	S. A. Doble	SA(4)	1972
4	P. A. Rossborough	F(4)	1974–75
4	W. N. Bennett	S(1), I(1), F(1), W(1)	1978–79
4	W. M. H. Rose	F(4)	1980–81
3	B. H. Black	W(2), S(1)	1930–31
3	J. Heaton	S(3)	1938–39
3	D. St. G. Hazell	F(2), S(1)	1954–55
3	D. Rutherford	W(2), S(1)	1959–60
3	R. W. Hosen	NZ 1st(2), NZ 2nd(1)	1963
3	D. Rutherford	W(1), F(2)	1964–65
3	R. Hiller	W(1), I(2)	1971–72
3	A. M. Jorden	I(1), F(2)	1972–73
3	A. G. B. Old	A 2nd(3)	1975
3	W. H. Hare	Arg 1st(1), Arg 2nd(2)	1981

INDIVIDUAL RECORDS

DATES

Dates of births and deaths of players have been obtained from several sources, but the works of the following have been invaluable in the compilation of this list: S. H. Lee and H. V. L. Stanton, compilers of the dates of births and deaths for *Wisden's Rugby Football Almanack*; C. J. B. Marriott, writer of the Obituary notices for the *Rugby Football Annual*; Captain W. Livingstone-Irwin, writer of the Obituary notices for *Playfair Rugby Annual*; Sir Andrew Noble, Bt., and A. R. McWhirter, authors of the *Centenary History of Oxford University R.F.C.*; A. R. McWhirter and U. A. Titley, authors of the *Centenary History of the R.F.U.*; and T. W. J. Auty, of Leeds, an industrious researcher who has corrected errors found in earlier sources and contributed innumerable dates and facts for this list.

Finally, grateful thanks are due to the staffs of Somerset House and General Register Office for their guidance and patience at all times. Any existing errors are the responsibility of the author, who would welcome any corrections and additions to this list. The births and deaths of a number of the earlier players have proved impossible to trace – any additional information from readers would be welcomed.

CLUBS

The intention has been to show all major clubs for which England players have appeared. For a player capped directly from a minor club, that club has also been identified. Where internationals have made significant contributions to Rugby football in the Services or at the hospitals, the relevant clubs have been recognised; while an effort has been made to indicate all England players who have attended Oxford and Cambridge Universities, even those who did not gain Rugby Blues.

DEBUTS

The following abbreviations have been used under this heading:

A	Australia	NZ	New Zealand
Arg	Argentina	NZN	New Zealand Natives
F	France	S	Scotland
I	Ireland	SA	South Africa
NSW	New South Wales	W	Wales

N.B. The England matches against Ireland in 1875–76 and Wales in 1882–83, denoted by the abbreviations I.1876 and W.1883, were played in December 1875 and December 1882 respectively.

456

CAPS

Numbers of caps were calculated from appearances in full international matches up to 30 April 1982. Figures in parentheses indicate number of matches played as a replacement.

SCORING ANALYSES

Scoring analyses have been obtained from the scoring summaries in the match reports. Inevitably, confusion existed concerning the identities of some scorers, but an attempt was made earlier to indicate alternative credits (see match reports). Three players, N. M. Hall (with dropped goals); A. Neary (with tries); and D. J. Duckham (also with tries) registered scores (after 1893) before and after the scoring values were altered. Asterisks will be found adjacent to their analyses to remind the reader of this fact.

POINTS TOTAL

Scoring values have been fairly constant since 1893–94 (see p 412) and points totals for players appearing in matches since that season were calculated in accordance with values prevailing at the dates of the matches. *However, in collecting points totals for players who scored in matches before 1893–94, the scoring values adopted between 1893–94 and 1904–05 have been used. This also applies to the career records appended to the players' section. Figures in italic in the final column of the career records for each player denote where the 'pseudo' calculation has been made.*

DUAL INTERNATIONALS						
ENGLAND RUGBY CAPS			**OTHER CAPS**			
Player	*Caps*	*Dates*	*Sport*	*Country*	*Caps*	*Dates*
R. H. Birkett	4	1871–1877	Soccer	England	1	1879
W. H. Milton	2	1874–1875	Cricket	South Africa	3*	1888–1892
A. N. Hornby	9*	1877–1882	Cricket	England	3*	1878–1884
G. F. Vernon	5	1878–1881	Cricket	England	1	1882–1883
C. P. Wilson	1	1881	Soccer	England	2	1884
A. E. Stoddart	10*	1885–1893	Cricket	England	16*	1887–1898
J. W. Sutcliffe	1	1889	Soccer	England	5	1893–1903
S. M. J. Woods	13*	1890–1895	Cricket	Australia	3	1888
			Cricket	England	3	1895–1896
J. H. Marsh	1	1892	Rugby	Scotland	2	1889
F. Mitchell	6*	1895–1896	Cricket	England	2	1898–1899
			Cricket	South Africa	3*	1912
R. O. Schwarz	3	1899–1901	Cricket	South Africa	20	1905–1912
R. H. Spooner	1	1903	Cricket	England	10	1905–1912
R. H. M. Hands	2	1910	Cricket	South Africa	1	1913–1914
F. W. Mellish	6	1920–1921	Rugby	South Africa	6	1921–1924
H. G. Owen-Smith	10*	1934–1937	Cricket	South Africa	5	1929
M. P. Donnelly	1	1947	Cricket	New Zealand	7	1937–1949
C. B. van Ryneveld	4	1949	Cricket	South Africa	19*	1951–1958
M. J. K. Smith	1	1956	Cricket	England	50*	1958–1972

* indicates that player captained his country.

Players' Career Records

	Dates	Clubs	Caps	Debut	T	C	DG	PG	Pts
Aarvold, C. D.	1907–	Cambridge U., West Hartlepool, Headingley, Blackheath	16	1928, NSW	4	—	—	—	12
Adams, A. A.	1880–1963	Otago (NZ), London H.	1	1910, F	—	—	—	—	—
Adams, F. R.	1853–1932	Richmond	7	1875, I	2	—	—	—	6
Adey, G. J.	1947–	Leicester	2	1976, I	1	—	—	—	3
Adkins, S. J.	1922–	Coventry	7	1950, I	1	—	—	—	3
Agar, A. E.	1923–	Hartlepool Rovers, United Banks, Harlequins	7	1952, SA	1	—	1	—	6
Alcock, A.	1882–1973	Guy's H., Richmond, Blackheath, Gloucester	1	1906, SA	1	4	—	—	11
Alderson, F. H. R.	1867–1925	Cambridge U., Hartlepool Rovers, Blackheath	6	1891, W	—	2	—	1	7
Alexander, H.	1879–1915	Birkenhead Park, Richmond	7	1900, I	—	—	—	—	—
Alexander, W.		Northern	1	1927, F	—	—	—	—	—
Allison, D. F.	1931–	Northern, Coventry	7	1956, W	—	—	—	5	15
Allport, A.	1867–1949	Guy's H., Blackheath	5	1892, W	—	—	—	—	—
Anderson, S.		Rockcliff	1	1899, I	—	—	—	—	—
Anderson, W. F.	1944–	Orrell	1	1973, NZ	—	—	—	—	—
Anderton, C.		Manchester Free Wanderers	1	1889, NZN	—	—	—	—	—
Archer, H.	1884–1946	Guy's H., Bridgwater Albion	3	1909, W	—	—	—	—	—
Armstrong, R.	1898–1968	Medicals, Northern	1	1925, W	—	—	—	1	3
Arthur, T. G.	1940–	West Hartlepool, Wasps, Moseley, Waterloo	2	1966, W	—	—	—	—	—
Ashby, R. C.	1937–	Wasps	3	1966, I	1	—	—	—	3
Ashcroft, A.	1930–	St Helens, Waterloo	16	1956, W	1	—	—	—	3
Ashcroft, A. H.	1887–1963	Cambridge, U., Birkenhead Park	1	1909, A	—	—	—	—	—
Ashford, W.	1871–1954	St Thomas's H., Richmond, Exeter	4	1897, W	—	—	—	—	—
Ashworth, A.	1864–1938	Oldham, Rochdale Hornets	1	1892, I	—	—	—	—	—
Askew, J. G.	1908–1942	Cambridge U., Durham City	3	1930, W	—	—	—	—	—
Aslett, A. R.	1901–1980	Blackheath, Army, Richmond	6	1926, W	2	—	—	—	6
Assinder, E. W.	1888–1974	Old Edwardians	2	1909, A	—	—	—	—	—
Aston, R. L.	1869–1930	Cambridge U., Blackheath	2	1890, S	—	—	—	—	—
Auty, J. R.	1910–	Headingley, Leicester	1	1935, S	—	—	—	—	—
Bainbridge, S. J.	1956–	Gosforth	2	1982, F	—	—	—	—	—
Baker, D. G. S.	1929–	Oxford U., Old Merchant Taylors	4	1955, W	—	—	—	—	—
Baker, E. M.	1874–1940	Oxford U., Moseley, Blackheath	7	1895, W	—	—	—	—	—
Baker, H. C.	1863–1934	Clifton	1	1887, W	—	—	—	—	—
Bance, J. F.	1925–	Cambridge U., Bedford	1	1954, S	—	—	—	—	—
Barr, R. J.	1907–1975	Leicester	3	1932, SA	—	1	—	—	2
Barrett, E. I. M.	1879–1950	Lennox	1	1903, S	—	—	—	—	—

Players' Career Records (*continued*)

	Dates	Clubs	Caps	Debut	T	C	DG	PG	Pts
Barrington, T. J. M.	1908–	Bridgwater Albion, Harlequins, Richmond, Bristol	2	1931, W	—	—	—	—	—
Barrington-Ward, L. E.	1884–1953	Oxford U., Edinburgh U.	4	1910, W	—	—	—	—	—
Barron, J. H.	1874–1942	Bingley	3	1896, S	—	—	—	—	—
Bartlett, J. T.	1924–1969	Liverpool U., Waterloo	1	1951, W	—	—	—	—	—
Bartlett, R. M.	1929–	Cambridge U., Harlequins	7	1957, W	—	—	—	—	—
Barton, J.	1943–	Coventry	4	1967, I	2	—	—	—	6
Batchelor, T. B.	1884–1966	Oxford U., Richmond, London H.	1	1907, F	—	—	—	—	—
Bateson, A. H.	1901–1982	Otley	4	1930, W	—	—	—	—	—
Bateson, H. D.	1856–1927	Oxford U., Liverpool, Blackheath	1	1879, I	—	—	—	—	—
Batson, T.	1852–1933	Oxford U., Blackheath	3	1872, S	—	—	—	—	—
Batten, J. M.	1853–1917	Cambridge U.	1	1874, S	—	—	—	—	—
Baume, J. L.	1920–	Northern, Headingley, Harrogate, Army	1	1950, S	—	—	—	—	—
Baxter, J.	1870–1940	Birkenhead Park	3	1900, W	—	—	—	—	—
Bazley, R. C.	1929–	Waterloo, Liverpool U.	10	1952, I	2	—	—	—	6
Beaumont, W. B.	1952–	Fylde	34(1)	1975, I	—	—	—	—	—
Bedford, H.	1866–1929	Morley, Batley	3	1889, NZN	2	—	—	—	6
Bedford, L. L.	1903–1963	Headingley	2	1931, W	—	—	—	—	—
Beer, I. D. S.	1931–	Cambridge U., Bath, Harlequins	2	1955, F	1	—	—	—	3
Beese, M. C.	1948–	Liverpool, Bath	3	1972, W	1	—	—	—	4
Bell, F. J.		Northern	1	1900, W	—	—	—	—	—
Bell, H.	1860–1935	New Brighton	1	1884, I	—	—	—	—	—
Bell, J. L.		Darlington	1	1878, I	—	—	—	—	—
Bell, P. J.	1937–	Blackheath	4	1968, W	—	—	—	—	—
Bell, R. W.	1875–1940	Cambridge U., Blackheath, Northern	3	1900, W	—	—	—	—	—
Bendon, G. J.	1929–	Wasps	4	1959, W	—	—	—	—	—
Bennett, N. O.	1922–	St Mary's H., U.S.	7	1947, W	1	—	—	—	3
Bennett, W. N.	1951–	Bedford, London Welsh	7(1)	1975, S	2	—	—	5	23
Bennetts, B. B.	1883–1958	Penzance, Devonport Albion, Redruth, Richmond	2	1909, A	—	—	—	—	—
Bentley, J. E.	–1913	Gypsies	2	1871, S	—	—	—	—	—
Berridge, M. J.	1923–1973	Northampton, Leicester	2	1949, W	—	—	—	—	—
Berry, H.	1883–1915	Gloucester	4	1910, W	2	—	—	—	6
Berry, J.	1867–1930	Tyldesley	3	1891, W	—	—	—	—	—
Berry, J. T. W.	1907–	Leicester	3	1939, W	—	—	—	—	—
Beswick, E.	1860–1911	Swinton	2	1882, I	—	—	—	—	—
Biggs, J. M.	1855–1935	U.C.H., Wasps	2	1878, S	—	—	—	—	—
Birkett, J. G. G.	1884–1968	Harlequins	21	1906, S	10	—	—	1	34

Players' Career Records (*continued*)

	Dates	Clubs	Caps	Debut	T	C	DG	PG	Pts
Birkett, L. H.	1853–1943	Clapham Rovers	3	1875, S	—	—	—	—	3
Birkett, R. H.	1849–1898	Clapham Rovers	4	1871, S	1	—	—	—	3
Bishop, C. C.	1903–1980	Cambridge U., Blackheath	1	1927, F	—	—	—	—	—
Black, B. H.	1907–1940	Oxford U., Blackheath	10	1930, W	2	6	—	4	30
Blacklock, J. H.	1878–1945	Aspatria	2	1898, I	—	—	—	—	—
Blakeway, P. J.	1950–	Gloucester	11	1980, I	—	—	—	—	—
Blakiston, A. F.	1892–	Cambridge U., Liverpool, Blackheath, Northampton	17	1920, S	2	—	—	—	6
Blatherwick, T.	1855–1940	Epsom, Manchester	1	1878, I	—	—	—	—	—
Body, J. A.	1846–1929	Gypsies	2	1872, S	—	—	—	—	—
Bolton, C. A.	1882–1963	Oxford U., U.S.	1	1909, F	2	—	—	—	6
Bolton, R.	1909–	Wakefield, U.C.H., Harlequins	5	1933, W	6	2	—	—	22
Bolton, W. N.	1862–1930	Blackheath	11	1882, I	—	—	—	—	—
Bonaventura, M. S.	1902–	Blackheath	1	1931, W	—	—	—	—	—
Bond, A. M.	1954–	Sale	6	1978, NZ	—	—	—	—	—
Bonham-Carter, E.	1870–1956	Oxford U., Blackheath	1	1891, S	—	—	—	—	—
Bonsor, F.	1861–1932	Bradford	6	1886, W	2	—	—	—	6
Boobbyer, B.	1928–	Oxford U., Rosslyn Park	9	1950, W	3	—	—	—	9
Booth, L. A.	1909–1942	Headingley, Bohemians	7	1933, W	—	—	—	—	—
Botting, I. J.	1922–1980	Oxford U., Leicester, Blackheath	2	1950, W	—	—	—	—	—
Boughton, H. J.	1910–	Gloucester	3	1935, W	—	1	—	4	14
Boyle, C. W.	1853–1900	Oxford U.	1	1873, S	—	—	—	—	—
Boylen, F.	1879–1938	Hartlepool Rovers	4	1908, F	—	—	—	—	—
Bradby, M. S.	1899–	Cambridge U., U.S.	2	1922, I	—	—	—	—	—
Bradley, R.		West Hartlepool	1	1903, W	—	—	—	—	—
Bradshaw, H.	1868–1910	Bramley	7	1892, S	2	—	—	—	6
Braithwaite, J.	1873–1915	Leicester	1	1905, NZ	—	—	—	—	—
Braithwaite-Exley, B.	1927–	Headingley	1	1949, W	—	—	—	—	—
Brettargh, A. T.		Liverpool O.B.	8	1900, W	1	—	—	—	3
Brewer, J.		Gypsies	1	1876, I	—	—	—	—	—
Briggs, A.	1871–1943	Otley, Bradford	3	1892, W	—	—	—	—	—
Brinn, A.	1942–	Gloucester	3	1972, W	—	—	—	—	—
Broadley, T.	1871–1950	Bingley, Bradford	6	1893, W	—	—	—	—	—
Bromet, W. E.	1868–1949	Oxford U., Tadcaster, Richmond	12	1891, W	1	—	—	—	3
Brook, P. W. P.	1906–	Cambridge U., Harlequins, Bristol	3	1930, S	—	—	—	—	—
Brooke, T. J.	1940–	Richmond	2	1968, F	—	—	—	—	—
Brooks, F. G.	1883–1947	Bedford	1	1906, SA	1	—	—	—	3

Players' Career Records *(continued)*

	Dates	Clubs	Caps	Debut	T	C	DG	PG	Pts
Brooks, M. J.	1855–1944	Oxford U.	1	1874, S	—	—	—	—	—
Brophy, T. J.	1942–	Liverpool	8	1964, I	—	—	—	—	—
Brough, J. W.	1903–	Silloth	2	1925, NZ	—	—	—	—	9
Brougham, H.	1888–1923	Oxford, U., Harlequins	4	1912, W	3	—	—	—	9
Brown, A. A.	1911–	St Helens, Headingley, Exeter	1	1938, S	—	—	—	—	—
Brown, L. G.	1888–1950	Oxford U., London H., Blackheath	18	1911, W	4	—	—	—	12
Brown, T. W.	1907–1961	Bristol	9	1928, S	—	—	—	—	—
Brunton, J.	1888–1971	North Durham, Army	3	1914, W	—	—	—	—	—
Brutton, E. B.	1863–1922	Cambridge U.	1	1886, S	—	—	—	—	—
Bryden, C. C.	1852–1941	Clapham Rovers	2	1876, I	—	—	—	—	—
Bryden, H. A.	1854–1937	Clapham Rovers	1	1874, S	—	—	—	—	—
Buckingham, R. A.	1907–	Leicester	1	1927, F	—	—	—	—	—
Bucknall, A. L.	1945–	Oxford U., Richmond	10	1969, SA	—	—	—	—	—
Budd, A.	1853–1899	Cambridge U., Blackheath	5	1878, I	1	—	—	—	3
Budworth, R. T. D.	1867–1937	Oxford U., Blackheath, London Welsh	3	1890, W	1	—	—	—	3
Bull, A. G.		Northampton	1	1914, W	—	—	—	—	—
Bullough, E.		Wigan	3	1892, W	—	—	—	—	—
Bulpitt, M. P.	1944–	Blackheath	1	1970, S	—	—	—	—	—
Bulteel, A. J.		Manchester	1	1876, I	—	—	—	—	—
Bunting, W. L.	1873–1947	Cambridge U., Moseley, Richmond	9	1897, I	—	—	—	—	—
Burland, D. W.	1908–1976	Bristol	8	1931, W	3	4	—	2	23
Burns, B. H.	1848–1932	Blackheath	1	1871, S	—	—	—	—	—
Burton, G. W.	1855–1890	Blackheath	6	1879, S	6	—	—	—	18
Burton, H. C.	1898–	Richmond	1	1926, W	—	—	—	—	—
Burton, M. A.	1945–	Gloucester	17	1972, W	—	—	—	—	—
Bush, J. A.	1850–1924	Clifton	5	1872, S	—	—	—	—	—
Butcher, W. V.	1878–1957	Bristol, Streatham	7	1903, S	—	—	—	—	—
Butler, A. G.	1914–	Harlequins	2	1937, W	1	—	—	—	3
Butler, P. E.	1951–	Gloucester	2	1975, A	—	2	—	2	10
Butterfield, J.	1929–	Northampton	28	1953, F	5	—	—	—	15
Byrne, F. A.	1873–	Moseley	1	1897, W	—	—	—	—	—
Byrne, J. F.	1871–1954	Moseley	13	1894, W	—	2	2	4	24
Cain, J. J.	1920–	Waterloo	1	1950, W	—	—	—	—	—
Campbell, D. A.		Cambridge U.	2	1937, W	—	—	—	—	—
Candler, P. L.	1914–	Richmond, Cambridge U., St Bart's H.	10	1935, W	2	—	—	—	6
Cannell, L. B.	1926–	Oxford U., Northampton, St Mary's H.	19	1948, F	2	—	—	—	6

Players' Career Records (continued)

	Dates	Clubs	Caps	Debut	T	C	DG	PG	Pts
Caplan, D. W. N.	1954–	Headingley, Northampton	2	1978, S	—	—	—	—	—
Cardus, R. M.	1956–	Roundhay, Wasps	2	1979, F	—	—	—	—	—
Carey, G. M.	1872–1927	Oxford U., Blackheath	5	1895, W	1	—	—	—	3
Carleton, J.	1955–	Orrell	16	1979, NZ	6	—	—	—	24
Carpenter, A. D.	1900–1974	Gloucester	1	1932, SA	—	—	—	—	—
Carr, R. S. L.	1917–	Old Cranleighans, Manchester, Moseley	3	1939, W	—	—	—	—	—
Cartwright, V. H.	1882–1965	Oxford U., Nottingham, Harlequins	14	1903, W	—	4	—	—	8
Catcheside, H. C.	1899–	Percy Park	8	1924, W	6	—	—	—	18
Cattell, R. H. B.	1871–1948	Oxford U., Moseley, Blackheath	7	1895, W	2	—	—	—	6
Cave, J. W.	1867–1949	Cambridge U., Richmond	1	1889, NZN	—	—	—	—	—
Cave, W. T. C.	1882–	Cambridge U., Blackheath	1	1905, W	—	—	—	—	—
Challis, R.	1932–	Bristol	3	1957, I	—	2	—	2	10
Chambers, E. L.	1882–1946	Cambridge U., Blackheath, Bedford	3	1908, F	—	—	—	—	—
Chantrill, B. S.	1897–	Weston-s-Mare, Bristol, Richmond, Rosslyn Park, Manchester	4	1924, W	—	—	—	—	—
Chapman, C. E.	1860–1901	Cambridge U.	1	1884, W	—	—	—	—	—
Chapman, F. E.	1888–1938	Westoe, Hartlepool Rovers	7	1910, W	1	7	—	1	20
Cheesman, W. I.	1889–1969	Oxford U., Old Merchant Taylors	4	1913, SA	—	—	—	—	—
Cheston, E. C.	1848–1913	Oxford U., Richmond	5	1873, S	1	—	—	—	3
Christopherson, P.	1866–1921	Oxford U., Blackheath	2	1891, W	2	—	—	—	6
Clark, C. W. H.	1856–1943	Liverpool	1	1876, I	1	—	—	—	3
Clarke, A. J.	1913–1975	Coventry	6	1935, W	—	—	—	—	—
Clarke, S. J. S.	1938–	Cambridge U., Bath, Blackheath	13	1963, W	1	—	—	—	3
Clayton, J. H.	1848–1924	Liverpool	1	1871, S	—	—	—	—	—
Clements, J. W.	1932–	Old Cranleighans, U.S., Cambridge U.	3	1959, I	—	—	—	—	—
Cleveland, C. R.	1866–1929	Oxford U., Blackheath	2	1887, W	—	—	—	—	—
Clibborn, W. G.		Richmond	6	1886, W	—	—	—	—	—
Coates, C. H.	1857–1922	Cambridge U., Yorkshire Wanderers, Leeds	3	1880, S	—	—	—	—	—
Coates, V. H. M.	1889–1934	Bridgwater Albion, Cambridge U., Bath, Leicester, Richmond	5	1913, SA	6	—	—	—	18
Cobby, W.	1877–1957	Cambridge U., Hull E.R., Castleford	1	1900, W	—	—	—	—	—
Cockerham, A.		Bradford Olicana	1	1900, W	—	—	—	—	—
Colclough, M. J.	1953–	Liverpool, Rosslyn Park, Angoulême	15	1978, S	—	—	—	—	—
Coley, E.	1903–1957	Northampton	2	1929, F	1	—	—	—	3
Collins, P. J.	1928–	Camborne	3	1952, S	—	—	—	—	—
Collins, W. E.	1853–1934	Old Cheltonians, St George's H.	5	1874, S	1	—	—	—	3

Players' Career Records (*continued*)

	Dates	Clubs	Caps	Debut	T	C	DG	PG	Pts
Considine, S. G. U.	1901–1950	Bath	1	1925, F	—	—	—	—	—
Conway, G. S.	1897–	Cambridge U., Rugby, Harlequins, Blackheath, Manchester	18	1920, F	1	11	—	—	25
Cook, J. G.	1911–1979	Bedford	1	1937, S	—	—	—	—	—
Cook, P. W.	1943–	Richmond	2	1965, I	—	—	—	—	—
Cooke, D. A.	1949–	Harlequins	4	1976, W	—	—	—	—	—
Cooke, D. H.	1955–	Harlequins	4	1981, W	—	—	—	—	—
Cooke, P.	1916–1940	Oxford U., Richmond	2	1939, W	—	—	—	—	—
Coop, T.		Tottington, Leigh	1	1892, S	—	—	—	—	—
Cooper, J. G.	1881–1965	Moseley	2	1909, A	—	—	1	—	4
Cooper, M. J.	1948–	Moseley	11(1)	1973, F	—	—	2	—	6
Coopper, S.F.	1878–1961	R.N.E.C. Keyham, Blackheath	7	1900, W	—	—	—	—	—
Corbett, L. J.	1897–	Bristol	16	1921, F	3	—	★	1	15
Corless, B. J.	1945–	Birmingham, Coventry, Moseley	10(1)	1976, A	1	—	—	—	4
Cotton, F. E.	1948–	Loughborough College, Sale, Coventry	31	1971, S	1	—	—	—	4
Coulman, M. J.	1944–	Moseley	9	1967, A	1	—	—	—	3
Coulson, T. J.	1896–1948	Gloucester, Coventry	3	1927, W	—	—	—	—	—
Court, E. D.	1862–1935	Oxford U., Blackheath	1	1885, W	—	—	—	—	—
Coverdale, H.	1889–1964	Hartlepool Rovers, Blackheath	4	1910, F	—	—	1	—	4
Cove-Smith, R.	1899–	Cambridge U., K.C.H., Old Merchant Taylors	29	1921, S	1	—	—	—	3
Cowling, R. J.	1944–	Gloucester, Leicester	8	1977, S	—	—	—	—	—
Cowman, A. R.	1949–	Loughborough College, Coventry	5	1971, S	—	—	2	—	6
Cox, N. S.	1877–1930	Sunderland	1	1901, S	—	—	—	—	—
Cranmer, P.	1914–	Oxford U., Richmond, Moseley	16	1934, W	1	—	2	1	14
Creed, R. N.	1945–	Moseley, Coventry	1	1971, P	—	—	—	—	—
Cridlan, A. G.	1909–	Oxford U., Blackheath	3	1935, W	—	—	—	—	—
Crompton, C. A.	1848–1875	Blackheath	1	1871, S	—	—	—	—	—
Crosse, C. W.	1854–1905	Oxford U.	2	1874, S	—	—	—	—	—
Cumberlege, B. S.	1891–1970	Cambridge U., Blackheath	8	1920, W	—	1	—	—	2
Cumming, D. C.	1903–1979	Cambridge U., Blackheath	2	1925, S	—	—	—	—	—
Cunliffe, F. L.	1854–1927	R.M.A. Woolwich	1	1874, S	—	—	—	—	—
Currey, F. I.	1849–1896	Marlborough Nomads	1	1872, S	—	—	—	—	—
Currie, J. D.	1932–	Oxford U., Harlequins, Bristol	25	1956, W	—	2	—	4	16
Cusworth, L.	1954–	Wakefield, Moseley, Leicester	3	1979, NZ	—	—	—	—	—
d'Aguilar, F. B. G.	1849–1896	R.M.A. Woolwich, Royal Engineers	1	1872, S	1	—	—	—	3

includes a goal from a mark ★

Players' Career Records (*continued*)

	Dates	Clubs	Caps	Debut	T	C	DG	PG	Pts
Dalton, T. J.	1926–	Coventry, Rugby	1(1)	1969, S	—	—	—	—	—
Danby, T.		Durham City, Harlequins	1	1949, W	—	—	—	—	—
Daniell, J.	1878–1963	Cambridge U., Richmond	7	1899, W	—	—	—	—	—
Darby, A. J. L.	1876–1960	Cambridge U., Richmond, Birkenhead Park	1	1899, I	—	—	—	—	—
Davenport, A.	1849–1932	Oxford U., Ravenscourt Park	1	1871, S	—	—	—	—	—
Davey, J.	1880–1951	Redruth, Coventry	2	1908, S	—	—	—	—	—
Davey, R. F.	1905–	Leytonstone, Exeter	1	1931, W	—	—	—	—	—
Davidson, Jas	1868–1945	Aspatria	5	1897, S	—	—	—	—	—
Davidson, Jos	1878–1910	Aspatria	2	1899, W	—	—	—	—	—
Davies, G. H.	1959–	Cambridge U., Coventry	8	1981, S	3	—	—	—	12
Davies, P. H.	1903–1979	Manchester, Sale	1	1927, I	—	—	—	—	—
Davies, V. G.	1899–1941	Harlequins	2	1922, W	—	—	—	—	—
Davies, W. J. A.	1890–1967	R.N.E.C. Keyham, U.S., Royal Navy	22	1913, SA	4	—	3	—	24
Davies, W. P. C.	1928–	Cambridge U., Cheltenham, Harlequins	11	1953, S	1	—	—	—	3
Davis, A. M.	1942–	Torquay Athletic, Harlequins	16	1963, W	—	—	—	—	—
Dawson, E. F.	1858–1904	R.I.E. College, Richmond	1	1878, I	—	—	—	—	—
Day, H. L. V.	1898–1972	Leicester, Army	4	1920, W	2	2	—	2	16
Dean, G. J.	1909–	Cambridge U., Harlequins	1	1931, I	—	—	—	—	—
Dee, J. M.	1938–	Hartlepool Rovers	2	1962, S	—	—	—	—	—
Devitt, Sir T. G.	1902–	Cambridge U., Blackheath, Army	4	1926, I	—	—	—	—	—
Dewhurst, J. H.	1863–1947	Cambridge U., Richmond, St Thomas' H.	4	1887, W	—	—	—	—	—
de Winton, R. F. C.	1868–1923	Oxford U., Marlborough Nomads, Blackheath	1	1893, W	—	—	—	—	—
Dibble, R.		Bridgwater Albion, Newport	19	1906, S	—	—	—	—	—
Dicks, J.	1912–	Northampton	8	1934, W	—	—	—	—	—
Dillon, E. W.	1881–1941	Oxford U., Blackheath, Richmond	4	1904, W	—	—	—	—	—
Dingle, A. J.	1891–1915	Oxford U., Richmond, Hartlepool Rovers	3	1913, I	—	—	—	—	—
Dixon, P. J.	1944–	Oxford U., Harlequins, Gosforth	22	1971, P	4	—	—	—	16
Dobbs, G. E. B.	1884–1917	Plymouth Albion, Llanelli, Devonport Albion, Army	2	1906, W	—	—	—	—	—
Doble, S. A.	1944–1977	Moseley	3	1972, SA	—	1	—	6	20
Dobson, D. D.	1880–1916	Oxford U., Newton Abbot, Devonport Albion	6	1902, W	3	—	—	—	9
Dobson, T. H.	1872–1902	Bradford	1	1895, S	—	—	—	—	—
Dodge, P. W.	1958–	Leicester	20	1978, W	1	1	—	3	15
Donnelly, M. P.	1917–	Oxford U., Blackheath	1	1947, I	—	—	—	—	—
Dovey, B. A.	1938–	Lydney, Cambridge U., Rosslyn Park	2	1963, W	—	—	—	—	—
Down, P. J.	1883–1954	Bristol	1	1909, A	—	—	—	—	—
Dowson, A. O.	1875–1940	Oxford U., Moseley, Manchester	1	1899, S	—	—	—	—	—

Players' Career Records (*continued*)

	Dates	Clubs	Caps	Debut	T	C	DG	PG	Pts
Drake-Lee, N. J.	1942–	Cambridge U., Leicester, Waterloo, Manchester	8	1963, W	1	—	—	—	3
Duckett, H.	1867–1939	Bradford	2	1893, I	—	—	—	—	—
Duckham, D. J.	1946–	Coventry	36	1969, I	10*	—	—	—	36
Dudgeon, H. W.	1874–1935	Guy's H., Northern, Richmond	7	1897, S	—	—	—	—	—
Dugdale, J. M.	1851–1918	Oxford U., Ravenscourt Park	1	1871, S	—	—	—	—	—
Duncan, R. F. H.	1896–	Guy's H.	3	1922, I	—	—	—	—	—
Dunkley, P. E.	1904–	Leicester, Harlequins	6	1931, I	—	—	—	—	—
Duthie, J.	1878–1946	West Hartlepool	1	1903, W	—	—	—	—	—
Dyson, J. W.	1866–1909	Huddersfield	4	1890, S	1	—	—	—	3
Ebdon, P. J.	1874–	Wellington	2	1897, W	—	—	—	—	—
Eddison, J. H.	1888–	Headingley	4	1912, W	1	—	—	—	3
Edgar, C. S.	1876–1949	Birkenhead Park	1	1901, S	—	—	—	—	—
Edwards, R.	1887–1951	Newport	11	1921, W	1	—	—	—	3
Elliot, C. H.	1861–1934	Sunderland	1	1886, W	—	—	—	—	—
Elliot, E. W.	1879–1931	Sunderland	4	1901, W	2	—	—	—	6
Elliot, W.	1910–	Royal Navy, U.S.	7	1932, I	1	—	—	—	3
Elliott, A. E.	1869–1900	Cambridge U., St Thomas's H.	1	1894, S	—	—	—	—	—
Ellis, J.	1912–	Wakefield	1	1939, S	—	—	—	—	—
Ellis, S. S.	1859–1937	Queen's-House, Blackheath	1	1880, I	1	—	—	—	3
Emmott, C.	1868–1927	Bradford	1	1892, W	—	—	—	—	—
Enthoven, H. J.	1878–	Richmond	1	1878, I	—	—	—	—	—
Estcourt, N. S. D.	1929–	Cambridge U., Blackheath	1	1955, S	—	—	—	—	—
Evans, E.	1921–	Loughborough College, Sale	30	1948, A	5	—	—	—	15
Evans, G. W.	1950–	Coventry	9(1)	1972, S	1	1	—	—	7
Evans, N. L.	1908–	R.N.E.C., Keyham, Devonport Services, Royal Navy	5	1932, W	—	—	—	—	—
Evanson, A. M.	1859–1934	Oxford U., Richmond	4	1883, W	1	3	—	—	6
Evanson, W. A. D.	1851–1934	Civil Service, Richmond	5	1875, S	1	—	—	—	3
Evershed, F.	1866–1954	Burton, Oxford U., Blackheath	10	1889, NZN	4	—	—	—	12
Eyres, W. C. T.		U.S., Richmond	1	1927, I	—	—	—	—	—
Fagan, A. R. St L.	1862–1930	Guy's H., Richmond	1	1887, I	—	—	—	—	—
Fairbrother, K. E.	1944–	Nuneaton, Coventry	12	1969, I	—	—	—	—	—
Faithfull, C. K. T.	1903–1979	Halifax, Devonport Services, Harlequins, Army	3	1924, I	—	—	—	—	—
Fallas, H.	1884–	Wakefield Trinity	1	1884, I	—	—	—	—	—
Fegan, J. H. C.	1872–1949	Cambridge U., Blackheath	3	1895, W	1	—	—	—	3
Fernandes, C. W. L.	1857–1944	Wakefield, Leeds, Yorkshire Wanderers	3	1881, I	1	—	—	—	3

*Note that the points-value for a try changed mid-way through Duckham's career**

Players' Career Records (*continued*)

	Dates	Clubs	Caps	Debut	T	C	DG	PG	Pts
Fidler, J. H.	1948–	Cheltenham, Gloucester	2	1981, Arg.					—
Field, E.	1871–1947	Cambridge U., Richmond, Middlesex Wanderers	2	1893, W					3
Fielding, K. J.	1949–	Moseley, Loughborough College	10	1969, I	1				3
Finch, R. T.	1857–1921	Cambridge U., Richmond, St George's H.	1	1880, S					—
Finlan, J. F.	1941–	Coventry, Moseley	13	1967, I			3		9
Finlinson, H. W.	1871–	Blackheath	3	1895, W					—
Finney, S.	1852–1924	R.I.E. College	2	1872, S	1				3
Firth, F.	1894–	Halifax	3	1894, W					—
Fletcher, N. C.	1877–1951	Cambridge U., Old Merchant Taylors, U.C.H.	4	1901, W					—
Fletcher, T.	1874–1950	Seaton,	1	1897, W					—
Fletcher, W. R. B.	1851–1895	Oxford U., Blackheath, Marlborough Nomads	2	1873, S					—
Fookes, E. F.	1874–1948	Sowerby Bridge, Taranaki (NZ)	10	1896, W	5				15
Ford, P. J.	1932–	Gloucester	4	1964, W					—
Forrest, J. W.		U.S., Royal Navy	10	1930, W		1			2
Forrest, R.	1878–1903	Blackheath, Taunton, Wellington	6	1899, W	1				3
Foulds, R. T.	1906–	Moseley, Waterloo	2	1929, W					—
Fowler, F. D.	1855–	R.I.E. College	2	1878, S					—
Fowler, H.	1857–1934	Oxford U., Walthamstow, Blackheath	3	1878, S					—
Fowler, R. H.		Leeds	1	1877, I					—
Fox, F. H.	1863–1952	Wellington, Marlborough Nomads	2	1890, W					—
Francis, T. E. S.	1902–1969	Cambridge U., Blackheath	4	1926, W		4			8
Frankcom, G. P.	1942–	Bedford, Headingley, Cambridge U., Bath	4	1965, W					—
Fraser, E. C.	1853–1927	Oxford U., Blackheath	1	1875, I					—
Fraser, G.	1878–1950	Richmond	5	1902, W					—
Freakes, H. D.	1914–1942	Oxford U., Harlequins	3	1938, W		1			2
Freeman, H.	1850–1916	Oxford U., Marlborough Nomads	3	1872, S			2		8
French, R. J.	1939–	St Helens	4	1961, W					—
Fry, H. A.	1910–1977	Liverpool, Fylde, Army, Waterloo, Rosslyn Park	3	1934, W	2				6
Fry, T. W.		Queen's House	3	1880, I	1				3
Fuller, H. G.	1856–1896	Cambridge U., Bath	6	1882, I					—
Gadney, B. C.	1909–	Richmond, Leicester, Headingley	14	1932, I	1				3
Gamlin, H. T.	1878–1937	Devonport Albion, Blackheath, Wellington	15	1899, W			1		3
Gardner, E. R.	1886–1954	Devonport Services	10	1921, W	1				3
Gardner, H. P.	1855–1908	Richmond	1	1878, I	1				3
Garnett, H. W. T.	1851–1928	Bradford	1	1877, S					—
Gavins, M. N.	1934–	Loughborough C., Middlesbrough, Moseley, Leicester	1	1961, W					—

Players' Career Records (*continued*)

	Dates	Clubs	Caps	Debut	T	C	DG	PG	Pts
Gay, D. J.	1948–	Bath, Harlequins	4	1968, W	—	—	—	—	—
Gent, D. R.	1883–1964	Gloucester	5	1905, NZ	—	—	—	—	—
Genth, J. S. M.		Manchester	2	1874, S	—	—	—	—	—
George, J. T.	1918–	Falmouth	3	1947, S	—	—	—	—	—
Gerrard, R. A.	1912–1943	Bath	14	1932, SA	—	—	—	—	—
Gibbs, G. A.	1920–	Bristol, Northern	2	1947, F	—	—	—	—	—
Gibbs, J. C.	1902–	Harlequins	7	1925, NZ	2	—	—	—	6
Gibbs, N.	1922–	Oxford U., Bristol, Harlequins	2	1954, S	—	2	—	—	4
Giblin, L. F.	1872–1951	Cambridge U., Blackheath	3	1896, W	—	—	—	—	—
Gibson, A. S.	1844–1927	Oxford U., Manchester	1	1871, S	—	—	—	—	—
Gibson, C. O. P.	1876–1931	Oxford U., Northern	1	1901, W	—	—	—	—	—
Gibson, G. R.	1878–1939	Northern	2	1899, W	—	—	—	—	—
Gibson, T. A.	1880–1937	Cambridge U., Northern	2	1905, W	—	—	—	—	—
Gilbert, F. G.		Devonport Services	2	1923, W	—	—	—	—	—
Gilbert, R.	c1885–	Devonport Albion	3	1908, W	—	—	—	—	—
Giles, J. L.	1910–1967	Coventry	6	1935, W	2	—	—	—	6
Gittings, W. J.	1939–	Coventry	1	1967, NZ	—	—	—	—	—
Glover, P. B.	1945–	R.A.F., Bedford, Bath	3	1967, A	—	—	—	—	—
Godfray, R. E.	1880–1967	Richmond	3	1905, NZ	—	—	—	—	—
Godwin, H. O.	1935–	Coventry	11	1959, F	—	—	—	—	—
Gordon-Smith, G. W.		Camborne School of Mines, Redruth, Blackheath	3	1900, W	1	—	1	—	3
Gotley, A. L. H.	1887–1972	Oxford U., Blackheath	6	1910, F	1	—	—	—	7
Graham, D.	1875–1962	Aspatria, Rochdale, New Brighton	1	1901, W	—	—	—	—	—
Graham, H. J.	1856–	Wimbledon Hornets	4	1875, I	—	—	—	—	—
Graham, J. D. G.	1856–	Wimbledon Hornets	1	1876, I	—	—	—	—	—
Gray, A.	1917–	Otley	3	1947, W	—	1	—	—	2
Green, J.	1881–1968	Skipton	8	1905, I	—	—	—	—	—
Green, J. F.	1846–1923	West Kent	1	1871, S	—	—	—	—	—
Greenwell, J. H.	1864–1942	Rockcliff, Tynemouth	2	1893, W	—	—	—	—	—
Greenwood, J. E.	1891–1975	Cambridge U., Old Alleynians, Leicester, Harlequins	13	1912, F	—	12	—	2	30
Greenwood, J. R. H.	1941–	Cambridge U., Waterloo, Coventry	5	1966, I	1	—	—	—	3
Greg, W.	1851–1906	Marlborough Nomads, Manchester	2	1876, I	—	—	—	—	—
Gregory, G. G.	1908–1963	Taunton, Bath, Bristol	13	1931, I	—	2	—	—	4
Gregory, J. A.	1923–	Wanderers, Blackheath, Clifton, Bristol	1	1949, W	—	—	—	—	—
Grylls, W. M.	1885–	Redruth	1	1905, I	—	—	—	—	—
Guest, R. H.	1918–	Liverpool U., Waterloo	13	1939, W	5	—	—	—	15

Players' Career Records (continued)

	Dates	Clubs	Caps	Debut	T	C	DG	PG	Pts
Guillemard, A. G.	1845–1909	West Kent	2	1871, S	—	—	—	—	—
Gummer, C. H. A.	1905–	Plymouth Albion, Moseley	1	1929, F	1	—	—	—	3
Gunner, C. R.	1853–1924	Marlborough Nomads	1	1876, I	—	—	—	—	—
Gurdon, C.	1855–1931	Cambridge U., Richmond	14	1880, I	—	—	—	—	—
Gurdon, E. T.	1854–1929	Cambridge U., Richmond	16	1878, S	1	—	—	—	3
Haigh, L.	1880–1916	Manchester	7	1910, W	—	—	—	—	—
Hale, P. M.	1943–	Moseley	3	1969, SA	—	—	—	—	—
Hall, C.		Gloucester	2	1901, I	—	—	—	—	—
Hall, J.		North Durham, Hartlepool Rovers, Blackheath	3	1894, W	—	—	—	—	—
Hall, N. M.	1925–1972	St Mary's H., Huddersfield, Richmond	17	1947, W	1	8	3*	4	39
Hamersley, A. St G.	1848–1929	Marlborough Nomads, Canterbury (NZ)	4	1871, S	1	—	—	—	3
Hamilton-Hill, E. A.	1908–1979	Harlequins	3	1936, NZ	—	—	—	—	—
Hamilton-Wickes, R. H.	1901–1963	Cambridge U., Harlequins	10	1924, I	4	—	—	—	12
Hammett, E. D. G.	1891–1947	Newport, Blackheath	8	1920, W	—	6	—	—	12
Hammond, C. E. L.	1879–1963	Oxford U., Harlequins	8	1905, S	—	—	—	—	—
Hancock, A. W.	1939–	Northampton	3	1965, F	1	—	—	—	3
Hancock, G. E.	1912–	Birkenhead Park	3	1939, W	—	—	—	—	—
Hancock, J. H.	1932–	Newport	2	1955, W	—	—	—	—	—
Hancock, P. F.	1865–1936	Cambridge U., Blackheath	3	1886, W	—	—	—	—	—
Hancock, P. S.	1883–	Streatham, Richmond	3	1904, W	—	—	—	—	—
Handford, F. G.	1884–	Manchester	4	1909, W	—	—	—	—	—
Hands, R. H. M.	1888–1918	Oxford U., Blackheath	2	1910, F	—	—	—	—	—
Hanley, J.	1901–	Plymouth Albion, Civil Service	7	1927, W	1	—	—	—	3
Hannaford, R. C.	1944–	Cambridge U., Bristol, Gloucester, Rosslyn Park	3	1971, W	1	—	—	—	3
Hanvey, R. J.	1899–	Aspatria	4	1926, W	—	—	—	—	—
Harding, E. H.	1899–1980	Devonport Services	1	1931, I	—	—	—	—	—
Harding, V. S. J.	1932–	Cambridge U., Sale, Harlequins, Edinburgh Wanderers, Saracens	6	1961, F	1	—	—	—	3
Hardwick, P. F.	1878–1924	Percy Park	8	1902, I	—	—	—	—	—
Hardy, E. M. P.	1927–	Army, Blackheath, Headingley	3	1951, I	—	—	—	—	—
Hare, W. H.	1952–	Notts., Leicester	14	1974, W	1	11	1	31	122
Harper, C. H.	1876–1950	Oxford U., Blackheath, Exeter	1	1899, W	—	—	—	—	—
Harris, S. W.	1893–	Blackheath	2	1920, I	1	—	—	—	3
Harris, T. W.	1906–1958	Northampton	2	1929, S	—	—	—	—	—
Harrison, A. C.	1911–	Hartlepool Rovers	2	1931, I	—	—	—	—	—

Note that the points-value for a dropped goal changed mid-way through Hall's career

468

Players' Career Records (continued)

	Dates	Clubs	Caps	Debut	T	C	DG	PG	Pts
Harrison, A. L.	1886–1918	U.S., Royal Navy	2	1914, I					—
Harrison, G.	1858–1894	Hull	7	1877, I					—
Harrison, H. C.	1889–1940	U.S., Royal Navy	4	1909, S		2			4
Hartley, B. C.	1879–1960	Cambridge U., Blackheath	2	1901, S					—
Haslett, L. W.	1900–	Blackheath	2	1926, I	1				3
Hastings, G. W. D.	1924–	Gloucester	13	1955, W	1	1		2	11
Havelock, H.		West Hartlepool	3	1908, F					—
Hawcridge, J. J.	1863–1905	Manningham, Bradford	2	1885, W	2				6
Hayward, L. W.	1886–	Cheltenham	1	1910, I					—
Hazell, D. St G.	1931–	Loughborough College, Leicester, Bristol	4	1955, W				3	9
Hearn, R. D.	1940–	Oxford U., Bedford	6	1966, F					—
Heath, A. H.	1856–1930	Oxford U.	1	1876, S					—
Heaton, J.	1912–	Liverpool U., Notts, Waterloo	9	1935, W		4		3	17
Henderson, A. P.		Cambridge U., Edinburgh Wanderers	9	1947, W	1				3
Henderson, R. S. F.	1858–1924	Edinburgh U., Blackheath, St Mary's H.	5	1883, W	1				3
Heppell, W. G.		Devonport Albion		1903, I					—
Herbert, A. J.	1933–	Cambridge U., Wasps	6	1958, F					—
Hesford, R.	1953–	Wasps, Bristol	4(2)	1981, S				3	9
Hetherington, J. G. G.	1932–	Cambridge U., Northampton	6	1958, A		1			2
Hewitt, E. N.	1924–	Coventry	3	1951, W					—
Hewitt, W. W.	1860–1920	Queen's House, Blackheath	4	1881, I					—
Hickson, J. L.		Bingley, Bradford	6	1887, W	2				6
Higgins, R.	1930–1979	Leeds U., Army, Liverpool	13	1954, W	2				6
Hignell, A. J.	1955–	Cambridge U., Bristol	14	1975, A		3		14	48
Hill, B. A.	1880–1960	Army, U.S., Blackheath	9	1903, I		5			10
Hillard, R. J.	1903–	Oxford U., Old Paulines	1	1925, NZ					—
Hiller, R.	1942–	Oxford U., Harlequins	19	1968, W	3	12	2	33	138
Hind, A. E.	1878–1947	Cambridge U., Leicester, Nottingham	2	1905, NZ					—
Hind, G. R.	1887–1970	Guy's H., Blackheath	2	1910, S					—
Hobbs, R. F. A.	1878–1953	Army, Blackheath	2	1899, S					—
Hobbs, R. G. S.	1908–	Army, Richmond	4	1932, SA					—
Hodges, H. A.	1886–1918	Oxford U., Nottingham, Blackheath	2	1906, W					—
Hodgson, J. McD.	1909–1970	Northern, Leicester	7	1932, SA					—
Hodgson, S. A. M.	1928–	Durham City	11	1960, W		2			—
Holmeyr, M. B.	1925–	Oxford U.	3	1950, W		2		1	7

Players' Career Records (continued)

	Dates	Clubs	Caps	Debut	T	C	DG	PG	Pts
Hogarth, T. B.	1877–1961	Hartlepool Rovers, West Hartlepool, Leicester, Durham City	1	1906, F	1	—	—	—	3
Holford, G.	1886–	Gloucester	2	1920, W	—	—	—	—	—
Holland, D.	1886–1945	Devonport Albion, Gloucester	3	1912, W	1	—	—	—	3
Holliday, T. E.	1898–1969	Aspatria	7	1923, S	—	—	—	—	—
Holmes, C. B.	1915–	Manchester	3	1947, S	1	—	—	—	3
Holmes, E.	1863–	Manningham	2	1890, S	—	—	—	—	—
Holmes, W. A.	1925–	Nuneaton	16	1950, W	—	—	—	—	—
Holmes, W. B.	1928–1949	Cambridge U., Richmond	4	1949, W	—	2	—	—	4
Hook, W. G.	1920–	Gloucester	3	1951, S	—	1	—	—	2
Hooper, C. A.	1869–1950	Cambridge U., Richmond, Middlesex Wanderers, Gloucester	3	1894, W	—	—	—	—	—
Hopley, F. J. V.	1883–1951	Cambridge U., Blackheath	3	1907, W	—	—	—	—	—
Hordern, P. C.	1907–	Oxford U., Newport, Gloucester, Blackheath	4	1931, I	—	—	—	—	—
Horley, C. H.	1861–1924	Swinton	1	1885, I	—	—	—	—	—
Hornby, A. N.	1847–1925	Preston Grasshoppers, Manchester	9	1877, I	1	—	—	—	3
Horrocks-Taylor, J. P.	1934–	Cambridge U., Halifax, Wasps, Middlesbrough, Leicester	9	1958, W	—	—	—	1	3
Horsfall, E. L.	1922–	Huddersfield, Bedford, Gloucester, Headingley, Harlequins, Percy Park, Cardiff	1	1949, W	1	—	—	—	3
Horton, A. L.	1938–	Blackheath	7	1965, W	—	—	—	—	—
Horton, J. P.	1951–	St Helens, Sale, Bath	9	1978, W	—	—	2	—	6
Horton, N. E.	1948–	Moseley, Toulouse	20	1969, I	1	—	—	—	4
Hosen, R. W.	1933–	Loughborough College, Plymouth Albion, Wasps, Cheltenham, Bristol, Northampton	10	1963, NZ	—	6	—	17	63
Hosking, G. R. d'A.	1922–	Devonport Services	5	1949, W	1	—	—	—	3
Houghton, S.	1870–1920	Birkenhead Wanderers, Runcorn	2	1892, I	—	—	—	—	—
Howard, P. D.	1908–1965	Oxford U., Old Millhillians	8	1930, W	—	—	—	—	—
Hubbard, G. C.	1867–1931	Blackheath	2	1892, W	1	—	—	—	3
Hubbard, J. C.	1902–	Blackheath, Harlequins	1	1930, S	—	—	—	—	—
Hudson, A.	1882–1973	Gloucester	8	1906, W	9	—	—	—	27
Hughes, G. E.	1870–1947	Barrow, Otley	1	1896, S	—	—	—	—	—
Hulme, F. C.	1881–	Birkenhead Park, Blackheath, Liverpool	4	1903, W	—	—	—	—	—
Hunt, J. T.		Preston Grasshoppers, Manchester	3	1882, I	—	—	—	—	—
Hunt, R.	1856–1913	Preston Grasshoppers, Manchester, Blackheath	4	1880, I	2	1	1	—	12
Hunt, W. H.	1854–	Preston Grasshoppers, Manchester	4	1876, S	—	—	—	—	—

	Dates	Clubs	Caps	Debut	T	C	DG	PG	Pts
Hurst, A. C. B.	1935–	Oxford U., Wasps	1	1962, S	—	—	—	—	—
Huskisson, T. F.	1914–	Old Merchant Taylors	8	1937, W	1	—	—	—	3
Hutchinson, F.	1885–1960	Old Leodiensians, Headingley	3	1909, F	—	—	—	—	—
Hutchinson, J. E.	1884–	Durham City	1	1906, I	—	—	—	—	—
Hutchinson, W. C.	1856–	R.I.E. College	2	1876, S	2	—	—	—	6
Hutchinson, W. H. H.	1849–1929	Hull	2	1875, I	—	—	—	—	—
Huth, H.	1859–1929	Huddersfield	1	1879, S	—	—	—	—	—
Hyde, J. P.	1930–	Northampton	2	1950, F	—	—	—	—	—
Hynes, W. B.	1889–1968	U.S., Royal Navy	1	1912, F	—	—	—	—	—
Ibbitson, E. D.	1882–1956	Headingley	4	1909, W	—	—	—	—	—
Imrie, H. M.	1877–1938	Durham City	2	1905, NZ	1	—	—	—	3
Inglis, R. E.	1863–1916	Oxford U., Blackheath	3	1886, W	—	—	—	—	—
Irvin, S. H.	1880–1939	Devonport Albion	1	1905, W	—	—	—	—	—
Isherwood, F. W.	1852–1888	Oxford U., Ravenscourt Park	1	1872, S	—	1	—	—	2
Jackett, E. J.	1882–1935	Falmouth, Leicester, Devonport Albion, Transvaal (SA)	13	1905, NZ	—	2	—	—	4
Jackson, A. H.		Guy's H., Blackheath	2	1878, I	—	—	—	—	—
Jackson, B. S.		Broughton Park	2(1)	1970, S	—	—	—	—	—
Jackson, P. B.	1930–	Old Edwardians, Coventry	20	1956, W	6	—	—	—	18
Jackson, W. J.	1870–	Gloucester, Halifax	1	1894, S	—	—	—	—	—
Jacob, F.	1873–1945	Cambridge U., Blackheath, Richmond, Cheltenham	8	1897, W	—	—	—	—	—
Jacob, H. P.	1902–	Oxford U., Blackheath	5	1924, W	4	—	—	—	12
Jacob, P. G.	1875–	Cambridge U., Blackheath	1	1898, I	—	—	—	—	—
Jacobs, C. R.	1928–	Northampton	29	1956, W	—	—	—	—	—
Jago, R. A.	1882–	Devonport Albion	5	1906, W	1	—	—	—	3
Janion, J. P. A. G.	1946–	Bedford, Richmond	12	1971, W	—	—	—	—	—
Jarman, J. W.	1872–1950	Bristol	1	1900, W	—	—	—	—	—
Jeavons, N. C.	1957–	Moseley	10	1981, S	1	—	—	—	4
Jeeps, R. E. G.	1931–	Northampton	24	1956, W	—	—	—	—	—
Jeffery, G. L.	1863–1937	Cambridge U., Harlequins, Blackheath	6	1886, W	1	—	—	—	3
Jennins, C. R.	1942–	Waterloo	3	1967, A	—	—	—	—	—
Jewitt, J.		Hartlepool Rovers	1	1902, W	—	—	—	—	—
Johns, W. A.	1882–	Gloucester	7	1909, W	1	—	—	—	3
Johnston, W. R.	1887–	Bristol, Gloucester	16	1910, W	—	—	—	—	—
Jones, F. P.	1873–1944	New Brighton, Birkenhead Park	1	1893, S	—	—	—	—	—
Jones, H. A.	1918–	Barnstaple	3	1950, W	—	—	—	—	—

Players' Career Records (*continued*)

	Dates	Clubs	Caps	Debut	T	C	DG	PG	Pts
Jorden, A. M.	1947–	Harlequins, Cambridge U., Blackheath, Bedford	7	1970, F	—	5	—	4	22
Jowett, D.	1866–1908	Heckmondwike	6	1889, NZN	—	1	—	—	2
Judd, P. E.	1934–	Coventry	22	1962, W	—	—	—	—	—
Kayll, H. E.	1855–1910	Sunderland	1	1878, S	—	—	—	—	—
Keeling, J. H.		Guy's H.	2	1948, A	—	—	—	—	—
Keen, B. W.	1944	Newcastle U., Northern, Moseley	4	1968, W	—	—	—	—	—
Keeton, G. H.	1878–1949	Cambridge U., Richmond, Leicester	3	1904, W	—	—	—	—	—
Kelly, G. A.	1914	Bedford	4	1947, W	—	—	—	—	—
Kelly, T. S.	1882–	Exeter, London Devonians	12	1906, W	—	—	—	—	—
Kemble, A. T.	1862–1925	Liverpool	3	1885, W	—	—	—	—	—
Kemp, D. T.	1910–	Blackheath	1	1935, W	—	—	—	—	—
Kemp, T. A.	1915–	Cambridge U., St Mary's H., Richmond, Manchester	5	1937, W	—	—	—	—	—
Kendall, P. D.	1878–1915	Cambridge U., Blackheath, Birkenhead Park	3	1901, S	—	—	—	—	—
Kendall-Carpenter, J. M. K.	1925–	Oxford U., Bath, Penzance & Newlyn	23	1949, I	1	—	—	—	3
Kendrew, D. A.	1910–	Woodford, Leicester, Army	10	1930, W	—	1	—	—	2
Kennedy, R. D.	1925–1979	Camborne School of Mines	3	1949, I	1	—	—	—	3
Kent, C. P.	1953–	Oxford U., Rosslyn Park	5(1)	1977, S	1	—	—	—	4
Kent, T.	1864–1928	Salford	6	1891, W	—	—	—	—	—
Kershaw, C. A.	1895–1972	Blackheath, U.S., Royal Navy	16	1920, W	2	—	—	—	6
Kewley, E.	1852–1940	Liverpool	7	1874, S	1	—	—	—	3
Kewney, A. L.	1883–1959	Rockcliff, Leicester	16	1906, W	2	—	—	—	6
Key, A.	1908–	Old Cranleighans	2	1930, I	—	—	—	—	—
Keyworth, M.	1949–	Swansea	4	1976, A	—	—	—	—	—
Kilner, B.	1852–1922	Wakefield Trinity	1	1880, I	—	—	—	—	—
Kindersley, R. S.	1858–1932	Oxford U., Exeter	3	1883, W	2	—	—	—	6
King, I.	1924–	Harrogate	3	1954, W	—	1	—	1	5
King, J. A.	1883–1916	Headingley	12	1911, W	—	—	—	—	—
King, Q. E. M. A.	1895–1954	Blackheath, Army	1	1921, S	1	—	—	—	3
Kingston, P	1951–	Moseley, Gloucester	5	1975, A	—	—	—	—	—
Kitching, A. E.	1889–1945	Cambridge U., Blackheath	1	1913, I	—	—	—	—	—
Kittermaster, H. J.	1902–1967	Oxford U., Harlequins	7	1925, NZ	3	—	—	—	9
Knight, F.	1908–	Devonport, Plymouth	1	1909, A	—	—	—	—	—
Knight, P. M.	1947–	St Luke's College, Bristol	3	1972, S	—	—	—	—	—
Knowles, E.	1868–1945	Millom	2	1896, S	—	—	—	—	—
Knowles, T. C.	1908–	Birkenhead Park	1	1931, S	—	—	—	—	—

	Dates	Clubs	Caps	Debut	T	C	DG	PG	Pts
Krige, J. A.	1897–1946	Guy's H.	1	1920, W	—	—	—	—	—
Labuschagne, N. A.	1931–	Western Province (SA), Guy's H., Harlequins, Natal (SA)	5	1953, W	—	—	—	—	—
Lagden, R. O.	1889–1915	Oxford U., Richmond	1	1911, S	—	2	—	—	4
Laird, H. C. C.	1908–	Harlequins	10	1927, W	5	—	—	—	15
Lambert, D.	1883–1915	Harlequins	7	1907, F	8	8	—	2	46
Lampkowski, M. S.	1953–	Headingley	4	1976, A	1	—	—	—	4
Lapage, W. N.	1883–1939	U.S., Royal Navy	4	1908, F	2	—	—	—	6
Larter, P. J.	1944–	R.A.F., Northampton, Weston-s-Mare	24	1967, A	1	—	—	1	6
Law, A. F.	1853–1921	Oxford U., Richmond	1	1877, S	—	—	—	—	—
Law, D. E.	1902–	Birkenhead Park	1	1927, I	—	—	—	—	—
Lawrence, Hon H. A.	1848–1902	Richmond	4	1873, S	—	—	—	—	—
Lawrie, P. W.	1888–1956	Leicester	2	1910, S	1	—	—	—	3
Lawson, R. G.	1898–1961	Workington	1	1925, I	—	—	—	—	—
Lawson, T. M.	1900–1951	Workington	2	1928, NSW	—	—	—	—	—
Leadbetter, M. M.	1947–	Broughton Park	1	1970, F	—	—	—	—	—
Leadbetter, V. H.	1924–	Cambridge U., Edinburgh Wanderers	2	1954, S	—	—	—	—	—
Leake, W. R. M.	1865–1942	Cambridge U., Old Alleynians, Harlequins	3	1891, W	—	—	—	—	—
Leather, G.	1881–1957	Liverpool	1	1907, I	—	—	—	—	—
Lee, F. H.	1855–1924	Oxford U., Marlborough Nomads	2	1876, S	1	—	—	—	*3*
Lee, H.	1882–1933	Cambridge U., Guy's H., Blackheath	1	1907, F	—	—	—	—	—
Le Fleming, J.	1865–1942	Cambridge U., Blackheath	1	1887, W	1	—	—	—	3
Leslie-Jones, F. A.	1874–1946	Oxford U., Blackheath, Richmond	2	1895, W	—	—	—	—	—
Lewis, A. O.	1920–	Bath	10	1952, SA	—	—	—	—	—
Leyland, R.	1912–	Liverpool U., Waterloo, Leicester, Richmond, Army	3	1935, W	—	—	—	—	—
Livesay, R. O'H.	1876–1946	Blackheath, Army	2	1898, W	—	—	—	—	—
Lloyd, R. H.	1943–	Clifton, Harlequins	5	1967, NZ	2	—	—	—	6
Locke, H. M.	1898–1960	Birkenhead Park	12	1923, S	1	—	—	—	3
Lockwood, R. E.	1867–1915	Dewsbury, Heckmondwike	14	1887, W	5	8	—	—	*31*
Login, S. H. M.	1851–1909	Royal Naval College	1	1876, I	—	—	—	—	—
Lohden, F. C.	1871–1954	Hartlepool Rovers, Blackheath	1	1893, W	1	—	—	—	3
Longland, R. J.	1908–1975	Bedford, R.A.F., Northampton	19	1932, S	—	—	—	—	—
Lowe, C. N.	1891–	Cambridge U., Blackheath, R.A.F., Old Alleynians, Richmond	25	1913, SA	18	—	—	1	58
Lowrie, F. W.	1868–1902	Batley, Wakefield Trinity	2	1889, NZN	—	—	—	—	—
Lowry, W. M.	1900–1974	Birkenhead Park, Old Leysians, Waterloo	1	1920, F	—	—	—	—	—

Players' Career Records (continued)

	Dates	Clubs	Caps	Debut	T	C	DG	PG	Pts
Luddington, W. G. E.	1894–1940	Devonport Services	13	1923, W	—	5	★	1	16
Luscombe, F.	1846–1926	Gipsies	6	1872, S	—	—	—	—	—
Luscombe, J. H.	1848–1937	Gipsies	1	1871, S	—	—	—	—	—
Luxmoore, A. F. C. C.	1876–1944	Cambridge U., Richmond	2	1900, S	—	—	—	—	—
Luya, H. F.	1918–	Waterloo, Headingley	5	1948, W	—	—	—	—	—
Lyon, A.	1852–1905	Liverpool	1	1871, S	—	—	—	—	—
Lyon, G. H. D'O	1883–1947	U.S., Royal Navy	2	1908, S	—	—	—	—	—
McCanlis, M. A.	1906–	Oxford U., O. Cranleighans, Gloucester, Northampton	2	1931, W	—	—	—	—	—
McFadyean, C. W.	1943–	Bristol, Loughborough College, Moseley	11	1966, I	4	—	1	—	15
MacIlwaine, A. H.	1889–	Hull E.R., U.S., Harlequins	5	1912, W	—	—	—	—	—
Mackie, O. G.	1869–1927	Cambridge U., Wakefield Trinity	2	1897, S	—	—	—	—	—
Mackinlay, J. E. H.	1850–1917	St George's H.	3	1872, S	—	—	—	—	—
MacLaren, W.		Manchester	1	1871, S	—	—	—	—	—
MacLennan, R. R. F.	1903–	Old Merchant Taylors, Headingley, London Scottish	3	1925, I	—	—	—	—	—
McLeod, N. F.	1856–1921	R.I.E. College	2	1879, S	—	—	—	—	—
Madge, R. J. P.	1914–	Exeter	4	1948, A	—	—	—	—	—
Malir, F. W. S.	1905–1974	Otley	3	1930, W	—	—	—	—	—
Mangles, R. H.	1874–1948	Richmond, Army	2	1897, W	—	—	—	—	—
Manley, D. C.	1932–	Exeter	4	1963, W	—	—	—	—	—
Mann, W. E.	1885–1969	U.S.	3	1911, W	1	—	—	—	3
Mantell, N. D.	1953–	Rosslyn Park	1	1975, A	—	—	—	—	—
Markendale, E. T.	1856–	Manchester Rangers	1	1880, I	1	—	—	—	3
Marques, R. W. D.	1932–	Cambridge U., Harlequins	23	1956, W	1	—	—	—	3
Marquis, J. C.	1876–1928	Birkenhead Park	2	1900, I	—	—	—	—	—
Marriott, C. J. B.	1861–1936	Cambridge U., Gipsies, Blackheath	7	1884, W	—	—	—	—	—
Marriott, E. E.	1857–1917	Manchester	1	1876, I	—	—	—	—	—
Marriott, V. R.	1938–	Harlequins	4	1963, NZ	—	—	—	—	—
Marsden, G. H.	1880–1948	Morley	3	1900, W	—	—	—	—	—
Marsh, H.	1850–1939	R.I.E. College	1	1873, S	—	—	—	—	—
Marsh, J.		Edinburgh Inst. F.P., Edinburgh U., Swinton	1	1892, I	—	—	—	—	—
Marshall, H.	1870–1929	Cambridge U., Sunderland, St Bart's H., Blackheath	1	1893, W	3	—	—	—	9
Marshall, M. W.	1853–1930	Blackheath	10	1873, S	—	—	—	—	—
Marshall, R. M.	1917–1945	Oxford U., Harlequins	5	1938, I	1	—	—	—	3
Martin, N. O.	1946–	Cambridge U., Harlequins	1(1)	1972, F	—	—	—	—	—
Martindale, S. A.	1905–	Kendal	1	1929, F	—	—	—	—	—

★ includes a goal from a mark

Players' Career Records (*continued*)

	Dates	Clubs	Caps	Debut	T	C	DG	PG	Pts
Massey, E. J.	1900–	Liverpool, Leicester	3	1925, W	—	—	—	—	—
Mathias, J. L.	1878–1940	Bristol	4	1905, W	—	—	—	—	—
Matters, J. C.	1879–1949	R.N.E. College, Keyham	1	1899, S	—	—	—	—	—
Matthews, J. R. C.	1922–	Guy's H., Harlequins	10	1949, F	—	—	—	—	—
Maud, P.	1870–1947	Royal Engineers, Blackheath	2	1893, W	1	—	—	—	4
Maxwell, A. W.	1951–	New Brighton, Headingley	7	1975, A	1	—	—	—	3
Maxwell-Hyslop, J. E.	1899–	Oxford U., Richmond	3	1922, I	1	—	—	—	3
Maynard, A. F.	1894–1916	Cambridge U., Harlequins, Durham City	3	1914, W	—	—	—	—	—
Meikle, G. W. C.	1911–	Cambridge U., Waterloo, Leicester	3	1934, W	4	—	—	—	12
Meikle, S. S. C.	1904–1960	Waterloo	1	1929, S	1	—	—	—	3
Mellish, F. W.	1897–1965	Blackheath, Western Province (SA)	6	1920, W	1	—	—	—	3
Merriam, L. P. B.	1894–1966	Oxford U., Blackheath	2	1920, W	—	—	—	—	—
Michell, A. T.	1853–1923	Oxford U., Ravenscourt Park	3	1875, I	1	—	—	—	3
Middleton, B. B.	1858–1947	Marlborough Nomads, Birkenhead Park	2	1882, I	—	—	—	—	—
Middleton, J. A.	1894–	Wanderers, Richmond, Army	1	1922, S	—	—	—	—	—
Miles, J. H.	1880–1953	Leicester, Northampton	1	1903, W	—	—	—	—	—
Millett, H.	1892–1974	Guy's H., Richmond, Harlequins	1	1920, F	—	—	—	—	—
Mills, F. W.	1849–1904	Marlborough Nomads, Bradford	2	1872, S	—	—	—	—	—
Mills, S. G. F.	1953–	Gloucester	2	1981, Arg.	—	—	—	—	—
Mills, W. A.	1912–	Devonport Albion	11	1906, W	4	—	—	—	12
Milman, D. L. K.	1884–1961	Cambridge U., Bedford, Edinburgh Wanderers	4	1937, W	—	—	—	—	—
Milton, C. H.	1885–1915	Camborne School of Mines	1	1906, I	—	—	—	—	—
Milton, J. G.	1854–1930	Bedford G.S., Camborne School of Mines	5	1904, W	—	—	—	—	—
Milton, W. H.	1872–1935	Marlborough Nomads	5	1874, S	—	—	—	—	—
Mitchell, F.	1865–1905	Cambridge U., Blackheath	6	1895, W	1	1	—	—	5
Mitchell, W. G.	1882–1917	Cambridge U., Richmond, Guy's H.	7	1890, W	—	—	—	—	—
Mobbs, E. R.	1850–1914	Northampton	7	1909, A	4	—	—	—	12
Moberley, W. O.	1862–1925	Oxford U., Clifton, Ravenscourt Park	1	1872, S	—	—	—	—	—
Moore, E. J.	1877–1938	Oxford U., Blackheath, St Bart's H.	2	1883, I	—	—	—	—	—
Moore, N. H.	1921–	Bristol	3	1904, W	2	—	—	—	6
Moore, P. B. C.	1921–	Oxford U., Blackheath	1	1951, W	—	—	—	—	—
Moore, W. K. T.	1951–	Devonport Services, Leicester	7	1947, W	—	—	—	—	—
Mordell, R. J.	1868–1954	Wasps, Rosslyn Park	1	1978, W	—	—	—	—	—
Morfitt, S.	c1890–1961	West Hartlepool, Hull Kingston Rovers	6	1894, W	3	—	—	—	9
Morgan, J. R.	1935–	Hawick	1	1920, W	—	—	—	—	—
Morgan, W. G. D.		Medicals, Newbridge, Percy Park	9	1960, W	—	—	—	—	—

Players' Career Records (continued)

	Dates	Clubs	Caps	Debut	T	C	DG	PG	Pts
Morley, A. J.	1950–	Bristol	7	1972, SA	2	—	—	—	8
Morris, A. D. W.	1883–1962	U.S., Royal Navy	3	1909, A	—	—	—	—	—
Morrison, P. H.	1868–1936	Cambridge U., Northern	4	1890, W	1	—	—	—	3
Morse, S.	1854–1929	Marlborough Nomads, Law Club	3	1873, S	—	—	—	—	—
Mortimer, W.	1874–1916	Cambridge U., Blackheath, Marlborough Nomads	1	1899, W	—	—	—	—	—
Morton, H. J. S.	1886–1955	Cambridge U., Blackheath, London H.	4	1909, I	—	—	—	—	—
Moss, F.		Broughton	3	1885, W	—	—	—	—	—
Mycock, J.	1916–	Sale, Vale of Lune, Harlequins	5	1947, W	—	—	—	—	—
Myers, E.	1895–1956	Headingley, Bradford, Leicester	18	1920, I	3	1	—	—	13
Myers, H.	1875–1906	Keighley	1	1898, I	—	—	—	—	—
Nanson, W. M. B.	1880–1915	Carlisle	2	1907, F	1	—	—	—	3
Nash, E. H.	1854–1932	Oxford U., Richmond	1	1875, I	1	—	—	—	4
Neale, B. A.	1923–	Rosslyn Park, Army	3	1951, I	—	—	—	—	—
Neale, M. E.	1886–1967	Blackheath	1	1912, F	—	—	—	—	—
Neame, S.	1856–1936	Blackheath, Old Cheltonians	4	1879, S	—	—	—	—	—
Neary, A.	1949–	Broughton Park	43(1)	1971, W	5*	—	—	—	19
Nelmes, B. G.	1948–	Bristol, Cardiff	6	1975, A	1	—	—	—	4
Newbold, C. J.	1881–1946	Cambridge U., Wanderers, Blackheath	6	1904, W	—	—	—	—	—
Newman, S. C.	1919–	Oxford U.	3	1947, F	—	—	—	1	3
Newton, A. W.	1879–	Blackheath, Army	1	1907, S	—	—	—	—	—
Newton, P. A.	1860–1946	Oxford U., Blackheath	1	1882, S	—	—	—	—	—
Newton-Thompson, J. O.	1920–1974	Oxford U.	2	1947, S	—	—	—	—	—
Nichol, W.	1868–1922	Brighouse Rangers	2	1892, W	1	—	—	—	3
Nicholas, P. L.	1876–1952	Oxford U., Exeter	1	1902, W	—	—	—	—	—
Nicholson, B. E.	1913–	Old Whitgiftians, Harlequins	2	1938, W	1	—	—	—	3
Nicholson, E. S.	1912–	Oxford U., Guy's H., Leicester, Blackheath	5	1935, W	—	—	—	—	—
Nicholson, E. T.	1871–1953	Liverpool, Birkenhead Park	2	1900, W	1	—	—	—	3
Nicholson, T.		Rockcliff	1	1893, I	—	—	—	—	—
Ninnes, B. F.	1948–	St Ives, Coventry	1	1971, W	—	—	—	—	—
Norman, D. J.	1897–1971	Leicester	2	1932, SA	—	—	—	—	—
North, E. H. G.	1868–1942	Oxford U., Blackheath	3	1891, W	—	—	—	—	—
Northmore, S.		Millom	1	1897, I	—	—	—	—	—
Novak, M. J.	1947–	Harlequins	3	1970, W	1	—	—	—	3
Novis, A. L.	1906–	Oxford U., Army, Headingley, Blackheath	7	1929, S	4	—	—	—	12

Note that the points-value for a try changed mid-way through Neary's career

Players' Career Records (*continued*)

	Dates	Clubs	Caps	Debut	T	C	DG	PG	Pts
Oakeley, F. E.	1891–1914	U.S., Royal Navy	4	1913, S	—	—	—	—	—
Oakes, R. F.	1873–1952	Hartlepool Rovers, Headingley	8	1897, W	—	—	—	—	—
Oakley, L. F. L.	1925–	Bedford	1	1951, W	—	—	—	—	—
Obolensky, A.	1916–1940	Oxford U., Rosslyn Park	4	1936, NZ	2	—	—	—	6
Old, A. G. B.	1945–	Middlesbrough, Leicester, Sheffield	16	1972, W	1	8	3	23	98
Oldham, W. L.		Coventry	2	1908, S	—	—	—	—	—
O'Neill, A.		Torquay Athletic	3	1901, W	—	—	—	—	—
Openshaw, W. E.	c1851–1915	Manchester	1	1879, I	—	—	—	—	—
Osborne, R. R.	1848–1926	Rochdale, Manchester	1	1871, S	—	—	—	—	—
Osborne, S. H.	1880–1939	Oxford U., Harlequins, St Bees	1	1905, S	—	—	—	—	—
Oughtred, B.	1880–1949	Hartlepool Rovers, Hull E.R., Barrow	6	1901, S	—	—	—	—	—
Owen, J. E.	1939–	Blackheath, Moseley, Cambridge U., Coventry	14	1963, W	1	—	—	—	3
Owen-Smith, H. G.	1909–	Oxford U., St Mary's H.	10	1934, W	—	—	—	—	—
Page, J. J.	1947–	Cambridge U., Bedford, Northampton	5	1971, W	—	—	—	—	—
Pallant, J. N.	1944–	Loughborough College, Notts.	3	1967, I	—	—	—	—	—
Palmer, A. C.	1887–1963	London H., Harlequins	2	1909, I	2	2	—	—	10
Palmer, F. H.	1877–	Richmond	1	1905, W	—	—	—	—	—
Palmer, G. V.	1900–1972	Army, N.I.F.C., Cross Keys, Harlequins, Richmond	3	1928, I	2	—	—	—	6
Pargetter, T. A.	1932–	Moseley, Coventry	3	1962, S	—	—	—	—	—
Parker, G. W.	1912–	Cambridge U., Gloucester, Blackheath	2	1938, I	—	6	—	4	24
Parker, Hon S.	1852–1897	Liverpool	2	1874, S	—	—	—	—	—
Parsons, E. I.	1912–1940	R.A.F., Hull E.R.	1	1939, S	—	—	—	—	—
Parsons, M. J.	1943–	Northampton	4	1968, W	—	—	—	—	—
Patterson, W. M.	1936–	Sale, Wasps	2	1961, SA	—	—	—	—	—
Pattisson, R. M.	1860–1948	Cambridge U., Gipsies, Blackheath	2	1883, I	—	—	—	—	—
Paul, J. E.		R.I.E. College	1	1875, S	—	—	—	—	—
Payne, A. T.	1908–1968	Bristol	2	1935, I	—	—	—	—	—
Payne, C. M.	1937–	Oxford U., Harlequins	10	1964, I	1	—	—	—	3
Payne, J. H.	1858–1942	Cambridge U., Broughton	7	1882, S	—	1	—	—	2
Pearce, G. S.	1956–	Northampton	8	1979, S	—	—	—	—	—
Pearson, A. W.	1854–	Guy's H., Blackheath	7	1875, I	4	—	—	—	8
Peart, T. G. A. H.	1936–	Blackheath, Hartlepool Rovers	2	1964, F	—	—	—	—	—
Pease, F. E.	1864–1957	Darlington, Hartlepool Rovers	1	1887, I	—	—	—	—	—
Penny, S. H.		Leicester	1	1909, A	—	—	—	—	—
Penny, W. J.	1875–1965	K.C.H.	3	1878, I	1	—	—	—	3
Percival, L. J.	1869–1941	Oxford U., Rugby	3	1891, I	1	—	—	—	3

Players' Career Records *(continued)*

	Dates	Clubs	Caps	Debut	T	C	DG	PG	Pts
Periton, H. G.	1901–1980	Waterloo	21	1925, W	6	—	—	—	18
Perrott, E. S.	1852–1915	Old Cheltonians	1	1875, I	—	—	—	—	—
Perry, D. G.	1937–	Harlequins, Cambridge U., Bedford	15	1963, F	2	—	—	—	6
Perry, S. V.	1918–	Cambridge U.	7	1947, W	—	—	—	—	—
Peters, J.	1880–1954	Bristol, Plymouth	5	1906, S	2	—	—	—	6
Phillips, C.	1856–1940	Oxford U., Birkenhead Park	3	1880, S	—	—	—	—	—
Phillips, M. S.	1936–	Oxford U., Fylde	25	1958, A	5	—	—	—	15
Pickering, A. S.	1885–1969	Headingley, Harrogate	6	1907, I	—	—	—	—	—
Pickering, R. D. A.	1943–	Bradford	2	1967, I	—	—	—	1	3
Pickles, R. C. W.	1895–	Bristol	2	1922, I	—	—	—	—	—
Pierce, R.	1874–	Liverpool	2	1898, I	—	—	—	—	—
Pilkington, W. N.	1877–1935	Cambridge U., Blackheath	1	1898, S	—	—	—	—	—
Pillman, C. H.	1890–1955	Blackheath	18	1910, W	8	1	—	—	26
Pillman, R. L.	1893–1916	Blackheath	1	1914, F	—	—	—	—	—
Pinch, J.	1871–1946	Lancaster	3	1896, W	—	—	—	—	—
Pinching, W. W.	1851–1878	Guy's H.	1	1872, S	—	—	—	—	—
Pitman, I. J.	1901–	Oxford U., Harlequins	1	1922, S	—	—	—	—	—
Plummer, K. C.	1947–	Bristol	4	1969, W	—	—	—	—	—
Poole, F. O.	1870–1949	Oxford U., Gloucester, Sunderland	3	1895, W	—	—	—	—	—
Poole, R. W.	1874–c1930	Hartlepool Rovers	1	1896, S	—	—	—	—	—
Pope, E. B.	1911–	Cambridge U., Blackheath	1	1931, W	—	—	—	—	—
Portus, G. V.	1883–1954	Oxford U., Blackheath	2	1908, F	1	—	—	—	3
Poulton, R. W.	1889–1915	Oxford U., Harlequins, Liverpool	17	1909, F	8	—	1	—	28
Powell, D. L.	1942–	Rugby, Northampton	11	1966, W	—	—	—	—	—
Pratten, W. E.	1907–	Blackheath	2	1927, S	—	—	—	—	—
Preece, I.	1920–	Coventry	12	1948, I	—	—	—	—	—
Preece, P. S.	1949–	Coventry	12(1)	1972, SA	—	—	—	1	3
Prentice, F. D.	1897–1962	Leicester	3	1928, I	—	—	—	—	—
Prescott, R. E.	1913–1975	Oxford U., Harlequins	6	1937, W	1	—	—	—	3
Preston, N. J.	1955–	Richmond	3	1979, NZ	1	—	—	—	4
Price, H. L.	1899–1943	Oxford U., Leicester, Harlequins	4	1922, I	2	—	—	—	6
Price, J.	1933–	Coventry	1	1961,	—	—	—	—	—
Price, P. L. A.		R.I.E. College	3	1877, I	—	—	—	—	—
Price, T. W.	1914–	Gloucester, Cheltenham	6	1948, S	—	—	—	—	—
Prout, D. H.	1942–	Redruth, Loughborough College, Northampton	2	1968, W	—	—	—	—	—
Pullin, J. V.	1941–	Bristol	42(1)	1966, W	1	—	—	—	3

Players' Career Records *(continued)*

	Dates	Clubs	Caps	Debut	T	C	DG	PG	Pts
Purdy, S. J.	1936–	Rugby, Fylde	1	1962, S	—	—	—	—	—
Pyke, J.	1866–1941	St Helens Recreation	1	1892, W	—	—	—	—	—
Pym, J. A.	1891–1969	Army, Blackheath	4	1912, W	1	—	—	—	3
Quinn, J. P.	1930–	New Brighton, Harrogate	5	1954, W	—	—	—	—	—
Rafter, M.	1952–	St Luke's College, Bristol	17(1)	1977, S	—	—	—	—	—
Ralston, C. W.	1944–	Richmond	22	1971, S	1	—	—	—	4
Ramsden, H. E.		Bingley	2	1898, S	—	—	—	—	—
Ranson, J. M.	1938–	Durham City, Rosslyn Park, Headingley	7	1963, NZ	2	—	—	—	6
Raphael, J. E.	1882–1917	Oxford U., Old Merchant Taylors	9	1902, W	1	—	—	—	3
Ravenscroft, J.	1857–1902	Oxford U., Birkenhead Park	1	1881, I	—	—	—	—	—
Rawlinson, W. C. W.	1855–1898	Blackheath	1	1876, S	—	—	—	—	—
Redmond, G. F.	1943–	Cambridge U., Bedford, St Luke's College, Weston-s-Mare	1	1970, F	—	—	—	—	—
Redwood, B. W.	1939–	Bristol	2	1968, W	1	—	—	—	3
Reeve, J. S. R.	1908–1936	Cambridge U., Harlequins	8	1929, F	5	—	—	—	15
Regan, M.	1929–	Liverpool, Blackheath	12	1953, W	1	—	—	—	3
Rew, H.	1906–1940	Exeter, Blackheath, Army	10	1929, S	—	—	—	—	—
Reynolds, F. J.	1916–	Old Cranleighans, Army, Blackheath	3	1937, S	1	—	1	—	7
Reynolds, S.	1874–1946	Richmond	4	1900, W	—	—	—	—	—
Rhodes, J.		Castleford	3	1896, W	—	—	—	—	—
Richards, E. E.	1905–	Penryn, Plymouth Albion	2	1929, S	—	—	—	—	—
Richards, J.		Bradford	3	1891, W	—	—	—	—	—
Richards, S. B.	1941–	Oxford U., Richmond, Bristol, Sheffield	9	1965, W	—	—	—	—	—
Richardson, J. V.	1903–	Oxford U., Birkenhead Park, Richmond	5	1928, NSW	1	8	1	—	23
Richardson, W. R.	1861–1920	Manchester G.S., Oxford U., Manchester	1	1881, I	—	—	—	—	—
Rickards, C. H.	1854–1920	Gipsies	1	1873, S	—	—	—	—	—
Rimmer, G.	1925–	Waterloo	12	1949, W	—	—	—	—	—
Rimmer, L. I.	1935–	Oxford U., Bath	5	1961, SA	—	—	—	—	—
Ripley, A. G.	1947–	Rosslyn Park	24	1972, W	2	—	—	—	8
Risman, A. B. W.	1937–	Manchester U., Loughborough College	8	1959, W	—	1	—	2	8
Ritson, J. A. S.	1887–1957	Northern	8	1910, F	2	—	—	—	6
Rittson-Thomas, G. C.	1926–	Oxford U.,	3	1951, W	1	—	—	—	3
Robbins, P. G. D.	1933–	Oxford U., Moseley, Coventry	19	1956, W	—	—	—	—	—
Roberts, A. D.	1887–	Cambridge U., Northern	8	1911, W	5	—	—	—	15
Roberts, E. W.	1878–1933	R.N.E. College, Royal Navy	6	1901, W	—	—	—	—	—
Roberts, G. D.	1886–1967	Oxford U., Harlequins, Exeter	3	1907, S	—	3	—	—	6

Players' Career Records (continued)

	Dates	Clubs	Caps	Debut	T	C	DG	PG	Pts
Roberts, J.	1932–	Old Millhillians, Sale, Cambridge U.	18	1960, W	6	—	—	—	18
Roberts, R. S.	1911–	Coventry	1	1932, I	—	—	—	—	—
Roberts, S.	1924–	Swinton	2	1887, W	—	—	—	—	—
Roberts, V. G.	1924–	Penryn, Swansea, Harlequins	16	1947, F	2	—	—	—	6
Robertshaw, A. R.	1861–1920	Bradford	5	1886, W	—	—	—	—	—
Robinson, A.	1865–1948	Cambridge U., Hartlepool Rovers, Blackheath	4	1889, NZN	—	—	—	—	—
Robinson, E.	1929–	Coventry	4	1954, S	—	—	—	—	—
Robinson, G. C.	1876–1940	Gosforth, Percy Park, Blackheath	8	1897, I	8	—	—	—	24
Robinson, J. J.	1872–1959	Cambridge U., Headingley	4	1893, S	1	—	—	—	3
Robson, A.	1896–	Northern	5	1924, W	—	—	—	—	—
Robson, M.	1908–	Heriot's F.P., Oxford U., Blackheath	4	1930, W	1	—	—	—	3
Rogers, D. P.	1935–	Bedford	34	1961, I	3	—	—	—	9
Rogers, J. H.	–1922	Moseley	4	1890, W	1	—	—	—	3
Rogers, W. L. Y.	1878–1948	Oxford U., Army, Blackheath	2	1905, W	—	—	—	—	—
Rollitt, D. M.	1943–	Loughborough College, Bristol, Wakefield	11	1967, I	1	—	—	—	3
Roncoroni, A. D. S.	1908–1953	West Herts, Richmond	3	1933, W	—	—	—	—	—
Rose, W. M. H.	1957–	Cambridge U., Leicester, Coventry	5	1981, I	1	2	—	11	41
Rossborough, P. A.	1948–	Coventry	7	1971, W	1	3	1	7	34
Rosser, D. W. A.	1940–	Manchester, Wasps, Cambridge U.	5	1965, W	—	—	—	—	—
Rotherham, Alan	1862–1898	Oxford U., Coventry, Richmond	12	1883, W	2	—	—	—	6
Rotherham, Arthur	1869–1946	Cambridge U., Richmond, St Thomas's H., Coventry, Middlesex Wanderers	5	1898, S	—	—	—	—	—
Roughley, D. F. K.	1947–	Liverpool	3	1973, A	—	—	—	—	—
Rowell, R. E.	1939–	Loughborough College, Leicester, Fylde, Waterloo	2	1964, W	—	—	—	—	—
Rowley, A. J.	1908–	Coventry	1	1932, SA	—	—	—	—	—
Rowley, H. C.	1854–	Manchester	9	1879, S	3	—	—	—	9
Royds, P. M. R.	1874–1955	Blackheath, U.S.	3	1898, S	1	—	—	—	3
Royle, A. V.		Broughton Rangers	1	1889, NZN	—	—	—	—	—
Rudd, E. L.	1944–	Liverpool, Oxford U.	6	1965, W	—	—	—	—	—
Russell, R. F.	1879–1960	Cambridge U., Leicester, Castleford, Cork	1	1905, NZ	—	—	—	—	—
Rutherford, D.	1937–	Percy Park, Preston Grasshoppers, Wasps, St Luke's College, Gloucester	14	1960, W	—	6	—	8	36
Ryalls, H. J.	1858–1949	New Brighton	2	1885, W	1	—	—	—	3
Ryan, P. H.	1930–	Cambridge U., Richmond	2	1955, W	—	—	—	—	—
Sadler, E. H.	1912–	Army	2	1933, I	1	—	—	—	3
Sagar, J. W.	1878–1941	Cambridge U., Castleford	2	1901, W	—	—	—	—	—

Players' Career Records *(continued)*

	Dates	Clubs	Caps	Debut	T	C	DG	PG	Pts
Sample, C. H.	1862–1938	Cambridge U.,	3	1884, I	—	1	—	—	2
Sanders, D. L.	1924–	Ipswich YMCA, Harlequins	9	1954, W	—	—	—	—	—
Sanders, F. W.	1893–1953	Plymouth Albion	3	1923, I	—	—	—	—	—
Sandford, J. R. P.	1881–1916	Oxford U., Marlborough Nomads	1	1906, I	—	—	—	—	—
Sangwin, R. D.	1937–	Hull and E.R.	2	1964, NZ	—	—	—	—	—
Sargent, G. A. F.	1950–	Lydney, Gloucester	1(1)	1981, I	—	—	—	—	—
Savage, K. F.	1940–	Northampton, Harlequins	13	1966, W	1	—	—	—	3
Sawyer, C. M.	1856–1921	Broughton	2	1880, S	1	—	—	—	3
Saxby, L. E.	1900–	Gloucester	2	1932, SA	—	—	—	—	—
Schofield, J. W.	1858–1931	Manchester	1	1880, I	—	—	—	—	—
Scholfield, J. A.	1888–1966	Cambridge U., Manchester, Preston Grasshoppers, Harlequins	1	1911, W	1	—	—	—	3
Schwarz, R. O.	1875–1918	Cambridge U., Richmond	3	1899, S	—	—	—	—	—
Scorfield, E. S.	1882–1966	Percy Park	1	1910, F	—	—	—	—	—
Scott, C. T.	1877–1965	Cambridge U., London H., Blackheath	4	1900, W	—	—	—	—	—
Scott, E. K.	1918–	Oxford U., Redruth, St Mary's H., Harlequins	5	1947, W	—	—	—	—	—
Scott, F. S.	1886–1952	Bristol	1	1907, W	—	—	—	—	—
Scott, H.	1926–	U.S., Manchester	1	1955, F	—	—	—	—	—
Scott, J. P.	1954–	St Luke's College, Rosslyn Park, Cardiff	23(1)	1978, F	1	—	—	—	4
Scott, J. S. M.	1935–	Birkenhead Park, Oxford U., Harlequins	1	1958, F	—	—	—	—	—
Scott, M. T.	1865–1916	Cambridge U., Northern, Blackheath	3	1887, I	—	—	—	—	—
Scott, W. M.	1870–1944	Cambridge U., Northern, Blackheath	1	1889, NZN	—	—	—	—	—
Seddon, R. L.	1860–1888	Broughton Rangers	3	1887, W	—	—	—	—	—
Sellar, K. A.	1906–	U.S., Blackheath, Royal Navy	7	1927, W	—	—	—	—	—
Sever, H. S.	1910–	Sale	10	1936, NZ	5	—	—	—	19
Shackleton, I. R.	1948–	Cambridge U., Richmond, Harrogate	4	1969, SA	1	—	1	—	3
Sharp, R. A. W.	1938–	Oxford U., Wasps, Redruth, Bristol	14	1960, W	2	4	3	1	26
Shaw, C. H.	1879–1964	Moseley	6	1906, S	—	—	—	—	—
Shaw, F.		Cleckheaton	1	1898, I	—	—	—	—	—
Shaw, J. F.	1878–1941	R.N.E. College	2	1898, S	—	—	—	—	—
Sheppard, A.		Bristol	1(1)	1981, W	—	—	—	—	—
Sherrard, C. W.	1848–1921	Blackheath, Royal Engineers	2	1871, S	—	—	—	—	—
Sherriff, G. A.	1937–	Saracens	3	1966, S	—	—	—	—	—
Shewring, H. E.	1882–1960	Bristol	10	1905, I	1	—	—	—	3
Shooter, J. H.	1875–1922	Morley	4	1899, I	—	—	—	—	—
Shuttleworth, D. W.	1928–	Roundhay, Blackheath, Headingley, Army	2	1951, S	—	—	—	—	—

Players' Career Records (continued)

	Dates	Clubs	Caps	Debut	T	C	DG	PG	Pts
Sibree, H. J. H.	1885–1962	Harlequins	3	1908, F	—	—	—	—	—
Silk, N.	1941–	Oxford, U., Harlequins, St Thomas's H.	4	1965, W	—	—	—	—	—
Simpson, C. P.	1942–	Ipswich, Harlequins, Army	1	1965, W	—	—	—	—	—
Simpson, T.		Rockcliff	11	1902, S	3	—	—	—	9
Sladen, G. M.	1904–	U.S.	3	1929, W	—	—	—	—	—
Slemen, M. A. C.	1951–	St Luke's College, Liverpool	29	1976, I	8	—	—	—	32
Slocock, L. A. N.	1886–1916	Liverpool	8	1907, F	3	—	—	—	9
Slow, C. F.	1911–1939	Leicester, Northampton	1	1934, S	—	—	—	—	—
Small, H. D.	1922–	Oxford U.	4	1950, W	—	—	—	—	—
Smallwood, A. M.	1892–	Cambridge U., Leicester	14	1920, F	7	—	1	—	25
Smart, C. E.	1950–	Newport	13	1979, F	—	—	—	—	—
Smart, S.	1888–	Gloucester	12	1913, SA	—	—	—	—	—
Smeddle, R. W.	1908–	Durham City, Blackheath, Cambridge U.	4	1929, W	2	—	—	—	6
Smith, C.		Gloucester	1	1901, W	—	—	—	—	—
Smith, D. F.	1890–1969	Richmond	2	1910, W	—	—	—	—	—
Smith, J. V.	1926–	Cambridge U., Stroud, Rosslyn Park	4	1950, W	4	—	—	—	12
Smith, K.	1952–	Roundhay	4	1974, F	—	—	—	—	—
Smith, M. J. K.	1933–	Oxford U.	1	1956, W	—	—	—	—	—
Smith, S. J.	1951–	Loughborough College, Sale	25(2)	1973, I	2	—	—	—	8
Smith, S. R.	1934–	Cambridge U., Richmond	5	1959, W	—	—	—	—	—
Smith, T.		Northampton	1	1951, W	—	—	—	—	—
Soane, F.	1866–1932	Bath	4	1893, S	—	—	—	—	—
Sobey, W. H.	1905–	Old Millhillians, Cambridge U.	5	1930, W	—	—	—	—	—
Solomon, B.	1885–1961	Redruth	1	1910, W	1	—	—	—	3
Sparks, R. H. W.	1899–	Plymouth Albion	9	1928, I	—	—	—	—	—
Speed, H.	1871–1937	Castleford	4	1894, W	—	—	—	—	—
Spence, F. W.	1867–	Birkenhead Park	1	1890, I	—	—	—	—	—
Spencer, J.	1939–	Harlequins, St Jean-de-Luz	1	1966, W	—	—	—	—	—
Spencer, J. S.	1947–	Headingley, Cambridge U.	14	1969, I	2	—	—	—	6
Spong, R. S.	1906–1980	Old Millhillians	8	1929, F	—	—	—	—	—
Spooner, R. H.	1880–1961	Marlborough Nomads, Liverpool	1	1903, W	—	—	—	—	—
Springman, H. H.	1859–1936	Liverpool	2	1879, S	—	—	—	—	—
Spurling, A.	1856–1945	Blackheath	1	1882, I	—	—	—	—	—
Spurling, N.	1864–1919	Blackheath	3	1886, I	—	—	—	—	—
Squires, P. J.	1951–	Harrogate	29	1973, F	6	—	—	—	24
Stafford, R. C.	1893–1912	Bedford	4	1912, W	—	—	—	—	—

Players' Career Records *(continued)*

	Dates	Clubs	Caps	Debut	T	C	DG	PG	Pts
Stafford, W. F. H.	1854–1942	Royal Engineers	1	1874, S	—	—	—	—	—
Stanbury, E.	1897–1968	Plymouth Albion	16	1926, W	—	5	—	1	13
Standing, G.		Blackheath	2	1883, W	—	—	—	—	—
Stanger-Leathes, C. F.	1881–1965	Northern	1	1905, I	—	—	—	—	—
Stark, K. J.	1904–	Old Alleynians	9	1927, W	—	1	—	1	5
Starks, A.	1873–1952	Castleford	2	1896, W	—	—	—	—	—
Starmer-Smith, N. C.	1944–	Oxford U., Harlequins	7	1969, SA	—	—	—	—	—
Start, S. P.	1879–1969	R.N.E. College, Royal Navy, U.S.	1	1907, S	—	—	—	—	—
Steeds, J. H.	1916–	Cambridge U., Saracens, Middlesex H.	5	1949, F	—	—	—	—	—
Steele-Bodger, M. R.	1925–	Cambridge U., Harlequins, Moseley, Edinburgh U.	9	1947, W	—	—	—	—	—
Steinthal, F. E.	1886–	Oxford U., Ilkley	2	1913, W	—	—	—	—	—
Stevens, C. B.	1941–	Penzance & Newlyn, Harlequins	25	1969, SA	2	—	—	—	8
Still, E. R.	1852–1931	Oxford U., Ravenscourt Park	1	1873, S	—	—	—	—	—
Stirling, R. V.	1919–	R.A.F., Leicester, Wasps	18	1951, W	1	—	—	—	3
Stoddart, A. E.	1863–1915	Blackheath, Harlequins	10	1885, W	2	1	★	—	12
Stoddart, W. B.	1871–1935	Liverpool	3	1897, W	—	—	—	—	—
Stokes, F.	1850–1928	Blackheath	3	1871, S	—	—	—	—	—
Stokes, L.	1856–1933	Blackheath	12	1875, I	—	17	—	—	42
Stone, F. le S.	1886–1938	Blackheath	1	1914, F	—	—	—	—	—
Stoop, A. D.	1883–1957	Oxford U., Harlequins	15	1905, S	2	—	—	—	6
Stoop, F. M.	1888–1972	Harlequins	4	1910, S	—	—	—	—	—
Stout, F. M.	1877–1926	Richmond, Gloucester	14	1897, W	1	1	—	—	5
Stout, P. W.	1875–1937	Gloucester, Bristol, Richmond	5	1898, S	1	—	—	—	3
Stringer, N. C.	1960–	Wasps	1(1)	1982, A	—	—	—	—	—
Strong, E. L.	1862–1945	Oxford U., Bath	3	1884, W	—	—	—	—	—
Summerscales, G. E.	1879–1936	Durham City	1	1905, NZ	—	—	—	—	—
Sutcliffe, J. W.	1868–1947	Bradford, Heckmondwike	1	1889, NZN	1	1	—	—	5
Swarbrick, D. W.	1927–	Oxford U., Blackheath	6	1947, W	—	—	—	—	—
Swayne, D. H.	1909–	Oxford U., Harlequins	1	1931, W	—	—	—	—	—
Swayne, J. W. R.	1906–	Bridgwater Albion, Harlequins	1	1929, W	—	—	—	—	—
Swift, A. H.	1958–	Fylde, Swansea	2	1981, Arg.	—	—	—	—	—
Syddall, J. P.	1956–	Waterloo	1	1982, I	—	—	—	—	—
Sykes, A. R. V.		Blackheath	1	1914, F	—	—	—	—	—
Sykes, F. D.	1927–	Huddersfield, Northampton	4	1955, F	1	—	—	—	3
Sykes, P. W.	1925–	Cambridge U., Wasps	7	1948, F	—	—	—	—	—

includes a goal from a mark ★

Players' Career Records (continued)

	Dates	Clubs	Caps	Debut	T	C	DG	PG	Pts
Syrett, R. E.	1931–	Wasps	11	1958, W	1	—	—	—	3
Tallent, J. A.	1911–	Cambridge U., Blackheath	5	1931, S	3	—	—	—	9
Tanner, C. C.	1908–1941	Cambridge U., Richmond	5	1930, S	1	—	—	—	3
Tarr, F. N.	1887–1915	Oxford U., Leicester, Headingley, Richmond	4	1909, A	2	—	—	—	6
Tatham, W. M.	1862–1938	Oxford U., Marlborough Nomads	7	1882, S	1	—	—	—	3
Taylor, A. S.	1859–1917	Cambrige U., Guy's H., Blackheath	4	1883, W	—	—	—	—	
Taylor, E. W.	1869–	Rockcliff	14	1892, I	2	3	★	—	16
Taylor, F.	1890–1956	Leicester	2	1920, F	—	—	—	—	
Taylor, F. M.	1888–1964	Leicester	1	1914, W	—	—	—	—	
Taylor, H. H.	1858–1942	St George's H., Blackheath	5	1879, S	6	—	—	—	18
Taylor, J. T.	1876–1951	Castleford, West Hartlepool	11	1897, I	1	1	—	—	5
Taylor, P. J.	1931–	Wakefield, Northampton, Loughborough College, Blackheath	6	1955, W	—	—	—	—	
Taylor, R. B.	1942–	Northampton	16	1966, W	2	—	—	—	6
Taylor, W. J.	1905–	Cambridge U., Blackheath	5	1928, NSW	2	—	—	—	6
Teden, D. E.	1916–1940	Richmond	3	1939, W	1	—	—	—	3
Teggin, A.	1860–	Broughton Rangers	6	1884, I	1	—	—	—	3
Tetley, T. S.	1856–1924	Bradford	1	1876, S	—	—	—	—	
Thomas, C.	1875–c1935	Barnstaple	4	1895, W	1	—	—	—	3
Thompson, P. H.	1929–	Headingley, Waterloo	17	1956, W	5	—	—	—	15
Thomson, G. T.	c1857–1889	Halifax	9	1878, S	1	—	—	—	3
Thomson, W. B.	1871–	Blackheath	4	1892, W	1	—	—	—	3
Thorne, J. D.	1934–	Bristol	3	1963, W	—	—	—	—	
Tindall, V. R.	1928–	Richmond, Liverpool U.	4	1951, W	—	—	—	—	
Tobin, F.	1849–1927	Cambridge U., Liverpool	1	1871, S	—	—	—	—	
Todd, A. F.	1873–1915	Cambridge U., Blackheath	2	1900, I	—	—	—	—	
Todd, R.	1847–1927	Manchester	1	1877, S	—	—	—	—	
Toft, H. B.	1909–	Waterloo	10	1936, S	—	—	—	—	
Toothill, J. T.	1866–1947	Manningham, Bradford	12	1890, S	1	—	—	—	3
Tosswill, L. R.	1880–1932	Marlborough Nomads, St Bart's H., Exeter	3	1902, W	—	—	—	—	
Touzel, C. J. C.	1855–1899	Cambridge U., Liverpool, Blackheath	2	1877, I	—	—	—	—	
Towell, A. C.		Leicester, Bedford	2	1948, F	—	—	—	—	
Travers, B. H.	1919–	Oxford U., Harlequins	6	1947, W	—	2	—	—	4
Treadwell, W. T.	1939–	Wasps, Guy's H.	3	1966, I	—	—	—	—	
Tristram, H. B.	1861–1946	Oxford U., Durham City, Newton Abbot, Richmond	5	1883, S	—	—	—	—	

★ includes a goal from a mark

484

Players' Career Records (*continued*)

	Dates	Clubs	Caps	Debut	T	C	DG	PG	Pts
Troop, C. L.	1910–	Richmond, Army	2	1933, I	—	—	—	—	—
Tucker, J. S.	1895–1973	Bristol	27	1922, W	2	—	—	—	6
Tucker, W. E.	1872–1953	Cambridge U., Blackheath, St George's H.	5	1894, W	—	—	—	—	—
Tucker, W. E.	1903–	Cambridge U., Blackheath, St George's H.	3	1926, I	—	—	—	—	—
Turner, D. P.	1846–1909	Richmond	6	1871, S	—	—	—	—	—
Turner, E. B.	1854–1931	St George's H.	3	1876, I	1	—	—	—	3
Turner, G. R.	1855–1941	St George's H.	1	1876, S	—	—	—	—	—
Turner, H. J. C.		Manchester	1	1871, S	—	—	—	—	—
Turner, M. F.	1921–	Old Whitgiftians, Cambridge U., Blackheath	2	1948, S	—	—	—	—	—
Turquand-Young, D		Richmond, Army	5	1928, NSW	—	—	—	—	—
Twynam, H. T.	1852–1899	Richmond	8	1879, I	4	—	—	—	12
Underwood, A. M.	1940–	St Luke's College, Exeter, Northampton	5	1962, W	—	—	—	—	—
Unwin, E. J.	1912–	Rosslyn Park, Army	4	1937, S	3	—	—	—	9
Unwin, G. T.	1874–1948	Oxford U., Moseley, Blackheath, Cheltenham	1	1898, S	—	—	—	—	—
Uren, R.	1926–	Waterloo	4	1948, I	—	2	—	1	7
Uttley, R. M.	1949–	Gosforth, Wasps, Fylde	23	1973, I	2	—	—	—	8
Valentine, J.	1866–1904	Swinton	4	1890, W	1	—	—	—	2
Vanderspar, C. H. R.	1852–1877	Richmond	1	1873, S	—	—	—	—	—
Van Ryneveld, C. B.	1928–	Oxford U.	4	1949, W	3	—	—	—	9
Varley, H.	1868–1915	Liversedge	1	1892, S	—	—	—	—	—
Vassall, H.	1860–1925	Oxford U., Blackheath, Marlborough Nomads	5	1881, W	3	—	—	—	9
Vassall, H. H.	1887–1949	Oxford U., Blackheath	1	1908, I	—	—	—	—	—
Vaughan, D. B.	1925–1977	Cambridge U., Headingley, Harlequins	8	1948, A	—	—	—	—	—
Vaughan-Jones, A.	1909–	U. S., Army	3	1932, I	—	—	—	—	—
Verelst, C. L.	1855–1890	Liverpool	2	1876, I	—	—	—	—	—
Vernon, G. F.	1856–1902	Blackheath	5	1878, S	—	—	—	—	—
Vickery, G.	1879–1970	Bath, Aberavon	1	1905, I	—	—	—	—	—
Vivyan, E. J.	1879–1935	Devonport Albion	4	1901, W	3	2	—	—	13
Voyce, A. T.	1897–1980	Gloucester, Cheltenham, Richmond, Blackheath	27	1920, I	5	—	—	—	15
Wackett, J. A. S.	1930–	Rosslyn Park	2	1959, W	—	—	—	—	—
Wade, C. G.	1863–1922	Oxford U., Richmond	8	1883, W	7	—	—	—	21
Wade, M. R.	1938–	Cambridge U., Leicester	3	1962, W	1	—	—	—	3
Wakefield, W. W.	1898–	Cambridge U., R.A.F., Leicester, Harlequins	31	1920, W	6	—	—	—	18
Walker, G. A.	1912–	Cambridge U., R.A.F.	2	1939, W	—	—	—	—	—
Walker, H. W.	1915–	Coventry	9	1947, W	—	—	—	—	—
Walker, R.	1846–1919	Manchester	5	1874, S	—	—	—	—	—

Players' Career Records (*continued*)

	Dates	Clubs	Caps	Debut	T	C	DG	PG	Pts
Wallens, J. N. S.	1879–1947	Waterloo	1	1927, F	—	—	—	—	—
Walton, E. J.	1874–1940	Oxford U., Castleford	4	1901, W	—	—	—	—	—
Walton, W.	1885–1963	Castleford	1	1894, S	—	—	—	—	—
Ward, G.		Leicester	6	1913, W	—	—	—	—	—
Ward, H.		Bradford	1	1895, W	—	—	—	—	—
Ward, J. I.	1858–1924	Gipsies, Richmond	2	1881, I	—	—	—	—	—
Ward, J. W.	1873–1939	Castleford	3	1896, W	—	—	—	—	—
Wardlow, C. S.	1942–	Carlisle, Northampton	6(1)	1969, SA	—	—	—	—	—
Warfield, P. J.	1951–	Durham U., Rosslyn Park, Cambridge U.	6	1973, NZ	—	—	—	—	—
Warr, A. L.	1913–	Moseley, Harlequins, Oxford U., Wakefield, Gloucester, Richmond	2	1934, W	1	—	—	—	3
Watkins, J. A.	1947–	Gloucester	7	1972, SA	—	—	—	—	—
Watkins, J. K.	1913–1970	Devonport Services, U.S.	3	1939, W	—	—	—	—	—
Watson, F. B.	1884–1960	Royal Navy, U.S.	2	1908, S	1	—	—	—	3
Watson, J. H. D.	1890–1914	Edinburgh U., London H., Blackheath	3	1914, W	1	—	—	—	3
Watt, D. E. J.	1938–	Bristol	4	1967, I	—	—	—	—	—
Webb, C. S. H.	1902–1961	Devonport Services, Royal Navy	12	1932, SA	—	—	—	—	—
Webb, J. W. G.		Northampton	3	1926, F	1	—	—	—	3
Webb, R. E.	1943–	Coventry	12	1967, S	2	—	—	—	6
Webb, StL. H.	1931–1978	Blackheath, Bedford	4	1959, W	—	—	—	—	—
Webster, J. G.	1946–	Moseley	11	1972, W	—	—	—	—	—
Wedge, T. G.		St Ives	2	1907, F	—	—	—	—	—
Weighill, R. H. G.	1920–	Birkenhead Park, R.A.F., Waterloo, Leicester, Harlequins	4	1947, S	—	—	—	—	—
Wells, C. M.	1871–1963	Cambridge U., Harlequins	6	1893, S	—	—	—	—	—
West, B. R.	1948–	Loughborough College, Northampton	8	1968, W	—	—	—	—	—
Weston, H. T. F.	1869–1955	Northampton	1	1901, S	—	—	—	—	—
Weston, L. E.	1947–	Loughborough College, West of Scotland, Rosslyn Park	2	1972, F	—	—	—	—	—
Weston, M. P.	1938–	Durham City, Richmond	29	1960, W	1	—	1	—	6
Weston, W. H.	1905–	Northampton	16	1933, I	—	—	—	—	—
Wheatley, A. A.	1908–	Coventry	5	1937, W	—	—	—	—	—
Wheatley, H. F.	1912–	Coventry	7	1936, I	—	—	—	—	—
Wheeler, P. J.	1948–	Leicester	33	1975, F	—	—	—	—	—
White, D. F.	1926–	Northampton	14	1947, W	2	—	—	—	6
Whiteley, E. C. P.	1904–1973	Old Alleynians	2	1931, S	2	—	—	—	6

Players' Career Records (*continued*)

	Dates	Clubs	Caps	Debut	T	C	DG	PG	Pts
Whiteley, W.	c1871–	Bramley	1	1896, W	—	—	—	—	—
Whitley, H.	1903–1975	Northern	1	1929, W	—	—	—	—	—
Wightman, B. J.	1936–	Loughborough College, Moseley, Coventry, Rosslyn Park	5	1959, W	—	—	—	—	—
Wigglesworth, H. J.	1861–1925	Thornes	1	1884, I	—	—	—	—	—
Wilkins, D. T.	1924–	Royal Navy, U.S., Roundhay	13	1951, W	—	—	—	—	—
Wilkinson, E.	1863–1896	Bradford	5	1886, W	2	—	—	—	6
Wilkinson, H.	1903–	Halifax	4	1929, W	2	—	—	—	6
Wilkinson, H. J.	1864–1942	Halifax	1	1889, NZN	—	—	—	—	—
Wilkinson, P.		Law Club	1	1872, S	—	—	—	—	—
Wilkinson, R. M.	1951–	Cambridge U., Bedford	6	1975, A	—	—	—	—	—
Willcocks, T. H.		Plymouth Albion	1	1902, W	—	—	—	—	—
Willcox, J. G.	1937–	Oxford U., Harlequins, Fylde, P.U.C., Headingley	16	1961, I	—	4	—	3	17
William-Powlett, P. B. R. W.	1898–	Royal Navy, U.S.	1	1922, S	—	—	—	—	—
Williams, C. G.	1950–	Lydney, Headingley, Gloucester	1	1976, F	—	—	—	—	—
Williams, C. S.	1887–	Manchester	1	1910, F	—	—	—	—	—
Williams, J. E.	1932–	Old Millhillians, Sale, Headingley, Harlequins	9	1954, W	1	—	—	—	3
Williams, J. M.	1927–	Cambridge U., Penzance & Newlyn, Richmond	2	1951, I	—	—	—	—	—
Williams, S. G.		Devonport Albion	7	1902, W	2	—	—	—	6
Williams, S. H.	1886–1936	Newport	4	1911, W	—	—	—	—	—
Williamson, R. H.	1886–1946	Oxford U., Blackheath	5	1908, W	2	—	—	—	6
Wilson, A. J.	1886–1917	Northern, Camborne, Camborne School of Mines	1	1909, I	—	—	—	—	—
Wilson, C. E.	1871–1914	Blackheath, Army	1	1898, I	—	—	—	—	—
Wilson, C. P.	1859–1938	Cambridge U., Marlborough Nomads	1	1881, W	—	—	—	—	—
Wilson, D. S.	1926–	Metropolitan Police, Harlequins	8	1953, F	4	—	—	—	12
Wilson, G. S.	1907–1979	Tyldesley, Manchester, Birkenhead Park	2	1929, W	—	2	—	—	4
Wilson, K. J.	1938–	Cheltenham, Gloucester	1	1963, F	—	—	—	—	—
Wilson, R. P.	1870–1943	St Bart's H., Liverpool O.B.	3	1891, W	2	—	—	—	6
Wilson, W. C.	1885–1967	Army, U.S., Richmond	2	1907, I	—	—	—	—	—
Winn, C. E.	1926–	Oxford U., Rosslyn Park	8	1952, SA	3	—	—	—	9
Winterbottom, P. J.	1960–	Exeter, Headingley	5	1982, A	—	—	—	—	—
Wintle, T. C.	1940–	Rosslyn Park, Cambridge, U., Northampton, St Mary's H.	5	1966, S	—	—	—	—	—
Wodehouse, N. A.	1887–1941	U.S., Royal Navy	14	1910, F	2	—	—	—	6
Wood, A.		Halifax	1	1884, I	—	—	—	—	—

Players' Career Records (*continued*)

	Dates	Clubs	Caps	Debut	T	C	DG	PG	Pts
Wood, A. E.	c1882–1963	Cheltenham, Gloucester	3	1908, F		4			8
Wood, G. W.	1886–1969	Leicester, Nuneaton	1	1914, W					—
Wood, R.	c1873–	Liversedge	1	1894, I					—
Wood, R. D.		Liverpool O. B.	3	1901, I					—
Woodgate, E. E.	1922–	Paignton	1	1952, W					—
Woodhead, E.	1857–1944	Edinburgh U., Huddersfield, Dublin U.	1	1880, I					—
Woodruff, C. G.	1920–	Harlequins, Cheltenham	4	1951, W					—
Woods, S. M. J.	1868–1931	Cambridge U., Wellington, Blackheath, Bridgwater A.	13	1890, W	1	1			5
Woods, T.	1883–1955	Bridgwater Albion	1	1908, S					—
Woods, T.		Devonport Services, Royal Navy, Pontypool	5	1920, S	1				3
Woodward, C. R.	1956–	Loughborough College, Harlequins, Leicester	15(1)	1980, I	4				16
Woodward, J. E.	1931–	Wasps	15	1952, SA	6			1	21
Wooldridge, C. S.	1858–1941	Oxford U., Blackheath	7	1883, W					—
Wordsworth, A. J.	1953–	Cambridge U., Harlequins	1(1)	1975, A					—
Worton, J. R. B.	1901–	Harlequins, Army	2	1926, W					—
Wrench, D. F. B.	1936–	Wilmslow, Harlequins, Cambridge U.	2	1964, F					—
Wright, C. C. G.	1887–1960	Cambridge U., Blackheath	2	1909, I					—
Wright, F. T.	1862–1934	Edinburgh Academy, Manchester	1	1881, S					—
Wright, I. D.	1945–	St Luke's College, Rosslyn Park, Northampton	4(1)	1971, W					—
Wright, J. C.	1910–	Metropolitan Police, Newport	1	1934, W					—
Wright, J. F.	1863–1932	Bradford	1	1890, W					—
Wright, T. P.	1931–	Blackheath, Penarth	13	1960, W					—
Wright, W. H. G.	1889–	Plymouth Albion	2	1920, W					—
Wyatt, D. M.	1949–	St Luke's College, Bedford, Bath, Oxford U.	1(1)	1976, S					—
Yarranton, P. G.	1924–	Wasps	5	1954, W					—
Yiend, W.	1861–1939	Hartlepool Rovers, Leicester, Keighley	6	1889, NZN					—
Young, A. T.	1901–1933	Cambridge U., Army, Blackheath	18	1924, W	2				6
Young, J. R. C.	1937–	Moseley, Oxford U., Harlequins	9	1958, I	2				6
Young, M.	1946–	Cambridge U., Gosforth	10	1977, S	1	4		1	15
Young, P. D.	1927–	Cambridge U., Clifton, Rosslyn Park, Wanderers	9	1954, W	1				3

LONGEST CAREER SPANS

Seasons	Player	Caps	Career span
13	J. Heaton	9	1934–35 to 1946–47
12	L. G. Brown	18	1910–11 to 1921–22
12	N. E. Horton	20	1968–69 to 1979–80
12	T. A. Kemp	5	1936–37 to 1947–48
12	J. E. Williams	9	1953–54 to 1964–65
11	F. E. Cotton	31	1970–71 to 1980–81
11	H. Coverdale	4	1909–10 to 1919–20
11	W. J. A. Davies	22	1912–13 to 1922–23
11	E. Evans	30	1947–48 to 1957–58
11	R. H. Guest	13	1938–39 to 1948–49
11	C. N. Lowe	25	1912–13 to 1922–23
11	J. V. Pullin	42	1965–66 to 1975–76

MOST CONSECUTIVE CAPS IN A CAREER

Caps	Player	Opponents
36	J. V. Pullin	*1968* W,I,F,S *1969* I,F,S,W,SA *1970* I,W,S,F *1971* W,I,F,S (1 + 2),P *1972* W,I,F,S,SA *1973* NZ,W,I,F,S,NZ,A *1974* S,I,F,W *1975* I
33	W. B. Beaumont	*1975* A (1 R + 2) *1976* A,W,S,I,F *1977* S,I,F,W *1978* F,W,S,I,NZ *1979* S,I,F,W,NZ *1980* I,F,W,S *1981* W,S,I,F,Arg. (1 + 2) *1982* A,S
29	W. W. Wakefield	*1920* W,F,I,S *1921* W,I,S,F *1922* W,I,F,S *1923* W,I,S,F *1924* W,I,F,S *1925* NZ,W,I,S,F *1926* W,I,F,S
28	J. Butterfield	*1953* F,S *1954* W,NZ,I,S,F *1955* W,I,F,S *1956* W,I,S,F *1957* W,I,F,S *1958* W,A,I,F,S *1959* W,I,F,S
27	A. T. Voyce	*1920* I,S *1921* W,I,S,F *1922* W,I,F,S *1923* W,I,S,F *1924* W,I,F,S *1925* NZ,W,I,S,F *1926* W,I,F,S
27	A. Neary	*1971* W,I,F,S (1 + 2),P *1972* W,I,F,S,SA *1973* NZ,W,I,F,S,NZ,A *1974* S,I,F,W *1975* I,F,W,S,A (1)
25	C. N. Lowe	*1913* SA,W,F,I,S *1914* W,I,S,F *1920* W,F,I,S *1921* W,I,S,F *1922* W,I,F,S *1923* W,I,S,F
24	M. A. C. Slemen	*1976* I,F *1977* S,I,F,W *1978* F,W,S,I,NZ *1979* S,I,F,W,NZ *1980* I,F,W,S *1981* W,S,I,F
23	R. W. D. Marques	*1956* W,I,S,F *1957* W,I,F,S *1958* W,A,I,F,S *1959* W,I,F,S *1960* W,I,F,S *1961* SA,W
22	J. D. Currie	*1956* W,I,S,F *1957* W,I,F,S *1958* W,A,I,F,S *1959* W,I,F,S *1960* W,I,F,S *1961* SA
22	C. W. Ralston	*1971* S (2),P *1972* W,I,F,S,SA *1973* NZ,W,I,F,S,NZ,A *1974* S,I,F,W *1975* I,F,W,S
22	P. J. Wheeler	*1977* S,I,F,W *1978* F,W,S,I,NZ *1979* S,I,F,W,NZ *1980* I,F,W,S *1981* W,S,I,F

MOST CAPS IN A CAREER

Caps	Player	Career span
43	A. Neary	1970–71 to 1979–80
42	J. V. Pullin	1965–66 to 1975–76
36	D. J. Duckham	1968–69 to 1975–76
34	D. P. Rogers	1960–61 to 1968–69
34	W. B. Beaumont	1974–75 to 1981–82
33	P. J. Wheeler	1974–75 to 1981–82
31	W. W. Wakefield	1919–20 to 1926–27
31	F. E. Cotton	1970–71 to 1980–81
30	E. Evans	1947–48 to 1957–58
29	R. Cove-Smith	1920–21 to 1928–29
29	C. R. Jacobs	1955–56 to 1963–64
29	M. P. Weston	1959–60 to 1967–68
29	P. J. Squires	1972–73 to 1978–79
29	M. A. C. Slemen	1975–76 to 1981–82
28	J. Butterfield	1952–53 to 1958–59
27	A. T. Voyce	1919–20 to 1925–26
27	J. S. Tucker	1921–22 to 1930–31
25	C. N. Lowe	1912–13 to 1922–23
25	J. D. Currie	1955–56 to 1961–62
25	M. S. Phillips	1957–58 to 1963–64
25	C. B. Stevens	1969–70 to 1974–75
25	S. J. Smith	1972–73 to 1981–82
24	R. E. G. Jeeps	1955–56 to 1961–62
24	P. J. Larter	1966–67 to 1972–73
24	A. G. Ripley	1971–72 to 1975–76
23	J. M. K. Kendall-Carpenter	1948–49 to 1953–54
23	R. W. D. Marques	1955–56 to 1960–61
23	R. M. Uttley	1972–73 to 1979–80
23	J. P. Scott	1977–78 to 1981–82
22	W. J. A. Davies	1912–13 to 1922–23
22	P. E. Judd	1961–62 to 1967–68
22	C. W. Ralston	1970–71 to 1974–75
22	P. J. Dixon	1970–71 to 1978–79
21	J. G. G. Birkett	1905–06 to 1911–12
21	H. G. Periton	1924–25 to 1929–30
20	P. B. Jackson	1955–56 to 1962–63
20	N. E. Horton	1968–69 to 1979–80
20	P. W. Dodge	1977–78 to 1981–82

MOST POINTS IN A CAREER

Pts	Player	Matches	Career span
138	R. Hiller	19	1967–68 to 1971–72
122	W. H. Hare	14	1973–74 to 1981–82
98	A. G. B. Old	16	1971–72 to 1977–78
63	R. W. Hosen	10	1963 to 1966–67

Pts	Player	Matches	Career span
58	C. N. Lowe	25	1912–13 to 1922–23
48	A. J. Hignell	14	1975 to 1978–79
46	D. Lambert	7	1906–07 to 1910–11
42	*L. Stokes	12	1874–75 to 1880–81
41	W. M. H. Rose	5	1980–81 to 1981–82
39	N. M. Hall	17	1946–47 to 1954–55
36	D. Rutherford	14	1959–60 to 1967–68
36	D. J. Duckham	36	1968–69 to 1975–76
34	J. G. G. Birkett	21	1905–06 to 1911–12
34	P. A. Rossborough	7	1970–71 to 1974–75
32	M. A. C. Slemen	29	1975–76 to 1981–82
31	*R. E. Lockwood	14	1886–87 to 1893–94
30	J. E. Greenwood	13	1911–12 to 1919–20
30	B. H. Black	10	1929–30 to 1932–33
28	R. W. Poulton	17	1908–09 to 1913–14
27	A. Hudson	8	1905–06 to 1909–10
26	R. A. W. Sharp	14	1959–60 to 1966–67
26	C. H. Pillman	18	1909–10 to 1913–14
25	G. S. Conway	18	1919–20 to 1926–27
25	A. M. Smallwood	14	1919–20 to 1924–25
24	J. F. Byrne	13	1893–94 to 1898–99
24	G. C. Robinson	8	1896–97 to 1900–01
24	W. J. A. Davies	22	1912–13 to 1922–23
24	G. W. Parker	2	1937–38
24	P. J. Squires	29	1972–73 to 1978–79
24	J. Carleton	16	1979–80 to 1981–82
23	J. V. Richardson	5	1927–28
23	D. W. Burland	8	1930–31 to 1932–33
23	W. N. Bennett	7	1974–75 to 1978–79
22	*W. N. Bolton	11	1881–82 to 1886–87
22	A. M. Jorden	7	1969–70 to 1974–75
21	*C. G. Wade	8	1882–83 to 1885–86
21	J. E. Woodward	15	1951–52 to 1955–56
20	F. E. Chapman	7	1909–10 to 1913–14
20	S. A. Doble	3	1972 to 1972–73

* See page 457

MOST TRIES IN A CAREER

T	Player	Matches	Career span
18	C. N. Lowe	25	1912–13 to 1922–23
10	J. G. G. Birkett	21	1905–06 to 1911–12
10	D. J. Duckham	36	1968–69 to 1975–76
9	A. Hudson	8	1905–06 to 1909–10
8	G. C. Robinson	8	1896–97 to 1900–01
8	D. Lambert	7	1906–07 to 1910–11
8	R. W. Poulton	17	1908–09 to 1913–14
8	C. H. Pillman	18	1909–10 to 1913–14
8	M. A. C. Slemen	29	1975–76 to 1981–82
7	C. G. Wade	8	1882–83 to 1885–86
7	A. M. Smallwood	14	1919–20 to 1924–25

T	Player	Matches	Career span
6	G. W. Burton	6	1878–79 to 1880–81
6	H. H. Taylor	5	1878–79 to 1881–82
6	W. N. Bolton	11	1881–82 to 1886–87
6	V. H. M. Coates	5	1912–13
6	W. W. Wakefield	31	1919–20 to 1926–27
6	H. C. Catcheside	8	1923–24 to 1926–27
6	H. G. Periton	21	1924–25 to 1929–30
6	J. E. Woodward	15	1951–52 to 1955–56
6	P. B. Jackson	20	1955–56 to 1962–63
6	J. Roberts	18	1959–60 to 1963–64
6	P. J. Squires	29	1972–73 to 1978–79
6	J. Carleton	16	1979–80 to 1981–82
5	R. E. Lockwood	14	1886–87 to 1893–94
5	E. F. Fookes	10	1895–96 to 1898–99
5	A. D. Roberts	8	1910–11 to 1913–14
5	A. T. Voyce	27	1919–20 to 1925–26
5	H. C. C. Laird	10	1926–27 to 1928–29
5	J. S. R. Reeve	8	1928–29 to 1930–31
5	H. S. Sever	10	1935–36 to 1937–38
5	R. H. Guest	13	1938–39 to 1948–49
5	E. Evans	30	1947–48 to 1957–58
5	J. Butterfield	28	1952–53 to 1958–59
5	P. H. Thompson	17	1955–56 to 1958–59
5	M. S. Phillips	25	1957–58 to 1963–64
5	A. Neary	43	1970–71 to 1979–80
4	H. T. Twynam	8	1878–79 to 1883–84
4	F. Evershed	10	1888–89 to 1892–93
4	W. A. Mills	11	1905–06 to 1907–08
4	E. R. Mobbs	7	1908–09 to 1909–10
4	L. G. Brown	18	1910–11 to 1921–22
4	W. J. A. Davies	22	1912–13 to 1922–23
4	H. P. Jacob	5	1923–24 to 1929–30
4	R. H. Hamilton-Wickes	10	1923–24 to 1926–27
4	C. D. Aarvold	16	1927–28 to 1932–33
4	A. L. Novis	7	1928–29 to 1932–33
4	G. W. C. Meikle	3	1933–34
4	J. V. Smith	4	1949–50
4	D. S. Wilson	8	1952–53 to 1954–55
4	C. W. McFadyean	11	1965–66 to 1967–68
4	P. J. Dixon	22	1970–71 to 1978–79
4	C. R. Woodward	15	1979–80 to 1981–82
3	H. C. Rowley	9	1878–79 to 1881–82
3	H. Vassall	5	1880–81 to 1882–83
3	H. Marshall	1	1892–83
3	S. Morfitt	6	1893–94 to 1895–96
3	E. J. Vivyan	4	1900–01 to 1903–04
3	D. D. Dobson	6	1901–02 to 1902–03
3	T. Simpson	11	1901–02 to 1908–09
3	L. A. N. Slocock	8	1906–07 to 1907–08
3	H. Brougham	4	1911–12
3	E. Myers	18	1919–20 to 1924–25
3	L. J. Corbett	16	1920–21 to 1926–27
3	H. J. Kittermaster	7	1924–25 to 1925–26

T	Player	Matches	Career span
3	D. W. Burland	8	1930–31 to 1932–33
3	J. A. Tallent	5	1930–31 to 1934–35
3	L. A. Booth	7	1932–33 to 1934–35
3	E. J. Unwin	4	1936–37 to 1937–38
3	C. B. van Ryneveld	4	1948–49
3	C. E. Winn	8	1951–52 to 1953–54
3	D. P. Rogers	34	1960–61 to 1968–69
3	R. Hiller	19	1967–68 to 1971–72
3	G. H. Davies	8	1980–81 to 1981–82

MOST CONVERSIONS IN A CAREER

C	Player	Matches	Career span
17	L. Stokes	12	1874–75 to 1880–81
12	J. E. Greenwood	13	1911–12 to 1919–20
12	R. Hiller	19	1967–68 to 1971–72
11	G. S. Conway	18	1919–20 to 1926–27
11	W. H. Hare	14	1973–74 to 1981–82
8	R. E. Lockwood	14	1886–87 to 1893–94
8	D. Lambert	7	1906–07 to 1910–11
8	J. V. Richardson	5	1927–28
8	N. M. Hall	17	1946–47 to 1954–55
8	A. G. B. Old	16	1971–72 to 1977–78
7	F. E. Chapman	7	1909–10 to 1913–14
6	E. D. G. Hammett	8	1919–20 to 1921–22
6	B. H. Black	10	1929–30 to 1932–33
6	G. W. Parker	2	1937–38
6	D. Rutherford	14	1959–60 to 1967–68
6	R. W. Hosen	10	1963 to 1966–67
5	B. A. Hill	9	1902–03 to 1906–07
5	W. G. E. Luddington	13	1922–23 to 1925–26
5	E. Stanbury	16	1925–26 to 1928–29
5	A. M. Jorden	7	1969–70 to 1974–75
4	A. W. Pearson	7	1874–75 to 1877–78
4	F. H. R. Alderson	6	1890–91 to 1892–93
4	V. H. Cartwright	14	1902–03 to 1906–07
4	A. E. Wood	3	1907–08
4	T. E. S. Francis	4	1925–26
4	D. W. Burland	8	1930–31 to 1932–33
4	J. Heaton	9	1934–35 to 1946–47
4	R. A. W. Sharp	14	1959–60 to 1966–67
4	J. G. Willcox	16	1960–61 to 1963–64
4	M. Young	10	1976–77 to 1978–79
3	A. M. Evanson	4	1882–83 to 1883–84
3	E. W. Taylor	14	1891–92 to 1898–99
3	G. D. Roberts	3	1906–07 to 1907–08
3	P. A. Rossborough	7	1970–71 to 1974–75
3	A. J. Hignell	14	1975 to 1978–79

MOST PENALTY GOALS IN A CAREER

PG	Player	Matches	Career span
33	R. Hiller	19	1967–68 to 1971–72
31	W. H. Hare	14	1973–74 to 1981–82
23	A. G. B. Old	16	1971–72 to 1977–78
17	R. W. Hosen	10	1963 to 1966–67
14	A. J. Hignell	14	1975 to 1978–79
11	W. M. H. Rose	5	1980–81 to 1981–82
8	D. Rutherford	14	1959–60 to 1967–68
7	P. A. Rossborough	7	1970–71 to 1974–75
6	S. A. Doble	3	1972 to 1972–73
5	D. F. Allison	7	1955–56 to 1957–58
5	W. N. Bennett	7	1974–75 to 1978–79
4	J. F. Byrne	13	1893–94 to 1898–99
4	B. H. Black	10	1929–30 to 1932–33
4	H. J. Boughton	3	1934–35
4	G. W. Parker	2	1937–38
4	N. M. Hall	17	1946–47 to 1954–55
4	J. D. Currie	25	1955–56 to 1961–62
4	A. M. Jorden	7	1969–70 to 1974–75
3	J. Heaton	9	1934–35 to 1946–47
3	D. St. G. Hazell	4	1954–55
3	J. G. G. Hetherington	6	1957–58 to 1958–59
3	J. G. Willcox	16	1960–61 to 1963–64
3	P. W. Dodge	20	1977–78 to 1981–82

MOST DROPPED GOALS IN A CAREER

DG	Player	Matches	Career span
3	W. J. A. Davies	22	1912–13 to 1922–23
3	N. M. Hall	17	1946–47 to 1954–55
3	R. A. W. Sharp	14	1959–60 to 1966–67
3	J. F. Finlan	13	1966–67 to 1972–73
3	A. G. B. Old	16	1971–72 to 1977–78
2	H. Freeman	3	1871–72 to 1873–74
2	L. Stokes	12	1874–75 to 1880–81
2	J. F. Byrne	13	1893–94 to 1898–99
2	P. Cranmer	16	1933–34 to 1937–38
2	R. Hiller	19	1967–68 to 1971–72
2	A. R. Cowman	5	1970–71 to 1972–73
2	J. P. Horton	9	1977–78 to 1980–81

MOST INDIVIDUAL APPEARANCES IN ONE POSITION

Position	Appearances	Player	
Full-back	19	R. Hiller	1968–1972
	16	W. R. Johnston	1910–1914
Wing	29	M. A. C. Slemen	1976–1982
	29	P. J. Squires	1973–1979
Centre	28	J. Butterfield	1953–1959
Fly-half	22	W. J. A. Davies	1913–1923
Scrum-half	25	S. J. Smith	1973–1982
	24	R. E. G. Jeeps	1956–1962
Prop	31	F. E. Cotton	1971–1981
	29	C. R. Jacobs	1956–1964
Hooker	42	J. V. Pullin	1966–1976
	33	P. J. Wheeler	1975–1982
	29	E. Evans	1950–1958
Lock	34	W. B. Beaumont	1975–1982
	25	J. D. Currie	1956–1962
Flanker	43	A. Neary	1972–1980
	34	D. P. Rogers	1961–1969
Number eight	24	A. G. Ripley	1972–1976

NB   D. J. Duckham, with 22 appearances on the wing and 14 in the centre, won most caps as a three-quarter.

MOST APPEARANCES IN COMBINATION

Position	Appearances	Players
Centre	15	M. S. Phillips, M. P. Weston
	12	P. W. Dodge, C. R. Woodward
	10	H. M. Locke, L. J. Corbett
	10	D. J. Duckham, J. S. Spencer
	9	J. Butterfield, W. P. C. Davies
Half-backs	14	W. J. A. Davies, C. A. Kershaw
	9	R. A. W. Sharp, R. E. G. Jeeps
	8	H. C. C. Laird, A. T. Young
	8	G. H. Davies, S. J. Smith
Front row	11	C. B. Stevens, J. V. Pullin, F. E. Cotton
	10	R. V. Stirling, E. Evans, W. A. Holmes
	9	C. R. Jacobs, E. Evans, G. W. D. Hastings
Second row	22	R. W. D. Marques, J. D. Currie
	12	W. B. Beaumont, M. J. Colclough
	11	W. B. Beaumont, N. E. Horton
Back row	12	P. J. Dixon, A. G. Ripley, A. Neary
	8	D. F. White, J. M. K. Kendall-Carpenter, A. O. Lewis

NB   The record 11 appearances for the front-row unit include one occasion when J. V. Pullin came on as replacement.

495

CLUB PAIRINGS

Position	Club	Players	First pairing
Centre	Oxford U.	F.A. Leslie-Jones, E. M. Baker	1895
	Oxford U.	F. N. Tarr, R. W. Poulton	1909
	Harlequins	J. G. G. Birkett, F. M. Stoop	1910
	Harlequins	J. G. G. Birkett, R. W. Poulton	1912
	Harlequins	R. W. Poulton, F. M. Stoop	1913
	The Army	A. R. Aslett, A. L. Novis	1929
	St Mary's H.	N. O. Bennett, E. K. Scott	1947
	Oxford U.	L. B. Cannell, C. B. van Ryneveld	1949
	Oxford U.	L. B. Cannell, B. Boobbyer .	1950
	Cambridge U.	D. W. A. Rosser, G. P. Frankcom	1965
	Wasps	D. W. A. Rosser, T. G. Arthur	1966
	Coventry	G. W. Evans, P. S. Preece	1973
	Leicester	C. R. Woodward, P. W. Dodge	1980
Half-backs	R.I.E. College	W. C. Hutchinson, P. L. A. Price	1877
	Manchester	F. T. Wright, H. C. Rowley	1881
	Bradford	C. Emmott, A. Briggs	1892
	Blackheath	H. Marshall, R. F. C. de Winton	1893
	Richmond	R. O. Schwarz, A. Rotherham	1899
	Blackheath	H. Coverdale, J. A. Pym	1912
	Royal Navy/U.S.	W. J. A. Davies, F. E. Oakeley	1913
	Leicester	F. M. Taylor, G. W. Wood	1914
	Royal Navy/U.S.	W. J. A. Davies, C. A. Kershaw	1920
	Harlequins	H. J. Kittermaster, J. R. B. Worton	1926
	Harlequins	H. C. C. Laird, J. R. B. Worton	1927
	Blackheath	C. C. Bishop, A. T. Young	1927
	Old Milhillians	R. S. Spong, W. H. Sobey	1930
	Leicester	C. F. Slow, B. C. Gadney	1934
	Blackheath/Army	E. M. P. Hardy, D. W. Shuttlewoth	1951
	Moseley	J. F. Finlan, J. G. Webster	1973
	Moseley	M. J. Cooper, J. G. Webster	1975
Midfield backs (two centres and fly-half)	Harlequins	F. M. Stoop, J. G. G. Birkett, A. D. Stoop	1910
	Harlequins	J. G. G. Birkett, R. W. Poulton, A. D. Stoop	1912
	St Mary's H.	N. O. Bennett, E. K. Scott, N. M. Hall	1947
	Leicester	P. W. Dodge, C. R. Woodward, L. Cusworth	1982
Second row	Harlequins	R. W. D. Marques, J. D. Currie	1956
	Coventry	T. A. Pargetter, J. E. Owen	1963
	Northampton	M. J. Parsons, P. J. Larter	1968

NB No club has yet given an entire threequarter line, front row or back row